Handbook of Old Gallatin County

Contents include
- Goodspeed's *History of Gallatin County* (1887)
- Early anecdotes from a variety of sources
- Military history of the county

Plus, over 250 Gallatin Co. biographies from the following:
- *Centennial Atlas of the State of Illinois* – 1876
- *History of White County* – 1883
- Goodspeed's *History of Gallatin County* – 1887
- *Memoirs of the Lower Ohio Valley* – 1905
- *History of Southern Illinois* – 1912

Jon Musgrave, Editor

IllinoisHistory.com
Marion, Illinois

Copyright ©2002 IllinoisHistory.com

All rights reserved. No part of this publication may be reproduced, stored in a retrieval system or transmitted in any form or by any means electronic, mechanical, photocopying, recording or otherwise, without the prior written permission of the publisher.

Published by
IllinoisHistory.com
PO Box 1142
Marion IL 62959

Cover
Bank of Illinois at Shawneetown in 1934
Historic American Buildings Record
Library of Congress

Library of Congress Control Number: 2002110936

International Standard Book Number (ISBN)
cloth: 0-9707984-0-7
paperback: 0-9707984-1-5

Printed in the United States of America
1st printing

*In dedication to those who have gone on before
in recording, preserving and interpreting
Gallatin County's history.*

George W. Smith, Clarence Bonnell,
Lucy Bender, Vernon H. Crest,

and

Lucille Lawler
(1908-2002)

who taught us it's never too late to learn.

Introduction

It's through. Thankfully!

It's over and there aren't any mistakes. However, I know better. There were mistakes — factual errors, misspellings and typos in the 1887 version — some of the old ones probably made it through for this 21st Century version. Regrettably, I may have even added some new ones.

I probably shouldn't open the introduction highlighting my mistakes, but it's the first thing to come to mind. I started researching Gallatin County's history seven or eight years ago, a process that hastened once I joined the team of Ron Nelson and Gary DeNeal in uncovering the story of the Old Slave House back in 1996.

The History of Gallatin, Saline, Hamilton, Franklin and Williamson Counties, Illinois is often referred to as the "1887 History" (the year of its publication) or the "Five-County History." Original copies are extremely rare. Twice reprinted in the last half century, its 1,200 or so pages are not an easy read, or even easy to hold; not to mention it contains information on four counties too many for most researchers.

My early goal consisted of republishing the Gallatin County portion. Then, I added additional biographies from other sources. I probably should have stopped there, but I didn't. Instead, I kept adding items.

I made the early decision to not change the wording. As a journalism instructor, the drive to edit copy is tremendous. This is particularly true for the clunky 19th Century writing that clogs up so many of the book's passages. Once I realized I couldn't — or wouldn't — change the sentences, any additions would have to be included in the footnotes. That became a problem. In some early drafts the footnotes became longer than the passages. That's when the idea for the second and third sections of this book came about. Titled "Early Anecdotes of Gallatin County" and "Military History of Gallatin County," everything new I found soon had a home. However, the word "new" probably isn't appropriate. Here it means simply found elsewhere in other, mostly 19th Century, works.

The only changes I did make are in the headings and the paragraphs. I added more headings to help make the book easier to follow and added paragraph breaks to break up the sometimes page-long original paragraphs, but only where it could be done without changing the original meaning.

As far as the language used in this volume, readers should keep in mind 19th Century attitudes when reading this work. It's not politically correct and is often insensitive to minorities, sometimes extremely so. However, in defense of the authors or editors of the 1887 edition, there is a surprising amount of history concerning Gallatin residents of African descent. Even the attitude expressed is downright enlightened when compared with the neighboring *History of Union County, Kentucky*, also published by Goodspeed just a year earlier.

However, certain words, particularly the pejorative form of the word Negro, have been kept in this volume for two reasons. First, while the layout and presentation of the 1887 history has been updated, the wording has not. Secondly, names like *Nigger Spring* while rightfully offensive, at least do acknowledge the role of blacks at the saltworks. This is more than the modern diluted name of *Saline Well*. A few years ago I had the pleasure of taking three faculty members from the Black American Studies department at Southern Illinois University at Carbondale on a tour of the saltworks area. At one point we visited the salt well a mile off of Route 1. I expressed my interest in encouraging the Forest Service to change the name to *Great Salt Springs*, the named used in the original Indian treaties, or at least to *Lower Lick*, a name in use for the site while the saltworks operated. Surprisingly, they disagreed with me, not that the generic name should be replaced with a historic one, but that the old name, the offensive one, would be better. That name, they explained, at least recognized their people had been there. *Saline Well*, as they saw it, simply wrote them out of the history.

There are footnotes throughout the book. Some are from the original book and are noted. Some of the new footnotes correct mistakes, provide alternative spellings for names, or add significant information. In the Anecdotes and Military History sections, footnotes at the end of a passage provide the source for the material. In those two sections, passages are taken verbatim from the original source. If a new introduction was needed, it was set apart typographically to distinguish it. The Index includes every name mentioned in this book with one exception. The long listing of the county's Civil War soldiers included in the Military History section is not indexed. However, they are in alphabetical order.

A project like this couldn't have been completed without the help of numerous folks including fellow Crenshaw Rascals Ron Nelson and Gary DeNeal, Betty Head, Nick Questell, Vernon H. Crest's granddaughter Kathie Crest Thatcher, the staff at the Gallatin County Clerk's and Circuit Clerk's office, George Sisk at the Old Slave House, the folks on the Gallatin County Genealogy list at Rootsweb.com, the Illinois State Archives, the Illinois State Historical Library and the Illinois History Survey at the University of Illinois, as well as the staff at Special Collections at Southern Illinois University's Morris Library and the Illinois Regional Archives Depository staff in Carbondale and Chicago. Also, I can't forget the staff and volunteers in the local history and genealogy collections at the public libraries in Shawneetown, Harrisburg, Eldorado, Marion and Mount Vernon as well as the Saline County Genealogical Society, the Williamson County Historical Society, the Genealogy Society of Southern Illinois and the Frankfort Area Historical Society.

Also, from the financial side in helping get this book published, I want to add a special thanks to the 100 or so folks who pre-ordered this book.

Enjoy.

Jon Musgrave
IllinoisHistory.com

Table of Contents

Introduction v
Table of Contents vii
Goodspeed's History of Gallatin County 1
   Geography 1
   Saltworks of Gallatin County 4
   Early settlement of the county 7
   Troubles with Indians 8
   Land entries 9
   Slaves and Indentured Servants 11
   Elections and Politics 22
   Railroad History 26
   The Agricultural Association 27
   Bench and Bar 27
   The County Commissioners' Court 33
   Location of County Seat 34
   The Circuit Court 37
   Military History 44
   Shawneetown 51
   The Press of the County 65
   Other Towns and Villages 66
   Presbyterian Church History 75
   Methodist Church History 80
   Catholic Church 81
   Social Brethren Church 83
   School History 83
Anecdotes of Early Gallatin County 91
   Early Outlaws and Other Crimes 91
   Wild Things 94
   Early Descriptions 94
   Early Saltworks 108
   Lafayette's Visit 113
   Cutting Gallatin Down to Size 115
   Linder's *Early Bench and Bar* 117
   Kidnappings 123
   Education 129
   Additional Church History 131

Bear Creek Township & Omaha	136
New Haven	139
More History of Shawneetown Floods	140
Sketch of the 1890 Grand Jury	143
Military History	149
French and Indian War	149
Indian Troubles/War of 1812	150
Black Hawk War	169
Mexican War	171
Civil War	174
Spanish-American War	203
Gallatin County Biographies	205
Bibliography	407
Index	411

Goodspeed's History of Gallatin County

Geography

Location and Boundaries

GALLATIN COUNTY is situated in the southeastern part of Illinois. It is bounded on the north by White County, on the east by Indiana and Kentucky, on the south by Hardin County and on the west by Saline County. It contains 313.44 square miles or 200,602.41 acres. The length of the county from north to south is 21 miles, its extreme width 19 miles, and its shortest width 12 miles, just below Shawneetown. The county, like all of the State of Illinois, is sectionalized and divided into townships, of which there are nine, only one of which Eagle Creek Township, in the southwest corner, is a congressional township. The streams are Saline River, which enters the county nearly two miles south of the northwest corner, and flowing in a south-southeasterly direction, enters the Ohio on the line between Gallatin and Hardin Counties; and numerous small creeks which flow into the Saline River from either side. In the northeastern part of the county are several bodies of water, as Big Fish Lake, Little Fish Lake, Woods Pond, Round Pond, Honey Moore Pond, Yellow Bank Slough, Mill Slough and Beaver Pond, and in the southeastern portion Big Lake.

Topography

Generally speaking, the surface of the county is gently undulating. Nowhere to the hills rise more than about 250 feet above the general level, and the elevations rising to this altitude are in Eagle Creek Township along Eagle Creek. The most marked feature, however, in the topography of this county is a ridge named Gold Hill Ridge,[1] extending in an east and west direction in the southern tier of sections in Township 9. This ridge attains an elevation of 342 feet above high water in the Ohio River, and as it approaches the Ohio, gradually descends until it is lost in the alluvial bottomlands back of Shawneetown. There is a low depression in Gold Hill Ridge at Island Riffle, in Section 36, Township 9, Range 8 east of the principal meridian, where it is crossed by the Saline River. Coal Hill is the name of a short range of hills commencing in Section 4, Township 10, Range 9, and terminating on Section 8, Township 10, Range 9. In the vicinity of Bowlesville is another short range of hills lying to the north of Gold Hill and terminating near Equality, on the west side of the North Folk of the Saline.[2] With the exception of the elevated narrow ridge, running nearly north and south along the road from Shawneetown to New Haven, terminating within three miles of the former place, the county north of the Gold Hill axis is without prominent hills.

---

[1] An original footnote at this spot notes: "Named after Calvin Gold, an old settler, but previously called Moreland Hill, after Hazel Moreland." In between Gold Hill and Coal Hill lies Kuykendall Valley.

[2] The reference to Bowlesville is misleading. Today this range appears on either side of Route 13.

Geology – Coals and Rock Strata

The rocks of Gold Hill Ridge belong to what is known in the geology of Illinois as the Chester Group, this group constituting the upper portion of the Subcarboniferous Period, the maximum thickness of which (the Chester Group) in Illinois is 800 feet, according to the State geologist's report. The most easterly exposure in Gallatin County is a little more than three miles west of Shawneetown, on Section 33, Township 9, Range 9 east. The following section of the rock was obtained:

	Feet
Covered slope to top of ridge	50
Conglomerate with pebbles	50
Irregular bedded sandstone	20
Covered sandstone and shale	90
Limestone with Archimedes	55
Covered to high water of the Ohio	40
	305

The Chester limestone exposure near the base is for the most part a coarse, crystalline, gray rock, filled with small entrochites (the petrified arms of star fishes), the organic structure of which is almost obliterated by crystallization. It is remarkably poor in other fossils, only some badly preserved specimens of archimedes, and a few fragments of a small spirifer being found besides. This same limestone crops out also up the Saline River on Section 27, Township 9, Range 8 east. Near this locality were the old salt works known as the "Nigger Works." Besides these two localities, the only other place in Gallatin County where the Chester limestone outcrops is in the southwestern corner, near the corner of Pope and Hardin Counties.

Above the Chester Group lie the coal measures proper of various and varying thickness and value, interspersed with sandstone, limestone, shale, fire clay, etc. The seams or veins of coal that exist in the general section of Illinois geology, are numbered from 1 to 10 includes, No. 1 being the lowest down, nearest the Chester limestone. Those that are worked in Gallatin County are Nos. 1, 2, 3, 4, 5, 6 and 7.

■ No. 1, half a mile above Sellers' paper-mill is ninety-five feet above low water, and at T. Rees & Co.'s mines it is 122 feet above.

■ No. 2, the "four foot seam," is reached by a shaft on the Saline River, at the Independent Coal Company's mines, where it is four feet thick and of excellent quality for steam and manufacturing purposes. The space between Nos. 1 and 2 is about 140 feet.

■ No. 3 is not so good as No. 2, because of the presence of sulphur.

■ No. 5 lies eight to 100 feet above No. 4, and has been reached by boring on Eagle Creek in Section 13, Township 10, Range 8. It has furnished fuel for Ross' mill at Equality, about two miles southwest of which place it has been worked by drifting into the hill, and where it furnished fuel to evaporate the brine of the salt works under Castle & Temple.

■ No. 5 is five feet thick, No. 6 two feet six inches, No. 7 four to seven feet, No. 8 two feet, and No. 9, consisting of shale and thin coal, three feet.

- No. 6 has not been worked of recent years.
- No. 7 outcrop on both sides of Coal Hill and has been opened in various places.

Coal was first mined in Gallatin County, above two miles from Equality, a little to the west of north, and hauled to that place over bad roads, it not being then known that every one could have a coal mine in his own door yard, if he so chose.

Above the coal measures in the upper carboniferous is the quaternary formation, represented by the drift and loess deposits. The drift occupies the hills and ridges all over the county and is from ten to twenty feet thick. It is composed chiefly of yellow clay, and contains occasionally a granite or trappean boulder. The largest stranger of this kind of the county is about one and one-half feet long and one foot broad. The loess is from ten to forty feet thick and occupies to the tops of the ridges from Shawneetown to New Haven. This deposit contains an abundance of land and fresh water shells, belonging most to species now living in this State.

There is an abundance of building stone all along the Gold Hill Ridge, along Eagle Creek and its tributaries, at Equality and at New Haven. A black septaria limestone is also found at Shawneetown, when the water in the Ohio River is low; but it obtainable in such limited quantities as to but little value in building. Quick-lime is derived from the Chester limestone in Gold Hill Ridge. Good brick clay is found in most parts of the county, and potters' clay, it is believed, may also be found.

Soil and Natural Productions

The soil in the eastern part of the county is derived from the washing of the quaternary and carboniferous strata, and by inundations of the Ohio. It is a sandy loam and is especially adapted to the raising of Indian corn. The other varieties of soil are the calcareous clay soil derived from the loess along the ridges between Shawneetown and the Little Wabash, which ranks next in fertility to the sandy loam of the river bottoms. The sedimentary clay loam along the main Saline and its principal tributary, the North Fork, which is compact and tenacious, and which in its native state is not adapted to either extremely wet or extremely dry seasons, could be brought by a thorough system of under-draining into a high state of cultivation; and the yellowish, gravelly clay land in the northwestern part of the county is derived from the drift, as the former is derived mainly from the argillaceous shale of the coal measures. This is particularly well adapted to the growth of all the cereals, grasses and clover.

There is an abundance of timber in this county. In the river bottoms large black walnut, oak and hickory are its principal trees. By some of the ponds and sloughs and in the low wetlands post oak prevails.

Saltworks of Gallatin County

The ancient salt works

Besides the above mentioned valuable beds of mineral wealth and other natural resources with which the county is supplied, the salt springs have in the past been sources of great wealth, and have had much to do with shaping the character of the population, not only in Gallatin county, but also to a limited extent that of the southern part of Illinois. The streams are fed by numerous saline springs, and Saline River was named from the fact that its tributaries are thus fed.

The only place, however, where profitable brine has been found in the county is on Section 19, Township 9, Range 8 East of the principal meridian, about a mile north of Equality and hear the Half Moon Lick, a semi-circular excavation made long before the settlement of the country by white people, by buffaloes and other wild animals, which assembled here in vast herds to lick the salty earth. This remarkable excavation is in the shape of a horseshoe, and is from twelve to sixteen feet deep. From point to point it is about 200 yards, and from a line connecting the points to the toe, or back of the curve, 250 yards. Descending into this lick are still to be seen deeply trodden buffalo roads. The measurements here given were made by B. Temple.

In the long ago when the present site of the salt works was an alluvial swamp, this locality was a favorite resort of the mammoth and the mastodon, for from time to time numerous bones of these extinct animals have been found. After the retirement of the mammoth and the mastodon from this region, or after their extinction, these salt springs, according to tradition sustained by abundant evidence as to its truth, were extensively worked by the native Indians.

The evaporating kettles used by them, a few entire, and innumerable fragments of broken ones, were found near the Negro Salt Well and the Half Moon Lick, when the brine first commenced to be evaporated in territorial times. These kettles were from three to four feet in diameter and were made of siliceous clay and pounded shells, and the innumerable fragments found over a large extent of territory and to considerable depths in the soil, suggest, if they do not prove, the prehistoric existence of an Indian pottery manufactory at this locality, to which, in the light of recent investigations by George E. Sellers, who now is living at Bowlesville, extraordinary interest attaches as being the place where, through his investigations, the problem of the method of making this pottery has been solved, and the solution through rather tardily, accepted by all the eminent archæologists of the present day.

They were made upon a mold of stones and clay in an inverted position, and polished smooth. From the laminated structure of the fragments, the clay and broken shell cement appear to have been put on this mold in layers, and every fresh layer firmly compressed upon the previous one until the desired thickness was obtained, when a thin layer or even a wash of river silt or mud was applied, and lastly a cloth was wrapped around the whole. When it became necessary to remove the cloth a slight surface moistening would accomplish the object without injury, and the river-silt was sufficiently siliceous to become in the process of time, when in contact with a body of lime cement, almost as hard as the cement itself. That this river silt was applied for this purpose seems to be fully established by the fact that in no instance was there found this coating or any impression of the cloth on the bottoms of the kettles.

The materials used in weaving this cloth were generally the fiber of bark, of flax, of hemp, of grass, etc., spun into thread of various sizes, or splinters of wood, twigs, roots, vines, porcupine quills, feathers and a variety of other animal tissues, either plaited or in an untwisted state, the articles woven consisting of mats, nets, bags, plain cloths and entire garments, such as capes, belts and sandals. The kettles or vessels, when sufficiently dry to be lifted from the mold, were so lifted by means of wedges driven under the edges, thus permitting the drying process to proceed without cracking the kettles, which were then thoroughly sun-dried before being used. That they were not baked in the fire is clear from the fact that it would thus be impossible to bake them evenly, and that when so heated and moisture afterward applied to them, they crumble into dust by the slacking o the lime in the broken shells of which they are in part composed.

Indian mounds

Numerous mounds still exist along the ancient trail from near New Haven to the Negro Salt Well, and up and down the Saline River on either side extending down into Hardin County.

One mound in this latter series named Dutton's Mound, just below the line of Gallatin, is one of the most interesting in the State. It is oval in form, and has a flat top about 80 feet long by 35 feet in width. The interesting feature of Dutton's Mound is this, that it was, when discovered, paved or covered with layers of stones all around its sides up to the truncated top, the layers forming terraces or steps, and the steps covered in such manner with smaller stones to fill up the angles, and render the sloping sides of the mound smooth. Mounds are found built in the same manner in Mexico and Central America, which seems to indicate that this southern Illinois mound was erected by the same tribe or nation as were those in the countries farther south.

The largest mound, however, in southern Illinois, is known as Boyd's Mound, situated nearly five miles north of Shawneetown. This mound, otherwise known as Sugar Loaf mound, was visited at least as early as 1809 by Stephen Fields and James Fields.

In 1855 its dimensions were taken and found to be: area of base four acres, and perpendicular height 55 feet. It is apparently filled with human skeletons, as pieces are constantly being taken out on the top and on the sides, suggesting the possibility of its having been built as an elevated sepulcher, increasing in height as the bodies of the dead were deposited upon it and covered up with earth, which appears to have been brought from a pond, now filing up, about three-fourths of a mile to the northward. The mound could not have been erected for an observatory, as there are hills to the south and southwest higher than the mound, and at no great distance; neither could it have been necessary to enable its builders to escape the overflow of the Ohio River, for the same reason; and there have been as yet no evidences found to is having been designed as a religious temple; though when opened, as is now the intention of Squire William J. Boyd, what discovered may be made within it is impossible to conjecture.

Government leases of the salt works

How long the Indians worked the salt springs mentioned above is not known; but on the 12th of February 1812, Congress set apart of tract of land six miles square[3] to support the works, and leased the springs to Phillip Trammel, mentioned elsewhere as one of the first legislators from Gallatin County. The work was performed mostly by Negroes from Kentucky and Tennessee, to which reference is made in the constitution of 1818, Article VI, Section 2, as follows:

> No person bound to labor in any other State shall be hired to labor in this State, except within the tract reserved for the salt works near Shawneetown; nor even at that place for a longer period than one year at one time; nor shall it be allowed there after the year 1825. Any violation of this article shall effect the emancipation of such person from his obligation to service.

Many of the Negroes engaged at these salt works, by extra labor, saved money enough to buy their freedom, and were the progenitors of the large number that lived in Gallatin and Saline Counties before the war. The salt manufactured here under the Government leases was sold at $5 per bushel, and found a ready market in Indiana, Kentucky, Tennessee, Alabama and Missouri. It was transferred by keel boats up the Tennessee and Cumberland Rivers, and also up the Mississippi to St. Louis.

Salt lands granted to the state

At the time of the admission of Illinois into the Union, Congress gave these lands to the State, which continued the lease system until about 1840, the last lease being made to John Crenshaw, December 9, of that year. Mr. Crenshaw became a very wealthy man, and exercised large political influence in the southeastern portion of the State. After the establishment of salt works on the Kanawha River in Virginia,[4] and at Pomeroy, Ohio, the mines in Gallatin County could no longer compete in the market. In 1847 the lands were sold, that portion containing the salt wells being purchased by the school trustees of Township 9, Range 9.[5]

---

[3] Although initially correct, Congress later increased the reservation to an area 12 miles from east to west (approximately from Eldorado to Ridgway on the north side) and 10 miles from north to south (the ridge of hills to the south), plus a "tail" attached on the southeast corner on both sides of the Saline River down to its mouth. The tail was anywhere from one to three miles in width.

[4] Now West Virginia.

[5] This is incorrect. The General Assembly passed legislation transferring ownership of the previously state-owned saline lands to the two boards of school trustees of Township 9 South, Range 7 East (which is now part of Saline County) and Township 9 South, Range 8 East (which is now Equality Township in Gallatin County). The 1852 auction date is also wrong. At a joint meeting of the two boards of township school trustees on April 16, 1853, Thomas Clark, John Slaten and Jonathan B. Moore of the western township, and Wm. D. Greetham, Abner Flanders and Wm. Siddall of the eastern township voted to auction off the lands two months later on June 16, 1853. [Source: V. H. Crest, trans. 1939. *Entries and Notes from Old School Records*. Unpublished MSS. 6.]

In 1852 the lands were sold at public auction, and in 1854 Castle & Temple, the present proprietors, commenced to bore a new and deeper well, and began the manufacture of salt by an improved system which had its origin in France. The first brine was struck at a depth of 108 feet, and at 1,100 feet, the boring stopped, the brine obtained marking 7.2° of Baume's saltometer, and requiring only seventy-five gallons to make a bushel of salt-fifty pounds. The State geologist believes that at this depth, 1,100 feet, the Chester limestone was struck, and it forms the basis of the muriatiferous rocks in this pat of the State. As late as 1870 it was no uncommon thing to see from three to four wagons, each drawn by from four to six mules, on the road from Equality to Shawneetown, laden with salt for the various markets in the South and West; but in 1873, in consequence of the panic, overproduction and ruinous prices, Castle & Temple closed the works, and on the same property engaged in mining and making coke.

Early settlement of the county

When the first white man arrived in Gallatin County to make a permanent settlement the Indians occupied it only occasionally, and then only as a hunting-ground. This first white man was in all probability Michael Sprinkle,[6] but where he came from can not be ascertained.[7] He settled on the present site of Shawneetown, about the year 1800. He was a blacksmith and gunsmith, and for this and other reasons was a great favorite among the roaming bands of Indians, as well as with the early settlers as they came straggling in. He resided in Shawneetown until about 1814, when he moved about four miles into the country, on the poorest piece of land he could have found in the county, if to live on poor land had been his desire, but the location was chosen not on account of the sterility of the soil, but because of the existence there of a never failing spring.

Among the early settlers were the following, most of whom were here previous to 1815: Jacob Barger, Samuel Hayes, Joseph Hayes, John Marshall, Michael Robinson, Humphreys

---

[6] Sprinkle is more accurately described as the first permanent American settler of Gallatin County in the 19th Century to have stayed around long enough for people to remember him. John McElduff, better known as Duff the counterfeiter lived in the area as early as the 1770s and had been removed by soldiers from Fort Massac for making salt at the salines prior to his death on June 4, 1799.

[7] Sprinkle is now believed to have moved to the site of Shawneetown from Vincennes (or that general area of Indiana). Earlier in 1792, he, his parents and siblings, lived at Red Banks, Kentucky, now the present site of Henderson, on the Ohio River above Evansville. On April 8, 1793, a small party of Indians killed Michael's 17 or 18-year-old brother Peter and kidnapped another brother George while they and three other youths tended livestock across the Ohio River from Red Banks. The Indians ransomed George at Fort Wayne about 1794. Another brother, John Sprinkle was the first permanent settler of Warrick Co., Ind., Born in Pennsylvania in 1772, he moved to Indiana in 1803, and settled at Newburg, Warrick County, where he died, 1821. John served as a major in the Kentucky militia. One source says the Indians captured his brother George, during the Miami war, about 1790, but the 1793 date is confirmed by the writings of one of the other boys captured. [Sources: Edmund L. Starling. 1887. *History of Henderson Co., Kentucky*. 104-105; *Indiana Magazine of History*. 24:308; and Hiram H. Hunter. 1839, Reprint 1904. *The Story of Isaac Knight, Indian Captive*. Overbrook, Kan.: The Overbrook Citizen. Accessed online at http://www.cumberland.org/hfcpc/minister/KnightI.htm.]

Leich, Stephen Fields, Thornton Tally, John Herrod, John Martin, Isaac Baldwin, Adrian Davenport, James Davenport, Michael Jones, Frederick Buck, William Akers, Andrew Slack, James M. Pettigrew, Abraham T. McCool, John Scroggins, O. C. Vanlandingham, John Walden, Henry Ledbetter and Dr. John Reid.

In the northwestern part of the county there were a Mr. Dunn, Mr. Hurd, Abraham Armstrong, Allen Dugger, John Kinsall, Charles Edwards, Sr., John Edwards, Benjamin Kinsall, Sr., James Trousdale and Mr. Orr. It is believed that the first settler on the present site of Omaha was a Mr. Perry. Zephrania Johns settled on the site of Omaha, in 1825. He sold his improvements to Rev. William Davis, who entered the land in 1833. The first post office in this region was at South Hampton, at the residence of David Keasler, the first postmaster. It was discontinued because of the railroads passing on both sides of it. The first election was held at the house of John Kinsall where Moses Kinsall now resides, a short distance east of Omaha.

Troubles with Indians

Indian Attack

From 1812 to 1815, the settlers in Southern Illinois were much troubled by the Shawnee tribe of Indians. About that time a boy by the name of Maurice Hyde was attacked in Reuben Beller's by two Indians, which was at the time occupied by an old man and some children, left alone because of a gathering in the neighborhood. The children were out playing Indian, when these two Indians came up; one of the boys gave the alarm, but Maurice thought it was only a pretended alarm, so was caught and carried away. The Indians were pursued by the rangers who captured one of the Indians and took his scalp, and ran the other into the river who soon afterward died. Maurice was recovered and restored to his friends.[8]

Shawnee – Kaskaskia Clash

Another incident was somewhat as follows: A portion of the Shawnee tribe, which was then living up on the Wabash, came to Shawneetown, and there met a portion of another tribe, believed to have been the Kaskaskias, the main body of which was living near the Mississippi. Between these two tribes there had been some difficulty,[9] and the chiefs of both these factions which met in Shawneetown, made a tour of the saloons and made earnest request of all not to sell to any of their warriors any fire water, knowing that if any of them should obtain fire water, trouble would be the result. All the saloon-keepers complied with this reasonable request but one living in the south part of the town. At this establishment some of the Indians secured some whisky, the old feud was fanned into a flame, a quarrel and a fight ensued, and one of the Shawnees was killed. The Kaskaskias engaged in the

---

[8] More information on Indian skirmishes and attacks can be found in the Military History section of his volume.

[9] See the "First Salt War" and "Second Salt War" stories later in this volume for a little on the "difficulties" between the Shawnee and Kaskaskia tribes.

killing immediately sought safety in flight, and other members of the tribe, in order to appease the Shawnees, proposed to pursue the murderers, and bring one of them back dead or alive. In due course of time they returned with the head of the Kaskaskia who had struck the fatal blow and peace was restored. After being fed by the citizens of Shawneetown, until this affair was settled the Indians all took their departure, much to the relief of the white people.

The Swapping of Alexander Reid

Still another was the following: Dr. John Reid mentioned elsewhere as an early settler, father of Mrs. S. C. Rowan, still living on the old homestead about two miles north of Shawneetown in what was then known as Sugar Grove, at the age of eighty-two, was one day away from home, when a part of Indians called at the house. Alexander Reid was then an infant, and Mrs. Reid had him nicely dressed and lying in the cradle. One of the squaws had her dirty little papoose strapped on her back, and all at once admiring little Alexander so neat and clean, exclaimed "me swap," and instantly made the exchange and the party started off for their camp, on the ridge in town.

Mrs. Reid being alone was helpless and was filled with astonishment and dismay. Dr. Reid soon came home and found his wife almost crazed with grief at the loss of her babe. But he was a man of resources, and after soothing his wife, suggested that she scrub up the little red stranger, put some good, clean clothes on him, and taken him into camp. Although it was an unpleasant task, it was the only course to pursue, so she polished up the little papoose, put on a clean frock, combed out his straight black hair, and made him look like a new creature. She then shouldered him and took him into camp, and exhibited him to his surprised mother, who when she saw him looking so neat and clean at once proposed to swap back, which Mrs. Reid was only to glad to do.

Land entries

While quite a number of settlers came early into the county the land office was not opened at Shawneetown until 1814, and then no land entries were made until July of that year. The following is a complete list of all the land entries made during the year 1814, showing the names of many of the early settlers and the locations in the county which they preferred. So far as was learned from the entry book, the first entry was made on July 7, 1814, by John Black, of the northwest quarter of Section 19, Township 10 south, Range 9 east; on the 19th of the month Jephthah Hardin entered the southwest quarter of Section 7, Township 9, Range 10; on the 21st of the month Warren Buck entered the southeast quarter of Section 17, Township 9, Range 10; Thomas McGehee, the southwest quarter of Section 33, Township 9, Range 9; and Jesse B. Thomas, the southwest quarter of Section 23, Township 9, Range 9. On the 25th, John Reid entered the northeaster quarter of Section 19, Township 9, Range 10; Michael Jones, the southeast quarter of Section 19, Township 9, Range 10; and Archibald Roberts, the southeast quarter of Section 23, Township 9, Range 9. On the 26th, M. Jones, the west half of Section 3, Township 10, Range 9, and , the southeast quarter of Section 34, Township 9, Range 9; on the 27th, Henry Boyer, the southeast quarter of Section 12, Township 9, Range 9; and on the 28th, Edward Farley, the northwest quarter of Section 19, Township 9, Range 10.

The entries in August were: On the 5th, Thomas Hayes, northwest quarter of Section 1, Township 9, Range 9; on the 10th, James Dillard southwest quarter of Section 14, Township 9, Range 9; on the 19th, Lewis Kuykendall, southeast quarter of Section 5, Township 10, Range 9; on the 24th, George Patterson, northeast quarter of Section 20, Township 7, Range 10; and Thomas M. Dorris, southeastern quarter of Section 24, Township 8, Range 9, and on the 25th, James Willis, northwest quarter of Section 33, Township 9, Range 9.

The following are the entries made in September on the 1st: Stephen Clautau, southwest quarter of Section 5, Township 10, Range 9; on the 5th William McCay, northwest quarter of Section 8, Township 9, Range 10; on the 9th, Thornton Talley, northwest quarter of Section 14, Township 9, Range 9; on the 10th, Michael Sprinkle, southwest quarter of Section 8, Township 9, Range 10, and on the 12th, Daniel McKinley, northeast quarter of Section 32, Township 9, Range 9.

In October the following: On the 6th, James Morris, southeast quarter of Section 1, Township 8, Range 9; on the 10th, James M. Pettigrew, northeast quarter of Section 8, Township 9, Range 10, and William Wheeler, southwest quarter of Section 9, Township 10, Range 9; on the 12th, Isaac Hagan, northeast quarter of Section 9, Township 10, Range 9, and Merrel Willis, northwest quarter of Section 5, Township 10, Range 9; on the 14th, William Kelly, northwest quarter of Section 9, Township 9, Range 10; on the 15th, White, Dawson & Brown, southeast, northeast and northwest quarters of Section 1, Township 10, Range 9, and John Forrester, northeaster quarter of Section 2, Township 10, Range 9; on the 17th, John Willis, northeast quarter of Section 3, Township 10, Range 9; and Meredith K. Fisher, northwest quarter of Section 23, Township 9, Range 9, who had entered the southwest quarter of the same section on the 4th; on the 18th, Littlepage Proctor, northwest quarter of Section 10, Township 10, Range 9; on the 19th, Cornelius Lafferty, southwest quarter of Section 35, Township 9, Range 9; on the 20th, Samuel Clark, southeast quarter of Section 2, Township 10, Range 9; on the 23d, Samuel Green, southwest quarter of Section 18, Township 9, Range 10; on the 25th, Baston Banewood,[10] southeast quarter of Section 22, Township 9, Range 9; Samuel Clark, northeast quarter of Section 23, Township 9, Range 9, Annesley Clark, east half of the northeast quarter of Section 2, Township 8, Range 9 and John Carter, southeast quarter of Section 13, Township 9, range 9; on the 29th, Thomas Dawson, northwest quarter of Section 2, Township 10, Range 9; on the 31st, John Groves, northwest quarter of Section 29, Township 7, Range 10, and Joseph Scott, east half of the northeast quarter of Section 15, Township 9, Range 9.

In November the following: On the 2d, Jerrett Trammel, southwest quarter of Section 19, Township 10, Range 9; on the 4th, William Castle, east half of the northeast quarter of Section 13, Township 9, Range 9; on the 7th, Daniel McKinley, southeast quarter of section 29, Township 9, Range 9; on the 12th, Peter Baker, southeast quarter of section 9, Township 10, Range 9; on the 14th, Warren Buck, east half of the southwest quarter of Section 15, Township 8, Range 10; Hazle Moreland, northwest quarter of Section 34, Township 9, Range 9, and James Moreland, west half of the northeast quarter of Section 23, Township 19, Range 9; on the 17th, James Weir, southwest quarter of Section 5, Township 9, Range 10;

---

[10] This probably should be Boston Daimwood.

Andrew Slack, southwest quarter of Section 4, Township 9, range 10, and Edward Gattu, southwest quarter of Section 10, Township 10, Range 9; on the 22^d, John Ewing, northeast quarter of Section 27, Township 9, Range 9; on the 25th, Frederick Buck, Section 22, Township 8, Range 10, and on the 26th, Moses M. Rawlings, southeast quarter of Section 4, Township 10, Range 9.

The following are the entries for December: On the 3^d, John Caldwell, west half of Section 19, Township 9, Range 10; Joseph M. Street, southeastern quarter of Section 5, Township 9, Range 10; Samuel W. Kimberly, northwest quarter of Section 35, Township 9, Range 9; on the 5th, Thomas M. Dorris, southwest quarter of Section 19, Township 8, Range 10; on the 8th, Stephen Fields, northeast quarter of Section 14, Township 9, Range 9; on the 14th, Housan Fletcher, southwest quarter of Section 4, Township 10, Range 9; on the 29th, Jephthah Hardin, fractional Section 30, Township 9, Range 10, and on the 31st, George Sexton, southeast quarter of Section 36, Township 9, Range 10.

In 1816 there were nearly 20 land entries made by different individuals, among them some of those whom we have already enumerated Michael Jones, John Reid and Joseph M. Street. The latter entered two and a quarter sections on the 25th of February: Sections 24 and 25, and the northeast quarter of Section 26, Township 9, Range 9, on which Shawneetown is located; and Michael Robinson, on the 23^d of September, entered the southwest quarter of Section 12 Township 9, Range 9.[11]

Some of those who made entries in 1817 were Robert Peeples, on May 22, the east half of the southeast quarter of Section 36, Township 7, Range 9; Rachael McGehee, December 18, the east half of the northwest quarter of Section 28, Township 9, Range 9, and R. Peeples and J. Kirkpatrick, January 11, the southwest quarter of Section 30, Township 7, Range 10.

In 1818 Ephraim Hubbard, on the 24th of April, entered the northwest quarter of Section 35, Township 8, Range 9, and Martin P. Frazier, on the 13th of May, entered the west half of Section 15, Township 10, Range 9. There were many other entries made, a list of which it is deemed unnecessary to give.[12]

Slaves and Indentured Servants

Most of the early settlers of this county came from some one of the Southern States: Kentucky, Virginia, Tennessee, and in some few instances from Georgia and Alabama. Many of those, but not all who came brought with them slaves, with transcripts of the evidence of ownership from the records of the counties from which they emigrated, which transcripts were duly recorded in Gallatin County. Some of those who brought slaves either upon or after arriving in the county, set them free, either in consideration of past faithful services, or of money. In this way large numbers of Negroes and mulattoes of different degrees of

---

[11] Although the original history gives the year 1816, at least some of these entries took place in 1815. Only Robinson's entry in September appears in the records as 1816. The dating appears to be correct in the next paragraph. Peeples did make his entry in 1817.

[12] Luckily for genealogists the Illinois State Archives has this information online in database form on the Illinois Secretary of State's website at www.sos.state.il.us.

darkness found themselves in southern Illinois, and resided here either as free persons, or as indentured servants, mostly of the time up to the breaking out of the war.

The following is a form of indenture usually employed, and the one given is the first one upon the records of Gallatin County:

> THIS INDENTURE made and entered into this 5th day of July, 1814, between William Killis, mulatto man about the age of 25, and Joseph M. Street, both of Shawneetown, Gallatin County, in the Illinois Territory, witnesseth, that for and in consideration of $200, by the said Joseph to the said William in had paid, the receipt whereof is hereby acknowledged, the said William hath placed and bound himself to the said Joseph as a servant for the full term of four years from the date hereof, or, in other words, until the 5th day of July, 1818, and the said Joseph agrees on his part to furnish the said William with everything proper for him, and the said William, on his part, agrees to act and demean himself in an orderly and proper manner in his capacity of servant.
>
> In testimony whereof we have hereunto set our hands and seals the day and year above written.
>
>   *His*
>   William *X* Killis.
>   *mark*
> Test: Joseph M. Street
> Thomas Posey.
> Fayette Posey.

Indentured servants always made their mark. The last record upon the books devoted to recording the movements and status of colored persons, was made September 1, 1862, and had reference to Carolina Sanders, late slave of Gen. Pillow, of the Rebel Army. She was brought to Shawneetown on that day by James B. Turner, and asserted her right to freedom under the confiscation act of the General Government. James B. Turner certified to the facts as asserted by Carolina, and gave bond to the county that she should not become a county charge.[13]

Because of the prejudices of many of the people then against the Negro, and of their frequent attempts to steal them and sell them into slavery in the Southern States, great trouble frequently arose; many cruelties and outrages upon their rights were perpetrated by persons, some of whom are still living, who would, with their present enlightened views of justice, crimson to the temples to see their names published in connection with the crimes they once thought it a duty to commit, but which names frequently appear on the records of the circuit court, in indictments for kidnapping.

It was frequently necessary for a free Negro to prove to the court that he was free. Following is the record of a case of this kind:

---

[13] Compare this act by Turner with his despicable tactics a month later in Saline County in the Anecdotes section.

Wednesday, September 11, 1839.

Mary Smith, a woman of color, vs. Benjamin Lafferty and John Cook. This day came the plaintiff by her attorneys, and the said defendants. The suit hath been brought by the plaintiff to establish her right and that of her children to freedom under the constitution and laws of the State. It was agreed by the defendants she and they are free so far as they know or believe, and they consent that the said plaintiff may have judgment accordingly, and that each shall pay their own costs. It is therefore considered by the court that the said plaintiff recover her freedom for herself and her said children as against the said defendants.[14]

Following is an illustration of the method of procedure when a Negro could not prove his freedom to the court.

Monday, September 14, 1840.

This day came into open court William Wilburn, a man of color, who produced to the court the certificate of the sheriff of this county, whereby it is shown to the court here that the said William was legally committed to the custody of the said sheriff as a runaway; that the said William produced no certificate or other evidence of his freedom to the said sheriff within the time limited by law; he, the said William, was regularly hired out from month to month for the space of one year, notice according to law frequently given; and it further appearing that due notice by publication in a public newspaper printed in said state has been given by the said sheriff, as required by the section of an act respecting free Negroes, mulattoes, servants and slaves approved January 17, 1829, and that no owner hath appeared to substantiate his claim to said Negro within one year from his commitment aforesaid; whereupon the said William moved the court that it be certified that he be henceforth deemed a free person, unless he shall be lawfully claimed by a proper owner or owners, hereafter, and it is by the court ordered to be and it is hereby ordered accordingly.

Regulators and Vigilantes

Excitement ran very high about 1840, and for a few years afterward about Negroes living in the State. The excited state of feeling resulted in the organization of a body of men calling themselves "Regulators," whose purpose was to force all Negroes without regard to age, sex or condition, to leave the county. This movement had its origin in the fact that some time previously John Crenshaw sold a family of Negroes to a Mr. Kuykendall. This Negro

---

[14] This Mary Smith is believed to be the same one whose children had been kidnapped and were the subject of a rescue effort being organized in 1840. Henry Eddy and Harrison Wilson played roles in this effort. This Mary Smith is also believed to be the sister of Bryant Smith, a free black minister living next to John Hart Crenshaw in the 1840 census when Crenshaw had moved to Cypressville (modern-day Junction).

family considered, it is believed, of indentured servants.[15] Kuykendall ran the Negroes out of the state, and as a result of this action by Kuykendall, both he and Crenshaw were indicted by the grand jury for kidnapping. At the term of court held early in 1842, Crenshaw was acquitted because the State's attorney could not prove that the Negroes were taken out of the Stated, although it was well known to the community to be the case. It was asserted in connection with this case that Negroes were the best laborers in the county, that they were no more frequently guilty of crimes than white people, and that when guilty they were most certainly punished. Some time previously, Benjamin Hardin had been cruelly murdered, and it was attempted to show that the Negroes had something to do with it, and while it was proved that the murder was committed by a Negro, who was hired to commit the crime by another Negro, yet it was believe then, and is now, by a large number of people, that a certain leading white man was the real instigator of the crime, yet, as the name of this leading business man was never connected with the case in law, it can not judiciously be connected with it in history. The murder of Hardin was characterized at the time as

> "the most wicked, the most cruel, the most cold-blooded and horrible ever committed in a civilized community—a murder so wanton, so deliberately planned and executed, so foul and atrocious that the Almighty, in his wrath, smote the spot upon which it was perpetrated and the country all around, involving in one sheet of flame, the forests, the fences, the houses, the grass of the ravine-the very post from which the murdered man fell, covering the entire premises with the black grapery of mourning, which may be seen unto this day-a mark of the indignation of the Most High—a memento of the fate of the unfortunate Hardin."[16]

The writer of the above characterization, Samuel D. Marshall, was one of the ablest editors and lawyers that ever resided in Shawneetown. He was sufficiently rational and just to wish to see crime punished but at the same time not so unreasonable as to condemn an entire race for the crimes of the individual; hence his position was that of a defender and protector of the oppressed. Hence, also, it was that in his paper, the *Illinois Republican*, he condemned the proceedings of the regulators as disgraceful and unjustifiable,

> "conspiring as they had done to drive all of the Negroes out of the country, good and bad, lazy and industrious, old and young; those who had property and those who had not-all must go, and with a notice of only a week. He were a vast

---

[15] The kidnapped members of this family included Maria Adams and seven or eight of her children. One of the children may have been Nancy Jane Adams. While Maria still had time left on her indenture, Crenshaw had only properly registered Nancy Jane's birth. Thus, he had no legal claim to the remaining children, or the right to sell them. Kuykendall took the family to Texas. Henry Eddy, John Marshall and others were involved in an attempt to rescue the family in the first part of 1847. It is unknown if they succeeded.

[16] It is not known how this Benjamin Hardin connects with the rest of the Hardin families in Illinois and Kentucky. Jephtha Hardin of Shawneetown served as executor of Benjamin's estate suggesting a family relationship, even as close as a son or nephew. This Benjamin is not Jephtha's half-brother, the great lawyer and orator Ben Hardin of Kentucky.

number of Negroes, many of them honest, industrious and good citizens, forced to sacrifice theirs lives or their property within seven days. No such procedure can ever be justified in a free country. Any combination which proposes to violate the laws of security in person and in property, guaranteed to all our citizens, white or black, which sets up its own arbitrary will in opposition to that of the people, subverts our form of government, and leads directly to anarchy and eventually to despotism."

In the list of regulators were the names of many young men who were otherwise men of respectability and character; but as a general thing the bands of regulators were composed of bad men, who wished to screen themselves from deserved punishment and have some one else punished for crimes of which they were guilty. The *Illinois Republican* argued forcibly that every man who loved liberty must adhere to law as the sheet anchor of his own security, as nowhere else, but in the law are liberty and security guaranteed. As instancing the character of the regulators the *Republican* recorded the fact that in March or April, 1842, several regulators went to the house of an old and inoffensive Negro for the purpose of "regulating him," that is, of whipping and terrifying him.

Among those thus visiting the old Negro was a man named John Moore, otherwise known as "Leather Moore," because of his having been tired and convicted of stealing leather in Gallatin County. Most of the "boys" with whom Moore was with when they arrived at the old Negro's house, thought it would be a shame to whip the old man and left without doing so, not withstanding that Moore was strongly in favor of the proceeding.

A redoubtable corps of regulators made a raid into Shawneetown, on Saturday, April 9, 1842, in battle array. The poor Negroes heard of the coming of the corps in time, and soon were as scarce as squirrels on a windy day. Not a single woolly head was anywhere to be seen, and it was not long before the brave regulators began to fear that their honorable services were not in need at that particular time and place, and that they would have to be contented with the laurels of the past. Soon, however first one and then another and finally several of the good citizens of the place began to take compassion upon them and addressed them thus:

"Gentlemen regulators we suppose you would be glad of a chance to regulate some Negroes."

"Yes, yes," they responded on all sides, and then from numerous persons in the town the invitation was extended to the brave and public-spirited citizens to go down to such and such houses, and "regulate" such Negroes as were there to be found. But the invitations were universally declined for prudential reasons, and after one of their number made the following speech they left the town:

"Gentlemen, we were merely passing through your town, and did not intent to stop. If you will drop the matter, we will."

Such outrages, however, carried with them to a considerable extent their own antidote. Violent proceedings were revolting to the majority of the best men in the community, and unsustained by public sentiment must necessarily cease. All reflecting men soon began to regard the lawless assumption of power by individuals as a direct blow at the liberties of all.

But these did not cease without calling into existence a band of vigilantes under the command of M. K. Lawler to operate against them, which band did noble work in aiding the Negro to enjoy his liberties in the southeastern counties of Illinois, and the services of Capt. Lawler and his men deserve a fitting tribute in the history of the times.

Case of the Prather Negroes

In 1851 an attempted murder was developed in connection with a case of kidnapping. Mrs. Prather, formerly from Weakley County, Tenn., having emancipated her slaves, they removed to Gallatin County. To this county they were followed by parties from their former home, who conspired to arrest them as fugitive slaves.[17] The United States District Court decided that the conspirators had no claim to the colored people. Connected with the conspirators was a man named Newton E. Wright, who had long been in the business of kidnapping, and who, while in Gallatin County, attempted to reclaim the Prather Negroes as fugitives, formed the acquaintance of another notorious kidnapper, named Joe O'Neal of Hamilton County. With O'Neal was associated Abe Thomas, a disreputable character. After this attempt in Gallatin County O'Neal stole three children from an old Negro in Hamilton County, named Scott, ran them off and sold them to Wright, partly on credit, who resold them at New Madrid to a man named Phillips. When O'Neal's note matured he sent Thomas to collect it, telling him further that Wright had business with him for which he would be well paid.

Arriving at Wright's he agreed to kill a Dr. Swayne of Hicco, Tenn., for $150, who had sued Wright for $8,000. If Dr. Swayne could be killed, Wright could successfully defend the suit by means of nicely forged receipts.

In May, 1850, a man calling himself Stewart rode up to the house of Dr. Swayne, with the request that he pay a professional visit to his father, who was sick a little distance from the Doctor's house. After proceeding some distance Stewart fell a little behind and shot the Doctor, the shot badly fracturing his arm. A cry of murder being raised, Stewart effected his escape, and every effort made failed to find the assassin.

In the next year two citizens of White County, John and Shannon Eubanks, father and son, went to Tennessee with a lot of horses for sale. While in the neighborhood of Dr. Swayne's they heard him relate the particulars of the attempt at his assassination and give a minute description of the attempted assassin. Shannon Eubanks knew the description applied to Abe Thomas, who was stopping at Joe O'Neal's in Hamilton County. Soon afterward Thomas was seized by some Tennesseans and taken to that State for trial.[18]

---

[17] The emancipation records identify Mrs. Prather as Martha Prather.

[18] An original footnote at this point in Goodspeed's History notes this the source of this as taken from Davidson & Stuve's *History of Illinois*. They in turn took the story from an 1851 issue of the *Shawneetown Mercury*. The attempted murder in this case did not take place in 1851 as Goodspeed's History implies, but in 1850. The newspaper didn't report the story until the following year when the Eubanks recognized the description of Thomas.

Last Attempt to Return Slaves

The last effort to return fugitive slaves was made in the latter part of 1862.[19] It was reported that there was a fugitive from labor harbored at the house of Stephen R. Rowan, and a few pro-slavery men determined that he should be returned according to the Fugitive Slave Law.

At that time the rebel forces had possession of that portion of Kentucky opposite Shawneetown, and they had made frequent threats to sack and burn the town, and for this reason the meeting was not harmonious, there being some present at the meeting bold enough to protest against the return of the fugitive to rebels in arms against the Government, and strong enough to prevent any attack upon Mr. Rowan. The fugitive, therefore, was never returned.[20]

Wild Animals and Reptiles

Wolves for many years infested the woods and made things very unpleasant for the early settlers. In order to get rid of them it was found necessary to make it the interest of as many as possible to make an unrelenting war upon them. To this end an address was drawn up in the following words.

> To the wolf hunters of Gallatin County, Ill. – April 22, 1846 – We, the undersigned, agree to bind ourselves severally to pay to any person who may kill the old wolves in the districts of country in the following bounds.
>
> Beginning at the mouth of Big Eagle Creek, thence up same creek to Z. Malingly's, thence to White's Mill on the Saline, thence down the Saline to the beginning at the mouth of Big Eagle Creek, of if the wolves are started in the above bounds it matters not where they are killed, we the undersigned will pay the amounts annexed to our names for each and every old wolf, started in the above bounds, in good trade or case on or before the 25th day of September next.
>
> Any person being a subscriber to this paper who may bring the scalp to the town of Equality on the 1st day of November next, and prove the boundary in

---

[19] Here's a slightly different version of this account written by D. W. Lusk, who lived in Shawneetown at the time and may have even been in the crowd. It's found in his 1884 book, *Politics and Politicians: A Succinct History of the Politics of Illinois from 1856 to 1884.*

"About the last effort to return a slave from this State to his master, under the fugitive slave law, was made at Shawneetown in the latter part of 1862. It was reported that there was a fugitive from labor harbored at the house of Stephen R. Rowan, a prominent citizens, but who was then known as a Black Republican, whereupon a few pro-slavery men were called together for the purpose of determining upon measures for the return of the fugitive at any cost. At that time the Confederates had possession of that part of Kentucky near Shawneetown, and frequent threats had been made to sack and burn the town. Under these circumstances, this meeting was not altogether harmonious, there being one spirit among the number bold enough to protest against the return of the slave, and strong enough to deter the others from molesting Mr. Rowan in the possession of the supposed fugitive slave."

[20] Although he's not mentioned here, based on the events involving Dr. Mitchell in Saline County during this same time, James B. Turner is probably lurking in the background of this story as well.

which the wolf was started, or make affidavit to the same if required, shall be entitled to the amount of this subscription for each scalp so started and killed.

Subscribers' names and amounts

Benjamin White	$5.00	William Dorsey	50
Walter White	1 00	Thomas Dorsey	50
I D Bemin	1 00	David Williams	50
Nancy White	1 00	William Baldwin	1 00
John Baker	50	Benjamin Seawell	50
James Pruet	1 00	Philip Garrall	50
John Dorsey	1 00	Caleb Baldwin	50
John Williamson	1 00	James Willis	50
William Black	1 00	James Dorsey	50
Archibald Willis	1 00	Will G. Seawell	50
Lewis Seawell	50	Edward Lenwell, Jr.	50
Francis Williams	50	Valentine Christian	—

The language of the above agreement is scarcely to be taken literally, for if it were intended precisely as written, the "starting and killing of wolf scalps" within the bounds named would have been exceedingly profitable, more so probably than the kidnapping of free Negroes, in which too many of the inhabitants of southern Illinois and Kentucky were unjust enough to engage. According to the terms of the above agreement, each wolf scalp would bring to the hunter who should bring it in about $20, provided Valentine Christian, intended to subscribe 50 cents with the rest, which is probable. It is said, however, by old settlers that the intention was to raise a fund out of which $1 should be paid for each wolf scalp, which is more likely than that each subscribed meant to promise to pay the amount annexed to his name for each wolf scalp brought in.[21]

Wolves, however, although the most numerous, were not the only wild animals in the woods which annoyed the early settlers and raided upon their stock. There were catamounts and panthers, for the scalps of the former of which 50 cents each was paid, for those of the latter $2 each. There were also plenty of black bears, but so far as the writer knows, no price was put upon them. Besides wild animals there were large numbers of snakes, poisonous as well as innocuous. Of the poisonous snakes there were rattlesnakes, water moccasins and copperheads. The water moccasins were of two kinds—black with red bells, and mottled-brown and yellow. Regarding the number of the various kinds of snakes, it used to be said that a man in clearing a piece of land could kill upon it snakes enough to fence it, and it may be that the term "snake-fence," as applied to the crooked rail fence, had its origin in this exaggeration. But strange as it may at first appear, notwithstanding the immense numbers of these poisonous reptiles, very few persons, if any, were bitten by them to death, not even by the copperhead, the most deadly of all. The explanation for this fact lies in the correlative

---

[21] Lewis Seawell, Benjamin Seawell, Will G. Seawell and Edward Lenwell, Jr. should most likely be Lewis Leavell, Benjamin Leavell, Will G. Leavell and Edward Leavell, Jr. All four of these brothers lived in the area of Leavell (Level) Hill southwest of the Island Ripple. The author of the 1887 history must have mistook the cursive "L" for an "S" which is quite easy to confuse on some of the early records. Most of the men on this list can be placed in the area south of the modern Wildcat Hills on either side of Illinois Route 1 and north of Eagle Creek.

fact that the early settlers familiar with, and always had handy, the various efficacious Indian snake-bite remedies.

St. Clair and Randolph Counties

In order clearly to perceive the position of Gallatin county, in the chronological order of the organization of the counties, it is necessary to present as briefly as many be the history of the organization of those counties older than this. When Gen. Arthur St. Clair, accompanied by Winthrop Sargent, arrived at Kaskaskia, March 5, 1790, the country comprising Illinois, extending as far northward as the mouth of Little Mackinaw Creek, on the Illinois River, was organized into one county, and named St. Clair, in honor of the governor. This county was divided into three judicial districts, a court of common pleas established, and three judges appointed, and Cahokia became the county seat. Randolph County was next organized by William Henry Harrison, governor of Indiana Territory, February 3, 1801, and embraced the territory within the following boundaries:

> Beginning on the Ohio River, at a place called the Great Cave, below the Saline Creek; thence by a direct north line until it intersects an east and west line running from the Mississippi, through the Sink Hole Spring; thence along the said line to the Mississippi, thence down the Mississippi to the mouth of the Ohio, and up the same to the place of beginning.[22]

The territory remained thus divided until 1809, when the following proclamation was issued:

> Kaskaskia, April 28, 1809
>
> A proclamation by Nathaniel Pope, secretary of the territory of Illinois, and exercising the government thereof.
>
> By virtue of the power vested in the governor for the prevention of crimes and injuries, and for the execution of process, civil and criminal, within the territory, I have thought proper to, and by this proclamation do, divided the Illinois Territory into two counties, to be called the county of St. Clair and the county of Randolph.
>
> The county of Randolph shall include all that part of the Illinois Territory lying south of the line dividing the counties of Randolph and St. Clair, as it existed under the government of the Indiana Territory, on the last day of February, 1809, and the county of St. Clair shall include all that part of the Territory which lies north of that line.
>
> Done at Kaskaskia, the 28th day of April, 1809, and of the Independence of the United States, the thirty-third.
>
> Nathaniel Pope[23]

---

[22] The Great Cave is of course Cave-in-Rock, the cavern, not the modern community. The east and west line through the Sink Hole Spring is the extension of the modern line dividing Madison and St. Clair counties.

[23] Pope created this county by executive order as the acting territorial governor. Newly appointed Territorial Gov. Ninian Edwards had not arrived from Kentucky yet. What Goodspeed's 1887 History fails to note is that from

Madison, Gallatin and Johnson Counties

No other counties were organized then until September, 1812, when Madison, Gallatin and Johnson were called into existence by Gov. Edwards, by the following proclamation:

>By Ninian Edwards, Governor of the Territory of Illinois.
>>Kaskaskia, September 14, 1812
>>A Proclamation
>
>>By virtue of the powers vested in the governor of the territory, I do hereby lay off a county or district to be called the county of Madison, to be included within the following bounds: To begin on the Mississippi, to run with the second township line above Cahokia, east until it strikes the dividing line between the Illinois and Indiana Territories, thence with said dividing line to the line of Upper Canada, thence with said line to the Mississippi, and thence down the Mississippi to the beginning. I do appoint the house of Thomas Kirkpatrick to be the seat of justice of said county.
>
>>I do also lay off a county or district to be called the county of Gallatin to be bounded as follow: to begin at the mouth of Lusk Creek, on the Ohio, running up with said creek to Miles' Trace, thence along said trace to Big Muddy, thence up Big Muddy to its source, thence north to the line of St. Clair County, thence with said line to the Wabash, thence down the Wabash and Ohio to the beginning. And I do appoint Shawnee Town, to be the seat of justice of Gallatin County.
>
>>And I do lay off a county or district to be called Johnson County to be bounded as follow: To begin at the mouth of Lusk Creek on the Ohio; thence with the line of Gallatin County to Big Muddy; thence down Big Muddy and the Mississippi to the mouth of the Ohio, and up the Ohio to the beginning. And I appoint the house of John Bradshaw to the seat of justice for Johnson County.
>
>>Done at Kaskaskia the 14th day of September, 1812, and of the Independence of the United States the thirty-seventh.
>>>By the Governor
>>>Ninian Edwards
>
>>Nathaniel Pope
>>Secretary.
>>[seal]

Gallatin County was named in honor of Albert Gallatin, a distinguished American statesmen and Secretary of the Treasury under Jefferson. The name was conferred upon the county, or at least suggested, by John Bradolette, register of the land office at Vincennes, and a countryman and admiring friend of Gallatin, and not, as had been stated by certain

---

1801 to 1809, the territory of modern day Gallatin County laid split between two counties; Randolph and Knox. Everything east of a line running north from Cave-in-Rock remained in old Knox County with its county seat of Vincennes. This territory included the eastern fourth of Hardin County, the mouth of the Saline River, as well as the area of Old Shawneetown and New Haven. The former Green House south of New Haven would have stood close to that county line. Besides this sliver of what is now Illinois, Knox County included almost all of Indiana.

historians, by John Caldwell, who was receiver of the land office at Shawneetown.[24] The county was reduced in size at several times. Franklin County was organized in 1818; White County in 1815; Hardin County in 1839, and Saline County in 1847, and finally made separate in 1852.[25]

Adjustment of Boundary Lines.

Although White County was organized, as just stated, in 1815, the boundary line between it and Gallatin County was not settled for many years. At the December term (1830) of the county commissioners court of Gallatin County, the surveyors of Gallatin, White and Hamilton Counties were required to meet on the 16th of August, 1831, to run and establish a line between said counties. They met according to this requirement, but could not determine the piece of ground upon which Boone's mill had stood.

The south line of White County was once described in law as "beginning in the eye of the millstone in Boone's mill, in New Haven," but when the surveyors arrived on the ground August 16, 1831, the mill had been removed, and of course after passing the act relative to the boundary. The surveyors, therefore, had five citizens, viz.; John Groves, Roswell H. Grant, Merritt Taylor, Samuel Dagley and Peter Slater, designate as nearly as practicable the point to commence from, which they did as follows: Beginning at a rock in the Little Wabash River, from which a black oak twelve inches in diameter bears south 60° east, distant seventeen links; thence running due west, to the corner of White and Hamilton Counties on the Gallatin County line, fourteen miles distant. The survey was completed August 23, 1831. The surveyors were David Stinson, of Gallatin County; John Storms, of White County, and Enos T. Allen, of Hamilton County.

On February 10, 1853, it was enacted by the Legislature that the section line running east and west, through the center of Township 7 south, in Ranges 5, 6, 7, 8, 9 and 10 east of the third principal meridian should constitute and stand for the county line dividing the two counties, Gallatin and White, for revenue and all other purposes; said line to commence at the southwest corner of Section 18, Township 7 south, Range — east, and run thence due east along and with the section line to the Little Wabash River.

On February 28, 1854, the Legislature amended the last clause of the above section so as to make it read,

> "Said line shall commence at the southwest corner of Section 18, Township 7 south, Range — east, and shall run thence due east on said section line to the southwest corner of Section 17, Township 7 south, Range 10 east, thence north to the northern line of said section in the center of the Little Wabash River, and down that stream to its confluence with the great Wabash River."

---

[24] At this point in the 1887 edition, an asterisk points to a footnote stating, "see biography of Albert Gallatin Caldwell." Caldwell's biography is present in this edition as well.

[25] Hamilton County split off from White in 1821. Williamson County split off from Franklin in 1839 and the eastern portion of Hardin County down to the great cavern at Cave-in-Rock, then known as the "Curtail" split off from Gallatin County and joined the rest of Hardin County in 1847.

Elections and Politics

List of County Officers

The county officers of Gallatin County have been as follows:

Sheriffs.—Marmaduke S. Davenport, George Robinson, Ephraim Hubbard, Dr. Henry Boyers, John Lane, 1833; Thomas Tong, 1842; John T. Walters, 1848; Joseph B. Barger, 1850; Richard Richeson, 1853; Thomas Wilson, 1854; James Davenport, 1855; James H. McMintry, 1857; John T. Walters, 1858; Parker E. Pillow, 1862; John M. Eddy, 1863; George B. Hick, 1865; W. L. Blackard, 1867; George B. Hick, 1869; Joel Cook, 1871; John Yost, 1875-80, inclusive; Robert J. Bruce, 1885-86, and J. F. Nolen, 1886 to the present time.[26]

Circuit Court Clerks.—Joseph M. Street, Leonard White, 1828; John E. Hall, 1848-56, when murdered; James Davenport, 1857-64; James R. Loomis, 1865-72; James W. Millspaugh, 1873-76; Joseph F. Nolen, 1877-94; Robert L. Millspaugh, 1885 to the present time (1887).

States Attorneys.—Under the constitution of 1848, the duties of States' attorneys extended over an entire circuit, hence a complete list of those attorneys practicing in Gallatin County, while that system was in vogue, would not be easy to form or perhaps even desirable.[27] Some of them were, however, as follows: William H. Stickney, Samuel S. Marshall, L. J. S. Turney, James Robinson, Thomas Smith, Milton Barley, C. M. Damron and F. M. Youngblood. The latter gentleman served from 1869 to 1872, both years inclusive. Under the constitution of 1870 this officer's duties are limited to his own county. Since 1872 the following have been state's attorneys of Gallatin County: William F. Crenshaw,[28] 1873-1876; E. D. Youngblood, 1877-80; D. M. Kinsall, 1881 to the present time.

Masters in Chancery.—The following is a partial list of these officers: William Hensley was appointed by Judge Duff, as also was Milton Bartley, who likewise served four years while Judge Tanner presided on this circuit, and Carl Roedel two years. Milton Bartley succeeded Carl Roedel, and served during the years 1878 to 1879; D. M. Kinsall then followed during the years 1880 and 1881, in which latter year E. D. Youngblood was appointed and still serves in that capacity.

Clerks of the County Courts.—Joseph M. Street, Leonard White, Calvin Gold, John E. Hall, Joseph B. Barger, from 1856 to 1882, and Silas Cook from 1882 to the present time.

County Treasurers.—John G. Daimwood, William McCoy, Joseph Hayes, Eli Adams, Benjamin Rice, Benjamin Thomas, W. Burnett, William Siddall, John Williamson, John W.

---

[26] John E. Hall served as sheriff for two years from 1846 to 1848, but is not listed. Who served as sheriff from 1880 to 1885 is not clear from this list.

[27] From the Franklin County portion of the 1887 History (p. 369-370)... State attorneys—Samuel Marshall, 1837-1839; Wm. H. Stickney, 1839-1841; Willis Allen, 1841-45; Wm. A. Denning, 1845-47; Samuel Marshall, 1847-50; Wm. K. Parrish, 1850-53; M. C. Crawford, 1854-54; John A. Logan (late United States Senator), 1854-57; M. C. Crawford, 1857-59; Edward V. Pearce, 1859-61; J. M. Cleminson, 1861-63; A. P. Corder, 1865-64; C. N. Damron, 1864-69; F. M. Youngblood, 1869-72. Caution: Franklin and Gallatin may not have always been in the same circuit and there may be state attorneys listed here that didn't serve in Gallatin County.

[28] Should be William T. Crenshaw.

Trousdale, Benjamin Bruce, William L. Blackard, Arad R. McCabe, Joseph A. Lane, S. M. Smyth, and W. W. Mayhew, the latter elected in 1886.

Congressional Districts

From the organization of the State up to 1832, Illinois constituted one Congressional District, of which of course Gallatin County formed a part, and John McLean, of Shawneetown was the representative during the first term of Congress after the admission of Illinois into the Union. In 1824, Hon. John McLean, was chosen to the United States Senate to fill out the unexpired term of Ninian Edwards. While in Washington Mr. McLean acted as correspondent of the Shawneetown paper, the *Illinois Gazette*, and here is a specimen of his work:

Senate Chamber, February 9, 1825
SIR—The votes for President are as follows: Mr. Adams, six, New England States, New York, Maryland, Ohio, Illinois, Missouri, and Kentucky. He is elected. The mail starts, I have time to write no more. Great God deliver us!
John McLean.

John McLean was again chosen to fill a vacancy in the United States Senate in 1829, that caused by the resignation of Jesse B. Thomas, but he died October 4, 1830.

From 1832 to 1843, Gallatin County was in the First Congressional District, seventeen counties having been constituted the Second District in 1832, but appears not to have been represented in either branch of Congress during that time. In 1843, under the new apportionment, the Second District was composed of Johnson, Pope, Hardin, Williamson, Gallatin, Franklin, Hamilton, White, Wabash, Edwards, Wayne, Jefferson, Marion and Massac, and John A. McClernand was elected to represent the district in Congress from 1843 to 1851. Samuel S. Marshall was representative from 1855 to 1859, and John A. Logan from 1859 to 1863; William J. Allen (deceased) was elected in 1862,[29] Samuel S. Marshall was again elected in 1864, and Green B. Raum in 1866. In 1868 John M. Crebs was elected, and again in 1870; in 1872 Samuel D. Marshall was elected. William B. Anderson then served one term when he was followed in 1877 by Hon. R. W. Townshend, who has been biennially elected ever since, and is a member of the L Congress.[30]

In 1852 the Ninth District was made to consist of the following counties: Alexander, Pulaski, Massac, Union, Johnson, Pope, Hardin, Gallatin, Saline, Williamson, Jackson, Perry, Franklin, Hamilton, White, Wayne, Edwards and Wabash.

In 1861 the Thirteenth District was composed of Alexander, Pulaski, Union, Johnson, Williamson, Jackson, Perry, Massac, Pope, Hardin, Saline, Gallatin, White, Edwards and Wabash Counties.

---

[29] It's not known what the "deceased" is supposed to mean in reference to Allen. The *Biographical Directory of the United States Congress* notes his death didn't occur until 1901. The author may have been confused by Allen's removal from Marion to Springfield in 1886 where he took an appointment of U.S. District Judge for the Southern District of Illinois the following April.

[30] That is the 50th Congress.

In 1872 the Nineteenth District was made to consist of Edwards, Franklin, Hamilton, Gallatin, Hardin, Jefferson, Richland, Saline, White, Wabash and Wayne Counties; and in 1881, when the State was divided into twenty congressional districts, the Nineteenth was composed of White, Hamilton, Gallatin, Saline, Hardin, Franklin, Jefferson, Marion and Clinton Counties.

Election Returns

Following are some election returns and political data without much attempt at systematic arrangement. Gallatin County was represented in the first territorial Legislature, which convened at Kaskaskia, November 25, 1812, by Benjamin Talbott as a member of the Council, and by Alexander Wilson and Philip Trammel in the House of Representatives. In the Second Territorial Legislature Benjamin Talbott was again a member of the Council, and Philip Trammel and Thomas C. Browne were members of the House. The Legislature convened November 14, 1814, and passed an act incorporating Shawneetown. In the Third Territorial Legislature, which convened December 2, 1816, Gallatin County was represented in the council by Thomas C. Browne, and by whom in the House the writer did not learn.

Members of the Constitutional Convention, Etc.

According to an act of Congress, passed April 18, 1818, the people of the Territory of Illinois elected delegates to a convention to form a State constitution, the convention to meet on the first Monday (the 3d) of August. Michael Jones, Leonard White and Adolphus F. Hubbard were members of the convention from Gallatin County. This first constitution was adopted, not by the people, but by the convention that framed it.

The First General Assembly of the State of Illinois convened Monday October 5, 1818, and there were present from Gallatin County as member of the Senate, Michael Jones, and as members of the House of Representatives, J. G. Daimwood, Adolphus F. Hubbard, John Marshall and Samuel McClintock.[31] The capital of the State was then as Kaskaskia; in 1820 it was removed to Vandalia, and when it was removed to Springfield Shawneetown received one vote.

The Second General Assembly convened at Vandalia, Tuesday, December 4, 1821, and upon the organization of the house John McLean was made speaker. When the second State government was inaugurated, Adolphus F. Hubbard, of Gallatin County, presided over the Senate. Lieut.-Gov. Hubbard also presided over the Senate during the term commencing Monday, January 2, 1826, and John McLean was speaker of the House. During the term of the General Assembly which convened Monday, December 4, 1826, John A. McClernand was a member and also during the session which commenced Monday, December 1, 1828. The General Assembly which put in operation the famous internal improvement system convened December 15, 1836, and contained many members who afterward attained to national distinction. During the session of 1835 William J. Gatewood was senator from Gallatin County. He was a man of eminent ability and earnestly opposed legislation in favor of railroads.

---

[31] Marshall resigned and Daimwood took his place.

Michael Jones' Ride

Michael Jones was a member of the House of Representatives. The session was to open on Monday morning, and Jones was still in Shawneetown when the sun was two hours high on Sunday morning. At that time there were no railroads, not even the Shawneetown & Alton had been built, and it was a matter of grave doubt as to whether Jones could reach Vandalia, 140 miles away, by the time of the opening of the Legislature Monday morning. Mr. Gatewood was anxiously looking all Sunday and late into Sunday night for Jones, but had to retire without the joyful sight of his Democratic features. Next morning, however, when Mr. Gatewood went down to breakfast, whom should his eyes behold but Michael Jones, as calmly seated at the breakfast table as if he had enjoyed the best of a night's sleep on a feather bed. Mr. Jones had successfully made the entire distance by relays of horses, 140 miles in twenty-two hours.

Election Returns

In 1858, John A. Logan was elected to Congress by a vote of 15,878 to 2,796 cast for David L. Phillips and 144 for William K. Parrish, and in 1860 John A. Logan was again elected by 20,683 votes to 5,207 for David T. Linegar and 165 scattering.

In the Constitutional Convention of 1862 Milton Bartley, a member from Gallatin County, received 4,290 votes for Congressman to 9,487 for William J. Allen (Democrat). In 1864 Andrew J. Kuykendall (Republican) was elected to Congress by a vote of 11,742 to 10,759 for William J. Allen (Democrat) and 57 for Milton Bartley. In 1866 Green B. Raum was elected by a vote of 13,459 to 12,890 for William J. Allen, and was defeated in 1868 by a vote of 14,261 to 14,764 for John M. Crebs.

In 1866 John A. Logan was candidate at large for Congress against T. Lyle Dickey receiving in Gallatin County 649 votes to 936 for Dickey. The Rebellion had made Logan a Republican, hence he was not so popular in Gallatin County. Logan's vote in the other counties, the histories of which are in this volume, was in Saline County 942 to Dickey's 988; Franklin County, 863 to Dickey's 1,049; Hamilton County, 602 to Dickey's 1,133, and Williamson County, 1,245 to Dickey's 1,197. Logan was, however, elected by a vote of 203,045 to 147,038 cast for Dickey.

In 1870 John M. Crebs was elected to Congress by a vote of 13,949 to 12,366 for David W. Munn (Republican). In 1872 Gallatin County was placed in the Nineteenth Congressional District and Samuel S. Marshall (Democrat) was elected to Congress over Green B. Raum by a vote of 13,297 to 11,282. In 1874 William B. Anderson (Greenbacker) was elected to Congress by a vote in the district of 8,293, Samuel S. Marshall receiving 7,556, and Green B. Raum, 5,485. At this election Gallatin County cast for Anderson 753 votes, for Marshall 737, and for Raum 400.

In 1876 Richard W. Townshend was elected by 12,720 votes to 8,558 for Edward Bonham (Republican) and 7,463 for W. B. Anderson. In 1878 Townshend's vote was 12,603 to 8,190 for Robert Bell, and 2,847 for Seth F. Crews; in 1880 it was 18,021 to 14,561 for C. W. Pavey (Republican) and 1,456 for Samuel Flannigan (Greenbacker); in 1882 it was 15,606 to 9,930 for George C. Ross. In 1884 he was elected again by a vote of 18,296 to 13,553 for Thomas S. Ridgway. In 1886. Mr. Townshend was elected by a vote of 16,326 to 11,974 cast for Martin, Republican candidate.

Other election returns limited strictly to Gallatin County have been as follows: In 1830 John Reynolds for governor received 672 votes; William Kinney, 372; Zadock Casey, for lieutenant-governor received 668; R. B. Slocumb, 349; for the State Senate: Timothy Guard, 656; Michael Jones, 366; for representative: J. E. Watkins, 747; W. J. Gatewood, 670; Jephtha Hardin, 316; Benjamin White, 285; for Sheriff: M. S. Davenport, 800; Harrison Wilson, 241.

In 1840 Van Buren received 1,283 votes for President; Harrison, 500. In 1842 Thomas Ford received 1,160 votes as candidate for governor; Joseph Duncan, 441; for State Senator Lane received 621; Leviston, 942; for representative John A. McClernand received 1,262 votes; Thomas S. Hick, 707; Flanders, 770; Stickney, 587; Elder, 578; Hopper, 338, and Rice, 373.

In 1859 Thomas S. Hicks was again a member of the House from Gallatin County, James B. Turner in 1863, C. Burnett in 1869; in 1871 Simeon K. Gibson was a member of the Senate, and William G. Bowman in the House of Representatives; in 1873 J. R. Loomis was elected to the House, and J. M. Wasson in 1875.

For governor in 1880 Gallatin county cast for S. M. Cullom 1,052 votes, Lyman Trumbull 1,567, and for A. J. Street (Greenbacker) 18.

In 1882 the vote for the various officers was—Congress: Townshend, 1,555; Ross, 986; State senator: Blanchard (Democrat) 1,448; Morris (Republican) 1,043; representatives: Bowman (Democrat) 2,358; Gregg (Democrat) 2,198; Boyer (Republican) 1,429; McCartney (Republican) 1,469; county judge: E. D. Youngblood (Democrat) 1,302; Milton Bartley (Independent Democrat) 700; Rhoades (Republican) 460; sheriff: Bruce (Democrat) 1,425; Yost (Republican) 1,077; clerk of the county court: Silas Cook, 2,247, no opposition; treasurer; Mayhew (Democrat) 1,182; Smyth (Republican) 1,292.

In 1886 the vote was as follows—State Treasurer: Ricker (Democrat) 1,579; Farmer (Republican) 1,240; Congressman: Townshend (Democrat) 1,722; Martin (Republican) 1,015; State senator: Richeson (Democrat) 1,454; Yost (Republican) 1,273; county judge Youngblood (Democrat) 1,413; Bartley (Republican 1,389; county clerk: Cook (Democrat) 1,671; Bailey (Republican) 1,142; sheriff: Hale (Democrat) 1,307; Nolen (Republican) 1,450; treasurer: Mayhew (Democrat) 1,433; Shaw (Republican) 1,392; county superintendent of schools: Proctor (Democrat) 1,511; Rodgers (Republican) 1,319; county commissioner: McLain (Democrat) 1,531; Allyn (Republican) 1,237; surveyor: Smyth (Democrat) 1,571; Smith (Republican) 1,268; for township organization, 1,189; against township organization, 1,343; for hogs and sheep running at large, 1,979; against the same, 628.

Railroad History

There are two railroads running into Gallatin County, and terminating at Shawneetown, the Louisville & Nashville and the Ohio & Mississippi, both using the same track from Cypress Junction.[32] In 1838 the road from Shawneetown to Alton was projected, and in 1840 John Crenshaw was awarded the contract on the section from Shawneetown and the grade

---

[32] This is modern-day Junction, Illinois.

was completed most of the way between Equality and Shawneetown. Afterward the Shawneetown and Eldorado Railway Company was chartered, and to this road was granted the right of way, bridges, culverts, etc., of the old road which failed.

In 1869 the St. Louis & Southeastern was chartered, and Joseph J. Castle became the owner of the Shawneetown & Eldorado Road from Shawneetown to Equality and gave that road to the St. Louis & Southeastern, and the county of Gallatin gave this latter company $100,000 in donations bonds and subscribed $100,000 to its stock, paying for the same in bonds.[33] In 1880 the road was changed to the Louisville & Nashville.

What is now called the Shawneetown Branch of the Ohio and Mississippi Railroad was built under the superintendency of Hon. Thomas S. Ridgway. Chief Engineer Rice made the first survey in 1868, and a second survey was made in 1870. To this railroad, which extends to Beardstown, Cass County, a distance of 226 miles, Gallatin County contributed $100,000 in bonds. Ten thousand dollars of the $200,000 has been paid, and the $190,000 remaining funded at 6 per cent interest.

The Agricultural Association

Gallatin County Agricultural and Mechanical Association was incorporated under an act approved April 18, 1872. M. M. Pool, John D. Richeson and A. M. L. McBane were the commissioners to open subscription books to the stock of the association, the stock amounting to $4,000. A meeting was held August 31, 1872, at which nine directors were elected and the following officers: President, M. M. Pool; vice-president, C. W. McGehee; secretary, A. M. L. McBane; treasurer, John D. Robinson. The only changes in the officers since have been that in 1874 John L. Robinson became secretary, and in 1886 George A. Lowe became treasurer. The association owns twenty-six acres of land in the edge of Shawneetown. It has held fifteen annual fairs, which have been largely attended by the farmers of the county, and have resulted in advancing all the various interests of the farming community; better stock, better farm machinery, improved methods of agriculture and superior results as to variety and value of farm products, are noticeable on every hand.

Bench and Bar

The common pleas court of Gallatin County held its first session in January 1813, but the records commence in March of that year, and are as follows:

> "Pursuant to an act of the territorial Legislature passed at their last session, held at Kaskaskia on the 12th of November, in the year 1812, 'regulating the time

---

[33] The first passenger rail service in Gallatin County began Monday, January 15, 1871. For 50 cents a person could ride the train from Equality to Shawneetown. A month later on Feb. 14, the St. Louis & Southeastern merged with the Evansville & Southern Illinois Railroad Company and the Evansville, Carmi & Paducah Railroad Company with the new corporation continuing the name of St. Louis & Southeastern. [Source: Jan. 13, 1871. *McLeansboro Times*.]

for holding the courts of common pleas in the several counties of said Territory and for other purposes,' the commission of his Excellency Ninian Edwards, governor of our said Territory, having been produced to Leonard White and Gabriel Greathouse, gentlemen, judges of our said court of common pleas for the county of Gallatin, by Joseph M. Street as clerk of said court of common pleas for the county of Gallatin in the Illinois Territory, and he having qualified as said clerk and entered into the office bound with sufficient security, is duly constituted the clerk of said court, and on the 21st of March, 1813, being the fourth Monday in said month and the day appointed by the before recited act for holding the court of common pleas for the county of Gallatin aforesaid, the sheriff and clerk met at the house of Joseph M. Street in Shawanoe Town in the said county of Gallatin, and a sufficient number of judges not attending to constitute the court, the sheriff adjourned the same until to-morrow; and now on the 22d of March, 1813, a sufficient number of judges not attending, court is adjourned until to-morrow; and now on the 23d of March, 1813, a sufficient number of judges not attending, court is adjourned until court in course."

    This court met according to adjournment, May 24, 1813, at the house of Gabriel Greathouse in Shawanoe Town. "Present, the Honorable John C. Slocumb and Gabriel Greathouse, gentlemen." On this day it was ordered by the court that the proceedings, had at a court of common pleas for this county, "on the fourth Monday in January last," and "on the 15th day of February, 1813, for a special purpose," for which the court convened was that of the appointment of Samuel Omelvaney commissioner to take a list of the taxable property in the county of Gallatin, and he was required to give an "office bond" for the faithful performance of his duties.

    On this same day the court, all of the judges being present, "Hon. J. C. Slocumb, Gabriel Greathouse and Leonard White, gentlemen," it was ordered that the following order of court of common pleas for the county of Randolph, in the Illinois Territory, made at the August term of said court in the year 1812, be renewed, and that Lewis Barker be entered in said order as one of the viewers instead of Col. Phillip Trammel. (Gallatin County Court of Common Pleas, May term, 1813, May 24.)

    On the petition of a number of the inhabitants of Rock and Cave Township, praying for the establishment of a road from Barker's ferry at the Rock and Cave on the Ohio River, the nearest and best way to intersect the road from Kaskaskia to the United States Saline Springs at Francis Jourdan's; also for the establishment of a road from said Barker's ferry to the United States Saline Works; and it appearing to the said court that the proper proofs were produced to the said court of Randolph County at their aforesaid term, that the notices required by law were duly given, it is ordered that Lewis Barker, Phillip Coon and Isaac Casey be appointed viewers on the route from the ferry to the United States Saline works and that Francis Jourdan, Joseph Jourdan and Chism Estes be appointed overseers on the route from the ferry to Francis Jourdan's, which said viewers are directed to view and mark out several routes for said roads on the nearest and best way and as near as may be to the request of the petitioners.

    On the next day, May 25, the court met pursuant to adjournment, present, Hons. Leonard White, John C. Slocumb and Gabriel Greathouse, gentlemen. The county was laid off into townships as follows: The bounds of the militia companies were constituted the boundaries of the several townships. Capt. Steel's boundary shall constitute one township to be known by the name of Granpier; Capt. McFarland's to constitute one township to be known by the name of Big Creek; Capt. Barker's to constitute one township to be known by the name Rock and Cave; the company lately commanded by Capt. Trousdale to constitute one township to be known by the name of Shawanoe; Capt. White's to constitute one township to be known by the name of Saline; Capt. Grove's to constitute one township to be known by the name of Pond; and Capt. McHenry's to constitute one township to be known by the name of Prairie Township.[34]

The following persons were then appointed constables for their respective townships: for Big Creek, Leonard Harrison; for Granpier, John Jackson; for Rock and Cave, Asa Ledbetter; for Shawanoe, John Forrester; for Saline, Seth Hargrave; for Pond, Joshua Beggs; and for Prairie Township, Reuben Bell.

Building of the Jail

It was then ordered that a jail be built on the "publick square" in Shawanoe Town, and a "stray pen" established. The plan of the jail was as follows:

> "to consist of two stories, the first to be eight feet and the second seven feet high in the clear, to be built of good, sound white oak logs hewed to ten inches square, and put up with a dove-tail at the corners. The first story to be ten feet square in the clear, surrounded by another wall of the same description as the first, leaving a space of ten inches between the two walls, into which timbers of ten inches in thickness are to be dropped endwise and as close side to side as they can be placed. The second story to be at least thirteen feet, four inches square in the clear to be made by running up the outer wall of the lower story perpendicularly to the height of seven feet, ten inches above the top of the first story; the floor of the first story, the floor of the second story, and the ceiling of the second story to be laid with good oak timbers ten inches in thickness let in with a shoulder upon the logs of the house."

Other and minute particulars were prescribed as to the roof, the platform, the windows, doors, etc., but the above will serve to show the strength of this first criminals' rendezvous of

---

[34] No detailed map of these townships has been found. Considering the area Gallatin County covered in 1813, only rough generalities can be made. Rock and Cave covered what's now eastern Hardin County including the community of Cave-in-Rock. Big Creek is the stream on the west side of Elizabethtown so that township would include the future site of that community. They named Granpier for Grand Pierre Creek that flows along the modern border of Hardin and Pope County. It definitely included Rosiclare and the bluff just upstream from Rosiclare. James Ford, the militia captain before James Steele, owned land there. That township would have stretched downriver to the county border at the mouth of Lusk Creek on the north side of Golconda. Shawanoe included modern Shawneetown. Saline included the saltworks in the Equality area. McHenry's blockhouses and territory include the modern area of Carmi and White County. Pond Township appears to be what's now southern White County.

Gallatin County. Alexander Wilson, Michael Jones, Joseph M. Street, Cornelius Lafferty and Henry Oldham were appointed commissioners to contract for the building of the jail and the "stray pen."

Phillip Coon was then appointed administrator upon the estate of George Coon, (deceased), late of this county, and tavern rates were then fixed according to law, as follows: Breakfast, dinner and supper each, 25 cents; lodging, 12½ cents; horse to hay or fodder one night, 25 cents; oats or corn per gallon, 12½ cents; whisky per one-half pint, 12½ cents; peach brandy, 25 cents; cherry bounce, 25 cents; French brandy, 50 cents; rum and tafia, 37½ cents; wine, 50 cents; gin, 25 cents; cider, per quart, 12½ cents; cider royal, 25 cents; strong beer, 25 cents, and small beer, 12½ cents.

Hazle Moreland was then granted a license to keep tavern at his house, "as it appeared to be the court that he was a man of good moral character and would probably keep an orderly house." His license was $7, the fee to the clerk $1, and his bond was $300. Gabriel Greathouse and Thomas M. Dorris were each granted licenses to keep tavern, the amount paid in each case being $12, and the clerk's fee being $1. Jephtha Hardin was admitted to practice law at this court, he having a certificate from two of the judges of the general court of the Territory, and was thus the first lawyer admitted to practice at this bar.

The next day, May 26, all the honorable gentlemen of the court being present, it was ordered among other things, that the rates of taxation for the year 1813 should be: For Negroes, $1 each; horses, 50 cents each; all the ferries on the Ohio River, $10 each; on the Saline, $5 each; those on the Big Wabash, $4 each; on the Little Wabash, $1 each, and that the next above the mouth of the Saline Creek, $2. It was then ordered that the order of the common pleas court of Randolph County, establishing a road from the ferry at Shawanoe Town, to the United States Saline Salt Works, be renewed, and that John Robinson, Sr., be appointed supervisor thereof from the Island Ripple to the said salt works, in the place of William Cheek, and that Hazle Moreland be appointment supervisor from the ferry in Shawanoe Town to the Island Ripple. Overseers of the poor were then appointed: in Prairie Township, John Hannah and Robert Lann; in Granpier Township, Isham Clay and Joseph Ritchy. It was then ordered that stocks be erected for this county, and that their erection be let at the same time and by the same persons as the jail and stray pen, "to be completed by the next term of this court."

The next term of this court commenced September 27, 1813, present, the "Hon. John C. Slocumb and Gabriel Greathouse, gentlemen." Charles Wilkins & Co. were granted a license to keep a tavern at the United States Saline Salt Works, by the payment of $12 to the county and $1 to the clerk. Belam May was license to keep a tavern at the Island Ripple, by the payment of $7, and John Davis to keep tavern at his house upon payment of $4. But the most important item of business transacted on this day had reference to the ferry at Shawneetown, and was as follows:

> On motion of Alexander Wilson the following order, bond and certificate of the court of common pleas of Randolph County was spread upon the records: Randolph County Court, December, 1810.—On the motion of Alexander Wilson, and satisfactory proof appearing to the court, it is ordered that the said Alexander Wilson be licensed and permitted to establish and keep a ferry across the Ohio River from the rocks near the upper end of Shawanoe Town and that he be

allowed to charge the same rates of ferriage at the said ferry as is established for Fritz Hoit's ferry across the Ohio, to-wit:

For each wagon and team consisting of not more than four horses or oxen	$1.50
For each wagon and team consisting of not more than two horses or oxen	1.00
Two-wheeled carriages, consisting of not more than two horses or oxen	75
Man and horse	50
Each person (children under seven excepted)	25
Each horse, mare, mule or ass	25
Each head of neat cattle	12½
Each head of sheep or hogs	06¼

I, William C. Greenup, Clerk of the Court of Common Pleas, of the County of Randolph, Illinois Territory, do hereby certify that the above is a true transcript from the records of the late County Court of Randolph, now in my office, and that the above named Alexander Wilson hath filed in my office a bond for the faithful discharge of his duty as the keeper of said ferry conditioned as the law directs. Given under my hand and the seal of the said Court, etc., this 3d day of August, 1813, etc.

William C. Greenup

On motion of James McFarland, made in court September 28, 1813, and on the petition of a number of a number of the inhabitants of Big Creek Township, praying for the establishment of a road from McFarland's ferry to the United States Saline Salt Works, William Frizzel, Elias Jourdan, Peter Etter and Lewis Watkins were ordered to mark out the several routes for said road upon the nearest and best way between the two points. The viewers of the last (May) term of court to mark out a road from Barker's ferry, at the Rock and Cave to the United States Saline Salt Works, made the following report:

"Agreeable to an order of the court of common pleas of Gallatin County, May term, 1813, to have a road viewed from Barker's ferry to the United States Saline, we, the viewers, Lewis Barker, Phillip Coon, and Isaac Casey, did begin at the said ferry and review from thence to Nathaniel Armstrong's; thence across Harris Creek to a large spring; thence to cross Eagle Creek just above the forks, and thence to the United States Salines."

Henry Ledbetter and John B. Stovall were appointed overseers of said road, with power to call out all the hands on each side of said road within six miles of it, to cut it out and keep it in repair. Henry Ledbetter from the Ohio to Harris Creek, and John B. Stovall from Harris Creek to the Saline.

On the next day James McFarland was licensed to keep a ferry across the Ohio River from where he resided on land belonging to the United States until the sale of said public lands, or other disposition by the United States, and Frederick Buck, Jonathan Hampton, Samuel Craig, Dennis Clay and John Rheburne were ordered to view and mark out a road from Rheburne's ferry, on the Wabash, to Shawanoe Town. The above is the sum and substance of the business transacted by the Gallatin County Court of Common Pleas during the first year of its existence, 1813. Its accomplishments during the subsequent years of its career must be more briefly noticed.

This court convened again January 19, 1814; present, "Hon. John C. Slocumb and Leonard White, Gentlemen." Russell E. Heacock's motion to grant an order for a ferry across the Ohio River on his improvement was continued to the next term of court and then overruled. The office of attorney or counsel for the courts was created, and Jephtha Hardin appointed to the position at an annual salary of $50. The road from McFarland's ferry to the United States Saline Salt Works was established as follows: Beginning at McFarland's ferry; thence to Absalom Estes; thence to Nathan Clamhit's; thence to where Betty Pankey lives on Big Creek; thence to Elias Jourdan's; thence to Lewis Watkins', taking the old road to Willis Hargrave's salt works.

Prison bounds were established—a circle drawn at 20 yards' distance from the common jail, so as to make the jail the center. The reviewers reported that they had viewed and marked the road from Rheburne's ferry, on the Wabash, to Shawanoe Town, to the best of their ability and knowledge, "the nearest and best way." Frederick Buck was appointed supervisor of this road, which was ordered to be cut sixteen feet wide, and fence viewers were appointed, three for each township.

On the 2d of May, 1815, Willis Hargrave, by Russell E. Heacock, his attorney, asked the court for the privilege of establishing a ferry in Shawanoe Town, opposite Lots Nos. 1210, 1211, 1212, and offered to prove by testimony the necessity of another ferry in Shawanoe Town, as a matter of public utility, but the court refused to hear the testimony, and also refused to hear proof that the petitioner had advertised according to law "being themselves fully settled in the conviction that one ferry was enough to do all the ferrying there was to be done, as it was in their own knowledge." The court on the same day found it necessary to exercise its authority in another direction by fining Jephtha Hardin, Thomas C. Browne, "for contempt offered this court."

On the 5th of September, a number of citizens having procured two lots in Shawanoe Town for the public square and for the erection of a courthouse and other public buildings, Lots No. 1113 and 1114. Thomas Sloo, John Caldwell and Joseph M. Street were appointed commissioners to let the building of the courthouse. Taxes for 1815 were fixed as follows: On each horse, mare, mule or ass, 50 cents; on all neat cattle above three years, 10 cents every bond servant or slave, $1; on water and wind mills, houses in town, town lots, and mansions in the country of the value of $200, on each $100 of the value thereof, 30 cents; ferries on the Ohio River $10, and on each on all other ferries, $5.

This court met February 20, 1816, at the house of Charles Hill, in Shawanoe Town; present, Hons. Leonard White and John Marshall. On this day John McLean was admitted to practice law. November 19, 1816, Stephen Hogg produced his commission from Gov. Ninian Edwards, as a judge of the Gallatin County Court. February 4, 1817, Hons. Stephen Hogg and Marmaduke S. Davenport held court. On November 23, 1818, the judges were Hons. John Marshall, John G. Daimwood and Andrew Wilkins. The next day there was present in addition to the above honorable gentlemen, Erastus Wheeler.

A special term of this court was begun and held at the house of Samuel Hayes in Shawanoe Town, January 4, 1819; present, "John Marshall, John G. Daimwood and Samuel Hayes, Esquires." The court adjourned to meet on the 6th instant, at the house of Ephraim Hubbard, to settle the accounts of the sheriff and clerk. The total amount due the county from Ephraim Hubbard, sheriff, was $1,508.83½, all of which he paid, except $316.56½, for which he gave his note. The total amount due the county from Joseph M. Street, clerk, was $454, and it was found that the county was in his debt $57.50. A court was held April 19, 1819, at the house of Samuel Hayes; present, "Jacob Sexton, Samuel Hayes, William McCoy and John Forrester, Esquires." The court proceeded to lay off the county into five townships or election districts, with judges of election, as follows: Rock and Cave Township, John Black, Asa Ledbetter, and Alexander McElroy; Shawanoe Township, Cornelius Lafferty, Andrew Stark and Samuel Hayes; Cane Creek, John Groves, Joseph Riley, and Mr. Stout; Saline Township, William Burnett, Eli Adams, and Coleman Brown; Monroe Township, Hankerson Rude, Hugh Robinson, and Chism Estes.

The County Commissioners' Court

This appears to have been the last official act of the old court of common pleas. It was succeeded by the present county commissioners' court, which held its first meeting on June 7, 1819, at the house of Samuel Hayes in Shawanoe Town. Present, John Forrester, John Lane and Robert Peeples, Esqs. Joseph M. Street, as clerk of the court, gave bond in the sum of $1,000, with Cornelius Lafferty and Marmaduke S. Davenport as sureties.

The first action of this new court was to appoint supervisors for the different roads: William McCoy, Brice Hannah, Martin Hitchcock, Joseph Riley, Frederick Buck, Christopher Robinson, Michael Bartlett, Meredith Fisher and Moses Rawlings on the various roads already laid out. On the 9th of June Thomas A. Spilman was appointed deputy clerk of the county commissioners' court. Tavern rates and rates of ferriage were fixed for the year. Constables were appointed: James Beal for Monroe Township: Michael Robinson for Shawanoe; Joseph Riley for Cave, and Arthur G. Young for Saline Township.

Isaac Baldwin, John Black, Neil Thompson and Alexander McElroy, reviewers appointed by the late county court, reported having laid out a road from Flinn's Ferry, on the Ohio River to the Saline tavern, and the court ordered that the road be established as a public highway. Hugh McConnell as appointed supervisor on this road from Powell's cabins to include the crossing of Beaver Creek; John Black from Beaver Creek to Eagle Creek, and Robert Watson from Eagle Creek to its intersection with the road from Shawanoe Town to the Saline tavern. Supervisors were appointed for other roads and reviewers to mark out new roads, the particulars of which would be burdensome to this volume. One other item should not be omitted, and that is that billiard tables were taxed $150 each.

A settlement was made March 11, 1820, with Marmaduke S. Davenport, sheriff of the county, the total amount due the county being $1,567.26½; and also with John G. Daimwood, county treasurer, whose total collections for the year had been $1,628.20 ½. The next year, in June, a settlement was made with the sheriff, which showed that he had collected $1,348.50, taxes due for 1820. In March, 1822, the treasurer's statement showed that he had handled $641.19½, but in 1812 the amount reached $2,564.97. Dr. William

McCoy was treasurer in 1825; and in 1826 Dr. Henry Boyer, sheriff, collected for the year previous, $2,070.21½.

Equality platted as new county seat

In 1827, in pursuance of an act entitled "An act requiring the county commissioners' court of Gallatin County to carry into effect an act entitled an act permanently to locate the seat of justice of Gallatin County," approved January 26, 1827, a county commissioners' court was held at the house of Emanuel Ensminger in the town of Equality, which was located and laid out under the provisions of said act, on the first Monday in March, 1827. The commissioners at that time were Andrew Slack, John Shearer and Charles Mick; and on the 6th of March they ordered that the county treasurer pay Josiah Solomon $572.62½ in specie, or its equivalent, for building a courthouse and jail.

The first writ of *ad quod damnum* issued by this court was on March 10, 1837. Orval Sexton made application to the court to confirm him in a "mill seat" on the Big Slough, running through fractional Section 32, Township 9, Range 10 east. James Bradford appeared and informed the court that he expected to be injured by the overflowing of his lands should the "mill seat" be confirmed. The verdict of the jury upon the case was that the application to confirm the mill seat be overruled, and that he pay the costs. Mr. Sexton then applied for a new writ of *ad quod damnum* on his aforesaid land, to be near the mouth of Big Slough, which was awarded him accordingly; the jury, deciding that the health of the neighborhood would not be injuriously affected, and believing that the mill would be of great public utility, agreed that he might build a dam at the mouth of Big Slough. Harvey Green was permitted to build a mill dam on the Running Slough, Section 3, Township 9, Range 10, and John Tanner on the Saline River, near the center of the northeast quarter of Section 19, Township 10, Range 5 east.

In 1840 John Lane, Thomas Tong and Joseph Hayes were appointed commissioners to let to the lowest, responsible bidders the building of a new jail at Equality, the county seat having been removed there. The building was to be similar to that already described as having been erected at Shawneetown, except that it was larger, 20 feet, 4 inches square. Benjamin Lafferty took the contract to build it for $1,300.

In 1843 it was ordered by this court that a poorhouse be established at the house of Turner Cook "for the purpose of trying the poorhouse plan of taking care of paupers for one year, to commence in March next," and an appropriation of $60 per annum was made for each pauper that should stay the full year.

Location of County Seat

The act establishing the county of Saline provided that in case the county of Saline was established in accordance therewith, elections should be held in the counties made by the division, on the first Saturday of September following for the location of the seats of justice for the two counties, and that previous to the election any number of voters not less than 50, should nominate places to be voted for, and file their nominations in the office of the count commissioners' court. John E. Hall and 61 others in Gallatin County, designated in writing, the northwest quarter of the southwest quarter of Section 5, Township 9, Range 9 east, land owned by Washington Sherwood, as a proper place for the seat of justice of Gallatin County, and the nomination was filed in the county commissioners' court as required by law, August 12, 1847. Robert H. Morrow and 114 others, in a similar manner, designated in writing and nominated as a proper place for the seat of justice, Lots Nos. 815 and 816 in the town of Shawneetown, and this nomination was accompanied with bond and security for the conveyance to the county of the title of said lots; and these were the only places in nomination for the county seat.

The election for the choice of one of these places was held on the first Saturday of September, 1847, and Daniel P. Wilbanks, clerk of the county commissioners' court, on the 10th of September, associated with himself Israel D. Towle and John T. Cook, justices of the peace, and they, as judges of the election, opened the poll books, compared the returns and certified to the result as being, that the place nominated by John E. Hall and 61 others had received 459 votes, while that nominated by Robert H. Morrow and 114 others had received but 21 votes. Hence, on the popular vote, Shawneetown was beaten for the county seat.

However, on the 26th of October, 1847, Samuel D. Marshall made a motion in the circuit court for a rule upon the circuit court clerk, requiring him to forthwith remove the circuit court records to Shawneetown, and in support of the motion produced a certificate of the clerk of county commissioners' court and two justices of the peace of Gallatin County, stating that Shawneetown had received a majority of the votes of said county for the seat of justice thereof, at an election by the people. At the same time Henry W. Moore produced against the motion, a certificate of entry on the records of the county commissioner's court, of said county, signed by the same two justices of the peace, setting for that that a tract of land therein described, donated by Washington Sherwood, had received the highest number of votes at the same election; and the motion of S. D. Marshall was disallowed.

At the March term in 1848 of the county commissioners' court the following proceedings were had with reference to this matter:

> "The circuit court of Gallatin County at its last term, having decided that Shawneetown was then the seat of justice of said county,[35] thereupon ordering the books, records, etc., pertaining to the various county offices required by law to be kept at the seat of justice, to be removed to Shawneetown, which decision has been reversed by the supreme court of the State; and this court being now, as heretofore, likewise of the opinion that Shawneetown is not the legally elected seat of justice, and therefore concurring entirely, as bound to do, in the decision of reversal of the supreme court and acquiescing in the other decision of said circuit court remaining unreversed by which at its last term it refused to hold the same at Shawneetown, deciding to hold said term wherever it might find the records thereof remaining pursuant to the offer of this court, and did accordingly hold said term at Equality, where the books, records, etc., now are, and where they should remain until the dispute concerning this matter shall be finally and conclusively adjudicated."

---

[35] A footnote in the 1887 history states "This decision was not found on the records."

And the sheriff was ordered to repair the courthouse and prepare it for the holding of the next term of court at Equality. A county commissioners' court was held at Equality, June 5, 1848, but a regular term of this court was held at the office of Isaac Cooper in Shawneetown, September 4, 1848. On the 8th John Reynolds was request to remove the records, books, and papers to Shawneetown, or his office would be declared vacant, and that after the 10th of September the room he occupied in the courthouse at Equality would be for rent. A similar notice was served on James Davenport, probate justice and Calvin Gold, clerk of the county commissioners' court, was authorized to rent a suitable building for the use of the circuit and county courts and for other offices for one year. On October 3, 1848, James T. Trousdale, county treasurer, was ordered to remove his office to Shawneetown or his office would be declared vacant, and Calvin Gold had entered into a contract with W. J. Durbin by which Durbin was to have the upper story of the depot ready for the occupancy of the courts by the 23d of October.[36] The county clerk was then instructed to notify D. P. Wilbanks, clerk of the circuit court, James Davenport, probate justice and John Reynolds, recorder, [that the county] had leased and held ready suitable rooms for the public offices when applied for.[37]

Thus the contest waged for years, until at length the Legislature passed an "act to create the county of Gallatin out of Gallatin and Saline," and in the same act provided that the county seat should be permanently located at Equality. This act was to take effect on the fourth Monday in April 1851. Samuel S. Marshall was then judge of the Twelfth Judicial Circuit, of which Gallatin and Saline Counties formed parts. Under this law, consolidating the two counties, Judge Marshall refused to hold a term of court in Saline County.

---

[36] This agreement was rediscovered by the editor and Ron Nelson in a collection of court documents in Nashville, Tenn., removed from the courthouse by a previous circuit clerk about the time of the 1937 flood. It's interesting because it is apparent that this depot served as the first Catholic church in Shawneetown. The Mr. Durbin mentioned is more properly remembered as Father Durbin, the Catholic priest. The agreement is as follows: "This article of agreement made and entered into this 23rd day of September A.D. 1848 between E. J. Durbin of Union County Kentucky, and Turner Cook, Charles Vinson and Isaac Cooper, acting County Commissioners, for the County of Gallatin, State of Illinois, witnesseth, for & in consideration of the covenants and agreements herein after to be done and performed, on the part of the said commissioners, the said E. J. Durbin, hath leased, demised and to form let, unto the said commissioners, for the use of said County, the following rooms, & portion of a certain building known as the Depot, situated in Shawneetown, county and state, aforesaid, to wit, all the second or upper story, except the two lower and back rooms, said contract to take effect from and after the 23rd day of October AD 1848, and to be, and continue, for the term of one year, from and after the said 23rd day of October 1848, the said E. J. Durbin, also agrees, by the said 23rd day of October 1848, to lathe and plaster over head, all of said rooms, except the large front room fronting the altar, as it now stands, and over said large room, to lay plank, on the joice above, so as to make the room as warm as possible without laying & jointing the floor, and the said Cook, Vinson & Cooper, commissioners, aforesaid, for and in consideration of the covenants and agreement, hereinto before stated, on the part of the said Durbin, to be done, agrees to pay unto the said Durbin, or his representatives the sum of one hundred dollars payable in orders of the County of Gallatin at par, and to be paid by the said Commissioners, quarterly or otherwise as the said Durbin may request, said Commissioners further agree to return said premises in as good order as they receive them, the usual wear and tear and unavoidable accidents excepted."

[37] Words in brackets not included in original 1887 version.

Thereupon William K. Stephenson, in the name of the people made an application to the supreme court for a peremptory mandamus, ordering the judge to hold court in Saline County, and upon a hearing of the cause, a peremptory mandamus was granted, the decision of the supreme court being based upon the clause of the constitution reading: "No territory shall be added to any county without the consent of a majority of voters of the county to which it is propose to be added." The Legislature, therefore, in June, 1852, passed an act amending the above act, providing for an election to be held the first Monday in August 1852, to test the question of reuniting the two counties and providing that if the election should result in favor of such reunion, then Equality should be the permanent county seat. However, the election resulted in the permanent separation of the two counties.

Under the constitution of 1848 the old county commissioners' court was superseded by the system of county judge and two associate justices. The first judge under this arrangement was James Davenport, elected in 1849; the next was William R. Rohrer, elected in 1853; A. W. Hamilton, 1857; R. P. Hinch, 1859; William G. Bowman, 1861; Angus M. L. McBane, 1865; Milton Bartley, 1869-82, and E. D. Youngblood from 1882 to the present time (1887). Under the constitution of 1870 the above system was so changed that a county was provided for, to consist of three commissioners, to manage the county affairs. These commissioners have been, in 1873, John T. Walters, Benjamin Kinsall and Thomas J. Tate; elected since, in 1874, James T. Colbert; 1875, Edgar Mills and Robert M. Trousdale; 1876, James T. Colbert and F. McClain; 1879, E. M. Smith and Isaac Smith; 1880, Thomas B. Logsdon; 1881, J. A. Lane; 1882, Simon Reeder; 1883, W. C. Trusty; 1884, Henry Hill; 1885, Simon Reeder, and 1886, F. McClain.

The Circuit Court

The first term of the circuit court system held in Gallatin County, so far as the records show, was convened at the house of Joseph M. Street, in Shawneetown, Monday, July 3, 1815, by the Hon. Stanley Griswold. This county was then in the Third Judicial Circuit; Jesse B. Thomas was judge the First Judicial Circuit and William Sprigg in the Second. Judge Griswold gave notice that in the course of the term he would prepare a paper consenting to the above arrangement, but remonstrating against the mode in which said arrangement was made, and saving himself from the effect of his present consent as a precedent to guide him in future allotments. Thomas C. Browne procured a commission from His Excellency Ninian Edwards, governor of the Territory, appointed the said Browne prosecuting attorney on behalf of the Territory to the district consisting of the counties of Edwards, Gallatin and Johnson, which commission, together with the endorsement of the governor, was recorded and Thomas E. Craig was empowered to administer the necessary oaths.

The first case in the circuit court was that of William Edwards vs. Daniel Bridgeman, in detinue. On motion of the plaintiff a dedimus was awarded him to take the deposition of William Edwards, Sr., and Matthew West, to be read on the trial, and all further proceedings were continued to the next term of court. The second case was that of John Carter vs. William Cheek, on a debt; the third was that of the United States vs. Buzel Lee, John G. Wilson and Moses M. Rawlings, on a recognizance. On motion of the plaintiff's attorney a *scire facias* was issued against the said defendants, returnable at the next term of court. The fourth and last case for that day was that of Frederick Buck vs. John Walls. The defendant moved for leave to file a plea which motion was greed to and the case continued until the next term of court. The grand jury was adjourned and the court adjourned until next day, July 4, when eight ordinary cases, such as for debt, trespass, etc., were disposed of. On July 5 there were ninety-three cases of various kinds and on the 6th only five, when court adjourned.

A circuit court was held at the house of Thomas M. Dorris, in Shawanoe Town, July 1, 1816, by Hon. Thomas Towles, with the same judges as before on the first and Second Circuits. Judge Towles laid down rules for the government of the court in the trial of causes. The November term was held at the same place by the same judge, as also were those of 1817. The March term, 1818, was held at the house of William Hardin by Judge Jephtha Hardin, as was also the July term. The May term, 1819, was held at the house of Samuel Hayes, in Shawnaoe Town, by Hon. Thomas C. Browne. At this term William Badger, William L. O. Ewing and Thomas A. Young were admitted to practice law. The October term was held at the house of Marmaduke S. Davenport by Hon. William Wilson. Most of the cases at this term were "upon an indictment," sued out in the name of the United States. The May term, 1820, was held at the house of Peeples & Kirkpatrick, in Shawanoe Town, by Hon. Thomas C. Browne, as was the October term, the May term, 1821, and the May and October terms, 1822. The April term, 1823, was held at the house of Moses M. Rawlings by the same judge. At this term the principal case was that of the President and Directors of the Bank of Illinois vs. John Seebolt. Then followed a number of cases for assault and battery, one for riot, one for usurpation in office, for debt, for trespass, for non-attendance as a juror, for slander, etc.

The first murder trial came on before Hon. Thomas C. Browne, judge of the Fourth Judicial Circuit, which then consisted of Franklin, Union, Johnson, Alexander, Pope, Jackson and Gallatin Counties, September 16, 1823. In this trial John Darr was tried for the murder of William Thomason. The grand jury was composed of Isaac Hogan, Michael Jones, Gardner Moreland, Stephen Fields, Robert Harding, Thomas Akers, William Robinson, James Willis, Sr., Coleman Brown, William Forester, James Logan, Robert Beale, William Wing, Andy Laughlin, Laban Robinson, Edward Shearwood, Townsend Cannon, David Gill and William Gardner, "good and lawful men of the county and circuit aforesaid."

The substance of the indictment was that "John Darr, late of the county of Gallatin, not having the fear of God before his eyes, but being moved and seduced by the instigation of the Devil, on the 7th day of September, 1823, with force and farms, feloniously, willfully and of his malice aforethought," made an assault upon William Thomason with a certain knife held in his right hand and did stab him in the right side to the depth of eight inches, of which wound William Thomason instantly died. James Hall prosecuted for the State. The jury for the trial were James Fields, Alexander Barnhill, John McAlister, Boston Daimwood, Lowery Hay, Thomas Addison, John B. Shoemaker, James Stephenson, Zadock Aydelotte, Pleasant Tally, Spencer Ellis and James McGhee. The verdict of the jury was "We, the jury, find the defendant, John Darr, guilty of murder in the manner and form as he stands indicted."

The next indictment for murder was found on the same day the above verdict was rendered, and was against Jordan Lacy. In this case the jury rendered a verdict of guilty of manslaughter, and sentenced Lacy to imprisonment in the jail for one year, and to pay a fine of $500, and to stand committed until the fine was paid. Then followed a number of ordinary cases—slander, false imprisonment, trespass *vi et armis*, assault and battery, replevin, *scire facias*, rape, etc.[38]

Case of John Doe v. Richard Roe

On March 14, 1825, the Hon. James Hall, judge of the Fourth Judicial Circuit, held court at the house of Richard Elliott in Shawanoe Town. Joseph M. Street was still clerk, bond $5,000; Henry Eddy, circuit attorney. An interesting case occurred at the July term (1825) of this court, in which the fictitious personages, John Doe and Richard Roe, were permitted to figure. It was that of "John Doe" vs. "Richard Roe;" Henry Eddy, attorney for the plaintiff, James Jones, date July, 1825. This was a suit for ejectment against tenants in possession of a farm, houses, etc., in the town of Shawnee, the tenants in possession being Henry Boyers, John Milne, John Reid and John Smothers. The suit was brought before Hon. E. Wattles, judge of the Fifth Judicial Circuit, and was continued until the next term of the court, which convened March 8, 1826. It was not heard by Hon. James Hall, judge of the Fourth Judicial Circuit. The same parties, as named above, were attached to answer Joe Doe of a plea whereupon they the defendants, with force and arms entered in five messuages,[39] five barns and five outhouses and the lot and grant and one acre of land with the appurtenances situated and being in Shawneetown, etc. This case was against until the next term of court, held at Equality May 22, 1827, by Hon. Thomas C. Browne, defendants entered a plea of not guilty, and both parties to the suit "put themselves upon the country," McLean & Grundy for defendants and Hardin & Eddy for plaintiffs. Whereupon plaintiffs' attorney filed a notice in the following words and figures to wit:

> Mr. McLean,
> Sir: you are required to produce in the trial of the case of *Doe vs. Henry Boyers et al.*, the certificate granted by the register of the land office at Shawneetown to John A. Wilson, assignee of the heirs of Alexander Wilson, deceased.
> Hardin & Eddy.

Thereupon came the following jury: Joseph Reynolds, William Mills, John Choisser, James Cairns, Robert Keith, Robert Henderson, A. T. McCool, T. Guard, John Crenshaw, A. P. S. Wight[40], John Seebolt and John Berry; but before the jury had time to render a verdict, the defendant filed a motion for a nonsuit, which being allowed, the court adjudged the costs against the plaintiff.

---

[38] Trespass *vi et armis* is usually translated as trespass by force of arms. Replevin is an action to recover personal property said or claimed to be taken illegally. *Scire facias* represents a judicial writ, based upon some matter of record, such as a judgment, that requires the person against whom it's brought to appear before the court and to show cause why the parties bringing it should not have advantage of such record or thing.

[39] Messuage is an old Middle English word that means premise; i.e., as in the suspect entered the premise.

[40] Should be A. G. S. Wight.

On the 12th of September, 1825, James O. Wattles sat as judge in consequence of Hon. James Hall being engaged in some of the cases before the court. John Norman, John Frazier, John Lincoln, John B. Ellis, John Ellis and James Davis were found guilty of rioting, and fined $15 each. Hon. James O. Wattles served until the close of the September term of that year, and on the second Monday of January, 1826, Hon. James Hall resumed his seat upon the bench. Hon. James O. Wattles presided again at the September term, 1826; at which term James Caldwell, a subject of the king of Great Britain, was naturalized, which was probably the first case in Gallatin county. The May term, 1827, was held at the courthouse in Equality, by Hon. Thomas C. Browne, Leonard White, clerk.

An important case was that of the president and directors of the State Bank of Illinois vs. Hazle Moreland for the foreclosure of a mortgage. This action was commenced by *scire facias* in the Gallatin Circuit Court on a mortgage executed to plaintiffs and recorded according to law. The defendant demurred to the *scire facias*, and judgment was rendered for the defendant. The case was then taken to the supreme court, Hon. William Wilson, chief justice; Theophilus W. Smith and Samuel D. Lockwood, associate justices. The supreme court quoted the 18th section of an act passed January 17, 1825, concerning judgments and executions as follows:

> If default be made in the payment of any sum of money secured by mortgage on lands and tenements duly executed and recorded, and if the payments be by installments and the last shall have become due, tit shall be lawful for the mortgagee to sue out a writ of *scire facias* from the Clerk's office of the Circuit Court, in which the said mortgaged premises may be situated on any part thereof.
>
> If language is comprehensive enough to authorize this proceeding by *scire facias*, the Legislature certainly employed it in this statute, and the supreme court decided that the mortgagee was allowed to proceed by *scire facias*. The case was, therefore, remanded to the Gallatin Circuit Court, which at its May term 1829, judged that the *scire facias* had been duly executed and that the plaintiff recover of the defendant $400, and that the southeast quarter of Section 34, Township 9, Range 9, be sold to satisfy the judgment.

The State Bank won a similar suit against Harrison Wilson. Hon. Thomas C. Browne presided in this circuit court from 1827 to 1834. April 6, Hon. Alexander F. Grant, judge of the Third Judicial Circuit, presided holding that term; Hon. Justice Harlan presided in October, and Judge Grant in November, 1835. April 4, 1836, Judge Jephtha Hardin began a term of this court; on the 5th Thomas Pickering was indicted for selling cards and for playing cards; Stephen Blackman for keeping a gaming house, and Jacob Cummins for playing cards. Thomas Pickering was on the 20th of July acquitted of selling cards, an on the 25th plead guilty of playing cards and gambling, and was fined $10. Hon. Walter B. Scates, held court at the April term, 1837, commencing April 3, and on the 8th Peter Hardin was found guilty of murder and sentenced to death. September 23 Isom Franklin was found guilty of manslaughter and the court passed the following sentence:

You are to be remanded to jail, to be taken thence to the penitentiary at Alton, there to remain two years and eleven calendar months at hard labor, and one calendar month in solitary confinement, and to be fined $1.

Hon. Walter B. Scates continued to preside in this court until 1846, when he was succeeded by Hon. William A. Denning in 1851, in which year Hon. Samuel S. Marshall became judge of the Twelfth Judicial Circuit. The May term, 1851, was held by Judge Marshall at the courthouse in Equality, and the September term, 1851, at the courthouse in Shawneetown.

About this time for a number of years, both before and after, there were numerous indictments against various parties for kidnapping, which crime may be found discussed in another place. A special term of this court was begun February 16, 1852, for the trial of chancery cases, Judge Samuel S. Marshall on the bench.

At the October term of 1854, Hon. Downing Baugh presided. On the 30th of this month Sanford Browning was found guilty of manslaughter and sentenced to the penitentiary for seven years at hard labor. At this term also H. K. Starkey was sentenced to be hanged, but was acquitted at a new trial. At the June term of 1855, Hon. Downing Baugh also presided, but was succeeded in October, 1855, by Hon. Edwin Beecher.

The Assassination of John E. Hall

At the May term of 1857, Hon. Wesley Sloan was judge. At this term was commenced one of the most remarkable murder trials that have taken place in any country, remarkable because of the almost if not quite absolute lack of provocation, because of the high standing of the murdered man, and of his family, and because of it being one of the first of the kind, since numerous cases in which the insane pleas of emotional insanity has resulted in a verdict of acquittal.

The murdered man, John E. Hall, at the time clerk of the circuit court, was without a moment's warning shot in the back by Robert C. Sloo in 1856. The jury before whom the case was tried was as follows: Joseph Grayson, George McMurchy, Jesse Jenkins, William Hargrave, Sterling Edwards, Wesley Brown, Jesse Johnson, A. H. Cook Bethuel Cook, William Williams, Andrew J. Cowan and Allen Robinett. Logan (John A.), Allen, Robinson and Posey were the attorneys for the people, and Davis, Swett, Crockett, Freeman and McCallen, for the defense. The verdict of the jury was as follows: "We, the jury, find the defendant not guilty;" it was therefore "ordered and adjudged by the court, that the defendant, Robert C. Sloo, is not guilty of the charge alleged in the indictment in this case against him, and that he be discharged without day."

Hon. Wesley Sloan continued to preside in this court until the May term, 1867, and was succeeded at the October term by Hon. Andrew D. Duff. The circuit of which this county formed a part was changed to the 19th vin 1863, and to the 26th vin 1867, and Judge Duff continued to preside until 1873. He was followed at the February term, 1874, by Hon. Tazewell B. Tanner, when the circuit became the 24th. At the November term, 1877, the circuit was changed to the 2nd, and Hon. James C. Allen presided in Gallatin County.

At the March term of 1878, the judge was Hon. John H. Halley, and at the May term, Hon. James C. Allen; at the November term, 1878, and the May term, 1879, Hon. T. B.

Tanner; at the September term, 1879 and the February term, 1880, Hon. William C. Jones; at the February term, 1881, the September term, 1881, the February and September terms, 1882, and the February term, 1883, Hon. Chauncey S. Conger; at the September term, 1883, Hon. William C. Jones; at the February term, 1884, Hon. Thomas S. Casey; at the September term, 1884, and the April term, 1885, Hon. Chauncey S. Conger; at the September term, 1885, and the February term, 1886, Hon. Carroll C. Boggs; at the September term, 1886, Hon. C. S. Conger; and the February term, 1887, Hon. Carroll C. Boggs.

To give a complete list of the murder trials in this county would be unnecessary in a volume of this character, as they have been quite numerous, indicating a much more than ordinarily perturbed condition of society, lasting through a long series of years.

Aiken Murder Trial

The Aiken murder trial, however, cannot be passed unnoticed. John Aiken killed Augustus Stewart in March 1864, in White County, and was committed to jail at Carmi, but broke jail and was not captured until 1877, and then through the efforts of Thomas I. Porter, sheriff of White County, one of the quietest and most courageous of men.[41] A change of venue was taken to Gallatin County, where the trial took place before the following jury: John B. Walters, John H. Crow, William Willis, Jasper Bowling, Thomas Frohock, Albert Hill, A. M. Hannah, James J. Williams, John M. Thomas, John Fitzgibbon, William R. Tate and John Wilde.

The verdict of the jury was as follows: "We, the jury, find the defendant guilty of murder and fix the punishment at death." A motion was made for a new trial, and on hearing of that motion it was developed that the jurors, before arriving at their verdict as recorded above, had all been in favor of finding him guilty of murder, but one of them was opposed to the infliction of the death penalty. As this one would not yield his opposition to this penalty, it was arranged that two members of the jury, the one opposed to hanging and another, unwilling to agree to anything else, should draw straws for the verdict, the long straw to win. The result of the drawing was that the juror unalterably in favor of hanging drew the long straw, and hence the fixing by the jury of the death penalty. Upon the development of this fact, a new trial was granted, and the jury which had adopted the novel methods recounted above of arriving at a verdict were punished as follows: the four engaged in the drawing of the straws, the one who procured them, the one who held them and the two who drew them were fined, three of them being fined $100 each, one of them $50 and the remainder of the jury were acquitted.

Upon the second trial the following were the jury: John Eskew, Samuel Simpkins, Thomas Martin, Richard Sweeney, Edward Young, Moses McDonald, James A. Jones, William Clayton, George B. Stilly, Price Williams, Charles Mock and Thomas McKee. They brought in a verdict of guilty of murder and fixed the punishment at imprisonment in the penitentiary at hard labor for life. The accomplices of Aiken, Henry and Charles Glide have not been apprehended.[42]

---

[41] See the *History of White County* for more details of this case.

[42] John Aiken was the son of George Aiken, a Williamson County man who opened a store at Blairsville in 1848. He also served in the ill-fated "Whang Doodle" 128th Regiment. "After George Aiken was frustrated in his

Legal Hangings

Three men have been hanged for murder in Gallatin County, the first of which occurred before the State was admitted into the Union. In this case Martin Frazier was hanged for the murder of Mr. Dryden. Frazier had been on criminally intimate terms with Mrs. Dryden and it was because of this intimacy that Dryden was killed. The murder was committed with an axe while Dryden was milking a cow. His body was buried under his smokehouse and such means as suggested themselves were taken by Mrs. Dryden to prevent the discovery of the body. At the expiration of about two weeks, during which time the entire community supposed he had voluntary left the county never to return, his body was found under the smokehouse, some say by means of an old lady's dream, others through the observations of some boys who noticed an unusual number of flies going down through and coming up through the cracks in the smokehouse floor.

Upon the discovery being made, Frazier, who had assiduously assisted to find traces of the missing man, immediately started on a full run for the woods, thus confessing himself the cause of Dryden's mysterious disappearance. Pursuit on foot and on horseback was promptly made by a number of citizens, who rode and ran rapidly towards the fords across Hardin Creek on the Saline Mines Road, and on the Tally's Ferry Road. Frazier made for the Big Bend between the two fords, but no one supposed it possible for him to escape because of the extremely soft nature of the sides and bottom of the creek, in which, as some have expressed it, "a mosquito would mire." Frazier ran with all possible speed toward a comparatively narrow place in the creek, where the banks on either side were high and dry, and to the surprise of all, made a running leap and cleared the creek, though the distance, as afterward measured, was a trifle over 22 feet from toe to heel. The then ran for a herd of cattle and, placing himself in a stooping posture on the opposite side of a large steer, endeavored thus covered to escape to a canebrake not far distant, and would have succeeded but the keen eyes of a boy who accompanied the pursuing party, and who remarked that "that old red steer, it seems to me, has too many fore legs." This led to a rapid chase by horsemen who succeeded in surrounding and capturing the fugitive, who was tried for the murder, convicted, sentenced to death and hanged.

Two other hangings for murder are all that have occurred in the county, though a large number of murders have been committed. The last murder trial was that of James Switzer for the killing of John J. Ramsey, the trial occurring at the February term, 1887, of the circuit court, and accused being convicted and sentenced to the penitentiary for 20 years.

---

efforts to sell out the One-Hundred and Twenty-Eighth, at Cairo, he went to Missouri, and got Allen Glide and Charley Glide, and came back here [Williamson Co.]. These, and his son John Aiken, are the ones supposed to compose the 'Aiken Gang.' This gang flourished here in the spring of 1863, in the north part of the county, during which time several murders were committed, and no less than fifty or our citizens robbed. Dr. Bandy was taken out and whipped unmercifully, and George Cox was attacked in his house and fired on several times. This band soon got so large that it became unwieldy, and they got to stealing horses. Several of them were arrested, tried and bailed, and left the county. Among the men arrested was James Cheneworth." [Source: Milo Erwin. 1876. *History of Williamson County*. Privately Published. 103.]

Early Lawyers

Some of the ablest attorneys furnished to the State of Illinois have been members of the Gallatin County bar. Among them may be mentioned Jephtha Hardin, the first one admitted to practice, as elsewhere appears; Henry Eddy, William J. Gatewood, S. D. Marshall, John A. McClernand; John McLean, one of the brightest minds of Illinois; Thomas C. Browne, later one of the supreme judges of the State; Russell E. Heacock, afterward a prominent lawyer of Chicago; Elias Kent Kane, John A. Logan, Robert G. Ingersoll, A. G. Caldwell, and, occasionally, Abraham Lincoln.

The present bar consists of E. D. Youngblood, Roedel & Sisson, Bowman & Pillow, Bartley & Son, Parrish Bros., D. M. Kinsall and R. W. Townshend, the latter member of Congress from the 19th District.

Military History

Mexican War

For the Mexican War Illinois raised six regiments, a larger number than was raised in any other State. The Third Regiment was composed of ten companies, one of which was raised in Gallatin County. Of this company, Michael K. Lawler was captain, and Samuel D. Marshall, major. The Third Regiment was commanded by Col. Forman. Subsequently Capt. Michael K. Lawler raised a company of dragoons in Gallatin County. Thus Gallatin County performed her full share in the war for the annexation of Texas.[43]

Civil War

When the slaveholders' Rebellion broke out there was, in southern Illinois, a large number of people in favor of peace so long as there was any hope in their minds of preventing a dissolution of the Union by peaceful measures; and besides these there was a large number of people who were so fully in sympathy with the Rebellion that they not only depreciated war upon the South to prevent secession being consummated, but they opposed the war with all their influence and even favored the secession of southern Illinois from the Union, and the union of its fortunes with those of the Southern States. This was owing to the fact that a large number of the early settlers were originally from the Southern States, as has been shown elsewhere, and they and their descendants were generally, though not universally, admirers of the chivalry of the South, and of the peculiar institution of slavery, and they were fully convinced that it was constitutional to destroy the Constitution, along with the Government of the Constitution, for the sake of the preservation of that peculiar institution; though, a was just intimated, there were Southern men, some from Kentucky, some from Virginia, who might be given, who expressed the opinion to leaders in the Southern movement, that the movement would not only fail, but that it would end in the

---

[43] Former Cypressville postmaster Edgar Bogardus also served as an officer from Gallatin County. See his biography for details.

death of slavery, in whose interest it was in part inaugurated. That southern Illinois did not join the Southern Confederacy, or, at least attempt to do so, is due as much to the attitude and patriotism of John A. Logan, as to the efforts of any other man, and it was also due to his influence that many of the counties in southern Illinois should have assumed the apparently paradoxical position of being so largely in favor of secession and yet, at the same time, furnishing so many soldiers to the Union Army as to avoid the drafts all through the war.

In 1861 the entire number of persons in the county subject to military duty was 1,314, and in 1862 it was 1,063. The quota of the county in 1861 was 214, and in 1862 it was 146. Under the calls of 700,000 men February 1, and March 14, 1864, it was 240, and under the call for 500,000 men July 18, 1864, it was 186. Prior to December 31, 1864, the entire quote of the county was, as enumerated above, 786, and the entire number furnished to the army by that time was 1,358, or 542 in excess of all calls. Prior to December 31, 1865, the entire quota of the county was 1,358, and the entire credit of the county 1,362, or just 4 in excess of the number called for by the Government. In 1865 the number of persons subject to military duty was 1,343.[44]

The soldiers who thus volunteered were distributed in larger or smaller numbers among the different regiments. Most of the soldiers who volunteered from this county joined the 18th Infantry, the 29th Infantry or the Sixth Cavalry, and it is deemed sufficient to present brief sketches of these regiments in this connection.

The Eighteenth Regiment

The 18th Regiment was originally officered as follows: Colonel, Michael K. Lawler, of Gallatin County; lieutenant-colonel, Thomas H. Burgess, of DuQuoin; major, Samuel Eaton. Col. Lawler was mustered in June 30, 1861, and promoted to brigadier-general April 14, 1863. He was brevetted brigadier-general November 29, 1862, and major-general March 13, 1865. Henry S. Wilson, of Shawneetown, became major of this regiment June 11, 1863, succeeding Samuel B. Marks, of Anna, who was promoted lieutenant-colonel. Lewis Lambert was the first chaplain of this regiment and Mordecai B. Kelly the second.

Company B of this regiment was raised almost wholly in Shawneetown. Its successive captains were Elias W. Jones, Henry S. Wilson and Cornelius C. Weaver; its first lieutenants, Cornelius C. Weaver, and Charles M. Edwards, and its second lieutenants, William Scanland, Emri C. Watson, Charles M. Edwards and James Orr. Of the private soldiers who lost their lives in the service in various ways were the following: William O'Brien, drowned August 18, 1861; G. W. Coad, died of wounds April 1, 1862; Franklin Collard, died August 2, 1861; John M. Fish, died January 13, 1862; Martin Fogle, killed at Shiloh, April 6, 1862; Reivas W. Greer, died October 15, 1863; Henry Hewitt, killed at Shiloh; John Henson, killed at Fort Donelson; Washington C. Jones, died March 29, 1862; John Kielbraid, died of wounds April 30, 1862; Elijah Morris, died at Elizabethtown, Ill.; Hiram Noye, died at Mound City, September 20, 1861; Nathan L. Newell, killed at Fort Donelson; Solomon

---

[44] At least nine Gallatin County residents of African descent fought for the Union cause as privates in the 29th U.S. Colored Infantry Regiment. They were James M. Bell, John S. Day, Cornelius Elliott, Timothy A. Guard, Peter Levell, Samuel Marshall, Elias McAllister, James H. Patton, and Jefferson Taburn.

Stanton, died at Mound City, November 14, 1861; Jasper Whitney, killed by guard December 24, 1863; Charles H. Wilson, killed at Fort Donelson.

Company D was raised in various parts of southeastern Illinois, but partly in Gallatin, Saline and Williamson Counties. Its first captain was Joseph T. Cormick, of Centralia, and its second Patrick Lawler, of Shawneetown. Its first lieutenants were Wilmer Bedford, of Centralia; John G. Mansker and Chalon A. Towle, of Harrisburg; Chalon A. Towle had been second lieutenant and previously sergeant. Daniel D. Mattice, of Harrisburg, was first sergeant. George W. Grant, of Crab Orchard, Williamson County, died at Jackson, Tenn., May 25, 1863; Garland W. Shackleford, of Williamson County, died at Cairo, October 9, 1861.

Company K, though mostly raised in Jackson County had numerous members from Franklin and Gallatin Counties. Those from the latter county, who died in the service, were Lee Sullivan Harris, Richard J. North of wounds March 30, 1862; William Russell, killed at Fort Donelson.

Briefly recited, the history of the regiment is as follows: It rendezvoused at Anna, Union Co., Ill., May 16, 1861; on May 19[45] it was mustered into State service for thirty days by U.S. Grant, and on the 28th of May was mustered into the United States service for three years, moved to Bird's Point, Mo., June 24, 1861, and remained there, mainly, until August 26, when it went to Mound City, Ill., to guard the building of gunboats; formed part of a command under Col. Oglesby sent to Bloomfield, Mo., to rout Jeff. Thompson and his command, after performing various duties February 3, 1862, when it went with the expedition under Gen. Grant up the Tennessee River; was among the first to enter Fort Henry, February 6. At the battle of Fort Donelson it lost 200 men, killed and wounded—Col. Lawler, himself, being wounded; went into camp at Pittsburg Landing March 23; participated in the battle of April 6, under command of Major Eaton, until he was wounded, and then under Capt. Rush, until he was twice wounded, and then under Capt. Anderson. Its loss was 75, killed, wounded and missing—Maj. Eaton died of his wound. It marched upon Corinth, and after the evacuation of that place, to Jackson, Tenn., from which place, as a base of operations, it did severe and valuable duty until May 30, 1863, when with General Kimball's division, it went to Memphis and thence to a position above Vicksburg, and up to Haine's Bluff, in the vicinity of which place it was occupied in assisting to prevent Johnston's army from raising the siege of Vicksburg, which lasted from May 18 to July 4, 1863, when Gen. Pemberton surrendered the city to Gen. Grant. July 24, went up the Mississippi, landing at Helena, Ark., on the 27th. Started from Helena, August 13, on the "Arkansas Expedition," and went into camp at Duvall's Bluff, August 24, and on September 2, went to Brownsville after remaining in Arkansas doing valiant service for the Union until May 28, 1864, when the term expired for those who had composed the regiment originally. All of these returned to Springfield, Ill., for pay and discharge, while all the re-enlisted men and recruits were formed into companies, and on the 14th of April, 1865, the regiment was composed of two veteran companies (B and C), one company (A) of three years' recruits, and seven companies of one year's recruits, assigned to it in March, 1865. The regiment was mustered out at Little Rock, Ark., December 16, 1865, and arrived at Camp Butler, Ill., on

---

[45] Book says May 9, but it must be May 19 to fit.

the 31st of the same month for pay and discharge. The entire number belonging to this regiment, rank and file, was 2,043.

The Twenty-Ninth Infantry

The 29th Infantry was raised largely in the counties of the histories of which are in this volume. Its first colonel was James S. Rearden, of Shawneetown, and its second, Moses Brayman, of Springfield. Charles M. Ferrill, of Elizabethtown, was its third colonel and Loren Kent, fourth. Its lieutenant-colonels were James E. Dunlap, of Jacksonville; Charles M. Ferrill, Loren Kent, John A. Callicott, of Shawneetown, and Elijah P. Curtis; majors, Mason Brayman, John A. Callicott, Elijah P. Curtis, Eli W. Green, and adjutants, Aaron R. Stout, of Shawneetown, Loren Kent, Richard M. Bozeman, Golconda and Pleasant G. Waters.

Company C was raised mainly in Gallatin County. John A. Callicott, Eli W. Green and Sanford B. Kannady were its successive captains; John M. Eddy, Thomas Rieling and Michael Hickey, first lieutenants, and Alfred De Witt, William Boswell and Sandford B. Kanady, second lieutenants. The non-commissioned officers and private soldiers who lost their lives in this company were Serg. Marion McCool, of Shawneetown, killed at Fort Donelson; Corp. Charles E. Vinson, died at Mound City, February 28, 1862; Corp. Alexander Norton, died May 2, 1863; Corp. Elijah J. Timmins, died at Cairo, January, 1862; Corporal John Fletcher, killed at Fort Donelson; Jackson J. Mangrum, died October 19, 1861; John Behan, died at Vicksburg, October 13, 1863; James Bradshaw, killed at Fort Donelson; William Fromley, died January, 1862; Edward Donley, died May 4, 1863; George W. Dupont, died February, 1862; Anderson England, died May, 1862; William H. Frame, died June 5, 1864; George Hughes, killed at Fort Donelson; Jacob Long, died October, 1861; Jesse L. Martin, killed at Fort Donelson; Robert Oskins, died October, 1861; George Farrell, died as prisoner of war, February 16, 1864; Alexander Seat, died at Vicksburg, December 7, 1863; Claiborne C. Vaught, died of wounds received at Shiloh; Joseph White, died May 2, 1863; Joseph Adkinson drowned near Memphis; Andrew J. Donovan, died December 11, 1863; Andrew Pate, died as prisoner of war, February 16, 1864, and James J. White died at home.

Company D was raised mostly in Gallatin County. Its captains were John S. Whiting, of Equality; James B. Hart and Eberlee P. H. Stone, both of New Haven. First lieutenants: James B. Hart; Benjamin F. Berry, of Indiana; Samuel Bagsley, of New Haven; John F. McCartney, and Robert W. Sherrod, of Saline County. Second lieutenants; Eberlee P. H. Stone; Pinckney B. Harris, of White County, and Augustus H. Melvin, of New Haven. The non-commissioned officers and private soldiers from Gallatin County, who laid down their lives in the service of the country, were Serg. William P. Davis, killed at Fort Donelson; Bogarth Wesley, died December 15, 1861; George R. Crawford, died of wounds February 18, 1862; Edward Brown, died at Natchez, January 15, 1864; William R. Crawford, died at Vicksburg, October 22, 1863; John B. Groves, died at St. Louis, March 17, 1862; Isaac Lackins, died March 4, 1862, of wounds received at Fort Donelson; Lewis Harvey, died at New Orleans, February 8, 1865; James Rochell, killed at Fort Donelson; Daniel Gaddes, died at Natchez, December 18, 1863; Samuel Bagley, at New Haven, first lieutenant of this company was killed April 29, 1863.[46]

The history of this regiment is briefly as follows: It was mustered into the service of the United States at Camp Butler, Ill., August 19, 1861, and was assigned to the brigade of Gen. John A. McClernand. After going to Bloomfield, Mo., under Col. R. J. Oglesby, it went into Kentucky under Brig-Gen. John A. McClernand in January, 1862. It participated in the battles of Fort Henry and Fort Donelson, and afterward went to Savannah, Tenn., and was engaged in the battle of Pittsburg Landing, engaged in the siege of Corinth, and after arduous services in Tennessee and Mississippi, eight companies of the regiment were surrendered by Col. R. C. Murphy at Holly Springs, December 1, 1862, to the rebel general Van Dorn. The eight companies captured were paroled and sent to Benton Barracks, where they remained until July, 1863, when, being exchanged, they returned to duty. The two other companies served in the Western Navy, and lost several men and one officer in running the batteries at Vicksburg and Grand Gulf. On the 19th of October, 1863, the 131st Illinois was consolidated with the 29th, and Lieut-Col. Kent was promoted colonel and placed in command of the regiment. The regiment re-enlisted in January, 1864, and after veteran furlough returned to duty in the field, serving at Natchez and Memphis, and afterward were sent to Paducah, Ky., to protect that State against rebel cavalry. In November, 1864, returned to Memphis; went to Mobile, after taking part in the siege of Fort Morgan, and then to Galveston, Tex., arriving there July 1, 1865. After serving in Texas until November 6, 1865, it was mustered out of the service and reached Illinois in November on the 26th and was paid and discharged November 28, 1865.

56th Illinois Infantry

Company D, of the 56th Regiment, was raised partly in this county. Its captains were David Slinger, of White County, and Sylvester R. Cone, of Gallatin County. Its first lieutenants were William F. Williams and Sylvester R. Cone, both of Gallatin, and Michael J. Dempsey, of White. Its second lieutenants were Cone and Dempsey. The non-commissioned officers and private soldiers of this county who died in the service were Corporal James Ayres, died in hospital; George Covey, died April 12, 1862; Benjamin Hickman, died at Corinth, July 1, 1862; James P. Hall, died July 26, 1862; George McClellan, died July 26, 1862; Elihu Milligan, died April 5, 1862; Benjamin F. Young, died at Corinth, September 24, 1862.

The Sixth Cavalry Regiment

The Sixth Cavalry Regiment was raised mainly in Gallatin, Saline and Hamilton Counties. Its field and staff officers were, however, with the exception of Thomas G. S. Herod, from other counties. Herod was from Shawneetown, and was major of the regiment from December 18, 1862, to November 2, 1863, when he was sentenced to the penitentiary for ten years for killing Lieut.-Col. Loomis in Memphis, Tenn.

---

[46] Should be Samuel Bagsley.

Company L of this regiment was raised mostly in Gallatin County. Its captains were Thomas G. S. Herod of Shawneetown, Mathew H. Staff, Firth Charlesworth, Wade W. McCoy of Shawneetown, and John J. Clark. First lieutenants, Benedict Crandle and Samuel A. Armstrong of Shawneetown, Mathew H. Staff, Firth Charlesworth, John W. Hughes, Wade W. McCoy, Willibald Yehie, and John J. Clark. Second lieutenants, Henry Stout, Armstrong, Staff, Charlesworth and Hughes, as above, and Joseph A. Davenport.

This regiment was organized at Camp Butler, November 19, 1861, and moved to Shawneetown, November 25, 1861, remaining until February, 1862, when it moved to Paducah, Ky., and then to Columbus, Ky., where it was divided, five companies going to Trenton, Tenn., and five to Memphis, two going to Paducah and Bird's Point. During the summer of 1862 the detachments operated against guerrillas and were in several engagements at Dyersburg, Olive Branch and Coldwater. In the fall of 1862 the regiment was reunited at Memphis, and moved with Sherman towards Grenada, Miss., and pursued Van Dorn after his raid upon Holly Springs, engaging him for seven consecutive days; went to La Grange in January, 1863. On March 29, was attacked while asleep, but got into position and repulsed the enemy; Lieut. Wilson and eight men were killed during the engagement, and Lieuts. Baker and Anderson and 29 men wounded. This regiment was in Grierson's famous raid through Mississippi and Louisiana. It operated under Banks at the siege of Port Hudson, and after the surrender of the place July 9, embarked for Memphis. In West Tennessee it was in the number of engagements, one with Gen. Forrest at La Grange and later at Moscow, Tenn., with the same forces. After a number of other engagements the regiment re-enlisted and returned home on veteran furlough. The veteran regiment participated in a large number of engagements, many of them battles, notably the Battle of Nashville, December 13-15, 1864, and after the victory gained there pursued the fleeing rebels to Florence, Ala. After service in Alabama until November 5, 1865, it marched to Selma and was there mustered out of service, and was finally discharged at Springfield, Ill., November 20, 1865.

Company E, 14th Illinois Cavalry

Company E, of the 14th Cavalry, was raised largely in Gallatin County. Its captain was Benjamin Crandle; first lieutenant, George W. Evans; and second lieutenants, John Hahr, George C. Smith, William M. Duvall (of Shawneetown, not mustered, died at prison at Wilmington, N. C., March 12, 1865) and Robert P. Simmons. The Gallatin County private soldiers who died in the service were Henry Artman, died at Louisville, April 10, 1864; Scott Awalt, died in rebel prison, Florence, S. C., October 18, 1864; James Dailey, killed in Battle at Camp Cetico, Tenn., May 27, 1864; Noah Friar, killed near Springfield, Tenn., December 9, 1864; Stephen Morgan, died at Glasgow, Ky., June 6, 1863; William Roleman, died at home, June 11, 1864.

120th Illinois Infantry

Company D, of the 120th Infantry, was raised mostly in Gallatin County. Its captains were Parker B. Pillow and Washington Canady, of Shawneetown. First lieutenant, Washington Canady, until promoted captain; and second lieutenant, Joshua D. Jennings, of

Shawneetown. The non-commissioned officers and private soldiers who died in the service were Corporals John Davis, at Memphis, June 19, 1863; William H. McCool, killed at Guntown, Miss., June 10, 1864; Albert N. Sketo, died at Memphis, August 21, 1863, and Isaac Hogan at Memphis, March 18, 1863. Private soldiers — Emriah J. Carter, at Memphis, June 19, 1863; Jackson Crabtree, at Memphis, June 19, 1863; Elisha C. Colbert, at Memphis, June 16, 1863; George W. Greer, died in Andersonville prison, November 3, 1864; grave numbered 11778; Charles M. Henry, at Lake Providence, July 15, 1863; George W. Hargrave, at Memphis, August 18, 1863; Fountain E. Harpool, at Lake Providence, July 9, 1863; Jacob Rice, at Memphis, June 19, 1863; John Sherwood, at Memphis, February 21, 1863; Edward Sherwood, June 12, 1863; Thomas Sanderson, killed at Greenville, Miss., May 11, 1863; William Thompson, died at Lake Providence, July 11, 1863; Alexander Thompson, at Memphis, November 20, 1862; Needham A. Warrick, in Andersonville prison, January 24, 1863, grave numbered 12392; James H. Watson, died of wounds at Mobile, July 12, 1864, while prisoner of war; William Brown, at Memphis, January 17, 1865; Alonzo Bennett, at Memphis, August 20, 1865; John Hooker, at Memphis, February 8, 1863; George W. Owen, at Memphis, May 22, 1865; Carr Owen at Andersonville prison, September 11, 1864, number of grave 8414.

Company H, of this regiment, was raised in Gallatin, Saline and White Counties. Its captains were David Porter, of White County, and General F. M. Bean, of Gallatin County. First lieutenants, William Wallers, and James A. Trousdale, both of White County. Second lieutenants, William L. Blackard and General F. M. Bean. The non-commissioned officers and private soldiers from Gallatin County who died in the service were Corporals Adam Mayhue, died at Memphis, March 12, 1863, and Charles E. Riley, at Memphis, January 26, 1863. Private soldiers: Joseph M. Bean, killed at Guntown, Miss., June 10, 1864; William C. Bean, died at Memphis, December 11, 1862; Francis M. Dillard, at Memphis, April 2, 1864; George F. Garrett, at Lake Providence, July 12, 1863; Israel Harget, at Memphis, December 27, 1862; David W. Lewis, at Camp Butler, in 1862; William T. Pritchett, at Memphis, October 28, 1863; John Vergel Mitchell, at Memphis, November 30, 1863.

131st Illinois Infantry

Company E of the 131st Infantry, was mostly from Gallatin County. Its captain was Cornelius W. Halley; first lieutenants, Amster B. Pate and Philip A. Pate, and second lieutenants, Sidney A. Pinney and Josiah Campbell. The company was mostly transferred to Company B of the consolidated regiment.

Company G of this regiment was raised very largely at Equality. Its captain was Edward H. McCaleb, first lieutenant, John Dailey, both of Equality, and second lieutenant, James A. Peter of Metropolis. The company was mostly transferred to Company D of the consolidated regiment.

Gallatin County Veteran Association

The first annual reunion of the soldiers of Gallatin County was held September 14, 15, and 16, 1886. A large number of soldiers was present and the Gallatin County Veteran Association was formed. The officers of this association are Col. John M. Bowling, of

Equality, president; J. L. Boyd, of Shawneetown, vice-president; L. E. Quigley, of Omaha, secretary; W. P. Aldridge, New Haven, treasurer.

The Mexican veterans present were John A. Callicott, Milton Bartley, Adam Stinson, G. W. Usselton, Charles A. Kaufman, G. H. W. Lawrence and W. H. Blades.

Gallatin County furnished three distinguished generals to the Union Army; Gen. M. K. Lawler, an excellent soldier; Gen. John A. McClernand, and Gen. James Harrison Wilson.

Gen. Grant's Horse, 'Egypt'

The following letter from Gen. Grant is worthy a place in the history of Gallatin County, and explains the transaction which it is desired to commemorate:

Chattanooga, Tenn., December 11, 1863

O. Pool, Esq.,

Dear Sir: The very elegant horse presented to me by the citizens of Gallatin, Pope, Saline and Hamilton Counties, Illinois, reached me during the absence of Gen. Wilson (at Knoxville) who was commissioned to make the presentation in the name of the citizens of the above named counties.

Permit me through you to thank them for their present which I accept as a token of their devotion to the cause of the union, and as a very great complement to me personally, as an agent of the loyal people in assisting in breaking down rebellions.

Very truly your obedient servant,
U.S. Grant, Maj. Gen. U.S.A.

This horse was christened "Egypt" by Gen. J. H. Wilson and others in honor of the people who presented him, and it was hoped by them that the horse, "Egypt," would become quite as famous as McDonald's "Selam."

Shawneetown

Shawneetown, the county seat of Gallatin County, is situated on the Ohio River, in longitude 88° 10', and latitude 37° 45', and is elevated 353 feet above the sea. It derives its name from the Shawnee Indians, located here and in the vicinity from about 1735 to about 1812 or 1815. It is one of the oldest places in the State, having contained a few scattered houses as early as 1804. It was first surveyed by the United States Government in 1810, in accordance with an act of Congress, and again in 1814. The first town plat was approved April 30, 1810, and the established of the land office in Shawneetown was approved February 21, 1812, but no land entries were made until July 1814. Shawneetown was laid off and established as a kind of trading post for the salt works then being established along the Saline River "by a few squatters who always precede civilization."

For a number of years salt-making roved a very profitable undertaking, and diffused activity and prosperity all around, and as a natural consequence Shawneetown acquired an important which departed after the salt works were closed.

Among the very early settlers in the place, after Michael Sprinkle, he being the first settler in the county and in Shawneetown, were W. A. G. Posey, Dr. Alexander Posey, and Thomas L. Posey. Thomas Sloo, first register of the land office, and his sons, Thomas and John; Dr. A. B. Dake, Dr. Shannon, Dr. John Reid, John Marshall, Marmaduke S. Davenport, James Davenport, Moses M. Rawlings, Samuel Hayes, Solomon Hayes, Richard Jones, James M. Jones, Jacob Barger, Peter C. Seaton, Samuel Seaton, John Rohrer, John Shearer, Mrs. Fatima McClernand, mother of John A. McClernand; Michael Robinson, John C. Reeves, Alexander Wilson and his sons, John Hilton, John McLean, James S. Beaumont, Robert Peeples, father of John McKee Peeples; James and Alexander Kirkpatrick, Joseph Logsdon and Joseph Reid.

A word or two comment about a few of these early settlers may not be out of place. Solomon Hayes was one of the innumerable army who have believed in their ability to discover perpetual motion; but different from most of them finally arrived at the rational conclusion that he could not succeed without overcoming or neutralizing friction. With friction overcome he believed he could succeed. Jacob Barger settled on a farm just outside Shawneetown, near the present roundhouse. John C. Reeves was cashier of the first bank established in Shawneetown, and used to sleep at night on top of barrels of silver in order to prevent its being stolen. He was the founder of the *Congressional Globe*. Alexander Wilson was the first to run a ferry across the Ohio River at Shawneetown. Dr. John Reid moved out of town and settled on the farm where now resides Mrs. S. C. Rowan.

Some of these, besides those mentioned above, moved out into the county and settled on farms. John Pool, father of Orval Pool, was also an early settler in Shawneetown, as was Joseph M. Street; Mrs. Catharine Shelby, a colored woman, whose husband was kidnapped during the times when "colored men had no right which white men were bound to respect," but who was rescued, came to Shawneetown in 1812 and is still living.[47]

John Marshall built the first brick house in Shawneetown; Moses M. Rawlings built the second, which was long known as the Rawlings House, still standing, and kept by Mr. Connor as a hotel.[48] Robert Peeples built the third, also still standing, and occupied as a residence by the widow of John McRoy Peeples, and standing just above E. F. Armstrong's hardware store on Main Street.[49] Joshua Sexton and his son Orville were also among the early inhabitants of Shawneetown.

Among the very early businessmen in Shawneetown were Weir & Vanlandingham (O. C.), afterward Mr. Vanlandingham alone, who kept a general store; for a short time a Mr. Patterson; Peeples & Kirkpatrick kept a general store. The first blacksmith was Michael Sprinkle, elsewhere mentioned; Hiram Walters was a blacksmith and wagon-maker, carrying on his trades where now stands Swafford Brothers' store, and Michael Kane also had a

---

[47] Mrs. Shelby's husband appears to have been Edmund Shelby, a native of Virginia born about 1792. The 1850 census finds the two of them together in their Shawneetown household. According to the census, Mrs. Shelby would have been around 16 when she came to Illinois from presumably her native state of Kentucky.

[48] This is incorrect. The Rawlings House already stood in November 1822 when Christine Holmes Tillson stayed there a week. During this time construction still continued on Marshall's house. See Tillson's account of Shawneetown in the Early Anecdotes section for more details.

[49] Peeples built his home in 1823 according to the building's National Register of Historic Places nomination form. His son John McKee Peeples built his home attached to the father's in 1846.

blacksmith shop between Hiram Walters' establishment and the river. _____ Tarleton kept a tavern in early days, down on the river bank, near where the present brick warehouse stands, originally built for a depot by John Crenshaw. Thomas M. Dorris was also an early tavern-keeper, and John Milne was the first silversmith in the place.

Widow 'Peggy' Logsdon

One of the most noted early settlers in Shawneetown was the widow, "Peggy" Logsdon, an excellent physician and midwife, to whose judgment and skill in the practice of obstetrics all the other early physicians deferred. It was her custom to ride on horseback to visit her patients, and no weather was too severe for her to venture out, nor obstacle too great for her to overcome. She practiced across the Ohio River in Kentucky as well as in Gallatin County, keeping a skiff in which she rowed herself across in answer to calls, which she could distinctly hear from the other side when at her house on "Sandy Ridge," in the southern extremity of Shawneetown.

One night after she had retired, a call came to her from the Kentucky shore. She answered back that she would be there as soon as she could dress and row across in her skiff. Going down to the river bank where her skiff was usually moored, she found it gone and not to be found, nor was any other in sight. She was, however, not to be daunted, so calling across again, she said she would be there as soon as she could swim the river. A log happened to be at hand with a short, stout limb standing perpendicularly in the air. Stripping of all her clothes, she tied them up tightly and suspended them upon the limb, then stepping into the water, she swam safely across, pushing the log before her. She had three sons (John, Joseph and Butler), and two daughters (Margaret and Nancy), and besides being an independent and hardy pioneer, she was a highly respected woman.

Bad Impressions

Besides these there were other worthy citizens, and besides, an over abundant supply of those who gave to the place a bad reputation for many years. Numerous early missionaries have left on record their recollections of Shawneetown. A Mr. Low, who was here in 1816, says:

> Among its two or three hundred inhabitants not a single soul made any pretensions to religion. Their shocking profaneness was enough to make one afraid to walk the street; and those who on the Sabbath were not fighting and drinking at the taverns and grog shops, were either hunting in the woods or trading behind their counters. A small audience gathered to hear the missionary preached, but a laborer might almost as soon expect to hear the stones cry out as to effect a revolution in the morals of this place.

Thomas Lippincott was here in January, 1818, and says: "We found a village not very prepossessing, the houses with one exception being set up on posts several feet from the earth," on account of the annual overflow.[50]

Mrs. Tillson was here nearly four years later, in November 1822. Referring to Shawneetown, she says:

> Our hotel,[51] the only brick house in the place, was made quite a commanding appearance from the river, towering as it did among the twenty, more or less, log cabins, and three or four box-looking frames. One or two of these were occupied as stores; one was a doctor's office, a lawyer's shingle graced the corner of one; cakes and beer another. The hotel lost its significance, however, on entering its doors. The finish was of the cheapest kind, the plastering handing loose from the walls, the floors carpetless, except with nature's carpeting-with that they were richly carpeted. The landlord was a whiskey keg in the morning and a keg of whisky at night; stupid and gruff in the morning, by noon could talk politics and abuse the yankees, and by sundown was brave for a fight. His wife kept herself in the kitchen; his daughters (one married and two single), performed the agreeable to strangers; the son-in-law, putting on the airs of a gentleman, presided at the table, carved the pork, dished out the cabbage, and talked big about his political friends. His wife, being his wife, he seemed to regard a notch above the other members of the family, and had her at his right hand at the table, where she sat with her long curls and her baby in her lap. Baby always seemed to be hungry while mamma was eating her dinner, and so little honey took dinner at the same time. Baby didn't have any tablecloth!—new manners to me.[52]

All of which serves to show the customs of the times-which, of course, still prevail in frontier places-and also the fastidiousness of the observer. Another incident which, however, happened somewhat earlier, shows the character of a portion of the people in a different phase. The great comet of 1811 spread consternation far and wide among the ignorant and superstitious, and it is related that when the first steamboat on the Ohio passed Shawneetown it was believed to be the comet-tail and all! If this be true, as it doubtless is, this first steamboat must have passed Shawneetown very soon after the disappearance of the comet, or while it was below the horizon.

---

[50] Lippincott (1791-1869) came from New Jersey and stopped at Shawneetown on his way to the Alton and Edwardsville area of Madison Co., Illinois, where he became a leading anti-slavery newspaper editor. He later became a Presbyterian minister and preached the funeral service of slain abolitionist leader Elijah P. Lovejoy in 1837.

[51] An original footnote at this point identified Mrs. Tillson's hotel as "The Rawlings' House." However, the innkeeper described is not Moses M. Rawlings but a man named Hilton, most likely John Hilton.

[52] See the Anecdotes section for the rest of Tillson's further adventures in Gallatin County.

Lafayette's Visit to Shawneetown

Another incident in the early history of Shawneetown will always be remembered with pride and pleasure—the visit of Lafayette in 1825. It was on the 14th of May when the boat, bearing this great friend of the United States, came in sight of the town; as it neared the landing a salute of twenty-four guns was fired. The people of the surrounding country had turned out en masse to great the hero of the day. Two lines were formed from Rawlings' Hotel to the river, calico having been previously spread upon the ground, upon which the Frenchman was to walk. Between the lines the committee of reception, town officials and other dignitaries, passed to the landing, received the nation's quest, and escorting him, returned to the hotel, and passed up again between the lines of silent, uncovered and reverent citizens. A large number of ladies was assembled at the door of the hotel, where the party halted, and an address of welcome was delivered by Judge James Hall.[53] Lafayette replied in a voice tremulous with emotion, thanking the people for their gratitude and affection. A collation was served, and a number of toasts were drunk appropriate to the occasion.

During the festivities an affecting incident occurred, worthy of record because worthy of Lafayette. A poor, and poorly clad, Frenchman stood at the door of the hotel, with his eyes resting on the General, but not venturing to approach. At length the General himself caught sight of the tattered form of the old soldiers, recognized him, and advanced to great him with extended hands. They rushed into each other's arms, and thus stood for some time in an affectionate embrace. The old soldier had once served on the body guard of Gen. Lafayette in a time of danger, and had been the means of saving his life. After a few hours spent in pleasant converse, the General was conducted back to the steamer, where he reluctantly took an affectionate leave of his friends, a salute being fired at his departure as a lasting farewell.

Early Shawneetown Merchants

Shawneetown for a good many years continued to grow in size and importance, on account of its location on the Ohio River, and the lack of railroads in the interior of the State. Following are the names of the principal business men of the place in 1842: Alexander Kirkpatrick, wholesale and retail dry goods; E. H. Gatewood, wholesale and retail dry goods, groceries, hardware and commission merchant; John Marshall & son, wholesale and retail dry goods; John T. Jones, dry goods, groceries and hardware; Jesse Kirkham, groceries, liquors, etc.; J. C. Carter, groceries and liquors; S. N. Docker, druggist; Thomas Morris, wholesale and retail groceries; W. A. G. Posey, wholesale and retail dry goods, groceries and hardware; W. A. Docker, wholesale and retail dry goods, groceries and hardware, and commission merchant. Henry Eddy and Samuel D. Marshall were then the leading attorneys at law.

Early and Other Banks

The first bank in the Territory of Illinois was established at Shawneetown, the act authorizing its establishment having been approved December 28, 1816. It was named the

---

[53] Hall's address can also be found in the Anecdotes section.

Bank of Illinois; its capital was not to exceed $300,000, one-third of which was to remain open to be subscribed by the Legislature of the Territory or of the State, when the State should be formed. Its charter was to continue until January 1, 1837, and its title was the "President, Directors and Company of the Bank of Illinois." The directors were to be twelve in number, to be elected on the first Monday in January annually. The rate of interest received by the bank was not to exceed 6 percent, and if the bank should refuse to redeem any of its bills in specie or to pay any of its depositors on demand, then such holder was authorized to receive the amount due with interest at the rate of 12 percent per annum from the time the demand was made. The bill was signed by Willis Hargrave, speaker pro tempore of the House of Representatives and by Pierre Menard, president of the Legislative Council, and was approved by Ninian Edwards, governor, on the date mentioned above.

In 1823 or 1824 this bank suspended operations, and on the 12th of February, 1835, and act was passed to extend the charter for twenty years from January 1, 1837, the name of the institution to be the State Bank of Illinois at Shawneetown. This bill was approved by Joseph Duncan, governor. The first officers of the bank were John Marshall, president, and John Siddall, cashier.

The State Bank of Illinois

From a point of time somewhat earlier than this, to one considerably later, the State Bank of Illinois at Shawneetown was a principal figure in the history of the town. Upon the recommendation of Gov. Joseph Duncan, elected in 1834, the Legislature passed an act chartering a new State bank with a capital of $1,500,000, with the privilege of increasing the capital $1,000,000 more. Six branches were authorized, one of these at Shawneetown, was to be a revival in a certain sense of the old Territorial Bank at this place, which was the first bank in the Territory that had been in a state of suspension over twelve years. The capital of this bank was fixed at $300,000.

By an act of March 4, 1837, the capital stock of this bank was authorized to be increased $1,400,000; $1,000,000 being reserved for the State, and $400,000 for private subscription. The bank was to have nine directors, and was authorized to established three branches, one at Jacksonville, one at Alton and one at Lawrenceville, each to have such an amount of capital as the mother bank could safely supply. Upon an attempt to dispose of the State bonds it was found they could not be negotiated at par, hence the banks took the bonds at par, amounting to $2,665,000. The bank at Shawneetown sold its share, $900,000. Soon after this came the financial revulsion of 1837, and although the banks were solvent, they could not stand the drain of specie caused by the presentation of their notes, and hence were compelled to suspend. The charters of the banks provided that if suspension of specie payments was continued for more than sixty days together the charters would thereby be forfeited and the banks should go into liquidation. Hence, in order to avoid the common ruin in which the State and its splendid scheme of internal improvements would be involved by a destruction of the banks, the canal commissioners urged the governor to convene the Legislature to legalize an indefinite suspension of specie payments. The Legislature met in special session July 10, 1837, and acted upon the governor's suggestion. The suspension was again made legal in 1839, but without attempting to follow in detail the trials and troubles of the banks, it may be said that it was found impossible even the most assiduous pains and care to keep them on their feet. In February, 1842, the entire institution, with a circulation of $3,000,000 and upward, fee. With reference to the bank at Shawneetown, its condition in November, 1841, when the crisis was impending, is shown by the following statement published at that time, to enhance its credit by promoting confidence in its stability:

Liabilities—State capital stock, $1,000,000; individual capital stock, $349,240; circulation, $1,309,996; United States Treasurer, $40, unclaimed dividends, $1,876.40; individual deposits, $70,708.28; due other banks, $7,497.78; discounts, exchange, interest, etc., $29,259.61; surplus fund, $115,463.35; branch balance, $2,317.59-total, $2,886,398.51.

Resources—Bills discounted, $1,312,070.11; bills of exchange, $295,795.47; suspended debt, $101,085.92; Illinois bonds, $369,998.68; Illinois scrip, $819.55; bank and insurance stock, $11,900; due from other banks, $178,472.49; real estate, $83,336.74; incidental expenses, $7428.34; cash (specie), $422,371.13; notes of other banks, $103,120-total, $2,886,398.51.

This bank had loaned to the State in the first place $80,000, to complete the new State house at Springfield, and early in the autumn of 1839, upon the earnest solicitation of Gov. Carlin, and upon his solemn promise to deposit as a pledge of security, $500,000, in internal improvement securities, it had loaned to the commissioners of public works $200,000, in order to prevent a cessation of their improvements, otherwise unavoidable. The deposit of the $500,000 security, however, was never made, neither was the $200,000 loan to the fund commissioners ever repaid, and as a consequence, although the directors had resolved to resume specie payments on the 15th of June, 1842, the bank finally collapsed during the same month with a circulation of somewhat over $1,300,000. The banks were compelled to go into liquidation in 1843.

The real estate enumerated in the above statement was worth $83,336.74, consisted of a lot on the north corner Main and Main Cross Streets, in Shawneetown, and the bank building is still standing and now occupied by the First National Bank. This building was erected in 1839-40. It is a massive stone structure, four stories high, with five massive corrugated, Doric columns in the front, built at a cost of $80,000.

The directors of this bank for the year 1835 were as followed, appointed by the stockholders: E. H. Gatewood, Alexander Kirkpatrick, W. A. Docker, W. A. G. Posey, Timothy Guard, Daniel Wood, M. M. Rawlings, P. Redman, Henry Eddy, James C. Sloo and O. C. Vanlandingham . Appointed on behalf of the State: Porter Clay, David J. Baker, H. H. West, J. K. Dubois, William Linn, William Sim, James Dunlap, E. B. Webb and Peter Butler.[54]

---

[54] One of the most fascinating stories in Southern Illinois folklore is the account of the Shawneetown bank turning down the City of Chicago for a loan. Throughout the 20th Century professional historians scoffed at the story, yet when archivists uncovered a stash of Chicago City Council documents long thought destroyed in the Great Chicago Fire, they found the bank's rejection letter to the city dated July 5, 1838.

"Your favor of the 15th Ult. was duly received and submitted to the Board of Directors this day — I am instructed to inform you that owing to the great demand for money in this section of the State, together with the prospect of an early resumption of specie payments, render it altogether out of the power of this Institution to make the loan to your City asked for, neither is it practicable to let you have the smaller amount mentioned as we have discontinued making any further loans for the present and expect not to [make any] more for some time.

First National Bank of Shawneetown

The bank building was afterward sold to Joel A. Matteson for $15,000, who, in 1853, started a bank under the free banking act, which was named the State Bank of Illinois, and had a capital stock of $500,000. R. E. Goodell, son-in-law of ex-Gov. Matteson, was president of the bank, and A. B. Safford, cashier for four years, when upon going to Cairo, Ill., he was succeeded by L. B. Leach. This bank was conducted by Mr. Leach until the breaking out of the War of the Rebellion, when it was closed, because of Gov. Matteson's fears that southern Illinois would be overrun by the rebel hordes.

From the same fears he sold the building to Thomas S. Ridgway, for the ridiculously small sum of $6,500, who bought it for a residence and has since occupied it as such, but 1865 himself and partner, John McKee Peeples, decided to establish The First National Bank of Shawneetown, and since then the building has been used for the business of this bank as well as for a residence.[55] The capital stock of the bank was in the first place $200,000, with five stockholders as required by law, William D. Phile, George A. Ridgway and A. K. Lowe, each holding $2,000, while Mr. Ridgway and Mr. Peeples held the balance in equal shares. In 1878 the capital of the bank was reduced to $50,000, because of the unjust policy of the assessors, who insisted on assessing the capital stock of the bank at its par value, while real estate was at the same time being assessed at from about 25 to 33 per cent of its cash value.

Mr. Peeples remained president of this bank until his death in 1879, when Mr. Ridgway, who had been cashier from the organization of the bank, became president, and William D. Phile, who had been assistant cashier from the establishment of the bank, became cashier, and these two remain the officers of the institution. The surplus fund is now $25,000, and the deposits range from $180,000 to $200,000.

Gallatin National Bank

The Gallatin National Bank was established in February 1871, with a capital of $250,000, and with the following directors and officers: Orval Pool, president; Henderson B. Powell, cashier; Dr. William M. Warford, John D. Richeson and Peter Smith, directors. In June 1871, Orval Pool died, and M. M. Pool, his son, was elected successor. At the same time Mr. Powell resigned as cashier and F. C. Crawford succeeded him. In 1872 Hon. R. W.

"We were well aware of the advantageous situation of your City for the location of a Branch of this Bank and fully appreciate the numerous invitations that we have received from respectable citizens of your City to locate a Branch there yet, at the same time we were bound by a law of the Legislature to establish three Branches at points designated which provided us from any choice in their location, and now owing to our limited means not having sold all the Bonds we are still prevented from establishing any other Branches at present, but so soon as it is convenient to do so, the question will be brought up, when the land of your City will be taken into consideration. —

"Respectfully Yours,
"John Siddall, Cash."

[Source: John Siddall. July 5, 1838. Letter to B. S. Morris Esq. City of Chicago. Chicago City Council Proceedings Files. 1833-1871. File 0660A. Illinois State Archives.]

[55] Ridgway and Peebles had actually started banking in 1862 under the firm Ridgway and Peebles. However they waited for the end of the Civil War to incorporate as the First National Bank.

Townshend was chosen vice-president of the bank, and upon the resignation of Mr. Crawford, became cashier. In 1874 the bank went into voluntary liquidation, because of the county, although it had at one time agreed to reduce the assessed value of its capital stock 25 per cent below its nominal value, yet receded from that position and insisted upon taxing the bank upon the face value of its stock. Upon closing out the affairs of the national bank, a private bank was organized under the firm name of M. M. Pool & Co. (the Co. being William B. Henshaw, of Union County, Ky.)

This bank is still in existence, on Main Street, nearly opposite the First National Bank.

The Floods

Shawneetown has suffered very much from floods at various times, from its earliest days to within a few years of the present time, but these vexatious and destructive visitations have not yet succeeded in depopulating the place. Morris Birbeck, writing under date of August 2, 1817, in "Notes on a Journey in America," thus refers to Shawneetown:

> "This place I account a phenomenon, evincing a pertinacious adhesion of the human animal to the spot where it has once fixed itself. As the lava of Mount Ætna can not dislodge this strange being from the cities which it has repeatedly ravaged by its eruptions, so the Ohio, with its annual overflow, is unable to wash away the inhabitants of Shawneetown. Here is the land office for the southeast district of Illinois, where I have just constituted myself a land owner by the payment of $720 as one-fourth of the purchase price for 1,440 acres. This, with a similar purchase made by Mr. Flower, is a part of a beautiful and rich prairie about six miles from the Big, and the same distance from the Little Wabash."

Construction of the Levees

These floods have been quite numerous, and sometimes rose to such a height that steamboats could navigate the streets. As the country became more generally denuded of its forests and more thoroughly and systematically drained, the floods kept rising to greater and greater heights. It is deemed sufficient for this history to enumerate the principal floods and to give briefly some account of the later ones with the means employed to protect the place.

The first disastrous flood was in 1832; the next in 1847 then one in 1853, and next in 1858, when it became apparent that something must be done to protect the town from destruction. Application was made to the Legislature for a charter with power to borrow money to build a levee. The charter was granted and the State agreed to grant aid in a sum equal to the State taxes of the city for twenty years equal to about $108,000. Work was commenced and a little done each year as money could be raised, until 1867, when the river again submerged the town, rising to the ridge poles of the smaller houses. Meetings were held, the issue of additional bonds voted, the work put under contract and carried forward to completion, until it was supposed the levee was ample to protect the town. A debt of $70,000 was incurred, and the State failed to fulfill its contract of a remissions of taxes for twenty years, because of the decision by the supreme court in 1874, deciding the law unconstitutional.

The old levee was built sufficiently high and strong, it was thought, to keep out the water for all future time, but on August 12, 1875, the levee broke and the town was filled in four hours. The levee was afterward repaired and served as a protection until 1882, when, on February 24, the levee broke at 5 o'clock a.m. and the water came to a level at 4 p.m. At its highest stage this time it was three and one-half feet deep inside E. F. Armstrong's hardware store. The next year, however, was to witness a still higher flood. On the 15th of February, the water rose over the lower levee at 12 midnight, came to a level at 10 p.m., continued to rise until the 25th, rose to the height of eight feet, two inches in Mr. Armstrong's store, filling the town to the depth of about fifteen feet on the average, carried away 108 houses, doing immense damage to the remainder. But in 1884, the water rose still higher than 1883. This year the levee broke on February 12, at 8 a.m.; the water came to a level at 10 p.m., and continued to rise until February 28, when it was eight feet, four and one-half inches deep in Mr. Armstrong's store. This flood, the highest known, rose to a height of something over sixty-six feet above low-water mark, which was established in October 1856. The edge of the water was then 518 feet from the front wall of Hall's brick house, known as "Rawlings' Brick," to an iron peg set in the rock at the water's edge, a few feet below a direct angle from the north gable end of said house.

In order to prevent, if possible, a repetition of such calamities as had befallen the city three years in succession, it was determined to raise the levee one foot higher than the flood of 1884, and to this end a contract was made in 1883 with the Ohio Mississippi Railway Company, May 6, 1884. This was additional to, or in place of, a similar contract made in 1883 with the same company, and rendered necessary by the later and higher flood. According to the first contract $30,000 was to be paid for a certain amount of work, and by the latter one $29,000 more was agreed upon, $15,000 of which was guaranteed by Ridgway and Carroll, and $14,000 by the city. When completed the levee was four and one-half miles long, contained 400,000 cubic yards of earth, was twelve feet wide on top and had a cost in the aggregate, including the old levee and the sewer, $200,000. The main trouble with the levee, as it stands, is that it is too steep on the outside, and that the material of which it is constructed, contains too much sand, and is, therefore, without the best of covering by rip-rapping or otherwise, too liable to wash away. The following statement shows the total cost of the levee and sewer up to the present time:

Work done under Norton & Hayden	$60,000
Work done on south levee	25,000
Work done on repairs on levee up to 1882	10,000
Work done on original contract in 1883 (for 200,000 cubic yards @ 15 cents)	30,000
Work done on contract of 1884	29,000
Tax for levee purposes since 1872	10,000
Tax for levee previous to 1872	6,000
Sewer, right of way and other expenses	20,000
Total	$190,000

Incorporation of the Town

Previous to 1825 Shawneetown was a mere settlement, or unorganized village. In that year the trustees of Shawneetown became incorporated by an act of the General Assembly entitled "an act concerning Shawneetown," approved January 10, 1825, and by acts amendatory thereto. One of the most important cases tried in the Gallatin Circuit Court was in connection with this incorporation and may be mentioned here. It was entitled "Ryan vs. the trustees of Shawneetown," and was brought by Ebenezer Z. Ryan, as assignee of the State Bank of Illinois, for the recovery of money loaned to the trustees, for the purpose of paving the wharf with rock. The loan was agreed to August 28, 1837, and was for $20,000, secured by mortgage on certain town lots. Under this agreement large sums were advanced to the trustees, and finally on settlement a note was given the bank, signed by W. A. Docker, president, and attested by J. M. Jones, clerk, for $38,311.39, dated January 1, 1841, and payable, "on or before the first day of January next."

The trustees abandoned their charger, and organized under Chapter XXV, of the revised statues, and after this act the suit on the above note was brought in the circuit court, decided against the assignee, and was carried by him to the supreme court, by which the circuit court was sustained,[56] on the ground that more than $20,000 had been loaned by the bank, that it did not appear that the mortgage given was given to secure the money that was actually loaned, and that the trustees had no authority to borrow money. Previous to this, however, that is on the 19th of October, 1848, W. A. Docker paid his proportions, $6,282.10

On the 27th of February 1847, an act was passed entitled "An act to incorporate the town of Shawneetown," under which the town was incorporated by the name of "The President and board of trustees of the town of Shawneetown," by which name they were granted perpetual succession. The boundaries of the town were to embrace "all in lots of said town as originally laid off by the United States survey upon the River Ohio." Five trustees were to be elected annually on the first Monday, and all white male inhabitants over twenty-one years of age who had resided in the town three months, and who were qualified to vote for members of the General Assembly, were entitled to vote for the trustees, who could not borrow money without the consent of a majority of legal voters of the town. The affairs of the town were conducted under this charter until 1861, when a new charter was obtained.

As the records of the town government under these trustees could not be found, and as no one could remember the names of the officers under the charter of 1847, a list of such officers is perforce omitted. The charter of 1861 was approved by Gov. Richard Yates, February 22, that year. It was entitled "an act to incorporate the City of Shawneetown, and to change the name." Section 1 incorporated the inhabitants of the town of Shawneetown, by the name and style of the City of Shawneetown, unless the name be changed to Shawnee City. Section 2 fixed the limits and jurisdiction of the City of Shawneetown as to included all that district of country situated in the county of Gallatin, embraced within the limits of the town of Shawneetown, according to the plat thereof, as may be embraced within a levee proposed to be built around said city. Section 4 provided for the divisions of the city into two wards. The officers were to be a mayor, and two aldermen from each ward. All free white male inhabitants of the city, over twenty-one years of age, who had been residents six months, were to be legal voters.

---

[56] An original footnote here reads, "See "Illinois Reports," Vol. XIV, p. 20."

Article IX provided, that the inhabitants of the city of Shawneetown are hereby exempt from State tax for the period of twenty years from the adoption and passage of this act for the purpose of enabling the said inhabitants to levee the city to prevent its frequent or periodical inundation from the overflow of the banks of the Ohio and Wabash Rivers, within and adjacent to the said town; and the city council was authorized to levy a levee tax, which should be equivalent to the tax which would have inured to the State of Illinois, had the exemption from the State tax not been made.

On the 20th of April, 1872, the salaries of the officers of the city were fixed as follows: Mayor, $200; alderman, $75 each; city collector, 3 per cent on all taxes and assessments collected by him and paid into the treasury; treasurer, city clerk and city attorney, each $100; city marshal, $200.

On the 11th of November, 1871, an ordinance was passed providing for the issuance of bonds to the amount of $50,000, for the purpose of building the north and front divisions of a levee around the city, in pursuance of the act of 1861, incorporating the city, and of a majority of the votes cast at an election legally held June 6, 1870, and on the 15th of the same month an ordinance was passed providing for the issue of bonds to the amount of $25,000, in favor of the St. Louis & Southeastern Railway Company, in payment to the city's subscription to the capital stock of the company to that extent. The boundaries of the city were fixed by ordinance, February 27, 1872, as follows: Commencing in the northeast boundary line of the town, as originally laid out and surveyed at the line dividing Out-lots Nos. 90 and 91, thence along said line to the line dividing the States of Illinois and Kentucky; thence along said line dividing said States to a point opposite the middle of the street between Out-lots No. 254 and No. 255, thence up that street until it intersects the line dividing Out-lots Nos. 87 and 94, thence along said line dividing Out-lots Nos. 87 and 984, to the beginning.

On the 10th of April 1872, an act was passed providing for the incorporated of cities and villages. Under this general act, the mayor and city council, upon petition of the requisite number of citizens, appointed May 22, 1874, the day of election to decide the question of incorporation under the law, which question was decided in the affirmative by a vote of 74 for, to 14 against. An ordinance was then passed June 13, 1874, dividing the city into three wards instead of two. The First Ward contains all that part of the city north of Second North Cross Street; the Second Ward, all that part between Second North Cross Street and Main Cross Street, and the Third Ward, all that part of the city south of Main Cross Street. The number of aldermen was increased from four to six, thus increasing the expense of maintaining the city government. Salaries were fixed June 29, as follows; Mayor, $200; aldermen $3, for each meting, but not to exceed $75, per annum; city attorney, $100; city clerk, $150; city treasurer, $100. An ordinance was then passed unanimously July 27, providing for the appointment by the council of a city marshal. This ordinance remained in force until October 14, 1878, when it was provided by ordinance that the city marshal should thereafter be elected annually, thus placing the choice of the officer who should preserve order in the city, in the hands frequently of the disorderly elements of society.

On the 17th of August, 1878, the city council deemed it prudent and indeed necessary to quarantine against yellow fever, and adopted regulations to the effect that no steamboat should land between the mouth of the Saline River and the mouth of the Big Wabash, on the Illinois side of the Ohio, which was supposed to have on board any passenger or freight from any place infected with yellow fever, and the same regulations were applied to all railroads coming to the city.[57]

Following is a list of the principal officers of the city since the adoption of the charter of 1861, with the date of election.

Mayors: James S. Rearden, 1861; Matthew Hunter, 1862; George Beck, 1864; William G. Bowman, 1866; J. B. Turner, 1867; J. W. Redden, 1868; John A. Callicott, 1869; J. W. Redden, 1871; John A. Callicott, 1872; H. O. Docker, 1873; A. K. Lowe, 1874; E. Mills, 1875; J. W. Millspaugh, 1880, and Carl Roedel, 1885.

Clerks: James Docker, 1861; James H. Hart, 1866; J. N. Wasson, 1866; C. G. Hughes, 1867; Carl Roedel, 1871; J. B. Perry, 1874; John M. Coop, 1875; W. S. Hazen, 1878; A. C. Millspaugh, 1881; L. W. Goetzman, 1883, and A. C. Millspaugh, 1885.

Treasurers: James H. Hart, 1861; A. K. McCabe, 1871; H. C. Barger, 1874; J. H. Hart, 1875; John P. Hopper, 1883; L. H. Adams, 1885.

City Attorneys: John Olney, 1864; C. G. Hughes, 1871; Carl Roedel, 1871, elected to fill vacancy; William L. Halley, 1875; C. G. Hughes, 1876; W. T. Crenshaw, 1877; D. M. Kinsall, 1879; D. O. Hause, 1881; W. T. Crenshaw, 1883; George W. Pillow, 1885.

The first directory of the city of Shawneetown was published by D. W. Lusk in 1872. According to that directory the principal business men then in the city were the following:

---

[57] In 1878, an outbreak of yellow fever in Cairo alarmed the state and led to quarantine measures that practically paralyzed traffic from the south. Known at the time as "the hot year," 1878 began with a mild winter followed by a hot spring and an excessively hot summer. The highly fatal yellow fever epidemic worked its way north along the Mississippi River Valley, pausing in Hickman, Kentucky, prior to its arrival in Cairo in August. Wanting to prevent yellow fever from entering the state at Cairo, state and local health officials moved to institute a quarantine in late July 1878. The quarantine order was the first time the State Board of Health had tested its power to enact and enforce rules and regulations to preserve the public's health. Armed guards patrolled the levees and all steamers and a physician visited trains from the south. If all was well, the steamers and trains were allowed to enter the city.

During the quarantine, a steamer from New Orleans landed in Cairo and discharged its crewmembers, one of whom died at a Cairo hospital on Aug. 12. In about a week, the steamer returned from St. Louis with several cases of yellow fever on board. Part of the crew again remained in Cairo and the steamer proceeded up the Ohio River. Ironically, yellow fever struck hard at the *Cairo Bulletin*, whose editor had been active in getting authorities to clean up the city and simultaneously trying to calm the fears of city residents. The father of the Bulletin's publisher and later the paper's editor and two printers died of the disease.

Many residents left town and did not return until the disease seemed to abate in late September. The schools reopened on Sept. 30, 1878; however, they were soon closed again when yellow fever reappeared in October. On Oct. 6 and 7, six people died, including a public school teacher. Another exodus occurred, with about one-third of the city's population fleeing. Business was suspended, except for those services deemed necessary for the people who remained at home. Those who left did not begin returning to Cairo until the latter part of October when a frost brought the outbreak to an end. A total of 80 cases, 62 of them fatalities, occurred during the yellow fever outbreak at Cairo. Five cases and three deaths occurred in Centralia, 100 miles north of Cairo, and a woman died at home in Rockford after contracting the disease in Decatur, Alabama. [Source: 2002. "124 Years Ago in IDPH History." Illinois Department of Public Health. http://www.idph.state.il.us/webhistory11.htm.]

Dry goods, Docker & Peeples, Waggener & Mills, George A. Ridgway and John D. Richeson; groceries, Bechtold & Webber, Wilson Bros., Adam Baker, Waggener & Mills, Joseph Ulmsnider & Son, George A. Ridgway and John D. Richeson; drug stores, Dr. J. W. Redden; marble yard, Gordon, Sterling & Greer; carriage-markers, Joseph P. Hull and J. A. Quick; butcher, James Litsey; saddles and harness, John A. Callicott; clothing store, James H. Hart; hardware, cutlery and farm machinery, Richeson & Winner; tailor, T. H. Sils; boots and shoes, Benjamin Hoelzle; cigars and tobacco, S. F. Herman; planing mill, Peeples & Karcher; carpenters, Karcher & Scanland; plasterer, Henry Scates; real estate, F. L. Rhoads; painter, W. J. Elwell; small fruits, A. Ellsworth; commission merchant, J. C. Ketchum; wharf masters, Howell, Millspaugh & Co.; attorneys at law, J. B. Turner, Bowman & Wasson, Silas Rhoads, Alexander H. Rowan, Carl Roedel, Milton Bartley and B. F. Brockett.

The present business interests of the town are conducted by the following individuals and firms: dry goods, groceries, etc., John D. Richeson, Charles Carroll, A. M. L. McBane, A. K. Lowe's Sons, Swoffard Bros., A. M. Lewis & Bro.; groceries, Jacob Bechtold, Ambrose Erwein, Joseph F. Noel, Lewis Weber, John Hopper, Goetzman Bros.; hardware, E. F. Armstrong, Robinson Bros.; dry goods and clothing, A. Mayer; clothing and gent's furnishing goods, M. Lyon, James H. Hart; drug stores, E. Eherwine, W. A. Howell, Robinson Bros.; harness and saddlery, J. A. Callicott & Son; tailor, Mr. Gallagher; blacksmiths, James A. Quick, Michael Golden, Charles Brozul and Burris; foundry and repair shop, A. D. Reddick; hotels, Riverside, Germania, Connor House, Farmers' Hotel, Fissinger's Hotel; jewelers, Feehrer Bros.; livery stables, Horace Martin, Smyth & Wiseheart, William J. Boyd; steam flouring mills, McMurchy & Bahr, L. Rowan & Son; planing mill, Karcher & Scanland; lumber and shingles, Seelinger & McDonald; millineries, Miss Alice Eddy, Miss Jennie Hair; cigar-makers, S. F. Herman, William Gregg; physicians, E. C. Colvard, M. S. Jones, Jacob Fair, _____ Cassidy, S. N. Docker; dentist, A. H. Cole; real estate and abstracts, John R. Boyd.

Following is a list of the postmasters at Shawneetown: John Marshall, John Stickney, Pleasant L. Ward, Joseph B. Barger, Calvin Gold, John Edwards, Mrs. Edwards, A. M. Sargent, Mrs. Edwards, the second time, and the present incumbent, William L. Loomis, appointed in 1886.

The Land Office

The land office at this place was established by act of Congress February 21, 1812, and the commissions of the register and receiver were sent from the general land office at Washington, D.C., April 30, 1814, their duties to commence July 1, 1814. Following are the names of the officers, and their periods of service:

Registers: Thomas Sloo, from July 1, 1814, to June 8, 1829; James C. Sloo, from June 8, 1829, to August 17, 1849; Andrew McCallen, from August 17, 1849, to May 3, 1853; John M. Cunningham from May 3, 1853, to May 2, 1856.[58]

Receivers: John Caldwell, from July 1, 1814, to October 9, 1835, when he died; Stephen R. Rowan, from October 30, 1835 to April 7, 1845; Braxton Parrish, from April 7, 1845, to

---

[58] An original footnote here noted, "Father of Miss Mary F. Cunningham, who was married to John A. Logan, at Shawneetown, Tuesday, November 27, 1855." Also, James C. Sloo was the son of Thomas Sloo.

July 18, 1849; John N. Notsom, from July 18, 1849, to May 3, 1853; Samuel K. Carey, from May 3, 1853, to December 20, 1854, and William L. Caldwell, from February 12, 1855 to May 2, 1856.

On May 2, 1856, the records of the office at Shawneetown were consolidated, with the office at Springfield, Ill., by direction of the Secretary of the Interior, under the provisions of Act of Congress, June 12, 1840, section 2, and the terms of the officers ended.[59]

Societies

M. K. Lawler Post, No. 337, G.A.R., was mustered in at the courthouse, October 12, 1883, by Capt. J. H. Vaught, special mustering officer for southern Illinois. All of those mustered in were charter members.

The Women's Christian Temperance Union was organized June 2, 1885, by Mrs. Mary H. Villars, with thirty members. The first officers were: president, Mrs. Addie A. Long; vice-presidents, Mrs. Almira James, Presbyterian; Mrs. Jennie Brooks, Methodist; Mrs. Ira Thomley, Christian; Mrs. Reubenacher, Catholic; corresponding secretary, Miss Mira Phile; recording secretary, Miss Eva Youngblood; treasurer, Mrs. Myra Lauderbaugh.

Gallatin Lodge, No. 1708, K. of H., was organized at Shawneetown, August 2, 1879. The officers were, Past Dictator, A. M. L. McBane; Dictator, T. H. Cossitt; Vice Dictator, L. H. Adams; Assistant Dictator, Carl Roedel; Reporter, James W. Millspaugh; Financial Reporter, W. D. Phile; Treasurer, D. L. G. Dupler; Chaplain, George H. Potter; Guide, Thomas J. Cooper; Guardian, J. R. Boyd; Sentinel, A. G. Richeson; Medical Examiner, J. T. Binkley.

The Press of the County

The first paper published in Shawneetown, and the second in Illinois, was the *Illinois Emigrant*, later the *Illinois Gazette* established and published for several years by Henry Eddy. Mr. Eddy was an early Whig, an able man, and edited an excellent paper, and it is to be regretted that a detailed history of it could not be obtained. One of the interesting items in connection with its history, however, was the receipt of the following bill:

```
                              Pittsburgh, June 25, 1819.
      Mess. Eddy & Kimmel.
              Bought of CRAMER & SPEAR
      18   Reams No. 4 @ 4.50        $81 00
       3   Reams  "  5 "  3.50         10 50
       1   Ream   " 4                   4 50
                                      $96 00
           Contra Cr.,
           By 9½ doz. Deerskins @ $6  $57 00
```

---

[59] An original footnote here noted, "The history of the Land Office was furnished by Hon. William A. J. Sparks, Commissioner of the Land Office at Washington, D.C."

$39 00
Received note @ 4 months for balance
CREAMER & SPEAR.

A large number of papers have been published in Shawneetown, among them the *Illinois Republican*, a Whig paper by Samuel D. Marshall. A very able paper, the *Southern Illinoisan*, was started by W. Edwards & Son, May 7, 1852, as a six-column folio Democratic paper, which so continued until the nomination of Bissell for governor, when it support him for that position, and James Buchanan for the presidency. After the election of Buchanan it became wholly Republican, W. Edwards having retired from the paper during the campaign. In 1860 it suspended publication, there not being sufficient demand for a Republican paper in southern Illinois.

The *Southern Illinois Advocate* was published for a few months as a daily, tri-weekly and weekly by L. J. S. Turney, but not being sufficiently well supported it was discontinued.[60] The *Western Voice* was published for some time, and continued as the *Shawneetown Intelligencer*, by W. H. McCracken & Co. The *Shawneetown Mercury* was published from 1860 to 1873, by D. W. Lusk, discontinued in 1873. The *Shawnee Herald* was started February 11, 1876, by Francis M. Pickett[61], and continued until 1879. The present papers in Shawneetown are the *Local Record*, established December 1, 1877, by Conrad O. Edwards and still published by him as a Democratic paper, and the *Shawnee News* as continued from the *Home News* of some years since, and now edited and published as a Republican paper by L. F. Tromley. It is an able paper, is thorough devoted to the interests of Gallatin county and favors the principle of prohibition in the treatment of the liquor question.

Other Towns and Villages

New Haven

New Haven is situated in the northeast corner of the county, on the Little Wabash River. It claimed to be the third oldest town in Illinois, and assuming that the town was started

---

[60] L. J. S. Turney died at his home at Benton, May 20, 1881, aged 61 years. Some of our older citizens will remember him as the publisher of the *Daily, Tri-Weekly* and *Weekly Southern Illinois Advocate* at this place many years ago. The office was situated in the old Rawlings building on the levee. [Noted as the house in which Lafayette once took his dinner while on his trip down the river during his visit to the United States. Bolts of calico were spread out from the boat to the house for him to walk upon.] The daily paper was a failure. Since then Mr. Turney, who was a lawyer, has had many ups and downs in the world, and has resided in various parts of the State. At one time accumulated considerably property in California, all of which he lost by fire. In 1862 he acted as Governor of Washington Territory. His life in many respects was remarkable. He leaves a wife and one son. Judge Turney was a member of the M. E. Church at the time of his death. — From his obituary published June 4, 1881, in *The Local Record* of Shawneetown.

[61] Pickett also started the *Saline County Register*, parent of the present-day newspaper of Harrisburg, *The Daily Register*, in March 1869.

when Jonathan Boone[62] first settled there, the claim is doubtless correct. Jonathan Boone was a brother of Daniel Boone, the famous first settler of Kentucky. Jonathan Boone made an entry of land under date of August 24, 1814, as follows: Southeast quarter of Section 17, Township 7 south, Range 10 east of the third principal meridian. A stockade was erected on the bank of the Little Wabash, enclosing considerable land, and the enclosure, with its protections, was called Boone's Fort. He also built a mill not now in existence, but always referred to as Boone's Mill. The steam mill now in New Haven, mentioned hereafter, stands within the limits of the ancient stockade. An interesting land-mark stands close to the south end of this steam mill, in the shape of a stout and an umbrageous catalpa tree, the result of the growth of a riding whip, carelessly stuck in the ground by one of Jonathan Boone's daughters, upon her return from a pleasure ride on horseback. Jonathan Boone came to this country in 1812, for in that year Samuel Dagley, Sr., moved to New Haven with his family of fifteen children, being attracted there by family relationship, one of his sisters being the wife of Jonathan Boone. Mr. Boone remained in New Haven but a few years, possibly because he could not tolerate the refinements of advancing civilization, and so moved again into the wilderness-this time into the wilds of Arkansas, where he died at an advanced age.

His successors in New Haven were Paddy Robinson and Roswell H. Grant, who bought his improvements and claim, and improved the waterpower.[63] A survey of the town was made either by Robinson or Grant or both, the original plat consisting of 261 lots, each 70 by 140 feet in size. It was laid out into regular streets running at right angles with each other, and those running nearest north and south, parallel with the Little Wabash. Water Street was 70 feet wide, the others 66. The principal street was Mill Street.

In 1834 Shawneetown parties purchased the town, and a second survey was made in 1845 or 1836, by Albert G. Caldwell; the name borne by the place was conferred in honor of New Haven, Conn., it is believed by Roswell H. Grant, who was from New England. This town has had three periods of activity and decay. During one of its active periods, lots sold for $500 that in ordinary times would not bring $100.[64]

In 1826 Roswell H. Grant was doing a flourishing business in the mercantile line, running a general store. Paddy Robinson also carried on a flourishing business, but not so extensive as Grant's.[65]

In 1833 William Parks, from Franklin County, Tenn., and an Englishman, whose name is not how recalled, were keeping store, as also Gatewood and Kirkham of Shawneetown,

---

[62] At this point in Goodspeed's History a footnote reads, "Not Joseph Boone as is published in the history of White County."

[63] This section on New Haven is taken nearly verbatim from the 1883 *History of White County* with some exceptions. At this point in the 1883 account the original writer described Grant as "a shrewd Yankee from Connecticut, and a son of A. S. Grant. He had been a trader with the Indians, carrying on several trading posts in the northern portion of the State and near the Galena lead mines. Records of his business in 1826 show him doing a good business. He died a bachelor in September, 1836." At another point the author added to his Yankee description, noting Grant, "as a Yankee, the genius of invention and master of circumstances."

[64] The *History of White County* adds: "An instance may be cited where $2,500 was paid for property on the corner of Mill and Water streets, by Mrs. Sheridan, that in the corresponding depression shrank at least $1,200."

[65] The *History of White County* noted Grant's "papers show a healthy trade. Of course Robinson was his contemporary to a certain extent, buying produce and shipping to New Orleans, but not running a general store."

and John Wood. There were two hotels, one kept by Hazle Moreland, the other by John Melvin, at the old Robinson House.[66]

In 1850 the businessmen were Thomas S. Hick, Hinch & McDaniel, James Dagley, Jr., H. P. Powell, and Mrs. John Sheridan. The blacksmiths were Henry Stone and John Ellis; Handmore & Galagher, steam saw and grist-mill; in 1870, Hick & Hinch, Decker Bros., and Abshier & Stone, general stores, and Hunter & Keister, steam saw and grist-mill, besides a few others.[67]

---

[66] The *History of White County* added: "Others were R. H. Grant, Gabriel Harrison (also from the East, and who went West a few years after,) Peter Slater, Ephraim H. Gatewood and Jesse Kirkham of Shawneetown (Gatewood & Kirkham) and John Wood. These gentlemen did a general business in the grocery line, exchanging their goods for the pioneers' produce, and skins and hides, the results of their hunts. There were also three small saloons kept by Robert Grant, Stephen Morris and "Johnny" Sheridan. A few years later another was opened by Jones & Mansfield.

"There were two hotels about that time, one kept by Hazel Moreland, in a frame house that long stood on the site just above Dr. Hicks' present drug-store [in 1883]. It was at times used as a school-house. It was burned in 1873, the sparks from which ignited the old mill. He kept a good house, and for many years was known as a genial hosteller. John Mervin had open doors at the old Robinson House. This old block house, standing as it does somewhat remote, demands a digression. It was built about 1823, and stands 'a silent sentinel of the old guard.' It was built to accommodate the workmen of Robinson. It is a large two-story log house, 30 x 40 feet, built of poplar logs; latterly it was sided. It contains eight large square rooms, with a ponderous New England-styled chimney in the center, opening into which were five fire places, with one for cooking purposes, capable of accommodating the largest kind of a back log. In the base of the chimney is a large brick oven, the whole showing it to have been built by Yankee hands."

[67] The *History of White County* again provides more information at this point filling in the years between 1850 and 1887: "Passing over a period of nearly twenty years we find the men in business in 1850 were: Thomas S. Hick, Hinch & McDaniel, Samuel Dagley, Jr., H. P. Powell, dry goods and groceries; Mrs. John Sheridan, groceries and a saloon; and Henry S. Line, John Ellis, blacksmith; Fletcher, a small tannery and boot and shoe store; Hanmore & Gallagher, the steam saw and grist mill and distillery above the town at the old ferry landing owned by Mrs. Sheridan; a gentleman called Major Powell packed pork in the long warehouse on lot No. 1. The hotel was kept by Dr. Jones Galbrieth. These people remained in business until their death, excepting Major Powell, who remained until 1859, moving to Shawneetown.

"In 1860 the business of the town had not materially increased. The firms read: Bailey & Hinch, Thomas S. Hick, Samuel Dagley & Co., Mrs. Sheridan, Felix Robinson. The Hanmores controlled the old mill; John H. Huse ran the steam mill; H. C. Catlin, the hotel. During this decade Richardson, of Shawneetown, established in 1854 the dry-goods and grocery store, with Griffith Garland as manager. About the same day Samuel Hayes, of Derby, Ind., did a small business in the grocery line, and also bought hoop poles, which at this time was quite a business. These poles were shipped South on flat-boats. The latter firm had a full load of goods confiscated while near New Orleans, the effects of which embarrassed them financially.

"In 1857 Nelson & Melville (J. L. Nelson and Andrew Melville) commenced a general mercantile business, succeeded by Hodge, Ulen & Nelson. They merged the business into that of grain. They closed as a firm in 1860.

"In 1870, resuming again, we find Hick & Hinch, representing the old firms of Bailey & Hinch and Thomas S. Hick; Decker Bros. (produce, provisions and general merchandise), representing Dagley & Co.'s store and warehouse; Abshier & Stone, general store, were in Hicks old stand; Hunter & Keister, store, saw and grist mill, at the ferry. In 1865 A. J. Lurguy erected the building corner of Mill and Vine, now occupied by the Swafford Brothers.

In 1887 the following are the business houses: Dry goods, groceries, etc., George Luther, Maurice Feehrer and W. A. Brounnelhouse & Co.; groceries, Matthias Epley; confectionery, Sumners & Co.; drug stores, Dr. Matthias Epley & Co. and James H. Hess & Co.; saloons, W. R. Flack and Charles Feehrer; blacksmiths, Theodore S. Smith and Henry White; millinery, Mary Hanmore; hotels, and Farley Housek, George W. Robinson. W. S. Dale, Nathan Stephens, Joel H. Grady, and lawyer, W. S. Sumner.

The Little Jim Roller Mill was erected in 1886, by Porter (D. M.) and Winterberger (Alois); it is three stories high, including basement, and has five full sets of rollers for grinding wheat, and one set of burrs for grinding corn. It is propelled by a thirty-horse power steam engine, and has a capacity of 45 barrels of flour each 24 hours.

The post office was established in 1820; some of the postmasters have been Col. Thomas S. Hick, John Wood, B. P. Hinch, Samuel Dagley, Thomas B. Hick; A. J. Surgery, W. P. Abshier, J. B. Hanmore, Victor Melvin, Lee Caruth, W. P. Aldrich, Dr. I. M. Asbury, James O'Neill and the present incumbent, Joseph E. O'Neill.

New Haven Lodge, A. F. & A. M., No. 330, was organized many years ago. Its charter members and first officers were James Edwards, W. M.; Sidney Pruney, S. W.; Jackson Abshier, J. W.; James Melvin, S. D.; E. W. Gaston, J. D.; John Hughes and William Glasscock.

New Haven has been incorporated twice, first in 1837 and the second time in 1873, under the general incorporation law approved April 10, 1872. The present board of trustees is composed of Leroy Hinch, president; J. P. Decker, James Dossett, George W. Gevney, Thomas A. Haley and Roley McFadden; Mathias Epley is treasurer; J. L. Greenlee, clerk; W. P. Aldridge, police magistrate, and W. S. Dale, village constable. The town contains about 400 inhabitants, and its present lack of prosperity is attributed by some to its saloons, but it is living in the memory of past, and in the hope of future glory, which will doubtless come after a railroad shall cross the Little Wabash at that point.

F. L. Rhoads Post, No. 586, G.A.R., was organized August 7, 1886, by J. F. Nolen, assisted by members of M. K. Lawler Post. The officers were I. M. Asbury, Commander; W. P. Aldridge, S.V.C.; G. W. Gerley, J.V.C.; McDonald Kincade, Adj.; Andrew P. Smith, Q.M.; P. P. Harris, surg.; J. C. Buttram, Cap.; L. P. Cubbage, O. D.; Alexander Mobley, O.G.; Thomas Pool, S. M.; Stephen Hendricks, Q.M.S. Twenty-three members united with the post.

He also had a hardware and tinsmith's shop. T. W. Rice in 1870 was doing business in a small way on the Dagley estate, and C. S. Hanmore had established himself where he is at present — keeping a good line of groceries. Stephen Callahan had succeeded Mrs. Sheridan. Robert Hargraves also kept saloon. The water mill had ceased; the new sixteen-foot dam was furnishing power for the new mill at that point that was run by Captain Ford, and through the new lock small boats passed to and from Carmi, loaded with grain for Evansville and other railroad points.

"In 1882 we find in the general merchandise line and buying country produce: Swafford Brothers, C. S. Hanmore, Mr. Luther, and Maurice Freeher; in the drug business: C. S. Hanmore, and Dr. Hick, with Lowry Hinch, assistant; Hinch & Epley keep the saloon; T. W. P. Aldrich is Postmaster; J. H. Grady, cooper; Barton & Co., wheelwrights and carriage manufacturers; Mrs. Dr. Hall, George Robinson, and James Farley are, respectively, proprietors of the three hotels. The steam saw-mill lies idle."

Above references from the *History of White County* are from pages 938 to 941.

Ridgway

Ridgway is a flourishing village of about 400 inhabitants located on the Ohio & Mississippi Railway one and one-half miles northwest of the center of the county. This first merchant in the place was John Hamersly, who opened his store in 1867. John McIlrath was the second and about one year after he established himself in business, W. A. Dickey in 1870, bought Mr. Hamersly's goods and continued in business until 1886. The next business established was a family grocery and saloon by Charles Evans.

Within the past year (1886) the place has very materially improved and merchants and others are now moving to Ridgway from the surrounding country and adjacent towns. The present business interests are being conducted by W. A. Peeples, dry goods, groceries, etc.; J. L. Boyd, general merchandise; John Kunn & Son, dealers in furniture; M. J. Moore, harness and saddle manufacturer; W. R. Rathbone, general merchandise (Mr. Rathbone, previous to establishing himself in business in Ridgway in 1876, had been engaged in the same business for ten years in Harrisburg, Saline County); W. H. Bowling, fancy groceries and queensware; Dr. F. F. Hanna, drugs, medicines and hardware; Charles F. Barter, hardware; Massey & Hemphill, confectionery, tobacco, cigars and country produce; Charles Swager, boots and shoes; B. F. Porter, livery, feed and sale stable. In August, 1886, W. W. Davidson established *The Central Star*, a newspaper independent in politics and "wide-awake to the interests of Gallatin County." There are three regular practicing physicians and one dentist. There are two blacksmith shops and one wood worker. A hotel was erected in 1881 by L. B. Cralley, the present proprietor.

The town, which was named for Thomas Ridgway of Shawneetown, contains two churches, a Cumberland Presbyterian and a Catholic, both having large membership, and the Catholic a resident priest. The public school has two teachers and about 135 scholars. The Catholic school, which is supported by subscription, employs two teachers and has a large attendance. A flouring-mill was built in 1884, which is well equipped with the new roller process and has a capacity of 100 barrels of flour per day.

The town was incorporated under the general law of 1872, in February, 1886, with boundaries as follows: Commencing at a point one-fourth of a mile due east of the junction of Main and Division streets, as originally laid out and recorded, in Section 30, Township 8, Range 9 east; thence running due south one-fourth of a mile; thence due west one-half a mile; thence due north one-half a mile; thence due east one-half a mile, and then due east to the beginning. Elections are held on the third Tuesday of April each year for the election of trustees and clerk. The police magistrate is elected for four years. The first president of the board of trustees was E. Mills, the second and present one W. S. Phillips. The first and only clerk was J. H. Hemphill; the first and present treasurer, F. H. Hannah; constable, William W. Abbott, and police magistrate, John A. Crawford. The village attorney is W. S. Phillips. Spirituous liquors are not allowed to be sold or given away within the limits of the corporation. The population of the village is estimated at 400 and is slowly but steadily increasing.

The *Central Star* was started here by W. W. Davidson, October 7, 1886. It is a seven-column folio paper, neutral in politics and has already (March, 1887), acquired a circulation of 380 copies each week.

Omaha

Omaha is situated on the Ohio & Mississippi Railway, in the northeast corner of Section 27, Township 7, and Range 8 east, about 18 miles from Shawneetown. It was laid out by Rev. R. M. Davis on part of his farm. The name was suggested by Henry Bearce, first baggage master on the St. Louis & Southeastern Railway, who had acted in the same capacity in Omaha, Neb. The first store in the place was J. C. Harrell's drug store, and the first dry goods store was established by Hall & Pemberton, of Saline County. The Omaha Flouring Mill was built by G. R. Pearce & Co. in 1878. In 1879 Mr. Pearce bought out the "Co.," Messrs. Porter and Rice, and sold a half interest to William Trusty. Soon afterward he sold the other half to Mr. Trusty, who then sold one-half to E. A. West.

In 1881 Trusty & West sold the mill to Latimer & Bryant, and in 1882 Mr. Bryant sold his interest to W. F. Harrell. The mill has the latest improved machinery and is propelled by steam. Geo. A. Lutz established a stave factory, which was run about four years, giving employment to a large number of hands and requiring a large quantity of timber. It was blown up by a keg of powder igniting in the boiler, placed there by an incendiary, and was not rebuilt. Dr. J. C. Harrell was the first postmaster, and has been succeeded by M. M. Davis, R. M. Davis, Samuel Davis, H. P. Blackard, and Benjamin Kinsall. The first hotel was built by J. B. Latimer. L. E. Quigley built a fine hotel in 1882 which is well fitted up and has excellent accommodations. Omaha has made rapid progress within the last few years, and hopes to be one of the most important inland towns in southern Illinois.

Omaha Lodge, No. 723, A.F.&A.M., was charged by the Grand Lodge of Illinois, at Chicago, October 7, 1874, with sixteen charter members. The present officers are James M. Gregg, W.M.; C. R. Gallaway, S.W.; H. P. Blackard, J.W.; W. E. Gregg, Sec.; J. H. Randolph, Treas.; L. L. McGehee, S. D.; W. J. Crabtree, J.D.; R. P. Caldwell, Tyler.

Omaha Lodge, No. 183, A.O.U.W., was chartered May 10, 181, with twenty-one members. The first officers were J. C. Harrell, P.M.W.; Thomas Martin, M.W.; A. M. Blackard, Foreman; A. H. Blackard, Overseer; Edward Rice, Recorder; M. M. Davis, Financier; M. H. Walters, Receiver; W. D. Pearce, Guide; Peter Edwards, I.W.; John Sarver, O.W. The present officers are V. A. Rau, P.J.W.; H. L. Rodgers, M.W.; A. H. Blackard, Recorder; R. G. Rice, Financiers; M. M. Davis, Receiver; W. W. Thompson, Foreman; Daniel M. Keiser, Overseer; E. A. West, Guide; Thomas Martin, I.W.; Peter Edwards, O.W.

The order of the Iron Hall was chartered August 13, 1886, with fifteen members, and the following officers: W. E. Ferrell, Chief Justice; R. S. Kinsall, Vice-Justice; J. H. Wilson, Accountant; George T. Crabtree, Cashier; J. H. Blackard, Adjuster; William Duckworth, Previtt; Solomon Duckworth, Herald; J. H. Utly, Watchman; J. W. Edwards, Videt. This order was established for life insurance purposes and sick benefits, furnishing as much as $1,000 insurance, and sick benefits in proportion to the amount of insurance carried. It is a branch of the Grand Lodge at Indianapolis, and is in a flourishing condition.

Order of the Eastern Star was instituted April 7, 1886, with 14 charter members. The elected officers are as follows: Miss Lulu S. Hall, W. M.; Lewis M. Price, W. P.; Miss Clemma Latimer, A. J.; Miss Jennie Davis, C.; Miss Mary Harrell, A. C.; Miss Mary Hall, Sec.; M. A. Baker, Treas. The appointed officers are Miss Jennie Kinsall, Ada; Mrs. M. C. Gregg, Ruth; Miss Emma Gregg, Esther; Mrs. Mary Keasler, Martha; Miss Connie Crabtree, Electra; H. P. Blackard, Warden; W. E. Gregg, Sentinel. Rev. R. M. Davis, Chaplain.

Omaha Lodge, No. 472, I.O.O.F., was instituted January 20, 1872, with seven members, by the Grand Lodge at Chicago. Its first officers were W. G. Hunter, N.G.; J. L. Garrett, V.G.; Thomas Bruce, Treas., and Charles Edwards, Sec. Its present officers are H. P. Caldwell, N.G.; I. T. Trusty, V.G.; H. L. Rodgers, Sec., and David Hidger, Treas.

Loren Kent Post, No. 523, G.A.R., at Omaha, was organized August 31, 1885, and up to February 1, 1886, had received sixty-eight members.

Omaha has no lawyer. The first physician was Dr. J. C. Harrell. The others have been James Porter, M. D.; J. M. Asbury, M.D.; J. H. Moore, M.D.; C. M. Hudgins, M.D., and J. C. Hall, M.D. Following are the business firms now in Omaha:

R. M. Davis & Sons, general merchandise; L. E. Quigley, proprietor of the Quigley House; Dr. Rodgers, drugs; Dr. J. C. Hall, drugs; W. C. Trusty, general store; ___. McCauley, grocer; Thomas Hardy, hardware; S. B. Lewis & Co., grocers; R. S. McGehee, dry goods; Sterling Edwards, undertaker; W. F. Himple, grocer, and J. S. Dixon, dry goods.

Cypress Junction

Cypress Junction is a very small place at the junction of the Louisville & Nashville Railroad with the Ohio & Mississippi Railroad. William Cremeens is the postmaster, and Charles Cremeens keeps a small store. There are two houses and a schoolhouse within about half a mile of the store.[68]

Equality

Equality is situated on the Louisville & Nashville Railway, in the western part of the county. It was laid off in ___,[69] its streets running at right angles with each other, its east and west streets running 20 degrees south of east and north of west. The streets are named Jackson, Clinton, Benton and Tazewell, while those running north and south are named Rowan, Calhoun, Van Buren, McDufie and McAvery. One block was reserved for the church, bounded by Jackson, Benton, McDufie and McAvery; one block and a half for the academy, bounded by Jackson, an alley between Benton and Tazewell, and by Rowan and the village limits. There were in the original plat 162 lots, generally 60 x 180 feet, and the area of the plat was 105 acres.

The first house was built mostly for an office for the salt works in the immediate vicinity. Samuel Ensminger, who lived about two miles below in the woods, moved in and opened a hotel, a store having been opened by Capt. John Lane, in his residence. Gen. Willis Hargrave, who obtained his title in the Black Hawk war, opened a hotel west of the old courthouse on Jackson Street. John Siddall built a large two-story frame house on the corner

---

[68] This community briefly used the name Cypress and Cypress Mills, until John Hart Crenshaw secured a post office at his story and mill site in 1840 under the name of Cypressville. After the mill and town burnt in 1842, the site can often be found in records as Burnt Mill. Cypress Junction came about when the two railroads came together at this place. By the 20th Century, as the cypress trees disappeared so did the word "Cypress" in the name. The community and post office are known today as simply Junction.

[69] The blank line is in the original and is due to the loss of the original survey of Equality from the courthouse. However, 1827 is likely the year.

of Calhoun and Clinton Streets, and Allen Redman built a house on the corner of Calhoun Street and the public square. It is stated that Joseph M. Street, as surveyor, laid off the town.

Equality was the county seat of Gallatin County for a number of years, both before and after the separation of Saline, and as such was the residence of numerous notable men, among them being William J. Gatewood, Edward Jones and M. K. Lawyer[70], and the most distinguished lawyers in the State then practiced at its bar, as John A. Logan, R. G. Ingersoll, S. A. Douglas and others. The business houses in Equality at the present time are the following: Dry goods and groceries, T. A. Davis, John W. Hales, A. F. Davenport, E. H. McCaleb, and C. W. Smith, who also keeps boots and shoes; drugs are kept by Dr. Isaac Bourland and E. H. McCaleb. The blacksmiths are Christian Helm and William Davenport, and the New Hotel is kept by Mrs. J. W. Hales. The churches in the place are the Methodist, Episcopal, Catholic, Missionary Baptist and Social Brethren.

Equality has been incorporated at various times. A meeting was held at James Caldwell's April 9, 1831. There were present the president and clerk of a former meeting held in pursuance of an act of the General Assembly of February 12, 1831, who produced the certificate of an election held April 4, 1831, that thirty-one votes had been cast for incorporation and none against it. At an election held on Saturday, March 9, 1833, Willis Hargrave, John Siddall, James Caldwell, Joseph L. Reynolds, and Leonard White were elected trustees. Willis Hargrave was chosen president and Allen Redman clerk and treasurer, and John Woods constable. Following are some of the presidents of the board of trustees from time to time — Willis Hargrave in 1835; Leonard White, 1838; William Hick, 1841; S. K. Gibson, 1854.

Under the general incorporation act of 1872, the first board of trustees was E. M. Wiederman, J. R. Hargrave, J. S. Bunker, E. B. Hargrave, John Donohue, William Davenport and J. W. Clifton, the latter being president, and W. H. Crawford, clerk subsequent presidents have been P. H. McCaleb, 1874; James R. Hargrave, 1875; Joseph J. Castle, 1876; J. S. Greer, 1877-78; Joseph Cook, 1879; P. Siddall, 180; William Davenport, 1881-82; J. W. Hale, 1883; C. E. Dupler, 1884; William McIntire, 1885; George W. Moore, 1886. The clerks have been E. D. Bailey, 1876; O. P. Spilman, 1878; Joseph G. Bunker, 1879; B. F. Hine, 1883, and Joseph G. Bunker, 1885.

The treasurers have been C. A. Caldwell, 1876-84; M. V. Baldwin, 1884, and John W. Hales, 1885 to the present time.

The Gallatin Academy was established in Equality in 1836. Its board of trustees was William J. Gatewood, Timothy Guard, William Hick and George Livingston. It was taught in a building erected for the Methodist Church, where Lucian Gordon now lives. It flourished for six or eight years and in it were taught the higher English branches and the classics, and its scholars came from quite a distance. Rev. Benjamin F. Spilman was the first teacher, and the later ones were a Mr. McIlvane from Kentucky, John Dixon and John McCullogh, who was the last.

---

[70] Should be M. K. Lawler.

Bowlesville

Bowlesville is a small town at the end of the railroad running from Shawneetown to the old Bowlesville coal mine, not now in operation. The town was the result of the operation of the mine, and inhabited mainly by miners and their families. Mr. Bowles purchased the land here in 1854 and in the same year the Western Mining Company, consisting of Mr. Bowles, Dr. Talbot and Thomas Logsdon, was formed and mining commenced. Dr. Talbot and Mr. Logsdon afterward sold out to Louisville parties, the name of the company remaining the same. Under this arrangement, however, very little coal was mined, and the land was permitted to be sold for taxes, Mr. Bowles buying it in and running it himself. When the war stopped the operations of the coal mines in Kentucky this mine had the entire demand and transacted an immense business, as many as nine steamboats being at the landing at one time, and slack selling for 10 cents per bushel and coal for 25 cents. No screening was done at that time. Mr. Bowles made a great deal of money, but died soon after the war. The property was then sold to Philadelphia parties, who, after operating the mine seven or eight years, have since let them remain idle. Bowlesville at its greatest prosperity contained one store, a grist-mill, blacksmith shop, carpenter shop, medicine shop, post office and about 350 people. It now contains about 50 inhabitants. F. H. Sellers is and has been the only postmaster of the town.

The Saline Coal & Manufacturing Company.

Not far from Bowlesville lies the property of the Saline Coal and Manufacturing Company, a company incorporated under the law of Illinois January 28, 1851, by Albert G. Caldwell, Joseph Bowles and their associates. These gentlemen assigned their interests to Hibbard Jewett, who associated with himself Joseph G. Castle, and they were granted power to organize. In 1854 George E. Sellers became president of this company, which had among its stockholders such distinguished men as William B. Ogden, Thomas Corwin, Andrew H. Green (partner of Samuel J. Tilden), Gen. J. D. Webster, Roscoe Conkling, M. Woodward and Joseph Alsop. The property of the company consisted of about 14,000 acres of land and included large areas of coal in Gallatin County and iron ore in Hardin County. It had a front of 18 miles on the Saline River and it was the original design of the projector of the company to develop both minerals and establish an iron manufactory on the property, for which where would seem to be one of the finest opportunities in the country. However, from various causes, nothing of importance beyond surveying the land and boring for coal, which was found in abundance, has been done.

Other Communities

Besides the towns above named there are a few other places, not villages dignified with names, among them, Bartley, Blackburn, Buffalo, Country Hampton, Crawford, Hell's Half Acre, Lawler, Leamington, Overton, Robinet, Seaville, South Hampton and Wabash. Irish Store, New Market and Elba have some pretensions to villages or towns.

Presbyterian Church History

Shawneetown Presbyterian Church

The first Presbyterian minister to visit the Illinois county was probably John Evans Finley, from Chester County, Penn., who arrived at Kaskaskia in 1797. He remained, however, but a short time, retiring from fear of enrollment in the militia. The next missionaries to arrive in this country were John F. Schermerhorn and Samuel J. Mills, who were sent out by the Massachusetts & Connecticut Missionary Society, and by local Bible societies. This was in the fall of 1812. In Illinois Territory there were then no Presbyterian nor Congregational ministers. Messrs. Schermerhorn and Mills touched at certain parts of the Territory, and went on the Mississippi River with Gen. Jackson to New Orleans.

The next exploring missionary tour was undertaken in 1814 by Samuel J. Mills and Daniel Smith, their expenses being borne by the Massachusetts Missionary Society, by the Philadelphia Bible Society and by the Assembly's committee of missions. From Cincinnati, Ohio, they passed through the southern portion of the Territories of Indiana and Illinois, and found only one Presbyterian minister in Indiana Territory—Rev. Samuel T. Scott, at Vincennes—and none in Illinois. On their way to St. Louis they passed through Shawneetown, where they found Judge Griswold, formerly from Connecticut; but they could not find a Bible nor a place in the Territory where a Bible could be obtained. On their return from St. Louis they again passed through Shawneetown and upon their second arrival in the place Judge Griswold informed them that an effort was being made to establish a Bible society for eastern Illinois.

A certain citizen, presumably of Shawneetown, informed these pious missionaries that for the previous ten or 15 years he had been trying to obtain a copy of the Bible, but up to that time of their visit without success. The missionaries recommended that 50 Bibles be sent to Shawneetown, and 50 also to St. Louis, and they expressed the opinion that it was of infinite important that one missionary, at least, should be maintained in each of the Territories—Indiana, Illinois and Missouri. These zealous missionaries were greatly disappointed and somewhat painfully shocked to find that the Presbyterians in the Territory of Illinois, from the neglect of their Eastern brethren, had become Methodists and Baptists, and said:

> "In all this Territory there is not a single Presbyterian preacher, and when we arrived we learned that considerable districts had never seen one before. Already have the interests of orthodoxy and of vital godliness suffered an irretrievable loss."

Soon after this, however, came a change; a Presbyterian Church was organized in what is now White County, and named the Church of Sharon, the first Presbyterian Church organized in the Territory of Illinois—in 1816, and probably in September, by Rev. James McCready, of Henderson, Ky. In this church building B. F. Spielman[71] was ordained and installed its pastor in November, 1824. The next Presbyterian Church organized in the

---

[71] Should be Benjamin F. Spilman.

Territory was at Golconda, October 24, 1819. With these two churches—Sharon and Golconda—B. F. Spielman began his ministerial labors as a licentiate in 1823, connecting with them also other places in southeastern Illinois, among them Shawneetown. It is believed he commenced his religious work in Shawneetown in December of that year, finding there upon his arrival but one member of the Presbyterian Church, and that one of course a woman—Mrs. Amira L. Marshall—and it was in her parlor that he preached his first sermon in the place.

Shawneetown, according to writers on that period of history of the Territory, was one of the most unpromising points for ministerial labors in the United States. For a period of between two and three years, Rev. Mr. Spilman could preach here not more than once a month, but at length in May, 1826, he succeeded in organizing a church, the first members of which were six or seven women—no men. The names of these women were Mrs. Amira L. Marshall and her two sisters, Mrs. Achsah Caldwell and Mrs. Hannah Gold, Mrs. Mary Oldenburgh, Mrs. Nancy Campbell, and Mrs. Dutton and her daughter. The first entry upon the records of the session was as follows:

> Shawneetown, November, 1827.
>
> The Sacrament of the Lord's Supper was administered to the church for the first time by Rev. Benjamin F. Spilman, and the following persons were recognized as members: James De Wolf, Amira Marshall, Achsah Caldwell, Hannah Gold, Mary Olden-burg, Lydia Dutton, Sr., Lydia Dutton, Jr., Ann B. Spilman, Mary Campbell, Judith Castle. Mr. and Mrs. Thompson were considered as members but did not commune. Of the above named Amira Marshall, Hannah Gold, Mary Oldenburg, Judith Castle and Lydia Dutton, Jr., were received into communion for the first time.   B. F. Spilman, Clerk

Mrs. Amira L. Marshall's house, in the parlor of which Mr. Spilman preached his first sermon in Shawneetown, stood and still stands on Front Street, a short distance below Mr. Charles Carroll's residence. The next place where religious services were regularly held was in one of the one-story frame houses known as Seabolt's Row on the north side of Main Cross Street where now stands Docker's "Riverside Hotel." The room used was rented by four ladies: Mrs. Amira L. Marshall, Mrs. Kirkpatrick, Mrs. Campbell and Mrs. Ruddick. Various other places were used until at length Mrs. Marshall and Mrs. Campbell determined upon building a church. Mr. John Marshall headed the subscription list and soon the two ladies had collected $65, including their own subscriptions. Mr. Kirkpatrick donated a lot on the Mound on Market Street in the upper part of the town on which to build it, the deed of which was so written that the property should always remain in the possession of the Old School branch of the Presbyterian church.

At length, in 1832, the church was completed, and "how truly grant it seemed!" It was of hewn logs and 20 x 30 feet in size. On the inside it had a gallery running across one end and long a part of the two sides for the colored people. It cost about $800. But in time the old church was outgrown; the town was improving, the streets were being paved, a splendid bank building was being erected, and the necessity had arisen for a more elegant church building more centrally located. The result was the present brick church edifice, completed in May 1842, at a cost of about $5,000. The parsonage stands on Main Street and commands from the upper story a fine view of the Ohio. It was purchased of E. J. Nicholson for $2,062.

The Rev. B. F. Spilman remained pastor of this church from December 1823, to 1845, when he temporarily retired. Rev. William G. Allen was pastor from 1846 to 1848, and Rev. J. M. McCord from 1848 to 1851, on November 23 of which year Rev. Mr. Spilman returned, was installed in June 1853, and remained until his death, May 3, 1859. He was succeeded by Rev. N. F. Tuck, who remained until August, 1860; Rev. Benjamin C. Swan from October, 1860, to the fall of 1862, when he became chaplain of the 13th Regiment of Illinois Volunteers. He returned to the church as supply pastor November 16, 1863, was installed November 20, 1864, and remained until August 1, 1868. Rev. Charles C. Hart began his labors as pastor in October, was installed November 12, 1868, and remained until October 9, 1871. Rev. A. R. Mathes was installed December 6, 1872, and remained until April 1875, and was succeeded by Rev. J. M. Green, who was supply pastor until the beginning of 1878, and the present pastor, Rev. John McCurdy Robinson, took charge June 1, and was installed November 14, 1878.

The following persons have been elders in this church: Washington A. G. Posey, John Siddall, George W. Cayton, Alexander Kirkpatrick, John Kirkpatrick, William H. Stickney, John L. Campbell, Allen Redman, Matthew Hunter, Thomas S. Ridgway, John McKee Peeples, Robert Reid, George A. Ridgway, Joseph W. Redden, Benjamin F. Brockett, Henderson B. Powell, Carl Roedel and Dr. L. H. Adams.

During the last year of Mr. Spilman's labor, 77 persons joined his church. In April 1870, there was a membership of 157; in 1878 there were 128, and at the present time 150. Large sums of money have been contributed by this church for benevolent and educational purposes, and their position upon the question of the morality of dancing is that "dancing, even in moderation and in private society, is not innocent."

The presbytery of Saline was organized by the synod of Illinois (Old School), October 8, 1858, and included most of the southeastern part of the state, 16 counties. At that time it had only four ministers and nine churches. This presbytery met at Shawneetown, April 5, 1860. John Mack was enrolled as licentiate, examined and ordained, *sine titulo*, April 8. This presbytery, in 1870, became the presbytery of Cairo.

Saline Mines Presbyterian Church

The Presbyterian Church of Saline Mines, was organized as a branch of Shawneetown Church, November 12, 1869, by Rev. C. C. Hart, pastor of Shawneetown Church, and three of his elders: J. M. Peeples, Matthew Hunter and Robert Reid. The Lord's Supper was administered and meetings continued, daily, for two weeks. On April 2, 1870, this branch church was organized as an independent church; Robert Reid and Robert Wright were made elders, and the name at the beginning of this paragraph was chosen. Religious services were, for several years, held by the leaders of the church, especially by Robert Reid. Services have continued until the present time by George H. Potter, and Elder Robert Reid, the latter of whom was ordained to the ministry, in September 1884. A frame church building 24 x 40 feet has been erected at a cost of about $700. It will seat about 175 persons. The Sunday-school consists of 50 scholars. Rev. Robert Reid is superintendent and J. M. Proctor, assistant.

Equality Presbyterian Church

Equality Presbyterian Church was organized May 26, 1832, by Rev. B. F. Spilman, and the church was under his care until 1845. During his absence in Madison and Randolph Counties, the church became somewhat reduced. On the 15th of December 1849, the following paper was adopted:

> "The undersigned members of the Presbyterian Church, at Equality, Ill., having, in some way, lost al of the records of the church, and being desirous still to continue the ordinance of God's house, do hereby agree to continue under the old style of Equality Presbyterian Church, under the care of the presbytery of Kaskaskia.
>
> "William C. Campbell, John L. Campbell, Timothy Guard, Alexander Guard, Andrew Stephenson, Martha E. Guard, Emily Herritt, Sarah Brown, Sarah Crawford, Apphia Flanders, Deborah Flanders, Israel D. Towl, Abner Flanders, Sr., Samuel C. Elder, Elizabeth Hayes, Ann V. Campbell, Martha Siddall, Mary A. Robinson, Mary Brown, Varanda J. White, Eliza Towl."

Israel D. Towl is said to have been the first elder and the only male member of the congregation at the time of its organization, but at that time there were ten female members. After the reorganization above recorded, the first elders were Israel D. Towl and John S. Campbell. Other elders have been as follows: C. C. Guard and J. S. Robinson, J. W. Clifton, William C. Campbell, Ephraim Proctor, Alexander Guard, William H. McComb, William T. Grimes.

Up to 1876 this church cannot be said to have prospered, the reason being frequent changes in the ministry. Among the ministers who have supplied have been Rev. John Mack in 1861, Rev. B. Leffler in 1862, Rev. J. B. McComb from March 1868, to October, 1870, and Rev. John Branch in 1873. Several others preached occasionally, but none very long at a time. Abner Flanders in 1865 gave a parsonage, worth about $500, to the church, and previous to the time mentioned above (1876), there had been connected with the organization more than 150 persons.[72]

Since 1876 the history of the church has been briefly as follows: It has been served by Revs. R. C. Galbreath, B. C. Swan and Robert Reid, and arrangements are now being made to erect a church building.

Eagle Creek Presbyterian Church

Eagle Creek Presbyterian Church is located on the Ford's road about one-half mile above Eagle Creek bridge, and eight miles south of Equality. It was started in 1875, by Elder George H. Potter, who preached there only once a month. The organization was effected in June 1876, with 19 members. Since then Elder Potter and Rev. Robert Reid have alternated in preaching for this church. The membership is now 45. A church building was erected in

---

[72] An original footnote in Goodspeed's History at this point reads, "From Norton's History of the Presbyterian Church in Illinois.

1878, 34x40 feet in size, which will seat 200 persons. It cost about $900. A. M. Gibson is the superintendent of the Sunday-school, which has 40 scholars.

Cumberland Presbyterian Churches

The Palestine Cumberland Presbyterian Church was regularly organized December 25, 1852. This organization was the result of a movement commenced in 1848, when a few of the pioneers agreed to build a house of worship if Rev. R. M. Davis would agree to preach. This house of worship was a neat hewed-log structure, which served its purpose for forty years. The present large, well-furnished, frame building was erected in 1868 at a cost of $3,000. Rev. R. M. Davis is the only pastor the church has ever had. The first elders were John Kinsell,[73] Eli Price, Lewis West and Allen Dugger. The present church is situated on a portion of Rev. Mr. Davis' land, donated by him to the organization, which has been remarkable prosperous, having received in all about 700 members into the fold, the present number being 300. The Sunday-school was organized in 1851, with John Kinsall as superintendent.

Hazel Ridge Cumberland Presbyterian Church was organized September 1, 1881, by Rev. R. M. Davis. The elders were L. Shain, J. B. Edwards and John Burns, and the number of original members was 12. A house of worship was erected in 1883, 30x50 feet in size, at a cost of $865. It was dedicated June 8, 1884, by Rev. Mr. Davis. The present membership is 70.

Liberty Cumberland Presbyterian Church, three miles northeast of Ridgway, was organized in 1855 by Rev. Gen. F. M. Bean. It flourished until his death, since which time it has had but meager success.

Concord Cumberland Presbyterian Church, two and one-half miles northwest of Ridgway, was organized in 1858, by Rev. Gen. F. M. Bean and M. Brown. After partially failing, it was reorganized by William E. Davis. It now has a supply of preaching and is doing very well.

New Haven Cumberland Presbyterian Church was organized in 1866, a church building having been erected in 1865. Rev. R. M. Davis was pastor until 1869; Rev. M. Green became pastor in 1885. The first elders of this church were Andrew Melvin, Joseph L. Purvis and Benjamin T. Mize, and the first membership amounted to 25.

In early days there was a large congregation of this denomination on Eagle Creek. Rev. R. M. Davis preached for them about six years. It is now but a small congregation.[74] There was also organized a church at Ringold, six miles south of Shawneetown, about 1860, which has been ministered unto by a number of preachers. The present minister is Rev. Mr. Fields, and the organization is just building a church.

The first Cumberland Presbyterian Church in Gallatin County was organized, it is believed by Joseph M. Street near Shawneetown, but the exact date could not be learned. It was afterward moved to "Dillard's Place," near the present site of New Market, and then in

---

[73] Should be John Kinsall.

[74] This is believed to be the Pisgah Cumberland Presbyterian Church. Its early records can be found at the Gallatin County ILGenWeb site. The Baldwin, Leavell and Peebels families are listed among its early members. The early records start in 1834 and continue to January 1847.

1830 moved to near the present site of Ridgway and there organized by Rev. David W. McLin as New Pleasant Cumberland Presbyterian Church. The place was known for some time as Crawford's Campground before there were any church buildings in the county, except, possibly, at Shawneetown. At the time of this organization or rather reorganization, there were two ordained ministers in Gallatin County of this denomination—John Crawford and Benjamin F. Bruce—and one licentiate, John Bennett. The ruling elders of this New Pleasant Church were James Dillard, Sr., John V. Sherwood, Isaiah W. Pettigrew, John Murphy, Sr., John Alexander, James Fleming and Isaac N. Hannah. With their election the organization was completed in September, 1830.

Oak Grove Cumberland Presbyterian Church, located about half way between Omaha and New Haven, and nearly on the county line, was organized March 31, 1862, by Rev. R. M. Davis with twenty-eight members. A frame church building was erected in 1869, costing $1,500. Its pastors have been rev. R. M. Davis, Rev. Martin Brown, and the present pastor, Rev. Z. T. Walker, of Norris City. It is a large and flouring organization.

Methodist Church History

Early Circuit Riders

The early ministers of this denomination in southern Illinois were mostly itinerants. In 1812 this part of the Territory was embraced in a district extending from near Cairo, upon the Ohio and Wabash Rivers to Mt. Carmel, and probably above this point and into Indiana, including several churches, with Peter Cartwright as presiding elder. Thomas S. Fills traveled a circuit embracing all of Southern Illinois south of Mt. Vernon, including Equality, and it is believed, Shawneetown. The Carmi Circuit was formed in 1825, with Robert Delap as the preacher. In 1831 the Shawneetown Circuit was formed, embracing about the same territory as the Carmi Circuit. Charles Slocumb, an earnest and eloquent man, was the preacher. He was again appointed to this circuit in 1833, with James Harsha as colleague. This year there were reported but five members, but this must have been a mistake, as in 1834, Slocumb and Harsha reported 555 members.

In 1834 John Fox was appointed to this circuit, and found John Crenshaw one of the main supporters of Methodism in this region. In 1835 G. W. Stribling was appointed to the circuit; in 1836, Isaac L. Barr and Christopher J. Houts, who returned 407 members; in 1837, Rev. Mr. Barr was appointed alone and returned 333 members; in 1838, James Hadley reported 346; in 1839, Thomas C. Lopas, 296, and in 1840, G. W. Stribling, 297.

In 1841, when on certain authority there were but two Methodists in Shawneetown, that place was made a station and George J. Barrett appointed to the charge. He was somewhat eccentric, but a fine speaker and very popular. In 1842 he reported fifty members, and in 1843, 100. Norris Hobart came in 1844, and had trouble about completing the church building commenced by Mr. Barrett. It was taken possession of under a mechanic's lien, but after some years was redeemed. Mr. Hobart returned forty-four members.

From 1844 for several years Shawneetown ceased to be a station, but was instead placed in a circuit called Shawneetown, and James M. Massey and James F. Jaques appointed thereto. In 1845 Joseph H. Hopkins was Massey's colleague. In 1846 Robert

Ridgway and Daniel Fairbank were appointed, and in 1847 Shawneetown was made a two weeks' circuit, Equality becoming the other principal point, the preacher residing at Equality. Charles W. Munsell was appointed in 1847, and in 1848 he was succeeded by R. W. Travis, who had for his colleague Ephraim Joy. In 1850 the name of the circuit was changed to Equality, which name was continued for a number of years, that being the residence of the preacher.

Shawneetown Church

Shawneetown was again made a station in 1858, with Thomas M. Boyle as preacher, who was succeeded by J. A. Robinson, who was followed by Z. S. Clifford, who preached both at Shawneetown and Equality for a number of years. B. R. Price lived at Equality and ministered at Shawneetown when the station was very weak. In 1868 F. L. Thompson was appointed; in 1870, W. J. Whitaker; in 1871, Jesse P. Davis; in 1862, Ephraim Joy; in 1873, G. W. Farmer, and in 1874, J. W. Van Cleve; in 1876 J. B. Thompson was appointed and remained three years; in 1879, V. C. Evers; in 1881, Rev. Mr. Maneer; in 1882, Olin B. Rippetoe; in 1884, L. M. Flocken, and in 1886, Rev. J. E. Nickerson. The church building, damaged by the floods to the extent of $500, has been repaired.

Smaller Methodist Churches

The Bethlehem Methodist Episcopal Church was organized and a house of worship erected in 1868, the dedication of the building taking place February 15 of that year. At this time there was a membership of 50.

The New Haven Methodist Episcopal Church was started in 1872. Among its pastors have been Revs. Mr. Fields, J. J. R. Reaf, C. W. Morris and A. W. Morris. The church is now in quite a flourishing condition.

The Omaha Methodist Episcopal Church was organized in 1879. A building has been erected at a cost of $800, which was dedicated September 16, 1882. At first there were 25 members. The pastors have been Revs. Mr. Hobbs, J. J. R. Reaf and C. W. Morris.

Catholic Church

First Catholic Church

The first Catholic immigrant to Gallatin County was John Lawler, who came from Ireland in 1830.[75] The late famous M. K. Lawler, a general in the Union Army during the war of the Rebellion, and Thomas Lawler, likewise a soldier, were his sons. A few more Irish

---

[75] This date is incorrect. John Lawler arrived in New York City in March 1816, moved a few months later to Fredericktown, Maryland where John Lawler applied for his citizenship on Nov. 7, 1819. Later that month the family traveled west, arriving in Shawneetown by flatboat on Dec. 31, 1819. [Source: William T. Lawler. 1978. *The Lawlers from Ireland to Illinois*. Privately Published. 1.]

families moved in soon after John Lawler and settled about half way between Shawneetown and New Haven, the settlement being known for a long time as the Pond settlement, but is now known as Waltonboro. Here the first Catholic Chapel was built about 1848 or 1849. The families then residing there were the Lawlers, Maloneys, McGuires, Murphys, Keanes, Dalys, Walshes, and Duffys. The Doherty brothers moved in a few years later. A new and stately frame church building, the larges now in Gallatin County, was erected in 1879.

Catholic Church at Shawneetown

In Shawneetown several Catholic families, mainly of Irish nationality, located as early as 1840, and later a few German Catholics came in. all the Catholics here were attended by Rev. Father Durbin from the church of the Sacred Heart at Uniontown, Ky., who is still living. The first baptism recorded here was on November 16, 1842. Numerous other priests paid visits to Shawneetown in the following years. Since the erection of the church building at that place, about thirty years ago, there has always been a resident priest at Shawneetown.

Among the first of these was Father Lewis Lambert, from 1860 to 1862. Father Lambert was a noted man and Catholics look with great pride upon his controversy, and other connections and contrasts, with another noted man, Col. Robert G. Ingersoll, who formerly was a resident and law student at Shawneetown. Father J. Rensmann, priest at Ridgway, says:

> "Lambert and Ingersoll two remarkable men. We meet both in Shawneetown, the one a priest, the other lawyer; we find them again on the same battlefield, the one as an army chaplain, the other as a colonel, and a third time they come before the public on religious battleground, Father Lambert the defender of the revealed truth, Col. Ingersoll its scoffer."

Father Lambert was author of "Notes on Ingersoll" and other works. After him came to Shawneetown Father S. Wagner, 1862-67; Francis Mueller, 1867-70; Anton Demming, 1870-74. Father Demming started the Catholic school named St. Mary's, the building for which was completed by his successor, J. Rensmann.

On May 16, 1874, a meeting was held at the church of the Immaculate Conception to protest against the removal of Rev. Father Anton Demming, it being thought that no successor could take up his work where he laid it down and carry it on to success. But the protest was of no avail; Father J. Rensmann remained with the church until October, 1879, when he was succeeded by Father Adam Leufgen, who remained one year, and was followed by Father William Krug, who remained until 1883.

In this year trouble arose in St. Mary's School because in the fall three colored children of Catholic parents were admitted thereto. Rev. Mr. Krug, upon the breaking out of the trouble, wrote to Bishop Baltes at Alton for instructions, and the Bishop in reply directed that the rules of the Catholic church, which make no different on account of color or nationality, be sustained. As a consequence it became necessary to close the school, and Father Krug left Shawneetown for Morganfield, Ky. The sister teachers also left the town. This trouble over the admission of colored children to the school, coupled with the damage caused by the floods, has prevented the school from being reopened. After a brief pastorate of six months by Rev. Father Joseph Poston, the present pastor, Rev. Carl Eckert, took charge of the church in April 1885. About 30 families are connected with the church of the Immaculate Conception.

Catholic Churches at Ridgway and Equality

In the meantime a Catholic Church was built at Ridgway, where the Devons, Drones, Braziers, Moores, Kaufmans, Bowleses and Wathens were the first Catholics, about 1875. This congregation has enjoyed a more rapid growth than the others. In 1879 Rev. J. Rensmann was called from Shawneetown. In 1883 a parochial school was built at Ridgway and taught by sisters. The school has also grown strong, and a second teacher is needed therein. The number of families in the congregation is about 72, and it is in contemplation to build a large brick church.

In Equality a Catholic Church was built in 1881. The congregation, numbering about thirty families, is attended from Ridgway.

Social Brethren Church

The Social Brethren[76] have three churches in Gallatin County; Green Valley Church, eight miles south of Equality, organized in 1875 by Rev. Hiram T. Brannon, has at present 64 members. Their services, conducted in turn by the different pastors of the denomination within the Southern Illinois Association, were held in the schoolhouse until 1887, when a church building was erected, 24 x 36 feet, at a cost of $500. Rocky Branch Church was organized in 1880, by Rev. Hiram T. Brannon. Its membership is now is now 55. This organization has a church building 24 x 36 feet in size, which cost $400. Equality Church of the Social Brethren was organized March 10, 1887, by Rev. Hiram T. Brannon, with ten members. The first meeting was held in the brick schoolhouse on the public square, where preaching is had once each month.

School History

Previous to the adoption of the common school law, which was approved in 1855, there were comparatively few public schools in Gallatin County, and those few were supported, of course, by private subscriptions. There were a few of these subscription schools in existence in 1820. The teachers were mostly foreigners who were prospecting through the western States and Territories, and who taught school when and because out of funds. One of those early schools was taught in the vicinity of the present site of Omaha, by a colored man

---

[76] An original footnote in Goodspeed's History noted, "For origin of this denomination of Christians see Saline County." That entry is included in this volume in the section of Early Anecdotes.

named Prof. Robinson, about 1820.[77] Sandy Trousdale taught on Sterling Edward's farm in 1826. The parents of the pupils usually paid at the rate of $1 per month per scholar, the teacher requiring about eighteen scholars to make up the school. Sometimes when the required number of scholars could not be found, one or more of the patrons of the school would pay for one or more scholars with the privilege of adding pupils to the school until his subscription was full. The teacher generally paid $1.25 per week for board.

In course of time settlers came in who were competent to teach and they naturally superseded the peripatetic pedagogues, through it is not claimed that any very marked improvement in methods was the result, but a beneficial change was made in adding one term of school each year. Under the new arrangement one term was taught in summer and one in the winter-the former exclusively for the small children, the latter being attended also by the larger boys and girls. The first teacher in the southern part of the county, whose name can now be ascertained, was a Mr. Stephenson, who taught in about 1822 or 1823. The building used was a large one originally erected for a barn. Afterward a floor was laid in it, and it was used for a dwelling house and then for a schoolhouse. It stood on high ground in the western part of Shawneetown.

John Cassidy's School

One of the early teachers of Shawneetown should not be forgotten; he was an educated Irishman named John Cassidy, and is well remembered. He taught about 1825 or 1826. John W. McClernand was one of his pupils as was Joseph B. Barger. Mr. Cassidy was a very irascible gentleman, as well as very learned; was very aristocratic in his feelings and hard to please, so much so that after the ladies of Shawneetown became familiar with these peculiarities none of them would take him to board. One other reason of his unpopularity with the ladies was that he would excuse no scholar's absence from school except upon the written request or explanation of the father, and the result of this animosity on the part of the ladies was that Mr. Cassidy kept "bachelor's hall" during nine of the 12 or 15 months of pedagogic sojourn in Shawneetown.

During these nine months he taught his scholars in a frame building standing on Main Street where now stands A. G. Richeson's hardware store. For common scholars he charged $3 per half year, while for those pursuing Latin his price was $1.50 per month. For truancy

---

[77] Hamilton County also has a story about an early black teacher. It may be the same man. The story comes from Job Standefer, an early settler who arrived in Hamilton County in 1816. He wrote the following in 1870. The *McLeansboro Era* published it in February 1878.

"About this time, somewhere between 1818 and 1820, we began to have prayer meetings. We had no preacher anywhere in reach. The people would come to these simple devotions for miles, always bringing their guns with them, and stacking them just outside of the house where the meeting was to be held, until the services were concluded.... At one of those meetings (prayer) an old colored man, an entire stranger, made his appearance and announced himself as a preacher. Of course no excuse would be taken and the old man had to preach! He did so, and preached the first sermon ever preached in Hamilton County. This sermon of the old colored man pleased the people so well that they determined that he should teach them at a school. A subscription was started and a little log house was provided. In a very short time, the colored preacher was engaged in training or teaching the first school ever taught in the county, and the writer of this was one of the little number that attended his school."

and failure to prepare lessons, punishment was not parsimonious, and was certain and severe. There was no compunction of conscience connected with it, and but little feeling, except on the part of the delinquent. The instrument of torture employed was a sole-leather strap about an inch and a half wide and three feet long. It had an exceedingly stimulating effect upon the student, and failure to prepare lessons was unusually rare. In fact, it is doubtful whether better lessons have ever been learned since the departure of this model Irish pedagogue. One remarkable thing about him was that notwithstanding his unpopularity with women, he was always popular with men. He was very intelligent, naturally sociable, had great conversational powers, and could rule their sons.

First Shawneetown Schoolhouse

After he had sought other climes a building was erected on purpose for a schoolhouse, a description of which it seems necessary to preserve. It was built of little, black hickory logs, about 10 inches in diameter, and was 18 x 20 feet in size. The floor was made of puncheons, and the fireplace extended entirely across one end of the room. For want of bricks a kind of mortar was made of clay, with which the logs were plastered to a height sufficient to protect them from the blaze. Logs were placed upon the fire from twelve to fifteen feet long, no short wood being used. For chimney there was nothing but a hole about three feet square, in the roof, directly over the fireplace, yet it is credibly related that this primitive chimney never smoked. For windows, holes about a foot square were cut in the walls, in each of which was fastened a piece of foolscap paper, greased. For desks upon which to write and lay their Webster's spelling books, boards were laid on pine driven into auger-holes bored into the walls, with a proper slant, and benches were made by splitting a log through the middle, and setting the half logs up on legs, driven into auger-holes bored into the rounding sides. These benches stood before the desks in such a position that to use the desks, the scholars sat with their faces to the wall.

Later Shawneetown Schools

Other buildings were erected from time to time, as they were demanded, similar to, or varying from this, according to circumstances and taste. It is typical, and no other of the kind need to describe. The first teacher in this temple of learning was named Gregory. He "boarded round" among his scholars who lived sufficiently near, but could not board with those who came six miles to school, as some of them did. For the balance of time he paid as high as $1.25 per week for board and washing. The next teacher was James Stinson, afterward surveyor of Gallatin County. As times improved, better schoolhouses were erected, and better educated teachers employed. In 1850, according to the United States census for that year, there were in the county twenty schools, with twenty teachers, and 896 scholars attending school. The public school fund amounted to $800, and other funds to $1,975. There was one school with an endowment of $60. The numbers of adult persons who could not read and writer were, of whites—male, 232; female, 331; and of colored-males, 69—females, 87; total, 719. The population was then as follows: white-male, 2,618; female, 2,477; colored-male, 153; female, 200; total population, 5,448.

The public school fund mentioned above was derived from the sale of lands set apart for school purposes, under the celebrated ordinances of 1787, usually the sixteenth section in each township, with occasionally other lands. Joseph Hayes was school commissioner, at least as early as 1834, for from June 1 of that year to March 1, 1836, he sold off 60 acres of land for $108.80. Up to March 15, 1838, he sold, in addition to the above, 1,300 acres for $1,720. On June 7, 1841, the school fund on hand amounted to $1,680. Samuel Elder succeeded Joseph Hayes as school commissioner, and according to his report, made September 7, 1844, he had paid out during the previous school year to the different townships $1,225.70¼. The lowest amount paid to any teacher was $1.20¼, and the highest amount $47.25½. The total number of scholars in the county, then, Saline County not having been set off, was 5,977. On the 26th of April, 1849, the school commissioners of Gallatin and Saline Counties were ordered to settle, and divide the school fund in accordance with the provisions of the act creating Saline County, each county to receive an equal share of what was then on hand, and no dividend was to be made to that portion of the county which had been cut off from Gallatin and attached to Hardin County, containing, it was thought, 385 children, until the taxes in that portion of the county should be paid for 1846, except by the commissioners, and in that case the commissioners of the two counties of Gallatin and Saline agree to pay and equal proportion of that fund.

Some of the provisions of the law establishing the present common-school system were as follows: That a school commissioner should be elected for two years; at that time he should report to the State superintendent each congressional township that was established a township for school purposes, and in each township there should be three trustees, and the townships were to be divided into school districts, each district to have three directors, also elected for two years. The State school fund was fixed at 20 cents on the $100, at which it remained until recently, when the law was so changed that a State common-school fund of $1,00,000 was established, the levy varying from year to year, according to the changes in the assessed value of property in the several counties, and the $1,00,000 raised is distributed to the several counties according to the number of school children in each county. In 1883 the State school tax in Gallatin County was 12 cents on the $100; in 1855 and 1886; it was 14 cents.

The directors in each district are authorized by law to levy a tax according to the necessities of their district, but not in any one year to exceed 20 cents on each $100, except for building purposes, when 30 cents additional may be levied, but not more.

County Superintendents

With reference to the county superintendency in its various forms it may be stated that it was established in 1829, the officer then being known as the school commissioner of lands. In 1840 this commissioner was required to distribute the school fund, and in 1841 he was first elected by the people. In 1845 it became a part of his duty to examine teachers, and in 1849 he was made an inspector of schools, but it was not until 1865 that he was known as county superintendent of schools. The following is believed to be a complete list of the school commissioners: Joseph Hayes, Samuel Elder, George W. Hise and Josiah E. Jackson, the latter of whom served from 1851 to 1864, and on the 6th of January, of this year, turned over the school fund amounting then to $1,076.83, to his successor, N. P. Holderby. During

Mr. Holderby's term as commissioner, the office of county superintendent was created, and be became the first superintendent, serving from 1865 to 1874. Thomas J. Cooper succeeded and served until 1881. H. P. Bozarth served during 1882, when Hugh C. Gregg was elected and was superintendent until 1886, when the present incumbent, Thomas J. Proctor, was elected.

Status of schools in 1883

The present condition of the schools is shown very nearly by the following facts and statistics taken from the superintendent's report for 1883. The total number of schools in the county was then 56, in three districts of which they are graded: Ridgway, Omaha and Equality. The number of schoolhouses belonging to the county was in that year 55, two of them brick, ten log and 43 frame. About one-half of them are good schoolhouses and in good repair, while the rest are indifferent or poor, and the apparatus is as yet inadequate to the necessities of the schools. In 1885 but one school was kept less than the constitutionally required time, 110 days; of the three graded schools, two were in session six months each and the other, nine months, and the ungraded schools were in session a trifle over six months on the average. The scholars enrolled in the graded schools numbered in one 65, in another 137, and in the third 373, a total of 575, and the number of teachers engaged in them was 11- three males and eight females. In the ungraded schools there were 52 male teachers and 22 females. The total number of scholars between the ages of six and 21, was, males, 2,149; females, 1,977, and the total number under 21 was, males, 3,296; females, 3,095, and the number between 12 and 21, unable to read and write was, males, 52; females, 22. The highest wages paid any male teacher was $111.10 per month, and the lowest $40, and the highest monthly wages paid any female teacher was $52.85, and the lowest $25. The total amount of money paid to male teachers was $11,596.16, and to female teachers, $5,798. The amount of district tax levy was $19,694.17. The estimated value of school property was $41,510, value of apparatus $1,978, and of the libraries $75. The bonded debt of the county was $10,150.

While the schools are in general making steady progress, yet it is evident to all that greater efficiency is desirable. One reason for the past inefficiency was doubtless the inadequate compensation of the superintendents. In 1882 the superintendent received but $218.15; in 1883 but $215.57; in 1884 but $306.10, and in 1885 but $309.31. Since then the office has become a salaried one, the salary now being $800 per year, and it is believed that it will have a tendency to attract men of greater ability and learning to the position.

The Shawneetown Public Schools

The first school directors in District No. 1, the Shawneetown district were A. B. Safford, Rev. B. J. Spilman and Joseph B. Barger, and much credit is due, especially to Rev. B. F. Spilman, for the establishment of the common-school system, and to all three of the directors for the successful initiation of the first free school in Shawneetown. A. B. Safford was its earnest and able advocate and main support. The first teachers were Dr. Mary E. Safford, now of Boston, Mass, and her sister, who performed noble duty for the schools. These schools were improved in their character from time to time, according to the ability and skill of the teachers employed, but were not systematically graded until 1882. For many years they were taught in a frame building near the corner of Market and Third North Cross Street, and until the completion of the brick building now in use. The principals of this school have been Daniel G. May in 1859; G. E. Smith, 1860-61; Edward Henry, 1862-63; David Smith, 1864-65; S. E. Willing, 1866; Rev. N. F. Tuck, 1867; Carl Roedel, 1868; James M. Carter, 1869-70; James H. Brownlee, 1871-73; Warner Craig, 1874-76; F. E. Callicott, 1877; George L. Guy, 1878-82, and C. J. Lemen, 1882 to the present time.

In 1875 a proposition was submitted to bond the district to the amount of $20,000, for the purchase of a schoolhouse site and the erection of a new schoolhouse, which carried by a vote of 154 for it to 35 against it; but this proposition was never reduced to practice. Another proposition was submitted to the people, November 15, 1881, which was to issue $10,000 to purchase a site with, and to erect a new school building. The site to be voted for or against, was described at Lots 19 to 24 inclusive, in Block 9, Pool's addition to Shawneetown. This location received 149 votes to eight votes for all other locations, and the new school house received 140 votes, and there were 34 votes against it. After the failure of a contract with R. H. Stanley, of McLeansboro, another contract was made with Peter Hyatt and Richeson & Cromwell to build the schoolhouse for $9,985, and afterward $835 was added to the price, thus making the new building cost about $11,000. This, added to the cost of the lots, $1,000, makes the cost of the school property $12,000. The clock was additional, and cost $800. The building is two stories high above the basement, and the rooms, four on each floor, are so arranged that they receive light from three sides; and each is capable of seating comfortably fifty pupils. The school is divided into six grades, the lowest grade being numbered 1 and the highest 6. Each grade comprises one year's study.

The enrollment for the district is 450, of which 87 are colored pupils. During the last five years the schools have very materially improved. In 1882 the percentage of attendance on enrollment was seventy-five; it is now from 90 to 94. In 1882 the number of cases of tardiness was 670; during the last year about 40. The teachers in the school for white children at the present time, 1887, are as follows: First grade, Miss Joanna Golden; second, Miss Ida Sisson; third, Miss Mary Hunter; fourth, Miss Jean Docker; fifth, Miss Alice Hunter, and sixth, C. J. Lemen. In the sixth grade there are about 40 pupils and usually about one-half of them are pursuing high school studies, as natural philosophy, physiology, zoology and botany, civil government, physical geography, rhetoric and algebra. No class in geometry has yet been formed. Thus far, these studies have been introduced only so far as could be done without interfering with the regular grammar school course.

Ridgway Schools

Ridgway has a new schoolhouse, built in the fall of 1880. It is a frame one-story building, with two rooms, and the school is divided into two grades, primary and principal, in each of which there are about 80 pupils. The first principal in this new building was W. S. Phillips in 1880. R. E. Brinkly was the principal teacher in 1881, 1882, and 1883, and the present principal, M. E. Fulk, has taught since 1885. Miss Mollie Hamilton was assistant in 1885, and Miss Mary Wathen in 1886, and is the present assistant.

Omaha Schools

Omaha has a large two-story schoolhouse and has had a graded school since 1874. The first principal was H. C. Bozarth, and he was succeeded by R. D. Kinsall, J. M. Kinsall, M. M. Robinson, A. H. Kinsall, W. E. Ferrell, H. P. Bozarth and W. E. Ferrell, the latter of whom was assisted by Miss R. Martin.

Equality Schools

The school in Equality was organized under the common-school law almost immediately upon its approval. The first principal was John L. Howell and his assistant was Mrs. E. J. Humphrey. Mr. Howell retired at the end of his first year because he had not the hardness of heart required to inflict the needed corporal punishment upon refractory pupils. He was succeeded by T. N. Stone, who remained but a part of the year 1856, Mrs. Humphreys still assistant. Dwite Spafford became principal in October, 1856.

Following are the names of the succeeding principals: James Ewing, commencing in 1859; J. Webster Childs, April, 1860; A. H. Morford, November, 1861; James Conner, 1862; T. J. Heath, 1865; Sullivan N. Gibson, 1868; C. F. Church, 1871; Oliver Edwards, 1872; T. L. McDouglass, 1878; J. B. Ford, 1880; J. F. Cassidy, 1881; George Burlingame, 1883; A. C. Rodgers, present principal, 1885. The school is divided into three grades: primary, intermediate and grammar, taught respectively by Miss Winifred Holderly, daughter of Nathaniel Holderly; Miss Alice M. Bailey and A. C. Rodgers. There are 70, 38 and 42 pupils in the three grades respectively, commencing with the primary.[78]

---

[78] For the history of New Haven schools from the *History of White County*, see the Anecdotes section.

Anecdotes of Early Gallatin County

The purpose of this section is to include additional tales and anecdotes recorded in other books and newspapers besides Goodspeed's history.

Early Outlaws and Other Crimes

The history of southeastern Illinois, including parts of Gallatin, is also that of the "ancient colony of horse-thieves, counterfeiters and robbers." Phillip Alston and presumably John Duff, or simply Duff the counterfeiter, are the first outlaws remembered. They joined up together at Cave-in-Rock in 1790. Alston soon left, but Duff stayed in the area. Local folklore puts him atop Gold Hill south of Shawneetown where he supposedly had a house, but long after their deaths their counterfeit descendants continued their trade.

Counterfeiters and Swindlers – 1819

For the past three or four weeks, strangers had been collecting here, in companies of two or three at a time, until the number had increased from twelve to twenty. The first who made their appearance were the family of Hagermans, consisting of an old woman, three young women, a young man, William Hagerman, two or three other young men, and perhaps some children. They rented a house and opened what they called a grocery. Others afterwards came and commenced boarding at this grocery — others boarded elsewhere — though Hagerman's was the common rendezvous, where they met every night to drink and dissipate, and swindle all who might fall into their clutches. But in this latter business they succeeded badly; their conduct being such, that they found few associates: and such, indeed, had excited some suspicion as to their character and designs. In this course of proceeding, however, they continued until a soldier, who had been lately discharged from the army, was drawn into their toils made drunk, and swindled of several hundred dollars—money which he had earned by a one years service of his country. After this, there was some stir among the citizens of this place, and an attempt made to recover back the money. A warrant was served upon one who was stated to be of the party, and who acknowledged he had won more than a hundred dollars of the money; and being unable to clear himself of the charge, was committed to jail.[79]

At this, some of the gang took the alarm and on the 16th last, set off towards St. Louis. Of these there was one they called Col. Johnson. He was about 6 feet high, and of a very decent appearance—rides in a handsome little wagon drawn by match sorrel horses. With

---

[79] An original footnote at the bottom of this article state, "From some facts that have since come to light, it is thought that he does not belong to the gang."

him in the waggon were a Mr. John Daily and William Hagerman; and on horseback accompanying them, a Mr. Nicholas Castleman. Daily is a thick, well set fellow, elegantly dressed—gray pantaloons and with a frock coat. Castleman rides a black horse—is a thick, well set, round faced, flat nosed, black looking fellow—5 feet 7 or 8 inches high. Hagerman is said to be lurking about this place. This part of the gang had only got to the Saline, 14 miles hence, when they began to offer notes altered from ones to tens and twenties, which being refused, they passed on about 15 miles further to Bridgman's, where they took up their head quarters, on the 18th, in the evening. While in this neighbourhood, they passed off a considerable quantity of notes, altered from ones to twenties. The notes are on the bank of Indiana at Vincennes, branch bank at Vevay, and Farmers' and Mechanicks' bank at Madison.

Our townsman, Mr. McLean,[80] being on his way to Vandalia, hearing of these proceedings, raised some men for the purpose of taking the rogue—which he effected, but having no proof of their guilt, was constrained to let them go again. Mr. McLean, (determined to break up their haunt in this place,) returned on Monday evening, raised another party, and went in pursuit of the others—three of whom (John S. Potter, Thomas Foster, and _____ Milburne) they found and brought before two of our magistrates for examination—. There was found on Potter, (besides much depreciated and uncurrent paper) one one hundred dollar note on the "Patriotick bank of Washington," D.C.—and on Foster two notes each of the same amount, on the same bank—all palpable forgeries. Nothing was found in Milburne's possession.

Note—The engraving of the place on which these notes were printed is a tolerable imitation of Murray, Draper, Fairman and Co.'s original, but the cashier's signature is very indifferently counterfeited.

It having been proved that Potter had attempted to pass some of his trash, he was committed to prison. The other two fellows, for want of sufficient proof, were acquitted—though little doubt is entertained as to their agency in circulating this spurious paper through the country.

Much credit is due to Mr. McLean for the prompt and determined manner in which he acted in this affair. We venture to predict, that Shawneetown will not be again infested with these men; and also, that the country would soon be rid of counterfeit money, if the people (as soon as they found such in circulation) would trace it to its source, and punish the makers to professed distributors thereof, with as much promptness and rigour as has been done in this case.

From a letter found in Foster's pocketbook, it would appear that Merrick Sturdivant, (the fellow who was taken up for passing counterfeit money about a year ago, at Golconda) resides at Manville Ferry (supposed to be on the Kaskaskia river,)[81] and that he is the head man of this horde of swindlers. The letter was from Potter to Sturdivant, introducing Foster

---

[80] This is John McLean (1791-1830) who had previously served in Congress but lost his re-election battle the year before. Possibly because of his good works in this case voters re-elected him to Congress the following year. He also later served as U.S. Senator from Illinois.

[81] Manville Ferry was located at New Athens, Illinois.

to the latter's acquaintance, and speaking of him as worthy of great confidence, and willing to engage in their "speculations."[82]

The Grindstaff Murder – 1870

To show the condition of society in that neighborhood, I get outside the Belt and Oldham factions into a third, and notice as cold-blooded and deliberate a murder as was ever perpetrated. Samuel Grindstaff was a miner, living in the southern portion of Gallatin County, the one next above Hardin. He was a drunken, worthless fellow, brutal and desperate, but the leader of a faction that existed more in spirit than in name. He had married a young girl, the stepdaughter of Jesse Davis, a southern refugee. The event about to be narrated occurred in 1870.

Mrs. Grindstaff, unable to endure longer the brutal ill treatment of her husband, had left him and taken refuge with Davis. Grindstaff saw Davis and demanded that Davis turn her away from his home so as to throw her on Grindstaff, and he agreed to treat her better. Grindstaff was not satisfied, but left reiterating his demand. When the next week came, the wife was at her step-father's, and Grindstaff wanted to know if Davis was going to make her leave. Davis repeated his former statement, whereupon Grindstaff drew a revolver and again made the inquiry. Davis became frightened and said that if Grindstaff could go to the house and persuade the girl to leave, he might have her. That would not suit Grindstaff. He wanted Davis to drive her away so as to compel her to return to his house and be at his mercy, and he grew imperative for an answer, yes or no. Davis saw at once that he was about to be murdered, and he began backing off, begging Grindstaff not to shoot, and saying he could have the girl if he could persuade her to go with him. They continued to converse until Davis had backed away about twenty feet, Grindstaff following him step by step. Grindstaff was accompanied by a notorious desperado named Kilgore, a man who ought to have been in the penitentiary long ago. At last Kilgore said "Grindstaff, do what you are going to do." Grindstaff took deliberate aim, and while the gray-haired old man was begging hardest for his life, Grindstaff shot him down dead. It was as atrocious, merciless and unprovoked a murder as was ever committed in this part of the State, and the jury sentenced the murderer to thirty-three years in the penitentiary. Gov. Beveredge commuted the term to twenty years, which with the good behavior allowance, will let him out in eleven years. Only a few weeks ago, the fiend had the audacity to apply to Gov. Cullom for a pardon, but the Governor refused to grant it. Efforts will no doubt be made with succeeding Governors to get him out, but the people in this part of the State will watch him closely. If any Governor does ever dare to lessen his punishment any more, it will cost him almost the entire lower tier of counties at a later election, so indignant are the people over the case. Grindstaff is a man of remarkable executive ability, and should he be released, he would no doubt head as desperate a band of ruffians as ever infested this district, and might begin by killing his wife.[83]

---

[82] Jan. 1, 1819. "Counterfeiters and Swindlers." (Shawneetown) *Illinois Gazette*.
[83] Shadrach "Shady" L. Jackson. 1888. *The Life of Logan Belt*. 101-103.

Wild Things

Bears – 1810s

Black Bear was also abundant [across the river from Shawneetown], and Mr. [Samuel H.] Neel remembers several stories of them that are quite interesting. Once he and his father [David M. Neele] and Mr. Solomon Blue were going to Shawneetown, and met a very large fat bear. Sammy and his father undertook to keep the bear at bay with the dog, while Mr. Blue proceeded to the ferry to get a gun. There was not gun at the ferry and he went onto Shawneetown but was so long returning that Mr. Neel left Sammy and the dog to guard the bear while he went in search of a gun. When the men returned, bruin had decamped, and was safely away in the cane. Mr. Neel declares this animal to have been the largest and fattest ever seen in that part.

In the years 1815 and 1816, Mr. Neel says the bear were especially numerous in the canebrake near Shawneetown. In the spring of the year he has seen fifty or sixty sunning themselves in the woods near this canebrake. They were soon killed off by the hunters.[84]

Squirrels – 1828

We understand from the farmers that great havoc is everywhere made and making by these mischievous animals — they were never seen before. A gentleman of veracity informed us, a day or two ago, that he killed upward of 400 in and about his field in one day, and the next morning they appeared as numerous as ever. They were constantly seen swimming backwards and forth across the Wabash, Ohio and Mississippi rivers, and are killed by the boys and sportsmen, in great numbers at their landings. It is not a fact to us in their natural history of these animals, that they could swim rivers from a mile to a mile and a half in width, but it everyday verified by the eyes of our inhabitants.[85]

Early Descriptions

Gov. Reynolds's Early History of Shawneetown

> The Increase of Population and the Extension of the Settlements in Illinois from 1805 to 1809... the Time of the Formation of Illinois Territory... Shawneetown Increased

The whole country on the margin of the Mississippi, Ohio, and Wabash Rivers, from the site where Alton now stands to Vincennes, commenced to improve. Within the present limits

---

[84] 1886. *History of Union County, Kentucky.* Evansville, Ind.: Courier Co., Printers, Binders and Engravers. 54.

[85] Sept. 7, 1828. (Shawneetown) *Illinois Gazette* as quoted by J. Ward Barnes. 1947. "The Saltworks and Pioneer Life." *Saline County: A Century of History, 1847-1947.* Harrisburg, Ill.: Saline County Historical Society.

of Gallatin, Johnson, and Union Counties, small colonies were formed. The Simpson, Stokes, and many other settlements, were established in this section of the country, while the country was under the jurisdiction of Indiana Territory. Some mills were erected on the Little Wabash River, near its mouth; and about this time the town of New Haven commenced near these mills. A talented and energetic merchant, then of Shawneetown, laid out New Haven, and erected a fine flour-mill in the vicinity.

The settlements around the Ohio Saline, in Gallatin County, increased considerably, and the business at the salt works was carried on with much prosperity and success. These settlements, around the margins of these large rivers, extended only a few miles in the interior; and within was a wilderness.

... During this period, Shawneetown, on the Ohio River, commenced to grow, and gave evidence then of becoming a large commercial town. Shawneetown made its first appearance in the years 1805 and 1806, and increased considerably for sometime. Great fleets of keel boats concentrated at this point, engaged in the salt, and other traffic, and diffused life and energy to the new colonies.

About the year 1804, La Bauissier, a Frenchman, located on the Ohio River; he fished, traded with the Indians, and kept a ferry.[86] E. Ensminger settled there about the same time, and was deputy-sheriff of Randolph County in 1808. Davenport, Wilson, Ellis, Hubbard, and others, located here a few years after.

Congress in 1810, and also in 1814, caused to be surveyed out two sections of land in lots, and sold many of them. After the sale a general jollification was enjoyed, and most of the old log-cabins in the town were burnt, so that new houses, larger, and built of better materials, would occupy the places of the squatter houses. The river, for several years, did not inundate the town, and everything seemed to prosper and advance the growth of the place—it soon contained a population of fifteen hundred inhabitants or more. The Indians were removed from the country near Shawneetown in 1811, and the immigrants flocked to the country in great numbers.

At the first settlement of Shawneetown, a number of extraordinary and highly gifted immigrants settled in it, and gave it a high standing and character throughout the country. Many of the pioneers reached, in after days, a high standing and fame in the public mind. Among many others, Isaac White, John Marshall, Moses M. Rallings, Leonard White, Willis Hargrove,[87] Henry Eddy, John McLean, Thomas C. Brown, A. F. Hubbard, Joseph M. Street, John Lane, Seth Guard, and many more.

In 1805, we computed the population of Illinois to be about five thousand souls; and in 1810, the census taken then returned 12,284 inhabitants in the territory of Illinois.[88]

---

[86] The late Southern Illinois historian Lowell Dearinger believed that LaBauisser was Labuxiere and a cousin to John Choisser, whose mother had been Marianne Labuxiere. Choisser was born in June 20, 1784 in Kaskaskia, Ill., He's remembered as an early salt maker at the salines and the one-time partner in the firm of Guard, Choisser & Co. which included brothers Timothy and Chalon Guard, and employed John Crenshaw.

[87] Probably should be Willis Hargrave.

[88] John Reynolds. 1879. 2nd Ed. *My Own Times*. Chicago: Chicago Historical Society. 61-63.

Traveler's Report of 1807

From the mouth of the Wabash, where there is only one settlement, you descend thirty miles, and arrive at Shawanese Town, an old Indian settlement on the right side of the river, situated a little above a small stream named Salina Creek. This town is now wholly abandoned by its ancient proprietors, and only occasionally visited by a few of them for the purpose of trading with five or six white families, who compose the whole of its settlement at present. Considerable quantities of salt are made on the aforementioned creek, and of a very good quality; the springs belong to the government, and are leased out to certain contractors, who are bound not to sell the salt higher than half a dollar a bushel at the works. These, therefore, have their private copartners, who buy all at the lawful price; and as the property has then apparently changed owners, they sell none at the store houses for less than two dollars a bushel.[89]

Bryant's Shawneetown in 1809

In October 1809, I [William Bryant] crossed the Ohio River at Shawneetown, and went to what was known as the Half Moon, a salt well, that being the only one in what is now known as the Saline Salt Works. This Half Moon is located on the South Fork of the Saline Creek, on the north bank of said Creek in Gallatin County, about twelve miles north-west of Shawneetown. On leaving this place, I started in a northwesterly direction, following the road that was then known as the Goshen road, leading to the Goshen hill, northwest of McLeansboro. About twenty miles from the Half Moon, I reached a settlement, which had been made by a man by the name of Hogg, in what was then White County, but now Hamilton...

...Shawneetown was the first settlement in this part of the state. When I first saw the place, in 1809, there was but two American born persons in it—one a widow woman by the name of Arbuckle, the other a colored man by the name of Simon Cade, whose occupation was that of selling whiskey. At that time there were living in Shawneetown a few French families and a few Indians of the Shawnee tribe. The next town settled was Carmi, and about the same time a small settlement was made in Gallatin County, on the Saline River.[90]

The Western Gazetteer's Description – 1817

Between two and three hundred thousand bushels of salt are annually made at the U.S. Saline, 26 miles below the mouth of the Wabash. These works supply the settlements of Indiana and Illinois. The salt is sold at the works at from 50 to 75 cents a bushel. Government has leased the works to Messrs. Wilkins and Morrison, of Lexington...

---

[89] Christian Schultz Jr. 1807. Letter to friend. *Journal of Travels into the Arkansas Territory*. Republished 1980. *The Saga of Southern Illinois*. "Letter From an Early Explorer." Summer. 7:2 24. Also republished 2002. "Journey Down the Ohio: Christian Schultz Jr. reports on new country." *Springhouse*. August. 19:3. 18-21.

[90] William Bryant. 1871. "Early Times in Illinois." *The* [McLeansboro, Ill.] *Era*. Reprinted in April 1982, Goshen Trails. Online at http://www.carolyar.com/Illinois/Bryant.htm.

...Shawannaetown, above the mouth of the Saline, containing 30 or 40 logs buildings; the inhabitants live by the profits of the salt trade. The growth of the town has been greatly retarded in consequence of the United States having reserved to themselves the property of the site of this place, the salt licks as well as the intermediate tract between this and Saline River, nine miles distant. It is a place of great resort for boats and in time twill no doubt become a place of consequence, as the lands in its vicinity are of a good quality. Here formerly stood an Indian village of the Shawannoe nation.[91]

Mrs. Tillson's Adventures in Gallatin Co. – 1822

We landed at Shawneetown early Monday morning; had expected to arrive there the Saturday previous.[92] We had a poor apology for a boat, and accommodations were only known by name. Captain Dent, who was also a passenger, decided to keep by the boat in hopes of finding a New Orleans boat at the mouth of the Ohio that would take him to St. Louis.[93] He said a great deal to us about the presumption of trying to cross Illinois by carriage, and thought we had better even go to New Orleans if we failed to meet a boat at Cairo, but your father seemed very hopeful, and besides we both felt as if we could go no farther until we had heard from Robert, from whom we had parted at Cincinnati, and had heard nothing for nearly two weeks.

Mr. Dent, in parting gave me a fatherly grip of the hand, with an assurance that he should feel interested in knowing that I was safely through all the bogs and bayous and corduroys that I might encounter. The swimming creeks and mire bottoms were all Greek to me, and his look so mysterious that I did not understand. I was able to interpret it before the end of my journey.

We walked from the boat landing to the hotel, a short distance, but it was raining hard and the mud was deed and adhesive, and I reached the house very much fatigued. It was before breakfast, and after getting me to the bar-room fire — the only one that never went out in the house — your father went to look after the "plunder," a western term for baggage. When he returned he thought I had better take some whiskey to ward off the effects of the morning's exposure. It was the first time I had ever tasted it and though always an impalatable beverage to me, I shall never forget how disgusted and outraged I was by that first taste off Shawneetown.

Our hotel,[94] the only brick house in the place, was made quite a commanding appearance from the river, towering as it did among the twenty, more or less, log cabins, and three or four box-looking frames. One or two of these were occupied as stores; one was a doctor's office, a lawyer's shingle graced the corner of one; cakes and beer another. The hotel lost its significance, however, on entering its doors. The finish was of the cheapest kind, the plastering handing loose from the walls, the floors carpetless, except with nature's

---

[91] Samuel R. Brown. *Western Gazetteer; or Emigrant's Directory.* Auburn, N. Y.: H. C. Southwice, 1817. 26-28.

[92] The Tillsons arrived in Shawneetown on Monday, November 11, 1822.

[93] Captain Dent's name was Frederick Fayette Dent. Four years later his wife gave birth to Julia Boggs Dent, the future wife of Ulysses S. Grant.

[94] The Rawlings' House.

carpeting-with that they were richly carpeted. The landlord was a whiskey keg in the morning and a keg of whisky at night; stupid and gruff in the morning, by noon could talk politics and abuse the Yankees, and by sundown was brave for a fight. His wife kept herself in the kitchen; his daughters (one married and two single), performed the agreeable to strangers; the son-in-law, putting on the airs of a gentleman, presided at the table, carved the pork, dished out the cabbage, and talked big about his political friends.[95] His wife, being his wife, he seemed to regard a notch above the other members of the family, and had her at his right hand at the table, where she sat with her long curls and her baby in her lap. Baby always seemed to be hungry while mamma was eating her dinner, and so little honey took dinner at the same time. Baby didn't have any tablecloth!—new manners to me

Your father's caution was always at hand, to try not to give them the impression that I was proud, with an illusion to the prejudice felt by this class of people toward the Yankees. We had a room fronting the street and could see everyone that came to the ferry, which was directly opposite the house, and my occupation from Monday until Friday was watching for Robert and the horses. We not only were in great haste to get away from such a disagreeable place, but were anxious for the safety of Robert, who had never before been left to do for himself. Indeed, we were all inexperienced and untried.

I can now recall the joy I felt when late in the afternoon on Friday, your father and Uncle Robert present themselves before the hotel. Your father had crossed the ferry several times each day, hoping to meet the long-looked for, it availed nothing, but for the want of something else to do, and to quiet his anxiety, he kept on the move. Robert had sold one of the horses, finding it tiresome and difficult to lead one while riding another, but had retained the best horse, "Charley." The first thing to be done was to buy a horse. Our landlord was quiet at ease as a horse-jockey, and early the next morning there appeared an array of men with their horses, each hoping to get a good bargain out of the green Yankees. After a few yours bantering it was decided that we were to have a little black pony, strangely contrasting with the noble bearing of our "Charley" horse.

Our landlord was very officious through it all, and finally closed up his morning's task by having a fight with one of the countrymen. I was at the open window and witnessed the whole disgraceful outbreak. I had often before heard of the western gouging and fighting, but never before saw a fight, and hope I never may again. I can now see the landlord, thin, tall, and erect, with his gray locks floating in the air, using the most unheard of profanity, "clinched," as they termed it, with a fat, squatty-looking beast of a being, each aiming at the other's eyes, and each showing that their dodging powers had been well trained. The desire of an ignorant western to stand up for his "right," as he called them, was the predominant feeling of his nature, and when these rights were encroached upon he knew no other redress than by strength of muscle; so when the countryman called the landlord "a pint-blank, mean liar," because he had not sold his horse to the Yankee, it was exasperating, but when the countryman saw your father counting out the bright "shiners" to one of his neighbors — the former owner of our pony — his wrath knew no bounds. He abused Hilton, who would not

---

[95] Peter C. Seaton is possibly the son-in-law mentioned by Mrs. Tillson. He married Lucretia Hilton on December 9, 1817, in Gallatin County. [Source: Illinois Statewide Marriage Index]. It's not certain if Lucretia is the married daughter mentioned in the article. She is the only Hilton wife listed for Gallatin County in the marriage index.

take abuse, hence the fight. Some half dozen of the lookers-on separated them, and old Hilton, after mopping his face with his shirt-sleeve, went into the house.

We then busied ourselves in getting ready to start as soon as possible, and I went to dinner light-hearted at the thought of its being the last meal at that place. Old Boniface didn't appear at dinner, and after going through the form I went to my room to put on my outer gear for the journey. I was standing with my back towards the door when I heard a voice behind me, and, looking around, there stood Hilton, with his face covered with plasters. It was always my weakness to scream when suddenly startled, so I perpetrated one of the most unearthly yells — which your father had not yet become acquainted with. He was coming to the room, and was near the door when the explosion took place. I do not know which one of the two was most puzzled to know what ailed me. As the landlord had only come to the room for the trunks, and we were hurrying to get away, not much explanation was necessary.

It was not in accordance with my ideas to start on a journey Saturday afternoon, but the thing had been talked over and the chances for Sabbath observance seemed less here than to launch out into one of the broad prairies. We thought perhaps we might come to some more congenial place; at least we should be relieved from the drunkenness and profanity for which Shawneetown was at that time noted; so about two o'clock we rode out of Shawneetown.

Before leaving, your father met a Mr. McClintock, who gave him a way-bill of the country through which we were to pass, with the names of the best places for meals and lodging. Mr. McClintock was a government surveyor, and had been all over the country, and we found it a great assistance to have his directions. The first place found on our bill was Brice Hanna's, where we could find good accommodations for man and beast.

I well remember the joyous freedom we realized after leaving Shawneetown. All were relieved from the anxiety caused by our separation, and were again at liberty to pursue our journey, and as it was my first introduction to the State which was to be my home I tried to make the dismally-looking bottom prairie through which we were passing look cheerful and homelike, merely because it was Illinois

Your father suggested that we should not make up our minds yet as to the beauty of a western prairie from what we saw of the "bottom lands," and as I could not succeed in finding anything to admire in the prospect around, I was willing to let the future take care of itself, and for variety started a song. The gentlemen were both singers, and I, putting in what power I possessed, we made the woods and prairies resound.

After riding about two hours we came to a horrible corduroy, and were relieved when that came to an end and we found ourselves at a running brook, where we stopped to give our horses water. After giving them due time to slake their thirst, and the signal was given to move on, we found them a fixture, and all the coaxing and whipping that was alternatively administered had no effect to produce a forward movement.

As "Charley" had always been so reliable, never having departed from his lofty bearing, the conclusion was that the new horse must be at fault, consequently a sound whipping was administered upon the poor darkey, who by plunging and trying to leap forward showed his willingness to obey. It then became evident that the trouble was with "Charley," who, when he was whipped, only floundered about in the water, and then settled himself down again.

Your father looked perplexed and troubled, and on closer examination discovered the stump of an old tree at the bottom of the water which he thought might be the cause of the difficulty. There being but one way to get out of it, he commenced another lashing of poor

"Charley." I felt like crying and I am not sure but that I gave myself up to indulgence. Your father seemed to feel every lash that he administered to his poor victim, who, finally, with one desperate leap freed himself from his anchorage, and it was found that one of his feet had been caught between two prongs of a stump, thereby holding him fast.

Joy came to us all when we found that although "Charley" came out with a ragged hoof and looking decidedly used up, he was able to walk and to take us on our journey. Your father had made up his mind — so he told us afterwards — that one of his legs was broken, and that he should be obliged to kill him, and leave poor "Charley" by the wayside, which would have been a most grievous thing to him. He had purchased him before going east with Mr. Collins in the spring; had rode from Illinois to Massachusetts on horseback, and then had driven him back to Illinois; and he was such a rare specimen of all that was reliable and elegant his loss would have been to us irreparable.

After the excitement was over — the carriage having been disengaged from the horses and drawn back on the corduroy — finding it would be some time before all could be in readiness to move again, I discovered myself not in high heart; that my enthusiasm for western prairies was vanishing; that I was approaching the extreme of what Captain Artus afterwards called "gaudiloupiness." So I concluded as my only resource to start off on a brisk walk, expecting the carriage would soon overtake me, but after losing sight of my companions, and looking about into the swampy surroundings, things looked dubious and the dismals were getting a good hold of my feelings when I heard a most unearthly yell coming through the forest, and the vivid recollection of a panther story I had heard not long before coming to my help, I turned back and with a quicker step than I could take now hastened towards the carriage, not knowing whether I was going from or approaching the dreaded foe. I had heard that their manner of attack was to perch themselves on the branch of a tree, and when within reaching distance pounce upon their prey. Every rustling of the branches assured me that a panther was on the watch for me with a hungry appetite.

At last I reached the brook, where a new difficulty was presenting itself. The horses had become so thoroughly frightened that no urging or driving could get them near enough to hitch to the carriage, and while trying to invent some way to draw it over two teamsters came along, each having a large Pennsylvania wagon drawn by four horses. One of the forward horses — which they called the leader — had a saddle on, on which sat the owner of the team, one of the men looking as lordly as if he was leading an army to battle. Your father asked them if they would take off their forward horses and draw out the carriage. The man nearest — the lordly looking one — said he would do it for a "droller." Your father not pretending to hear him, went on trying his own horses. The man again called out: "Stranger, I say, I'll do it for a droller." Your father told him he was in difficulty and would be much obliged to anyone who would help him. The wagoner looked sulky, and the man in the rear wagon called out: "See here, Brice, you move along, it isn't me that leaves a stranger in a fix like this;" so the "dollar" man moved on and the other drove up, unhitched his horses, and putting them to our carriage drew it out of the water. The whole performance did not occupy ten minutes. When the man was on his horse again and ready for a start, your father bestowed many thanks on him, and we were soon on our way. We soon overtook the teams and inquired how far it was to Brice Hanna's, and were answered by the man who had helped us. We also asked if it was a good place to stop. Imagine our surprise when he pointed to the other man and said, "That is Brice Hanna." Brice pretended not to hear.

... Brice Hanna was a tall, well-formed man with good features, and but for his surly expression might have been called handsome. When we arrived at his house he dismounted, came up to the carriage, and told us there was another house on the other side of the swamp where we could stay; that he had been home all the week; that his wife was sick, and that we could not be accommodated *anyhow*. Your father told him that it was nearly sunset, and that he should not attempt to go through a five-mile swamp until he could do it by daylight, so we unpacked ourselves and moved towards the house, and with much fear and trembling I set my foot on the threshold of Brice Hanna's cabin.

There was but one room in the main cabin, which I at once perceived was unusually clean for an establishment of that kind. There were two beds nicely made, with clean pillows and handsome bed-quilts, the floor clean, and the coarse chairs looking as if they had just been scrubbed. In a large, open fire-place was a cheerful fire of oak logs, which were supported by one old iron andiron and a stone on the other side. But what most puzzled me was a pretty woman — who did not seem to be more than twenty — sitting with her feet on a chair, and with pillows around her, and holding her infant in her lap. Her skin was very fair, and she had an abundance of jet black, curly hair, and bright, black eyes. She had on a pretty pink calico dress, which with her baby's gear had the appearance of thorough cleanliness. She looked a little annoyed when we first went in, but politely asked us to be seated, and by her manner we concluded that she was mistress of the mansion.[96]

Brice had not made his appearance, but he finally came in bringing a stone, which he threw down with an oath, saying he had had his eye on that rock for some time, and thought it would be a match for the one in the fire-place. He commenced pulling out the andiron, swearing at the fire for being too hot. His wife looked on tremblingly, and asked why he was not willing to have the andiron remain, as it was "a heap handier than the stone." With another string of oaths he jerked out the poor andiron, and taking it to the door he threw it as far as he could into the yard. Such things might do for the broadcloth gentry, but he did not belong to the gentry; at the same time giving one of his menacing glances at us. He went out, but returned in a few minutes to say to his wife that the woman she had there — who, with her husband and boy, occupied a little cabin in the yard — "should not stay in his diggings another night," and with another oath said, "clare them out."

"Well, what is the matter?" asked the trembling wife.

"Matter! Why the cursed——" a list of epithets too fearful to repeat; "infernal fool has let the hogs and cows get into my corn-field and destroy more corn and potatoes than thar eternally cursed necks are worth; so I'll clare them out," finishing off his sentence with another string of oaths not to be outdone by Sancho Panza's proverbs.

The poor wife would shrink down when the blast was heaviest, but after he had gone would brighten up again. When one of the storms had subsided and he had gone out to

---

[96] The third wife described by Tillson was the former Celia Tade, daughter of David Tade. She had given birth to Dolphes Brice Hanna just days before on October 11, 1822. "His father, who was a substantial business man engaged in trade and forwarding, died in the spring of 1823, leaving a wife and two children, one boy and one girl. He left considerable estate, consisting of personal property. John McLaughlin and the widow were appointed to administer the estate; and, as usual, McLaughlin did the work, pocketed the entire proceeds of the estate, and then left for parts unknown." [Source: 1889. *History of the Pacific Northwest: Oregon and Washington.* Portland, Ore.: North Pacific History Co. 2:362-363.]

anathematize the man and boy with curses loud and heavy, I ventured to ask her how long she had been a cripple. She said only a few months; that just before her baby was born she fell into the well and broke some of her bones, and was so hurt all over that she had not been able to walk since, and if it had been God's will she should have wished never to have come out alive. She was ignorant, but pretty, and with a sweet expression; so much truthfulness was manifested in all she said that my heart went out to her with a compassion that I cannot express.

After awhile the fiend again made his appearance with a large slice of bacon and corn bread in his hand, and with his foot he kicked along a chair until he reached his wife, and seating himself by her side he took out a long bowie knife and commenced eating. Looking at her with something of a subdued tone, he said: "This is the first corn bread and bacon I have tasted since I went from here."

"Too bad," she remarked, pleasantly; "and what did you eat all the week?"

"Why, you see, I was hauling for Marshall; Marshall is building a big house; and I have been hauling brick and timber.[97] When I gits to the house Marshall will call to that infernal old black cook of his'n to get my supper, and the ___ ___ " usual list of expletives, "fool goes and makes me some coffee as black as her darned old face, and some of them 'are cussed light Yankee biscuits, and some beef that was just warmed through as the old bull was when he was running alive and bellering, and when you put your knife inter hit by thunder the blood would run. Haven't had a bite of pone, or corn-dodger, or hog meat, not any since last Monday morning."

"Too bad; didn't they give you any milk?"

"Jest so; axed for milk, and the old black devil brought me some jest from the cow; haven't seen a sip of buttermilk or clabber."

"Too bad."

She looked pleased that he had become sufficiently subdued to bear soothing.

We had previously called for supper, and were summoned into the cabin in the yard, which was used for a kitchen and dining-room. The woman of all work — the wife of the man who didn't keep the hogs out of the cornfield — was standing at a side table where we were to be seated for our evening repast. I have forgotten what we had for food, but remember the cleanliness of the rough furnishing, and that a saucer standing on the table, filled with lard, with a strip of white cloth laid in it and one end raised up at the side of the saucer, burning, served to light the table and the whole room.

We went back from our supper to where the happy pair were still seated, he looking as if he had blown another blast and had settled down to sulk, and the wife trying to look happy, and smiling through her tears. He sat awhile as if trying to think of something disagreeable to say or do. All at once a happy thought seemed to occur to him, and looking at us with malicious satisfaction he commenced a furious rubbing and scratching, pushing up his sleeves and looking at his wrists. He turned suddenly around and asked us if we had any beds of our own to stretch on for the night. He had seen all we took from the carriage, and knew that we had no beds along, and looked satanically happy when he announced that we would all get the itch, as all in the house had it, and swore that the cursed old fellow who

---

[97] This would be John Marshall. The house being built would have been what's remembered as the first bank building in Shawneetown, now relocated and owned by the Gallatin County Historical Society.

couldn't keep the cows out of the corn-field had brought the itch to them. Such startling information would have been fearful had I not looked at the honest face of the poor wife, who, without uttering a word, showed plainly that it was news to her, and I felt sure it was only a scheme of his own to make us uncomfortable. He seemed disappointed that he had not made a greater sensation, and as no one replied to his last effort he settled himself to think of something else disagreeable.

At last, with a more extended swear than before, he said he was tired, and was going to bed; it would do for gentry, who could stay in bed as long as they pleased, to sit up late, "but I'm no gentry, and I'm going to bed." There were two beds in the room, standing foot to foot, on the side opposite the fire-lace. One was for us, the other for Brice, wife and baby, your Uncle Robert making his bed on the floor with the carriage cushions and a buffalo robe which had been purchased at Shawneetown. He evidently felt relived that he was not under the necessity of getting into the infected beds. Although I did not believe there was any danger, I took the precaution to spread some pocket-handkerchiefs over the pillows, and by only removing my outside garments and putting on gloves, a thing I could not induce your father to do, felt pretty secure as to infection, but not quite comfortable as respected the mood of mine host. Being very tired I thought I would life down, but not allow myself to sleep. Our trunks were deposited in the same room were we were, and I imagined that there had been a suspicious eyeing throughout the evening, and that the inside as well as the out might prove attractive; as we were so evidently in close quarters with a mad man, was not altogether at ease about our personal safety. I was very tired, and Morpheus finally overcame all my resolutions and made me forgetful of danger.

I do not know how long I had slept, when aroused by the crying of baby and the coarse swearing of the father. He scolded his wife for letting it cry, and then cursed the "little imp; imp of the devil." The wife said the child needed caring for, and would not go to sleep without it; that it must be taken to the fire and made dry an comfortable, but he swore he would gag the squalling brat. After a while he sprang out of his bed and pulling the child from under the bed clothes, declared he would roast it.

There was in the fire-place a large fire, made of oak logs, which were all aglow and gave light to the whole room. He took the baby under one arm, and with two or three bounds was at the fire-place. He commenced raking open the coals, still holding baby under his arm, swearing he would make a back-log; "yes, I'll brile ye."

I kept both eyes open and trembled for the fate of the baby, when, to my surprise, he seated himself, carefully warmed the dry linen that was hanging by the fire, and in the most handy manner performed all that a good nurse or mother could have done. And now that baby was dry and there was no good reason for crying, and swearing did not soothe, he pressed "the brat, imp of the devil," to his breast, and commenced singing a good Methodist hymn in a soft, subdued voice, and had it been my first impression I should have supposed him a most devout Christian. A more sudden change from the profane to the devotional could not be imagined.

This scene occurred forty-eight years ago, and now it is as fresh to my mind as at that time, but perfectly to describe it would be impossible. The most provoking part of the last performance was that I had to enjoy it alone; no one to share with me the ludicrous climax of the closing hymn, your father and Uncle Robert being asleep.

As soon as it was light we were up and ready for a leave-taking. At the five-mile house on the other side of the swamp we found a plane, decent family, who gave us a breakfast of "common doings," corn bread and bacon, without any attempt at "wheat bread and chicken fixings," and from them we heard more of Brice Hanna. The man told us that Brice had a good farm and in his way kept his family comfortable, took price in having the best wagon and horses in the county. He had always been proud of his wives, the one we saw being his third, but his greatest pride was in his peculiar capacity for swearing. He once took an oath that he would not swear again for two years, from the fact that he had found a man down in "Shawnee" who could out-swear him, and he said he felt mean ever after. He was true to his vow, but when the two years had expired commenced with renewed vigor.

The gossip of the settlement was that his first wife died of a broken heart, that he had poisoned the second, and that the poor young creature whom we saw had jumped into the well to drown herself, but the water not being deep, was pulled out with nothing but bruises for her effort. The man did not believe the story of his having poisoned his second wife, but thought what was reported of the last night be true.[98]

Duke of Wurttemburg's trip up the Ohio – 1823

Picturesque bluffs of limestone form the northern bank of the river above Horrican [Hurricane] Island. Abrupt, tower-like shapes, rising from the bed of the Ohio, present bold, wild groups pleasing to the observer. Among these limestone masses I also saw the much admired cave formations described by many travelers under the name of Cave-in-Rock (La Grande Caverne). Despite my desire, I had to give up the wish to examine more carefully the inner formation and structure of the dropstone and had to content myself with a superficial and fleeting look at this masterpiece of nature.

The cave is formed on a perpendicular cleft, extending to a height of more than one hundred feet, running in parallel layers of limestone. It does not contain as many remains of petrified sea and shell-bearing animals as the limestone formations at the falls of the Ohio, at Cincinnati, or in the mountains of Kentucky. The traces of bones of prehistoric mammals are said to have disappeared from these caves. However, there can be no doubt that more careful investigation and excavation would bring many of them to light.

During high water a great part of the cave is flooded by the river. At average low water, however, it is dry and can easily be reached and therefore explored. The cave has frequently been used as a place of refuge on the part of travelers meeting with an accident or seeking to escape inclement weather. The Indians are reported to have made use of it as a hiding place while on war expeditions, sallying forth from it to attack passersby and molest the colonists. Like all stories dealing with the aborigines, these theme is a favorite subject to the Americans and as unbelievable as other adventurous stories that have been told me about this place.

The summit of the rocky elevation on the north bank of the Ohio near the cave is overgrown with the American [eastern red] cedar (*Juniperus virginianus* [virginiana]), its roots penetrating into the clefts and fissures of the limestone and protruding in bunches. This

---

[98] Christiana Holmes Tillson; Milo Milton Quaife, ed. 1919, Reprint 1995. *A Woman's Story of Pioneer Illinois.* Carbondale, Ill.: Southern Illinois University Press. 46-65.

evergreen covering the rock banks of the upper Mississippi and Missouri, and there attaining a considerable height, prefers to grow on limestone cliffs. Its growth becomes more and more vigorous as one goes north. Forming small clumps of forest, this variety breaks the monotony of the desolate prairies along the river in the northwest.

Passing several dangerous rocks called Battery Rock Bar during the night, we landed early on the morning of April 21 near the Saline at Shawneetown. Here is a very important salt factory supplying the great part of the United States with this important product.[99]

The little settlement of Shawneetown derives its name from the Shawnee (Chuoanous) nation, which had one of its principal village here. This Indian tribe had not disappeared entirely, but by frequent intermixture of white blood has departed more from the customs of its ancestors than have the other neighboring tribes. Roaming about restlessly, the Shawnees and the half-bloods who assume this name live on the banks of the Ohio and in the states of Indiana and Illinois, do some agriculture, but mostly hunt and fish. Excepting the Iroquois and Algonquians, whom I only know slightly, they are one of the few tribes living within the inhabited parts of northeastern America inclined to accept the ways of the immigrated European races.[100]

Beck's Gazetteer – 1823

Shawneetown. A post town, and the seat of justice of Gallatin County, situated on the Ohio River, nine miles below the mouth of the Wabash, in Section 6, of Township 10 south, in Range 10, east of the 3rd p.m. the bank of the Ohio at this place has a gradual ascent, but is annually subject to inundation. On account of the peculiar situation of this town, it commands a fine view of the river for several miles above and below. It contains a bank, a printing office, from which a weekly paper is issued, a land office of the district, and about 100 dwelling houses a great proportion of which are built of wood. The whole town extends along the river about half a mile, but has rather the appearance of decline. This may be owing to the inundations of the river, and the unhealthiness which they occasion.

Mr. Birkbeck, in his *Notes on a Journey in America*, remarks: "This place I account as a phenomenon, evincing the pertinacious adhesion of the human animal to the spot where it once has fixed itself. As the lava of Mount Etna cannot dislodge this strange being from the cities which have been repeatedly ravaged by its eruptions, so the Ohio, by its annual overflowings, is unable to wash away the inhabitants of Shawneetown. Once a year for a series of successive sprints, it has carried away the fences from the cleared, lands, till at length they have surrendered and ceased to cultivate them. Once a year, the inhabitants make

---

[99] At this point an original footnote reads: "In the United States the common salt or sodium chloride in combination with potassium salt and calcium salt occurs most frequently in the rich springs on the Kanawha, the Little Sandy River, at Shawneetown, Boone's Lick at Franklin on the Missouri, the saline near Ste. Genevieve in whose salt beds I found bones of the American mastodon and in the salt springs of Riviere a la Mine. One should also read on this point Major Long's, *Account of an Expedition from Pittsburgh to the Rocky Mountains*, Vol. I, page 34."

[100] Paul Wilhelm, Duke of Wurttemberg. *Travels in North America, 1822-1824.* Translated by W. Robert Nitske. Edited by Savoie Lottinville. Norman, Okla.: University of Oklahoma Press, 1973. 155-156 (April 20-21, 1823).

their escape to higher lands, or take refuge in their upper stories, until the waters subside, when they recover their position on this desolate sand bank."[101]

Flint's Description – 1832

Shawneetown is situated on the Ohio, 9 miles below the mouth of the Wabash. The great United States Saline, situated 12 miles back of this town, contributes to give it consequence. It is the seat of justice for its county, has a bank with a large capital, and a Land Office. Golconda and America are inconsiderable villages on the Ohio. America, from its position, it should seems, must become one day of consequence. It is a point to which large steam boats can ascend from below, to wait for the smaller boats, that ascend the Ohio in low stages of the water. [102]

John Mason Peck's Gazetteer – 1837

Gallatin County joins the Wabash and the Ohio, in the southeastern corner of the state, and was organized in 1812. It is bounded north by White county; east by the states of Indiana and Kentucky; south by Pope County; and west by Pope, and Franklin counties.

It is from thirty to thirty-six miles long, and with a medium width of twenty-seven miles — containing about 760 square miles.

Its eastern boundary is washed by the Wabash and Ohio rivers, and the interior watered by the Saline creek and its tributaries.

Sand predominates the soil of this part of the state. The basis rock generally is sandstone, lying probably upon a stratum of clay slate.

This county is mostly covered with timber, amongst which are various kinds of oak, walnut, poplar, mulberry, hickory, beech, cypress, and other kinds found in this part of the state.

The salines, in the vicinity of Equality, are sources of wealth; and furnish large quantities of salt for home consumption.

Other articles of export, are horses, beef, pork, cattle, lumber, some tobacco, etc. About one half of the salt manufactured at the salines is exchanged for corn, corn meal, flour, beef, pork, potatoes and every species of produce raised in the country, to support the establishment.

This part of the state is well adapted to the growth of stock.

Gallatin County contains about 9,750 inhabitants. It is attached to the third judicial circuit, and sends three members to the House of Representatives, and one member to the Senate.

Shawneetown is an important commercial town on the Ohio.

The seat of justice is *Equality*.

---

[101] Lewis Caleb Beck (1798-1853). 1823, 1975 Reprint. *A Gazetteer of the States of Illinois and Missouri.* New York: Arno Press. 155.

[102] Timothy Flint. 1832, 2nd Ed. *The History and Geography of the Mississippi Valley.* Cincinnati: E. H. Flint and L. R. Lincoln. 1:327-328.

Bankstone's Fork, in Gallatin county, rises in the interior, runs a southeastern course, and enters the South Fork of Saline creek, fourteen miles above Equality. It has a fine country on its borders, and a large settlement.

Bear Creek, a small stream that rises in the north part of Gallatin county, runs south, and enters the North Fork of Saline creek, ten miles above Equality. Here is much good land, and a large settlement.

Cypress, a sluggish creek in Gallatin County, between Equality and Shawneetown, which runs into the Saline creek. The land in the vicinity is generally good and heavily timbered.

Devil's Anvil is a singular rock, of considerable elevation, and the top jutting over its base, near the road from Equality to Golconda. The surrounding country is very hilly, with rocky precipices, and exhibits all the desolation and wildness of a mountainous region.

Dillard's is a large settlement in Gallatin County, eight miles northwest of Shawneetown. The land generally is good.

Eagle Creek, a small stream in Gallatin County. It rises in the interior, runs south, and enters the Saline creek near its mouth. Some broken, and some good land, and a large settlement are on this stream.

Equality, the seat of justice for Gallatin County, situated on the north side of Saline creek, on section fifteen, nine south, eight east. It has nine stores, four groceries, two taverns, a brick courthouse forty feet square, two stories high, and neatly furnished, a number of mechanics of different trades, and about seventy or eighty families. It is situated in the vicinity of the salt manufactories, fourteen miles south of Shawneetown. The adjacent country south and west is broken and rough; north and east is much good land.

Ford's Ferry, in Gallatin county, on the Ohio, twenty miles below Shawneetown, and twenty-five miles south of Equality. It is on the great road from the southern parts of Kentucky and Tennessee to Illinois and Missouri.

Grable's Settlement, in Gallatin County, is sixteen miles west from Equality, on the road to Frankfort.

Harris's Creek rises in the bluffs of the Ohio River, in Gallatin County, runs a north course, and enters Saline creek, fifteen miles below Equality. Much of the land on its borders is rough and broken, interspersed with tracts of good soil.

Little Saline, in Gallatin County, rises in the bluffs of the Ohio River, runs a north course, and enters the South fork of the Saline creek, eighteen miles above Equality. It waters a tolerably good country, with a scattering population.

Logan's Settlement is in a good tract of country, in Gallatin county, eighteen miles northwest from Shawneetown.

Lollard's Settlement is ten miles northwest from Shawneetown, in Gallatin County, and contains much good land.

Rector's Fork, in Gallatin county, is a branch of the North fork of Saline creek, which it enters fifteen miles above Equality.

Saline, a navigable stream in Gallatin county, that enters the Ohio river twelve miles below Shawneetown, on section five, eleven south, ten east. It is made by three principal branches distinguished as the North, South and Middle forks, which unite near Equality. The North fork rises near McLeansboro' in Hamilton county, and runs a southerly course. The South fork rises on the borders of Johnson and Franklin counties, takes an easterly course, and unites with the North fork. The Middle fork rises on the east side of Franklin County, takes a southeasterly course, and unites with the South fork a few miles above Equality. Saline creek is navigable for steamboats to Equality, fourteen miles.

Shawneetown is the principal commercial town in the southern part of the state. It is situated on the Ohio River, about ten miles below the mouth of the Wabash, in section six, of township ten south, in range ten east of the third principal meridian, in latitude thirty-seven degrees forty minutes north.

The bank of the Ohio at this place has a gradual ascent, but is subject to inundation at the extreme floods. Between the town and the bluffs the surface is still lower, and more frequently submerged. Though no considerable sickness has prevailed in this town for some years past, it cannot but be regarded as less healthy than the more elevated portions of the state.

Considerable commercial business is transacted at this place, both in the wholesale and retail line. It has eight or ten stories, several groceries, two public houses, and six or seven hundred inhabitants.

The land office for the district is in Shawneetown. A printing office is here which publishes a weekly paper called the "*Illinois Advertiser*." There is also a bank here which was chartered by the territorial legislature, and which has lately recommenced doing business, after a suspension of several years.[103]

Early Saltworks

The French and Gallatin Salines – 18th Century

Equality, so far as tradition goes, was settled during the last years of the 17th Century by a military expedition which was sent here three years after the founding of Kaskaskia to trade with the Indians for salt. It proved, however, that no regular supply could be obtained from them and after an abortive attempt or two of this kind a military expedition was dispatched which was to organize a post and boil salt, the product of the summer work to be hauled overland in the fall, leaving a garrison of three or four men during the winter.

The Shawnee Indians, who were the Bedouins of America, soon attacked them and wiped out all but one, who escaped to Kaskaskia. He was absent from the post when the attack was made, it seems, after which a stronger party was sent and relieved semi-annually. (NOTE: I am of the opinion that the above massacre was incorrect - and has been confused with an attack made at Ft. Massac — unless the incidents were almost identical in result. V.H.C.)

These posts had been at the "Half Moon," or "Flitter Ford" as it was variously called, about a mile southwest of town. Early in the 17th century, and unexpectedly high water came and the garrison was driven out into the hands of the savages and a few survivors escaped to Kaskaskia. After this a block-house and stockade were erected on the property now known as the Bailey property. This block-house stood for years and the settlement

---

[103] John Mason Peck. 1837, 2nd Ed. *A Gazetteer of Illinois*. Philadelphia: Grigg & Elliot, 1837. 104-105, 152-307.

extended along where the L & N railroad now runs, toward North Fork railroad bridge and westward toward the old depot.

The late Wm. H. Crawford, Esq., gave the above information to the writer, he obtaining it from Gen. Leonard White who was U.S. salt commissioner from 1814 until 1834, until the government land office was closed and the lands turned over to the state in 1834, if I am not misinformed.

The late Rev. Bernard Hoter also gave me information which he obtained from a part of the old French records, which, I believe, he told me were at some Catholic institution at Belleville and in St. Louis. It is known that many of the French records were never obtained by the state, the wife of a French commandant, when it was captured by Gen. George Rogers Clark, secreted the records and afterwards laced them in the hands of the priests.

A part of the order for this first settlement were couched in these words, as I remember: "This expedition shall be made in order that the loyal subjects of his Most Catholic Majesty, King Louis XI who need salt shall have a regular supply of this commodity." This expedition was dispatched to the "Salines of the Oubatche."

I have before me a printed report of the year 1814 in which General White deplores the rascality of previous commissioners who had beaten the government out of dues for many years previous, and also refers to his report of 1810.

(NOTE: Gen. Leonard White was placed in complete charge of the Salt Works upon the death of Capt. – later, General – Isaac White, who was killed in the battle of Tippecanoe in December 1811 – V. H.C.)

This same General White was, during his time, offered the position of land commissioner at Fort Dearborn, now Chicago, and he declined with the statement that he had lived all his earlier life in the backwoods, never having had the opportunities of civilization, and now that this country was getting opened up, he'd be damned if he moved his children into the backwoods again, and if that was the best the administration could do for him they could go to the devil. I have never heard what became of the administration, but the general lived out his life here.

(Note: General White was a fixture here — and I think that this made his decision as it was, V.H.C.)[104]

Isaac White prepares to duel Capt. Butler

An incident occurred some time after [Isaac White's] appointment as colonel which shows at once the tenderness of the love he bore to his family and his coolness and courage. It seem that, unlike most Virginians of that age, he was morally opposed to dueling; but, like many men of the present day, he felt that occasions may arise when that mode of settling grievances is alone possible. Such an occasion actually arose in his life, and the preparations he made to meet it are partly told in the following letter to his wife, written a day or two after a brief visit to his family, who were then at Vincennes:

United States Saline, May, 23, 1811.

---

[104] Dr. L. W. Gordon. "Early History of Equality." As transcribed by Vernon H. Crest. Undated. Vernon C. Crest Collection in possession of Kathie Crest Thatcher.

Dear and Loving Wife: I got home this day about ten o'clock, after a great deal of fatigue and danger with the high water. I had liked to have strangled in the North Forke.

When you receive this I expect I shall be mingled with the dust. The day after to-morrow I am to fight a duel with Captain Butler. He gave me the first insult, and on my retorting he challenge me. I accepted it. We are to fight at six feet distance, and I expect we both will fall. But death to me has not the terrors that it is represented to have.

I am very anxious for the welfare of you and my dear children. O, did you but know the pangs I felt at parting with you and them. When my poor little son cried, I had hard work to smother my grief. You, I have no doubt, will be tender and kind to them; try and keep me in their remembrance. * * * I have left you the Negroes, and have tried to induce John Justice to stay with you until he is of age. You will have to sell Sukey and the children. Bob will stay with you his life-time. With the money you get for Sukey and children you can buy you one that is held in slavery in the Territory. I think that you had better have the house finished and live to yourself. I shall leave everything in the care of your brother Francis, who, I have no doubt, will act with tenderness and care towards you.

My sword, epaulettes, and watch and dirk I want left to George. In making my will I was actuated by the best of motives, and if I have not left you as much as you think I ought not have left you, you will forgive me when you reflect that what hat not been left to you I leave to your children, with a small exception, I repeat, again, * * * I cannot say more on this subject. So farewell, my dearest, forever! I am yours,

    Isaac White.
To Sally White.
Kiss George, Harriet and Juliet a thousand times for me.

The following is a copy of a will of Colonel White, which, giving as it does, some indication of the extent of his possessions, and conveying indirect information concerning the existence of slavery in Indiana, is of both personal and historical interest. In connection with this will there are two circumstances, who which special attention may not inappropriately be called: The first is that it was written by Colonel White himself, which, considering its lawyer-like accuracy and precision, gives some idea of his education and business intelligence; the second is that it was written on the same day as was the letter to his wife, hereinbefore quoted-a fact which, remembering that he was on the eve of a duel, that he had every reason to believe would result fatally to himself, show his coolness and perfect self-possession:

In the name of God, Amen! I, Isaac White, of the United States Saline, do make, ordain, and declare this instrument, which is signed with my own hand, to be my last will and testament, declaring at the same time that it is the first and only one that I have made.

All my debts, of which these are but few and none of magnitude, are to be punctually paid, and the legacies bequeathed are to be discharged as soon as circumstances will permit, and in the manner directed hereinafter.

To my dearly beloved wife, Sarah White, I give and bequeath all my household and kitchen furniture, all my stock and farming utensils, and all my Negroes, except as it hereafter excepted, to her and her heirs forever. I also give to her during her natural life the tract of land which I purchased of Daniel Smith and George Leech, containing two hundred acres; but if she, my wife, accedes to this my will, it is also my will that she shall raise my three children, George Washington White, Harriet G. White, and Juliet G. White, without any expense to my estate, except so much as will pay for their schooling.

It is my will that my son George have a classical education; that he may be taught fencing and dancing; and that he may be sent one year to a Military School; and that after he be sot aught he be allowed to follow the profession or occupation that he himself may choose. It is further my will that my daughters Harriet and Juliet have a good English education.

I give and bequeath to my son, George Washington White, all my estate, real and personal (except that part which I have given to my wife and hereafter excepted) he paying to his sister Harriet, at the time she becomes of age or gets married fifteen hundred dollars, and unto his sister one thousand dollars at the time she becomes of age or gets married, after paying for their schooling.

I give and bequeath to my nephews, Charles White and John Justice, a tract of land containing 464 acres and 70 poles, one moiety to each of them, to be so divided according to quality and quantity, providing that after John Justice goes to school this year, he goes home and continues to live with his aunt, Sarah White, until he is 21 years of age; if now, the moiety that was intended for him to revert back to George Washington White.

I give and bequeath to my niece, Betsy White, one mare, saddle and bridle, to be worth one hundred dollars in cash, to be paid when she becomes of age or gets married.

Should it happen that any of the legatees except George W. White should die before they are by this my last will to receive their legacies, that then and in that case the whole of the said legacies are to revert to the said George W. White. But should it please God that he should die before he comes of age, or after he becomes of age without issue, I will that then and in that case the whole of the estate, both real and personal, is to be divided equally between his sisters, Harriet G. and Juliet White.

I give and bequeath to Francis Leech all my books, maps, and backgammon table.

It is further my will that my executors collect all the debts that are due me, together with what may hereafter become due, and after paying my debts, &c., to vest the balance in bank stock.

Should Thom White wish to improve the tract of land which I have given to his son Charles, I hereby request that my executors devise it in the manner before mention.

I give and bequeath to George Leech, junior, my two-year-old colt called the Phaeton.

I constitute George Leech, John Marshall and Francis Leech, or any two of them, executors of this my last will and testament.

In witness of all and each of the things herein contained, I have set my hand and seal this 23d day of May, 1811.

The tract of land which I have bequeathed my nephews Charles White and John Justice, lies on the south side of White River, and is the one I purchased of Toussaint Dubois.

Isaac White.

In presence of —
G. C. Harlt,
Francis Leech.

The meeting which Col. White speaks of in the above letter actually took place, according to agreement between the parties, at a place now called Union Springs, in Kentucky, opposite Shawneetown; but the result of it was rather different from what he expected. Both parties were on time; but when the seconds finally announced that the weapons selected were horse-pistols and the distance six feet, the challenging party protested that such an arrangement was murderous, and gave no chance for life on either side. Colonel White's friends and himself, however, were determined, and insisted on the arrangement, when the challenger left the field, whole in body, and no doubt less included to offer challenges thereafter.[105]

Early lease of saltworks to John Bate – 1814

On this day Gov. Ninian Edwards of the Illinois Territory acting under the authority of the President of the United States signed a three-year lease of the saltworks near the mouth of the Wabash Saline with John Bate of Jefferson Co., Kentucky. Edwards signed the lease under the authority given the president by Congress on March 3, 1803.

The lease includes the salt spring known as the Saline Spring or Lick and the Half Moon Lick, "together with such number of acres of grounds around each of the said springs or licks for the purpose of erecting the necessary furnaces and buildings for the manufacture and extracting of salt from the said springs or licks." The rent of 10,025 [not certain about figure in the hundreds and tens column] bushels of "good dry merchantable salt weighing at least 50 pounds per bushel" every three months. Under the terms of the contract Bate is required to produce a minimum of 150,000 bushels a year (with a bushel weighing at least 50 pounds). The lease sets a maximum price of $1.25 per bushel and requires that Bate sell salt at that rate to everyone who applies.

In a section dealing with salt kettles, Bate agreed to purchase any sound kettles from the previous lessees, which were Jonathan Taylor, Charles Wilkins and James Morrison. In an

---

[105] George Fauntleroy White (grandson of Col. Isaac White). 1889. *Sketch of the Life of Colonel Isaac White, of Vincennes, Indiana. Killed at the Battle of Tippecanoe, November 7, 1811.* Washington: Gibson Bros., Printers and Bookbinders. 12-13, 22-24.

interesting section the lease reads, "whereas from the uncommon high waters and repeated Earthquakes[106] that have lately occurred at the said Saline there is a number of kettles necessary to the manufactory on the leased premises but not set in the furnaces the said John Bates doth further covenant and agrees to and with the United States that he will receive and pay for all the sound and undamaged kettles that may be necessary to set all the furnaces upon the premises aforesaid and on demand produce to the governor of the Illinois Territory a receipt for the same from the said Taylor, Wilkins and Morrison to the United States.

The next section gives Bate the right to cut timber and mine stone coal for use at the salines. Robert Ferry (possibly Terry) and James Barbour gave Joseph Owen a power of attorney to bind them as securities for the contract. Also, James Smally Bate and John and James Bradshaw also gave Joseph Owens a power of attorney to bind themselves as securities for the contract on behalf of John Bate. The total security pledged is $120,000. The contract is signed by Ninian Edwards, John Bate, Robert Ferry (or Terry), Phillip Barbour, James S. Bate, John & James Bradshaw, by Joseph Owens, their attorney in act, Joseph Owen and Thomas Ramsey.[107]

Lafayette's Visit

Judge Hall's Address Welcoming Lafayette

Sir:[108] — "The citizens of Shawneetown and its vicinity, avail themselves with infinite pleasure, of the opportunity which is this day presented to them, to discharge a small portion of the national debt of gratitude. The American people are under peculiar obligations to their early benefactors. In the history of governments, revolutions have not been unfrequent, nor have the struggles for liberty been few; but they have been too often incited by ambition, conducted by violence, and consummated by the sacrifices of the noblest feelings and dearest rights. The separation of the American colonies from the mother country was impelled by the purest motives, it was effected by the most virtuous means, and its results have been enjoyed by wisdom and moderation.

"A noble magnanimity of purpose and of action, adorned our conflict for independence; no heartless cruelty marked the footsteps of our patriot warriors, no selfish ambition mingled in the councils of our patriot sages. To those great and good men we owe, as citizens, all that we are and all that we possess; to them we are indebted for our liberty — for the unsullied honor of our country — for the bright example which they have given to an admiring world.

"Years have rolled away since the accomplishment of those glorious events, and few of the illustrious actors remain to partake of our affection. We mourn our Hamilton — we have wept at the grave of our Washington; but heaven has spared Lafayette to the prayers of a grateful people.

---

[106] New Madrid Earthquakes of 1811-1812. Tremors were felt for a number of years after the major quakes.

[107] *Gallatin County* (Ill.) *Deed Record A*. 9-18. Note, Bate's name is spelled both Bate and Bates in the record.

[108] This address was repeated in full by Mr. C. K. Roedel, May 14, 1925. Mr. Roedel impersonated Judge Hall at the Centennial observance of the visit of Lafayette to Shawneetown, May 14, 1825.

"In you, sir, we have the happiness of recognizing one of those whom we venerate — the companion of those whom we deplore. We greet you as the benefactor of the living, we greet your as the compatriot of the dead. We receive you with filial affection as one of the fathers of the Republic. We embrace with eager delight an opportunity of speaking our sentiments to the early champion of our rights — but we want language to express all we feel. How shall we thank thee who have so many claims upon our gratitude? What shall we call thee who have so many titles to our affection? Bound to us by a thousand fond recollections; connected with us by many endearing ties — we hail thee by every name which is dear to freeman. Lafayette — friend — father — fellow-citizen — patriot — soldier — philanthropist — we bid thee welcome. You were welcome, illustrious sir, when you came as our champion; you are thrice welcome as our honored guest. Welcome to our country and to our hearts — to our firesides and altars.

"In your extensive tour through our territories, you have doubtless beheld many proofs that he who shared the storms of our infancy, has not been forgotten amid the genial beams of a more prosperous fortune. In every section of the union our people have been proud to affix the name of Lafayette to the soil, in fighting for which that name was rendered illustrious. This fact, we hope, affords some testimony that although the philosophic retirement in which you were secluded might shelter you from the political storms which assailed your natal soil, it could not conceal you from the affectionate solicitude of your adopted countrymen. Your visit to America has disseminated gladness throughout the continent, but it has not increased our veneration for your character, nor brightened the remembrance of those services which were already deeply engraven on our memories.

"The little community which has the honor, today, of paying a small tribute to republican virtue, was not in existence at the period when that virtue was displayed in behalf of our country. You find us dwelling upon a spot which was then untrodden by the foot of civilized man; in the midst of forests whose silent echoes were not awakened by the tumults of that day. Around us are none of the monuments of departed despotism, nor any of the trophies of that valor which wrought the deliverance of our country. There is no sensible object here to recall your deeds to memory — but they dwell in our bosoms — they are imprinted upon monuments more durable than brass. We enjoy the fruits of your courage, the lesson of your example. We are the descendants of those who fought by your side — we have imbibed their love of freedom — we inherit their affection for Lafayette.

"You find our state in its infancy, our country thinly populated, our people destitute of the luxuries and elegancies of life. In your reception we depart not from the domestic simplicity of a sequestered people. We erect no triumphal arches, we offer no exotic delicacies. We receive you to our humble dwellings, and our homely faire —we take you to our arms and our hearts.

"The affections of the American people have followed you for a long series of years — they were with you at Brandywine, at York, at Olmutz, and at LaGrange — they have adhered to you through every vicissitude of fortune which has marked your virtuous career. Be assured, sir, that you still carry with your our best wishes — we fervently desire you all the happiness which the recollection of a well spent life, and the enjoyment of a venerable age, full of honor, can bestow — we pray, that health and prosperity may be your companions, when you shall be again separated from our embraces, to exchange the endearments of a people's love, for the softer joys of domestic affection, and that it may please heaven to preserve you many years to us, to your family, and to the world."[109]

Cutting Gallatin Down to Size

When created in 1812, Gallatin County included not only the present county, but also all of Hardin, parts of Pope, Saline, Williamson, Franklin, Jefferson, all of Hamilton, all of White County and parts of the counties even north of Hamilton and White. The creation of White County in 1815, Pope County in 1816, and Franklin County in 1818, set the stage for another for whole generation of Gallatin County residents. From 1818 to 1847, the county included all of the modern county, plus all of Saline and about one-third of what is now Hardin County. While the northern boundary would be adjusted slightly to match the section lines and Gallatin County kept its basic shape for nearly three decades. The county boundaries reflected tremendously the shape of the original U.S. Saline Reservation. But just because it took 29 years for the General Assembly to cut Gallatin County down to its modern size, doesn't mean others didn't try before.

Proposal for a New County at New Haven

The developers of New Haven pushed for the new proposal sometime in 1819 or later. Their proposal would have taken land from the northern part of Gallatin as well as land from the southern part of White County and make a new county with a county seat of New Haven. They didn't propose a name, just a county seat.

The evidence comes from a letter sent to the editors of the *Illinois Gazette* in Shawneetown. Although legal notice hasn't been found, the original letter remains in the Henry Eddy Collection at the Illinois State Historical Library in Springfield.

This proposed county would have ran 17 miles north to south on its east end. Besides New Haven it would have included the future sites of Cottonwood and Omaha, but would have left New Market, Ridgway and Elba still in Gallatin County. The diagonal lines for the southern boundary probably represented an attempt to avoid taking the county line across the boundary of the Saline Reservation set aside for the saltworks.

The following is the proposed notice. Presumably, the editors at the *Gazette* would have corrected the spelling before publication.

> Notice
> Is hereby given to all those concerned—that the Citizens of Gallatin and White Countys will present Petitions to the Legislater of the State of Illinois, at their next Sission to have a—new County formed out of a part of Gallatin & White Countys—and to have the new County Seat, located at New haven on the little Wabash River. Bounded as follows: Beginning on the Big Wabash at the SE corner of Section No 27 Township 8 Range 10 thence on a direct line to the SE corner of Section No 18 Township 8 Range 9 from thence to intersect the SE

---

[109] 1926. *Transactions of the Illinois State Historical Society.* Springfield, Ill.: Illinois State Historical Society.

corner of Hamilton & White Countys, thence North on the dividing line of Hamilton & White Co 7 miles from thence East on a direct line to the Big Wabash River thence down the Big Wabash to the place of beginning by request of the people

    Mr. Tobart [or Foliart] Sr
    P Slater

P. Slater, the postmaster at New Haven continued in his letter and asked the editors to publish the notice four times and forward the bill to them. The postmaster sent the letter for free, without postage. It is postmarked October 2, but no year is given.[110]

Proposal for Ohio County

The second known effort to split the county focused on an early version of Hardin County called Ohio County. The boundaries included almost all of modern day Hardin County except a pie-piece shaped wedge in the southwestern corner. The proposed county line would have extended from a point just downstream of Elizabethtown northwestward through Herod and Thacker's Gap to the west side of Eagle Mountain. Thus it would have contained a sliver of modern Pope and part of the southeastern township of Saline County. Also, the boundaries would have included all of the Eagle Creek settlement including the headwaters of Eagle Creek that are now in Saline County. These lands on the east side of Eagle Mountain are even today still associate more with Gallatin County due to the road networks and remain a part of the Gallatin County Unit School District.

> To All Whom It May Concern
>   TAKE NOTICE
> THAT Application will be made to the Legislature of the State of Illinois, at the Special Session, to be held on the 1st Monday of January, 1826, for a new County, beginning at the Mouth of the Saline Creek, thence up said Creek to the Mouth of Big Eagle, thence up same to the Saline Reserve, thence North and West with said Reserve to the S.W. Corner of Section 6, T. 10. R. 7.— thence, in a direct Line, to a Pointe West of the Mouth of Big Creek, on the Ohio River, and where the Line, dividing Sections 33 and 34, intersect the same, and thence up the said Ohio to the place of beginning.
> October 31, 1825.

Although hundreds signed petitions in favor of this county, a similar number argued against the proposal. In the end, the General Assembly did not act on the suggestion.[111]

---

[110] Slaton to Editors, Illinois Gazette. [no date] Henry Eddy Papers. Illinois State Historical Library, Springfield.
[111] "Take Notice." Folder 242. Legislative Papers 1826/27. Illinois State Archives.

Linder's *Early Bench and Bar*

William Jefferson Gatewood

The next name I propose to introduce here is that of William[112] J. Gatewood, better known by the name of "Jeff" Gatewood. I became acquainted with him at Carmi, Ill., on my first trip around my circuit. He was introduced to me by Col. A. P. Field. This was in 1836. Gatewood lived at Shawneetown, and was an eminent lawyer, and known as such by the bar all over the State. He stood in the front ranks of the legal profession. I have incidentally alluded to him in the sketch I have given of Jephtha Hardin. He was a large man, portly and good looking; had as fine a head as was ever placed upon any man's shoulders. I frequently met him at Vandalia and Springfield. He practiced law in the Supreme and Federal Courts of this State, and no lawyer stood higher with the court than Jeff. He was for a good many years a Senator in our State legislature. He was a splendid speaker, and would have risen to great national distinction had not death cut his career short in the very prime of life, he not being over forty years of age at the time of his demise. He had a very fine voice, which was full of melody. He was a remarkable for the originality of his views, borrowing nothing from books or men, seldom perpetrating a quotation, unless when he told a story, which he frequently did, and no man could tell a better one than Jeff. He was the very life and soul of every social and convivial party of which he made a member.

In his earlier career as a politician Jeff was a Whig, but as that party had little or nothing to bestow by way of preferment, Jeff finally concluded that there was richer pasturage on the other side of the fence, so he jumped over, expecting to feed on delicious Democratic clover. The Democrats were very glad to number Jeff as one of their party, but they did not seem to be in any haste to give him any high or lucrative place in their ranks.

I have heard a good story told of Jeff, which runs as follows: Being in a Democratic caucus at Springfield, where they were parceling out the offices amongst the various politicians of their party, they forgot to name Jeff as one of them, and when they got through Jeff said to them: "But what in the h--l are you going to do for Jeffy?" This remark struck them with such force that they changed their programme, and did provide for Jeff.

The last time I remember to have seen Jeff was when I was on the way to Kaskaskia in 1841. I fell in with him and Field at some little town about halfway between Charleston and Kaskaskia. I stopped at the hotel where they were, and we took dinner together.

Poor Jeff! He had his faults, but they were not crimes. I am not the man to unveil them, but would rather throw the broad mantle of charity over them; my maxim being *"Nihil mortuis nisi bonum."*

Jephtha Hardin

The first court that I attended in the spring of 1836, was at Lawrenceville, in Lawrence county. It seemed that some good genius attended me, for I got into almost immediate practice wherever I went, which increased from year to year until I quit the circuit. From

---

[112] The author of this passage, Gen. Linder Usher repeatedly referred to Gatewood as Thomas Jefferson Gatewood rather than the correct William Jefferson Gatewood.

Lawrenceville we went to Mt. Carmel; from there to Carmi, where we often met with lawyers from Shawneetown circuit — such as Gatewood, Eddy, Mapes, Samuel Marshall, and William H. Stickney, now of Chicago. But let me not forget to make especial mention of my distinguished friend, Jephtha Hardin, whom we frequently met at this court. He was a brother of the distinguished Benjamin Hardin, of whom I have spoken in a former part of these memoirs. He reminded me very much of his brother Ben, in looks and disposition. Of course he was not the equal of Ben, but not greatly his inferior.

Jephtha Hardin, like his brother Ben, of Kentucky, had a very good opinion of himself. Finding that I had been personally acquainted with his brother Ben, he seemed somewhat anxious to know what opinion I entertained of him. I told him Hardin was an able lawyer, so regarded by all who knew him—exceedingly sarcastic, as I had a good right to know; that I had felt the merciless inflictions of his coarse satire full many a time, and that I was even yet sore in the remembrance thereof; that as he was almost the counterpart of his brother in physical and mental stature—being large and ungainly in size and coarse in speech—I was only sorry that there was no case in court where we were on opposite sides, that I might liquidate the debt I owed to the Hardin family.

"The thing, by G-d," said he, "of all others I most desire. Well," added he, "there is a case of hog-stealing here. I know the defendant. I will see the young man who is defending, and get him to let me assist him. You must see the State's Attorney, and become his sole prosecutor, and I'll be d----d if I don't give you the worst dressing down you ever had in your life."

The matter was not difficult to arrange, either with the young man or the State's Attorney. So into the case we went, after the evidence was through, which was very strong against the accused. I opened with a plain statement of the facts and the law, telling, the jury that the most they would have to do would be to agree upon the time he should serve in the penitentiary, but I would take the liberty to tell them that the accused would be defended by the distinguished Jephtha Hardin, of Shawneetown, brother to the distinguished Ben Hardin, of Kentucky, of world-wide renown, who, being scarcely less distinguished than his brother, proposed to add new luster to this laurels by the castigation he was going to give me. I gave a brief statement of the fact that I had challenged him to the combat, for the purpose of paying off a debt I owed to the Hardin family. He immediately rose and replied to me at considerable length and with marked bitterness, and seemed unwilling to give me credit for a very moderate share of ability. He succeeded in getting off some pretty good laughs at my expense. When he closed and it was my turn to reply, the court adjourned to dinner.

During the recess the circumstance of our legal duel became known to everybody, so at the meeting of the court I had a full house, and quite a number of ladies to grace the occasion. I never entertained the least doubt of getting the better of him. I was not bitter, for indeed I entertained none but the kindest feelings toward Judge Hardin; but I indulged in many a ludicrous comparison, and drew from the crowd the most uproarious laughter; and when I was about closing, turning to Judge Hardin, I said, "Gentlemen of the jury, I have now settled with the Hardins in full the debt I owed."

"But I have not with you, by God, sir," observed Hardin, in quite an audible voice, which caused everybody to laugh to the splitting of their sides.

I went on to say, after the crowd had become quiet, "Gentlemen of the jury, you may now take leave of your old and distinguished friend, Jephtha Hardin; his face you'll see no more; the start that shone with undimmed luster had disappeared from its place in the heavens, but another shall take its place, of brighter sheen and more resplendent luster."

I sat down, leaving the crowd enjoying a hearty laugh, and friend Jephtha in a terrible bad passion. We parted, however, good friends, though I have never seen him since; but I will do him the justice to say that he was a man of kind disposition, great tenderness of heart, and eminently social.

I will next give some very amusing and interesting anecdotes of "Old Jephtha," and then take up some other distinguished man of that day, whose history will not be uninteresting to the present generation.

The Hardin Family

I will now relate some interesting anecdotes illustrative of the character and peculiarities of my friend Jephtha Hardin, the half brother of Ben Hardin, of Kentucky. But as my readers doubtless are not as well acquainted with the Hardin family as I am, I will take occasion here to say that they were the most distinguished family of Kentucky. They were a race of giants, physically and intellectually. Ben Hardin was the most distinguished of the family, not only as a lawyer but as an advocate. His wit and humor were scarcely inferior to that of Curran. When in Congress, where he served for some thirteen or fourteen years, everybody – even Randolph – acknowledged his prowess. Randolph compared him to a coarse kitchen butcher-knife whetted upon a brick-bat. The late General Thornton, of Shelby county, Illinois, who knew him well, and how lived in Washington at the time Hardin was a member of Congress, told me that when it was known that he was going to address the House of Representatives, he could gather the largest audience of any member of the House; not even Randolph or Clay could gather a larger. He said, when it was known that Hardin was going to speak, he has seen Negroes and boys running along the streets and avenues of Washington crying at the top of their voices, "Hardin has got the floor! Hardin has got the floor! Hardin has got the floor!" and in less than no time the streets would be filled with hacks and every sort of vehicle, carrying the eager crows to the Capitol to hear one of Kentucky's rarest and most gifted sons address the House of Representatives.

The late lamented John J. Hardin, of Illinois, the son of Gen. Martin D. Hardin, of Frankfort, Ky., was a near relative of Ben's. All the Wickliffes, from Charles A. down, had Hardin blood in their veins, and were all distinguished for their talents. My opinion is, that General John J. Hardin, of whom I have already spoken, who fell fighting at Buena Vista, under General Taylor, was not inferior to either Lincoln or Douglas. I knew him well, and he and Lincoln and Douglas and myself served in the Legislature of Illinois in 1836 and '37, at old Vandalia.

I have now given the reader as good an idea of the Hardin family as it is in my power to do. I shall therefore, return for a short period to my old friend, "Jep." I have already said that he was eminently social. I will add that he was garrulous—the never-failing weakness of old age. Mr. Stickney, of this city, told me that on one occasion they slept together in the same bed at a hotel, and Hardin talked him to sleep, recounting the scenes of his early life, and he supposed he had slept about two hours and awoke, and found Hardin rattling away, perfectly unconcerned as to whether Stickney was asleep or awake.

He and Michael Jones, of Shawneetown, had a deadly feud, and Jones threatened that if he outlived Hardin he would dig his bones up out of the grave and hang him in chains on a tree at some cross-roads in Gallatin county, of which threat Hardin was apprised; and being satisfied, from the character of Jones, that he would execute it, when he came to die he had a clause inserted in his will that they should dig his grave fifteen feet deep, and fill it up four feet above the surface of the earth with solid masonry; which I understand was done.

Jeffy Gatewood and Jep's 'Little Court'

One more anecdote in regard to my old friend Jephtha, and I will dismiss him. While he was presiding as judge at Shawneetown, the distinguished Jefferson Gatewood, of whom I have already spoken, with whom Hardin was not on very good terms, had a case before him in which the Judge ruled against him. Gatewood, thinking the ruling wrong, turned to some brother lawyer and in an undertone (which Hardin nevertheless heard) said, "I will elevate this case and take it out of the hands of the is little court."

Hardin, immediately addressing Gatewood, said, "What is that you say, Jeffy Gatewood-did you say little court? *You*, Jeff say little court! I'll show you whether this a little court or not! I'll fine you, and send you to jail into the bargain, sir! Clerk, enter a fine of fifty dollars against him!"

By this time the great drops of sweat, as big as beads, were rolling down Gatewood's forehead; he rose to his feet and undertook to explain. Hardin said, "Sit down, Jeffy, the court will hear no explanation from you. *You* say little court! Clerk, enter a fine of fifty dollars more against him; I'll show *you* how little a court this is. I'll thrash you, Jeffy, and you know I can do it. Sheriff, adjourn court till after dinner."

After the Judge had eaten a good hearty dinner of roast turkey and other accompaniments, he opened court at 2 o'clock. Being in excellent humor, he remitted Gatewood's fine, and proceeded with business as usual. I am informed that Gatewood never again intimated that Hardin's court was a *little court*. A. P. Field, a lawyer at that time of great distinction, who was present on the occasion, and from whom I gathered the foregoing facts, told me that in all his life he never witnessed such an amusing and ludicrous scene.

My dear reader, if I have wearied you with the account I have given you of my old friend Jephtha, attribute it to an old man's love of gossip, as I shall now dismiss him from these pages, hoping I have said nothing that will give you a bad opinion of him; for really he was a very good and an exceedingly kind-hearted man, and would cry like a child at a picture of sorrow or dress. Farewell, Jephtha! Peace to they ashes! *"Requiescat in pace."*

Note: Later on in his writings, Linder featured a sketch on Alexander P. Field that relates to the incident between Jephtha Hardin and Gatewood. Here it goes:

Field was not only a splendid orator, political debater, advocate and lawyer, but he could sing a good song and tell a good story. I remember at the Carmi Circuit Court he perfectly thrilled and electrified me by singing that beautiful song to be found in *Moore's Melodies*, commencing thus:

> "So slow our ship her foaming track
>   Against the wind was cleaving,
>   Her trembling pennant still look back

To that dear isle 'twas leaving."

My readers doubtless remember the balance of this beautiful song, and suffer me to say that it lost none of its beauties from the style, manner and voice in which Field sung it. It was upon this occasion, Jeff Gatewood, of Shawneetown, being present, that Field relate the reencounter between judge Jephtha Hardin and Jeff, in which Jeff used the words "little court," which I have related in the sketch I have given of Judge Hardin.

Samuel S. Hayes

The next person I intend to introduce into these pages is Samuel S. Hayes, of Chicago.[113] My acquaintance with him commenced sometime in 1840 — I think it was at Carmi, White County, the most southern county on my circuit.

S. S. Hayes is a very remarkable man. He acquired a thorough knowledge of the German and French languages in the course of a single winter, without a tutor or instructor, save the books which he purchased for that purpose. Bat Webb told me he was a perfect prodigy in the acquisition of languages.

I do not know at what precise time Mr. Hayes came to the bar, but I think it was somewhere about 1846, but I cannot speak positively. When I first knew him he lived in Shawneetown. I think he was not fully grown at that time. He came up from Shawneetown to Carmi at the term of the court which I was attending there. It was the first time I ever saw him. I took him then to be about seventeen years of age. He was introduced to me by my friend Henry Eddy, who told me privately that he was a young man of great promise, which in after life I found to be true.

Hayes had been a druggist, as I understood from himself, but he finally studied law and settled in White county, Ills., and represented that county in the lower House of the legislature in 1846. I was a member of that body at that time. Our relationship the character of members was very pleasant. We had some little difficulties in after years which I do not choose to mention here.

Hayes has been a fortunate and prosperous man. He was originally a Whig, and almost worshipped at the shrine of Henry Clay, which nearly all young lawyers did at that day; but finding that the road to preferment did not lay in that direction, he turned a political somersault and became a Democrat. He is now, and for a long time has been, Comptroller of the city of Chicago, and is a man, I understand, of fine financial abilities.

Mr. Hayes is the son-in-law of Col. E. D. Taylor, still living, and a man who has done more perhaps to bring about the success of the Illinois and Michigan Canal than any man now living.[114]

I will not extend my remarks any further on S. S. Hayes, only to say that he is a good lawyer and a self-made man. Though his education was liberal, it was acquired through his

---

[113] Before moving to Chicago, Hayes lived in White and Gallatin counties.

[114] Col. Taylor was the son of Giles Taylor; the first schoolteacher remembered in Saline County and was the brother-in-law of John Hart Crenshaw. He too started out in the saltworks working for the Guard family. He eventually moved northward and found success. D. W. Lusk remembered him in the mid 1880s as the last of the original salt manufacturers left alive in the state.

own ambition and industry. He was first appointed to the office of comptroller under Frank Sherman, then Mayor of the city of Chicago. In that capacity he discharged the duties thereof to the satisfaction of everybody, I believe.

Mr. Hayes is a man who might fill any diplomatic or other position under our national government with credit to himself and advantage to the country.

I ought to say before I close these remarks, that Mr. Hayes is a good public speaker and also a good writer.

Henry Eddy and the Legislature of 1846-47

One of the most distinguished men of that day, as a lawyer, was Henry Eddy, of Shawneetown. I first met him at Carmi, in 1836. I also met him at the Supreme Court repeatedly. He was employed in the largest cases that came up from Southern Illinois. When he addressed the court, he elicited the most profound attention. He was a sort of walking law library. He never forgot anything that he ever knew, no matter whether it was law, poetry or *belles lettres*. He often would quote whole pages of Milton and Shakespeare, when he felt in a genial mood. He was the son-in-law of John Marshall, of Shawneetown, president of the Shawneetown bank, and brother-in-law of Major Samuel Marshall, one of the most talented men in the State of Illinois. I served a term in the legislature of Illinois with Eddy, in 1846 and '7, and we roomed together during the whole of that winter.

On one occasion Eddy got very "high," and while in that condition, he rose in the House and made a few remarks, and it became obvious to us all that Eddy was not in a fit condition at that time to address the House. Some of his friends who sat near him whispered to him and advised him to postpone his remarks till the next day, which he did. That night four or five of his friends got together and determined to have some fun out of him, and we concocted this story, which each one of us was to tell him when the others were not present. I was the first one to open the dance, next morning, when Eddy was perfectly cool and at himself. I went to him with great gravity, with sorrow expressed in my face and said, "Eddy, you mortified your friends very much on yesterday, in attempting to speak when you were so much intoxicated." He confessed that he had been overtaken, and was very much intoxicated. He said that he had been to a saloon, and it being a cold morning, had taken a stiff horn of "Tom and Jerry,"[115] which, when he got into the warm Hall of Representatives, close to the stove, flew to his head, and he had really no recollection of what he had said.

"Ah, but Eddy, there lies the rub. You cursed and swore like a trooper."

"What did I say, Linder? Do you remember the words?"

---

[115] Before that famous cat and mouse cartoon duo of the mid 20th Century, the 1821 British novel, *Life in London, or The Day and Night Scenes of Jerry Hawthorn, Esq., and his elegant friend, Corinthian Tom, accompanied by Bob Logic, the Oxonian, in their Rambles and Sprees through the Metropolis*, brought to life this irrepressible well-remembered duo. As part of the publicity, the author Pierce Egan adapted a recipe for eggnog and named it the "Tom and Jerry." The spirituous winter holiday-time drink consisted of an ounce of rum, an ounce of brandy, a tablespoon of eggnog batter containing of eggs, sugar, cinnamon, allspice and ground cloves. This mixture would be added to a mug topped off with either boiling water or hot milk. The exact recipe used around the 1846 Christmas holiday in the Springfield establishments has not been determined (or even researched) by the editor.

"Yes, Eddy, I do, and I shall never forget them. You said, "Mr. Speaker, this subject by G-d, sir, is very far from being exhausted, and I'll be G-d d-----d, if I don't intend to ventilate it myself,' and at that point we got you by the coat tail and pulled you into your seat."

"O! my God!" said he, "is that so? As soon as the House meets, I will make my apology. I never did such a thing before, but for the d----d 'Tom and Jerry' would not have done it then."

The rest of our conspirators all met him, and, seriatim, told him the same story; and he actually started to the House to make his apology, but meeting with Rheman, a member from Vandalia, on his way to the House, told him what he was going to do. Rheman, not being in our plot, told him that he was present and heard what he said, and that he was perfectly respectful, and that there was not a word of profanity in what he had said. Eddy said, "I smell it now; the boys have laid a trap for me, but they haven't caught me this time."[116]

Kidnappings

The Lost Story of the Old Slave House

EDITOR'S NOTE: Clarence Bonnell wrote this in 1920 for publication in the *Transactions of the Illinois State Academy of Science*. Years later while writing *Illinois Ozarks* (published in 1947), he noted he first learned of the stories surrounding Crenshaw's mansion four decades earlier after his arrival in Harrisburg in 1903. At the time of this writing Bonnell taught science at Harrisburg High School. He later also served as vice-principal at the school.

This is titled the "lost story" because few in the area actually read it in the academic journal and those that had forgot about this small portion of Bonnell's larger article. It came out six years before tourists are remembered first coming to the house in sizable numbers. Bonnell wrote this a decade before the Sisk family decided to charge admission in an effort to stifle the growing numbers of visitors. That didn't work. The site became a bigger tourist attraction. For years critics of the site dismissed the stories told there by stating the family had just made them up for the tourists. Had someone remembered this article recording the stories before there were tourists, the Sisk family could have saved themselves a lot of grief.

On a personal note, as a researcher focusing on the house in 1996, it could have saved us a lot grief if we'd found this and recognized its importance before we did three years of research. Other than the years constructed, Bonnell's source for the story remembered the events fairly accurately. Now, in 2001, six years of research shows that all of the basic stories told at the Old Slave House are based on real events. In other words, the folklore is really the history — even the ghost stories.

> Stories come to me of an "Underground Railroad" station about four miles southeast of Equality in Gallatin County. Upon a hilltop, stands a large two-story frame house conspicuous for its many large windows. It is a plain rectangular

---

[116] Gen. Usher F. Linder. 1879 2nd Ed. *Reminiscences of the Early Bench and Bar of Illinois*. Chicago: The Chicago Legal News Company. 44-54, 207-208. 313-315.

block of a house, with a well pitched roof having a deck something like twelve feet wide running the entire length. Just under the edge of the deck there are windows corresponding to the ventilators of a railway car. The gables have large window. The attic is said to have been reached by a narrow stairway. Along each side of the attic hall just under the sloping part of the roof there are bunks arranged, bunks just as the beds are situated in a Pullman car.

One man relates that apparatus resembling stocks were seen the rubbish of this attic. The story is that it was built between 1838 and 1844 and was owned by Johnny Crenshaw. Some metal ornaments on the house are said to have come from England. Instead of this being an "underground" station for escaping slaves, so the story goes, this one was once used by a band operating as the automobile thieves of today. A free Negro or one escaping by flight, if found by this gang, was overpowered and conveyed by night under guard from farther north to this station. Another night journey took him to and across the Ohio River where his word was not accepted in court and where undisputed possession was evidence of ownership.

The price that Negroes brought in those days was great enough to justify the risk taken by the captors. Some who have owned this house and lived in it tell this story as true. Others who were children in that day and lived only a few miles away claim no knowledge of such use of the property. This is explained on the ground that great secrecy was maintained by the owners. True or untrue, here is a story to stir the imagination.[117]

Kidnapper's mode of operations

The crime of seizing free blacks, running them south and selling them into slavery from this State, for a long time was quite common.... [P]ortions of southern Illinois for many years afforded a safe retreat to those kidnapping outlaws. We cannot cite the numerous cases of kidnapping.

...[I]n the majority of cases the poor ignorant blacks, by fraud and deceit, were inveigled into a trip south on a flat boat, or other errand, and at some pre-arranged point on the river, they would be turned over to confederates, forcibly and rapidly taken to the interior and there sold into slavery... Another mode was to seize a black and forcibly convey him to a rendezvous either on the Ohio or Mississippi, but not out of the State, where a confederate would appear and carry him beyond.[118]

---

[117] Clarence Bonnell. Winter 1921. "The Lore of the Illinois Ozarks." *Transactions of the Illinois State Academy of Science*. Springfield, Ill.: Illinois State Academy of Science. 14:1. 56-57.

[118] Alexander Davidson and Bernard Stuvé. 1876. *A Complete History of Illinois from 1867 to 1873; Embracing the Physical Features of the country; its Early Explorations; Aboriginal Inhabitants; French and British Occupation; Conquest by Virginia; Territorial Condition and the Subsequent Civil, Military and Political Events of the State*. Springfield, Ill.: Illinois Journal Company. 318-321.

Wilson Fights the Kidnappers – late 1840s

The decade after the Mexican War was a turbulent one in southeastern Illinois. The closing of the salt works had let loose a large number of rough operatives, white and black. Gambling, drinking, horseracing, and gun-fighting prevailed, the slavery question came to the front as it had done once before, and kidnapping became common along the border of the slave states. Among the first victims was a colored girl who had belonged to the Wilson family. She was taken to the Red River, but as soon as she could be located my father [Harrison Wilson] went for her, and after much legal formality and trouble, brought her home in triumph. After a similar service in another case of the same sort, which aroused the public conscience, under his leadership, he had the satisfaction of seeing all forms of violence vindicated and the rowdies and kidnappers brought to punishment or driven out of the state.[119]

An Attempt to Kidnap Richard Yates – 1860

This campaign was one of the most hotly contested struggles ever witnessed in Southern Illinois, and the incident of which we write occurred in Gallatin County, which was then regarded as the fountainhead of pure Democracy. It had been the early home of many of the great lights of the party, and every attempt to dispute its authority was regarded as an invasion of sacred rights. Indeed, the people were so devoted to the cause of the Democracy, that an outspoken Republican was held in extreme contempt. But in this campaign the political world was moving, and the Democracy were thoroughly aroused to the necessity of disputing every inch of ground with their Republican adversary. The Republicans, few as they were in number, were equally in earnest, and there was hot blood in every quarter. The Democracy opened the campaign at Shawneetown with a grand barbecue. It was a great meeting, and was addressed by Gov. A. P. Willard of Indiana, John A. Logan, candidate for Congress, and Lewis W. Ross, candidate for Lieutenant-Governor, in the order in which their names appear. The speech of Mr. Willard, who at that time was regarded as the ablest and most eloquent champion of the Democratic party of the Northwest, was a powerful arraignment of the Republican party, and it caused many of the new converts to waver in their devotion to the cause they had so lately espoused, and to have judged the situation from the temper of that meeting would have been to predict a signal victory for the Democratic party.

But weak as the Republicans were, they were not to be overwhelmed by this single blow, and they set themselves about to hold a similar meeting upon the identical spot. Preparations were made for a barbecue, and a cordial invitation was extended to the people from far and near to be present, and hear Republican principles discussed from a Republican standpoint. Richard Yates, the Republican candidate for Governor, was positively announced to address the meeting. He was then in the very prime of manhood. The Democrats were afraid of his power on the stump, and it was determined by a few of the most daring of that party, that he should be kidnapped, and thus prevent his appearance at the meting (The

---

[119] James Harrison Wilson. 1912, reprint 1971. *Under the Old Flag*. Westport, Conn.: Greenwood Press Publishers. 5.

writer[120] was then a resident of Gallatin county, and was one of those who did not wish to hear Mr. Yates speak). He had spoken the day before at Carmi. The road on which he was expected to arrive was carefully guarded, and every precaution taken to make sure of his capture. An all-night watch was kept up, but in an unguarded moment the sentinels slept, and Yates, unconscious of their designs upon his liberty, arrived safely during the night in company with Robert Kirkham, (now Colonel) and next day he appeared in due time as the fearless champion of the Republican party.

The meeting was fully as large as that held by the Democracy, but there were comparatively few Republicans present. Many came through curiosity; others for mischief. Yates had hardly taken his seat on the stand before a series of hideous groans rent the air. But when the speaker was formally introduced the noise and confusion knew no bounds, and it continued until Daniel Jacobs, a life-long Democrat, mounted a spring wagon which stood in the midst of the throng, and declared in a tone loud enough to be heard by all, that the distinguished speaker should be heard, or he himself would be taken from the grounds a corpse and then and there, announced his abandonment of the Democratic party. This bold and daring declaration brought order out of confusion, when Mr. Yates proceeded with his address without further interruption, save an occasional question from some of the advanced thinkers of the Democratic party as to his position upon the "black laws" and Negro equality, subjects which were the stock in trade of the Democratic leaders of that section. But time brings many changes in politics. Some of the very men[121] who were foremost in the effort to break up that meeting are now leaders in the Republican party; and the name of Yates is held in dear remembrance by many who heard him on that memorable occasion.[122]

Last Slave Registered in Illinois – 1862

The reader has been made aware that prior to the emancipation proclamation colored persons could not permanently settle in Illinois without first giving bond that they would not become charges upon the State. Here is, perhaps, the last instrument of the kind executed in Illinois. It was made at the time slaves were known as "contrabands of war," and the colored person in question was brought from Cairo to Shawneetown to be employed in the family of her bondsman, as a servant:

> Know all men by these presents, that we, Caroline Sanders and James B. Turner, of Shawneetown, Illinois, are held and firmly bound unto the People of the State of Illinois, for the use of Gallatin County, in the sum of one thousand dollars, good and lawful money of the United States, to be paid to said State for the use of said county, to which payment well and truly to be made we bind ourselves, our heirs and administrators firmly by these presents. Sealed with our seals, and dated this 1st day of September, 1862.

---

[120] D. W. Lusk.

[121] The next to last reference about GOP leaders could refer to John A. Logan who changed parties during the Civil War.

[122] D. W. Lusk. 1884. *Politics and Politicians*. Springfield, Illinois: D. W. Lusk. 106-108.

The condition of this is such, that whereas, the above bounden Caroline Sanders is a free person of color, at least she asserts herself to be free, and is desirous of settling in Gallatin county, Illinois: now if the said Caroline Sanders shall not at any time become a charge to said county, or to any other county in the State, as a poor person, and shall at al times demean herself in strict conformity of the laws now enacted and that may hereafter be enacted in this state, then this obligation to be void, otherwise to be and remain in full force and effect.

       Caroline *her* X *mark* Sanders, (seal)
       James B. Turner, (Seal.)
Signed and sealed in the presence of
       Mary A. Richeson
State of Illinois,
  Gallatin County, } SS.

I, Silas Cook, county clerk of the county and State aforesaid, do hereby certify that the above and foregoing is a true and correct copy of the original bond now on file in my office. Given under my hand and official seal, this 20th day of April, A. D. 1883.

       Silas Cook,
       County Clerk.[123]

Contraband Negroes – 1862

The prejudices of a portion of the people of Saline County [and Gallatin as well] to the war and toward the Negro, whom they could clearly see would in all probability be benefited by the success of the Union arms, is illustrated by their course with reference to the introduction of Negro laborers into the county during the war. At first citizens, without respect to party, brought into different counties of southern Illinois contrabands, as laborers, because the absence from home of so many of the people in the army rendered labor scarce and dear.

Reference to this history of Gallatin County will show the reader the course of James B. Turner, of Shawneetown, with reference to Carolina Sanders. James B. Turner was a Democrat, and other Democrats had taken this reasonable course to procure domestics and laborers. Among others who had brought in Negroes was Dr. John W. Mitchell, known to be a strong Republican. He had imported two families of contrabands, and put them to work upon his farm. It was not long before everyone in the surrounding country knew o the presence of these Negroes, and their introduction was an outrage that many of the citizens could not permit to go unpunished.

But Hon. William J. Allen and other leading members of the Democratic party who were opposed to the war, and who desired to carry the next election, determined that the fight must be made upon the Negro question, and Mr. Allen, in company with Mr. Turner who was a candidate for the Legislature, visited Harrisburg for the purpose of advising their friends as to the line of action.

---

[123] D. W. Lusk. 1884. *Politics and Politicians: A Succinct History of the Politics of Illinois from 1856 to 1884.* Springfield, Ill.: H. W. Rokker. 347-348.

On the 25th of October a meeting of the people was held in the courthouse at Harrisburg, at which the following resolutions were adopted:

> At a mass meeting of the citizens of Saline County, Ill., held in the courthouse, on the 25th day of October, 1862, the meeting was organized by electing J. W. Russell, Esq., president, and Jackson Dodd and Archibald Blackburn, secretaries. J. L. Riley, being called on, explained the object of the meeting to be to consult upon the propriety, or impropriety, of contraband Negroes being brought within the limits of Saline County, showing that it was an infringement upon State rights form them to be sent within the State, and bringing black labor in competition with white labor.
>
> Upon motion the chair appointed J. L. Riley, James B. Barker, David Stiff, John Ledford and David Roper, a committee to draft resolutions expressive of the sense of this meeting. After a short absence the committee returned and reported the following preambles and resolutions, through their chairman, J. L. Riley.
>
> Whereas, the constitution of Illinois prohibits Negroes and mulattoes migrating to, and settling within, the State, and
>
> Whereas, the people of the State at a recent election re-endorsed the section containing said prohibition by over one hundred thousand majority, and
>
> Whereas, numerous hordes of contrabands have been sent within the limits of the State, which we regard as an infringement upon State rights, and
>
> Whereas, a number of said contrabands have been recently brought within the limits of Saline County, contrary to the wishes of a large majority of our citizens, therefore.
>
> Resolved, that we, the citizens of Saline County, in mass assembled, respectfully ask that said contrabands be sent or taken without the limits of said county forthwith.
>
> Resolved, that if any other person has in contemplation to bring more of said contrabands into the county, we entreat such a one, in the name of the constitution and of humanity, to desist the thought at once.
>
> Resolved, that these proceedings be signed by the officers and published in the *Harrisburg Chronicle*.
>
> Upon motion the preambles and resolutions were adopted unanimously.
>
> Upon motion the meeting adjourned.
>
>   James W. Russell,
>   President
>
> Jackson Dodd,   }
> Archibald Blackburn} Secretaries.

Of the committee on resolutions, James B. Barker, David Stiff and David Roper, and both the secretaries of the meeting were unable to read or write.

After the adoption of the resolutions the chairman of the meeting was requested to appoint a committee to wait upon Dr. Mitchell, who was upon his farm, and inform him of the actions taken by the "citizens of Saline County in mass assembled" with reference to contrabands, and to inform him that he "forthwith" remove said contrabands from the county or suffer the consequences. But it being well known to all that Dr. Mitchell was prepared for any emergency, no committee could be found with sufficient courage to notify him to remove the contrabands.

At length, after several attempts to secure a committee to perform this dangerous service had failed, one of the members who, however, was never in favor of the Rebellion, suggested that he believed Dr. Mitchell could read, that he could read print any way, and that if the resolutions were published it would be sufficient notification. Thus the Gordian Knot of the situation severed and the meeting adjourned.

But whether Dr. Mitchell ever read the printed notice or not, he did not remove the contrabands in accordance therewith, and a second meeting was held, a similar performance gone through with, and threats boldly made that if Dr. Mitchell did not remove the contrabands his life and property would be destroyed; but the Doctor bravely stood his ground, and a second failure on the part of the brave resolves was the result.

This failure caused calmer counsels to prevail, and upon the convening of the circuit court[124] [Dr. Mitchell] was indicted under the "black laws" of the State, and this indictment was not disposed of until the Constitution of 1870, from which the word "white" is omitted, came into effect, when the indictment was stricken from the docket.[125]

Education

Three Attempts to Educate Black Students

Both black and white residents of Gallatin County made at least three attempts to establish schools for black students in the years before the 14th Amendment.[126]

On January 25, 1844, Benjamin F. Spilman, John Siddall, Edmond J. Michelson and George W. Cayton, trustees of the Presbyterian Church of Shawneetown leased to Samuel McAllister, Samuel Bird and Henry Bell, trustees of the African Methodist Episcopal Church, the old Presbyterian church house on Shawneetown In-Lot 858. The lease allowed the A.M.E. trustees to use and occupy the church for 10 years as a place of public worship and a school house.[127]

This may be where the Colored Emancipation Baptist Church held worship as well. After the 10 years were over, the trustees of the Presbyterian Church transferred the property to the township school trustees to develop a female academy. At that time in 1855, the lot

---

[124] In August 1862, no circuit court was held because of the absence of Judge Andrew D. Duff, who had been arrested by Union troops on charges of disloyalty. The next session of court took place in March 1863, with Duff back presiding. A. P. Corder served as state's attorney pro tem filling in for J. M. Clementson or Clemison. Previously, the fill-in state's attorney, A. P. Corder, had been the same man who precipitated the events leading up to the would-be Battle of Goodall's Bridge southeast of Marion.

[125] 1887. *History of Gallatin, Saline, Hamilton, Franklin and Williamson Counties, Illinois*. Chicago: Goodspeed Publishing Company. 170-172, 194.

[126] This story is written by this Handbook's editor, Jon Musgrave.

[127] *Gallatin County* (Ill.) *Deed Record M*. 317.

contained an Indian mound as well as the brick grave of Alexander Kirkpatrick who had originally transferred the property to the Presbyterian Church in 1833.[128]

The second attempt took place on November 2, 1850, when for the sum of $20, John Hart Crenshaw and his wife Sina, sold to Robert Porter, Osborn Bently, Samuel Day, Louisa Lewis, George Taylor and Jesse Chambers Lot 25 in the First Addition to Equality for the purpose of a church house and school house. The first three buyers are supposedly the trustees of the school. The last three are listed as trustees of the Concord Regular Old Side Baptist Church for People of Color. They filed the deed June 7, 1851.[129]

Lot 25 is located on the north side of Lane Street between modern-day Walnut and McHenry streets. Crenshaw laid out the lot originally as 125 feet on the street and 180 feet deep back to a 20 feet wide alley that separated the First Addition to Equality with the original plat. A 15 feet-wide alley was on the east side. This is 3 and ½ blocks west of Calhoun Street that ran north to the courthouse.

It is not know whatever became of this school or church. The third attempt is actually incorrectly recalled as the first attempt at a school for black children in Gallatin County.

> The first attempt to establish a school for colored children in this State was made at Shawneetown, after the proclamation of freedom, by Miss Sarah Curtis, of Evansville, Ind. After a hard struggle she obtained a small room in which to open her school, and for a time she taught with great energy and apparent satisfaction, but she was so ostracized by white women that after a few months she gave up the work in utter disgust, and returned to her former home.[130]

New Haven Schools

In 1848 or '49, Lizzie Boyd had a subscription school, in an old log house on what is now platted as Main street, corner of Front and Main, between lots 37 and 52. The next school was in another log house, in 1851, near the old post oak tree, on lot 167, Mill street, and was taught by Samuel Murray, who had been a soldier and sailor, and whose stories amounted to more than his teaching. He was a popular man with the children, as he always catered to their pleasures.

Another school was taught in the same house about 1853 or '54, by Levi. H. Hitchcock, a Methodist Episcopal preacher from Ohio. He left as mysteriously as he came.

The following year an Irishman named Roger Frame taught in the same house. He was a good scholar, but not a strict disciplinarian, especially on Monday mornings, after his Saturday and Sunday potations.

In the spring of 1855 William Thomas taught another term of school on the hill. He also was a disciple of Bacchus more than the arts and sciences, or even of the common branches. In the following summer Jesse Fuller, a young man from Mississippi, taught a term in the town hall; then Lucy Rowe, and lastly, under the old subscription plan, William Carter.

---

[128] *Gallatin County* (Ill.) *Deed Record P.* 399-402.

[129] Nov. 2, 1850. *Gallatin County* (Ill.) *Deed Record O.* 547.

[130] D. W. Lusk. 1884. *Politics and Politicians: A Succinct History of the Politics of Illinois from 1856 to 1884.* Springfield, Ill.: H. W. Rokker. 350.

In the spring of 1856 the township was organized under the act of 1855, and elected a Board of three Directors, whose jurisdiction included all the territory of 7 south, 9 east, in Gallatin County; and Captain E. P. H. Stone, taught the first school under the free system.

In the fall and winter of 1856-'57, a six months' school was kept.

The next teacher was Walter H. Bunn, of Otsego County, N. Y., who was here in 1857. George W. Cortwright commenced the next term, but died before the term was finished, and was followed by William Wallace, of Hamilton County. Other teachers who then followed were: McMasters; John Malden, who taught several six-month terms, up to 1861; Fitzsimmons, who died while teaching and was followed by James S. Perkins; Geo. B. Knight; Winslow Bailey, who taught until 1866, assisted by his wife a portion of the time, and also by Miss Julia Boyd. Then, in the fall of 1866, Rev. John McIlreth, a Presbyterian minister, taught a fine classical school several years. Geo. H. Phar taught two years, and was the first to teach in the new school-house, in 1870. Then George F. Eaton, James R. Campbell (Miss Wilson, of McLeansboro, assistant), James Kinsoll, ___ Watkins, of the vicinity of Shawneetown, John G. Ferrell, J. C. Wooten, who failed, and the term was finished by Miss Prudence H. Bozeman, now the wife of Maurice Feehrer, and the present teacher.

The school now [1883] has about sixty pupils in the winter time, and fifty in the summer.

The school-house was built in 1870, corner of Main and Market streets, on lots 138 and 148. It is 24 x 70 feet, and two stories high, well furnished, and cost $3,300. It has a belfry, with bell.

The present Directors are Captain Stone, Lowry Hinch and George W. Overton.[131]

Additional Church History

Early Baptist History

One can only assume that the person responsible for writing the section on Baptist churches for Goodspeed's History failed to complete his assignment since the 1887 history doesn't mention the faith at all. Yet, the first Baptist church in the region, the first church to organize period in southeastern Illinois, organized on July 19, 1806, along the waters of Big Creek in what is now Hardin County, but then Randolph and later Gallatin Counties:

> We whose names are hither unto subscribed, having our lots providentially cast together in Randolph County, Indiana Territory — and professing to be Baptists of the United order, and having a desire to live together in a church capacity, do covenant and agree to give ourselves up to the Lord and to one another, to watch over each other in love, and to take the Word of God for the man of our counsel and rule of our lives and practices — for which purpose and our mutual health and satisfaction do agree to constitute on the following principles of faith, having called elders William Jones and Stephen Stilley, a

---

[131] 1883. *History of White County, Illinois*. Chicago: Inter-State Publishing Co. 941-943.

presbytery for that purpose and said presbytery did constitute us are hitherto annexed a gospel church July the 19th A. D. 1806.

        Elders William Jones, Stephen Stilley.

The organizing members of Big Creek Church included Benjamin Rogers, James Lee, Priscilla Lee, Jacob Self, Isham Clay, Aaron Neal, Nancy Neal, Joseph Eubanks, along "with others not recollected."[132] As the many of the earliest settlers moved farther along the trail they ended up settling in the western portion of old Gallatin County in what is now Saline. They did so to be close to the civilized comforts and protection of the saltworks, yet also be outside of the boundaries of the Saline Reservation so they could enter land. For that reason, that probably explains why all but one of the early Baptist churches in early Gallatin County are located in the area that became Saline.

Island Ripple Church appears to be the first Baptist church located within the modern boundaries of Gallatin. The Muddy River Baptist Association welcomed Island Ripple to its ranks in 1821.[133] With the saltworks going strong at this time, the congregation located themselves just east of the saltworks on the south side of Gold Hill a couple of miles east of Island Ripple, the crossing point over the Saline River for the Shawneetown to Equality road. On the west side of the ripple, pronounced "riffle" even today in Gallatin County, the road joined the older Flynn's Ferry, or later best known as the Ford's Ferry Road. Together the road rounded Leavell Hill and followed the route of the ancients to the Great Salt Springs before approaching Equality and Half Moon Lick.

Presumed church members Benjamin Jolly and his wife Mary deeded one acre of their farm to the church trustees Joseph Wathen and Thomas Barlow, for a meeting and schoolhouse as well as a burial yard. William McGehee staked out the north end and Benjamin Jolly staked out the other three sides. John Lockhart and Thomas Smith witnessed the deed.[134] It's not clear how long Island Ripple lasted, but they remained members of the Muddy River Association at least through 1844.[135]

In the 1820s, Baptist churches throughout the country, but particularly in the west, debated the role of missions, missionaries, Bible tract societies, and the like. Eventually, most of the churches in southeastern Illinois split over this issue in the 1830s. The anti-missions churches eventually took the name Regular Baptists, and are known today as Primitive Baptists. Before the split, the Muddy River Association included five churches in old Gallatin County; Island Ripple plus four in what is now Saline County. Those included Bethel's Creek near Raleigh, Wolf Creek near modern Eldorado, Bankston's Fork in the western part of the county, and Middle Fork of Saline River church, later known as "Old Ruff" located in the extreme northwest corner of Saline County. In 1833, the last year before the split, the association's minutes reported the following members at the churches:

---

[132] Ralph Harrelson, trans. Big Creek Church Minutes. Ron Nelson collection.

[133] Myron D. Dillow. 1996. *Harvesttime on the Prairie*. Illinois State Baptist Association. Franklin, Tenn.: Providence House Publishers. 122

[134] *Gallatin County* (Ill.) *Deed Record A*. 323-324. The land is described as one acre in the NE¼ Section 5 South, Range 9 East of the Third Principal Meridian.

[135] Phone interview with church historian Ron Nelson, January 1, 2002.

Bankston's Fork, 28; Bethel's Creek, 37; Island Ripple (didn't attend because of sickness); Middle Fork Saline River, 17; Wolf Creek, 31.

Another church, Block House Creek attempted to join that year, but refused entry for its decision to support missions. This one might have been located near Mitchellsville in southern Saline County, as Battle Ford Creek was then known as Blockhouse Creek. Bankston's Fork joined with the missionary side and left the association, making at least two pro-mission churches in what was then still the western part of Gallatin County.

In July 1833, the Lick Creek Church extended an arm to a new group known as the Lick Boundary Church, which used a school house near Crenshaw's Mill on the North Fork of the Saline River. The following July, the church formally organized and Lick Creek dismissed its members William Harget, Betsy Harget, Sister Ambers, Joseph Easley, Sister Easley, James Sands, Sister Sands, and Hepsy Willis to constitute the new church.[136] At the 1837 meeting of the association, the minutes include a report from Lick Boundary showing the church with 20 members. Joseph Easley and William Harget served as the church's messengers that year. That church continued to appear at least through 1840.[137]

While the existing churches fought the missionary movement within its congregation, a new movement that not only combined missionary fervor but with anti-slavery energy, began to sweep through the area. In May 1832, a group of families who lived southwest of what would become Harrisburg started to worship together. Later, in September they organized Liberty Baptist Church led by Eli Barbre and John Choudin or Shadowen. A few years later, John Mason Peck, a correspondent for the *Baptist Banner and Western Pioneer* in Illinois described Barbre in the February 20, 1840.

> In 1829, he immigrated to Illinois, at which time he was connected with that class of Baptists who oppose missionary and other benevolent organizations, yet he could not sympathize in this mode, while the worlds and many of the churches were destitute of the gospel. He left this connection and became united to a church now connected with the Saline Association in Gallatin county. About seven years ago last September, he was ordained.

The Saline Association took its name from the river and nearby saltworks. Yet, while slavery weaved its poison throughout the saltworks, this association instead joined with "The Baptized Churches of Christ, Friends to Humanity," in opposition to slavery and the release of those enslaved. Less than four years later Liberty helped organize Grassy Creek Church in western Williamson County. The following year, that church extended an arm and organized Hurricane Creek Church in between what are now the communities of Herrin and Carterville.[138] That same year in 1837, Island Ripple Church expelled its minister Stephen

---

[136] Robert Webb. 2001. "Church and Family Research Assistance for Gallatin County, Illinois." The Primitive Baptist Library. http://www.carthage.lib.il.us/community/churches/primbap/FamHist-Gallatin.html.

[137] Ron and Doris Nelson. *Minutes of the Muddy River Baptist Association of Illinois, 1820-1840.* Online at http://freepages.religions.rootsweb.com/~jgholson/minutes.htm.

[138] Ronald L. Nelson, Doris Nelson and Ralph S. Harrelson. 1996. *History of Liberty Baptist Church.* Utica, Ky.: McDowell Publications. 6-7, 43.

Stilley for supporting the missionary movement.[139] While it is not known if he ever joined the Emancipation Baptists, members of his family did so. Later in December, Eagle Creek Church organized six miles south of Equality. A report in *The Baptist Banner* on March 7, 1837, noted Elder W. J. Coolley helped constitute the church with 13 members. He ordained Edmund Vinson to the ministry and W. Jones and J. Hayle as deacons.[140]

Six months later on May 30, 1838, Stilley's son-in-law Michael Sowerheaver deeded the two acres where the Eagle Creek Church meeting house and graveyard stood. The deed gave the following terms:

> [That the] present Society that have regular preaching there now by ____ Vinson now regular pastor, to have the preference to days every month, the balance of the time the house to be occupied by all or any denomination that may think fit to occupy the same to have due regard to orderly Christian conduct. The ground for the graveyard to be sacredly held for the purpose and the meeting house used only if necessary to teach school in.

Ironically, the land for this anti-slavery church stood on a tract of land adjacent to John Hart Crenshaw's original homestead. Crenshaw, of course, is remembered as one the most pro-slavery men in old Gallatin County. It is located on the east side of Eagle Mountain and the upper end of Eagle Creek Valley. Jones Cemetery in Mountain Township in Saline County designates the spot of this church. In the succeeding years three more Emancipation Baptist churches would be organized in the region: Rock Creek Church in 1842 in eastern Williamson County (the parent of modern-day Coal Bank Springs and Indian Camp churches), Mineral Springs Church in 1843 at Herod in northeastern Pope County, and Big Saline Church in 1844 on the opposite side of Eagle Mountain from Eagle Creek at Somerset in Saline County.[141]

The Emancipationist activity showed up in the development of black churches too. The Shawneetown Colored Emancipation Baptist Church appears in the records in 1843, when it sent messengers to its association's conference. The minutes list Robert Casey and Elijah Campbell as the ordained ministers from the Shawneetown church. No data is listed for members other than the total number of 15. In another place Elder Elijah Campbell is listed from New Albany, Iowa.[142] On the other side of the Baptist split over missions, there appears the Concord Regular Old Side Baptist Church for People of Color in Equality in 1850 and 51. The only reference found to it is a deed where they purchased a lot from John Crenshaw to build a church and school.[143]

---

[139] Myron D. Dillow. 1996. *Harvesttime on the Prairie*. Illinois State Baptist Association. Franklin, Tenn.: Providence House Publishers. 101.

[140] Ronald L. Nelson, Doris Nelson and Ralph S. Harrelson. 1996. *History of Liberty Baptist Church*. Utica, Ky.: McDowell Publications. 44-45.

[141] Ronald L. Nelson, Doris Nelson and Ralph S. Harrelson. 1996. *History of Liberty Baptist Church*. Utica, Ky.: McDowell Publications. 44-49. The tract's description for Eagle Creek is W½ NE¼ 11-10s-7e.

[142] 1843. *Minutes of the Colored Baptist Association... August 11, 12, 13, & 14, 1843*. Alton, Ill.: Alton Telegraph.

[143] Nov. 2, 1850. *Gallatin County* (Ill.) *Deed Record O.* 547.

Social Brethren Denomination

Editor's Note: Although the Social Brethren movement technically started in Saline County, it nevertheless played an important role in the religious life in western Gallatin County. The following is from the Saline County portion of the 1887 Goodspeed's History:

The Social Brethren — This peculiar denomination of Christians had its origin in Saline County August 29, 1867, in contentions which arose between members of various denominations with reference to certain points of doctrine; the questions being as to whether these disputed and controverted points were in accordance with the Scripture. It being impossible for all to unite upon a decision, it became necessary for those who differed in option from the main body of the churches to which they belonged to withdraw their membership and to unite themselves together in a new sect.

The first meeting of these dissatisfied ones, who desired to promulgate the truth as it is found in the Word of God, was held on the date above given, Francis Wright, from the Methodist Episcopal Church South, being elected moderator; Hiram T. Brannon, from the Methodist Episcopal Church, clerk; William J. C. Morrison, from the Presbyterian Church and William Holt were also there, the latter moving that William J. C. Morrison and Hiram T. Brannon be ordained ministers of the church. These, therefore, were the first two ministers ordained by the Church of the Social Brethren. Business was then suspended for the purpose of listening to a sermon delivered by Rev. William J. C. Morrison, which was the first sermon delivered by an ordained ministered of the Church of the Social Brethren. The text was the latter clause of St. John xix, 5.[144]

After the sermon was finished the Organic Law of the Social Brethren was adopted. It provides that an organization may be established by a covenant body of five members — three males and two females — which organized body may call an ordained minister to constitute the church to appoint a clerk for the church. After providing for the discipline of members who shall be filled with all unrighteousness, such as fornication, wickedness, covetousness, maliciousness, envy, murder, debate, deceit, malignity, whispers, backbiting, hatred of God, despitefulness, pride, boasting, invention of evil things, disobedience to parents and the use of spirituous liquors to excess — the penalty being that if members guilty of such unrighteousness shall refuse to comply with the requirements of the church, they shall be expelled — a confession of faith was adopted expressing belief in the Trinity, that the Holy Scriptures contain all things necessary to salvation and that whatsoever is not read therein nor proved thereby is not required to be believed, that the Old Testament is not contrary to the New, that salvation is by the atonement of Christ, that baptism and the Lord's Supper are ordinances of Christ and that baptism may be by pouring, sprinkling or immersion, but that none but true believers are proper subjects of baptism, and that ministers of God are called to preach the gospel and that only, and other less important doctrines.

The Social Brethren disdain the idea of political preaching or anything else outside the gospel, and at all times stand ready to prove that other denominations differing from them with respect to any of the articles of their confession of faith are not Scriptural. They lay

---

[144] The founders of the Social Brethren movement met just east of the old Eagle Creek Emancipation Baptist Church on the road leading south from Equality through Horseshoe Gap and past the modern Glen O. Jones Lake. A block church still stands at this location. The Jones Cemetery, immediately to the west down a short lane is the site of the original Eagle Creek church.

great stress on the following features of their faith: baptism of believers only, preaching of the gospel only and non-belief in fatality.

There are now three church organizations of this denomination in Saline County: Pleasant Grove, organized in 1874, which now has a membership of ninety and a church building 30x40 feet, which cost $800; Mt. Pleasant No. 2, two miles northwest of Raleigh, organized in 1883, now having forty-four members, and the Raleigh Church, organized in 1884 with seven members and now having nineteen, but no property. These three churches with the three in Gallatin County and two in Pope County constitute the Southern Illinois Association of the Social Brethren. This association held its fourteenth annual session in October 1886, at Pleasant Grove Church in Saline County, belonging to it there are now thirteen ministers, eleven licentiates and twelve exhorters.[145]

Bear Creek Township & Omaha

Township 7 south is divided in the center by the line between White and Gallatin counties. It is undulating ridge land and is well adapted to farming. It is watered by the north fork of the Saline River on the southwest, Bear Creek in the center, and Kane Creek on the east. The portion lying in range 8 east, Gallatin County, was first settled by former residents of White County. Zephaniah Johns settled on the present site of Omaha, about 1805. He sold his improvements to Rev. William Davis, who entered the land in 1833. Mr. Dunn, Mr. Hurd, Abraham Armstrong, Allen Dugger, Charles Edwards, Sr., John Edwards, Benjamin Kinsall Sr., John Kinsall, James Trousdale, and Mr. Orr were among the first settlers of the township.

The first school in the township was taught in 1838 by Abraham Armstrong, on Moses Kinsall's farm. The first school under the free-school system was taught by Benjamin Kinsall, about 1848. The first house for school purposes was built on John Williams' farm, about 1840. There are now four school-houses in the township, valued at $1,525; there are 412 children of school age.

The first post office was at South Hampton. David Keasler was the first Postmaster and the office was at his residence. It was discontinued on account of the railroads passing on each side of it. The first election was held in 1805, at the house of John Kinsall, where Moses Kinsall now resides, just east of Omaha.

Religious

The Palestine Cumberland Presbyterian Church was regularly organized Dec. 25, 1852. Two years previous, in 1818, a few of the pioneers agreed to build a house of worship if Rev. R. M Davis, then a young minister, would preach for them, and erected a neat structure of hewed logs. In 1868 the present large, well-furnished frame building was erected at a cost of $3,000. Rev. R. M. Davis is the only pastor the church has ever had.

---

[145] 1887. *History of Gallatin, Saline, Hamilton, Franklin and Williamson Counties, Illinois.* Chicago: Goodspeed Publishing Co. 231-233.

The first Elders were John Kinsall, Eli Price and Lewis West. The present Elders are Benjamin Kinsall, D. B. Rogers, William Kiser and John Blackard. It has been remarkably prosperous, having received in all about 450 members. The Sunday-school was organized in 1851 with John Kinsall as Superintendent.

Hazel Ridge Cumberland Presbyterian Church was organized in September, 1881, by Rev. R. M. Davis. The Elders are L. Shain, J. B. Edwards and John Burns. The church numbers about forty members and has been under the leadership of Revs. W. E. Davis and Franklin McQuay. They have a prosperous Sabbath-school, and are contemplating building a new church soon.

The Bethlehem Methodist Episcopal Church was organized and the house of worship dedicated Feb. 15, 1868. They had a membership of fifty.

Omaha

The town was laid out by Rev. R. M. Davis on part of his farm, west of the railroad and about a mile east of the center of the township. The name was suggested by Henry Bearce, first baggage master on the St. Louis & Southeastern Railroad, who had acted in the same capacity in Omaha, Neb. The first store was Dr. J. C. Harrell's drug store. The first dry-goods store was established by Hall & Pemberton, of Saline County, Ill.

The Omaha flour-mill was built by G. R. Pearce & Co., in 1878. Mr. Pearce bought out the company, Messrs. Porter and Rice, of Roland, in 1879, and sold one-half interest to William C. Trusty, and in the same year, 1879, sold out to Mr. Trusty, who in turn sold one-half to E. A. West. In 1881 Trusty & West sold the mill to Latimer & Bryant, and in 1882 Mr. Bryant sold his interest to W. F. Harrell. The firm of Latimer & Harrell, by the assistance of their experienced miller, C. R. Galloway, are doing a good business. The mill has the latest improved machinery, and is run by steam-power.

George A. Lutz, of St. Louis, established a stave factory, which was ran about four years. He employed a number of hands and cut a large quantity of timber. It was finally blown up by a keg of powder in the boiler igniting, being placed there by an incendiary. It was never rebuilt. Messrs. Harrell & Johnson have a new patent brick machine, by which they manufacture a great many bricks, and one or two tile kilns will be established soon.

Omaha has a large two-story school-house, and has had a graded school since 1874. The first Principal was H. P. Bozarth, followed by R. D. Kinsall, J. M. Kinsall, M. M. Robinson, A. H. Kinsall, W. E. Ferrell, H. P. Bozarth and W. E. Ferrell, the present incumbent, who is ably assisted by Miss R. Martin.

Rev. R. M. Davis preached the first sermon in the village. The only church immediately in the village is the Methodist Episcopal, which was begun in 1878, and finished at a cost of $800. It was dedicated Sept. 16, 1882. The church was permanently organized in 1879, with twenty-five members, and has now thirty. The pastors have been J. J. R. Reaf and C. W. Morris.

Dr. Jas. C. Harrell was the first Postmaster. He was followed by M. M. Davis, Rev. R. M. Davis and Samuel Davis.

The first hotel was built by J. B. Latimer. The house is at present kept by A. D. Brockett. L. E. Quigley built a fine hotel in 1882, which is well fitted up with excellent accommodations. Omaha has made a wonderfully rapid growth in the last three years, and bids fair to be one of the most important inland towns of Southern Illinois.

Societies

Omaha Lodge, No. 723, A.F &A.M., was chartered by the Grand Lodge of Illinois, at Chicago, Oct. 7, 1874, with sixteen charter members. The present officers are: C. Harrell, W.M.; J. T. Hogan, S.W.; S. T. Webber, J.W.; Thomas Kinsall, Treasurer; Wm. F. Price, Secretary; John M. Crunk, S.D.; Charles Duckworth, J.D. The presiding officers in the order of their election are as follows: J. W. Meador, Dr. I. M. Asbery, L. E. Quigley, Dr. J. C. Harrell. This lodge is in a thriving condition.

Omaha Lodge, No. 183, A.O.U.W., was chartered May 10, 1881, with twenty-one charter members. The first officers were: J. C. Harrell, P. M.W.; Thomas Martin, M.W.; A. M. Blackard.; Foreman; A. H. Blackard, Overseer; Edward Rice, Recorder; M. M. Davis, Financier; W. H. Walters, Receiver; W. D. Pearce, Guide; Peter Edwards, I.W.; John Sarver, O.W. The present officers are: A. P. Caldwell, P.M.W.; Edward Rice, M.W.; J. B. Latimer, Foreman; J. C. Harrell, Overseer; S. D. Lewis, Recorder; Thomas Martin, Financier; J. P. Robinson, Receiver; W. H. Waters, Guide; Peter Edwards, I.W.; John Sarver, O.W.; J. C. Harrell, District Deputy.

Omaha has no lawyers. The first physician was J. C. Harrell. The other physicians have been James Porter, I. M. Asbery, J. H. Moore and C. M. Hudgins, all here at present except I. M. Asbery.

Business Directory

The following are the principal business men of Omaha: Barter & Kinsall, blacksmiths; H. P. Bozarth, real-estate agent and Notary Public; A. D. Brockett, proprietor of the Omaha House, livery and feed stable; Bruce & Young, groceries; C. Cook & Son, general merchandise; R. M. Davis & Sons, general merchandise; A. Derham, Notary Public; Duncan & Burks, meat market; Peter Edwards, druggist; John Gregg, boots and shoes; Harrell Bros., drugs, etc.; C. M. Hudgins, physician and surgeon; Harrell & Johnson, brick and lumber dealers; Thomas Kinsall, general merchandise; Charles Moore, hardware; J. H. Moore, physician and druggist; J. H. Porter, physician and surgeon; Quigley & Crabtree, blacksmiths; L. E. Quigley, proprietor of the Quigley House; Martin Rice & Co., general merchandise; Swafford Bros., general merchandise.[146]

---

[146] 1883. *History of White County*. Chicago: Inter-State Publishing Co. 957-960.

New Haven

Religious

The Cumberland Presbyterian Church has been a large organization, with R. M. Davis, of Omaha, as pastor. The building, a substantial and commodious structure, was built in 1865 by popular subscription. C. B. Bayley, Samuel Dagley, Jr., and J. L. Purvis were the first Trustees. The society, as an organization, has been rather inactive for a year or so.

The Methodist Church building was erected in 1872 by contribution. Among its pastors have been the Revs. Mr. Fields, who officiated two years; Mr. Reef, also two years, and Mr. Morris, present pastor.

Physicians

New Haven has had the unenviable reputation of being the very hot-bed of malaria and fever. This its citizens of to-day strongly contradict. It certainly has no modern cemetery. The disciples of Esculapius have been quite numerous. Among them we mention, Dr. Gilpin who was in practice for many years, Drs. Galbraith, two Halls, Lemon, Hudgins. The present doctors are all men well read in their profession, and doing a successful business.

A Banking Town

In the days of State Banks and wild-cat paper, New Haven ranked second in the State, at one time being the location of as many as five. This was in 1856. The idea was to have the location as far as possible from the business centers, in some small, unknown town, the object being to avoid the frequent runs made by brokers and speculators, who made a business of buying up, at a large discount, all bills found floating in the business circles of New York, Philadelphia, Boston, etc. The bills were issued, signed and cut, and circulated from the principal points, no business but that of redemption being brought up at New Haven.

Colonel Hick was President of "The Illinois State Bank." To him the agents of the brokers would come twice a month, with their gripsacks full of the discounted paper for redemption. The formality of presenting the bills was not gone through with until the gold was not forthcoming, whereupon a complaint was made to the Secretary of State, and the amount was paid from the State bonds deposited by the stockholders of the banks. The agents, while at New Haven, were always on the best of terms with Hick, playing cards evenings, smoking, and joking, and laughing over their hot punches. At one particular time the bankers of Chicago obtained definite information that a certain run was to be paid at a certain time. To outwit and general them several hundred dollars of five-cent silver pieces were hastily dispatched to Hick, with instructions to deal them out. Upon the arrival of the agents and their presentations, they were kindly treated, day after day, to redemption in earnest. Mistakes on the part of the joke-loving president were frequent, and a day's work was thought to be well done if $20 were redeemed. Banking hours, from ten a.m. until three p.m. This continued several days, but it was the winding up of a systematic course of scalping.

Miscellaneous

The first marriage in the town is said to have been that of Captain Samuel Dagley to a Miss Webb. The ceremony was performed by Squire Groves.

The first death was that of a child belonging to Boone. The first blacksmith was a Mr. Harper.

There is a ferry at this point, that has been in use for many years. The town is free of debt, with some $600 in the treasury.

The Stage Route was established at a very early day as a post route, extending from Shawneetown to Vincennes, from which point other routes diverged to all principal points. It was a tri-weekly route via New Haven, Carmi, Phillipstown, Grayville, etc., with a large patronage. The present routes are from Omaha to Carmi, via New Haven, and New Haven and Shawneetown, three miles daily.

The Post office was established about 1820. Some of the men who have held the position of Postmaster have been: Colonel Thos. S. Hick, 1837; John Wood, 1840; B. P. Hinch, 1845-'55; Samuel Dagley, 1855-'64; John Hick, 1863-'64; Thos. B. Hick, A. J. Surguy, W. P. Abshier, J. B. Hanmore, Victor Melvin; Lee Carruth, September, 1880; Victor Melvin, February, 1882; W. P. Aldrich, present incumbent.

The Telephone Exchange, of Evansville, established an office at this point in 1882, with office at the post office. W. P. Aldrich, operator. The citizens, being awake to its advantages, subscribed a large sum of money for its establishment. By this they have telegraphic communications at Mt. Vernon and also at Shawneetown.

Masonic.—The New Haven Lodge of A. F. & A. M. was organized many years ago, and, through some mistake, received a number far too high for the date of its application. The charter members and first officers were: James Edwards, W. M.; Sidney Pinney, S. W.; Jackson Abshier, J. W.; James Melvin, S. D.; E. W. Gaston, J. D.; John H. Hughes and Wm. Glasscock. Considering the size of the town, the lodge (No. 330) is in good condition.[147]

More History of Shawneetown Floods

Levee Construction in the 1880s

In 1884 the city was flooded the water rising 56.4 feet above low water mark. More money was spent and the levees raised. By 1888 or 1890 there were four and a half miles of levees, built at a cost of $200,000.[148]

---

[147] 1883. *History of White County*. Chicago: Inter-State Publishing Co. 944-946.

[148] George W. Smith. 1912. *A History of Southern Illinois: A Narrative Account of its Historical Progress, its People, and its Principal Interests*. Chicago, Ill.: Lewis Publishing Co. 1:469-474.

Song: 'Flood of Shawneetown' – 1898

G. B. Fields wrote the words and music to this song, "Flood of Shawneetown, or Broken Hearts and Homes." Fields dedicated the music to "G. R. Galloway, who lost a wife and two daughters in the great disaster of April 3rd '98." Previously he had authored "The Tattler," and "Dream of the Forrest Queen," He privately published the music in Fairfield, Ill.

Nearly half a century after this music came out; someone in Saline County borrowed the tune for the Saline County Centennial song in 1947.

VERSE 1

In the town of Shawneetown as the evening shades came down,
   On a quiet Sabbath evening cold and gray,
While the people walked the street or in dear communion sweet,
   Sat within their peaceful homes at close of day.
All at once the bells were ringing, with a wild and awful din,
   While the fearful fact breaks over one and all,
That the fateful levees broke pale the lips of those who spoke,
   While the roaring, crashing, awful flood comes in.

VERSE 2

On it came with mighty force, spoiling all within its course,
   Wrecking homes and snatching loved ones from their friends,
Where they found a wat'ry grave, 'neath the cold and silent wave,
   To be covered over by the drifting sands,
Tongue nor pen ne'er describe the hopeless anguish and despair,
   Of the poor survivors of that awful flood,
And they'll ne'er forget the day Shawneetown was washed away.
   Till they rest beneath the cold and silent sod.

VERSE 3

There were heroes too that day: Franklin Robinson they say,
   With his boat brought many safely to the shore,
While they struggled with the wave he row'd out their life's to save,
   Working bravely 'till the awful flood was o'er,
Father Bikeman saw it coming like a giant mountain high,
   And he knew what danger in his pathway lay;
But he did his duty well while he boldly rang the bell
   Warning all within the dangerline to fly.

VERSE 4

There are broken hearts and homes, there is sorrow, there are groans,
   There is trouble there is anguish and despair,
Where was once all smiles and light there is naught but darkest night,
   Where was once a happy city wrecks appear,
Let us rally to their succor from the city hill and plain,
   Give out sympathy and money to their aid;

Soon calamity may fall on our loved ones, homes and all,
May be separated ne'er to meet again.

Final Report of Relief Committee – 1898

Memorable will remain with the people of Shawneetown the terrible calamity which visited their city on the evening of April 3rd, 1898. At about 5 p.m. the north levee gave way at Locust Street. The high stage of the river registered 53.3 feet on the gauge. However, no general fears had been entertained against the soundness of the levee, and hence no efforts had been made by the people and the business men to place in safety any personal property. The damage which resulted was therefore so enormous. Few could forecast the destructive power of such a volume of water should it break into town. When the alarming news of the break was sentinelled many imagined themselves secure in the second stories of their dwellings and made no attempt to escape to safe refuge on the front levee, which they could easily have reached. Had it not been for this sense of security no lives would have been lost. But the force and the volume of water entering town carried with it death and destruction.

The unfortunate refugees perished with their houses. Twenty-five persons were drowned, among them some of our most prominent and respected citizens: Col. John A. Callicott, W. C. Callicott, Mrs. W. C. Callicott, Charles Clayton, Sr., Mrs. Charles Clayton, Sr., Gertrude Clayton, Grant Clayton, Jesse Clayton, Myrtle Clayton, Mrs. Edward Fleck, Mrs. C. R. Galloway, Dora Galloway, Mary Galloway, Mrs. John Halley, Mrs. Ellen McAllister, (col.) Mrs. Mary McAllister, (col.) Mrs. Paul Phalen, Minnie Phalen, Annie Rheinhold, Charles Rheinhold, Ella Rheinhold, Noah Welsh, Mrs. Noah Welsh, Mrs. Mary Eastwood and child, visitors at W. C. Callicott's.

The grief for the dead absorbed us. It could not permit us to weigh the losses sustained by damage done to property. Heroic efforts were made to rescue the distressed, and our community cherishes a grateful memory of those gentlemen who risked much to save the lives of their distressed fellow citizens. Whilst presence of mind prevailed to accomplish the first work of rescue, consternation followed. Some refugees had found their way to the hills, others had crowded in the Public School, the Court House, and second stories of some dwellings and business houses, but the greater majority had gathered in the Riverside Hotel, where Mr. Moody and wife exerted themselves to provide for them. A realization of the losses of the people gradually dawned upon them; their thoughts rambled into the future, the outlook was gloomy.

Telephonic and telegraphic connections had been cut off so that the news of our distressing situation could not be conveyed to the world. Immediate relief was necessary. We were obliged to appeal to the charity of the public for instant relief. After a short consultation held in the hotel, five gentlemen volunteered to go to Junction City that night, and if necessary, to Ridgway, to dispatch an appeal for relief. The people were informed that the delegation would dispatch for them such messages as they might wish to send to relatives and friends. With a bundle of messages, among them some from our Mayor to the Governor of our State, and to our Congressman, the delegation left town over the south levee about 10 p.m. and reached Junction City at midnight. The wires at that place were also under water, and it was here that a mile's width of deep water and no skiff cut the delegation off from the next telegraphic station, Ridgway. Fortunately after sometime a train from Ridgway arrived at the water's opposite edge. It conveyed several of the town's citizens who had been sent to ascertain the situation of our people. With the skiff which they had brought along, the delegation crossed the water and by the kindness of the B & O. S.W. crew were at once transferred to Ridgway, where they arrived at 2:20 the next morning.[149]

Levees after the 1898 Flood

In 1898, or thereabouts, the levees broke above the city and great damage was done property by the enormous current which swept through the city. Many homes were swept away and more than a score of lives were lost. The general government appropriated $25,000 with which to repair the break in the levee, and thousands of dollars in money, clothing and food poured into Shawneetown from every hamlet, village and town. In 1907 another severe test arose, the water reaching 52.8 feet. By prompt and vigilant attention by the city the threatened danger was averted.

A few years ago the state created an Internal Improvement Commission. This commission has expended many thousands of dollars of state appropriates in an effort to strengthen the Shawneetown levees. An effort is also on foot to get help from Congress, and there is reason to believe, since the high water of April 1912, that the levees are proof against the waters of the Ohio.[150]

[Note: George Washington Smith wrote this in 1912. High water broke through the levee the following year in 1913.]

Sketch of the 1890 Grand Jury

The Gallatin County Grand Jury must have been busy during the winter of 1890. The local newspaper ran a story entitled, "Our Grand Jury: A sketch of the Gentlemen who Have Been for the Past Two Weeks Delving into the Wickedness of Gallatin County." What wickedness took place isn't known, but here's what the newspaper wrote about the jury members themselves.

Joseph Ulmsnider

Joseph Ulmsnider, the foreman of the grand jury, was born in the State of Wittenberg, Germany, in 1816 and came to America with his parents in 1832. The family located at York, Pa., where they remained for two years and then removed of Mansfield, Ohio, the home of the Shermans. There Uncle Joe cast his first vote which was challenged by the now celebrated Gen. Sherman. In 1842 Uncle Joe came to Shawneetown and located on a farm for a few years, then went into the distillery business. In 1850 he became connected with

---

[149] Executive Relief Committee. 1900. *The Shawneetown Flood, April 3rd, 1898: Final Report of the Executive Relief Committee.* Shawneetown, Ill.: Executive Relief Committee.

[150] George W. Smith. 1912. *A History of Southern Illinois: A Narrative Account of its Historical Progress, its People, and its Principal Interests.* Chicago, Ill.: Lewis Publishing Co. 1:469-474.

Orval Pool's pork house as superintendent and remained there 16 years. After severing his connection with that enterprise he was engaged in butchering and groceries until 1877 when he was elected Justice of the Peace which office he held until Dec. 1889. During this time he tried 4,378 cases to say nothing of the business of acknowledgments, &c. He was at one time a prominent member of the Odd Fellows and Good Templars, fighting whiskey when some of our now leading temperance people were dealing in that article. He is a leading Democrat and a member of the Catholic Church. He is peculiarly fitted for the foremanship of this body and has given good satisfaction. It would be an injustice to close this sketch without referring to the fact that Uncle Joe was one of the prime movers in creating the Gallatin County Agricultural Society and has since been one of the leading spirits in making it so successful.

Fred Brasier

Of French descent and inheriting the characteristic courtesy and gentlemanly principles of his fathers, Mr. Ferd Brasier of Junction City is a popular member of the jury. He was born in Brown County, Ohio, in 1849, and came to Illinois in 1855. He is a farmer by occupation, living on a splendid farm of 120 acres. Politically he is an unwavering Democrat. Religiously he is a faithful member of the Catholic Church. He has never held office and has no higher ambitions than to remain a good and patriotic citizen with his family in the quietude of farm life.

John N. Bruce

Without stating his location any one acquainting with the history of Gallatin County would unhesitatingly place Mr. John N. Bruce's habitation in Bear Creek. Mr. Bruce was born in White county in 1833 and removed to this county in 1850. He is an honored member of one of the largest and best-known families in Southern Illinois and has all the characteristics of that family – good citizenship, morality and pure Democracy. He is a farmer and devoted to his occupation. Of a rather retiring disposition, Mr. Bruce does not impress on upon first sight with the firmness, ability and amiability which he possesses, but upon further acquaintance one learns of and admirers these qualities. He is also a devoted member of the M. E. church.

Mike Golden

The most striking member of this body is Mike Golden of North Shawneetown. While Mike is decidedly the largest man on the jury, yet he is the most amiable, being as Bill Nye would say "child like and bland" in his disposition. Mike is one of the few men whom everybody likes. By occupation he is a blacksmith, and from his strong right arm, sturdiness and general good cheer, might well represent Goldsmith's celebrated character. Born in Shawneetown in 1846, he is yet a young man. He is a Democrat with all the word implies and for 8 years was a member of our city council. He is also a member of the Catholic Church and a good citizen.

E. M. Smith

One of the best-known men in this county is Asbury's representative, E. M. Smith. He is a native Sucker, having been privileged to be born in White County in 1840. About 32 years ago seeing the superior advantages of Gallatin County he crossed the line into Asbury precinct where he owns a large and valuable farm. Mr. Smith is so thoroughly imbued with the principles of Democracy that one soon learns his politics and what is better he is a reading man and always ready to give reasons for his party preference. Mr. Smith was a member of the Board of County Commissioners in the seventies and for a number of years was township treasurer of 8-10. He is a positive man and hence a successful man and popular.

George Barnett

With honesty, courage and industry sticking out of every line of his face, Geo. Barnett of Eagle Creek would be recognized by any one as belonging to that class of sturdy yeomanry who have done so much toward turning our county from a wilderness into almost one vast farm. Born in this county in 1841, he has passed through 49 years of development of the best county in the state. Mr. Barnett is primarily a Democrat but is not a partisan and frequently affiliates with the Republicans. He owns a good farm of 140 acres and shows that by industry and thrift he is now able to live well. He is a good member of the body.

Joel F. Downey

One of the best natured looking members of the body is Joel F. Downey of White Oak, a native of Posey County, Ind., where he first saw light in 1830 and is now three score years old. He followed the avocation of farming in his native county until about 12 years ago when he removed to White Oak precinct in this county and bought a farm. Mr. Downy has never held office although well qualified to do so. He is a Jacksonian Democrat and a member of the Adventist church, two qualities which ought to make any one a good citizen.

J. M. Bean

One of the characters of the jury is Uncle Jimmy Bean of Ridgway. He was born in this county, near where he now resides, in 1832. Uncle Jimmy is one of the best farmers in Southern Illinois and now owns and lives upon one of the most beautiful farms in the county, containing 320 acres adjoining the town of Ridgway. In politics he is a thoroughbred Republican, always taking a lively interest in his party. He has been a devoted member of the C. P. Church since boyhood and believes in the prohibition of liquor traffic. As an evidence of moral tendencies he has never in all his 58 years tasted a drop of whisky, played cards or taken the name of God in vain. Uncle Jimmy also served his country three years and four months in the late rebellion as a member of the 131st and 29th Illinois regiments.

H. L. Turner

That gentleman with a long but pleasant appearing face and a patriarchical look is H. L. Turner of Equality and one of the very best members of the body. Born in Hamilton County, Ohio, near Cincinnati, he is naturally refined and courtly in his conduct and language. He was born in 1832 and removed to this county in 1881 where he is recognized as one of our very best citizens. This is his first service on the grand jury and he has never served on a criminal jury but once. By occupation he is a farmer, politically a Democrat of the Gov. Campbell type, and religiously a Missionary Baptist. We would be glad to have Ohio send us many more such citizens as Mr. Turner.

W. H. Holbrook

One of the working members of the grand jury is genial W. H. Holbrook of Junction City. Will was born in Jennings County, Ind., and removed to Flora, Clay County, in 1862. In 1870 he came to Shawneetown on the first train that came over the S. & I. S. E., now the O. & M. and has since resided in this county. He was a member of the city council of this city in 1882 and 1884 and took the initiative in securing the building of our levee. He is now engaged in farming and has proven that broom corn growing is a profitable farming interest in this county. Politically he is a red hot Republican and religiously a devotee of the tenets of the General Baptist church. He is also a firm believer in the future prosperity of Junction City.

E. P. Fowler

Perhaps the best-looking man on the jury, next to Mike Golden, is E. P. Fowler of Equality. He is low of stature, stout and has a head and face that would command attention anywhere. Mr. Fowler was born in Dearborn County, Ind., in 1835 and removed to this county in 1857. Few farmers have been more successful than he, and he owns 254 acres of the riches land in the county. He lives a few miles this side of Equality in one of the handsomest residences and on one of the best-improved farms in Egypt. He is a man of firm will power, an active member of the Missionary Baptist church and an unwavering Republican. It is such sturdy men as Mr. Fowler that are making Southern Illinois the garden spot of the West.

James J. Welch

At a glance one would recognize the nativity of this sturdy son of the Green Isle. James J. Welch of Waltonboro was born in County Limerick, Ireland, about the year 1840 and came to this country in 1857, locating in Waltonboro precinct where he has since resided. He owns a fine farm of 120 acres in a high state of cultivation. Like so many others of his patriotic countrymen Mr. Welch gave three years and four months of his life to his adopted country in the late war. He is an honored member of the Catholic Church and an earnest Democrat. Mr. Welch has never held office but his work on this jury would indicate that should he ever be honored with one he would give honorable and energetic service.

John A. Trousdale

Tall, dignified and intelligent looking, one would readily suppose Mr. John A. Trousdale of White Oak to be a leader in his neighborhood, which he is. He is a native of Gallatin County, having been born near the present town of Ridgway, Dec. 30, 1847. He is a man above the average, in point of ability and education. By occupation a farmer, yet always taking a deep interest in public affairs. He is an elder of the Ridgway C. P. Church and has been twice a candidate for member of the General Assembly of our State. He has been for several years a school trustee for 8-8. Politically, Mr. Trousdale is an unflinching republican, being ready at all times to obey the commands of his party.

John L. Allen

One of the youngest members of the grand jury is John L. Allen of Bear Creek. He was born in Posey County, Ind., in 1857 and removed to this county in 1886. He has been engaged in farming all his life and owns the farm upon which he lives. He is a staunch Republican in politics, firm in the faith of the principles of that party. Mr. Allen is a zealous and earnest member of the General Baptist church, taking a deep interest in the cause of religion and morality in his neighborhood.

W. B. Gilpin

When the jury organized they naturally selected W. B. Gilpin of New Haven for clerk on account of his evident ability to perform the duties of the position. Mr. Gilpin was born in New Haven in 1860 and is consequently one of the youngest members of the body. He is engaged in merchandising, having for several years been connected with H. M. Peeples in that business. He is of a pleasant, courteous and gentlemanly disposition, qualities which have made him very popular in his part of the county. He is a zealous working Republican and has been a member of the New Haven town board.

Cass Talbott

Saline Mines is represented on the jury by a genial pleasant gentleman in the person of Mr. Cass Talbott, a native of his precinct where he was born in 1851. He is a farmer by occupation, a Republican in politics and a good citizen. He has never sought for or held any public office and is content to live among his neighbors with simply their esteem.

Alfred D. Potts

The youngest member as well as one of the most unassuming is Alfred D. Potts of Eagle Creek. He was born in this county April 7, 1861, and lives on his own farm of 80 acres. In politics he is a Republican though not active being content to show his adherence to his party's tenets by his votes.

Cave McCord

The junior member from South Shawneetown is Mr. Cave McCord, a plain unassuming farmer. He was born in Graves Co., Ky., in 1822, and now lives about two miles south of town on a farm of 124 acres. Mr. McCord is a staunch Democrat though not an active worker in the party. He is a good member of the jury as well as a useful citizen.

Alex Mobley

New Haven has in the person of Mr. Alex Mobley a native member of this body. Mr. Mobley was born in 1837. He is a characteristic representative of that sturdy race of the native Illinoisan, being plain in manner, frank in expression and honest in his dealings. He is a farmer, a Democrat and an active member of the M. E. church. He also served his country for 13 months in the army during the war.

William Wiseheart

Every lover of good stock in Southern Illinois knows William Wiseheart of North Shawneetown. He was born in this county in 1832 and is one of our best farmers, living 4 ½ miles north of town where he owns 413 acres of the finest land in the county. Uncle will was a pioneer in the introduction of Norman and Clydesdale horses in this part of the country. Believing in the principles of right and justice to all, he is an active Democrat. He has served in the capacity of school trustee, and has ever taken a lively interest in our fair of which he was for several years Gen. Superintendent and is now a director.[151]

---

[151] Feb. 14, 1890. "Our Grand Jury." *Gallatin Democrat* (Shawneetown, Ill.).

Military History

French and Indian War

The First Salt War – 1754

The events that led to the Salt War, as it was called, were these: A tribe called the Salt Boilers had occupied the salt springs country for many years, centuries may be.[152] Some Frenchmen at Vincennes went down there with kettles aiming to have a monopoly on the salt. The Indians attacked them, and killed one or two. The rest left, and told their friends at Kaskaskia, and a war party went over there to punish the Salt Boilers, who had enlisted the support of the Shawnees. The two tribes met at the depot of Julius de Rouche, which was on the hill now called Frankfort Heights.[153] The Kaskaskia were outnumbered and fled, with the Shawnee in pursuit. At the bank of the Au Vase (Big Muddy) there was a scrap. The Kaskaskia escaped to the east bank of Little Muddy, at the old "Battle Mound," took shelter behind it and received the Shawnee with much slaughter. They were routed, but the Shawnee did not pursue farther. This took place about the year 1754, just prior to the French and Indian War.

This last portion is mere tradition. A near neighbor of ours in my teens was Gilbert Browning who was past 70 and had been a pioneer in the community. He said that he knew and traded with the Frenchman, de Rouche and had from him the story of the Salt War, with its location, etc.[154]

Kickapoos capture Croghan's party – 1765

In the year 1765, Col. George Croghan, a commissioner, was sent out West to conciliate the Indians, after the cession of the country to the British. He descended the Ohio River, and was at the falls of the Ohio on the 1st June 1765. The party came to the mouth of the Wabash, where they discovered some Indian fortifications. They still descended to an old Shawnee village, the same that retains the name of Shawneetown, in Gallatin County, on the north bank of the Ohio River. Col. Croghan and party remained there six days, making friendly arrangements with the Wabash Indians.

On the 8th of June, they were attacked by eighty warriors, mostly of the Kickapoo and Mascouten tribes, and many of the whites were killed and more wounded; and all made prisoners.

The party from this point went to Vincennes, by land, where they found eighty or ninety French families. From the Shawnee village, Col. Croghan sent messengers to Lord Frazier,

---

[152] The author of this story, William Moyers, believed that the 1802 Salt War story was false. However, the editor of this book is including both stories as if there were two Salt Wars, which is just as likely.

[153] West Frankfort, Ill.

[154] William Moyers. Jan. 19, 1939. Letter to Barbara Hubbs. Barbara Burr Hubbs Collection. Marion Carnegie Library. Marion, Ill.

who had been sent to Fort Chartres; and also dispatches were forward to Saint Ange at the same fort. After remaining at Vincennes several days, Col. Croghan went up the Wabash 210 miles, to Ouiatenon, the Weas Town, as the Americans called it, and on by the Miami post to Detroit, where they arrived on the 17th August. At Ouiatenon there were fourteen families and at Detroit about eighty houses of all sorts.[155]

Indian Troubles/War of 1812

Second Salt War – 1802

That portion of the Territory lying between the Big Muddy on the west, and the Wabash on the east, was for over thirty years inhabited by the Shawnee tribe of Indians. And that [time] west of Big Muddy, to the Mississippi, was occupied by the Kaskaskia Indians.

In the year 1802, a battle occurred between the two tribes.[156] These tribes would occasionally trespass upon the hunting grounds of each other, from which quarrels ensued, and finally the battle above mentioned. It was fought by agreement on the half-way ground, in Town Mount Prairie, in the edge of Franklin County, about three miles southwest of Frankfort. The Kaskaskia were under the command of their chief John DuQuoin, then quite an old man, and a good friend to the whites. The Shawnees were commanded by a chief of a treacherous nature, which was probably the cause of the fight. As to the duration of this battle, we have no means of knowing; but the battleground itself, though under a high state of cultivation, can yet be located by marks. The farms occupied by L. D. Throop and the Dennings, are at the extremes of the battlefield, the main fight taking place a little south of Mr. Throop's residence. A large number of the Shawnee were slain, and the remainder driven to the Big Muddy River, at a point about a quarter of a mile below the bridge, on the Frankfort and DuQuoin road, where, in attempting to cross they were nearly all butchered, and the tribe annihilated. The Kaskaskia after that held undisputed sway, until the encroachments of the whites drove them beyond the Mississippi.[157]

Jordan's Fort – 1804

In consequence of the difficulties that existed among the Indians, there were no settlers this side of Equality until the year 1804, when seven brothers by the name of Jordan, John and William Browning, Joseph Estes and a man named Barbrey, a brother-in-law to the Jordans, from Smith County, Tenn., located in this county, and built a fort and blockhouse where the residence of Judge William Elstun now stands. These settlers were all related.

---

[155] John Reynolds. 1852, 2nd 1887. *Pioneer History of Illinois*. Chicago: Fergus Printing. 79-80.

[156] This battle is referred to here as the Second Salt War since Moyers is so certain that it is wrong and should be placed around 1754. It's possible that these are two distinct battles between the two tribes fighting over similar causes over similar battlefields. This is especially true considering France and Germany fighting over the same territory in both World War I and World War II.

[157] Milo Erwin. 1876. Reprint 1976. *The History of Williamson County, Illinois*. Marion, Ill.: Williamson County Historical Society. 11-12.

John Browning's mother was Mollie Jordan, sister to the seven Jordan brothers. John Browning was the father of James and Levi, who were well known to nearly all citizens of the county... Elias Jordan, the father of Moses, was one of the seven brothers. William Browning died in 1817. From the time of the building of the fort until about the year 1815, little or no attempt was made to cultivate the soil, the settlers subsisting almost entirely on game, honey, and a little corn, which they, by close watching, succeeded in raising and preventing the Indians from stealing.[158]

Indian kills John Rector – 1805

At the present site of the Town House of the Town of Rector, toward the northeast part of [Saline] county, were three [Indian] campgrounds near Rector Creek, and all within one mile. One of the sites is north of Rector Creek, and two of the sites are south of the creek. It was in this neighborhood that a lone Shawnee slew John Rector in the year 1805, when he was surveying the township lines while employed by the Federal Government in the survey of this part of the Northwest Territory. Rector was a Revolutionary war soldier and a relative of the surveyor general of the new republic...

The first, perhaps, of the Revolutionary War veterans to die in Saline County, was John Rector. He was engaged in surveying the township lines in this part of the Northwest Territory, and was killed by an Indian, while working at his surveying duties, in what is now Rector Township, in Saline County. This companions buried him on the spot, under a cedar tree, and then, methodically, set down in their records, a surveyor's technical description of the location of his grave.[159]

Karnes' Blockhouse – 1806

[On the trail from the saltworks at Equality to Jordan's Fort in Franklin] Jacob Karnes built a block house it is claimed in 1806 on the S ¼ SW ¼ Sec. 5, Town 8, Range 6 and on the same trail the Browns built [one in 1812] and about six or seven miles west of the Brown block house, and three miles northwest of where the village of Raleigh now stands.[160]

A Rumor of War – 1807

A gentleman lately being in the company with a party of Shawnese and Delaware tribes of Indians, on the Saline creek, near the Saline Saltworks, and as the Indians had been at the Saltworks drinking and quarreling with the white people, there was one who assumed the title of Captain Jonny and another Captain Sam Lewis, who appearing very much irritated at

---

[158] 1887. History of Gallatin, Saline, Hamilton, Franklin and Williamson Counties, Illinois. Chicago: Goodspeed Publishing Company. 338-339.

[159] Clarence Bonnell, ed. 1947. *Saline County: A Century of History, 1847-1947*. Harrisburg, Ill.: Saline County Historical Society. 32, 293.

[160] John J. Jones, Sr., to G. W. Smith. Jan. 15, 1912. George W. Smith Papers. Special Collections. Morris Library. Southern Illinois University-Carbondale.

the usage they received at the like, caused the to speak freely, and said as soon as the leaves fell the Indians intended to move their wives and children over the big river Mississippi and the warriors were to join Frenchman, (who was the name of Golang, as this gentleman understood) that there were seven tribes had mark'd a long paper which Frenchman had, to go to war with the Kentuckians, to wit: the Shawanese, Delewares, Miahues, Peankeshaws, Musceogas, Kickapoos; and the White River tribe; that a great Captain was coming to join Captain Frenchman who would give the Indians all their country; and that Captain Frenchman was going to make big houses to fight in, and to put the women and children in, and would get all the warriors over the big river to mark his good paper, and that before the leaves get big again, they would kill all the Kentuckians and live in their houses and eat their cattle.[161]

Residents warn Harrison of impending Indian troubles

Randolph, Illinois, Aug. 6, 1810
[Harrison Papers 338-341.]

Sir:

The people inhabiting in the Prairie and adjoining thereto between the Big and Little Wabash have been very much fluctuated of late concerning a talk of an Indian War, the occasion of this disturbance was owing to the discourse of an old Muscoga Indian named Peter who told a man living here (one Jesse Bowman) that the Shawonese Indians intended to go to war with this whites this Moon and advised Bowman to provide for the safety of his family, and requested him to tell the same to some more people whom the old Indian had a friendship for. This Indian has lived about two years with the Whites and has got the confidence of most of the people; he also said that eleven Indians tribes had or were going to join the Shawonese, the names we are unable to inform your Excellency; this discourse has so operated on the minds of the people that out of forty-two families or more only fifteen families have determined to stay. Some of the remainder have moved, others making preparation to stay have proceeded to the erection of a Fort, what we request of your Excellency is to inform us by Mr. Wm. McHenry whether you think there is any such danger and should your Excellency have reason to fear there is, we shall feel grateful to be informed of the same, that we may be upon our guard. We hope the urgency of the case needs no apology with your Excellency for the trouble we give you and beg leave to subscribe ourselves.

Your Excellency's Friends and Fellow Citizens,

Henry Jones, James Garrison, Thomas Upton, Nathan Young, Ephraim Blackford, Alexander Hamilton, P. T. B., Wm. McHenry, Danl. McHenry, Reuben Blackford, Peter Kuykendall, Robt. Land.[162]

---

[161] Aug. 29, 1807. "A Caution to the Western People." *The* (Russellville, Ky.) *Mirror*.

[162] Logan Esarey, ed. 1922. *Governors Messages and Letters: Messages and Letters of William Henry Harrison. Vol. 1. 1800-1811*. Indianapolis: Indiana Historical Commission. 455.

Jordan builds fort – 1810

This brings me to the first settlement, which occurred in 1810. Frank Jordan built a fort in Northern Precinct.[163] It was a stockade enclosing about one acre of land, and contained four log cabins and a well, and was about fifty yards from Pond Creek. It is now [in 1876] known by the name of the "Old Station," and in 1820 half the stockade was standing and the cabins were occupied by James Howe and Mr. Parks. An old doctor by the name of John Dunlap was with the Jordans in this fort. He claimed to have been captured by the Indians when a boy and brought up by them to the practice of medicine. He lived a great many years and followed his profession, and always got his medicine out of the roots and herbs in the woods.[164]

Moore settles on Goshen – 1810

There seems to be no doubt that Andrew Moore was the first white man to settle in Moore's Prairie — or in Jefferson County, as to that matter. He erected a double cabin on the Goshen Road and there he resided with his family when there were none to molest or make afraid, except occasional bands of roving Indians. He must have settled there as early as 1810 and Crusoe on his lonely island was not more alone than Moore and his family. He seemed to be a pioneer in the true mould — yearning for freedom in its rawest sense. He was self-exiled from civilization, seeking the solitudes of the pathless woods. He did not burn the bridges behind him, simply because there were none to burn. He fished, hunted, cut bee trees and raised a truck garden, strictly for home consumption, seemed to have no fear of wild beasts or Indians and felt as secure in his cabin as he would in a fortified castle.

Moore and his ten-year-old boy one day went to the Jordan settlement many miles away to have some corn made into meal, expected to get back that night. But they never came. Mrs. Moore, after waiting all next day in vain, took the other children and set out for the Jordan mill to learn what had happened to her loved ones. She never learned. They had got their grinding and started home on time and that was the last seen of them. The woods were scoured, but no trace could be found. Mrs. Moore — heart-broken and desolate, returned to her cabin but could not stand it — she removed with her little ones to the Saline Salt Works settlement, but a few years later returned and occupied the old cabin, together with others who came to locate. A few years later a hunting party found a human skull, which Mrs. Moore recognized as her husband by a missing tooth. She took it to her home and cherished it as long as she lived. No other intelligence of Moore and son was ever received by the family and there seemed to be no doubt that they were killed by Indians and devoured by wild beasts.[165]

---

[163] This is near Corinth in Williamson Co., Illinois.

[164] Milo Erwin. 1876. Reprint 1976. *The History of Williamson County, Illinois.* Marion, Ill. Williamson County Historical Society. 20-21.

[165] William Nelson Moyers wrote in 1931 about the French voyageur station called Macedoin, near Macedonia. The hutte at this post was still standing well into the 1800s. Moyers wrote that Elder Hosea Vise used to point out the location of the building where Andrew Moore and his son had taken shelter the night they were murdered by Indians, near Macedonia. [Source: William Nelson Moyers. 1931. "A Story of Southern Illinois." *Journal of the Illinois State Historical Society.* 24:1.]

Tradition gives us the sequel to his horrible tragedy. It has been said that Moore and some of his friends from the Saline settlement were out in the woods splitting some board timber, when a couple of painted redskins came upon them and it looked like something must done to get rid of them. Moore was driving a wooden wedge into the log, which they expected to make into boards. By signs, Moore showed his apparent anxiety to get the log open by pulling while his friend mauled.

Finally the Indians showed signs of wanting to help. They took a good grip on either side of the log with their fingers well down in the aperture, when Moore, by a dexterous stroke of the maul, kit the wooden wedge, causing it to fly out — catching the fingers of the redskins so as to hold them fast in the closed fissure of the log. As soon as possible, Moore and his friends relieved them but they went away with revenge (the Indian characteristic) depicted on their faces, and it was believed that they waited for a chance to "get even" with Moore and over did the thing by killing him.[166]

Settlers build blockhouse near Marion – 1811

In 1811 John Phelps settled Phelps' Prairie. Jay and McClure settled at the Odum Ford. Joseph and Thomas Griffee settled at Ward's Mill. William Donald settled the Hill place. John Maneese and his son James settled on Phelps' Prairie.[167] During this year these settlers and some from down on Cache, built a blockhouse on the John Davis place, west of Marion. It was built of hewed logs, was twenty feet square, covered with slabs, and had port-holes eight feet from the ground. They all went into this fort at night, and had 19 white dogs for guards on the outside. The tracks of Indians were often seen around in the morning.[168]

Isaac White at Tippecanoe – 1811

Shortly after Colonel White's sale of his interest in the Illinois Salt works and his return to Vincennes, he had been initiated and passed as an apprentice and fellow-craft mason in the Masonic Lodge at Vincennes, then under the jurisdiction of the Grand Lodge of Kentucky, and on the 18th of September, 1811, he was raised to the degree of a Master Mason by his friend, the celebrated Colonel Jo. Daviess, Grand Master of Kentucky, who had come to Vincennes to offer his services to Gen. Harrison, in an expected campaign against the confederation of Indians which Tecumseh and his brother, the Prophet, were industriously endeavoring to form as a means of preventing the further advance of white settlements.[169]

---

[166] John A. Wall. 1909. *Wall's History of Jefferson County, Illinois.* Indianapolis: B. F. Bowen & Co., Publishers. 213-214.

[167] These places are centered around Marion, Ill. Phelps Prairie existed in the area now taken up by the Robert L. Butler Industrial Park on the west side of Marion south of Illinois Route 13 and the Williamson County Airport. Ward's Mill and Odum Ford are to the south and southeast of Marion. At Gallatin County's creation, these sites in what is now Williamson County would have been at the western edge of the Gallatin County.

[168] Milo Erwin. 1876. Reprint 1976. *The History of Williamson County, Illinois.* Marion, Ill. Williamson County Historical Society. 21-22.

[169] Letter of Judge Jno. Law to Isaac T. White:

Evansville, Ind., July 19, 1867.

To Dr. Isaac T. White,

The troubles arising out of the machinations of these two chiefs had then reached a point when active measures by the Territorial authorities became imperative, and Harrison, determining that an invasion of the Indian country was necessary, was busy with his preparations therefore. In the force that was to be raised for this expedition, Colonel White had earnestly requested to have his regiment included, or at least as much of it as could be readily made available; but Gen. Harrison, felling that, with the regular troops he had ordered to Vincennes, enough militia was already on hand to serve his purposes, and indeed not being certain that any severe fighting would be necessary, felt compelled to decline the request. Colonel White was not the man, however, to give up, for this reason, his determination to take part in the expedition. With the consent of his friend Col. Daviess, he enrolled himself as a private in the battalion of dragoons which Harrison had placed under that officer's command, and when the expedition started, on the 26th of September — eight days after he had been made a Master Mason — White accompanied it.

An affecting incident in connection with the enlistment of Colonel White was an exchange of swords between him and Colonel Daviess — an exchange to which Fate gave an awful solemnity when, afterwards, on the field of Tippecanoe, the weapon of White was found buckled on the belt of Daviess, and the sword of Daviess was held in the iron grip of his friend.

It will be remembered that the expedition of General Harrison, which culminated in the victory of Tippecanoe, left Vincennes on the 26th of September, 1811, and that on the afternoon of the 6th of November following the little army encamped on the banks of Burnet's Creek, seven miles north of the present city of Lafayette, and a short distance from the Prophet's town, where a large body of Indians were supposed to be on the war-path. The battle began early on the morning of the 7th by a sudden attack of the Indians on that portion of the camp were Daviess and his battalion were stationed. Part of the fire of the Indians, proceeding from a clump of trees some distance in front, was do deadly that Daviess was ordered to dislodge them, which, at the head of a detachment of twenty picked men from his force, hw at once proceeded gallantly to do; but, unhappily, his ardor was too great, and the little force with him, which included Colonel White, was driven back, Daviess and his friend both being mortally wounded they died upon the battle-field and were buried side by side—

(Keller & White),
Evansville, Indiana.

My Dear Sir: In examining the records of the Vincennes Lodge, No. 1, which was the first Lodge ever instituted in Indiana, and I might with truth say from the Miami River to the Pacific Ocean (the Lodge was organized at Vincennes September 1, 1808), I find the Col. Joseph H. Daviess, Grand Master of the Grand Lodge of Kentucky (the Lodge at Vincennes then being under the jurisdiction of the Grant Lodge of Kentucky), was at Vincennes, and that on the 18th of September, 1811 (two months before the battle of Tippecanoe), he presided over the Lodge at Vincennes.

I further find that on September 19, 1811, as Master of the Lodge, he conferred the degree of Master Mason on your grandfather, Isaac White. It is a little singular that in two months afterwards your grandfather, who received the degree, and Colonel Daviess, who conferred it, should both have fallen on the battle-field of Tippecanoe. I think it is a circumstance worthy of remembrance, by his descendants, and probably unknown to them.

Very truly yours,
John Law.

the temporary inequality of rank, of which the noble nature of both men had hardly suffered them to be conscious, being thus forever removed.[170]

Panic follows Battle of Tippecanoe – 1811

[Elder Wilson Thompson and wife] were then in Illinois. I will mention that the night before we had stayed at the Saline Salt Works, and while we were there a messenger came with the news that General Harrison had been surprised at Tippecanoe General and was defeated with great loss, and that the Indians were desolating the whole country. A council was called to determine what they could so — whether to abandon the salt works and go to Kentucky, or send out spies to ascertain what was best for them.[171]

Humphrey's Blockhouse – 1812

[In 1812] Charles Humphreys settled at the Stancil ford [on the Big Muddy River], and commenced to keep a ferry.[172] He built him a small blockhouse, but the Indians sometimes got so bad he had to remove his family to Jordan's fort for safety. One night, James Herrein, who had come out here on a visit, stayed in the house with the ferryman. It thundered and lightened terribly, and they could see the Indians around when it lightened. But they were all gone before day.[173]

[There may have been a second attack on the fort based on stories heard by W. N. Moyers who had an uncle who married into the Humphrey family.]

I recall that Chas. Humphrey's wife was called Aunt Betty Humphrey and the old people told the story that around 1812 or 1814 there was considerable Indian trouble in all of this southern Illinois country. Upon one occasion a Shawnee Indian came to Humphrey's and asked for water or food; he became ill and Aunt Betty and her husband cared for him until he was well. After that he stayed around the place some time and upon one occasion the house was attacked by three Kickapoo Indians; Chas. Humphrey and the Indian, using the cracks between the logs for portholes, with Aunt Betty loading the guns, soon gave the

---

[170] George Fauntleroy White (grandson of Col. Isaac White). 1889. *Sketch of the Life of Colonel Isaac white, of Vincennes, Indiana. Killed at the Battle of Tippecanoe, November 7, 1811.* Washington: Gibson Bros., Printers and Bookbinders. 15-16, 22.

[171] Wilson Thompson. 1873. *Autobiography of Elder Wilson Thompson.* Cincinnati: Wilstach, Baldwin & Co., Printers. 150. Reprinted in 1979 by Ron Nelson.

[172] The ferry is believed to have been located at the intersection of Miles' Trace and the Big Muddy River near Blairsville, Ill., in northwestern Williamson County. When Pope created Gallatin County later in 1812, this ferry crossing became the westernmost point in Gallatin County, the borders on the west side at the time being in part, Miles' Trace and the Big Muddy River.

[173] Milo Erwin. 1876. Reprint 1976. *The History of Williamson County, Illinois.* Marion, Ill. Williamson County Historical Society. 22-23.

Kickapoos such a warm reception that they left in a hurry. I do not remember many of the details of the story, but it is only one on many that I used to hear told.[174]

Attack on Jordan's Fort – 1812

In consequence of the difficulties that existed among the Indians, there were no settlers this side of Equality until the year 1804, when seven brothers by the name of Jordan, John and William Browning, Joseph Estes and a man named Barbrey, a brother-in-law to the Jordans, from Smith County, Tenn., located in this county, and built a fort and blockhouse where the residence of Judge William Elstun now stands. These settlers were all related. John Browning's mother was Mollie Jordan, sister to the seven Jordan brothers. John Browning was the father of James and Levi, who were well known to nearly all citizens of the county. Elias Jordan, the father of Moses, was one of the seven brothers. William Browning died in 1817. From the time of the building of the fort until about the year 1815, little or no attempt was made to cultivate the soil, the settlers subsisting almost entirely on game, honey, and a little corn, which they, by close watching, succeeded in raising and preventing the Indians from stealing. While these settlers were thus fortified, and in the year 1812, James Jordan and Mr. Barbrey, while out of the fort gathering wood, were fired upon by the Indians. Barbrey was killed and scalped. James Jordan was wounded in the leg. After obtaining re-enforcements from Frank Jordan's fort, which was then located in what is now Williamson County, about three miles south of the first named fort, the whites started in pursuit of the Indians and followed them as far as the Okaw River, but did not succeed in overtaking them. Barbrey was buried at the fort and his grave still remains near the residence of Judge William Elstom. This was the starting of the first graveyard in Franklin County.[175]

The Jordan settlement was made in what is now Cave Township [Franklin Co.].[176]

Indians attack in Hardin Co. – 1812

That part of the County now embraced in Monroe Precinct, was settled about or perhaps a little later than that embraced in Rose Clare precinct, of which we have written.[177] As late as 1812 the country was infested by savages, and during that year a man by the name of James Jourdan, was wounded by them in defense of a block house situated near the north

---

[174] W. N. Moyers. May 12, 1937. Letter to Nannie Gray Parks. Nannie Gray Parks Collection. Williamson County Historical Society. Published Spring 2002. *Footprints in Williamson County, Illinois*. 5:1. Marion, Ill.: Williamson County Historical Society. 3-4.

[175] An original footnote at this point reads: "From the Centennial address delivered in Benton in 1876, by Judge W. H. Williams, the historical facts of which are by permission introduced into this history."

[176] 1887. *History of Gallatin, Saline, Hamilton, Franklin and Williamson Counties, Illinois*. Chicago: Goodspeed Publishing Company. 338-339.

[177] Monroe Township was the northwestern township in Hardin County. The most concentrated early land entries are about two to three miles north of the Illinois Iron Furnace along Big Creek. The 1807 Squatters List shows Joseph Jordan claiming the east half of Section 33, Township 11 South, Range 8 East, about four miles south of Karbers Ridge.

boundary of the county.[178] The early settlers in that portion of the county were mainly from Tennessee, Kentucky and Virginia; among them were Daniel Vinyard, Henry Rose, Ezekiel McCoy and Myers Singleton.[179]

Construction of Farm Fort – 1812

Sometime in 1812, settlers in Capt. Grove's militia district, built a fortification in the center of the northwest quarter of Section 6, Township 8 South, Range 10 East, just over three miles south of New Haven. It stood about a mile southeast of Asbury Church and a half-mile northwest of the Green House Inn. Although remembered best as Farm Fort and described as simply a blockhouse,[180] it carried the early name of the Pond Settlement Fort, which would indicate it probably included multiple blockhouses and a stockade. William Ellis living in the eastern portion of modern Hardin County joined Capt. Barker's company around April 1, 1813. He spent the next three months guarding against Indian attacks and helping settlers build forts along the Ohio, Wabash and Skillet Fork frontier. He mustered out on June 1, at the Pond Settlement Fort.

The fort stood just west of the modern Shawneetown-New Haven Road, then the road leading from Shawanoe Town to Boon's Mill. County historian Glen Minor noted the fort also stood near the crossroads with an ancient Indian trail running from Fred Buck's Ferry near Indian Camp Creek on the Wabash River southeastward to the saltworks at Half Moon Lick at Equality.[181] Gov. William Henry Harrison described that trail in 1807 as follows: "The old trace that runs near the Ohio River crossing the Wabash and on the saline regions of the Illinois has been a regular pass way for Indians from time when none know."[182]

---

[178] This is probably the same James Jordan attacked in Franklin County. The Jordan family spread about from the Ohio River through Saline County to what is now Williamson and Franklin Counties all in the decade prior to the War of 1812. Though it is interesting that Jordan gets attacked at two blockhouses. It brings up the possibility that either Hardin County or Franklin County folklore is recalling the same event, but just at different locations. On the other hand, very little is known concerning any forts or blockhouses in what is now Hardin County. What's remembered as the Sturdivant Fort at Rosiclare probably was built during this period of frontier war. Another three-sided fort is recalled at Lamb in eastern Hardin County. The location mentioned in this story would be along the original Ford's Ferry Road that ran from the ferry site at Rosiclare north along Big Creek through the modern Garden of the Gods Wilderness Area before crossing through Horseshoe Gap on its way to Equality.

[179] Jan. 26, 1967. "Historical Sketch of County From Earliest Settlement to 1876." (Elizabethtown, Ill.) *Hardin County Independent*. (The article bears an original date of July 4, 1876 from a historical committee chaired by L. F. Twitchell.)

[180] Glenn Sneed. *Ghost Towns of Southern Illinois*. The fort also appears in the 1876 *Atlas of Illinois*.

[181] Glen Miner. 1979, 2nd. 1984. *Cemeteries of Gallatin County, Illinois, and a History of the County*. Vol. 2. Online at http://homepages.rootsweb.com/~davidca/Gall-cem/Book2.htm.

[182] Logan Esarey, ed. 1922. *Governors Messages and Letters: Messages and Letters of William Henry Harrison. Vol. 1. 1800-1811*. Indianapolis: Indiana Historical Commission. 267-268.

Fortifications in White Co. – 1812

While this war was in progress the people of the settlement, afterward organized as White County, were protected by a squad of 12 to 14 mounted "rangers," United States troops or volunteers, who had their headquarters in the "Big Prairie" east of where Carmi now is. Nevertheless, many of the inhabitants took fright and fled to older settlements in the South and East. Among the volunteers were Captain William McHenry, who had settled near where Grayville now is, and Daniel Boultinghouse, who had located at Williams' Ferry in 1810 and moved out to the prairie near the northern limits of the county, where he was afterward killed by an Indian. After him "Boultinghouse Prairie," in the southern part of Edwards County, was named. During this war one other man from White County was killed and two wounded, between Carmi and Grayville. Colonel Hosea Pearce, who had been a soldiers under General Jackson in the South, settled in this county about fifteen miles south of Carmi.

Block-Houses

The block-houses in [what is now] White County during the war of 1812, were these:[183]

On the Tanquary land, the northeast quarter section 16, township 5 south, 10 east, built by Captain Wm. McHenry in the summer of 1812. The year previous he had erected a horse-mill at the same place.

2. On the Starkey place, built by Hardy Council in 1813.[184]

3. On the east side of the prairie, built by Aaron Williams in 1813, near where the red house has since stood.[185]

4. A little south of George Hanna's house, and built by John Hanna.[186]

5. About 200 yards east of where Matthew Land now owns, built by Robert Land, who lived in it during the war.[187]

6. East of Thomas Logan's farm, erected by John Slocumb.[188]

---

[183] See "Residents warn Harrison of impending Indian troubles" a few pages earlier.

[184] There is no land entry for a Hardy Council. The earliest entry by a Council is by an Elizabeth Council on March 10, 1815. Elizabeth Council entered the northeast quarter of Section 19, Township 5 South, Range 10 East. This is on the east bank of the Little Wabash about a mile southeast of Carmi.

[185] On Aug. 4, 1814, Aaron Williams entered the southeast quarter of Section 22, Township 5 South, Range 10 East. On the same day a Thomas Williams entered the southwest quarter of the same section. This is about four miles east-southeast of Carmi.

[186] John Hanna entered the northwest quarter of Section 33, Township 5 South, Range 10 East, on Oct. 14, 1814. This is adjacent to the north of Robert Land's original land entry.

[187] On Aug. 1, 1814, Robert Land entered the southwest quarter of Section 33, Township 5 South, Range 10 East. This section contains a relative high point in this flat area east of the Little Wabash about four miles southeast of Carmi.

[188] Presumably in the northeast quarter of Section 20, Township 6 South, Range 10 East, or about one mile north-northeast of the little town of Emma in the modern township of the same name. This is in the flatlands between the Little Wabash and the main Wabash rivers. This quarter section is the first one purchased by John C. Slocumb on July 20, 1814. On the same day his son Samuel Slocumb entered the quarter section immediately to the south and another son Charles Slocumb entered the next quarter section (NE 29-6S-10E) [Source: *Shawneetown Land District Records 1814-1820.*]

These fortifications were a good protection against the Indians, who best weapons were poor rifles.

In March, 1815, before it was known in this region that peace had been declared between the hostile countries, a draft of men for the soldiery was made in this county. None of these, of course, entered the army, but a few went out toward St. Louis a distance and returned.[189]

Boone's Fort – 1812

Not much can be found about Boone's Fort in New Haven other than it existed. From the name it can be assumed it included a stockade and a number of blockhouses.

Saline Co. Fortifications – 1812-1815

There is no one source that list all six blockhouses and forts built by the early settlers within the bounds of the present day Saline County. Of course, during the War of 1812, all this territory was part of the center of Gallatin County.

The Saline County portion of Goodspeed's History notes "there was a blockhouse built on Hankerson Rude's farm, to which the surrounding settlers would retreat in case of danger, and then one on Hampton Pankey's farm."[190]

These were two of the three forts in the southern part of the county. Another three stretched out along the early trail from Shawneetown to Kaskaskia. The Jordan Fort in what is now Franklin County served as the fourth fort along this stretch.

Hankerson Rude located his farm on the northwest quarter of Section 19, Township 10 South, Range 7 East, in what is now Mountain Township on an early trail from the saltworks to the southwest. He entered his land ownership on Sept. 3, 1814. Later that December both Hampton Pankey and John Pankey entered quarter-sections in Township 9 South, Range 5 East, west of Harrisburg. Hampton took the southeast quarter of Section 28 and John took the northwest quarter of Section 34.[191] While the writer in 1887 described Rude's fortification as a blockhouse, an early 20th Century historian talked with two elderly women of the area who could recall the remains of two blockhouses and a part of a stockade wall. That would seem to indicate likely a standard fort.

> As it was told to me by an old lady by the name of Anna Owens, and another old lady we knew as Aunt Rit Crabb; they remembered seeing the ruins of the old fort, and had attended services in the church which was built in conjunction with the fort. These old ladies were in their seventies when I first met

---

[189] 1883. *History of White County*. Chicago: Inter-State Publishing Co. 450-451.

[190] 1887. *History of Gallatin, Saline, Hamilton, Franklin and Saline Counties, Illinois*. Chicago: Goodspeed Publishing Company. 157.

[191] 1887. *History of Gallatin, Saline, Hamilton, Franklin and Saline Counties, Illinois*. Chicago: Goodspeed Publishing Company. 153.

them forty-one years ago. They both, told about the block houses on the corners, and the palisades between which were made by setting logs on end.[192]

In between Rude and Pankey someone must have been another fort in what is now Independence Township, or Township 10 South, Range 6 East. The stream now known as Battleford Creek showed up on an 1876 state atlas as Blockhouse Creek.[193] While local tradition indicates the modern name for the creek is derived from the site of an early militia mustering grounds, it would seem that the name in 1876 indicates someone had a blockhouse alongside this stream. And that would further indicate if someone did have a blockhouse there, then the name "Battle Ford" could likely be taken literally as the site where a battle took place at a ford across the stream. The location of a militia mustering ground would be logical. It already had a military history and as a ford, it would have been a natural crossing point, meaning an early road or trail crossed at the site making it fairly convenient. But the question remains, if there was a blockhouse in this section, who built it? The land records don't provide much help. Unlike neighboring townships, no one made a land entry here until 1818, four years after settlers started entering land nearby. Plus, for the vast majority of the acreage in the township, no one patented the lands until the 1850s when they were sold off as Swamp Lands. Thus the blockhouse and possible battle site remains a mystery.

The north side of the county is better documented and remembered. It should be considering the settlers situated the forts along the Shawneetown-Kaskaskia Trail and the three forts roughly align with the modern communities of Eldorado, Raleigh and Galatia. The brothers Coleman, John, and Thomas Brown built a blockhouse near Wolf Creek on the west side of Eldorado (SW¼ 17-8s-7e) in 1812.[194] This would have protected the area along the Shawneetown-Kaskaskia Trail between the fort at Equality and Jacob Karnes's 1806 blockhouse on the ridge northwest of Raleigh at the later site of Bethel Church. On the other side of Karnes' fortification, William Gasaway built further to the west near Galatia.[195] A writer for Saline County's Centennial history described these types of blockhouses:

> These blockhouses were built square, and constructed from hewn logs, which were assembled with great care in order that there not be no opening through which the hand or weapon of the enemy could be thrust. The doors were usually made of thick puncheons, and were held in place with heavy wooden beams. At a height of about seven or eight feet, so as to be above the head of a man, there were portholes on each side for firing on an enemy. There were two

---

[192] Clarence Bonnell. [Undated]. Old Block House Fort. Published in The Shawnee. Winter 1999. Harrisburg, Ill.: Saline County Genealogical Society. 14:2. 33. Bonnell didn't move to Harrisburg until about 1904 and died in 1947, which indicates he wrote his notes sometime in the 1940s, probably in preparation for Saline County's centennial in 1947. By backdating it makes the women's memories of the church and fort date at the earliest to the late 1830s.

[193] Warner & Beers. 1876. "Saline County." *Illustrated Historical Atlas of the State of Illinois*. Union Atlas Co.

[194] John J. Jones, Sr., to G. W. Smith. Jan. 15, 1912. George W. Smith Papers. Special Collections. Morris Library. Southern Illinois University-Carbondale.

[195] Grace Collier. 1947. "Transportation Over a Century." *History of Saline County*. 228.

stories to these houses, and the second story projected over the first in order to have openings for rifles in the floor of the second story, through which to shoot any Indian who tried to force his way into the building. These houses for defense were usually built in a clearing, or at the edge of a natural prairie. If it were necessary to necessary to use a wooded place, the timber was cut for quite a distance on each side, in order that an attacking Indian, or band of Indians, could not be hidden from the sight of pioneers inside the building, or that a fire that might be set to the brush by the foe would not consume the blockhouse.[196]

The Battle of the Long Ridge – 1813

Note: The traditions from which this article is written are as told to the late Josephine Rubennaker by either the late Elizabeth Grayson or the late Emily Hewitt, or both. These in turn are said to have heard the stories direct from some of the participants themselves, such as Gens. White, McHenry, Hargrave and Dan Curtin.[197]

V.H. Crest

General Leonard White came to the Salines of the Wabash about 1795, while he was still a very young man. According to the best available traditions he was born in the Carolinas a little before the beginning of the Revolutionary War. At the time that young White arrived at the Saline, Col. Philip Trammell was the principal official in this area.

White was assigned to Dan Curtin, Chief Scout of the Salt Trails — a veteran scout of the George Rogers Clark Expedition. Curtin was a keen judge of men and almost at once recognized the great natural abilities of leadership so manifest in his protégé.

But to the rapid expansion of the salt industry Col. Trammell found it necessary to appoint a man to be military captain, that he himself might devote his whole time to the administration of the great salt industry. The Military Captain would have active charge of the Militia, of the Forest Rangers and of the Fort and Stockade.

As might be expected, Col. Trammell offered the position of Military Captain to his trusted friend and advisor, Dan Curtin. Curtin however, explained that he would be of far greater service to the Salines as Chief Scout than as Military Captain, and begged to be allowed to decline the proffered honor and promotion. Upon Curtin's urgent recommendation, Leonard White was appointed Military Captain and immediately assumed his duties as such.

Capt. Leonard White, though young, earned the respect of the elder older officers and men under his command. Possessed of a fair education for his times, Capt. White devoted his energies to improving the Fort and Stockade and in consulting with Col. Trammel, Dan

---

[196] Talitha E. Aaron. 1947. "Early Settlements in Saline County." *History of Saline County: A Century of History, 1847-1947.* Harrisburg, Ill.: Saline County Historical Society. 59-60.

[197] What is not mentioned in this account is the massacre of at least six persons in the area of Mound City, Illinois, by 10 Creek Indians led by two of their chiefs on February 9, 1813. It's possible that this event may have led to the Battle of the Long Ridge. The massacre did lead to the start of the Creek Civil War.

Curtin and others about further measures that might be taken to insure the safety of the inhabitants in case of Indian attack — an ever-present peril of the times.

White recognized the disadvantages of having the militiamen, rangers and citizens crowding pell mell into the Stockade at the sound of the Indian alarm bell. He determined to have the defenders assemble at a rendezvous at a point some distance from the Fort, there to receive their orders from the Commanding Officer and assume such positions of outer defense as the conditions might demand. In this manner the civilians and slaves could move chattels and valuables from the many homes and cabins to the Fort and Stockade in a more orderly manner.

Tradition tells that Capt. White made known his plans to a young Indian Maiden—who but for her untimely murder shortly afterward might have gone down in history as Madame White, wife of General Leonard White.

It is said that she selected the large oak tree in what is now the west part of the Old Cemetery in Equality, for the meeting-place of the Militia. Immediately after she had made the selection, Capt. White named the tree the "Mustering Oak" and issued military orders assigning it as the assembling point of the military forces of the Salines.

For almost two decades, at frequent intervals, both by day and by night, the armed forces of the surrounding area hastened on horseback or afoot to the shades of this tree upon the sound of the alarm bell on the old Fort — there to receive the orders of the young Commander. Not all of these meetings of the Military were mere drills. More than once they went forth under the command of Leonard White and his sub-officers to do battle in the defense of the Salines.

On a cold day in February 1813, the Mustering Oak and its surrounding grove witnessed the largest assemblage of armed forces sever to meet in the area of the old Salines. Bodies of armed men came from Shawneetown, from the Boone Settlement in New Haven, and from the Rock-in-Cave — (now Cave-in-Rock) — and many other points to join the forces of the U.S. Salines, preparatory to the last battle with the Shawnee Indians.

All through the day the military preparations were carried on within the area of the settlement behind the curtained protection of roving cavalry units under the direct command of Capt. William B. McHenry and Capt. Willis Hargrave.

During the late hours of the night Leonard White personally led the attack upon the camp of the hostile Shawnees. By dawn the battle of the Long Ridge had become history and the Indian peril had been permanently removed from Southern Illinois.[198]

In the late evening of the next day, amidst the shouts of victory and the moans and groans of the wounded and dying, those of the army who remained assembled in the gloom beneath the now leafless branches of the mustering oak to be honorable mustered out of service by their leader.

---

[198] In his "History of Equality" manuscript, Crest notes the following: "The site of the battle was on the northwest slope of the Long Ridge — a low lying hill to the west of town — the battle site being but a few hundred yards from the present home of Mr. I. W. White — and about two and a half miles west of Equality." This site is now in Saline County south of Route 13. The easiest way to locate it is to find Deer Lane and follow it south until it ends at a "T" intersection. Opposite this intersection is an obvious home place (though the White home has disappeared). Ironically, this White family is not related (at least closely) with either Isaac White or Leonard White who made salt in the general area. This battle may also be remembered as White's Massacre.

Few knew at the time that the tall dark man who had dismissed them had been painfully wounded in the leg near the beginning of the battle and that he had carried through on iron nerve alone. Cold and infection had aggravated the wound. During the night an emergency amputation was performed as the only hope of saving Leonard White's life.

Before the Commander recovered, however, news of the great victory had spread to the Territorial Capital of Kaskaskia. A grateful territorial governor, Ninian Edwards signed Leonard's White's commission as General of the Territorial Militia of Illinois.

In the years to come, two other brave officers who assembled with their cavalry units under the Mustering Oak at the time of the Battle of the Long Ridge also became Generals. Capt. McHenry became a General at some time prior to the Black Hawk War. Near the outbreak of the Black Hawk War, Capt. Willis Hargrave temporarily left his peace time position as President of the First Village Board of Equality, in the summer of 1832 and led his volunteer cavalry to Northern Illinois to engage in the Black Hawk War. In the intervening years, his old friend, Capt. McHenry, now General McHenry had removed to White county, where he organized a volunteer cavalry unit — also riding with Capt. Hargrave to the War.

It was fitting, and records show that General Leonard White, the one-legged hero of the Battle with the Shawnee was chosen as President Pro Tem of the Village Board during the interim until the Black Hawk War was ended with victory for the militia and Willis Hargrave returned to his people as General Willis Hargrave.

The Mustering Oak still stands, proud and sheltering over many graves of persons not yet born at the time that it played its heroic role in the stirring days of Indian peril before Statehood.[199]

Indians Attack Nelson Rector – c. 1814

About 12 or 14 years ago [from 1828] a gentleman named Rector, a brother of the late Surveyor General, was traveling from St. Louis to Shawanoe Town, when he fell into an ambuscade of hostile Indians, within 20 miles of the latter place.[200]

He was not aware of his danger until he saw himself surrounded by the foe, and heard the appalling war-whoop of the painted warriors, who issued, like the followers of Roderick Dhu, from every shade. Directly in the path, but a few paces before him, stood a savage, who as he discharged his rifle, laughed loud with a diabolical expression of malignant triumph, as if sure of his victim.

The ball passed through Rector's body, who still retained sufficient presence of mind to endeavor to escape. The path which he travelled was completely closed behind him; before him was a deep miry creek, whose high perpendicular banks overhanging the channel, seemed to render a passage impossible at any place but the ford to which he had been hastening, and the path to which was occupied by the enemy.

---

[199] V. H. Crest. [undated] "The Mustering Oak." MSS in possession of granddaughter Kathie Crest Thatcher. Crest's writings are believed to have appeared in an Equality newspaper in the late 1930s or early 1940s.

[200] The Rector in this story is Nelson Rector. Indians killed his brother John, also a surveyor, in 1805 at the same location where Nelson had been ambushed. John Rector was buried near the creek, which is named after him.

He could only give the rein and the spur to his horse, and trust to Providence. The gallant steed, who was also badly wounded, quitting the path, rushed to the bank of the stream and with a desperate leap, plunged to the bottom, and extricating himself from the mire, ascended the steep bank on the opposite side, and soon bore his master, now entirely insensible, beyond the reach of danger. The Indians, fearing pursuit, fled in contrary directions.

The unconscious Rector kept his seat for several miles, while the noble horse, as if tender of his charge, carried him safely through the thick and busy forest. At length Rector fell off, but the horse continued to fly at full speed until he reached the Saline, about six miles from the scene of the disaster. Here a few persons resided, engaged in making salt; to whom the bleeding wounds of the horse readily conveyed the intelligence of what had happened; but they were too few to oppose the enemy, nor did they dare to leave their families exposed. One of them was sent express to Shawanoe Town, who quickly returned with a party of eight or ten men. These, reinforced by the people at the Saline, pursued the tract of the horse, which was readily traced through the snow, which lay deep on the ground.

They found Rector, cold, still, and apparently dead: a rifle ball had passed through his breast. Happily one of the party was a physician, through whose care and skill the sufferer was resuscitated, and eventually recovered. Leaving a few of the first party with the wounded man, the remainder proceeded to the scene of action. Here they found the tracts of a considerable number of Indians; they traced the horse from the path to the edge of the bank; they saw where he had leaped down a descent of about 20 feet to the surface of the water, had broken through the ice in the middle of the creek, and had clambered up an almost perpendicular bank on the other side.

Had not the new fallen-snow, the tracts of the horse's feet, and the blood-drops which marked his whole course, rendered all this as plain as demonstration, those who then stood upon the margin of the rivulet would have thought it impossible for a horse to effect a passage at that spot; yet Rector's horse accomplished it, bearing a heavy burden, and himself wounded in a vital part.

One of the balls received by this fine animal passed through his breast immediately behind the shoulders. Several of those who inspected him, who had been accustomed to hunting all their lives, and were well acquainted with the formation of quadrupeds, and the effect of gun-shot wounds, have assured me that nine out of ten would have died instantly of such a wound; yet the horse recovered to entire health, and was cherished during life with the gentlest care, by his grateful master. The Indians were pursued for a considerable distance, but not overtaken. This stream, which empties itself into the Saline River, is called Rector's Fork.[201]

Indians attack Cannon Family – 1814

[Years later during the Black Hawk War, the settlers] would often relate the massacres that were inflicted upon the settlement on the Wabash. One instance occurred in 1814, about

---

[201] James Hall. 1828. *Letters from the West*. London.

one mile beyond the railroad bridge over the Bonpas Creek. [202] South of the residence of the late George W. Henekin was a family named Cannon, living in a cabin. The Indians tomahawked the whole family except Mrs. Cannon and her daughter; these they made captives and took away. The others, three or four in number, were cruelly butchered and left upon the premises to be devoured by wild beasts or the ravens. The rangers from Big Prairie settlement went up and buried the remains of all in one grave. A large cottonwood tree sprang up as a monument to that grave, and stood until a few year ago, when some person cut it down.[203]

Indians raid north of New Haven – 1814

Again, while some men from the settlement above New Haven were engaged in shelling corn one dark night in a cabin that stood 200 yards east of Uncle Sam Potter's house, they were startled by the presentation, through openings in the chimney, of eight or ten guns, which were instantly discharged, killing outright Hezekiah Davis, and mortally wounding a Mr. Seabolt, and breaking Richard Davis' thigh. James B. Davis, a brother of Hezekiah, and son of Richard Davis, sprang into the fire and stamped the burning corn-cobs and put out the only light in the cabin, thus preventing the Indians from taking the second deadly aim. One of the party made his way through the roof of the cabin and leaped to the ground in the midst of the Indians, but Dunlap made good his escape amidst a shower of bullets sent after him by the Indians' rifles. A stampede took place and the Indians fled, taking with them one blind horse out of a lot of seven or eight fine animals. It was the opinion of Richard Davis, that had it not been for the desertion of Dunlap, the whole company would have been massacred; the Indians mistook his maneuver, and beat a hasty retreat. The horses were immediately saddled, and the party, minus Hezekiah Davis, mounted and road to Big Prairie that night. Seabolt was held on his horse by some of the party, but died in a few days from the effect of his wound. Richard Davis' shattered thigh was very painful, and the disabled leg would lap around the saplings as he rode for the stockade at New Haven that night.

An armed burial party was sent up to bury young Davis, and his remains rested in that sepulcher until 1858, when "Uncle Dicky" Davis departed this life, and by his request, his son Hezekiah's bones were buried in the same grave with his father. The occasion was a very solemn one. When the grave was Hezekiah was opened, but slight evidence of the body remained. Some portion of the clothing could be seen, and the pewter buttons that were upon this coat, were in a good state of preservation; and four or five pieces of cut silver coin were found in the grave in the same state of preservation as on that fatal night forty-four years before, when that young man's spirit passed through the valley and shadow of death at the hands of the red men of the forest.[204]

---

[202] Bonpas Creek enters the Wabash River at Grayville near the corners of White, Edwards and Wabash counties.

[203] 1883. *History of White County*. Chicago: Inter-State Publishing Co. 452.

[204] 1883. *History of White County*. Chicago: Inter-State Publishing Co. 452-453.

Indians kill Daniel Boultinghouse's son – 1814

A son of Daniel Boultinghouse was killed and scalped by the Indians about the same time of the Cannon massacre, while herding hogs some three or four miles southwest of Albion, near Boultinghouse prairie.[205]

Attack on Brown's Blockhouse – 1815

Stories have been handed down of two attacks at the Coleman Brown blockhouse. One, when the barking of the dogs kept for protection, apparently frightened the attackers away, leaving their foot-prints in the frost to be found the next morning. The second occasion for alarm came while the men were in the dense forest trying to recover their horses that had strayed too far from the settlement. The men heard the click of the rifles and actually saw the Indians moving through the woods. They decided it would be better to run for safety than to fight, since they had no way to estimate the number the size of the band of attackers. Coleman Brown, his brother, and others built this house in the spring of 1815, even though his land was not entered land until January 1, 1816.[206]

Attack on the Pond Settlement – 1817

About 1815 a man named John Pond opened a clearing in what is now Indian Creek Township [White County]. In a few years[207] he had neighbors and the community was called the "Pond Settlement." One day in October, Pond was called away from home to help some newcomer raise a cabin. He left his wife and two little boys at home and was absent all day. On returning at night he found his wife killed and scalped in the cabin, and his two little boys scalped and lying the corner made by the old-fashioned stick-and-mud chimney joining the cabin wall. All three were lying in pools of blood which had poured form their ghastly wounds. Pond lost no time in calling on his neighbors, and before midnight a pursuing party of vengeance was formed. It was learned that three Indians of the Pe-anke-shaw tribe had been skulking about the settlement; and as this tribe was then living out in the western part of the State, in the vicinity of the Okaw (Kaskaskia) River and Big Muddy Creek, the chased promised to be a long one.

Three men — Pond, Hosea Pearce and Trousdale — were the party of men who proposed to have retribution. They were well mounted while the Indians were on foot. From indications it appeared that the killing had been done in the morning; and as this pursuing party could not start until the following marooning, the Indians had twenty hours start. The trail was found by noticing the disturbed condition of the wild pea-vines in the little prairie westward. With eager heart and piercing eye the men pushed forward. The woods in those

---

[205] 1883. *History of White County*. Chicago: Inter-State Publishing Co. 453.

[206] Talitha E. Aaron. 1947. "Early Settlements in Saline County." *History of Saline County: A Century of History, 1847-1947*. Harrisburg, Ill.: Saline County Historical Society. 59-60.

[207] Although the author gives the month, no exact year is given but a "few years" after 1815. One of the players in this account, Hosea Pearce didn't move to the region until 1817, providing the earliest date of October 1817.

days were open underneath; there being but little underbrush, and the pursers soon reached the Okaw. On the prairies the grass grew high, and a fugitive could be easily followed through them.

Not, however, until the fourth day did the party discover "fresh sign." The next morning at sunrise they found in the Okaw Bottom three Indians making their breakfast off a wild turkey. Each white man picked out his Indian, and fired at him. One of the guns missed fire; two Indians fell dead. They hunted for the other Indian all day, but failed to find him, as he made for the river and they lost his track. The white party therefore had to return to their homes with their vengeance but partially satisfied.

A few years later the white population around Mr. Pond became too dense for him, and he moved farther west. The incident of the massacre and the pursuit faded away from the memories of the old settlers, amid the bustle of the incoming civilization. But years afterward still, when one of the actors in the foregoing scene, Hosea Pearce, had become an old man, he, too, felt that the country was becoming too thickly settled for his comfort, and emigrated to Western Missouri, where lands were cheap, of which he could obtain a plenty for the "boys." One of Trousdale's sons was with him. These two were away from home one day, and at night stopped at the house of a middle-aged man, living on a fine and well-furnished farm. After supper, in the course of conversation, the host ascertained the county where Pearce formerly lived.

"Do you know any one in the Pond Settlement?" inquired the host.

"Why, that is right where I lived," required Pearce.

"Did you ever know John Pond?"

"Yes, sir."

This started Pearce to talking, and told all about Pond and the killing of his wife and boys, the pursuit, etc. Pearce was an interesting narrator, and he told the story as vividly as the facts would allow. Then the man said; "Well, stranger, I reckon that story is about as true as any you ever told." And as he said this is about as true as any you ever told." And as he said this he stepped to the high mantelshelf on which stood a clock; this he opened and took out a little parcel wrapped in whitish paper that showed the marks of age and much careful handling. While he was doing this Pearce was getting mad at the doubt thrown on this veracity by the words of the man, who, as he stood slowly opening the little parcel and noticing the change in Pearce's countenance, said: "Now don't get excited at what I said. I only meant it to prove what I am going to show you is true."

By this time he had taken from the paper a little tuft of flaxen hair which seemed to be grown from a piece of skin the size of a dollar. As he held it up he said. "Here is the scalp of one of John Pond's boys;" and bowing down his head and parting the hair from the crown, revealing a shining bald scar, and placing his finger on the spot, he added, "and there is where it came from!"

Old Hosea had forgotten that while both boys had been scalped only one was killed, although both were left for dead. He had forgotten, too, that among the trophies of the dead Indians the things most highly prized by Pond were his boys' scalps, which he recovered.[208]

---

[208] 1883. *The History of White County, Illinois.* Chicago: Inter-State Publishing Co. 293-295.

Black Hawk War

At least four companies of soldiers organized in Gallatin County for the two summers of fighting during the Black Hawk War of 1831 and 1832.

First Brigade (Staff)

General
Posey, Alexander

Orderly
Wood, John

Quartermasters
Jones, James M.
McClelland, John
Rawlings, Marshall

Paymaster
Wallace, William

Wagoner
Hargrave, Lee

First Regiment/First Brigade (Staff)

Colonel
Hargrave, Willis

Lt. Colonel
Gatewood, William J.

Major
Hampton, James

Quartermasters
Dunn, James
Hardin, Benjamin

Surgeons
Dunn, Tarlton
Jameson, William H.

Paymaster
Jones, Edward

Adjutant
Reed, Lewis

Sgt. Major
Ritchey, Robert

James Caldwell's Co., First Regiment, First Brigade

Captain
Caldwell, James
Holliday, Joel

1st Lieutenants
Cook, Turner

2nd Lieutenant
Dean, John J.

Sergeants
Dewel, Robert R.
Hubbs, Bani
Kinsall, Benjamin
Right, Linzey
Swearengin, Thomas V.

Corporals
Hubbs, Beni
Kinsall, David

Newman, John
Puckett, E. B.

Privates
Adams, J.
Barker, Jessee G.
Barker, William
Bish, George
Bozarth, David
Braddley, Joshua
Brooks, Samuel West
Brown, Adonijah
Brown, James
Burris, Thomas
Clayton, William
Cressap, James
Cusack, James
Dake, Arnold B.
Dawson, John
Edwards, Philip

Fouch, John
Fouch, Levi
Harlston, William
Haskins, James R.
Hays, Solomon
Heraldson, William
Herod, John W.
Hughston, Jonathan
Hutchcraft, Elijah
Johnson, James B.
Jones, Jonathan
Keeny, Jonathan
Lafferty, William
Luther, Ezra G.
Morrow, Forquer
Morrow, Thomas
Nelson, Stephen
Newman, John
Patilloe, Alexander
Powel, Thomas

Quigly, Aaron
Rawls, Nathaniel
Reynolds, Joseph L.
Sampson, William
Samson, William
Sherwood, Hugh B.
Sherwood, Thomas
Shoemaker, William
Smith, Peter
Stiff, Richard
Tally, Amos
Thompson, Matthew
Trousdale, James
Vinson, Charles
Westbrooks, Samuel
Williams, Henry B.
Williams, James
Wood, Mason

J. Hampton's Co., First Regiment, First Brigade

Captain
Coffey, Archilaus

1st Lieutenants
Botright, Daniel

2nd Lieutenant
Stricklin, Willis

Sergeants
Aden, Varner
Chossier, William
Garner, John
Karns, Samuel

Corporals
Gazaway, Hamilton

Grable, David A.
Rhyon, John
Roberts, Wiley

Privates
Abner, Henry
Alshear, Anderson
Barger, Isaac
Bond, George
Bond, Stephen
Carder, James K.
Carney, David
Cox, John
Coy, John
Fletcher, Wesley
Garret, William
Hall, Johnathan

Hawkins, James
Hawse, Peter
Hedge, James
Isom, Richard
Karnes, James
Karns, George
Karns, John
Lewis, Abraham
Martin, Jason
Medling, Nedum
Morris, Richmond
Oldham, Thomas
Pogue, James
Prier, Anderson
Rhyon, William
Richey, John P.
Smith, John

Smith, John H.
Spruel, Pleasant
Strickland, Henry
Strickland, William
Tongue, Thomas
Upchurch, John
Upchurch, Johnathan
Upchurch, Thomas
Ware, Robert
Whiteside, Thomas

A. Coffey's Company
Corporal
Gasway, Hamilton

Private
Kearny, David

David Russell's Co., First Regiment, First Brigade

Captain
Russell, David B.

1st Lieutenants
Pankey, William

2nd Lieutenant
Vinson, Edward

Sergeants
Henderson, Claiborne
Keath, George P.
Mitchell, Stephen F.
Pickering, Thomas

Corporals
Cook, Jourdan
Dodds, Thomas
Hampton, Edward
Mitchel, Robert

Bugler
Hall, Jesse

Privates
Abney, Matthew
Blackman, Josiah
Burchum, Joseph
Cook, Cullen
Cotner, Duncan
Covington, John

Duncan, Thomas
Dunn, Isham
Dunn, Squire
Fleming, Zachariah
Gaskins, William H.
Griffin, James S.
Griffin, John
Gulley, Thomas
Hall, John
Hampton, David
Harris, Aulsey
Harris, Gillam
Hide, William
Hill, Allen
Holland, James
Holms, Jacob

Hope, James
Howell, John
Howell, Riley
Hutchison, William G.
Ingram, Timothy
Johnston, John J.
Pierson, Henry
Robinson, Mark
Rood, Harvey
Russell, John
Shoat, Levi
Smothers, John
Stanley, Thomas
Stiff, Lewis
Waggoner, John
Wise, William

J. Watkins's Co., First Regiment, First Brigade

Captain
Bays, John

1st Lieutenants
Robertson, William

2nd Lieutenant
Wood, Daniel

Sergeants
Brown, John T.
Davenport, Adran H.
Dawson, John
McCloud, Sollomon

Corporals
Green, Reuben
Petigrew, Isaiah W.
Smothers, Thomas
Woods, John

Privates
Baker, Edmon
Bays, David, Jr.
Briant, John B.
Bridges, James
Bridges, Thomas L.
Brown, Daniel

Brown, Samuel
Cummons, William M.
Elder, John
Garner, Garret
Giles, William
Hamons, William
Hargraves, Carter
Hargraves, Willis, Jr.
Henderson, Benjamin
Hutson, John
Johnson, William
Kenrick, James
Levil, Lewis
McCaslin, James B.

Mundine, Thomas J.
Niswonger, Jefferson
Pruit, James
Reed, Green
Robinnet, John
Sands, John
Tadlock, Green
Thorn, Alexander
Vaughn, Thomas
Williams, Ebenezer
Wrinkle, George

Harrison Wilson's Co., First Regiment, First Brigade

Captain	Hood, Charles	Barger, Richard A. S.	Huston, Even
Wilson, Harrison	Sidle, Robert	Burnet, Hirun	Jacobs, Page
		Caldwell, John	Jones, Fawntainee W.
1st Lieutenants	*Corporals*	Clack, John T	Kirkindol, Robert
Logston, John	Coffee, Horatio	Coop, William	Logston, Joseph
	Crabtree, Isaac	Cox, William	Peeples, James C.
2nd Lieutenant	Keaton, William	Davis, Francis	Pool, Orvel
Willis, John	Talton, Richard	Davis, James M.	Scrogins, Bartin
		Ellis, William	Taylor, Washington
Sergeants	*Privates*	Giberson, William	Wadle, Andrew
Alexander, Mastin	Alexander, Rheubin	Hogin, Richard	Willis, Jacob
Brown, Solaman	Baker, James	Holey, Henry	

Mexican War

Company G, Third Illinois Infantry

The soldiers of Company G, Third Illinois Infantry Regiment, elected Michael K. Lawler captain on June 6, 1846. Gov. Thomas Ford signed off on the rank two weeks later on June 17. By July 4, the Gallatin County soldiers had arrived at the rendezvous point at Alton and were mustered into service on July 8. The Third Regiment left Alton on the steamers *Glencoe* and *John Aull* bound for New Orleans on July 22. Gen. James Shields commanded the Third. Arriving in New Orleans the troops learned that the both the Third and Fourth Illinois Regiments would be transferred to join Gen. Zachary Taylor on the Rio Grande. The troops traveled by steamer to Point Isabel, Texas. The Third ended up encamping close to the town of Matamoras on the banks of the Rio Grande.

On March 19, 1847, the Third finally marched to battle, taking up positions one mile outside the wall of Vera Cruz, Mexico. After the fall of Vera Cruz, the Third remained there until April 9, when the army began its march on Mexico City. Before they arrived, the battle of Cerro Gordo began on April 17. Two days later the troops began their march to Jalapa. By this time, the end of the soldiers' 12-month enlistment could be felt on the horizon. On May 4, Gen. Winfield Scott ordered the Illinois troops back to Vera Cruz. The Third began their return trip two days later on May 6. The Third officially discharged on May 21, 1847 in New Orleans. Out of an original 905 men, only 450 mustered out. Some 140 had died because of disease or battle (mostly disease), and 399 had been discharged due to illness.

Headquarters Company, 3rd Ill. Inf. Reg.

Colonel	*Major*	*Sergeant Major*	*Assistant Surgeon*
F. Forman	Marshall, Samuel D.	Hamilton, Henry	Turney, D.
Lt. Colonel	*Adjutants*	*Surgeons*	*Quartermaster*
Willey, W. W.	Everett, C., Jr.	O'Niel, J.	*Sergeant*
	Stapp, J. T. B.	Mahan, J.	Willbanks, J.

Assistant Quartermaster
Parker, Nathaniel

A.A.S.U.
Burch, J.

A.C.S.
Bradford, J. S.

Campbell, J. M.
Hackleton, S.

Principal Musicians
Caton, W. W.

Lamburth, James
Mapes, Thomas
Wiley, A.

Company G, 3rd Ill. Inf. Reg.

Captain
Lawler, Michael K.

1st Lieutenants
Pool, Alexander W.
Proctor, Samuel. S. M.

2nd Lieutenants
Rearden, James S.
Sticklin, William

1st Sergeant
Roberts, Hanson Q.

Sergeants
Eddy, Safford B.
Howard, John
Ingram, Timothy
Karnes, Alfred
Scully, Patrick

Corporals
Boyd, Robert A.
Jones, Edward
Sketoe, Isaac M.
Weed, George M.

Musicians
Creed, James

Privates
Addison, Sir Sidney
Baker, David P.
Barnett, David C.
Baugher, John J.
Bennett, Joseph C.
Bennett, Thomas I.
Bond, William
Bramlet, Alfred J.
Brazier, Riley
Cain, James M.
Carpenter, William
Choisser, Attallas
Choisser, Edmund
Creed, Robert
Crenshaw, Abraham
Cummings, Jacob
Davenport, William
Davis, John B. M.
Daws, Edmund
Donovon, James
Duncan, Stephen
Emory, Jacob
Evans, William G.

Fugate, John M.
Gaston, Wesley W.
Grayson, Jesse F.
Griggs, Hubbard A.
Hamilton, James
Hardin, Joseph
Harmons, George
Henrick, Americus
Hill, James
Holt, William
Hubbs, James
Hudgins, James
Ingram, John W.
Jones, John W.
Karnes, David B.
Lewis, Charles
Lowrey, Charles
Lynch, Logan
Mann, John
McCauslin, John
McChiskey, Hiram
Moody, John
Moore, Ransom
Oxberry, James
Page, William W.
Paisley, Joseph P.
Parker, John

Porter, Robert W.
Powell, John
Price, Berry
Proctor, Giles
Reid, Johnson
Reynolds, Thomas
Scarborough, John
Sisk, Albert
Sisk, Benjamin
Sitles, Henry
Skelton, William J.
Slavens, A. Calvin
Smith, John
Smith, William T.
Sneed, Eldridge
Stiff, Nathaniel
Stricklin, J. Garner
Taylor, Henry
Vinson, Stokely
Wamack, Shepherd F.
Warren, Charles M. C.
Weaver, Stokeley
Weddle, Andrew
Weddle, William
Williams, John
Williams, William G.

Marmaluke Legion

After being mustered out in 1847, Lawler traveled to Washington before returning to Gallatin County. Once back home he raised a new independent company of mounted troops known as the "Marmaluke Legion," and officially as the Third Independent Company of Illinois Mounted Volunteers. Gov. Augustus C. French commissioned Lawler captain of the company on Aug. 13, 1847. Of the 114 officers and men in this company of dragoons, only two veterans of Company G, joined up with Lawler: 2nd Lt. Samuel L. M. Proctor and Private Abraham Crenshaw, a first cousin to Lawler's wife.

Lawler's company traveled by river again and boarded the steamers *Fashion* and *Major Tompkins* at Baton Rouge and proceeded to Vera Cruz. Upon arriving in Mexico, Lawler's company engaged in scouting duty for the Department of Tampico with the mission of harassing the Mexican guerillas and keeping open the road from the Gulf of Mexico to Mexico City. Sometime prior to Dec. 10, 1847, Lawler's men skirmished with Mexican cavalry at Horcasitas. Lawler's company continued their activity for most of 1848, not returning home until the fall. Part of the company arrived at Cairo by Oct. 5. Others followed. The company officially mustered out at Shawneetown later in October. Thirteen of the men died in Mexico. [209]

Roster – 3rd Ind. Co. of Illinois Volunteers

Captain
Lawler, Michael K.

1st Lieutenant
Clark, Walter S.

2nd Lieutenants
Proctor, Samuel L. M.
Ridgway, John G.

Sergeants
Cadle, John
Lockhart, Theodore L.
Peeples, Robert M.
Sloo, Howell
Umsnider, Elias
White, George F.

Corporals
Mitchell, John C.
Powell, Thomas J.
Proctor, Samuel H. T.
Stone, Lorenzo W.

Buglers
Cockran, Sanford
Gatewood, William J.

Ferriers
Crandle, Benedict

Privates
Baker, William
Becraft, John
Berry, Charles
Boyer, William L
Bozman, Phineas
Bramlet, Sanford
Bruce, James
Buckner, Edwin
Burrel, Mars
Burrel, William
Burrell, John
Calicoat, John
Campbell, Chalon G.
Catt, Levi B.
Catt, Pilate S.
Caughman, Charles J.
Caughman, John
Cayton: William W.
Chapman, Isaac
Christian, Rufus
Clark, Josiah
Conyers, Isaac
Crenshaw, Abraham
Crissup, Thomas
Davis, James B.
Dorsey, William
Eastman, Jacob I.
Eaton, William H.
Ensminger, Stephen
Eubanks, George W.
Fowler: James
Gaston, John
Gaston, Robert
Gates, William
Gillerson, Patterson H.
Greathouse, Tevis
Greer, Peyton
Hair, James
Harget, William
Hargrave, Thomas
Henso, Elijah
Hill, Edward
Hill, Morris
Hood, James
Hood, William
Hudgins: Ambrose
Hudson, Sanford
Hughes, Alexander
Hughes, Cephas G.
Hughes, Champ T.
Hughes, George
Jameson, John D.
Jones, Richard M.
Jones, William H.
Kennedy, Daniel
Leavell, Benjamin
Linderman, Isaac
Lynchm John Q. A.
Mahoney, Cornelius
McCarty, Charles
McClusky, Daniel
Miller, John W.
Morris, Robison B.
O'Neil, Peter
Overbee, John
Pelham, John
Pennell, Willis Y.
Perrym Washington
Pillow, Parker B.
Pipe, Thomas
Pool, Thomas
Rawson, Thomas
Rearden, Henry T.
Reeves, Jeremiah H.
Renwick, John G.
Reynolds, Isaac
Reynolds, Thomas
Ritchey, Francis P.
Roark, David H.
Robison, John
Sharp, Holmes
Shirley, Nimrod
Sinks, Zachariah
Spivey, Lindley M.
Stickney, George W.
Sumpter, William
Trimble, John
Turner, John
Vaughn, Thomas B.
Walters, William
Watts, Lewis F.
Webb, Asa B.
White, Benjamin F.
White, Joseph
Wolf, Stephen
Wright, Alanson G.
Wright, Robert

---

[209] Jane W. Crichton. 1965. *Michael Kelly Lawler: A Southern Illinois Mexican War Captain and Civil War General*. Master's Thesis. SIU-Carbondale.

Civil War

New Haven and the War – 1861

On the 12th day of April, 1861, the Southern leaders, who had long threatened to secede from the Union, ordered the bombardment of Fort Sumter. The excitement in New Haven, as elsewhere, was intense. Although the citizens of New Haven, as well as those throughout Gallatin and White counties, were descendants of Southern families, "Southern" in customs and sympathies, and also warm Democrats, and who had been accused of sympathizing with the Southern cause of State rights, etc., nearly every able-bodied man sought enlistment. It is said this portion of the North — these two counties — furnished the largest number of volunteers, for the population, of any section in the North. The question was not, "Who will go?" but, "Who will be allowed to go?" In a surprisingly short time full companies were raised, mustered into service, and hurried to the front.

Company D, of the Twenty-ninth, was mustered into service Aug. 14, 1861, Lieutenants Hart and Stone. This was raised inside of one week's time. The Seventh Illinois Cavalry, Company G, was sworn in Sept. 7. This company was commanded by Captain Trafton, a brave and efficient officer. The Lieutenants were Hardin and Styles. In 1862 Company E, of the One Hundred and Thirty-first Infantry, was organized by J. L. Purvis with Lieutenants Haley and Pate. Purvis was afterward elected Major.[210] There were also men who enlisted in the Fifty-sixth and Eight-seventh Infantries, and Sixth and Fourteenth Cavalries. Others enlisted in Indiana regiments.[211]

Gallatin County Cavalry – 1861

[On July 9, 1861, the Gallatin County Cavalry mustered in as Company B of the First Illinois Cavalry with James Foster, a southerner, elected captain.]

The First Cavalry was organized — that is, seven companies, A, B, C, D, E, F, and G — at Alton, in 1861, and was mustered into the United States service July 3. Companies I, H and K, were not mustered in with the Regiment, nor did they operate in the field as a part of the Regiment proper.

From Alton the Regiment moved to St. Charles, Mo., where Colonel U. S. Grant was then in command. After remaining at this point a few days drilling, and receiving arms and uniforms, the Regiment moved in a westerly direction until it arrived at Jefferson City; remained there but a few days; from thence it moved to Mexico; from Mexico to Hannibal; and from Hannibal to Lexington. While on the way to Lexington, Company C, commanded by Captain Mitchell, encountered a rebel force, under command of Colonel McGoffin, at Georgetown, in which the command lost 1 man killed and 4 wounded: Captain Mitchell was

---

[210] Here are the full names of the officers mentioned: Lt. James B. Hart (later promoted to captain), Lt. Eberlee P. H. Stone (later promoted to captain), Capt. George W. Trafton; 1st Lt. Richard Hardin; Lt. William H. Stiles (later promoted to captain), Maj. Joseph L. Purvis, Lt. Cornelius W. Halley (later promoted to captain) and either Lt. Amster B. Pate or Lt. Philip A. Pate, both of whom served as first lieutenant in Company E, 131st Ill. Inf.

[211] 1883. *History of White County*. Chicago: Inter-Ocean Publishing Co. 943.

among the latter. The rebels retreated but Colonel McGoffin was captured and held as a prisoner of war until after the battle of Lexington.

The Battle of Lexington was the principal engagement in which the Regiment took part though it was ever on the alert and did much scouting and valuable service in various ways.

At Lexington the Regiment was joined by the Irish Brigade, under command of Colonel James Mulligan, and a small body of Missouri home guards.

The battle of Lexington really commenced on Monday, September 11, at which time an advance force of 3,000 men under General Harris advanced upon the place. The First Cavalry and the 13th Missouri were ordered out to meet them. A decisive action occurred which resulted in considerable loss to the Confederacy. After this there was little of moment until the 18th, each party anxiously watching the re-enforcements and Colonel Mulligan making his position as strong as possible.

Colonel Mulligan met the attack of the enemy with undaunted bravery and almost overwhelmed with a greatly superior force it was only after 52 hours of hard and uninterrupted fighting he surrendered the place. Colonel Mulligan's force all told, numbered less than 2,500 men while that of the enemy was 10,000 or more. The surrender took place on the 20th of September.

The officers were put on parole while the privates were given their choice of taking an oath to not again take up arms until they were exchanged or to remain prisoners of war. They chose to take the oath and they were escorted to the railroad where they took passage for Quincy and from thence to St. Louis, where they remained until they were joined by the officers of the Regiment a week later.[212]

The Regiment was paid off at St. Louis about the last of September, and returned to their homes to await an exchange. In November, however, the Governor having failed to affect an exchange of the non-commissioned officers and privates, ordered them to Springfield and discharged them.[213]

The commissioned officers were exchanged in December, and were ordered to re-organize the regiment and it was also ordered that such of the non-commissioned officers and privates as wished might return with their respective companies and draw pay as if they had remained continuously in the service, and to complete the re-organization by the enlistment of recruits. With this understanding the Regiment was re-organized at Benton Barracks in June 1862. Quite a number of the non-commissioned officers and privates of the original organization returned to their respective companies.

The Regiment remained at Benton Barracks a month or more when it was moved westward and was engaged for a time in guarding supply trains and supply depots at Rolla, Houston, Westplains and other places.

In the re-organization of the regiment there were one or two vacancies in nearly if not all the companies; some of the officers having been promoted or assigned to other regiments while others had resigned.

---

[212] This included Capt. James Foster, a son-in-law of John Hart Crenshaw of the Old Slave House fame. On Oct. 9, 1863, voters in Equality Township elected Foster as a township school trustee.

[213] Around 43 members of Company B., the former Gallatin County Cavalry were among these paroled prisoners discharged. On Monday, Nov. 4, 1861, Capt. Foster and his company left Shawneetown for Springfield, where the entire company could be paid off and the paroled members discharged.

In attempting to fill these vacancies a great dissatisfaction ensued throughout the entire Regiment which culminated in an order from the war department disbanding and mustering out of service the officers and men, which took place at Benton Barracks July 14, 1862.[214]

USS Conestoga heads to Shawneetown – 1861

On Oct. 24, 1861, the *U.S.S. Conestoga* and 300 infantry, on orders from Evansville steamed up the Ohio River, from Paducah to below Shawneetown, to intercept 70 "Knights of the Golden Circle" reported to be leaving Illinois to join Confederate army. The boat and troops were back to Paducah by early Oct. 25.[215]

'Aunt Lizzie' Aiken at Shawneetown – 1861

In 1861 Mrs. [Eliza N. (Atherton)] Aiken was fired with the spirit of her revolutionary sires and offered her services as nurse to Major Niglas, head surgeon of the Sixth Illinois Cavalry, and also known throughout the state as "Gov. Yates" Legion."

In November, 1861, the regiment was ordered to Shawneetown and Mrs. Aiken accompanied it. Here "Aunt Lizzie" won her sobriquet. As she passed from cot to cot ministering to the comfort of the suffering soldiers, one of the patients asked Major Niglas:

"What shall we call this kind woman?"

"You may call her Aunt Lizzie," answered the surgeon. She was never known by any other name during the entire war.

The winter of 1861 was severe, and accommodations for the soldiers inadequate, giving the nurses, two in number, plenty of work. The number of patients ranged from twenty to eighty every day, and the heroic women worked day and night each taking charge of the hospital for six-hour watches. In January, 1862, "Aunt Lizzie" wrote to a friend as follows:

> "Quite a little incident took place yesterday; we, as nurses, were sworn into the United States service. Dr. Niglas tells me I have saved the lives of more than 400 men. I am afraid I hardly deserve the compliment. General Grant, General Sturgis and General Sherman paid us a visit. All join in saying that we excel all other hospitals in being attentive to our sick and in cleanliness. They suggested my going to Cairo. Dr. Niglas spurned the proposition, and I did too. I cannot tell you how well this work suits this restless heart of mine; my great desire to do something to benefit my fellow creatures is gratified in my present occupation."

Would you know more of the experiences of Aunt Lizzie in the Army? Ask the patriots of 1861 and 1865. They will tell you in broken sentences as they lay upon their cots in the hospitals of Memphis or Paducah, of the tender care that saved their lives or of the pleading prayer that saved their souls. Aunt Lizzie has always been an honored guest and speaker at all of the G. A. R. encampments which she has attended.[216]

---

[214] First Illinois Cavalry Regiment History. Adjutant-General's Report. State of Illinois.
[215] *Official Records of the War of Rebellion, Naval.* I. 378.
[216] Excerpted from a 1906 memorial for Mrs. Aiken. Online at "Aunt Lizzie Aiken of Peoria."

Confederates raid Saline Landing area – 1861

[On or about Nov. 7, 1861] "Secessionists" from Union County charged with crossing the Ohio to the Mouth of the Saline River, killing cattle they find there and removing same in skiffs back to Kentucky. Col. Kirkman at Shawneetown to send some men to watch for them.[217]

Confederates threaten Shawneetown – 1864

In late April, guerrillas on the Kentucky shore, both above and below Shawneetown, fired on two boats. Mayor Hunter of Shawneetown called by letter (on the 23rd) upon Porter for aid, stating the guerrillas threatened to cross the river and destroy the town. The Shawneetown Committee included Aaron B. Stout, D. W. Lusk, J. McKee Peeples and F. LeRhodes.[218]

Johnson Raids near Shawneetown – 1864

On August 13, Col. Adam "Stove-Pipe" Johnson, commanding Confederate guerrillas, crossed the Ohio River below Shawneetown at Saline Bar (just above the mouth of the Saline River), attacked three stranded steamers, and destroyed their cargoes. One steamer got away. The other two he captured and ransomed. As a major part of the foraging raid he took the cattle from all three, which the soldiers swam across to the Kentucky shore.

The Shawneetown Artillery arrived and at least attempted to halt Johnson's effort to cross the river. About 100 Home Guards gathered at the Mouth of the Saline and fired across at the Confederates who were well out of range. At some point, Johnson crossed at least 100 men at the mouth (though reports claim 700 to 1,500 men).

Over the next two days through the 15th, he continued to attack steamboats from the riverbank near Curlew Mines and maintained a pseudo blockade of the river. On the 15th he reported, "We have captured and secured 28,000 pounds of bacon, 37,000 bushels of corn, 18,000 bushels of oats, 830 fat cattle, 43 boxes of army clothing and seven transports with supplies."

The following steamboats are the ones supposedly involved in Johnson's raid: *Kate Robison* (lost cargo of cattle,) *Arcola* (dumped cargo of cattle and escaped), *Clara Poe* (dumped cargo and cattle and escaped, losing barge), *Cottage* (boarded and searched then released), *Charmer* (presumed captured), *Carrie* (presumed captured), and the *Gem*, (presumed captured).

Johnson's forces consisted of Sypert's and Chenoweth's regiments as well as part of the 10th Kentucky Cavalry under the command of Lt. Col. Napier.[219]

---

http://www.alliancelibrarysystem.com/Projects/IllinoisWomen/files/pe/htm1/aiken.htm.

[217] Nov. 7, 1861. *Shawneetown Weekly Mercury.*

[218] *Official Records of the War of Rebellion, Naval.* I. 26: 265, 272

[219] *Official Records of the War of Rebellion.* I 39/1, 462. Johnson. *The Partisan Rangers of the Confederate States Army: Memoirs of Adam R. Johnson.* 170. Ellis. 9; *Evansville Daily Journal.* Aug. 15, 16, 1864; and George

Troops Arrest Shawneetown Editor – 1864

Immediately following Johnson's raid, around Aug. 16, 1864, an undercover Federal detective posing as an escaped Confederate officer duped James G. Blewett, editor of the *Gallatin County Democrat* at Shawneetown into joining either the Order of American Knights or the Sons of Liberty. On Aug. 23, 1864, or thereabouts, Gen. Paine at Cairo ordered Blewett and two others arrested on charges of disloyalty and taken to Paducah and held in a guardhouse. Blewett had formerly served as an officer in the 8th Kentucky Cavalry and came to Shawneetown six months earlier to start a paper.[220]

Gallatin County Soldiers in the Civil War

Compiled from the Illinois Civil War Veterans Database published by the Illinois State Archives. This is the only section of this book whose names have not been included in the index. This only includes Illinois soldiers in Illinois units and may have missed any recruits into Indiana or Kentucky units as well as any Gallatin County men who may have fought for the Confederacy.

Name	Rank	Co.	Unit	Residence
Aarons, George W.	Private	H	120th Ill. Inf.	Gallatin County
Abbott, Francis M.	Private	K	131st Ill. Inf.	Gallatin County
Abbott, Sterling H.	Private	L	6th Ill. Cav.	Shawneetown
Ackelson, Ebenezer	Private	F	28th Ill. Inf.	New Market
Ackelson, Jacob	Private	F	28th Ill. Inf.	New Market
Adams, Alexander	Private	G	7th Ill. Cav.	New Haven
Adams, James	Sergeant	L	6th Ill. Cav.	Shawneetown
Adams, John D.	Private	D	56th Ill. Inf.	Gallatin County
Adams, Stephen	Private	G	7th Ill. Cav.	New Haven
Adams, Taylor	Private	E	14th Ill. Cav.	Gallatin County
Adams, William	Recruit	I	118th Ill. Inf.	Shawneetown
Adams, William D.	Private	I	118th Ill. Inf.	Shawneetown
Adcock, John	Private	B	1st Ill. Cav.	Equality
Akens, Henry F.	Private	D	56th Ill. Inf.	Gallatin County
Akens, Henry F.	Recruit	K	56th Ill. Inf.	Gallatin County
Akin, William J.	Recruit	G	29th Ill. Inf.	Equality
Albert, Robert B.	Private	L	6th Ill. Cav.	Shawneetown
Aldridge, George D.	Recruit	G	7th Ill. Cav.	New Haven
Alexander, Charles G.	Private	I	118th Ill. Inf.	Shawneetown
Allen, Joseph H.	Private	G	7th Ill. Cav.	New Haven
Allen, Samuel	Private	L	6th Ill. Cav.	Shawneetown
Allyn, Edward R.	Corporal	F	56th Ill. Inf.	Shawneetown
Ambros, Marcus D.	Recruit	D	29th Ill. Inf.	Gallatin County
Ambrose, Dempsey	Corporal	E	131st Ill. Inf.	Gallatin County
Ambrose, Marcus	Private	E	131st Ill. Inf.	Gallatin County
Ambrose, Marcus	Private	B	131st Ill. Inf.	Gallatin County
Anderson, James	Private	D	120th Ill. Inf.	Gallatin County
Anderson, John A.	Private	B	18th Ill. Inf.	Shawneetown
Andrews, John M.	Private	L	6th Ill. Cav.	Shawneetown
Andrews, Presley	Private	B	56th Ill. Inf.	Shawneetown

Ticknor Curtis. [1864-1865]. *The true conditions of American loyalty: a speech delivered by George Ticknor Curtis, before the Democratic union association, March 28th, 1863.* New York. 15.

[220] Aug. 26, 1864. (Springfield) *Illinois State Journal.*

Name	Rank	Co.	Unit	Location
Andrews, William L.	Private	G	56th Ill. Inf.	Shawneetown
Anglow, Timothy	Corporal	B	18th Ill. Inf.	Shawneetown
Anselment, John	Private	B	1st Ill. Cav.	Equality
Appel, Casper	Private	B	1st Ill. Cav.	Equality
Armstrong, Samuel A.	1st Lt.	L	6th Ill. Cav.	Shawneetown
Arnold, Reuben	Private	E	131st Ill. Inf.	Gallatin County
Artman, Henry	Recruit	E	14th Ill. Cav.	Shawneetown
Artman, Henry B.	Corporal	B	1st Ill. Cav.	Equality
Ashton, Perry	Corporal	C	56th Ill. Inf.	Shawneetown
Atchison, James	Private	I	118th Ill. Inf.	Shawneetown
Awalt, Scott	Recruit	E	14th Ill. Cav.	Shawneetown
Ayers, Green	Private	D	56th Ill. Inf.	Gallatin County
Ayres, James	Corporal	D	56th Ill. Inf.	Gallatin County
Bagsley, Samuel	1st Lt.	D	29th Ill. Inf.	New Haven
Bain, Riley W.	Corporal	B	1st Ill. Cav.	Equality
Bain, William H.	Recruit	B	1st Ill. Cav.	Equality
Baker, Benjmain F.	Private	L	6th Ill. Cav.	Shawneetown
Baker, Cornelius	Recruit	B	18th Ill. Inf.	Shawneetown
Baker, William C.	Private	D	120th Ill. Inf.	Gallatin County
Baldwin, Thomas	Private	D	120th Ill. Inf.	Gallatin County
Ballard, Cassius M. C.	Recruit	G	29th Ill. Inf.	Equality
Ballard, Martin H.	Recruit	K	131st Ill. Inf.	Gallatin County
Barnes, Thomas	Private	L	6th Ill. Cav.	Gallatin
Barnes, Thomas P.	Private	L	6th Ill. Cav.	Shawneetown
Barnett, Ezra	Private	F	6th Ill. Cav.	Gallatin County
Barnett, Joseph	Private	F	6th Ill. Cav.	Gallatin County
Barr, John W.	Recruit	E	3rd Ill. Cav.	Shawneetown
Bartel, Augustus	Recruit	E	14th Ill. Cav.	New Market
Bayley, James W.	Recruit	G	29th Ill. Inf.	New Haven
Beam, Jacob W.	Corporal	K	131st Ill. Inf.	Gallatin County
Beam, James M.	Private	K	131st Ill. Inf.	Gallatin County
Beam, Jasper N.	Private	K	131st Ill. Inf.	Gallatin County
Bean, Bryson	Private	H	120th Ill. Inf.	Gallatin County
Bean, General F. M.	Captain	H	120th Ill. Inf.	Gallatin County
Bean, James M.	Private	B	131st Ill. Inf.	Gallatin County
Bean, James M.	Recruit	C	29th Ill. Inf.	Gallatin County
Bean, James W.	Private	H	120th Ill. Inf.	Gallatin County
Bean, Joseph M.	Private	H	120th Ill. Inf.	Gallatin County
Bean, William	Private	B	1st Ill. Cav.	Equality
Bean, William	Private	H	120th Ill. Inf.	Gallatin County
Bean, William C.	Private	H	120th Ill. Inf.	Gallatin County
Beck, William L.	Private	B	1st Ill. Cav.	Equality
Beektold, Edward	Sergeant	B	18th Ill. Inf.	Shawneetown
Behan, John	Private	C	29th Ill. Inf.	Shawneetown
Bell, James M.	Private	D	29th U.S. Col. Inf.	Shawneetown
Bellah, Samuel	Sergeant	B	1st Ill. Cav.	Equality
Bellah, William D.	Private	G	29th Ill. Inf.	Gallatin County
Bennett, James A.	Private	E	131st Ill. Inf.	Gallatin County
Bennett, James A.	Private	B	131st Ill. Inf.	Gallatin County
Bennett, James A.	Recruit	D	29th Ill. Inf.	Gallatin County
Berry, John R.	Recruit	B	18th Ill. Inf.	Shawneetown
Bingamon, Solomon	Private	E	131st Ill. Inf.	Gallatin County
Black, David M.	Private	I	118th Ill. Inf.	Shawneetown
Black, John	Sergeant	I	118th Ill. Inf.	Shawneetown
Black, John	Private	E	131st Ill. Inf.	Gallatin County
Black, William W.	Corporal	G	7th Ill. Cav.	New Haven
Blackard, John L.	Private	H	120th Ill. Inf.	Gallatin County
Blackard, William L.	2nd Lt.	H	120th Ill. Inf.	Gallatin County
Blakemore, Franklin M.	Private	B	1st Ill. Cav.	Equality

Name	Rank	Co.	Unit	Location
Bogarth, Wesley	Corporal	D	29th Ill. Inf.	Gallatin County
Bolden, Stephen J.	Private	D	120th Ill. Inf.	Gallatin County
Boneshong, Henry	Sergeant	B	18th Ill. Inf.	Shawneetown
Bontwell, Lona	Private	E	131st Ill. Inf.	Gallatin County
Bontwell, Lona	Private	B	131st Ill. Inf.	Gallatin County
Boon, Jonathan	Private	E	131st Ill. Inf.	Gallatin County
Border, James D.	Private	B	18th Ill. Inf.	Shawneetown
Boston, John	Private	F	131st Ill. Inf.	Gallatin
Boswell, William	2nd Lt.	C	29th Ill. Inf.	Shawneetown
Bouls, William	Private	I	56th Ill. Inf.	Gallatin County
Boutwell, Lana	Recruit	D	29th Ill. Inf.	Gallatin County
Bowling, John	Private	D	56th Ill. Inf.	Gallatin County
Boyd, George L.	Corporal	D	29th Ill. Inf.	Gallatin County
Boyd, Thompson L.	Private	E	131st Ill. Inf.	Gallatin County
Boyer, Calvin	Private	G	7th Ill. Cav.	New Haven
Boyer, Samuel	Private	G	7th Ill. Cav.	New Haven
Boyle, Thomas	Private	B	1st Ill. Cav.	Equality
Bozarth, David	Corporal	B	1st Ill. Cav.	Equality
Bradley, Harvey	Recruit	E	14th Ill. Cav.	Shawneetown
Bradley, Harvey	Private	I	14th Ill. Cav.	Shawneetown
Bradley, Haughey	Recruit	B	1st Ill. Cav.	Equality
Bradley, Jesse D.	Private	F	28th Ill. Inf.	New Market
Bradley, Robert	Private	B	1st Ill. Cav.	Equality
Bradley, William M.	Private	F	28th Ill. Inf.	New Market
Bradshaw, Moses	Private	E	14th Ill. Cav.	Shawneetown
Bradshaw, Moses	Private	C	29th Ill. Inf.	Shawneetown
Bradway, John E.	Private	K	16th Ill. Cav.	Shawneetown
Bradway, John E.	Private	B	18th Ill. Inf.	Shawneetown
Brady, Willis	Private	F	59 Ill. Inf.	Cottonwood
Bragg, John T.	Private	G	131st Ill. Inf.	Equality
Bragg, John T.	Private	D	131st Ill. Inf.	Equality
Branden, Lemuel M.	Private	H	120th Ill. Inf.	Gallatin County
Brandon, James L.	Private	D	120th Ill. Inf.	Gallatin County
Brannon, Elias H.	Recruit	B	1st Ill. Cav.	Equality
Branon, William	Private	D	120th Ill. Inf.	Gallatin County
Branson, William C.	Private	B	1st Ill. Cav.	Equality
Branston, William Cook	Private	C	56th Ill. Inf.	Equality
Brant, William	Private	F	14th Ill. Cav.	Shawneetown
Brasier, Charles	Private	D	120th Ill. Inf.	Gallatin County
Brasier, Edward	Private	D	120th Ill. Inf.	Gallatin County
Brazier, John	Recruit	E	14th Ill. Cav.	Equality
Brazier, John	Private	I	14th Ill. Cav.	Equality
Brewner, John W.	Recruit	E	3rd Ill. Inf.	Shawneetown
Bridges, Daniel S.	Private	K	73rd Ill. Inf.	Gallatin
Brinkley, Henry H.	Recruit	E	14th Ill. Cav.	Shawneetown
Brinkley, Henry H.	Private	I	14th Ill. Cav.	Shawneetown
Brinkley, John	Private	K	131st Ill. Inf.	Gallatin County
Bromley, Charles	Private	C	29th Ill. Inf.	Shawneetown
Bromley, William	Private	C	29th Ill. Inf.	Gallatin County
Brooks, James	Private	L	6th Ill. Cav.	Shawneetown
Broughton, Mason	Private	G	131st Ill. Inf.	Equality
Brown, Edward	Private	K	131st Ill. Inf.	Gallatin County
Brown, Edward	Private	D	29th Ill. Inf.	Gallatin County
Brown, Edward B.	Private	B	131st Ill. Inf.	Gallatin County
Brown, Edward B.	Recruit	E	29th Ill. Inf.	Gallatin County
Brown, Jesse	Private	K	131st Ill. Inf.	Gallatin County
Brown, Oliver C.	Private	G	131st Ill. Inf.	Equality
Brown, Thomas	Recruit	E	29th Ill. Inf.	Gallatin County
Brown, Thomas J.	Private	K	131st Ill. Inf.	Gallatin County

Name	Rank	Co.	Unit	Location
Brown, Thomas J.	Private	B	131st Ill. Inf.	Gallatin County
Brown, W. G. H.	Recruit	B	1st Ill. Cav.	Equality
Brown, William	Farrier	B	1st Ill. Cav.	Equality
Brown, William H.	Private	F	28th Ill. Inf.	New Market
Brown, William J.	Private	K	131st Ill. Inf.	Gallatin County
Brown, William J.	Recruit	E	14th Ill. Cav.	Shawneetown
Browne, Phillip	Private	B	18th Ill. Inf.	Shawneetown
Bruce, Benjamin F.	Private	H	120th Ill. Inf.	Gallatin County
Bruce, George	Corporal	C	29th Ill. Inf.	Shawneetown
Bruce, Robert J.	Private	H	120th Ill. Inf.	Gallatin County
Brumer, William	Private	D	120th Ill. Inf.	Gallatin County
Bryant, William S.	Recruit	E	14th Ill. Cav.	Shawneetown
Burdick, John	Recruit	D	29th Ill. Inf.	Gallatin County
Burdock, John	Private	E	131st Ill. Inf.	Gallatin County
Burdock, John	Private	B	131st Ill. Inf.	Gallatin County
Burdock, Reuben	Private	E	131st Ill. Inf.	Gallatin County
Burnet, Woodson B.	Private	D	29th Ill. Inf.	Gallatin County
Burnett, Richard W.	Private	E	131st Ill. Inf.	Gallatin County
Burns, Joseph M.	Private	C	56th Ill. Inf.	Shawneetown
Burrell, William W.	Wagoner	D	29th Ill. Inf.	Gallatin County
Burris, George	Private	D	56th Ill. Inf.	Gallatin County
Burris, George	Recruit	K	56th Ill. Inf.	Gallatin County
Burroughs, Thomas W. M.	Sergeant	D	120th Ill. Inf.	Shawneetown
Burwittar, Andrew	Recruit	B	18th Ill. Inf.	Shawneetown
Bush, William	Private	B	1st Ill. Cav.	Equality
Bushong, Henry D.	Private	C	18th Ill. Inf. Reorg.	Shawneetown
Bushwan, Augustus H.	Corporal	B	18th Ill. Inf.	Shawneetown
Bushwan, John	Private	B	18th Ill. Inf.	Shawneetown
Butler, Franklin	Private	E	131st Ill. Inf.	Gallatin County
Butler, Franklin	Private	B	131st Ill. Inf.	Gallatin County
Butler, Franklin	Recruit	D	29th Ill. Inf.	Gallatin County
Butler, James	Private	E	131st Ill. Inf.	Gallatin County
Butler, James	Private	B	131st Ill. Inf.	Gallatin County
Butler, James	Recruit	E	29th Ill. Inf.	Equality
Butler, James	Recruit	D	29th Ill. Inf.	Gallatin County
Butler, William S.	Recruit	B	1st Ill. Cav.	Equality
Byrd, George W.	Private	D	120th Ill. Inf.	Gallatin County
Byrd, William	Private	C	29th Ill. Inf.	Gallatin County
Cain, Daniel	Recruit	I	29th Ill. Inf.	Gallatin County
Cain, William J.	Recruit	F	87th Ill. Inf.	Shawneetown
Callcott, John A.	Captain	C	29th Ill. Inf.	Shawneetown
Callicot, Washington C.	Recruit	E	14th Ill. Cav.	Shawneetown
Callicott, John A.	Lt. Colonel	HQ	29th Ill. Inf.	Shawneetown
Callicott, Samuel W.	Private	E	131st Ill. Inf.	Gallatin County
Callicott, Washington C.	Private	I	14th Ill. Cav.	Shawneetown
Cameron, Nathan	Private	B	1st Ill. Cav.	Equality
Campbell, John W.	Recruit	C	56th Ill. Inf.	Gallatin County
Campbell, Josiah	2nd Lt.	E	131st Ill. Inf.	Gallatin County
Cane, Daniel	Private	I	131st Ill. Inf.	Gallatin County
Cane, Daniel	Private	B	131st Ill. Inf.	Gallatin County
Cane, Edward	Recruit	C	29th Ill. Inf.	Gallatin County
Carney, Joseph B.	Private	G	131st Ill. Inf.	Equality
Carney, Joseph B.	Private	D	131st Ill. Inf.	Equality
Carney, Joseph B.	Recruit	G	29th Ill. Inf.	Equality
Carr, John W	Private	B	18th Ill. Inf.	Shawneetown
Carrews, William	Recruit	G	29th Ill. Inf.	Equality
Carson, Charles B.	Private	B	1st Ill. Cav.	Equality
Carson, Charles T.	Private	F	6th Ill. Cav.	Equality
Carson, John	Buglar	F	6th Ill. Cav.	Equality

Carson, Samuel T.	Private	F	6th Ill. Cav.	Gallatin County
Carter, David S.	Private	I	131st Ill. Inf.	Gallatin County
Carter, David S.	Private	B	131st Ill. Inf.	Gallatin County
Carter, David S.	Recruit	F	29th Ill. Inf.	Gallatin County
Carter, Emriah J.	Private	D	120th Ill. Inf.	Gallatin County
Carter, Miles R.	Private	I	131st Ill. Inf.	Gallatin County
Carter, Miles R.	Private	B	131st Ill. Inf.	Gallatin County
Carter, Miles R.	Recruit	I	29th Ill. Inf.	Gallatin County
Carter, Thomas	Private	K	131st Ill. Inf.	Gallatin County
Caruth, Lee	Private	D	29th Ill. Inf.	New Haven
Cash, Benjamin	Private	D	120th Ill. Inf.	Gallatin County
Cash, Robert	Private	C	29th Ill. Inf.	Gallatin County
Catlin, Horace C.	Qmtr. Sgt.	G	7th Ill. Cav.	New Haven
Chaffin, John H.	Recruit	B	1st Ill. Cav.	Equality
Cheek, James W.	Private	I	131st Ill. Inf.	Gallatin County
Church, Benjamin	Private	H	120th Ill. Inf.	Gallatin County
Church, Franklin	Private	I	131st Ill. Inf.	Gallatin County
Clark, Jonathan	Private	D	56th Ill. Inf.	Gallatin County
Clark, Thomas	Private	I	118th Ill. Inf.	Shawneetown
Clarry, Thorndike	Private	C	3rd Ill. Cav.	Shawneetown
Clayton, Thomas	Wagoner	B	1st Ill. Cav.	Equality
Clayton, Thomas	Farrier	E	14th Ill. Cav.	Shawneetown
Cleaveland, Micager	Private	B	131st Ill. Inf.	Gallatin County
Cleghorn, Robert A.	Private	L	6th Ill. Cav.	Gallatin County
Clements, Gustavus A.	Corporal	B	18th Ill. Inf.	Shawneetown
Clifford, John W.	Corporal	D	29th Ill. Inf.	Gallatin County
Clifford, Leonidas H.	Recruit	D	29th Ill. Inf.	New Haven
Clifford, Zelotes S.	Chaplain	HQ	29th Ill. Inf.	New Haven
Cluck, George W.	Recruit	D	6th Ill. Cav.	Shawneetown
Coad, G. W.	Private	B	18th Ill. Inf.	Shawneetown
Coats, Berry	Private	G	7th Ill. Cav.	New Haven
Coats, William	Private	G	131st Ill. Inf.	Equality
Cockerill, Montgomery	Recruit	C	56th Ill. Inf.	Gallatin County
Colbert, Elisha C.	Private	D	120th Ill. Inf.	Gallatin County
Coleman, Bailey	Private	F	56th Ill. Inf.	New Market
Coleman, Isom B.	Recruit	E	14th Ill. Cav.	Shawneetown
Coleman, John	Private	F	56th Ill. Inf.	New Market
Coleman, Patrick	Private	E	14th Ill. Cav.	Shawneetown
Coleman, William S.	Private	D	120th Ill. Inf.	Gallatin County
Collard, Franklin	Private	B	18th Ill. Inf.	Shawneetown
Collins, Andrew	Private	L	6th Ill. Cav.	Shawneetown
Combs, Ephraim	Blacksmith	F	6th Ill. Cav.	Gallatin County
Combs, Trenton	Recruit	E	14th Ill. Cav.	New Market
Combs, Trenton	Private	I	14th Ill. Cav.	New Market
Conse, Sylvester R.	Captain	D	56th Ill. Inf.	Gallatin County
Consley, James	Private	G	131st Ill. Inf.	Equality
Consley, James	Corporal	D	131st Ill. Inf.	Equality
Conslin, James	Recruit	G	29th Ill. Inf.	Equality
Consstable, Benjamin	Private	I	131st Ill. Inf.	Gallatin County
Consstable, Benjamin F.	Recruit	K	131st Ill. Inf.	Gallatin County
Cook, Elijah	Corporal	E	131st Ill. Inf.	Gallatin County
Cope, Thomas	Recruit	K	56th Ill. Inf.	Shawneetown
Corbin, Alfred H.	Recruit		118th Ill. Inf.	Shawneetown
Cosebone, Henry	Private	K	9th Ill. Inf.	Shawneetown
Cover, Henry	Private	C	29th Ill. Inf.	Gallatin County
Cover, Jacob F.	Recruit		14th Ill. Cav.	Shawneetown
Cover, William R.	Recruit	E	14th Ill. Cav.	Shawneetown
Cover, William R.	Private	I	14th Ill. Cav.	Shawneetown
Covey, George	Private	D	56th Ill. Inf.	Gallatin County

Covey, James	Private	D	56th Ill. Inf.	Gallatin County
Covey, James	Recruit	K	56th Ill. Inf.	Gallatin County
Cowen, James	Private	G	7th Ill. Cav.	New Haven
Cowen, Wesley	Private	G	7th Ill. Cav.	New Haven
Cox, Andrew J.	Private	F	56th Ill. Inf.	New Market
Cox, Benjamin	Private	H	120th Ill. Inf.	Gallatin County
Cox, John G.	Private	K	56th Ill. Inf.	Gallatin County
Cox, Jonathan	Private	F	56th Ill. Inf.	New Market
Cox, Joseph N.	Private	H	120th Ill. Inf.	Gallatin County
Crabtree, Jackson	Private	D	120th Ill. Inf.	Gallatin County
Crandle, Benedict	1st Lt.	L	6th Ill. Cav.	Shawneetown
Crandle, Benjamin	Captain	E	14th Ill. Cav.	Shawneetown
Crawford, Alexander Marion	Musician	C	56th Ill. Inf.	Gallatin County
Crawford, Dawson T.	Private	I	131st Ill. Inf.	Gallatin County
Crawford, George N.	Private	K	6th Ill. Cav.	Gallatin County
Crawford, George R.	Corporal	D	29th Ill. Inf.	Gallatin County
Crawford, James R.	Private	I	118th Ill. Inf.	Shawneetown
Crawford, William R.	Private	D	29th Ill. Inf.	Gallatin County
Creek, Abraham	Private	I	131st Ill. Inf.	Gallatin County
Creemeans, Henry	Private	I	146th Ill. Inf.	Shawneetown
Cremeens, Asa	Private	F	6th Ill. Cav.	Gallatin County
Croake, John M.	Recruit	B	54th Ill. Inf.	Cottonwood
Crofford, William	Private	D	56th Ill. Inf.	Gallatin County
Crofford, William	Recruit	F	56th Ill. Inf.	Gallatin County
Cronk, Abraham	Private	E	14th Ill. Cav.	Shawneetown
Crosser, John D.	Recruit	F	56th Ill. Inf.	Gallatin County
Crosser, John F.	Private	D	56th Ill. Inf.	Gallatin County
Crow, Edward B.	Private	G	131st Ill. Inf.	Equality
Crow, Edward B.	Private	D	131st Ill. Inf.	Equality
Crow, Edward B.	Recruit	G	29th Ill. Inf.	Equality
Dailey, Amos	Private	B	1st Ill. Cav.	Equality
Dailey, Henry	Corporal	G	131st Ill. Inf.	Equality
Dailey, Henry	Recruit	G	29th Ill. Inf.	Equality
Dailey, James	Recruit	E	14th Ill. Cav.	Shawneetown
Dailey, James	Private	I	14th Ill. Cav.	Shawneetown
Dailey, John	1st Lt.	G	131st Ill. Inf.	Equality
Dailey, William	Recruit	E	14th Ill. Cav.	Shawneetown
Dailey, William	Private	I	14th Ill. Cav.	Shawneetown
Daily, Daniel	Recruit	K	87th Ill. Inf.	Shawneetown
Daily, Henry	Private	B	1st Ill. Cav.	Equality
Daily, Henry	Private	D	131st Ill. Inf.	Equality
Daily, John	1st Lt.	D	131st Ill. Inf.	Equality
Daily, John	Captain	G	29th Ill. Inf.	Equality
Daimwood, William H.	Musician	HQ	56th Ill. Inf.	Gallatin County
Dairnwood, William H.	Musician	H	56th Ill. Inf.	Gallatin County
Darnel, Robert L.	Private	H	120th Ill. Inf.	Gallatin County
Datton, Andrew J.	Recruit		118th Ill. Inf.	Shawneetown
Davenport, Joseph A.	2nd Lt.	L	6th Ill. Cav.	Shawneetown
Davenport, Thomas	Private	B	1st Ill. Cav.	Equality
Davenport, Thomas	Private	C	56th Ill. Inf.	Equality
Davidson, William	Private	L	6th Ill. Cav.	Gallatin County
Davis, Andrew J.	Private	L	6th Ill. Cav.	Shawneetown
Davis, Benjamin	Recruit	E	14th Ill. Cav.	Equality
Davis, Benjamin	Private	I	14th Ill. Cav.	Shawneetown
Davis, Henry J.	Recruit	E	14th Ill. Cav.	Shawneetown
Davis, Henry J.	Private	I	14th Ill. Cav.	Shawneetown
Davis, John	Corporal	D	120th Ill. Inf.	Gallatin County
Davis, John	Private	E	131st Ill. Inf.	Gallatin County
Davis, John E.	Private	K	131st Ill. Inf.	Gallatin County

Name	Rank	Co.	Unit	Location
Davis, John E.	Corporal	B	131st Ill. Inf.	Gallatin County
Davis, John E.	Recruit	C	29th Ill. Inf.	Gallatin County
Davis, Phelix G.	Private	E	56th Ill. Inf.	Gallatin County
Davis, Spivy D.	Private	D	29th Ill. Inf.	Gallatin County
Davis, William P.	Sergeant	D	29th Ill. Inf.	Gallatin County
Dawsey, Alden	Private	D	56th Ill. Inf.	Gallatin County
Dawsey, Alden	Recruit	K	56th Ill. Inf.	Gallatin County
Dawson, Andrew J.	Private	B	18th Ill. Inf.	Shawneetown
Dawson, William H.	Private	D	29th Ill. Inf.	Gallatin County
Day, John S.	Private	D	29th U.S. Col. Inf.	Shawneetown
Day, Wilson W.	Recruit		118th Ill. Inf.	Shawneetown
Dayton, Green B.	Private	F	6th Ill. Cav.	Gallatin County
Deavers, Michael J.	Recruit	F	56th Ill. Inf.	New Market
Deck, Stinson D.	Private	B	1st Ill. Cav.	Equality
Decker, Asa	Corporal	L	6th Ill. Cav.	Shawneetown
Decrow, Crairy	Recruit	C	6th Ill. Cav.	Shawneetown
Dempsey, Doctor D.	Private	G	131st Ill. Inf.	Equality
Dempsey, Doctor P.	Private	D	131st Ill. Inf.	Equality
Dempsey, Edward M.	Private	G	131st Ill. Inf.	Equality
Dempsey, Edward M.	Private	D	131st Ill. Inf.	Equality
Dempsey, John	Private	D	120th Ill. Inf.	Gallatin County
Dempsey, John D.	Private	G	131st Ill. Inf.	Equality
Dempsey, Thomas	Private	G	131st Ill. Inf.	Equality
Dempsey, William	Private	G	131st Ill. Inf.	Equality
Dempsey, William	Private	D	131st Ill. Inf.	Equality
Dempsey, William	Recruit	G	29th Ill. Inf.	Equality
Denson, James	Private	C	29th Ill. Inf.	Gallatin County
Denson, Leonard	Private	I	6th Ill. Cav.	Shawneetown
Desper, James	Private	C	120th Ill. Inf.	Gallatin County
Desper, James W.	Recruit	D	120th Ill. Inf.	Gallatin County
Detson, Ezekiel	Recruit	D	29th Ill. Inf.	Gallatin County
Deuson, Lewis	Private	I	14th Ill. Cav.	Shawneetown
Deuson, Louis	Recruit	E	14th Ill. Cav.	Shawneetown
Deven, Michael J.	Private	B	1st Ill. Cav.	Equality
Devers, Ezekiel	Musician	F	56th Ill. Inf.	Shawneetown
Devoy, Dennis	Recruit	F	87th Ill. Inf.	Shawneetown
Dewitt, Alfred	2nd Lt.	C	29th Ill. Inf.	Gallatin County
Dickey, James A.	Private	K	131st Ill. Inf.	Gallatin County
Dickey, James A.	Private	B	131st Ill. Inf.	Gallatin County
Dickey, John L.	Private	K	131st Ill. Inf.	Gallatin County
Dickey, John L.	Sergeant	B	131st Ill. Inf.	Gallatin County
Dickey, John L.	Recruit	C	29th Ill. Inf.	Gallatin County
Dickson, James	Recruit	B	1st Ill. Cav.	Equality
Dickson, James	Private	E	131st Ill. Inf.	Gallatin County
Dickson, James W.	Private	B	131st Ill. Inf.	Gallatin County
Dillard, Austin	Private	F	56th Ill. Inf.	New Market
Dillard, Charles	2nd Lt.	K	131st Ill. Inf.	Gallatin County
Dillard, David	Recruit	B	1st Ill. Cav.	Equality
Dillard, David M.	Recruit	H	120th Ill. Inf.	New Market
Dillard, Eli	Private	K	131st Ill. Inf.	Gallatin County
Dillard, Frances M.	Recruit	B	1st Ill. Cav.	Equality
Dillard, Francis M.	Private	D	120th Ill. Inf.	Gallatin County
Dillard, Francis M.	Private	H	120th Ill. Inf.	Gallatin County
Dillard, James M.	Recruit		120th Ill. Inf.	New Market
Dillard, Osborn	Private	K	131st Ill. Inf.	Gallatin County
Dillard, Osborn	Private	B	131st Ill. Inf.	Gallatin County
Dillard, Osborn	Recruit	C	29th Ill. Inf.	Gallatin County
Dillard, Samuel	Private	K	131st Ill. Inf.	Gallatin County
Dillard, Samuel	Private	B	131st Ill. Inf.	Gallatin County

Dillard, Samuel	Recruit	C	29th Ill. Inf.	Gallatin County
Dillard, Stephen B.	Recruit	H	120th Ill. Inf.	New Market
Dillard, Wesley	Corporal	F	56th Ill. Inf.	New Market
Dillinger, Herman F.	1st Lt.	F	56th Ill. Inf.	Shawneetown
Dillon, James	Private	F	6th Ill. Cav.	Gallatin County
Dimm, Ferdinand A.	1st t.	D	101st Ill. Inf.	New Haven
Dobbs, Howel	Private	D	56th Ill. Inf.	Gallatin County
Dobbs, Howell	Recruit	K	56th Ill. Inf.	Gallatin County
Dodd, Charles M.	Private	D	29th Ill. Inf.	Gallatin County
Dodson, Ezekiel	Private	E	131st Ill. Inf.	Gallatin County
Donahoe, James	Private	A	56th Ill. Inf.	Gallatin County
Donelson, Francis A.	Private	K	131st Ill. Inf.	Gallatin County
Donley, Edward	Private	C	29th Ill. Inf.	Shawneetown
Doom, Francis	Recruit	E	14th Ill. Cav.	New Market
Dorman, Jesse	Corporal	B	1st Ill. Cav.	Equality
Dorman, Michael	Recruit	C	29th Ill. Inf.	Shawneetown
Dorman, Samuel	Recruit	C	29th Ill. Inf.	Shawneetown
Dorman, William	Private	B	1st Ill. Cav.	Equality
Dorris, William	Private	G	7th Ill. Cav.	New Haven
Dorsey, Nicholas	Private	D	120th Ill. Inf.	Gallatin County
Dotson, Ezekiel	Private	B	131st Ill. Inf.	Gallatin County
Dougherty, John	Private	I	118th Ill. Inf.	Shawneetown
Douglas, Charles H.	Recruit		14th Ill. Cav.	Shawneetown
Downing, William C.	Recruit	E	14th Ill. Cav.	Shawneetown
Doyle, Jacob	Private	E	131st Ill. Inf.	Gallatin County
Doyle, Jacob	Private	B	131st Ill. Inf.	Gallatin County
Doyle, Michael	Recruit		14th Ill. Cav.	Shawneetown
Doyle, Michael	Private	I	14th Ill. Cav.	Shawneetown
Drone, Francis	Private	F	14th Ill. Cav.	New Market
Duffey, Edward	Private	B	131st Ill. Inf.	Gallatin County
Duffey, Edward	Recruit	C	29th Ill. Inf.	Gallatin County
Duffey, Patrick	Private	B	131st Ill. Inf.	Gallatin County
Duffey, Patrick	Recruit	C	29th Ill. Inf.	Gallatin County
Duffy, Charles	Private	B	1st Ill. Cav.	Equality
Duffy, Edward	Private	E	131st Ill. Inf.	Gallatin County
Duffy, Patrick	Private	E	131st Ill. Inf.	Gallatin County
Duncan, William	Private	G	7th Ill. Cav.	New Haven
Dunlap, Albert	Recruit	K	6th Ill. Cav.	Equality
Dunn, Charles	Private	E	14th Ill. Cav.	Shawneetown
Dunn, William A.	Private	D	120th Ill. Inf.	Gallatin County
Dunning, John M.	Private	F	6th Ill. Cav.	Gallatin County
Dupont, George W.	Private	C	29th Ill. Inf.	Shawneetown
Dupuy, William	Recruit	K	87th Ill. Inf.	Shawneetown
Durell, Thomas	Sergeant	C	28th Ill. Inf. Cons.	New Market
Duvall, William M.	2nd Lt.	E	14th Ill. Cav.	Shawneetown
Eakle, W.	Private	L	6th Ill. Cav.	Shawneetown
Earheart, George	Recruit	B	1st Ill. Cav.	Equality
Earley, Jaems	Private	G	7th Ill. Cav.	New Haven
Earnst, Louis	Private	B	18th Ill. Inf.	Shawneetown
Eastman, Stephen P.	Recruit	C	87th Ill. Inf.	Shawneetown
Eddy, Francis M.	Qmtr. Sgt.	HQ	120th Ill. Inf.	Shawneetown
Eddy, Francis M.	Sergeant	D	120th Ill. Inf.	Shawneetown
Eddy, John M.	1st Lt.	C	29th Ill. Inf.	Gallatin County
Edmondson, William	Private	L	6th Ill. Cav.	Shawneetown
Edwards, Charles	Private	G	29th Ill. Inf.	Gallatin County
Edwards, Charles M.	1st Lt.	B	18th Ill. Inf.	Shawneetown
Edwards, Joseph W.	Private	H	120th Ill. Inf.	Gallatin County
Edwards, Leonard	Recruit	B	1st Ill. Cav.	Equality
Edwards, Milton	Private	G	29th Ill. Inf.	Gallatin County

Name	Rank	Co.	Unit	Location
Edwards, Thomas G.	1st Sgt.	B	18th Ill. Inf.	Shawneetown
Ehterton, Lewis F.	Recruit	E	14th Ill. Cav.	Equality
Eilenstine, Oscar	Private	C	56th Ill. Inf.	Gallatin County
Elder, Robert S.	Private	K	131st Ill. Inf.	Gallatin County
Elder, Samuel	Private	D	56th Ill. Inf.	Gallatin County
Elliott, Aaron	Private	F	28th Ill. Inf.	New Market
Elliott, Cornelius	Private	D	29th U.S. Col. Inf.	Shawneetown
Ellis, John	Recruit	E	14th Ill. Cav.	Shawneetown
Ellis, John	Recruit		14th Ill. Cav.	Shawneetown
Ellis, Thomas	Private	G	131st Ill. Inf.	Equality
Ellis, Thomas	Private	D	131st Ill. Inf.	Equality
Ellison, John W.	Private	E	131st Ill. Inf.	Gallatin County
Ellison, John W.	Corporal	A	131st Ill. Inf.	Gallatin County
Ellison, John W.	Recruit	D	29th Ill. Inf.	Gallatin County
Emery, James	Recruit	E	14th Ill. Cav.	New Market
Emery, James	Private	I	14th Ill. Cav.	New Market
Endecott, Zephaniah	Recruit	B	1st Ill. Cav.	Equality
Endicott, Newton I.	Private	G	131st Ill. Inf.	Equality
England, Anderson	Private	C	29th Ill. Inf.	Shawneetown
Epley, George W.	Private	G	7th Ill. Cav.	New Haven
Eshenbach, James A.	Recruit	F	87th Ill. Inf.	Shawneetown
Etherton, Reuben F.	Private	K	6th Ill. Cav.	Gallatin County
Evans, David R.	Sergeant	B	1st Ill. Cav.	Equality
Evans, George	Qmtr. Sgt.	B	1st Ill. Cav.	Equality
Evans, George W.	Comm. Sgt.	HQ	1st Ill. Cav.	Equality
Evans, George W.	1st Lt.	E	14th Ill. Cav.	Shawneetown
Evans, Jacob	Private	F	6th Ill. Cav.	Gallatin County
Evans, John R.	Corporal	B	1st Ill. Cav.	Equality
Evans, William	Private	F	6th Ill. Cav.	Gallatin County
Farmer, Amos	Private	C	29th Ill. Inf.	Shawneetown
Farmer, George N.	Private	C	29th Ill. Inf.	Gallatin County
Farmer, Robert S.	Recruit	C	29th Ill. Inf.	Shawneetown
Farmer, Samuel W.	Private	C	29th Ill. Inf.	Gallatin County
Farmer, William S.	Private	C	29th Ill. Inf.	Gallatin County
Felps, Ezekiel	Private	K	1st Ill. Artillery	Shawneetown
Fenn, Joseph R.	Recruit	I	118th Ill. Inf.	Shawneetown
Fergusson, William	Recruit	B	18th Ill. Inf.	Shawneetown
Fields, William A.	Recruit	E	14th Ill. Cav.	Shawneetown
Filbrick, Francis B.	Recruit	F	28th Ill. Inf.	New Market
Finigan, Michael	Recruit	E	3rd Ill. Cav.	Shawneetown
Finn, Marcus R.	Private	I	118th Ill. Inf.	Shawneetown
Finn, Thomas H.	Sergeant	D	56th Ill. Inf.	Gallatin County
Fish, John M.	Private	B	18th Ill. Inf.	Shawneetown
Flaherty, William	Musician	F	28th Ill. Inf.	New Market
Fleetwood, Charles W.	Corporal	D	120th Ill. Inf.	Gallatin County
Flemings, Finis	Private	E	131st Ill. Inf.	Gallatin County
Flemmings, James T.	Private	B	18th Ill. Inf.	Shawneetown
Fletcher, Franklin	Private	F	56th Ill. Inf.	Gallatin County
Fletcher, John	Corporal	C	29th Ill. Inf.	Shawneetown
Fliar, Henry J.	Private	C	18th Ill. Inf. Reorg.	Shawneetown
Flood, Martin	Private	B	18th Ill. Inf.	Shawneetown
Floyd, Isaac E	Private	I	131st Ill. Inf.	Gallatin County
Fogle, Martin	Private	B	18th Ill. Inf.	Shawneetown
Fogsdon, G. A.	Private	L	6th Ill. Cav.	Shawneetown
Folkerson, Thomas	Private	L	6th Ill. Cav.	Shawneetown
Forrest, Charles	Private	K	73rd Ill. Inf.	Equality
Fortner, William H. H.	Recruit	H	87th Ill. Inf.	Shawneetown
Foster, James	Captain	B	1st Ill. Cav.	Equality
Fowler, Benjamin	Musician	K	131st Ill. Inf.	Gallatin County

Fowler, Benjamin	Recruit	F	56th Ill. Inf.	Gallatin County
Fowler, Benjamin T.	Private	B	1st Ill. Cav.	Equality
Fowler, George W.	Private	G	131st Ill. Inf.	Equality
Fowler, George W.	Recruit	G	29th Ill. Inf.	Equality
Fowler, Jesse	Private	L	6th Ill. Cav.	Shawneetown
Fowler, Moses M.	Private	G	131st Ill. Inf.	Equality
Fowler, Moses M.	Private	D	131st Ill. Inf.	Equality
Fowler, Moses M.	Recruit	G	29th Ill. Inf.	Equality
Fowler, William P.	Private	K	131st Ill. Inf.	Gallatin County
Fox, Charles	Private	B	1st Ill. Cav.	Equality
Fox, Patrick	Private	B	1st Ill. Cav.	Equality
Freels, John	Private	C	56th Ill. Inf.	Gallatin County
French, John N.	Recruit	E	14th Ill. Cav.	Shawneetown
Friar, Noah	Recruit	E	14th Ill. Cav.	Shawneetown
Friday, George	Private	B	18th Ill. Inf.	Shawneetown
Frier, Henry J.	Private	B	18th Ill. Inf.	Shawneetown
Frier, Noah	Private	I	14th Ill. Cav.	New Market
Frier, Noah	Private	L	6th Ill. Cav.	Shawneetown
Fuller, Benjamin F.	Recruit	E	14th Ill. Cav.	New Market
Fuller, Benjamin F.	Private	I	14th Ill. Cav.	New Market
Fuller, Benjamin F.	Private	C	29th Ill. Inf.	Shawneetown
Funkhouser, Young	Private	K	131st Ill. Inf.	Gallatin County
Gaddes, Daniel	Recruit	D	29th Ill. Inf.	Gallatin County
Gaddis, Daniel	Private	E	131st Ill. Inf.	Gallatin County
Gaddis, Daniel	Private	B	131st Ill. Inf.	Gallatin County
Gaddis, William R.	Private	E	131st Ill. Inf.	Gallatin County
Gailord, James	Private	F	6th Ill. Cav.	Gallatin County
Gain, Jacob P.	Private	K	131st Ill. Inf.	Gallatin County
Gallaher, James T.	Private	I	131st Ill. Inf.	Gallatin County
Garey, Jerome B.	Private	K	6th Ill. Cav.	Gallatin County
Garrett, George G.	Private	H	120th Ill. Inf.	Gallatin County
Gasken, John	Private	D	131st Ill. Inf.	Equality
Gaskins, Leroy	Recruit	B	18th Ill. Inf.	Shawneetown
Gaskins, William	Private	F	6th Ill. Cav.	Gallatin County
Gaston, John	Private	G	131st Ill. Inf.	Equality
Gates, Joseph B.	Private	D	120th Ill. Inf.	Gallatin County
Gatewood, Isaac	Recruit	B	18th Ill. Inf.	Shawneetown
Gatewood, Isaac	Recruit	I	31st Ill. Inf.	Equality
Gentry, Sidney L.	Recruit	I	87th Ill. Inf.	Shawneetown
Gerralds, Thomas N.	Private	I	118th Ill. Inf.	Shawneetown
Gholson, Reuben E.	Private	I	131st Ill. Inf.	Gallatin County
Glass, James A.	Private	K	131st Ill. Inf.	Gallatin County
Glasscock, James L.	Recruit	H	120th Ill. Inf.	New Haven
Gleeson, John	Recruit	E	14th Ill. Cav.	Shawneetown
Glen, Edward	Recruit	K	87th Ill. Inf.	Shawneetown
Glisson, James	Recruit	K	56th Ill. Inf.	Shawneetown
Glisson, John	Private	F	56th Ill. Inf.	Gallatin County
Glisson, John	Recruit	K	56th Ill. Inf.	Gallatin County
Glover, Daniel	Private	G	131st Ill. Inf.	Equality
Glover, Daniel	Private	G	7th Ill. Cav.	New Haven
Glover, Laton	Saddler	F	6th Ill. Cav.	Gallatin County
Glover, William	Private	E	131st Ill. Inf.	Gallatin County
Glover, William	Corporal	A	131st Ill. Inf.	Gallatin County
Glover, William	Recruit	D	29th Ill. Inf.	Gallatin County
Glover, Zaddock	Recruit	D	29th Ill. Inf.	New Haven
Glover, Zadock	Recruit	L	6th Ill. Cav.	Shawneetown
Goad, Elias R.	Corporal	G	7th Ill. Cav.	New Haven
Goforth, James A.	Private	B	1st Ill. Cav.	Equality
Goforth, Thomas C.	Private	E	131st Ill. Inf.	Gallatin County

Name	Rank	Co.	Unit	Location
Goodman, Elisha O.	Musician	D	120th Ill. Inf.	Gallatin County
Goodwin, Samuel	Private	G	131st Ill. Inf.	Equality
Goodwin, Samuel	Private	D	131st Ill. Inf.	Equality
Goodwin, Samuel	Recruit	G	29th Ill. Inf.	Equality
Gott, Benjamin F.	Private	G	29th Ill. Inf.	Gallatin County
Gott, John W.	Private	G	29th Ill. Inf.	Gallatin County
Gould, Solon H.	Private	B	18th Ill. Inf.	Shawneetown
Graham, Samuel	Private	B	18th Ill. Inf.	Shawneetown
Graham, Samuel	Private	C	18th Ill. Inf. Reorg.	Shawneetown
Graham, Sanford	Private	B	1st Ill. Cav.	Equality
Graves, John A.	Private	G	131st Ill. Inf.	Equality
Graves, John A.	Private	D	131st Ill. Inf.	Equality
Graves, John A.	Recruit	G	29th Ill. Inf.	Equality
Graves, Joseph	Private	F	6th Ill. Cav.	Gallatin County
Gray, John	Private	H	128th Ill. Inf.	Equality
Gray, Samuel	Private	H	128th Ill. Inf.	Equality
Grayson, John R.	Recruit	B	1st Ill. Cav.	Equality
Green, Eli W.	Major	HQ	29th Ill. Inf.	Shawneetown
Green, Elijah W.	Recruit	K	56th Ill. Inf.	Gallatin County
Green, Elisha	Private	F	56th Ill. Inf.	Gallatin County
Green, James	Private	G	131st Ill. Inf.	Equality
Greer, George W.	Private	D	120th Ill. Inf.	Gallatin County
Greer, Reivas W.	Private	B	18th Ill. Inf.	Shawneetown
Greeson, Jonathan	Recruit	B	54th Ill. Inf.	Cottonwood
Gregg, John	Saddler	L	6th Ill. Cav.	Shawneetown
Griffin, Harvey	Private	G	131st Ill. Inf.	Equality
Griffin, Hervey	Private	D	131st Ill. Inf.	Equality
Griggs, George O.	2nd Lt.	C	56th Ill. Inf.	Shawneetown
Gross, James	Private	I	131st Ill. Inf.	Gallatin County
Grounds, George W.	Private	D	120th Ill. Inf.	Gallatin County
Groves, John B.	Private	D	29th Ill. Inf.	Gallatin County
Guard, Charles C.	Surgeon	HQ	29th Ill. Inf.	Equality
Guard, Timothy A.	Private	D	29th U.S. Col. Inf.	Shawneetown
Haaran, William	Private	B	18th Ill. Inf.	Shawneetown
Hafford, Charles	Private	H	120th Ill. Inf.	Gallatin County
Hainey, Leonard	Private	C	29th Ill. Inf.	Shawneetown
Hale, John W.	Recruit	B	1st Ill. Cav.	Equality
Hales, John W.	Recruit	E	14th Ill. Cav.	Equality
Hales, John W.	Private	I	14th Ill. Cav.	Equality
Hall, James P.	Private	D	56th Ill. Inf.	Gallatin County
Hall, Joseph	Recruit	F	56th Ill. Inf.	New Market
Hall, Joseph	Private	K	73rd Ill. Inf.	Equality
Hall, Thomas J.	Private	B	1st Ill. Cav.	Equality
Halley, Cornelius W.	Captain	E	131st Ill. Inf.	Gallatin County
Hamberg, William	Corporal	B	18th Ill. Inf.	Shawneetown
Hamby, William	Private	D	56th Ill. Inf.	Gallatin County
Hamphill, John F.	Corporal	K	131st Ill. Inf.	Gallatin County
Hancock, Benjamin F.	Private	G	131st Ill. Inf.	Equality
Hancock, Jacob W.	Recruit		14th Ill. Cav.	New Market
Hancock, James M.	Private	G	131st Ill. Inf.	Equality
Hancock, John J.	Private	F	56th Ill. Inf.	New Market
Hancock, John W.	Private	C	29th Ill. Inf.	New Market
Haney, John	Private	G	29th Ill. Inf.	Gallatin County
Haney, Leonard	Recruit	G	7th Ill. Cav.	Shawneetown
Happerin, James	Private	B	18th Ill. Inf.	Shawneetown
Harden, Cormack	Private	D	29th Ill. Inf.	Gallatin County
Harden, William	Recruit	L	6th Ill. Cav.	Shawneetown
Hardin, Aaron	Private	E	131st Ill. Inf.	Gallatin County
Hardin, Edmund	Comm. Sgt.	HQ	29th Ill. Inf.	Gallatin County

Hardin, Edmund	Private	C	29th Ill. Inf.	Gallatin County
Hardin, James K. P.	Recruit	B	18th Ill. Inf.	Shawneetown
Hardin, Richard	1st Lt.	G	7th Ill. Cav.	New Haven
Hardin, Solomon	Private	B	1st Ill. Cav.	Equality
Hardin, Solomon	Musician	F	56th Ill. Inf.	New Market
Hardin, William	Recruit		14th Ill. Cav.	New Market
Harget, Israel	Private	H	120th Ill. Inf.	Gallatin County
Hargrave, George W.	Private	D	120th Ill. Inf.	Gallatin County
Hargrave, Willis B.	1st Lt.	E	3rd Ill. Cav.	Equality
Hargraves, George W.	Private	B	1st Ill. Cav.	Equality
Harman, James	Private	F	28th Ill. Inf.	New Market
Harper, Andrew J.	Corporal	H	56th Ill. Inf.	Gallatin County
Harper, Will C.	Private	H	56th Ill. Inf.	Gallatin County
Harpool, Fountain E.	Private	D	120th Ill. Inf.	Gallatin County
Harrelson, William	Sergeant	E	131st Ill. Inf.	Gallatin County
Harris, Thomas W.	Colonel	HQ	54th Ill. Inf.	Shawneetown
Harris, William B.	Sergeant	D	131st Ill. Inf.	Equality
Harris, William B.	Recruit	A	29th Ill. Inf.	Equality
Harris, William C.	Sergeant	G	131st Ill. Inf.	Equality
Harris, William D.	Private	B	18th Ill. Inf.	Shawneetown
Hart, James B.	Captain	D	29th Ill. Inf.	New Haven
Harvey, Lewis	Recruit	D	29th Ill. Inf.	New Haven
Harvey, Warren	Recruit	D	29th Ill. Inf.	New Haven
Hatchel, Newton J.	Corporal	H	120th Ill. Inf.	Gallatin County
Haughey, Samuel W.	Sergeant	C	29th Ill. Inf.	Shawneetown
Hayden, Hayes	Private	F	28th Ill. Inf.	New Market
Hayden, Hays	Corporal	C	28th Ill. Inf. Cons.	New Market
Hayden, Samuel	Private	D	56th Ill. Inf.	Gallatin County
Haynes, Albert	Recruit	C	87th Ill. Inf.	Shawneetown
Haynes, Charles C.	Private	D	29th Ill. Inf.	Gallatin County
Hazen, Daniel Thorn	1st Sgt.	L	6th Ill. Cav.	Shawneetown
Heard, Thomas H.	Private	I	56th Ill. Inf.	Gallatin County
Heath, Augustus	Private	K	131st Ill. Inf.	Gallatin County
Heath, Augustus N.	Private	B	131st Ill. Inf.	Gallatin County
Heath, Augustus N.	Recruit	C	29th Ill. Inf.	Gallatin County
Heath, Henry F.	Private	K	131st Ill. Inf.	Gallatin County
Heath, Henry F.	Private	B	131st Ill. Inf.	Gallatin County
Heath, William	Recruit	C	29th Ill. Inf.	Gallatin County
Heath, William M.	Private	K	131st Ill. Inf.	Gallatin County
Hedger, David	Recruit	B	1st Ill. Cav.	Equality
Hedger, David	Private	H	120th Ill. Inf.	Gallatin County
Hedger, Pleasant W.	Private	G	29th Ill. Inf.	Gallatin County
Hedger, Silas	Private	K	131st Ill. Inf.	Gallatin County
Hedger, Silas W.	Private	B	131st Ill. Inf.	Gallatin County
Hedger, Silas W.	Recruit	C	29th Ill. Inf.	Gallatin County
Hedger, William	Private	G	29th Ill. Inf.	Gallatin County
Heifner, Henry	Private	E	131st Ill. Inf.	Gallatin County
Hemphill, Samuel A.	Private	K	6th Ill. Cav.	Gallatin County
Hendricks, Samuel	Private	G	7th Ill. Cav.	New Haven
Hendrix, George	Private	D	29th Ill. Inf.	Gallatin County
Henry, Charles M.	Private	D	120th Ill. Inf.	Gallatin County
Henry, William	Private	H	56th Ill. Inf.	Gallatin County
Henry, William	Private	I	56th Ill. Inf.	Gallatin County
Hensen, Dennis	Private	G	7th Ill. Cav.	New Haven
Henson, Edwin B.	Private	E	131st Ill. Inf.	Gallatin County
Henson, James	Recruit	D	29th Ill. Inf.	New Haven
Henson, James	Recruit	G	7th Ill. Cav.	New Haven
Henson, John	Private	B	18th Ill. Inf.	Shawneetown
Henson, Rapheus	Private	D	29th Ill. Inf.	Gallatin County

Name	Rank	Co.	Unit	Location
Herod, Thomas G. S.	Major	HQ	6th Ill. Cav.	Shawneetown
Herod, Thomas G. S.	Captain	L	6th Ill. Cav.	Shawneetown
Hess, Francis N.	1st Sgt.	G	131st Ill. Inf.	Equality
Hess, John	Private	D	56th Ill. Inf.	Gallatin County
Hess, John T.	Sergeant	G	131st Ill. Inf.	Equality
Hess, John T.	Sergeant	D	131st Ill. Inf.	Equality
Hester, Jacob	Recruit	E	14th Ill. Cav.	New Market
Hester, Jacob	Private	F	14th Ill. Cav.	Shawneetown
Hewitt, Henry	Private	B	18th Ill. Inf.	Shawneetown
Hick, Thomas B.	Recruit	G	7th Ill. Cav.	New Haven
Hickey, Michael	1st Lt.	C	29th Ill. Inf.	Gallatin County
Hickman, Benjamin	Private	D	56th Ill. Inf.	Gallatin County
Hicks, Christopher C.	Private	I	118th Ill. Inf.	Shawneetown
Hicks, James	Private	I	118th Ill. Inf.	Shawneetown
Hicks, John W.	Sergeant	C	28th Ill. Inf. Cons.	New Market
Hill, William R.	Private	E	131st Ill. Inf.	Gallatin County
Hines, Joseph	Private	L	6th Ill. Cav.	Shawneetown
Hirst, Joseph H.	Recruit	B	1st Ill. Cav.	Equality
Hise, George W.	Private	K	131st Ill. Inf.	Gallatin County
Hise, George W.	Private	B	131st Ill. Inf.	Gallatin County
Hise, George W.	Recruit	C	29th Ill. Inf.	Gallatin County
Hise, Jacob H.	Corporal	K	131st Ill. Inf.	Gallatin County
Hise, John H.	Private	K	131st Ill. Inf.	Gallatin County
Hise, John W.	Corporal	K	131st Ill. Inf.	Gallatin County
Hise, William	Recruit	B	1st Ill. Cav.	Equality
Hise, William	Private	K	131st Ill. Inf.	Gallatin County
Hise, William	Private	B	131st Ill. Inf.	Gallatin County
Hise, William	Recruit	C	29th Ill. Inf.	Gallatin County
Hise, William J.	Private	K	131st Ill. Inf.	Gallatin County
Hise, William J.	Private	B	131st Ill. Inf.	Gallatin County
Hise, William J.	Recruit	C	29th Ill. Inf.	Gallatin County
Hodges, John	Private	I	118th Ill. Inf.	Shawneetown
Hodson, Edmund A.	Private	B	18th Ill. Inf.	Shawneetown
Hogan, Isaac	Corporal	D	120th Ill. Inf.	Gallatin County
Holder, Marion	Buglar	L	6th Ill. Cav.	Shawneetown
Holderfield, Joseph R.	Recruit	B	6th Ill. Cav.	Shawneetown
Holland, Lambert P.	Recruit	G	7th Ill. Cav.	Cottonwood
Holland, Shandy A.	Recruit	I	87th Ill. Inf.	Shawneetown
Holland, Thomas	Recruit	E	14th Ill. Cav.	Shawneetown
Holland, Thomas	Private	I	14th Ill. Cav.	Shawneetown
Holley, Smithing A.	Recruit	B	6th Ill. Cav.	Shawneetown
Holt, William	Sergeant	F	6th Ill. Cav.	Gallatin County
Hooker, John	Private	G	120th Ill. Inf.	Gallatin County
Hool, John D.	Private	E	14th Ill. Cav.	Shawneetown
Hornsby, William	Recruit	G	7th Ill. Cav.	Shawneetown
Hough, John	2nd. Lt.	G	29th Ill. Inf.	Equality
Howe, John	Sergeant	B	18th Ill. Inf.	Shawneetown
Hoyer, Frederick	Sergeant	B	18th Ill. Inf.	Shawneetown
Hubbs, Zadoc	Private	I	118th Ill. Inf.	Shawneetown
Hucheson, Elisha	Private	C	29th Ill. Inf.	Gallatin County
Hudgins, James H.	Private	G	131st Ill. Inf.	Equality
Hudgins, Sebern N.	Private	G	131st Ill. Inf.	Equality
Huff, John	Private	G	131st Ill. Inf.	Equality
Huff, John	1st Sgt.	D	131st Ill. Inf.	Equality
Huffine, Henry	Recruit	D	87th Ill. Inf.	Shawneetown
Huffine, Joseph	Recruit	D	87th Ill. Inf.	Shawneetown
Hughbanks, George	Private	B	18th Ill. Inf.	Shawneetown
Hughes, George	Private	C	29th Ill. Inf.	Shawneetown
Hughes, John W.	1st Lt.	L	6th Ill. Cav.	Shawneetown

Name	Rank	Co.	Unit	Location
Hughey, John P.	Private	B	18th Ill. Inf.	Shawneetown
Hull, Marion E.	Corporal	B	18th Ill. Inf.	Shawneetown
Hutchinson, Alex	Private	G	131st Ill. Inf.	Equality
Hutchinson, Alex	Private	D	56th Ill. Inf.	Gallatin County
Hutchinson, John R.	Private	B	1st Ill. Cav.	Equality
Ingermonson, Morris	Recruit	L	14th Ill. Cav.	Shawneetown
Ingleton, William	Private	E	131st Ill. Inf.	Gallatin County
Inman, William	Private	E	131st Ill. Inf.	Gallatin County
Irvin, William	Recruit	D	29th Ill. Inf.	Gallatin County
Isaacs, David A. M.	Recruit		56th Ill. Inf.	Shawneetown
Isham, James M.	Corporal	I	118th Ill. Inf.	Shawneetown
Israel, Samuel	Private	B	18th Ill. Inf.	Shawneetown
Jackson, Andrew	Private	F	131st Ill. Inf.	Gallatin County
Jackson, Francis M.	Private	K	131st Ill. Inf.	Gallatin County
Jackson, Francis M.	Private	B	131st Ill. Inf.	Gallatin County
Jackson, Francis M.	Recruit	E	29th Ill. Inf.	Gallatin County
Jackson, M. L.	Recruit	E	29th Ill. Inf.	Gallatin County
Jackson, Michael L.	Private	K	131st Ill. Inf.	Gallatin County
Jackson, Michael L.	Private	B	131st Ill. Inf.	Gallatin County
Jacobs, George W.	Private	B	18th Ill. Inf.	Shawneetown
James, John	Private	G	131st Ill. Inf.	Equality
Jamison, Andrew M.	Private	D	56th Ill. Inf.	Gallatin County
Jammeson, A. M.	Private	I	118th Ill. Inf.	Shawneetown
Jarrell, Wilson	Recruit	I	118th Ill. Inf.	Shawneetown
Jarrett, Daniel B.	Private	D	120th Ill. Inf.	Gallatin County
Jarrett, Daniel B.	Recruit	K	6th Ill. Cav.	Shawneetown
Jenings, William F.	Recruit	F	56th Ill. Inf.	Gallatin County
Jenings, William M.	Corporal	D	56th Ill. Inf.	Gallatin County
Jenkins, James	Recruit	E	14th Ill. Cav.	Shawneetown
Jenkins, James	Private	F	14th Ill. Cav.	Shawneetown
Jennings, Joseph D.	2nd Lt.	D	120th Ill. Inf.	Shawneetown
Johnson, Alexander	Private	D	29th Ill. Inf.	Gallatin County
Johnson, James	Recruit	D	29th Ill. Inf.	New Haven
Johnson, James	Recruit	L	6th Ill. Cav.	Shawneetown
Johnson, John H	Recruit	B	18th Ill. Inf.	Shawneetown
Johnson, Joseph W.	1st Sgt.	B	1st Ill. Cav.	Equality
Johnson, Robert	Private	L	6th Ill. Cav.	Shawneetown
Joiner, John	Private	D	131st Ill. Inf.	Equality
Jones, Elias W.	Captain	B	18th Ill. Inf.	Shawneetown
Jones, James	Recruit	L	6th Ill. Cav.	Shawneetown
Jones, Jonathan	Private	B	1st Ill. Cav.	Equality
Jones, Thomas	Recruit	L	6th Ill. Cav.	Shawneetown
Jones, Washington C.	Private	B	18th Ill. Inf.	Shawneetown
Kaine, John	Private	E	131st Ill. Inf.	Gallatin County
Kanady, Garland M.	Private	K	131st Ill. Inf.	Gallatin County
Kanady, Garland M.	1st Sgt.	B	131st Ill. Inf.	Gallatin County
Kanady, Garland M.	2nd Lt.	I	29th Ill. Inf.	Gallatin County
Kanady, John A.	Private	K	6th Ill. Cav.	Gallatin County
Kanady, John M.	Private	C	29th Ill. Inf.	Gallatin County
Kanady, Sanford B.	Captain	C	29th Ill. Inf.	Shawneetown
Kanady, Washington	Captain	D	120th Ill. Inf.	Shawneetown
Kane, Edward	Private	B	131st Ill. Inf.	Gallatin County
Karnes, Harvey C.	Recruit	B	1st Ill. Cav.	Equality
Karnes, William D.	Recruit	B	1st Ill. Cav.	Equality
Karnes, William M.	Corporal	K	73rd Ill. Inf.	Equality
Karns, William	Musician	HQ	1st Ill. Cav.	Equality
Karns, William	Musician	B	1st Ill. Cav.	Equality
Keaton, Cornelius	Corporal	D	131st Ill. Inf.	Equality
Keatons, Cornelius	Recruit	H	29th Ill. Inf.	Equality

Name	Rank	Co.	Unit	Location
Kerkham, John W	Corporal	F	56th Ill. Inf.	Shawneetown
Keyton, Cornelius	Corporal	G	131st Ill. Inf.	Equality
Killbraid, John	Private	B	18th Ill. Inf.	Shawneetown
Killian, William Barnabas	Recruit	F	28th Ill. Inf.	New Market
Killion, Barnabus	Private	C	28th Ill. Inf. Cons.	New Market
Killion, Emanuel M.	Private	F	28th Ill. Inf.	New Market
Kimbrow, John	Private	K	131st Ill. Inf.	Gallatin County
Kimbrow, William	Private	K	131st Ill. Inf.	Gallatin County
King, Floyd	Private	B	1st Ill. Cav.	Equality
King, Floyd	Recruit	E	14th Ill. Cav.	Shawneetown
King, Floyd	Private	F	14th Ill. Cav.	Shawneetown
Kingston, John	Private	L	6th Ill. Cav.	Equality
Kinsall, Daniel	Private	B	18th Ill. Inf.	Shawneetown
Kinsall, David M.	Private	H	120th Ill. Inf.	Gallatin County
Kirk, Alexander	Private	E	131st Ill. Inf.	Gallatin County
Kirk, Alexander	Private	B	131st Ill. Inf.	Gallatin County
Kirk, Alexander	Recruit	D	29th Ill. Inf.	Gallatin County
Kirk, Henry	Private	E	131st Ill. Inf.	Gallatin County
Kirk, William	Private	E	131st Ill. Inf.	Gallatin County
Kirkham, Robert	Colonel	HQ	56th Ill. Inf.	Shawneetown
Kisar, Daniel	Private	G	29th Ill. Inf.	Gallatin County
Kittinger, William M.	Recruit	B	1st Ill. Cav.	Equality
Klingfield, Charles F. T.	Recruit	C	2nd Ill. Artillery	Shawneetown
Kopp, John	Recruit	C	29th Ill. Inf.	Shawneetown
Lacefield, Albert M.	Private	B	1st Ill. Cav.	Equality
Lacefield, Albert M.	Recruit	E	14th Ill. Cav.	Shawneetown
Lacey, George	Private	C	56th Ill. Inf.	Gallatin County
Lackins, Isaac	Private	D	29th Ill. Inf.	Gallatin County
Lafferty, William	Corporal	D	56th Ill. Inf.	Gallatin County
Lam, Newton R.	Private	G	29th Ill. Inf.	Gallatin County
Lam, William F.	Private	H	120th Ill. Inf.	Gallatin County
Lamb, James M.	Private	B	1st Ill. Cav.	Equality
Lamb, Joel	Corporal	K	131st Ill. Inf.	Gallatin County
Lamb, Joseph	Private	K	131st Ill. Inf.	Gallatin County
Lamb, Nathan	Private	K	131st Ill. Inf.	Gallatin County
Lamb, William	Private	K	131st Ill. Inf.	Gallatin County
Lamb, William H.	Private	D	29th Ill. Inf.	Gallatin County
Lamb, William M.	Private	B	131st Ill. Inf.	Gallatin County
Lambert, Aaron	Qmtr. Sgt.	L	6th Ill. Cav.	Shawneetown
Lambert, Aaron	Recruit	L	6th Ill. Cav.	Shawneetown
Landingham, Zach	Recruit	E	29th Ill. Inf.	Gallatin County
Lanham, Zachariah	Private	B	131st Ill. Inf.	Gallatin County
Lanningham, Zacariah	Private	E	131st Ill. Inf.	Gallatin County
Lapperty, Alexander	Private	B	18th Ill. Inf.	Shawneetown
Lapperty, William	Private	B	18th Ill. Inf.	Shawneetown
Lastur, John	Private	L	6th Ill. Cav.	Shawneetown
Lawler, Michael K.	Colonel	HQ	18th Ill. Inf.	Gallatin County
Lawler, Patrick	Captain	D	18th Ill. Inf.	Shawneetown
Lawless, Thomas R.	Sergeant	E	14th Ill. Cav.	Equality
Ledbetter, William Washington	Private	G	7th Ill. Cav.	New Haven
Ledford, John B.	Private	B	18th Ill. Inf.	Shawneetown
Leming, Seaberry	Private	D	120th Ill. Inf.	Gallatin County
Leonbarger, Fredrick	Recruit	G	29th Ill. Inf.	Equality
Level, William	Recruit	K	56th Ill. Inf.	Gallatin County
Levell, Edward	Private	D	120th Ill. Inf.	Gallatin County
Levell, Peter	Private	D	29th U.S. Col. Inf.	Shawneetown
Levil, William	Private	D	56th Ill. Inf.	Gallatin County
Lewis, David W.	Private	H	120th Ill. Inf.	Gallatin County

Name	Rank	Co.	Regiment	Location
Lewis, James	Private	D	131st Ill. Inf.	Equality
Lewis, James	Recruit	G	29th Ill. Inf.	Equality
Lightfoot, Walker F.	Private	G	7th Ill. Cav.	New Haven
Like, Joel	Private	E	131st Ill. Inf.	Gallatin County
Likens, William B.	Private	K	131st Ill. Inf.	Gallatin County
Likens, William B.	Private	B	131st Ill. Inf.	Gallatin County
Likens, William B.	Recruit	D	29th Ill. Inf.	Gallatin County
Litchfield, Alexander	Private	E	131st Ill. Inf.	Gallatin County
Litsey, William	Corporal	L	6th Ill. Cav.	Shawneetown
Little, Charles	Private	C	87th Ill. Inf.	Gallatin County
Lofton, John	Private	E	131st Ill. Inf.	Gallatin County
Logan, David A.	Private	D	120th Ill. Inf.	Gallatin County
Logan, John R.	Private	D	120th Ill. Inf.	Gallatin County
Logsdon, George A.	Recruit	L	6th Ill. Cav.	Shawneetown
Logsdon, T. B.	Sergeant	L	6th Ill. Cav.	Shawneetown
London, John	Recruit	L	14th Ill. Cav.	Shawneetown
Long, Jacob	Private	C	29th Ill. Inf.	Shawneetown
Loomis, Cobb	Recruit	L	14th Ill. Cav.	Shawneetown
Lowe, Marcus C	Private	B	1st Ill. Cav.	Equality
Lucas, George W.	Wagoner	C	29th Ill. Inf.	Shawneetown
Lutes, Marens	Private	D	120th Ill. Inf.	Gallatin County
Luther, Alexander	Recruit	D	29th Ill. Inf.	New Haven
Luther, George M.	Private	D	29th Ill. Inf.	Gallatin County
Luther, James M.	Private	D	29th Ill. Inf.	Gallatin County
Lyon, John	Private	E	14th Ill. Cav.	Equality
Lytle, George	Recruit	B	54th Ill. Inf.	Cottonwood
Mage, Robert F.	Recruit	E	29th Ill. Inf.	Gallatin County
Mahoney, John	Recruit	B	1st Ill. Cav.	Equality
Mahoney, John	Corporal	G	131st Ill. Inf.	Equality
Mahoney, John	Private	D	131st Ill. Inf.	Equality
Mahoney, John	Recruit	C	29th Ill. Inf.	Gallatin County
Mahue, William	Recruit	B	1st Ill. Cav.	Equality
Malladay, Martin V.	Recruit	F	6th Ill. Cav.	Shawneetown
Maloney, Daniel	Private	E	131st Ill. Inf.	Gallatin County
Maloney, Daniel	Private	B	131st Ill. Inf.	Gallatin County
Maloney, Daniel	Recruit	C	29th Ill. Inf.	Gallatin County
Maltby, Christopher C.	Saddler	B	1st Ill. Cav.	Equality
Maltby, Thomas E.	Recruit	B	1st Ill. Cav.	Equality
Mangrem, Ephraim C.	Private	E	6th Ill. Cav.	Shawneetown
Mangrum, Burral	Recruit	E	14th Ill. Cav.	Shawneetown
Manheart, George	Private	G	29th Ill. Inf.	Gallatin County
Manley, Thomas	Private	B	18th Ill. Inf.	Shawneetown
Mann, Isaac	1st Lt.	D	30th Ill. Inf.	New Haven
Mappin, John J.	Private	F	28th Ill. Inf.	New Market
Margilen, Eli	Private	G	7th Ill. Cav.	New Haven
Marooney, John	Private	B	18th Ill. Inf.	Shawneetown
Marshall, Samuel	Private	D	29th U.S. Col. Inf.	Shawneetown
Martin, Benjamin F.	Private	L	6th Ill. Cav.	Shawneetown
Martin, George B.	Private	I	118th Ill. Inf.	Shawneetown
Martin, Jesse L.	Private	C	29th Ill. Inf.	Shawneetown
Martin, Joseph	Private	B	18th Ill. Inf.	Shawneetown
Martin, Rufus	Private	C	29th Ill. Inf.	Gallatin County
Martin, Thomas R.	Corporal	D	120th Ill. Inf.	Gallatin County
Mason, Jonathan F.	1st Sgt.	D	120th Ill. Inf.	Shawneetown
Mattie, Daniel D.	Recruit	B	18th Ill. Inf.	Shawneetown
Mattingley, Archibald	Private	C	29th Ill. Inf.	Gallatin County
Maugrim, Levi	Private	G	7th Ill. Cav.	Shawneetown
Mayfield, John	Private	K	131st Ill. Inf.	Gallatin County
Mayfield, John	Private	B	131st Ill. Inf.	Gallatin County

Mayfield, John	Recruit	E	29th Ill. Inf.	Gallatin County
Mayhue, Adam	Corporal	H	120th Ill. Inf.	Gallatin County
Mayhue, Benjamin F.	Recruit	G	29th Ill. Inf.	Equality
McAllister, Elias	Private	D	29th U.S. Col. Inf.	Shawneetown
McBrarthy, John	Private	C	29th Ill. Inf.	Shawneetown
McCaleb, Edward H.	Captain	G	131st Ill. Inf.	Equality
McClain, John S.	Private	B	1st Ill. Cav.	Equality
McClellan, George	Private	D	56th Ill. Inf.	Gallatin County
McCluskey, John	Recruit	B	1st Ill. Cav.	Equality
McCool, Franklin	Private	D	120th Ill. Inf.	Gallatin County
McCool, Marion	Sergeant	C	29th Ill. Inf.	Shawneetown
McCool, William H.	Corporal	D	120th Ill. Inf.	Gallatin County
McCoy, Adam C.	Private	E	14th Ill. Cav.	Shawneetown
McCoy, Wade W.	Captain	L	6th Ill. Cav.	Shawneetown
McCoy, William	Private	E	14th Ill. Cav.	Shawneetown
McDade, Andrew	Private	B	18th Ill. Inf.	Shawneetown
McDonald, Alexander H.	Private	F	56th Ill. Inf.	Shawneetown
McDonald, James	Private	E	131st Ill. Inf.	Gallatin County
McDonald, James	Private	B	131st Ill. Inf.	Gallatin County
McDonald, James	Recruit	D	29th Ill. Inf.	Gallatin County
McEwing, Thomas	Private	B	18th Ill. Inf.	Shawneetown
McGehee, Francis M.	Recruit	C	29th Ill. Inf.	Shawneetown
McGhee, Thomas	Recruit	D	29th Ill. Inf.	New Haven
McGhee, Thomas C.	Private	G	29th Ill. Inf.	Gallatin County
McGill, David	Private	F	6th Ill. Cav.	Gallatin County
McGowan, William	Recruit	E	14th Ill. Cav.	Shawneetown
McGowan, William	Private	I	14th Ill. Cav.	Shawneetown
McGowan, William	Recruit	L	6th Ill. Cav.	Shawneetown
McGowen, Henry	Recruit	G	29th Ill. Inf.	Equality
McGuire, Burnell	Recruit		14th Ill. Cav.	Shawneetown
McGuire, Edward	Private	E	131st Ill. Inf.	Gallatin County
McGuire, James	Recruit	B	1st Ill. Cav.	Equality
McGuire, James J.	Recruit	E	14th Ill. Cav.	Shawneetown
McGuire, James J.	Private	F	14th Ill. Cav.	Shawneetown
McHenry, Thomas P.	Recruit	E	14th Ill. Cav.	Shawneetown
McIntier, William	Private	D	131st Ill. Inf.	Equality
McIntire, William	Private	G	131st Ill. Inf.	Equality
McIntyre, William	Recruit	G	29th Ill. Inf.	Equality
McKeaig, George W.	Colonel	HQ	120th Ill. Inf.	Shawneetown
McKee, John	Private	L	6th Ill. Cav.	Shawneetown
McKee, Joseph	Private	B	18th Ill. Inf.	Shawneetown
McKee, Thomas	Corporal	B	18th Ill. Inf.	Shawneetown
McKernan, Charles	Private	B	1st Ill. Cav.	Equality
McKernon, L. W.	Corporal	B	1st Ill. Cav.	Equality
McMahon, Hirma	Recruit	F	56th Ill. Inf.	Gallatin County
McMan, William	Private	D	131st Ill. Inf.	Equality
McMann, William	Corporal	G	131st Ill. Inf.	Equality
McMillen, William	Private	C	120th Ill. Inf.	Gallatin County
McMuechy, George	Private	B	18th Ill. Inf.	Shawneetown
McMullen, Nathaniel	Private	G	7th Ill. Cav.	New Haven
McMurtry, William P.	Adjutant	HQ	120th Ill. Inf.	Shawneetown
McNamara, John	Private	G	131st Ill. Inf.	Equality
McNanamire, John	Private	D	131st Ill. Inf.	Equality
McPeeters, David	Private	B	18th Ill. Inf.	Shawneetown
Meadows, Isom	Corporal	E	131st Ill. Inf.	Gallatin County
Meeker, William B.	Private	F	28th Ill. Inf.	New Market
Mellon, Charles	Recruit	K	87th Ill. Inf.	Shawneetown
Melton, James	Private	H	120th Ill. Inf.	Gallatin County
Melton, James H.	Private	B	1st Ill. Cav.	Equality

Name	Rank	Co.	Unit	Location
Melvin, Augustus H.	2nd Lt.	D	29th Ill. Inf.	New Haven
Melvin, Jonathan H.	Sergeant	E	14th Ill. Cav.	Shawneetown
Melvin, Thomas A.	Corporal	D	29th Ill. Inf.	Gallatin County
Meyhew, Benjamin F.	Private	G	131st Ill. Inf.	Equality
Miers, William	Recruit	E	14th Ill. Cav.	Shawneetown
Milburn, William D.	Private	B	18th Ill. Inf.	Shawneetown
Miles, William H.	Private	C	29th Ill. Inf.	Gallatin County
Miligan, Elihu	Private	D	56th Ill. Inf.	Gallatin County
Miller, Edon	Wagoner	D	120th Ill. Inf.	Gallatin County
Miller, Harrison	Recruit	E	3rd Ill. Cav.	Shawneetown
Miller, Jacob	Private	D	120th Ill. Inf.	Gallatin County
Miller, John M.	Private	B	18th Ill. Inf.	Shawneetown
Miller, John W.	Farrier	G	7th Ill. Cav.	New Haven
Miller, Peter B.	Private	G	56th Ill. Inf.	New Haven
Miller, William	Private	D	120th Ill. Inf.	Gallatin County
Mills, David	Private	E	131st Ill. Inf.	Gallatin County
Miner, Daniel	Private	K	131st Ill. Inf.	Gallatin County
Minor, Robert J.	Private	K	131st Ill. Inf.	Gallatin County
Mitchell, John Vergel	Recruit	H	120th Ill. Inf.	Gallatin County
Mobley, Alexander	Sergeant	E	131st Ill. Inf.	Gallatin County
Mobley, James R.	Recruit	C	87th Ill. Inf.	Shawneetown
Mobly, Francis M.	Private	D	29th Ill. Inf.	Gallatin County
Modglin, Ely J.	Private	G	131st Ill. Inf.	Equality
Modglin, John	Private	D	56th Ill. Inf.	Gallatin County
Modglin, John	Recruit	K	56th Ill. Inf.	Gallatin County
Moore, Abner R.	Recruit	E	14th Ill. Cav.	New Haven
Moore, Daniel W.	Private	C	120th Ill. Inf.	Gallatin County
Moore, James	Private	E	131st Ill. Inf.	Gallatin County
Moore, James	Private	B	131st Ill. Inf.	Gallatin County
Moore, John C.	Private	H	120th Ill. Inf.	Gallatin County
Moore, Pleasant	Private	D	120th Ill. Inf.	Gallatin County
Moore, William	Private	E	131st Ill. Inf.	Gallatin County
Moore, William H.	Corporal	D	120th Ill. Inf.	Gallatin County
Moreland, John B. F.	Private	E	131st Ill. Inf.	Gallatin County
Morgan, Richard	Recruit	F	28th Ill. Inf.	New Market
Morgan, Richard	Private	C	28th Ill. Inf. Cons.	New Market
Morgan, Stephen	Recruit	B	1st Ill. Cav.	Equality
Morgan, Stephen	Recruit	E	14th Ill. Cav.	Shawneetown
Morgan, Stephen	Private	F	14th Ill. Cav.	Shawneetown
Morris, Elijah	Private	B	18th Ill. Inf.	Shawneetown
Morris, Ezekiel	Private	G	131st Ill. Inf.	Equality
Morris, Ezekiel	Private	D	131st Ill. Inf.	Equality
Morris, Ezekiel	Recruit	H	29th Ill. Inf.	Equality
Morris, Henry M.	Private	F	6th Ill. Cav.	Gallatin County
Morris, John C.	Private	F	6th Ill. Cav.	Gallatin County
Morris, Jordan	Recruit	G	29th Ill. Inf.	Equality
Morris, Jordan	Private	G	7th Ill. Cav.	New Haven
Morris, Owen M.	Private	K	131st Ill. Inf.	Gallatin County
Morris, Thomas	Private	G	131st Ill. Inf.	Equality
Morris, William W.	Private	K	131st Ill. Inf.	Gallatin County
Morris, William W.	Private	B	131st Ill. Inf.	Gallatin County
Morris, William W.	Recruit	E	29th Ill. Inf.	Gallatin County
Morrow, Farrierquer	Farrier	L	6th Ill. Cav.	Shawneetown
Morrow, Thomas	Private	L	6th Ill. Cav.	Shawneetown
Morton, Daniel B.	Recruit	E	3rd Ill. Cav.	Shawneetown
Morton, John	Recruit	E	3rd Ill. Cav.	Shawneetown
Morton, Sanford B.	Sergeant	C	29th Ill. Inf.	Shawneetown
Moses, Charles	Private	D	29th Ill. Inf.	Gallatin County
Move, Robert F.	Private	K	131st Ill. Inf.	Gallatin County

Name	Rank	Co.	Unit	Location
Moye, Robert F.	Private	B	131st Ill. Inf.	Gallatin County
Munday, Hiram	Corporal	D	120th Ill. Inf.	Gallatin County
Munson, Albert	Private	B	18th Ill. Inf.	Shawneetown
Murphy, Ignatius	Recruit	B	1st Ill. Cav.	Equality
Murphy, John	Private	E	131st Ill. Inf.	Gallatin County
Murray, James W.	Recruit	E	3rd Ill. Cav.	Shawneetown
Murray, John	Corporal	E	131st Ill. Inf.	Gallatin County
Musgraves, Eli	Recruit	D	120th Ill. Inf.	Gallatin County
Myers, John	Private	B	18th Ill. Inf.	Shawneetown
Neighbours, John	Private	C	29th Ill. Inf.	Gallatin County
Nelson, Samuel	Corporal	G	7th Ill. Cav.	New Haven
Newell, Nathan L.	Private	B	18th Ill. Inf.	Shawneetown
Nichols, Elijah S.	Recruit	F	28th Ill. Inf.	New Market
Nicholson, Marmaduke	2nd Lt.	F	56th Ill. Inf.	Shawneetown
Nolen, James M.	Private	B	1st Ill. Cav.	Equality
Nolens, Joseph F.	Recruit		15th Ill. Cav.	Gallatin
Norris, Moses	Recruit	K	131st Ill. Inf.	Gallatin County
Norton, Alexander	Corporal	C	29th Ill. Inf.	Shawneetown
Norton, Charles	Private	D	120th Ill. Inf.	Gallatin County
Noye, Hiram	Private	B	18th Ill. Inf.	Shawneetown
O'Brien, Henry	Private	K	73rd Ill. Inf.	Equality
O'Brien, William	Corporal	B	18th Ill. Inf.	Shawneetown
Ogden, Samuel	Private	C	29th Ill. Inf.	Gallatin County
Oglesby, John R.	Recruit	G	29th Ill. Inf.	Equality
Oliver, Thomas	Private	C	56th Ill. Inf.	Gallatin County
Olney, John	1st Lt.	F	18th Ill. Inf.	Shawneetown
Onyett, Lorenzo C.	Sergeant	D	120th Ill. Inf.	Shawneetown
Orr, James	2nd Lt.	B	18th Ill. Inf.	Shawneetown
Orr, James	Private	C	18th Ill. Inf. Reorg.	Shawneetown
Oskins, Robert	Private	C	29th Ill. Inf.	Shawneetown
Overbee, John	Musician	D	120th Ill. Inf.	Gallatin County
Owen, Carr	Recruit	D	120th Ill. Inf.	Shawneetown
Owen, George W.	Recruit	D	120th Ill. Inf.	Shawneetown
Owens, John P.	Private	G	131st Ill. Inf.	Equality
Owens, John P.	Recruit	C	29th Ill. Inf.	Equality
Owins, John P.	Private	D	131st Ill. Inf.	Equality
Oxford, Isaac N.	Private	I	118th Ill. Inf.	Shawneetown
Oxford, Phillip	Private	I	118th Ill. Inf.	Shawneetown
Oyment, Mcdonald	Recruit	D	18th Ill. Inf.	Shawneetown
Ozee, William D.	Private	C	29th Ill. Inf.	Gallatin County
Pace, Nelson	Private	C	29th Ill. Inf.	Gallatin County
Page, Francis M.	Recruit	B	54th Ill. Inf.	Cottonwood
Palmer, Calvin H.	Corporal	G	131st Ill. Inf.	Equality
Palmer, Calvin H.	Private	D	131st Ill. Inf.	Equality
Palmer, Calvin H.	Recruit	G	29th Ill. Inf.	Equality
Palmer, Thomas J.	Corporal	G	131st Ill. Inf.	Equality
Palmer, Thomas J.	Corporal	D	131st Ill. Inf.	Equality
Palmer, Thomas J.	Recruit	G	29th Ill. Inf.	Equality
Parker, Newton C.	Private	K	131st Ill. Inf.	Gallatin County
Parks, Carroll	Recruit	B	1st Ill. Cav.	Equality
Pate, Amster B.	1st Lt.	E	131st Ill. Inf.	Gallatin County
Pate, Andrew	Private	B	131st Ill. Inf.	Gallatin County
Pate, Andrew	Recruit	C	29th Ill. Inf.	Gallatin County
Pate, James	Private	L	6th Ill. Cav.	Shawneetown
Pate, James R.	Private	B	131st Ill. Inf.	Gallatin County
Pate, James R.	Recruit	C	29th Ill. Inf.	Gallatin County
Pate, Omster B.	Sergeant	L	6th Ill. Cav.	Shawneetown
Pate, Philip A.	1st Lt.	E	131st Ill. Inf.	Gallatin County
Patillo, Milton C.	Sergeant	D	120th Ill. Inf.	Gallatin County

Name	Rank	Co.	Unit	Location
Patrick, Christopher C.	Private	C	56th Ill. Inf.	Gallatin County
Pattillo, Lemuel J.	Private	C	56th Ill. Inf.	Gallatin County
Pattils, Andrew P.	Corporal	F	6th Ill. Cav.	Gallatin County
Patton, James H.	Private	D	29th U.S. Col. Inf.	Shawneetown
Payton, Delbert	Private	B	1st Ill. Cav.	Equality
Pearce, William D.	Corporal	H	120th Ill. Inf.	Gallatin County
Peart, Isaac	Private	C	29th Ill. Inf.	Shawneetown
Peeples, George Washington	Corporal	C	56th Ill. Inf.	Shawneetown
Peeples, Robert	Corporal	L	6th Ill. Cav.	Shawneetown
Peers, William	Private	I	73rd Ill. Inf.	Shawneetown
Peers, William	Recruit	K	73rd Ill. Inf.	Shawneetown
Pellham, John	Corporal	L	6th Ill. Cav.	Shawneetown
Perdue, Joseph M.	Private	G	131st Ill. Inf.	Equality
Perkins, David H.	Private	D	29th Ill. Inf.	Gallatin County
Perry, James R.	Private	F	56th Ill. Inf.	Equality
Philbrick, Francis B.	Corporal	C	28th Ill. Inf. Cons.	New Market
Philips, Zephaniah	Musician	B	1st Ill. Cav.	Equality
Phillips, Zephaniah	Private	F	56th Ill. Inf.	Equality
Phillips, Zepheniah	2nd Lt.	F	120th Ill. Inf.	Equality
Pierson, Henry C.	Recruit	C	29th Ill. Inf.	Shawneetown
Pillow, Parker B.	Captain	D	120th Ill. Inf.	Shawneetown
Pinney, Sidney A.	2nd Lt.	E	131st Ill. Inf.	New Haven
Piper, Thomas M.	Private	B	1st Ill. Cav.	Equality
Pistole, Joel H.	Private	D	120th Ill. Inf.	Gallatin County
Pohd, Charles	Private	L	6th Ill. Cav.	Shawneetown
Poindexter, John	Asst. Surg.	HQ	87th Ill. Inf.	New Haven
Poindexter, Randall	Asst. Surg.	HQ	56th Ill. Inf.	Shawneetown
Pool, David N.	Corporal	G	7th Ill. Cav.	New Haven
Powell, Henry A.	Private	B	18th Ill. Inf.	Shawneetown
Powell, Robert W.	Private	F	6th Ill. Cav.	Gallatin County
Powers, Jesse H.	Recruit	B	54th Ill. Inf.	Cottonwood
Powers, Seth H.	Corporal	B	18th Ill. Inf.	Shawneetown
Prewet, Benjamin F.	Recruit		14th Ill. Cav.	Shawneetown
Price, Guilford	Private	D	120th Ill. Inf.	Gallatin County
Price, Lofton	Farrier	B	1st Ill. Cav.	Equality
Pritchett, Isaac C.	Private	H	120th Ill. Inf.	Gallatin County
Pritchett, William T.	Private	H	120th Ill. Inf.	Gallatin County
Proctor, Henry D.	Recruit	B	1st Ill. Cav.	Equality
Proctor, Samuel L. M.	Captain	B	1st Ill. Cav.	Equality
Pruit, Assen G.	Private	D	29th Ill. Inf.	Gallatin County
Pursell, Jesse	Corporal	B	1st Ill. Cav.	Equality
Quigley, Leonard E.	1st Lt.	G	29th Ill. Inf.	Gallatin County
Quigley, Phillip C.	Private	G	29th Ill. Inf.	Gallatin County
Raber, Levi	Sergeant	K	131st Ill. Inf.	Gallatin County
Raber, Levi	Sergeant	B	131st Ill. Inf.	Gallatin County
Raber, Levi	Recruit	I	29th Ill. Inf.	Gallatin County
Railing, John W.	Private	L	6th Ill. Cav.	Shawneetown
Rearden, James S.	Colonel	HQ	29th Ill. Inf.	Shawneetown
Reddick, Alverson	Private	B	18th Ill. Inf.	Shawneetown
Redman, John A.	Musician	C	29th Ill. Inf.	Shawneetown
Reebinacker, John	Corporal	L	6th Ill. Cav.	Shawneetown
Reeden, Wasner	Private	E	14th Ill. Cav.	Shawneetown
Renfro, Thomas	Recruit	F	87th Ill. Inf.	Shawneetown
Reynolds, Joseph B.	Private	B	1st Ill. Cav.	Equality
Reynolds, Richard	Private	D	56th Ill. Inf.	Gallatin County
Rice, Jacob	Private	D	120th Ill. Inf.	Gallatin County
Rice, James A.	Recruit	B	18th Ill. Inf.	Shawneetown
Rider, Edgar M.	Corporal	B	131st Ill. Inf.	Gallatin County
Rider, Edgar M.	Recruit	C	29th Ill. Inf.	Gallatin County

Name	Rank	Co.	Unit	Location
Riders, Edward M.	Private	K	131st Ill. Inf.	Gallatin County
Riley, Charles E.	Corporal	H	120th Ill. Inf.	Gallatin County
Riley, Hugh	Recruit	E	14th Ill. Cav.	Shawneetown
Riley, Hugh	Private	F	14th Ill. Cav.	Shawneetown
Rine, James	Private	A	56th Ill. Inf.	Shawneetown
Rinehold, George	Private	G	7th Ill. Cav.	Shawneetown
Roarch, Christopher C.	Recruit	D	29th Ill. Inf.	Gallatin County
Roark, Christopher C.	Private	B	131st Ill. Inf.	Gallatin County
Robbnett, Joseph	Sergeant	I	118th Ill. Inf.	Shawneetown
Robinson, James	Private	G	7th Ill. Cav.	New Haven
Robison, William F.	Recruit	K	56th Ill. Inf.	Gallatin County
Rodman, William	Private	G	7th Ill. Cav.	New Haven
Roger, John U.	Private	C	29th Ill. Inf.	Shawneetown
Rogers, Elijah	Private	C	29th Ill. Inf.	Shawneetown
Rogers, George	Private	D	56th Ill. Inf.	Gallatin County
Rogers, Joseph A.	Private	H	120th Ill. Inf.	Gallatin County
Roleman, Spencer	Private	D	120th Ill. Inf.	Gallatin County
Roleman, William	Recruit	E	14th Ill. Cav.	Shawneetown
Rollman, George	Corporal	K	131st Ill. Inf.	Gallatin County
Rollman, George W.	Corporal	B	131st Ill. Inf.	Gallatin County
Rollman, George W.	Recruit	C	29th Ill. Inf.	Gallatin County
Rollman, McDonald	Private	B	131st Ill. Inf.	Gallatin County
Rollman, Mcdonald	Recruit	C	29th Ill. Inf.	Gallatin County
Rolman, John	Private	K	6th Ill. Cav.	Gallatin County
Rolman, Mcdonald	Private	K	131st Ill. Inf.	Gallatin County
Rolman, William S.	Recruit	B	1st Ill. Cav.	Equality
Rose, John C.	Recruit	F	56th Ill. Inf.	New Market
Rountree, Marcus L.	Private	G	56th Ill. Inf.	Shawneetown
Rountree, William J.	Private	G	56th Ill. Inf.	Shawneetown
Rowark, Jonathan	Recruit	E	14th Ill. Cav.	New Market
Roy, William	Bugler	G	7th Ill. Cav.	New Haven
Ruddic, James	Private	C	29th Ill. Inf.	Shawneetown
Runnions, John	Private	B	131st Ill. Inf.	Gallatin County
Runnions, John	Recruit	C	29th Ill. Inf.	Gallatin County
Runyon, Isaac	Recruit	F	56th Ill. Inf.	New Market
Russ, James J.	Private	B	1st Ill. Cav.	Equality
Russ, James J.	Bugler	E	14th Ill. Cav.	Shawneetown
Russ, Wilson	Private	F	14th Ill. Cav.	Shawneetown
Russ, Wilson T.	Recruit	E	14th Ill. Cav.	Shawneetown
Russell, George G.	Corporal	H	120th Ill. Inf.	Gallatin County
Ryman, George	Private	D	120th Ill. Inf.	Gallatin County
Sallions, Thomas	Recruit	F	87th Ill. Inf.	Shawneetown
Sanders, Francis M.	Recruit		14th Ill. Cav.	Shawneetown
Sanders, Harmon	Recruit	L	14th Ill. Cav.	Shawneetown
Sanders, James T.	Private	E	131st Ill. Inf.	Gallatin County
Sanders, James T.	Private	B	131st Ill. Inf.	Gallatin County
Sanders, James T.	Recruit	D	29th Ill. Inf.	Gallatin County
Sanderson, James	Private	C	22nd Ill. Inf.	Shawneetown
Sanderson, John	Private	C	22nd Ill. Inf.	Shawneetown
Sanderson, Thomas	Private	D	120th Ill. Inf.	Gallatin County
Sanderson, William C.	Private	K	56th Ill. Inf.	Equality
Sartin, James	Private	B	18th Ill. Inf.	Shawneetown
Sauls, Abram	Sergeant	E	131st Ill. Inf.	Gallatin County
Sauls, Henry	Corporal	E	131st Ill. Inf.	Gallatin County
Sauls, James	Corporal	E	131st Ill. Inf.	New Haven
Scanland, William	2nd Lt.	B	18th Ill. Inf.	Shawneetown
Scates, Henry	Private	B	1st Ill. Cav.	Equality
Schellenger, W. S.	Recruit	F	6th Ill. Cav.	Shawneetown
Schoonover, William	Private	G	131st Ill. Inf.	Equality

Name	Rank	Co.	Unit	Location
Schreifer, Frederick	Musician	B	18th Ill. Inf.	Shawneetown
Scott, Samuel	Recruit	B	54th Ill. Inf.	Cottonwood
Seat, Alexander	Private	C	29th Ill. Inf.	Shawneetown
Seat, James	Private	C	29th Ill. Inf.	Shawneetown
Seaton, Silas P.	Private	D	120th Ill. Inf.	Gallatin County
Seats, Hardin	Private	B	1st Ill. Cav.	Equality
Seely, Samuel	Private	C	56th Ill. Inf.	Shawneetown
Seets, Hardin	Private	D	56th Ill. Inf.	Gallatin County
Seets, Hardin	Recruit	F	56th Ill. Inf.	Gallatin County
Seets, John H.	Private	D	56th Ill. Inf.	Gallatin County
Segars, Isaiah	Recruit	D	29th Ill. Inf.	Gallatin County
Segars, James	Private	D	29th Ill. Inf.	Gallatin County
Sells, Abraham	Recruit	C	29th Ill. Inf.	Shawneetown
Shafer, Jacob	Private	D	120th Ill. Inf.	Gallatin County
Shane, Howell T.	Private	H	120th Ill. Inf.	Gallatin County
Sharon, Huston	Private	D	120th Ill. Inf.	Gallatin County
Shaw, Edmund	Private	B	18th Ill. Inf.	Shawneetown
Shaw, John T.	Private	H	120th Ill. Inf.	Gallatin County
Shaw, John W.	Recruit	B	1st Ill. Cav.	Equality
Shelton, Preston C.	Recruit	D	87th Ill. Inf.	Shawneetown
Sheppard, David	Recruit	B	54th Ill. Inf.	Cottonwood
Sherwood, Edward	Private	D	120th Ill. Inf.	Gallatin County
Sherwood, John	Private	D	120th Ill. Inf.	Gallatin County
Sherwood, John C.	Private	C	29th Ill. Inf.	Shawneetown
Sherwood, Thomas	Private	F	6th Ill. Cav.	Gallatin County
Shreeves, William	Private	B	1st Ill. Cav.	Equality
Shrieve, James A.	Private	F	14th Ill. Cav.	Shawneetown
Shrives, James A.	Recruit	E	14th Ill. Cav.	Shawneetown
Simmons, Benjamin	Private	K	131st Ill. Inf.	Gallatin County
Simmons, James C.	Private	I	131st Ill. Inf.	Gallatin County
Simmons, James C.	Recruit	K	131st Ill. Inf.	Gallatin County
Simmons, Robert P.	2nd Lt.	E	14th Ill. Cav.	New Market
Simmons, Samuel	Private	B	1st Ill. Cav.	Equality
Simmons, Samuel	Private	B	131st Ill. Inf.	Gallatin County
Simmons, Samuel	Recruit	D	29th Ill. Inf.	Gallatin County
Simonds, William	Private	G	131st Ill. Inf.	Equality
Simons, Robert D.	Private	B	1st Ill. Cav.	Equality
Simons, Samuel	Corporal	K	131st Ill. Inf.	Gallatin County
Simpson, Robert	Private	K	73rd Ill. Inf.	Equality
Simpson, William	Recruit	G	29th Ill. Inf.	Equality
Sisk, John K.	Recruit	H	120th Ill. Inf.	Gallatin County
Sisney, Elias	Private	C	120th Ill. Inf.	Gallatin County
Sivels, George	Private	L	6th Ill. Cav.	Shawneetown
Sketo, Albert N.	Corporal	D	120th Ill. Inf.	Gallatin County
Slaten, Charles E.	Private	G	56th Ill. Inf.	Equality
Slatten, John W.	Private	K	13th Ill. Cav. Cons.	Gallatin
Sloan, Carson	Recruit	B	1st Ill. Cav.	Equality
Sloan, Franklin	Recruit	B	1st Ill. Cav.	Equality
Smiley, William	Recruit	B	1st Ill. Cav.	Equality
Smiley, William	Private	G	131st Ill. Inf.	Equality
Smith, Charles M.	Private	B	18th Ill. Inf.	Shawneetown
Smith, David R.	Private	G	7th Ill. Cav.	New Haven
Smith, Dennis	Private	K	131st Ill. Inf.	Gallatin County
Smith, Foster	Recruit	E	14th Ill. Cav.	Shawneetown
Smith, Foster	Private	F	56th Ill. Inf.	New Market
Smith, George O.	Asst. Surg.	HQ	53rd Ill. Inf.	Shawneetown
Smith, George W.	Private	E	131st Ill. Inf.	Gallatin County
Smith, George W.	Recruit	G	7th Ill. Cav.	New Haven
Smith, Henry	Private	D	120th Ill. Inf.	Gallatin County

Name	Rank	Co.	Unit	Location
Smith, Hezekiah	Recruit	B	1st Ill. Cav.	Equality
Smith, James	Recruit	E	87th Ill. Inf.	Shawneetown
Smith, James A.	Recruit	F	87th Ill. Inf.	Shawneetown
Smith, Jasper N.	Private	H	120th Ill. Inf.	Gallatin County
Smith, John B. F.	Corporal	G	29th Ill. Inf.	Gallatin County
Smith, Samuel	Private	A	33th Ill. Inf.	New Market
Smith, Stevens A.	Private	D	29th Ill. Inf.	New Market
Smith, Virginius M.	Private	D	29th Ill. Inf.	Gallatin County
Smith, William	Private	K	131st Ill. Inf.	Gallatin County
Smith, William C.	Private	L	6th Ill. Cav.	Shawneetown
Snodgrass, John W.	Recruit	B	54th Ill. Inf.	Cottonwood
Sollars, Frederick	Captain	K	131st Ill. Inf.	New Market
Solomon, James	Private	I	118th Ill. Inf.	Shawneetown
Spears, James N.	Private	B	1st Ill. Cav.	Equality
Spears, Joseph	Recruit	B	1st Ill. Cav.	Equality
Spencer, James	Recruit	E	14th Ill. Cav.	Shawneetown
Spencer, James	Private	F	14th Ill. Cav.	Shawneetown
Spencer, Lafayette	Recruit	B	18th Ill. Inf.	Shawneetown
Spencer, Peleg H.	Sergeant	B	1st Ill. Cav.	Equality
Spencer, Pelige H.	Qmtr. Sgt.	E	14th Ill. Cav.	Shawneetown
Stafford, John	Corporal	C	29th Ill. Inf.	Gallatin County
Stambach, Henry	Recruit	F	87th Ill. Inf.	Shawneetown
Stanton, Solomon	Private	B	18th Ill. Inf.	Shawneetown
Stapleton, James	Recruit	D	14th Ill. Cav.	Shawneetown
Starkey, Hugh K.	Private	K	56th Ill. Inf.	Gallatin County
Starkey, Jesse	Private	G	29th Ill. Inf.	Gallatin County
Stephenson, Andrew P.	Sergeant	B	1st Ill. Cav.	Equality
Stephenson, David W.	Private	B	1st Ill. Cav.	Equality
Stewart, Alonzo	Private	E	131st Ill. Inf.	Gallatin County
Stewart, Henry	Private	E	131st Ill. Inf.	Gallatin County
Stewart, Jesse M.	Recruit	I	87th Ill. Inf.	Shawneetown
Stewart, John A.	Recruit	D	29th Ill. Inf.	New Haven
Stewart, Wellington	Private	E	131st Ill. Inf.	Gallatin County
Stewart, Wellington	Corporal	A	131st Ill. Inf.	Gallatin County
Stewart, Wellington	Recruit	D	29th Ill. Inf.	Gallatin County
Stilley, James A.	Private	D	120th Ill. Inf.	Gallatin County
Stinneth, William I.	Corporal	L	6th Ill. Cav.	Shawneetown
Stinnett, William	Private	L	6th Ill. Cav.	Shawneetown
Stockwell, James	Private	B	18th Ill. Inf.	Shawneetown
Stone, Eberlee P. H.	Captain	D	29th Ill. Inf.	New Haven
Stone, William H.	Sergeant	G	7th Ill. Cav.	New Haven
Story, George W.	Private	D	56th Ill. Inf.	Gallatin County
Stout, Aaron R.	Adjutant	HQ	29th Ill. Inf.	Shawneetown
Stout, Henry	2nd Lt.	L	6th Ill. Cav.	Shawneetown
Sturgill, Fielding	Private	G	7th Ill. Cav.	New Haven
Sutton, William	Private	G	120th Ill. Inf.	Gallatin County
Swinney, Wiley B.	Recruit	B	1st Ill. Cav.	Equality
Taburn, Jefferson	Private	D	29th U.S. Col. Inf.	Shawneetown
Tally, Amos	Recruit	E	14th Ill. Cav.	Shawneetown
Tanger, Van Buren	Private	C	29th Ill. Inf.	Gallatin County
Tant, William D.	Corporal	E	131st Ill. Inf.	Gallatin County
Tarrant, James A.	Corporal	H	120th Ill. Inf.	Gallatin County
Tarrant, William	Recruit	B	1st Ill. Cav.	Equality
Tate, John W.	Private	E	13th Ill. Cav. Cons.	Gallatin
Tatum, George	Private	B	1st Ill. Cav.	Equality
Tatum, George	Corporal	D	56th Ill. Inf.	Gallatin County
Tatum, George	Recruit	F	56th Ill. Inf.	Gallatin County
Taylor, George W.	Private	I	118th Ill. Inf.	Shawneetown
Taylor, John H.	Private	G	7th Ill. Cav.	New Haven

Name	Rank	Co.	Unit	Location
Taylor, Oliver	Private	I	73rd Ill. Inf.	Shawneetown
Taylor, Oliver	Recruit	K	73rd Ill. Inf.	Shawneetown
Taylor, William J.	Private	E	131st Ill. Inf.	Gallatin County
Teacher, William W.	Private	E	131st Ill. Inf.	Gallatin County
Teachnor, William W.	Private	B	131st Ill. Inf.	Gallatin County
Thomas, George	Recruit	E	6th Ill. Cav.	Shawneetown
Thomas, Hezekiah	Private	D	56th Ill. Inf.	Gallatin County
Thomas, Tipton B.	Buglar	L	6th Ill. Cav.	Shawneetown
Thomasson, Nathaniel	Private	D	18th Ill. Inf.	Equality
Thompson, Alexander	Private	D	120th Ill. Inf.	Gallatin County
Thompson, George	Private	D	120th Ill. Inf.	Gallatin County
Thompson, John	Private	L	6th Ill. Cav.	Shawneetown
Thompson, William	Private	D	120th Ill. Inf.	Gallatin County
Thompson, William J.	Private	I	118th Ill. Inf.	Shawneetown
Timmons, Elijah J.	Corporal	C	29th Ill. Inf.	Gallatin County
Trafton, George W.	Lt. Colonel	HQ	7th Ill. Cav.	New Haven
Trafton, George W.	Captain	G	7th Ill. Cav.	New Haven
Tremble, John	Sergeant	D	56th Ill. Inf.	Gallatin County
Trimble, John	Recruit	F	56th Ill. Inf.	Gallatin County
Tucker, G. W.	Private	B	18th Ill. Inf.	Shawneetown
Tunnel, Woodford	Corporal	B	1st Ill. Cav.	Equality
Twyman, Edward B.	Qmtr. Sgt.	HQ	56th Ill. Inf.	Gallatin County
Twyman, Edward B.	Private	E	56th Ill. Inf.	Gallatin County
Tyler, John F. M.	Private	D	29th Ill. Inf.	Gallatin County
Vance, Oscar D.	Recruit	B	15th Ill. Cav.	Shawneetown
Vance, Oscar D.	Corporal	C	29th Ill. Inf.	Shawneetown
Vanover, James	Private	L	6th Ill. Cav.	Shawneetown
Venters, George	Private	C	29th Ill. Inf.	Shawneetown
Venters, John	Private	G	7th Ill. Cav.	New Haven
Vickery, Richard	Recruit	B	1st Ill. Cav.	Equality
Vincent, James	Private	B	1st Ill. Cav.	Equality
Vines, Thomas	Private	G	7th Ill. Cav.	New Haven
Vineyard, John	Private	K	131st Ill. Inf.	Gallatin County
Vinson, Charles E.	Corporal	C	29th Ill. Inf.	Shawneetown
Vinson, Levi D.	Private	G	7th Ill. Cav.	Cottonwood
Vinson, Samuel H.	Private	D	29th Ill. Inf.	Gallatin County
Vinyard, John	Private	B	131st Ill. Inf.	Gallatin County
Walker, Andrew J.	Private	K	131st Ill. Inf.	Gallatin County
Walker, Andrew J.	Private	B	131st Ill. Inf.	Gallatin County
Walker, Andrew J.	Recruit	E	29th Ill. Inf.	Gallatin County
Walker, Jefferson	Private	B	18th Ill. Inf.	Shawneetown
Wallace, Isaiah H.	Private	F	14th Ill. Cav.	Shawneetown
Wallis, James	Private	H	120th Ill. Inf.	Gallatin County
Walls, Francis M.	Private	E	131st Ill. Inf.	Gallatin County
Walsh, James	Sergeant	A	131st Ill. Inf.	Gallatin County
Walsh, James	Recruit	C	29th Ill. Inf.	Gallatin County
Ward, Patrick	Private	I	131st Ill. Inf.	Gallatin County
Warner, Edwin H.	Recruit	F	5th Ill. Cav.	Cottonwood
Warrick, Needham A.	Private	D	120th Ill. Inf.	Gallatin County
Watson, Emri C.	2nd Lt.	B	18th Ill. Inf.	Shawneetown
Watson, James	Private	D	56th Ill. Inf.	Gallatin County
Watson, James	Recruit	F	56th Ill. Inf.	Gallatin County
Watson, James H.	Private	D	120th Ill. Inf.	Gallatin County
Watson, Joseph	Private	D	120th Ill. Inf.	Gallatin County
Watson, Robert C.	Recruit	G	7th Ill. Cav.	Shawneetown
Weaver, Cornelius C.	Captain	B	18th Ill. Inf.	Shawneetown
Webb, Coleman H.	Private	E	131st Ill. Inf.	Gallatin County
Webb, Edward	Private	D	29th Ill. Inf.	Gallatin County
Webb, James	Private	G	7th Ill. Cav.	Cottonwood

Name	Rank	Co.	Unit	Location
Webb, Moses	Private	L	6th Ill. Cav.	Shawneetown
Webb, Samuel	Private	G	7th Ill. Cav.	Cottonwood
Webster, James	Recruit	E	14th Ill. Cav.	Shawneetown
Welch, James	Corporal	E	131st Ill. Inf.	Gallatin County
Welch, Michael	Recruit	E	14th Ill. Cav.	Shawneetown
Welsh, Pinckney J.	Major	HQ	56th Ill. Inf.	Shawneetown
Welsh, Pinckney J.	Captain	C	56th Ill. Inf.	Shawneetown
Welte, Jacob	Private	B	18th Ill. Inf.	Shawneetown
Wengler, John	Private	B	18th Ill. Inf.	Shawneetown
Wesenfelder, Peter	Private	C	120th Ill. Inf.	Gallatin County
West, Joseph F.	Private	E	131st Ill. Inf.	Gallatin County
Wheeler, Burton	Private	D	120th Ill. Inf.	Gallatin County
Whitaker, William	Private	D	131st Ill. Inf.	Equality
White, Charles W.	Private	B	1st Ill. Cav.	Equality
White, George W.	Private	K	131st Ill. Inf.	Gallatin County
White, George W.	Private	B	131st Ill. Inf.	Gallatin County
White, George W.	Recruit	C	29th Ill. Inf.	Gallatin County
White, Joseph	Recruit	E	14th Ill. Cav.	Shawneetown
White, Joseph	Private	C	29th Ill. Inf.	New Market
White, Leonard	Recruit	K	6th Ill. Cav.	Equality
White, William	Private	K	6th Ill. Cav.	Gallatin County
White, William D.	Recruit	D	87th Ill. Inf.	Shawneetown
Whiticker, William	Recruit	G	29th Ill. Inf.	Equality
Whiting, James	Private	D	29th Ill. Inf.	Gallatin County
Whitmore, Frank G.	Private	L	6th Ill. Cav.	Shawneetown
Whitney, Jasper	Private	B	18th Ill. Inf.	Shawneetown
Whittaker, William	Private	G	131st Ill. Inf.	Equality
Whittaker, William	Recruit	L	6th Ill. Cav.	Shawneetown
Whitten, Henry	Private	B	18th Ill. Inf.	Shawneetown
Whitten, Henry W.	Private	L	6th Ill. Cav.	Shawneetown
Whitting, John S.	Captain	D	29th Ill. Inf.	Equality
Wilburn, Oliver	Corporal	E	29th Ill. Inf.	Gallatin County
Wiliamson, William	Private	B	131st Ill. Inf.	Gallatin County
Wilkerson, John	Recruit	B	1st Ill. Cav.	Equality
Wilkerson, John	Private	D	131st Ill. Inf.	Equality
Wilkison, John	Corporal	G	131st Ill. Inf.	Equality
Willford, Wilson	Recruit		118th Ill. Inf.	Shawneetown
William, George	Private	B	18th Ill. Inf.	Shawneetown
Williams, Chesby R.	Private	H	120th Ill. Inf.	Gallatin County
Williams, David	Sergeant	D	56th Ill. Inf.	Gallatin County
Williams, David	Recruit	K	56th Ill. Inf.	Gallatin County
Williams, George W.	Private	G	56th Ill. Inf.	Shawneetown
Williams, Isaac B.	Private	G	29th Ill. Inf.	Gallatin County
Williams, James H.	Recruit	B	1st Ill. Cav.	Equality
Williams, James N.	Private	B	1st Ill. Cav.	Equality
Williams, John	Private	I	118th Ill. Inf.	Shawneetown
Williams, John A.	Private	D	29th Ill. Inf.	Gallatin County
Williams, John M.	Private	D	131st Ill. Inf.	Equality
Williams, John M.	Recruit	G	29th Ill. Inf.	Gallatin County
Williams, John N.	Corporal	G	131st Ill. Inf.	Gallatin County
Williams, John W.	Recruit	E	3rd Ill. Cav.	Shawneetown
Williams, Marmaduke	Recruit	I	29th Ill. Inf.	Gallatin County
Williams, Mcdonald	Private	G	29th Ill. Inf.	Gallatin County
Williams, Philip C.	Private	B	1st Ill. Cav.	Equality
Williams, Phillip C.	Private	D	56th Ill. Inf.	Gallatin County
Williams, William	Recruit		56th Ill. Inf.	New Market
Williams, William F.	1st Lt.	D	56th Ill. Inf.	Gallatin County
Williamson, Joseph	Recruit	K	131st Ill. Inf.	Gallatin County
Williamson, Joseph	Recruit	I	29th Ill. Inf.	Gallatin County

Williamson, Joseph A.	Private	B	131st Ill. Inf.	Gallatin County
Williamson, Joseph W.	Private	I	131st Ill. Inf.	Gallatin County
Williamson, William	Private	K	131st Ill. Inf.	Gallatin County
Williamson, William	Recruit	I	29th Ill. Inf.	Gallatin County
Williamson, William, Jr.	Recruit	B	1st Ill. Cav.	Equality
Willis, Daniel M.	1st Lt.	K	131st Ill. Inf.	Gallatin County
Willis, Moses	Recruit	I	87th Ill. Inf.	Shawneetown
Willis, Thomas	Recruit	D	29th Ill. Inf.	New Haven
Wilmoth, Benjamin	Private	E	13th Ill. Cav. Cons.	Gallatin
Wiloford, Wiley	Private	F	56th Ill. Inf.	Shawneetown
Wilson, Bluford	Adjutant	HQ	120th Ill. Inf.	Shawneetown
Wilson, Charles H.	Private	B	18th Ill. Inf.	Shawneetown
Wilson, David C. A.	Private	K	6th Ill. Cav.	Gallatin County
Wilson, Henry S.	Major	HQ	18th Ill. Inf.	Shawneetown
Wilson, Henry S.	2nd Lt.	A	18th Ill. Inf.	Shawneetown
Wilson, Henry S.	Captain	B	18th Ill. Inf.	Shawneetown
Wilson, James M.	Private	F	6th Ill. Cav.	Gallatin County
Wilson, William S.	Private	B	18th Ill. Inf.	Shawneetown
Winbrow, Joshua T.	Private	C	29th Ill. Inf.	Gallatin County
Winterberger, Alvis	Private	C	120th Ill. Inf.	Gallatin County
Winters, Granville	Blacksmith	L	6th Ill. Cav.	Shawneetown
Wollam, George	Recruit	B	1st Ill. Cav.	Equality
Womack, David	Private	C	29th Ill. Inf.	Gallatin County
Wood, Ira	Private	G	131st Ill. Inf.	Equality
Wood, Ira	Private	D	131st Ill. Inf.	Equality
Wood, Ira	Recruit	G	29th Ill. Inf.	Equality
Woodall, William	Private	D	56th Ill. Inf.	Gallatin County
Woods, Ezekiel	Recruit	K	131st Ill. Inf.	Gallatin County
Woods, Ezekiel W.	Private	E	131st Ill. Inf.	Gallatin County
Woodward, Samuel L.	1st Lt.	G	6th Ill. Cav.	Shawneetown
Wooly, Hiram	Private	F	131st Ill. Inf.	Gallatin County
Wright, James	Recruit	E	6th Ill. Cav.	Shawneetown
Wright, Jesse L.	Sergeant	G	131st Ill. Inf.	Equality
Yancey, Thomas G.	Recruit	C	6th Ill. Cav.	Shawneetown
Yates, James A.	Private	G	29th Ill. Inf.	Gallatin County
Yates, Jonathan H.	Private	K	6th Ill. Cav.	Gallatin County
Yocum, John	Recruit	B	54th Ill. Inf.	Cottonwood
Yost, Casper	1st Lt.	B	1st Ill. Cav.	Equality
Yost, John	2nd Lt.	B	1st Ill. Cav.	Equality
Young, Benjamin F.	Private	D	56th Ill. Inf.	Gallatin County
Young, Henry	Private	D	29th Ill. Inf.	Gallatin County
Young, James M	Private	D	29th Ill. Inf.	Gallatin County
Young, John	Private	G	131st Ill. Inf.	Equality
Young, John	Private	D	131st Ill. Inf.	Equality
Zimmerman, John	Private	F	28th Ill. Inf.	New Market
Zimmerman, John	Private	C	28th Ill. Inf. Cons.	New Market
Zook, Abraham	Private	B	131st Ill. Inf.	Gallatin County
Zook, Abraham S.	Recruit	F	29th Ill. Inf.	Gallatin County
Zuck, Abraham	Sergeant	K	131st Ill. Inf.	Gallatin County

Spanish-American War

The following men from Gallatin County served in the Spanish-American War in 1898-1899.

Ninth Illinois Infantry – Company B

Captain
Townshend, Orval P.   Shawneetown

First Lieutenant
Gregg, James G.   Omaha

Second Lieutenant
Willis, Jacob   Ridgway

First Sergeant
Bahr, Charles   Shawneetown

Sergeants
Heath, Thomas S.   Shawneetown
Johnson, George A.   Cottonwood
Nation, Thomas C.   Equality
Rubenacker, Edward E.   Shawneetown
Wright, Robert E.   Equality

Corporals
Carroll, Henry D.   Omaha
Cluck, Joseph E.   Equality
Hale, Robert   Shawneetown
Joiner, Robert W.   Ridgway
Kinsall, Dan M.   Omaha
Mace, Edward   Shawneetown
McDaniel, Edward T.   New Haven
Smith, George W.   Equality
Weigant, William A.   New Haven
Wood, Walter W.   New Haven

Wagoner
Bellah, Thomas F.   Omaha

Privates
Allen, Samuel   Shawneetown
Armstrong, Elias A.   Omaha
Bean, General F. M.   Ridgway
Blackard, Edward S.   Omaha
Bruce, James M.   Ridgway
Burrell, Charles   Equality
Butler, William W.   Equality
Clayton, Alex   Shawneetown
Colvard, Charles   Shawneetown
Cox, Charles D.   Shawneetown
Davis, John W. F.   Ridgway
Davis, Thomas G.   Ridgway
Dolph, Hiram   Shawneetown
Elder, George R.   Equality
Farmer, Joseph D.   Equality
Ford, Clarence T.   Shawneetown
Goodpaster, Franklin   Equality
Goodpaster, John   Equality
Hemphill, Rufus M.   Ridgway
Holleman, Henry H.   Omaha
Jones, James   Shawneetown
Kannady, Thomas J.   Ridgway
Kingston, Jeff   Equality
Kinsall, Edward J.   Cottonwood
Logan, Moses M.   Shawneetown
Logsdon, John W.   Shawneetown
Mayfield, John L.   Ridgway
Murrap, Ed C.   Ridgway
Penberton, James A.   Equality
Reeves, William D.   Cottonwood
Rineholdt, George   Junction City
Rollman, William T.   Ridgway
Sturman, Robert L.   Omaha
Swan, Walter N.   Cottonwood
Talty, Eugene   Shawneetown
Talty, Lawrence   Shawneetown
Wild, John H.   Shawneetown
Williams, John   Omaha
Williamson, Daniel   Ridgway

Ninth Illinois Infantry – Misc. Companies

Company D (privates)
Ginger, Lacy Lee   Saline Mines
Locklar, Samuel   Equality
Moore, Otis C.   Ridgway
Slayton, Samuel S.   Kedron
Vinyard, John T.   Equality

Company E (privates)
Keagy, Charles   Shawneetown
Sanks, George D.   Shawneetown
Venters, Pete   Shawneetown

Company I (privates)
Williams, Herbert   New Haven

Company K (privates)
Gholson, George   New Haven
Routh, William V.   New Haven

Company M (privates)
Bryan, Simon P.   New Haven
Rice, Benjamin   Ridgway
Rice, Robert   Ridgway

Gallatin County Biographies

The following biographical sketches are derived from a variety of sources. The year following the name provides the date of publication. The source of the sketch is provided at the end of each one. Occasionally, the word (deceased) follows the name. This indicates that the person profiled had died prior to publication. As typical of the time period, nearly everyone of the biographies are of white men, very few woman had their biography printed, and only one African-American biographical sketch could be found from this period.

Jackson Abshier – 1883 208	Charles Carroll – 1905 234
F. M. Aldridge, M.D. – 1883 208	Robert B. Cash – 1905 235
William P. Aldridge – 1883 208	George P. Cassidy, M.D., (deceased) – 1905 235
John C. Anderson – 1905 209	James T. Colbert – 1905 236
J. W. Armstrong – 1883 210	Henry A. Cole, M.D. – 1876 237
I. M. Asbury, M.D. – 1883 210	G. W. Combs – 1887 237
Calvin M. Baker – 1905 211	George Washington Combs – 1905 237
George D. Barger – 1887 211	Charles Cook – 1883 239
J. B. Barger – 1887 212	Silas Cook – 1883 239
Jacob Barger – 1905 212	Silas Cook – 1887 239
Joseph Barnett – 1887 214	Prof. Thomas Jefferson Cooper – 1876 240
John S. Barter – 1883 214	John A. Crawford – 1887 240
Henry M. Bean – 1905 214	John Hart Crenshaw – 1905 241
James M. Bean – 1905 215	Rev. Nathaniel Crow, D.D. – 1912 241
James M. Bishop – 1887 216	John Daily – 1905 243
Harvey P. Blackard – 1905 216	William S. Dale – 1883 244
James S. Blue – 1905 217	A. F. Davenport – 1887 244
Edgar Bogardus – 1878 218	Abner F. Davenport – 1905 245
Isaac N. Bourland, M.D. – 1905 219	Rev. Robert Macklin Davis – 1883 245
Capt. John M. Bowling, M. D. – 1905 220	Rev. Macklin Davis – 1887 246
John William Bowling – 1905 221	Robert M. Davis – 1905 247
William Granville Bowman – 1876 222	J. Louis Devous – 1905 249
John R. Boyd – 1887 223	Joseph Devous – 1905 250
W. J. Boyd – 1887 223	Jonathan Dillard – 1905 251
William James Boyde – 1876 224	Martin Doherty – 1905 252
H. P. Bozarth – 1883 224	Felix Downen (deceased) – 1905 253
Harmon Pinnell Bozarth – 1905 225	Joseph Drone, Jr. – 1887 253
Alanson D. F. Brockett – 1883 227	Marion N. Drone – 1912 254
George W. Bruce – 1883 227	Charles E. Dupler – 1887 255
Robert J. Bruce – 1883 227	Notley Duvall – 1887 255
Robert J. Bruce – 1905 227	Henry Earnshaw – 1887 255
William M. Bruce – 1883 228	Lt. J. M. Eddy – 1887 256
T. W. M. Burroughs – 1887 229	Conrad O. Edwards – 1887 256
Albert Gallatin Caldwell – 1887 229	George T. Edwards – 1905 257
Frank E. Callicott – 1905 230	Leonard Edwards – 1905 258
William Campbell, M. D. – 1905 232	William G. Edwards – 1905 258
M. Carney – 1905 233	Mathias Epley – 1883 259

205

Name	Page
James Farley – 1883	259
Maurice Feehrer – 1883	259
William Ezra Ferrell – 1883	260
Judge Ajax Fillingin – 1887	260
Capt. James Ford – 1883	261
Thomas K. Ford – 1883	261
Isaac A Foster – 1905	261
Joseph Foster – 1905	262
Thomas J. Frohock – 1905	263
Charles R. Galloway – 1883	263
J. B. Gates – 1887	264
William Jefferson Gatewood – 1887	264
Richard Gill – 1887	265
Thomas H. Glasscock – 1905	265
Lucien Winslow Gordon, M. D. – 1905	266
Francis A. Gregg – 1905	267
H. C. Gregg – 1905	268
Hugh C. Gregg – 1883	269
William E. Gregg – 1883	269
Anthony Gross – 1887	270
John Grumley – 1905	270
Amariah Gwaltney – 1905	271
J. W. Hales – 1905	271
James Hall – 1856	272
Mary H. Hall – 1912	276
Charles S. Hanmore – 1883	278
Willis B. Hargrave – 1887	279
W. C. and B. R. Harsha – 1887	279
George Harrelson – 1905	280
James C. Harrell – 1883	280
William Finley Harrell – 1883	281
H. Harrington – 1887	281
John W. Harrington – 1905	281
James H. Hemphill – 1887	282
Thomas B. Hick, M.D. – 1883	283
Thomas B. Hick, M.D. – 1905	283
Thomas S. Hick (deceased) – 1883	284
Henry Hill – 1887	285
J. A. Hinch – 1883	285
Lowry Hinch – 1883	285
John T. Hogan – 1905	286
Richard M. Holland – 1905	286
George L. Houston – 1905	287
Will A. Howell – 1905	288
Frederick Adolphus Hubbard – 1895	290
Columbus M. Hudgins – 1883	292
William Inman – 1905	292
Daniel Jacobs – 1876	293
Dr. M. S. Jones – 1887	293
Moses Kanady – 1887	294
Lt. Wash. Kanady – 1887	294
Victor Karcher – 1887	295
Benjamin Kinsall – 1883	295
Benjamin Kinsall – 1887	295
D. M. Kinsall – 1887	296
David M. Kinsall – 1905	297
Monroe Douglas Kinsall – 1883	298
Prof. William M. Kinsall – 1887	299
Christian Kratz – 1905	299
Prof. R. A. Lamb – 1887	300
Marshall E. Lambert – 1905	300
James S. Lasater – 1883	301
John B. Latimer – 1883	301
Raphael E. Lawler – 1905	302
Prof. C. J. Lemen – 1887	303
Samuel D. Lewis – 1883	304
David A. Logan – 1905	304
John R. Logan – 1905	305
J. E. Logsdon – 1887	305
J. J. Logsdon – 1887	306
James J. Logsdon – 1905	306
Joseph Logsdon – 1905	307
Joseph E. Logsdon – 1905	309
Thomas B. Logsdon – 1905	309
William Hick Loomis – 1887	310
John Marshall – 1883	310
Thomas Martin – 1883	311
Judge Angus M. L. McBane – 1887	312
Angus M. L. McBane – 1905	312
Josiah McCue – 1905	318
C. W. McGehee – 1887	319
F. M. McGehee – 1887	319
W. S. McGehee – 1887	320
W. Smith McGehee – 1905	320
Dr. J. T. McIlrath – 1887	321
William McIntire – 1905	321
William R. McKernan – 1905	322
Franklin McLain – 1887	323
Peter McMurchy – 1887	323
Edgar Mills – 1887	324
Edgar Mills – 1905	324
Albert C. Millspaugh – 1912	326
James W. Millspaugh – 1887	327
R. L. Millspaugh – 1887	327
James Mitchell – 1905	328
John G. Mobley – 1905	329
George W. Moore – 1905	329
John S. Moore – 1887	330
Joseph H. Moore – 1883	331
Fredrick Mossman – 1887	331

William T. Moxley – 1887 331
Frederick Naas – 1905 332
J. F. Nolen – 1887 333
James O'Rourke – 1905 333
Granville R. Pearce – 1883 334
J. McKee Peeples – 1887 334
W. A. Peeples... 335
W. S. Phillips – 1887 335
Winfield Scott Phillips – 1905 335
Winfield S. Phillips – 1912 337
M. M. Pool – 1887 338
Marshall Mason Pool – 1876 339
Orval Pool (deceased) – 1876 339
General Thomas Posey (deceased) – 1912 339
George H. Potter – 1887 340
Joseph L. Purvis – 1883 340
Simon Baptiste Questell (deceased) – 2000 340
James A. Quick – 1905 341
Leonard E. Quigley – 1883 342
Philip C. Quigley – 1883 342
Moses M. Rawlings – 1883 342
Dent Reid – 1905 345
Rev. Robert Reid – 1905 345
James August Rensmann – 1887 346
Edward Rice – 1883 346
Edward Rice – 1905 347
George W. Rich – 1887 347
Albert G. Richeson – 1905 348
John D. Richeson – 1876 349
John D. Richeson – 1887 349
Edgar Rider – 1905... 350
Thomas S. Ridgway – 1876 351
Hon. Thomas S. Ridgway – 1887 351
Blueford Robinett – 1905 352
George W. Robinson – 1883 353
Hon. Carl Roedel – 1887 354
Carl Roedel – 1912 354
John W. Rogers – 1905 355
Robert Monroe Rudolph – 1905 356
Frank N. Sanders – 1905 357
William J. Sanders – 1905 358
Henry G. Sanks – 1905 359

Wiilliam M. Satterley – 1905.. 360
F. H. Sellers – 1887 360
Amaziah Morgan Sergeant – 1876................................... 361
J. P. Siddall – 1905 361
Amos L. Siebman – 1905.. 362
Virginius W. Smith – 1912 363
J. E. Speer – 1887 365
Allen T. Spivey – 1905 365
Allen Thomas Spivey – 1912 366
Capt. W. H. Stiles – 1887 369
William Henry Stiles – 1905 369
Gen. Joseph Montfort Street – 1918 371
H. C. Strickland – 1887 375
E. L. Tadlock – 1905 375
Joseph W. Towle – 1912 376
Richard Wellington Townshend – 1876 377
Richard W. Townshend – 1887 377
L. F. Tromly – 1887 380
Isaac T. Trusty – 1883 381
James B. Turner (deceased) – 1905 381
Peter J. Valter – 1912 382
George J. Vineyard – 1887 383
John B. Walters – 1905 383
William H. Walters – 1883 384
John T. Wathen – 1887 384
Ellen B. White – 1887 385
Isaac White (deceased) – 1889 385
J. W. Wilkins – 1905 392
W. J. Wilks – 1905 392
Aaron Wilson (colored) – 1887 393
Alois Winterberger – 1905.. 399
Marshall Wiseheart – 1905 400
R. J. Wiseheart – 1887 401
Richard J. Wiseheart (deceased) – 1905 401
Samuel Wiseheart (deceased) – 1887 402
James W. Young (deceased) – 1905............................... 402
Edmund D. Youngblood – 1876 403
Hon. E. D. Youngblood – 1887 403
Christian Zinn – 1887 404
William J. Zirkelbach – 1905 404
Gallatin County Bank – 1912 405

Jackson Abshier – 1883

JACKSON ABSHIER, born Jan. 8, 1815, the day of the memorable battle of New Orleans, was a son of Thomas and Nancy A. (Perryman) Abshier, natives of North Carolina. Their parents moved to Adair County, Ky., when they were both quite young and they were married there, about 1812, and moved to Murray County, Tenn.

They resided in Tennessee till 1829, when, with a family of ten children, they moved to Franklin Co., Ill. In 1833 the children that were living and unmarried and their mother came to New Haven, where they have since resided. The names of his father's family were — Elizabeth, Anderson, Jackson, Elias, Malinda, Milly L., now living. Anderson was in the Black Hawk War. He lives in Thompson, Franklin Co., Ill. Elizabeth married Wesley Fletcher and lives in Saline County. Washington lives at Tipton, Mo. Maria married J. L. Purvis, of New Haven.

— *History of White County, Illinois.*

F. M. Aldridge, M.D. – 1883

F. M. ALDRIDGE, M.D., the well-known physician and surgeon, was born near Mount Vernon, April 14, 1843, and was a son of Eli and Lavina (Kivit) Aldridge, both natives of North Carolina.

His professional education commenced under Dr. E. V. Spencer, physician and surgeon of Mt. Vernon, as preceptor, which took three years of study. One course of lectures was taken at Ann Arbor, and the graduating ones at the Western Reserve Medical College, Cleveland, Ohio, graduating in March, 1868. Previous to this he had been a farmer, and was married to Mary J. Black daughter of James and Nancy Black, of Posey County. It was after her death that he commenced to study for his profession. After his graduation he located in New Haven, where he married Fatima A. Hinch, daughter of Benjamin P. Hinch, by whom he had two children — Spencer (deceased), and Frances. Here he practiced for three years, gaining reputation and honor. When his wife died, in 1872, he south travel for his health and to partly savage his grief.

For three years or more he was in Texas, sometimes in business and at others solely for pleasure. Returning he re-established himself in New Haven, and is today a leading surgeon. For many miles around, in White, Gallatin and Posey counties, his services are sought when cases of dangerous surgical operations require the hand of a skilled surgeon, and are usually attended with the most satisfactory results.

— *History of White County, Illinois.*

William P. Aldridge – 1883

WILLIAM P. ALDRIDGE, born in Emma Township, White County, Ill., April 16, 1844, is a son of Russell D. and Sarah (Smith) Aldridge. Russell D.'s father was a Scotchman by birth and came to this country about 1800, locating in North Carolina, where Russell D. was born, in 1811. Their family consisted of seven children — Peter, Warren,

John, Russell D., Eliza, Patsy and Harriet. They moved to Posey County, Ind., being of the earliest settlers. The descendants live in that vicinity today.

Russell D. was married in White County and settled in Big Prairie Precinct. His family consisted of four children — Permelia (Mrs. N. McMullen, deceased), William P., George D., and Harriet (Mrs. Joel Clark). He was in the Mexican War. William P. Aldridge was married in 1867 to Mary, daughter of George and Emily Hantchel. They had four children - Sarah (died in infancy), Clara B., Minnie R. and Charles. Mrs. Aldrich died in November, 1878. In June 1881, Mr. Aldrich married Harriet, daughter of William and Mary Downes, of Posey County, Ind. Her father died when she was a young girl, and her mother married William McDaniel and moved to Emma Township, White County, Ill. Mr. and Mrs. Aldridge have one child - William.

Mr. Aldridge moved to New Haven in 1877. He has been deputy sheriff of Gallatin County four years; was marshal of the town three years, til 1880; has been a township trustee five years; was appointed postmaster of New Haven in February, 1882. At the post office is located the Evansville Telephone Exchange, of which Mr. Aldridge is operator. Mr. Aldridge enlisted in 1862, when 18, in Company. A, 65th Indiana Infantry. He was with Sherman on his March to the Sea, and was in East Tennessee under Foster. He was in 42 battles and skirmishes. He was mustered out at Greensboro, N.C.

— *History of White County, Illinois.*

John C. Anderson – 1905

JOHN C. ANDERSON, a farmer and stock dealer, living near Omaha, Ill., is a descendant of one of the oldest families in that portion of the Lower Ohio Valley. His grandfather, Solomon Anderson, was born in South Carolina, Feb. 8, 1806, his parents being James and Polly Anderson. On May 5, 1830, Solomon Anderson was married to Margaret Williams of Kentucky, she being at the time of her marriage but fifteen years of age, and soon afterward settled in Posey county, Ind., on the site of the village of old Springfield. There he followed the occupations of farming and shoemaking, and achieved quite a reputation as a hunter and trapper. The children of Solomon and Margaret Anderson were William N., Urbane, Asa C., Nancy, Martha, Margaret, Mary E., John and Elias.

William N. was born Sept. 2, 1831, and died Dec. 26, 1857. He married Mary A. Rusher, daughter of Jerry Rusher, who came from North Carolina in pioneer days and settled in Posey county. This couple were the parents of John C. Anderson/, the subject of this sketch, who was born in White county, Ill., Dec. 20, 1854. When he was but three weeks old his parents removed to Posey county, and there he grew to manhood on his father's farm.

At the age of twenty-one years he started out for himself. On Sept. 6, 1877, he was married to Miss Hannah Downen and in October came to Gallatin county, locating on the farm where he now lives, only thirty acres of which was at that time under cultivation. For two and a half years he lived in a log cabin, when he built a better house, and by his own industry he has cleared 125 acres of land, leaving only about twelve or thirteen acres of his farm that is not now under cultivation. Mr. Anderson buys and ships a great deal of live stock, most of which is shipped from Omaha. He has followed this business in addition to his farming interests for about fourteen years, and has been very successful as a stock dealer. He is a member of the Ancient Order of United Workmen and in politics is independent, voting for the man rather than for the candidate of any particular party. He and his wife have the following children: William L., Bertha, Stella M., Julia H., Mary A., Dora and Audrey.

— *Memoirs of the Lower Ohio Valley.*

J. W. Armstrong – 1883

J. W. ARMSTRONG was born in Indian Creek Township, White Co., Ill., Dec. 24, 1824. He was a son of Abraham L. Armstrong, and grandson of Lancelot Armstrong, who was one of the earliest settlers of North Carolina, and who served through the war of the Revolution, being in the service seven years. He was held in captivity by the Indians two years. Mr. Armstrong's father was a native of White County, Va. He emigrated to Kentucky, from there to Tennessee, and then to White County, Ill., in 1819. He was a journeyman hatter and worked at his trade a number of years in the vicinity of New Haven. He married Mary Lamb, daughter of John Lamb, a Revolutionary patriot. He was Justice of the Peace 28 years with an interim of but one term. He served in the war of 1812 under General Jackson.

J. W. Armstrong was married in 1855 to Margaret S. Blackard. They have a family of seven sons and three daughters, all living in this vicinity.

— *History of White County, Illinois.*

I. M. Asbury, M.D. – 1883

I. M. ASBURY, M.D., was born in McLeansboro, Hamilton Co., Ill, July 6, 1848. He was a son of Wesley and Susan M. (Mitchell) Asbury. His father was a native of North Carolina, and came to this State in 1844; at present engaged in farming. His mother is a native of Illinois. Her father, Ichabod Mitchell, was among the earliest settlers of Hamilton County, and was elected the first Treasurer of the county.

The subject of this sketch was reared in his native town, where he received an elementary school education. When 16 years of age he enlisted in the 60th Illinois Infantry, Company A, and remained until the close of the war. He was with Sherman's army in the grand March to the Sea. After the war he attended the High School of McLeansboro, and in the mean time read medicine with Dr. David Barry as preceptor. In 1868 he was in Minnesota, where he was employed in a drug store, and at the same time continued his medical studies. He returned to Illinois in two years, where he was again under the tuition of his former preceptor. In 1871 Dr. Asbury attended lectures at the Cincinnati Eclectic Medical College, graduating Mary 19, 1873. He practiced in Springfield for some time with good success, and has since been in practice in and about New Haven. Dr. Asbury has been a close student and thoroughly in love with his profession. The Doctor is a member of the Masonic order, and has represented his lodge in McLeansboro, as Master Mason, for several years.

He married, Jan. 1, 1877, Miss Mary Webb, daughter of John Webb, of Hamilton County, where she was born. The Doctor has find literary tastes, is a close student, and a conscientious, Christian gentleman.

— *History of White County, Illinois.*

Calvin M. Baker – 1905

CALVIN M. BAKER, a farmer near Equality, Gallatin County, Ill., is one of the oldest residents in that section of the state. He was born in Walker County, Ala., Dec. 27, 1824, his parents being William and Phoebe (Collinsworth) Baker.

In 1828 William Baker loaded one wagon with his worldly goods and with his wife and children came overland to Shawneetown. He located at the John Crenshaw salt works, where he was employed for about two years. He then entered 40 acres of land on Eagle Creek, built a log cabin and devoted the rest of his life to agricultural pursuits.

He died near Equality in 1841, aged 52 years. His wife died some time later at the age of 55. Of their children but three are now living, viz.: Calvin M., the subject of this sketch; Sarah, widow of William Dorsey, and William, who lives in Arkansas. Those dead are Elizabeth, who married Wallace McKenney, and lived to be 87 years old; Preston, who died at the age of 23 years; Covington, died at the age of seven years; Henry, died when he was about 20 years old; Phoebe, died in early childhood; James and Felix, who each died when about two years old; and Caroline, who married Thomas Scudmore.

When Calvin M. Baker was about 17 years old he commenced the battle of life by renting a farm, raising a crop in the summer months and working at the Illinois Iron Works in the winter time. He continued in this way for a few years, when on Jan. 10, 1850, he was married to Miss Frances Calvert[221] and for the next four years lived in Hardin County. He then returned to Gallatin County and bought a tract of 120 acres of land, upon which, to use the old familiar expression, "there was not a stick of timber amiss." This place has been his home for 50 years, though he has added to his original farm until he now owns 360 acres. Here he has seen his children grow to maturity, marry and found homes of their own, and here in 1879 be lost his wife by death, after nearly 30 years of happy married life.

Their children are Sarah, widow of Wiley Rose, now living at Elizabethtown, Ill.; William, who lives near his father; Phoebe, wife of John Harvey, also living in the neighborhood; Rena, deceased; Mary, wife of Harry Pearson, living near Harrisburg, Ill.; Lucy, wife of Charles Walsen, also living near Harrisburg; Effie, wife of John Brown, living near Equality.

Mr. Baker has been one of the successful farmers and stock raisers of Gallatin County for many years. He is a Democrat and cast his first presidential vote for Lewis Cass in 1848. Since then he has always been a stanch defender of Democratic principles, though he has many warm personal friends among those of the opposite political belief because of his sympathetic nature and genial disposition.

— *Memoirs of the Lower Ohio Valley*.

George D. Barger – 1887

GEORGE D. BARGER, a pioneer and farmer, was born in Shawneetown in 1832. He is the youngest of seven children of Jacob and Elizabeth (Seaton) Barger. The father, of German origin and born in Pennsylvania, was the son of Geo. Barger, Sr. He went to Breckenridge County when a young man, and learned the carpenter's trade. He married in 1809. And after 1815 he was a farmer and carpenter of Shawneetown, and died in 1847. The

---

[221] This should be Frances Colbert. See James Colbert biography.

mother was born in Kentucky in 1787, and died in 1860. She was a member of the Regular Baptist Church. Educated at Shawneetown, our subject, in 1854, was married to Lucy E., daughter of Henry A. and Ann Floyd of Union County, Ky., where she was born in 1830. Four of their seven children are living: Jos. T., Lucy G., Maud E. and Nathaniel B. After 1865 he moved from near Shawneetown to his present fine farm of 80 acres in Section 22, four and one-half miles from that city. Always a Democrat, he first voted for Buchanan. He and his wife are members of the Methodist Episcopal Church.

— *History of Gallatin, Saline, Hamilton, Franklin and Williamson Counties, Illinois.*

J. B. Barger – 1887

J. B. BARGER, farmer, was born in Breckenridge County, Ky., February 2, 1814, one of seven children – two living – of Jacob and Elizabeth (Seaton) Barger. The father, born in Pennsylvania in 1784, was the son of Geo. Barger, of Germany, who, on account of religious persecution, became a pioneer of Breckenridge County, Ky. The father was poorly educated, and married in 1809, and in 1815 came to Shawneetown, when, after several years as carpenter, he spent the remainder of his life as a farmer He was a trustee of Shawneetown for some time, and died in 1847. The mother, a native of Kentucky, was born in 1787 and died in 1860, a member of the Baptist church. She was a half sister of Gen. McClernand, and her mother was an early pioneer of Gallatin County.

Our subject was educated at Shawnee and engaged as clerk and in flat boating. In March, 1834, he married Louisa M., a daughter of John Carter, who was born in Kentucky about 1814. She died in 1861, a member of the Methodist Episcopal Church. Two of their seven children are living: George and Jacob.

In l847 President Polk commissioned him as postmaster at Shawneetown, and in 1850 he was elected sheriff, serving two years, and also some time as deputy. From 1854 to 1856 he was bookkeeper of the State Bank of Illinois. In 1836 he was elected county clerk, which position he held for twenty-six years, at the end of which time the citizens presented him, as a recognition of his faithfulness, a gold headed cane. Since his official life closed he has lived in retirement. He has always been a Democrat, and is a Mason and a member of the Methodist Episcopal Church. Besides town real estate, he owns the old homestead of 258 acres.

— *History of Gallatin, Saline, Hamilton, Franklin and Williamson Counties, Illinois.*

Jacob Barger – 1905

JACOB BARGER, a prominent citizen and member of the board of aldermen of Shawneetown, Ill., is a descendant of one of the early settlers of Gallatin county. The Barger family originally came from Germany. The first of the name to come to America was George Barger, who settled in Pennsylvania prior to the Revolutionary war. Later he removed to Kentucky and became one of the pioneers of Breckenridge county. His son Jacob was born in Pennsylvania in 1784. After receiving a limited education there he went to Breckenridge county, Ky., where he learned the carpenter's trade and worked at it for a number of years there.

In 1815 he removed to Illinois, locating at Shawneetown on the first day of May of that year. There he entered three hundred acres of land, though for several years he continued to work at his trade before he settled down to farming. He was prominent in local affairs and was for some time trustee of Shawneetown. He died in 1847. In 1809 while still living in Kentucky he was married to Miss Elizabeth Seaton. She was a native of Kentucky, was born in 1787, and was a half-sister of Gen. John A. McClernand, who won distinction in the Union army during the Civil war. She died in 1860. The seven children born to this couple are all dead. One of the sons, Joseph B. Barger, was born in Breckenridge county, Feb. 2, 1814, and was little more than one year old when his parents came to Shawneetown. As he grew up he attended the schools of the town and began life as clerk in a store. Subsequently he engaged to some extent in flatboating on the Ohio and Mississippi rivers. In 1847 he was appointed postmaster of Shawneetown by President Polk and served until 1850, when he was elected sheriff of the county, holding the office for a term of two years. Front 1854 to 1856 he was bookkeeper in the State Bank of Illinois, and in the latter year was elected county clerk. This office he continued to hold by repeated re-elections for twenty-six consecutive years. When he retired from the office his fellow-citizens presented him with a fine gold-headed cane in token of their appreciation of his efficient services, his uniform courtesy to every resident of the county, and his fidelity to his duty. Upon retiring from his long and honorable career as a public official he lived a quiet life until his death, which occurred Oct. 19, 1900.

In March, 1834, he was married to Miss Louisa M. Carter, who, like himself, was a native of Kentucky and about the same age. She died in 1861. They had seven children, viz.: Elizabeth, Richard, Harrison O., George, Jacob, Josephine, and one who died in infancy. Of these children Jacob is the only one now living. He was educated in the Shawneetown public schools and at the age of seventeen years went into the office of county clerk as a deputy. He served four years under James R. Loomis; four years under Joseph F. Nolen; was then two years with Mr. Nolen in the sheriff's office, and two years with S. M. Smith in the treasurer's office. Mr. Barger then removed with his family to the old homestead which his grandfather had entered, and which has ever since been in possession of the family, and there lived for about ten years, when he returned to Shawneetown. He still manages the farm of 204 acres, making frequent trips to it during the spring and summer seasons. Mr. Barger is a member of Lodge No. 838, Independent Order of Odd Fellows, and No. 638, Knights of Pythias, and has gone through the chairs in both orders. For the past eight years he has been one of the aldermen of the city and may properly be called a man of affairs. Politically he is a Democrat, and comes from old Kentucky Democratic stock.

He has been twice married. His first wife was Miss James Ella Parks, a daughter of James S. and Adeline (Goodwin) Parks, of Shawneetown, though natives of Tennessee. To this marriage there were born two children: Louise, now deceased, and James S. Mrs. Barger died in 1896, and in January, 1898, he married his second wife, Miss Anna Lawler, a daughter of Thomas B. and Sally Lawler, and a niece of Gen. M. K. Lawler. No children have been born to this union.

— *Memoirs of the Lower Ohio Valley.*

Joseph Barnett – 1887

JOSEPH BARNETT, farmer and stock dealer, was born in 1843, in Gallatin County, Ill., one of six children of Zadok and Malinda (Choat) Barnett. The father, a farmer, born about 1809 in Tennessee, came to Gallatin County when a young man, and afterward owned 240 acres on part of which our subject now lives, and remained until his death in 1859. The mother, born in 1809 in Gallatin County, died in 1851.

Our subject owns 120 acres of fine land. In 1868 he was married to Sidney A., daughter of Thomas and Lutitia Patton, and born in 1848 in Hardin County, Ill. She died in Gallatin County, Ill., April 2, 1879. Their five children are Albert C., Mary, Sarah J., Mellie M. and John T. In October, 1861, enlisting in Company F, Sixth Illinois Volunteer Cavalry, he was, on account of disability, honorably discharged in April 1862. He is a Republican, and his wife is a member of the Cumberland Presbyterian Church.

— *History of Gallatin, Saline, Hamilton, Franklin and Williamson Counties, Illinois.*

John S. Barter – 1883

JOHN S. BARTER – John H. Barter, senior partner of John H. Barter & Sons, the well-known carriage and wagon manufacturers, was a son of John F. Barter, a native of England. John F. was at one time in the English navy, and in 1812 was a Home Guard. He was a blacksmith, as has been his son and grandsons. John H. was born in Brooklyn, where his father was working at the time. He commenced business life in Mt. Vernon, by making trips down the Ohio and Mississippi in flat-boats carrying along a blacksmith's paraphernalia, stopping at plantations and doing work for steamboats, etc. Mt. Vernon was then known as McFadden's Bluff. From this small beginning has sprung the present works so well known throughout Indiana, Ohio, Kentucky and Southern Illinois. His business takes now a force of 150 men, and the steam mill and buildings occupy the group of 280 x 140 feet, and are three stories high. He turns out 100 wagons, 50 buggies, 300 plows, 100 harrows, etc., annually. He married Mary F. Ashworth, daughter of William Ashworth, of Posey County. They had $40 and one cow to commence married life with. The children born to them were—Charles A., Emma M., William (married Mattie Hutcherson, daughter of Philo Hutcherson, present Recorder Posey County), Ethel May. John H. married for his second wife Elizabeth J. Depriest. They have four children — Arthur, Ella, John A. and Fred. The New Haven Branch of John H. Barter & Sons was established in 1880, with William A., as manager. They are doing good work and are of great convenience to the county round about. Repairing is well and quickly done, and they always have a good supply of wagons, buggies or agricultural implements in their repository warehouse.

— *History of White County, Illinois.*

Henry M. Bean – 1905

HENRY M. BEAN, a prominent farmer living near Ridgway, Ill., was born on a farm adjoining that town, March 13, 1850, his parents being Henry and Margaret (Rise) Bean. (For account of ancestry see sketch of James M. Bean.) Henry M. Bean received all the schooling he ever got before he was ten years of age. Since then he has by his own efforts managed to secure as good an education as that of the average man. He grew to manhood on the place where he was born, the old house still standing, but not being occupied.

On March 13, 1870, he was married to Miss Jemima Kimbrough, a native of Gallatin county and a daughter of Calvin and Nancy Kimbrough, both natives of Tennessee. Mr. and Mrs. Bean began their married life on the old home place and lived there until 1902, when he built a modern, up-to-date home near the old one but inside the corporate limits of the town of Ridgway. Mr. Bean was supervisor for two years, and was for a long time a member of the school board. His farm at the present time consists of over 300 acres of fine land, all under cultivation, which he manages and oversees, making a specialty of Hereford cattle and Poland-China hogs. He is regarded as one of the best and most progressive farmers in the county, and consequently is one of the most prosperous. In addition to his farming interests he has for twenty years been one of the leading threshermen of Southern Illinois.

He and his wife are both members of the Cumberland Presbyterian church. Their children are: George L., living near Ridgway; Laura, now Mrs. Fulkerson, of Beechwood, Ill.; Charles, Marshall H. and Stella., at home with their parents.

— *Memoirs of the Lower Ohio Valley.*

James M. Bean – 1905

JAMES M. BEAN, a well known farmer of Gallatin county, Ill., living near the town of Ridgway, is a descendant of one of the pioneer settlers of that locality. His grandfather, Jonathan Bean, was born in the State of Tennessee, but in the spring of 1832 came with his family to Gallatin county, where he bought land and followed farming the remainder of his life, living to an advanced age. He married Catherine Skeef, a native of Tennessee, and they were the parents of the following children: William, Henry, John, James, Nancy, and Elizabeth, all now deceased.

Henry Bean, the second of the family, was born in Tennessee in 1809, and was therefore twenty-three years of age when his parents removed to Illinois. He became a farmer and at the time of his death in 1852 was the largest land owner in Gallatin county. His wife was a Miss Margaret Hise, a native of Tennessee, and a daughter of Jacob Hise, who removed from South Carolina to Tennessee and later to Illinois, where he died at the age of 103 years and six months. His wife, who was of German extraction, lived to be 101 years and six months old. Henry and Margaret Bean were the parents of ten children, viz.: Jacob, Turana, James M., Catherine, Jane, Jasper, Elizabeth, George, Margaret, and Henry. James M. is the subject of this sketch; Jasper died in the army during the war; Margaret is the wife of George Dillard, of Gallatin county; Henry lives in Ridgway; and the others are deceased.

James M. Bean was born near Ridgway, April 10, 1832, and has passed his whole life in Gallatin county. He received a good common school education and upon reaching manhood became a farmer, in which occupation he has ever since continued, being regarded as one of the progressive farmers of the county. On Aug. 13, 1862, he enlisted as a private in Company K, One Hundred and Thirty-first Illinois infantry, and served with that command until Nov. 15, 1863, when he was transferred to Company C, Twenty-ninth Illinois infantry, where he remained until the close of the war. He was in the siege of Vicksburg, the engagement at Arkansas Post, and in numerous minor skirmishes.

After the war he returned home and again took up the duties of farm life, in which he has continued ever since. Mr. Bean has been a member of the Cumberland Presbyterian church ever since he was fifteen years of age, and his entire life has been consistent with the teachings of his religious faith. He was married in 1854 to Miss Mary, daughter of James Glass, an old resident of Gallatin county. She died on July 15, 1893, the mother of nine children, viz.: Monroe, now living in Gallatin county; Nazarene, wife of Elijah Nelson, of Kansas; Jerome, a resident of Ridgway; Josephine, wife of Harvey Hemphill, of Enfield, Ill.; Sherman, living in Gallatin county; Fastina Ellen, wife of Jacob Willis, of Ridgway; Logan Grant and Belle, deceased, and Susan Catherine, wife of William Hatfield, of Ridgway.

— *Memoirs of the Lower Ohio Valley.*

James M. Bishop – 1887

JAMAS M. BISHOP, postmaster, was born in Saline County, April 4, 1842, the son of William and Mary (Davis) Bishop, natives respectively of Tennessee and Virginia, and both in their 85th year. They have been among the esteemed citizens of Saline County for over a half century.

Reared to manhood on his father's farm, and with a common school training, our subject, in August, 1861, enlisted in Company E, Third Illinois Cavalry, serving as bugler until the close of the war. He was wounded at Pea Ridge, and fought at Cotton Plant, Ark., Vicksburg, Jackson, then on to New Orleans, to Shreveport, La., on the Red River expedition under Gen. A. J. Smith, at Memphis when Forrest raided there, and finally was mustered out at Springfield, Ill.

He then farmed near Eldorado until 1879 when he came to Ridgway where he has been engaged in selling agricultural implements. He is an unswerving Democrat in politics, and for two years was constable. February 17, 1887, he was appointed to his present position of postmaster at Ridgway, by President Cleveland, and is giving satisfaction. November 18, 1864, he married Eliza J. Margrave, a native of Saline County. Mr. Bishop is a Mason and a member of the G. A. R. He and his wife are members of the Missionary Baptist Church, and among the best citizens of Ridgway.

— *History of Gallatin, Saline, Hamilton, Franklin and Williamson Counties, Illinois.*

Harvey P. Blackard – 1905

HARVEY P. BLACKARD, proprietor of the Omaha Flour mills, Omaha, Ill., is of Scotch-Irish extraction (See sketch of Felix G. Blackard for account of ancestry.) His grandfather, Thomas Blackard, was one of five brothers who came from Tennessee to Illinois some time in the decade between 1820 and 1830, where he entered government land near the line between White and Gallatin counties, and there followed farming the remainder of his life.

His son Alfred married Polly A., daughter of Jesse and Polly (McGehee) Pierce, and to this union there were born. two sons and three daughters. The daughters, Mollie, Sarah and Emma, are all deceased, and the two sons, Alexander H. and the subject of this sketch, both live in Omaha.

About 1877 Alfred Blackard removed with his family to Texas, where he died soon after his arrival. The mother returned to Illinois and located on a farm in Gallatin county, where she lived a few years, after which she removed to Omaha, and there she died in 1892.

H. P. Blackard attended the district schools in his boyhood and remained at home until the death of his mother, being employed during that time in various occupations. In 1882 he engaged in the grocery business in Omaha and followed that for about two years; was then in the tin and hardware business for a similar length of time; was appointed postmaster at Omaha under Cleveland's first administration, but resigned at the end of two years to become associated with the mercantile firm of R. M. Davis & Sons. In 1893 he purchased the flour mills, which he still conducts, making the well known brands of family flour — Jersey Cream, Kitchen Queen, and Old Times.

Mr. Blackard is one of the brightest Masons in Southern Illinois. He is now serving as worshipful master of Omaha Lodge, No. 723, for the fourteenth term, which has made him a representative to the Grand Lodge at Chicago for that number of times, and is a member of Saline Chapter, No. 165, Royal Arch Masons, of Harrisburg. Politically he is a Prohibitionist. In 1892 he was united in marriage to Miss Jennie V., daughter of Rev. Robert M. and Polly (Sharp) Davis, and to this union there have been born five children, three of whom, Leroy, Reece L. and Mansford W., are still living. Mr. and Mrs. Blackard are both members of the Cumberland Presbyterian church, in which he is also a ruling elder.

— *Memoirs of the Lower Ohio Valley.*

James S. Blue – 1905

JAMES S. BLUE, a well known grocer of Morganfield, Ky., and mayor of the city, was born in Caldwell County, Ky., Jan. 29, 1848. His parents, John R. and Pemesia (Glenn) Blue, were both natives of the same County, where the father was a farmer and a prominent Whig before the war. He died in 1864, the mother having died some ten years before. They had four children, all of whom are living.

The paternal grandfather, James Blue, lived in Union County in the early part of the 19th century. He was sheriff of the county along in the twenties and in 1830 removed to Caldwell County, where he died in 1848.[222] The maternal grandfather was David Glenn, a native of Lyon County, Ky., but who died in Caldwell County in 1864. James S. Blue received his education in the common schools of Caldwell County, where he lived until he reached his majority. In January 1871, he came to Union County and there farmed for several years, after which he located in Morganfield. He was marshal of the city for two years, constable for four years, and sheriff for three years. For the last eleven years he has been in the grocery business, and is now serving his third year as mayor of the city. Politically Mr. Blue is an unswerving Democrat, always willing to do his part to achieve a victory for his party, and in 1904 was nominated for sheriff of the County. He is a member of Morganfield Lodge No. 66, Free and Accepted Masons, and he and his wife belong to the Presbyterian church.

---

[222] Blue's grandfather was active in the lodging business in Gallatin County as early as the territorial days. His son-in-law Isaiah L. Potts is believed to be the basis for the legend of Billy Potts. The Blue family once held the deed for the Potts Inn on the Ford's Ferry Road.

Mr. Blue was married in April 1878, to Miss Lou Hughes, of Union County, and to this marriage there were born five children. Two sons died in infancy and those living are Bessie G., Camille, and Willis. Mrs. Blue departed this life in March 1888, and in the succeeding October Mr. Blue was married to Miss Bessie Hughes, a sister of his first wife. Four children have been born to this marriage, viz.: James Barber, George E., Charles David, and Sarah McGoodwin.

— *Memoirs of the Lower Ohio Valley.*

Edgar Bogardus – 1878

EDGAR BOGARDUS. Ypsilanti, [Michigan] is a descendant of the old Knickerbocker family, and was born at Catskill, New York, April 5, 1813. His father was Egbert, and his mother Elsie (Comfort) Bogardus. He attended the district schools, receiving an ordinary education. After leaving school, he went to New York City, where he entered a store in the capacity of clerk, remaining in this position until 1830, when he went to the coal regions of Pennsylvania and engaged in the mercantile business.

Seven years later, he removed to Illinois, where he engaged in constructing a railroad, and also took contracts for building mills. He had accumulated considerable property in the meantime, but, in 1842, it was consumed by fire, leaving him nearly destitute.[223] In 1846 he was elected Judge of Probate, and soon after received a commission as Captain in the 14th Infantry, under General Scott. While James K. Polk was President, Mr. Bogardus was very active in the Mexican War; he took part in the battles of Contreras, Molino del Rey, and Chapultepec, in which he was disabled.

After his return from Mexico, he went to California, where he engaged in the mining business on a very extensive scale, and also kept a trading-post. In 1854 he was elected to the Legislature for El Dorado County, California, remaining in office one year. In 1856 he was elected Sheriff for the same county, and occupied the position two years. He was one of the few who started the telegraph across the mountains to Salt Lake City. Mr. Bogardus has been connected with the Masonic Fraternity ever since he attained his majority, and has been an active worker in helping to build up lodges; he has held many important offices in that society, among which was that of Senior Grand Warden. He returned from California in 1859, and soon after went to Europe, where he remained six months. In 1859 he came to Ypsilanti, where he had, previous to this, established a banking business.

Mr. Bogardus was reared in the Episcopalian faith, and still adheres to the doctrines of that church. He has always been a stanch Democrat. In 1833 he married Miss Adeline Smith, who died fourteen months later. In 1835 he was united in marriage to Miss Elizabeth

---

[223] Bogardus moved to Gallatin County to help build the Shawneetown and Alton Railroad. He partnered with John Crenshaw in the firm of Crenshaw, Bogardus & Co., and served as postmaster of Cypressville from 1840 until 1842. The fire mentioned is the one that destroyed Crenshaw's sawmill while he was on trial for the kidnapping of Maria Adams and her children as mentioned earlier in the county history. It came out in the trial that Bogardus had witnessed the note between Crenshaw and Lewis Kuykendall that led to kidnapping and transaction between the two men over the Adams family. He unsuccessfully ran for county clerk in 1843 as well as sheriff the following year in a three-way race in which he took a distant third place.

Whiting, whose death occurred in 1846.[224] Mr. Bogardus has retired from active life, and devotes the greater portion of his time to reading.[225]

— *American Biographical History of Eminent and Self-Made Men.*

Isaac N. Bourland, M.D. – 1905

ISAAC N. BOURLAND, M.D., a physician and druggist of Equality, Ill., was born at Cottage Grove, Saline county of that state, Jan. 5, 1858. The founder of the family in America came from Ireland during the Colonial period. William Bourland, the grandfather of Dr. Bourland, was a native of South Carolina. He served in the war of 1812, after which he lived for a short time in Kentucky, and then located in Saline county. He had learned the trade of bricklayer before leaving South Carolina. In 1829 he entered a tract of government land in Saline county and followed farming, in connection with his trade, the rest of his life. He was also interested in the manufacture of charcoal. The first brick building in Equality was erected by him. It is still standing and in a good state of preservation. He married Rachel Slaten, a native of Kentucky, and died at the age of seventy-three years. She lived to be ninety-four, and died at the home of her daughter, Mrs. Susan Moore. Of their children, Ebenezer, John and Francis are deceased; Susan is a Mrs. Moore, living in Gallatin county, Ill., and the others live in Saline county. William Bourland and his wife were members of the Old School Baptist church.

James A. Bourland, a son of William and Rachel Bourland, was born on the old homestead in Saline county, Nov. 30, 1830. He received a limited education in the schools of that day, married Nancy Strong, a native of Kentucky, and commenced farming on the place adjoining his father's. There he lived until the death of his father, when he removed to the old home farm where he was born, and where he is now living. Of the children born to James A.

---

[224] After his wife's death, he sent his son Francis Pembrook Bogardus, then nine years of age, to live with his uncle Isaac N. Conklin of Ypsilanti, Michigan. After his father returned from Europe and the son joined his father's banking business in 1860, "under the firm name of E. & F. P. Bogardus. This firm existed seven years, when it was consolidated with the First National Bank, and Mr. [F. P.] Bogardus assumed its management, as Cashier. Mr. Bogardus was a man of strong, independent character, and has contributed in many ways to the growth and prosperity of Ypsilanti. He has been Treasurer of the city, filling the office with credit for several years. He has been Alderman of the First Ward six years, and Mayor two terms. He took a very active part in locating the State Normal School at Ypsilanti. Through his efforts, the iron bridge and many other improvements were completed.

In 1859 he became a Mason, and has passed through the chapter and commandery, having held many offices of trust and importance. Mr. Bogardus attends the Episcopal Church. He is a Democrat, but always votes for the man best adapted for the office, irrespective of party.

In September, 1858, he married Sarah E. Hall, a lady of English descent. They have three children. Mr. Bogardus is a man of many talents, thoroughly domestic and hospitable, delighting in his children, and gathering his friends about his fireside. He possessed few early advantages, and the position he now holds has been gained by integrity, perseverance, and good judgment, directed by a thoroughly independent spirit." [Source: 1878. *American Biographical History of Eminent and Self-made Men.* Michigan Volume. Cincinnati: Western Biographical Publishing Company. 2:12-13.]

[225] 1878. *American Biographical History of Eminent and Self-made Men.* Michigan Volume. Cincinnati: Western Biographical Publishing Company. 2:12.

and Nancy Bourland, Gabriel A. lives in Equality; Emma is a Mrs. Proctor, of Mount Vernon, Ill.; Isaac N. is the subject of this sketch; Timothy D. lives on the old home place; Elizabeth is a Mrs. Guard, of Equality, and Gertrude a Mrs. Pierce, living in Saline county. The mother of these children died in 1869. She was a member of the Methodist Episcopal church. The father is hale and hearty for one of his age and still takes considerable interest in politics as a Democrat.

Dr. I. N. Bourland attended the common schools of his neighborhood in his youth, and afterward attended the Harrisburg high school, and Ewing college in Franklin county. He then taught one term, after which he remained at home on the farm until 1880, when he commenced the study of medicine. In 1884 he was graduated from the Miami Medical college of Cincinnati and commenced practice in the vicinity of his father's home. Six months later he went to Eldorado, where he practiced for about fourteen months, at the end of which time he came to Equality. While at Eldorado he became interested in the drug business, and upon removing to Equality he brought his stock of drugs to that place, where he still continues to conduct a drug store in connection with his practice. Dr. Bourland is a member of the American and the Illinois State Medical associations, and of the Gallatin County Medical society, of which he now holds the office of president. He is medical examiner for several of the leading life insurance companies, and is one of the most popular physicians in the town. Politically he is a Democrat, and in fraternal matters is a member of the Free and Accepted Masons, now holding the office of treasurer in Lodge No. 2. In 1875 he was married to Miss Ella A. Greer, who was born in Equality, and to this union there have been born the following children Allie, Frank, John A., Anita G. and Herbert C., twins, and Bernardine. The last named is deceased and the others live at home with their parents.

— *Memoirs of the Lower Ohio Valley.*

Capt. John M. Bowling, M. D. – 1905

CAPT. JOHN M. BOWLING, farmer and stock dealer, living four miles northeast of Equality, Ill., was born in Boyd county, Ky., March 4, 1830. His grandfather, William Bowling, was a native of the eastern shore of Maryland, and was of French descent. He married Elizabeth Roman, a native of Virginia of Scotch extraction, and after his marriage lived in Virginia, where he followed mercantile pursuits all his life. He had two sons, John and James, both of whom were small when their father died. Their mother married again, her second husband being David Hogan, and after their marriage they removed to Kentucky, where John Bowling grew to manhood. Beginning in, early life he learned the trade of gunsmith, working at that occupation in, connection with farming until 1842, when he started with his family to Missouri, but died before reaching his destination. The widow returned to Kentucky and lived there until her death in 1868. They had six children, viz.: William, James, Elizabeth, John M., Jasper and Mary. The three eldest are dead; Jasper lives near Eldorado, Ill., and Mary is the wife of a Mr. Willis, of Greenup county, Ky.

Captain Bowling attended the subscription schools in his boyhood, after which he took a course in Duff's Mercantile college at Pittsburg, Pa., and then attended Washington college, beginning teaching when he was seventeen years of age to get funds to pay for his education. In 1855, he came to Gallatin county, Ill., where for several years he taught in the public schools. In 1858 he removed to the place where he now lives, beginning with ten acres, but now has 554 acres, all under cultivation except about 100 acres.

On Aug. 14, 1861, he enlisted in Company E; Third Illinois volunteer cavalry. The regiment was mustered in at Camp Butler and soon afterward was sent to Missouri on scout duty. After the battle of Pea Ridge, Ark., it returned to St. Louis, where it was assigned to provost duty. Mr. Bowling was promoted to second lieutenant on March 2, 1862, and in January, 1863, was sent into Illinois to pick up deserters. When he got to his old home he raised a company, of which he was elected captain, but on account of some irregularity the regiment was not mustered into service and he returned to his old command, with the rank of first lieutenant, to which he had been promoted March 4, 1863. Rejoining his regiment in front of Vicksburg he participated in the siege and surrender of that place, afterward taking part in all the engagements in which his command played a part, among which may be specially mentioned Pea Ridge, Cache River and Cotton Plant, Ark.; Arkansas Post, Grand Gulf, Port Gibson, Magnolia Hill, Jackson, Miss.; Big Black River, second battle of Jackson, and Nashville, Tenn. The regiment was mustered out in 1864, but he, being a veteran, was assigned to duty at Camp Butler, looking after conscripts and substitutes, where he remained until May 23, 1865, before receiving his discharge. Captain Bowling still carries a gold watch that was presented to him by his friends at Camp Butler.

After the war he returned to his farm, where he has ever since lived, giving his attention to his agricultural interests and dealing extensively in stock. He is one of the solid Republicans of Gallatin county, and with his family belongs to the Methodist Episcopal church. Captain Bowling has been twice married. His first wife, to whom he was married in 1857, was Miss Mary Ransbottom, a native of Connecticut. Their children were: William H., now living near his father; Flora, now Mrs. Riley, of Ridgway; Julia Ann, a teacher in Chicago; John E., deceased, and Maggie, now Mrs. Donahue, living near Equality. The mother of these children died March 25, 1879, and in February, 1881, he was married to Miranda, daughter of Riley and Mary Ann Bain, one of the old families of Gallatin county. To this marriage there have been born four children: Anna M., John M., Florence B. and Benjamin H., all at home with their parents.

— *Memoirs of the Lower Ohio Valley.*

John William Bowling – 1905

JOHN WILLIAM BOWLING, M.D., one of the leading physicians of Shawneetown, Ill., was born near Catlettsburg, Boyd county, Ky., Jan. 21, 1862. His father, Jasper Bowling, was also a native of Boyd county, and of Irish and English parentage. He was born Oct. 17, 1833, and grew to manhood near Catlettsburg, where he obtained a common school education, afterward graduating from the Cincinnati business college. For several years he was deputy clerk of Boyd county. During the war he was provost marshal, stationed at Catlettsburg, and for some time immediately after the war he served as deputy internal revenue collector. He was also interested in farming operations.

In the fall of 1868 he removed with his family to Gallatin county, Ill., making the trip by river, and upon locating there taught school for about three years, after which he bought a good farm in North Fork township, where he still lives. He continued to teach during the winter months for about twelve years, served for several years as justice of the peace, and also as township treasurer. He was married in 1861 to Miss Pauline Crow, a native of Northeastern Kentucky. She died in the spring of 1885, the mother of seven children, viz.: Dr. John W., the subject of this sketch; Eudora, who died in 1877 at the age of twelve years; Philip S. died in 1896 at the age of twenty-five; Abraham L., a farmer in Gallatin county; Edwin, a school teacher in the same county; Addie, wife of Louis McLain, of Halliday, Ark.; and Hattie, at home. Some time after the death of the mother of these children Mr. Bowling was married to Miss Jane Stinson, of Saline county, Ill., and one daughter, Helen, has been born to this second marriage.

Dr. John W. Bowling was about seven years of age when his parents came to Gallatin county. After a preliminary education in the district schools he spent one year at the Southern Illinois college, located at Carmi, and one year at Ewing college in Franklin county. He then taught for three years, studying medicine in the meantime as opportunity presented. He then took three courses of medical lectures; one year at Evansville, Ind., and two years in the College of Physicians and Surgeons, of Keokuk, Ia., from which he was graduated with the class of 1887. Returning to Illinois he commenced the practice of his profession at Omaha, in Gallatin county, and soon built a lucrative business. In the winter of 1901-2 he took a post-graduate course in the Post-Graduate school of Chicago, and in the latter year removed to Shawneetown, where he has ever since been engaged in general practice. In recent years he has devoted considerable attention to general surgery, in which he has performed some noteworthy operations. Dr. Bowling is a member of the American, the Illinois State, the Southern Illinois, and the Ohio Valley Medical associations, and the Medical society of Gallatin county. He is surgeon for both the Louisville & Nashville and the Baltimore & Ohio Southwestern railways; was county physician for eight years; is examiner for all the reputable old-line insurance companies doing business in Southern Illinois; and is a member of the pension examining board of Shawneetown. In politics he has always been a stalwart Republican; was a member of the county central committee from the time he attained his majority until his removal to Shawneetown; served for ten years as secretary of the committee, and has several times been called upon to serve as a delegate to state conventions. He is a member of the Masonic fraternity and the Modern Woodmen, in both of which he is popular because of his many sterling qualities. In 1885 he was united in marriage to Miss Eliza Davis, a native of Posey county, Ind., and to this union there have been born three children: Albert Leslie, Emory Emmons and Ethel Gail.

— *Memoirs of the Lower Ohio Valley.*

William Granville Bowman – 1876

HON. WILLIAM GRANVILLE BOWMAN, lawyer, Shawneetown, was born in Pulaski County, Kentucky, January 7, 1829. His parents were J. Winston and Mary Bowman. At the age of 14 he left home, and having learned the printer's trade at Independence, Missouri, became editor of the *Western Expositor* of that city in 1848 & 1849. He then taught school in Kentucky, Tennessee and Illinois.

He studied and was admitted to the bar at Shawneetown in 1856; was judge of Gallatin County Court two terms; elected member of the Constitutional Convention in 1869, and elected to the State Legislature in 1871. Mr. Bowman has always been a Democrat, and has been influential in securing the local lines of railway centering at Shawneetown, and developing the coal, iron and salt mines in that region.

— *Illustrated Historical Atlas of the State of Illinois.*

John R. Boyd – 1887

JOHN R. BOYD, abstractor of titles, and real estate and insurance agent, was born in Gallatin County in 1848, the eldest of nine children of Thompson and Martha (Langford) Boyd. The father of Scotch-Irish origin, and born in Maysville, Ky., in 1820, was a son of John Boyd, a native of Ohio, and a brick mason and plasterer by trade. Thompson went to Illinois with his parents when a young man, and in 1847 married in White County, and spent his life in the northeastern part of Gallatin County as a farmer and plasterer, and an esteemed and respected citizen. He was postmaster at Cottonwood from its establishment until his death, since which time it has been under the charge of Mrs. Boyd.

Our subject, educated in the home schools began the plasterers' trade at thirteen, under his father's instruction. He taught for eight years after his 20th year, and farmed during his vacations. October 7, 1869, he married Virginia, daughter of Jonathan B. and Catherine Dagley, of White County, where she was born in 1849. Their children are Samuel O., Thannie, Arthur L., Thompson, Jr., and Ethel.

In 1875 he was elected county treasurer and assessor, and re-elected in 1877, during which terms he made his present abstracts. He has since also been engaged successfully in real estate. He is a Democrat, and first voted for Seymour. He is a Mason, a Knight of Honor, and is a prominent member of the Presbyterian Church. Altogether he owns about 3,300 acres — 120 in Polk, and the rest in Gallatin and White Counties — one of the largest landowners in the county.

— *History of Gallatin, Saline, Hamilton, Franklin and Williamson Counties, Illinois.*

W. J. Boyd – 1887

W. J. Boyd, farmer and a pioneer, was born in Mason County, Ky., about 1823, a son of J. and L. C. (Bailey) Boyd. The father, of Irish origin was born in Kentucky in 1794, a son of Archibald Boyd, a native of Harper's Ferry. Archibald was a soldier of the Revolution, and a pioneer of Kentucky, where he served as sheriff of Louis County many years. The father was reared in Mason and Louis Counties, and married in 1819. In 1837 he removed to Gallatin County and resumed his work of brick laying. He died in 1846. The mother, born in Summit County, Md., in 1796, died December 5, 1857. She was a daughter of Bowdoin Bailey, a soldier of the War of 1812, in the commissary department, and one of the "Baltimore Blues." Returning to Kentucky in 1815, he then went to White County, Ill., in 1826.

Our subject was limited in school advantages, and in 1847 married Jane daughter of James and Margaret Bradford, and born in Ireland. Two of their six children are living: Rebecca, wife of James Rice (deceased) and Laura C. He was then living in New Haven, engaged in the tanning, saddlery and harness business. With the exception of the years from 1874 to 1885 in Shawneetown in a livery and feed stable in connection with the Riverside Hotel, he has, since 1853, resided on his present farm which he carved out of the early wilderness. It has 240 acres besides which he has another farm aggregating in all about 370 acres, and town property in addition. He has served for about 22 years, since 1846, as justice of the peace, in Asbury Precinct, and in his present home, beginning in 1854 in the then Wabash Precinct. He is one of the few now living who were citizens of the county in early life. He is a Democrat first voting for Polk. He is a Mason. His parents were Presbyterians, and his grandfather an elder who organized the church at Cabin Creek, Louis Co., Ky.

— *History of Gallatin, Saline, Hamilton, Franklin and Williamson Counties, Illinois.*

William James Boyde – 1876

WILLIAM JAMES BOYDE, Esq., born in Maysville, Kentucky, April 30, 1824, was the son of John and Leah C. Boyd, natives respectively of Kentucky and Maryland. At 13, he came to Gallatin County, Illinois. In 1846, he commenced business in New Haven, Illinois, and for seven years carried on an extensive tan-yard and boot and shoe manufactory.

He then removed to Nettle Bottom, Gallatin County, where he has developed one of the largest and best cultivated farms in the county. March 24, 1847, he was married to Miss Jane Bradford, and has two daughters. Mr. Boyd built himself a fine residence and livery establishment, in 1874, and carries on an extensive business in livery farming.

— *Illustrated Historical Atlas of the State of Illinois.*

H. P. Bozarth – 1883

H. P. BOZARTH, born in White Oak Precinct, Gallatin Co, Ill, Feb 2, 1852, is the son of Franklin and Lucretia Bozarth. His paternal ancestors were from France and Ireland. His mother's ancestors, the Pinnells, were from England and Scotland. All emigrated to America in the early Colonial times. His Grandfather Bozarth was among the first pioneer settlers in the vicinity of Equality, Gallatin Co., Ill. His father entered government land at $1.25 per acre, and by hard work and economy succeeded in making a fine farm of 200 acres.

Mr. Bozarth labored on the farm in summer and attended the public schools in winter. He made good use of his time and succeeded in becoming proficient in Ray's Third Arithmetic at the early age of 13 years. He obtained a portion of his education by study at home, frequently taking his book to the field to study while his team was resting. He began teaching in the common schools of Pope County, Ill., at the early age of 17, and has taught almost continually since that time. In 1872 he entered the Ewing High School in Franklin County for one term. In 1873 he attended Prof. John Turrentine's school at Enfield in the autumn of the same year he assisted Prof. W. I. Davis in his select school at Omaha, Ill.

He was married April 9, 1874, to Sarah M. Wolfe, of Hamilton County, Ill. In the fall of 1874 he entered the Omaha public school as principal; held that position two terms, and has taught select schools four terms. Taught one select school at Norris City, and three terms in the public schools at Roland, White Co. In 1875 he moved his family to Carbondale and attended the Southern Illinois University a year. In 1881, Mr. Bozarth was appointed Superintendent of Schools of Gallatin County for one year.

Mr. Bozarth is the owner of two improved farms in White County, besides some lands in Gallatin. He has some nice property in Omaha, where he now resides. He has a fine library and a pleasant home, and family of wife and three children — Jonnie, Charles Edwin, and Willie, aged respectively seven, four, and one. Mr. Bozarth has been for several years a member of M.E. church, A.F.&A.M. and I.O.O.F.

— *History of White County, Illinois.*

Harmon Pinnell Bozarth – 1905

HARMON PINNELL BOZARTH, attorney at law and insurance underwriter, of Omaha, Ill., can trace the origin of his family in America to a French soldier of that name who came over with La Fayette and fought in the Revolution. After the war he received a grant of land in Virginia from the new government, and passed the remainder of his life in the country whose freedom he had helped to establish. He reared a large family of children, and one of his sons, Elihu Bozarth, crossed the mountains and located in Central Kentucky. There he entered a tract of land, became a well-to-do farmer and reared a family of children.

Israel Bozarth, a son of Elihu, was born in Kentucky, received a common school education there, and in 1815 came to Illinois, locating near the present village of Equality, in Gallatin county. He entered government land, cleared a farm and lived there for several years, after which he removed to Miller county, Mo., and died there. His wife was a Miss Wilson, also a native of Kentucky and a very successful physician.[226] She had a large practice in Gallatin county and continued to practice after removing to Missouri. She died at the advanced age of eighty-seven years, the mother of eight children: Bryant, Tilford, Stephen, Jonathan, Finis, Franklin, Mary and Nicinda, all now dead with the possible exception of Stephen and Mary, who, if living at all, reside somewhere in Missouri.

Franklin P. Bozarth, the youngest son of the family, was born while they lived near Equality, and passed his whole life in Gallatin county. He received a limited education, entered land from the government, and became a farmer. At the age of thirty years he was stricken with total blindness, but notwithstanding this discouraging handicap he continued to manage his farm and between that time and the age of forty-seven he had cleared 200 acres and accumulated considerable personal property. It was his greatest satisfaction at that age to know that he had not become a burden to his friends because of his misfortune, and that he did not owe a dollar in the world. He died in 1866, as he had lived, out of debt and with a large number of friends. About 1848 he was married to Lucretia, the daughter of Wiley Pinnell, an old settler of Saline county, Ill.

Wiley Pinnell was born in Kentucky, his father having been a French soldier who fought under La Fayette. While still a young man he was married to Elizabeth Easley and located in Saline county, where they reared a family of children, viz.: Lucretia, Willis, William A., Gilbert, Greene, Juda, Harmon, Carlin, Nancy, Ambrose and Wesley.

During the Mexican war Wiley Pinnell held the rank of captain in the American army, and at the commencement of the Civil war, although sixty-six years of age offered his services to his country, passed a physical examination, was appointed sergeant and served for two and a half years. At the second battle of Atlanta he was overcome by the heat, was sent home to recover, but died a few months later. He was one of the few men in that great

---

[226] The Illinois Statewide Marriage Index shows an Israel Bozarth marrying a Polley Wilson in Pope County on February 16, 1820.

contest that came of a family three generations of which were on the firing line. Besides his own enlistment he had four sons, Willis, Gilbert, Ambrose and Carlin, and two grandsons, John W. Bozarth and Carroll Pinnell, in the Union army. Truly, a remarkable military record!

Franklin P. Bozarth and his wife had a large family of children, only four of whom are now living; John W. is a farmer in Missouri, Harmon P. is the subject of this sketch, Lucy is the wife of William M. Davis, of East St. Louis, and Alice is the wife of R. M. Edwards, of Gallatin county.

Harmon P. Bozarth was born on a farm near where he now lives, Feb. 2, 1852. As he grew up he worked on a farm during the summer months and attended the district schools in the wintertime. He made good use of his time in school and at the age of thirteen could boast that he had "gone through" Ray's third book in arithmetic, which in that day was the height of mathematical ambition of the average school-boy. Much of his early education was obtained by self-study. Frequently he could be seen taking a book to the field with him, in order that he might snatch a few moments study while his team was resting. At the age of seventeen he commenced teaching and for seventeen years taught in the common schools of Pope county. In 1872 he attended one term at Ewing college in Franklin county; spent one term in the Enfield high school the following year, and in 1875 attended the Southern Illinois Normal school at Carbondale.

In 1881 a change was made in the county superintendent law, which left a year unprovided for and he was appointed by the board of education of Gallatin county to fill the interim. This was done by a board of the opposite political faith to Mr. Bozarth, several members of the board expressing their belief that he was the best and most progressive teacher in the county. Mr. Bozarth continued to teach until 1886, having in the meantime taken up the study of law.

In 1886 he retired to the farm, engaged in agricultural pursuits and in pursuing his legal studies until 1892, when he was admitted to the bar. It has been a maxim of Mr. Bozarth's life to do thoroughly whatever he undertakes. The judges who examined him for admission said afterward that he was one of the best-informed men in the basic principles of law that they had ever examined. He at once began the practice of his profession at Omaha, in which he still continues. In addition to his law practice he has a large fire insurance business, and he has always taken an interest in public affairs. In 1890 he was the census enumerator for Omaha, and for two terms held the office of justice of the peace. At the beginning of the Spanish-American war he raised a company, of which he was commissioned captain, but the war closed before it could be mustered into service.

Mr. Bozarth owns a fine fruit farm in White county, a fine residence and other property in Omaha. He is a member of the Masonic fraternity, the Independent Order of Odd Fellows, the Court of Honor, the Loyal Americans, and belongs to the Methodist church. Mrs. Bozarth is a Presbyterian. He was married on April 9, 1874, to Miss Sarah M. Wolfe, the youngest daughter of Dr. A. A. Wolfe, of Hamilton county, and today they have the following children John A., a freight conductor, living at El Paso, Texas; Charles Edwin, at home; William Franklin, who enlisted May 31, 1901, in Company A, Twenty-eighth United States infantry, was mustered at Vancouver barracks in the State of Washington, sailed for the Philippines in November, served there a little over two years, being present at the capture of General Melvar, was made corporal for bravery in action, and was the youngest noncommissioned officer in the regiment. He is now at home. The others are Fred D., Minnie May, Pearl, Lillian and George, all at home.

— *Memoirs of the Lower Ohio Valley.*

Alanson D. F. Brockett – 1883

ALANSON D. F. BROCKETT, son of James and H. A. Brockett, was born in White County, Ill., April 28, 1820. He received only a limited education, having to go three miles to attend the early subscription schools. He removed to Gallatin County in 1861 and purchased 142 acres of rich, black bottomland. He resided there twenty years and was a very successful farmer. In 1881 he moved to Omaha, and is now, with the help of his family, running the Omaha House and a livery and feed stable, and also carrying on his farm.

— *History of White County, Illinois.*

George W. Bruce – 1883

GEORGE W. BRUCE was born in Tennessee, April 10, 1834. He came to Gallatin County and settled near Shawneetown. He enlisted in 1861 in the late war and served eight months, but was obliged to retire on account of ill health. After his return he settled near Omaha and engaged in farming, he went to Missouri and staid ten years. He then returned to Omaha, and is now in partnership with Mr. Young in the grocery business. Mr. Bruce is a son of Henry Bruce and grandson of Walker Bruce, the first man buried in Palestine cemetery.

— *History of White County, Illinois.*

Robert J. Bruce – 1883

ROBERT J. BRUCE, son of William M. and Maria Bruce, was born Jan. 25, 1838. His early days were spent on the farm in summer and attending the district schools in winter. He was very studious and was prepared to teach at an early age. He has taught about nine years. He enlisted in the late war and after his discharge invested his money in the find farming lands known as the "Thorn Thicket," and has at this time one of the finest farms in Gallatin County. He was married April 5, 1866, to Huldah C. Campbell. They have four sons and one daughter. Mr. Bruce is serving his second term as Sheriff, having defeated at the last election one of the most popular men in the county. He is worth about $15,000.

— *History of White County, Illinois.*

Robert J. Bruce – 1905

ROBERT J. BRUCE, a well known citizen of Omaha, Ill., now deputy sheriff of Gallatin county, was born near Norris City, White county, Ill., Jan. 25, 1836. His grandparents, Robert and Sallie (Bantam) Bruce, were natives of Tennessee, were married in that state, came to Gallatin county about 1820, removed soon afterward to White county and there passed the remainder of their lives. Robert Bruce was a cooper by trade, but after settling in White county he followed farming the rest of his life. He was an ardent Democrat in his political views, and both himself and wife were members of the Methodist Episcopal church. He died at the age of seventy-six years and she at the age of seventy-eight. Their three children are all deceased.

William M. Bruce, one of the sons of this couple, was born in Tennessee, Nov. 12, 1812. He came to Illinois with his parents and lived with them until his marriage to Sallie Millspaugh, a native of Hamilton county, Ill., after which he lived until 1848 on a farm near Norris City. He then removed to Gallatin county, bought a farm near Omaha, where he and his wife both died some years later. They both lived to a good old age, the father being seventy-six at the time of his death and the mother eighty. Of their six children five are still living. Robert J. is the subject of this sketch; Benjamin F. lives at Ridgway; Margaret J. is now a Mrs. Shaw, of Omaha; Isaac T. is deceased; Solomon S. lives at Omaha; and Sallie is a Mrs. Rollman, of Evansville, Ind.

In his day William M. Bruce was a man of prominence in the community where he lived. Soon after his removal to Gallatin county he was elected justice of the peace, an office which he held altogether for twenty-six years. He was active in politics, being one of the leading Democrats of the county, and was eight years judge of the county court. He and his wife were both consistent members of the Methodist Episcopal church.

Robert J. Bruce acquired his education in the public schools and lived with his parents until the commencement of the Civil war. On Aug. 15, 1862, he enlisted as a private in Company H, One Hundred and Twentieth Illinois volunteer infantry, and was mustered in at Camp Butler. The regiment was on guard duty at Memphis until April 1, 1863, when it was ordered to Vicksburg and took part in the siege and surrender of that place. After the fall of Vicksburg Mr. Bruce fought with his company at Ripley, Guntown, East Point, Miss., and in numerous minor engagements, being mustered out as second sergeant, Aug. 22, 1865.

After the war he returned home and took up the occupations of farming and teaching school. On April 5, 1866, he was married to Miss Hulda C. Campbell, who was born July 10, 1841, in White county, and they located on a farm near Omaha, where they lived until 1898, when he removed to another farm nearer the town, and the following year took up his residence in Omaha, living a retired life with the exception of directing the management of his farm. In 1880 Mr. Bruce was elected sheriff of the county, was re-elected two years later and held the office for four years in all. He was for three years marshal of Omaha, has held other minor offices, and for the years twelve years has been deputy sheriff. Few Democrats in the county are more active in behalf of their party, and in campaigns he is always consulted by the party leaders as to how to will a victory. Mr. Bruce is a member of the Cumberland Presbyterian church and belongs to Lodge No. 423, Free and Accepted Masons, in which he holds the office of tiler. His wife died on Sept. 1, 1902, leaving six children: Oscar F., John T., Otis T., Sarah M., Tillis and Eslie. All are living in Omaha. Sarah married a Mr. Lamb.

— *Memoirs of the Lower Ohio Valley.*

William M. Bruce – 1883

WILLIAM M. BRUCE was born in Sumner County, Tenn., March 19, 1814. His father came to Illinois in 1817, and settled near the present site of Norris City, White County. Mr.

Bruce came to Gallatin County in 1849 and entered 80 acres of government land at $1.25 per acre. He now owns 250 acres of fine, well-improved farming land near the north fork of the Saline River.

Mr. Bruce was elected associate justice of the County Court of Gallatin County, in 1857; was Justice of the Peace 21 years, always serving the public with fidelity and justice. He was married March 5, 1835. Mr. and Mrs. Bruce reared a family of four boys and two girls. Two sons, Robert and Franklin, were in the late war. Robert and Thomas were schoolteachers for a number of years. Robert has been elected for the second time sheriff of Gallatin County. Mr. Bruce has been a member of the Methodist church for the past 40 years, and has been found ready to do his part in the work of the church.

— History of White County, Illinois.

T. W. M. Burroughs – 1887

T. W. M. BURROUGHS, farmer, was born in Union County, Ky., in 1831, one of three children of George and Martha (Coleman) Burroughs. The father, born in Maryland in 1793, and a farmer, after his marriage moved to Union County. In 1838 he came to Gallatin County, and for six years carried on a wood yard. He served several years as justice. The mother, born about 1796, died in Union County about 1837.

Beginning life as a poor boy, in 1866 he became the owner of his present improved farm of 120 acres. In 1850 he married Martha J., daughter of William and Mary F. Baldwin, and born in 1834 in Gallatin County. Their nine children are George, Mary, William H., Martha E., Caroline D., Charles R., Victoria, Emily N. and James M.

In September, 1862, enlisting as orderly sergeant in Company D, 120th Illinois Volunteer Infantry, he was, among others, actively engaged at the siege of Vicksburg, and honorably discharged in September, 1865. Politically a Republican, his first vote was for Scott, in 1852. He and his wife are members of the Presbyterian Church.

— History of Gallatin, Saline, Hamilton, Franklin and Williamson Counties, Illinois.

Albert Gallatin Caldwell – 1887

ALBERT GALLATIN CALDWELL (deceased), attorney at law, was born in 1817, in Shawneetown, the son of John Caldwell, a native of Brownsville, Penn., and who married Sarah, a daughter of John Badollet, a Frenchman. The latter and Albert Gallatin (not our subject) were schoolmates together in Geneva, Switzerland, the former coming to America in 1786 and the latter in 1780, both locating in Pennsylvania. In 1802 Gallatin was Secretary of the Treasury under Thomas Jefferson, and secured Badollet's appointment as register of the land office at Vincennes, Ind., and John Caldwell obtained the same office at Shawneetown. Badollet's privilege of naming the fourth county in Illinois Territory, resulted in this county having its present name, Gallatin, in honor of his old friend and schoolmate. John Caldwell died in 1835. His children are Eliza, wife of Alexander Kirkpatrick;[227] John

---

[227] Prior to marrying Alexander Kirkpatrick, Eliza married James Reed on April 15, 1828 in Gallatin County. After his death she married Kirkpatrick in Gallatin County on January 4, 1843. Previously, Kirkpatrick had married

B., teller of the State Bank at Shawneetown for a time and afterward a farmer, who died in 1856; our subject; William L. (deceased), a Shawneetown merchant; Margaret, widow of John Caldwell of Indianapolis, and Martha, who lives with the last mentioned sister.

Our subject was educated in Shawneetown. In 1841 he married Eleanor, daughter of Joseph Castle of Philadelphia, and born in 1822 in the latter place. Their children are Charles, and Sarah, wife of George Ridgway.

Mr. Caldwell was one of the leading members of the county bar, and an eloquent speaker. In 1850 he was elected to represent his county in the Legislature, and the following year he died, passing away in his prime, leaving many friends to mourn his loss. He was a Mason and an Odd Fellow.

— *History of Gallatin, Saline, Hamilton, Franklin and Williamson Counties, Illinois.*

Frank E. Callicott – 1905

FRANK E. CALLICOTT, one of the largest landowners in Gallatin county, Ill., living three miles west of Shawneetown, is a descendant of one of the oldest families in America. His ancestry can be traced back to an Englishman of that name, who came to this country and settled in Virginia, long before the Revolution. He had three sons, John, Beverly, and Harrison, all of whom fought in the Revolution, John being a captain in Washington's command and present at the surrender of Lord Cornwallis. Beverly Callicott was born in 1752. He married and reared a family of eight children, viz.; John, Beverly, William, Samuel, Jordan, Dicey, Nancy, and Polly.

Samuel, the fourth child, was born in Virginia in 1797. He married a Miss Anderson, whose father was a major under General Marion, and in 1829 came with his wife and family to Gallatin county, settling in the Pond settlement about eight miles north of Shawneetown, where they passed the remainder of their lives and are buried in the Callicott cemetery. Their children were Aggie, Claiborne, John, Polly Ann, Harrison, Talitha, Wade, and Washington. In those pioneer days he was a noted hunter, was twice married but no children were born to the second marriage.

John A. Callicott, the third of the family, was born in Smith County, Tenn., March 31, 1824. He received his education in the old-fashioned subscription schools and about the time he reached his majority went to Shawneetown and served an apprenticeship with Orvil Poole and Jobe Smith at harness making. At the breaking out of the Mexican war he enlisted in Capt. M. K. Lawler's company of dragoons and served through the entire war. After being mustered out he returned to his trade of harness making which he followed for several years, then becoming interested in transporting grain by flatboat on the Ohio and Mississippi rivers. The last trip he made to New Orleans was just at the beginning of the Civil War, and he lost his load of corn which he had taken down the river.

Upon his return home he, with John Eddy and others, raised a company of volunteers, of which he was elected captain and Eddy first lieutenant, and which was mustered in as Company C, 29th Illinois infantry. The regiment was attached to McClernand's division of Grant's army and fought at Forts Henry and Donelson, Pittsburg Landing, Corinth, around

---

Elizabeth Marshall in Gallatin County on January 15, 1824. Dates for the three marriages are taken from the Illinois Statewide Marriage Index.

Vicksburg, and toward the close of the war assisted in the reduction of Spanish Fort and Fort Blakely, after which it was sent to Texas, where it was mustered out in November, 1865.

At Fort Donelson, Captain Callicott was wounded five times and sent home to recover. He rejoined his regiment in time to take part in the fight at Pittsburg Landing, and remained under Grant until the latter was assigned to the command of the Army of the Potomac. Captain Callicott was soon promoted to major, then to lieutenant colonel, and during the last three years of service was in command of the regiment. After being discharged he returned to Shawneetown, where he engaged in the saddlery business until 1875, when he again took up flatboating and followed that occupation for about four years. He then turned his attention to agricultural pursuits until his death, which occurred on April 3, 1898, when he and his brother Washington fell victims to the great flood that did so much damage about Shawneetown, twenty-six lives being lost. He was buried on his farm in what is known as the Kanady graveyard.

In 1850 he was married to Miss Sarah, daughter of John Ellis, whose father, William Ellis, was with Jackson in the war of 1812, and settled in Gallatin county about 1815. He entered a large tract of land and was the first county surveyor. His children were William, Abner, John, Caleb, Benjamin, James and Nancy. All married and reared large families, so that at the present time a large number of his descendants are living in Southern Illinois. The sons, like the father, took a deep interest in public affairs, and the family played an important part in shaping the early destinies of the county. The widow and one son, William, lived to be over 100 years old.

John Ellis, the father of Mrs. Callicott, married Letitia McCool, daughter of Abraham McCool, who was an officer under General Marion in the Revolution. After the death of William Ellis his widow married a man named Hogan, after whom the Hogan graveyard near Bowlesville was named, and where William Ellis and a number of his descendants are buried. After the death of Abraham McCool in North Carolina, his son, also named Abraham, with his mother and her children came to Gallatin County. Two of his sons, William and Marion, were killed while serving in the Union army during the war, one at Fort Donelson and the other at Guntown.

To the marriage of John A. Callicott and Sarah Ellis was born one son, Frank E., the subject of this sketch. His mother died in 1854, when he was only about one year old, and his father in 1856 married Eliza Hamilton, but no children were born to this union. The second wife died in 1860, and in 1865 he married Hester Kanady. To this marriage there were born four children: Rebecca, now Mrs. McGhee, living five miles west of Shawneetown; Mary (deceased); William B. (deceased), and one who died in infancy. The mother of these children died in 1872. For many years John A. Callicott was prominently identified with the civic life of Gallatin county. He was one of the first four men to vote the Republican ticket in that county in 1856, and for nearly half a century afterward took an interest in political affairs. After the war he served two terms as mayor of Shawneetown and held other offices, in all of which he made a creditable record. He belonged to the Independent Order of Odd Fellows, more for the good that he could do others than for the benefits he might receive.

Frank E. Callicott was born April 18, 1853, in the house now occupied by Mrs. Frank Eddy in Shawneetown. His early education was acquired in the public schools of his native town, and he still cherishes very highly a number of books awarded him by his teachers as prizes for good conduct, the highest scholarship, and regular attendance. Afterward he graduated from Miami University at Oxford, O., with the class of 1873, standing at the head of his class, and receiving the degrees of Bachelor and Master of Arts. He then took up the work of teaching and was for four years the principal of the Shawneetown schools. During that time he studied law, and in 1878 was admitted to the bar. He never practiced his profession, however, as he had become interested in farming operations in 1876, and from the time of his admission until 1893 was in partnership with his father. In 1877 he also engaged in the harness and implement trade, and while in this business had the distinction of introducing into Gallatin county some of the modern farm implements, among which might be named the twine binder, the disc harrow, the corn planter, the traction engine and the drilled well. In 1900 he sold out this business and the following year removed to the place where he now lives, and where he owns about 2,500 acres of land, most of which is under cultivation. To oversee this large farm requires most of his time and attention. All of this property has been accumulated by his own industry and business sagacity, and he is regarded as one of the most successful men in the county in whatever he undertakes. During the war he was with his father's regiment for a while each year, thus becoming acquainted with military movements, an experience he still vividly remembers. He is a member of the Independent Order of Odd Fellows and the Knights of Pythias, and as a Republican takes an active part in political affairs, though he has never held any office, either by election or appointment, although well qualified for almost any position. In his younger days he was a member of the Illinois National Guard as a member of Captain Nolen's company, and participated in their drills, encampments and sham battles. In his youth he took great delight in athletic cycling, but in later years his time has all been taken up with his business affairs, though he still enjoys athletics as a spectator. He has never married.

— *Memoirs of the Lower Ohio Valley.*

William Campbell, M. D. – 1905

WILLIAM CAMPBELL, M.D., who has practiced medicine at Equality, Ill., for almost forty years, was born two and a half miles west of that town Nov. 12, 1842. His father, William C. Campbell, was born in Virginia about 1789 and came in early childhood to Kentucky with his parents, who settled near Lexington. There he grew to manhood, married Mary Guard, and soon afterward came to Gallatin county, Ill. His wife died shortly afterward and he subsequently married Mrs. Sallie Gillette Hewitt, the widow of William Hewitt, and a native of Vermont. They continued to live on the farm until 1858, when they removed to Equality and there spent their declining years. He died at the age of eighty years and she at eighty-two. Of their two children Doctor Campbell is the only one living.

Dr. William Campbell received his elementary education in the public schools of Equality, and began his business career as a clerk in a store. While thus employed he commenced the study of medicine, and after 1864 devoted his entire time to the acquirement of a professional education. In 1867 he was graduated from the Cincinnati College of Medicine, and soon afterward opened an office in Equality, where he has ever since practiced his profession. Doctor Campbell is one of the oldest practicing physicians in his section of the state, has a lucrative business, is recognized as one of the successful men in the treatment of diseases, and stands high with both the public and his brother physicians. He was one of the organizers of the Gallatin County Medical Society, to which he has belonged ever since its formation. As a member of Lodge No. 19, Independent Order of Odd Fellows, he has filled all the chairs, and has taken considerable interest in promoting the good works of the Methodist Episcopal church, of which he is a member.

In 1867 he was married to Miss Rose Norcross, a native of Evansville, Ind., and they have three daughters and a son living. The three daughters live at Equality, where Nellie is a Mrs. Purcell; Mary a Mrs. Dempsey, and Nora a Mrs. Wathen. The son, William A., is an engineer on the railroad and lives at Danville, Ill. Doctor Campbell is one of the public spirited men of the town, and as a Democrat takes a keen interest in political questions, though he is not what could be called a practical politician.

— *Memoirs of the Lower Ohio Valley.*

M. Carney – 1905

M. CARNEY, an old resident and prominent businessman of Shawnee-town, Ill., was born June 24, 1856, not far from Athens, O., and is of Irish extraction. His grandparents both lived and died in Ireland, and his father, whose name was John Carney, was born in the County of Tipperary in, 1830. In 1852 he came to the United States and located at Circleville, O., where he worked as a stone mason on railroad construction for some time, after which he located at Big Run, in Athens county. There he lived until 1869, when he came to Shawneetown, where he continued to follow railroad building until his death at the age of fifty-seven years. With the exception of a short residence in Cairo he lived at Shawneetown from the time he first came there until his death. Soon after coming to America he was married to Margaret Euright, who was born in County Limerick, Ireland, and came to this country in 1851 with a brother. Of the children born to this marriage Mary and Ellen are deceased; William lives in Cincinnati; the subject of this sketch; and Josephine is a Mrs. Ward, of Danville, Ill. The mother of these children died in 1875.

Mr. Carney was denied the privilege of attending school, for at the age of nine years he began life as a driver of a cart in railroad building. However, he has by self-study kept up with the world's progress, and today has a more practical education than many whose opportunities far excelled his own. He continued to drive carts on the railroad for three years, and when he came to Shawneetown in February, 1869, he was employed as a teamster on the Springfield & Illinois Southeastern, now part of the Baltimore & Ohio Southwestern railroad, which was then under construction. From that time until now he has been connected with the road in various capacities, though he is also interested in other enterprises.

On Jan. 1, 1901, he was made general superintendent of the Bruns-Bowersox Lumber Company at Shawneetown, which position he still holds. He has also been engaged in the grocery business, and dealer in coal and ice. For several years he was superintendent of the Bowlesville Coal Company, and owns and oversees several farms. Although Mr. Carney had the misfortune to lose his left leg by an accident, he is one of the most active men in Shawneetown, and successfully conducts his various interests.

In political matters he is a Republican, and has held the following offices: Tax collector, 1892; alderman, 1893-97; mayor, 1897 to 1901. His administration as mayor was marked by the big flood of April, 1898, which did great damage to Shawneetown and vicinity, a number of lives being lost. In this emergency Mayor Carney was prompt to devise measures for the relief of the sufferers, and the progress of the city since that unhappy event is due in a great degree to his wise course at the time.

He is a member of Lodge No. 838, Independent Order of Odd Fellows, in which he is popular for his genial disposition and many good qualities. On April 15, 1879, Mr. Carney and Miss Belle Ward, a native of Ohio, were united in marriage. They have three children, Charles H., William F. and John all at home with their parents.

— *Memoirs of the Lower Ohio Valley.*

Charles Carroll – 1905

CHARLES CARROLL, a well known merchant of Shawneetown, Ill., and the only surviving child of James and Judith M. (Williamson) Carroll, was born at Lynchburg, Va., Feb. 25, 1833. About 1824 three brothers, Patrick, John, and James Carroll, came to America and located at Richmond, Va., where they established themselves in the mercantile business. There Patrick died and some five years later the other two brothers removed to Lynchburg.

In 1828 James was married to Judith M. Williamson, of an old Virginia family, and in 1834 removed to St. Louis, Mo. In 1836 he went to St. Charles, Mo., and died there in the fall of that year. He and his wife had two sons, John, who died in infancy, and Charles. After the death of her husband Mrs. Carroll went to Louisville, Ky., and in 1837 removed with her son, then some four years old, to Shawneetown. There she was married in 1839 to John D. Richeson, by whom she had one son and two daughters. Elenora married Judge J. D. Turner and died in 1899. Albert G. is now a merchant in Shawneetown, and Mary is the wife of Judge McBane of the same place. The mother of Charles Carroll died on Sept. 6, 1856.

As Charles Carroll grew up he attended the schools of Shawneetown, where he received his primary education. In 1846 he entered Cumberland college at Princeton, Ky., and studied in that institution for three years. Returning to Shawneetown in 1849 he entered the law office of Albert G. Caldwell as a student, and continued to study law until 1852. He then went into the wholesale and retail dry goods business in partnership with his step-father, under the firm name of Richeson & Carroll. This partnership was dissolved in 1868, and since that time Mr. Carroll has been engaged in conducting a general store at Shawneetown. For a number of years he was also a large operator in grain and tobacco, and was interested in river navigation.

In connection with Thomas S. Ridgway and Charles A. Beecher he was one of the projectors of the Illinois & Southeastern railway (now a part of the Baltimore & Ohio Southwestern), and supervised its construction from Shawneetown to Beardstown, Ill., a distance of two hundred and twenty miles. Mr. Carroll is president of the Gallatin county agricultural board, and under his management very successful fairs have been held for several years past. He takes a lively interest in all political affairs, but has never been a seeker for public office. Notwithstanding this he was nominated by the Democratic party for the office of state treasurer in 1874, but he was defeated along with the rest of the ticket by the usual Republican majority.

In 1856 he was married to Miss Elizabeth K., eldest daughter of the late Henry Eddy, who was for many years regarded as the leading lawyer of Shawneetown. To this marriage there have been born the following children: Charles Jr., now mayor of Shawneetown; Mary Eddy, wife of E. R. Sisson, a lawyer at Storm Lake, Ia.; Judith Mimms, wife of William

Ridgway, a lumber dealer in Chicago; and Bessie, wife of William R. Higgins, formerly a grain dealer of Chicago, but now in the real estate business at Spencer, Ia.

— *Memoirs of the Lower Ohio Valley.*

Robert B. Cash – 1905

ROBERT B. CASH, a native and old resident of Gallatin county, Ill., was born at Shawneetown, the county seat of that county, Dec. 9, 1843. His father, William T. Cash, was one of the early settlers in that section of the state. In August, 1861, Robert B. Cash enlisted as a private in Company C, Twenty-ninth regiment Illinois volunteer infantry, and was mustered in at Springfield. He received his baptism of fire at Fort Donelson, and at Shiloh was severely wounded by a gun shot in the left thigh. He was placed on board a transport and sent to St. Louis, where he soon afterward received a furlough for fifty days to come home and recover. As soon as his furlough expired he rejoined his command. His next engagement of any consequence was at Holly Springs, Miss., where he was captured, but was paroled, sent to St. Louis, and was soon afterward exchanged. Again he joined his regiment, fought at Spanish Fort and Fort Blakely, then at Mobile, after which the regiment was sent to Texas and kept on duty there until the close of the war, not being mustered out until November, 1865. He was at Mobile when a large quantity of captured ammunition exploded and assisted in taking the dead and wounded from the ruins, and in moving the debris.

Upon receiving his discharge he returned home, and in 1867 bought the farm where he now lives. He was married in that year to Miss Serena Hall, of Tennessee, and to this marriage there have been born nine children.

Mr. Cash is a member of the Ridgway Post, Grand Army of the Republic, and of Junction Lodge, No. 434, Independent Order of Odd Fellows. In his political views he is a Republican and takes an active interest in winning victories for his party.

— *Memoirs of the Lower Ohio Valley.*

George P. Cassidy, M.D., (deceased) – 1905

GEORGE P. CASSIDY, M.D., (deceased), late a prominent physician of Shawneetown, Ill., was born, on a farm near that city, June 6, 1860, and died at Shawneetown, May 15, 1903. His parents, John A. and Bridget Cassidy, were natives of Ireland. Both are now deceased.

Dr. Cassidy received his early education, in the public schools. At the age of sixteen years he entered the Notre Dame, Ind., university, and graduated in the class of 1881. The following year he entered the Miami Medical College of Cincinnati, where he continued until he had taken three full courses of lectures, when he traveled south to Cuba and the surrounding islands for about a year. He then re-entered the medical college and graduated with the degree of M.D. in the class of 1885. From that time until his death he practiced his profession in Shawneetown, winning the reputation of being one of the most progressive and successful physicians in the place. After graduating from the Miami College he took a special course in diseases of the eye and ear. In his untimely death the profession lost one of its most brilliant members. He was the founder and first president of the Gallatin County Medical Society; was a member of the State Medical Society; and also of the Southern Medical Society. In all these organizations he was ever to be found working for the advancement of the profession.

In his religious views he accepted the faith of his parents and belonged to the Catholic Church. On April 18, 1893, Dr. Cassidy and Miss Olive Grattan were united in marriage. She is a native of Saline County, Ill., and a descendant of one of the first families. Three children were born to Dr. and Mrs. Cassidy: Grattan, Claudia, and one who died in infancy.

— *Memoirs of the Lower Ohio Valley.*

James T. Colbert – 1905

JAMES T. COLBERT, a well-to-do farmer, living near Equality, Gallatin County, Ill., was born in the neighborhood where he now lives, May 3, 1827. His father, James Colbert, was born in Alabama about 1792. When he was a young man he came with his brothers, Henry, Drury, and Hiram, to Illinois, and after working for a while at the salt works entered 80 acres of government land and passed the rest of his life as a farmer. This farm is now in the possession of the subject of this sketch, and it was there that he was born.

James Colbert fought in the Black Hawk War and died in 1834. His children were: Allen B., William, Nancy J., Elisha, Hiram, James T., Thomas and Frances. Allen died at the age of 35 years; William lived to be 77; Nancy married Robert Pinson and after his death Johnson Kanady, and died at the age of 75; Elisha died in 1862 while serving in the 120th Illinois infantry; Hiram died in 1834; Thomas died in 1890; and Frances is the wife of Calvin Baker. The mother of these children died at the age of 76 years.

James T. Colbert commenced life on his own account when he was 20 years old, his only capital being an ax, a fiddle, and a determination to succeed. His education had been acquired in the old subscription schools, in a log house with no floor but the ground and split saplings for seats. From the time he was twenty until he was thirty years of age he followed farming during the summer seasons and worked at the Illinois Iron Works in the winter time, devoting all his leisure time to self-study, until today he is one of the best informed men in his locality. He has also prospered in the accumulation of this world's goods. When he was first married in 1847 he went to housekeeping in a log cabin, about a mile from where he now lives. He remained there until 1891, when he removed to his present location, where he has a well-improved farm, all the improvements having been made by himself. He now owns 800 acres of fine land, five hundred acres of which are under cultivation, and has given something like four hundred acres to his children. As a stock raiser Mr. Colbert has been quite successful, though the greater part of his attention has been devoted to a general farming business. He takes an interest in public affairs and has served as County commissioner, to which office he was elected on the Democratic ticket, having affiliated with that party ever since he became a voter.

Mr. Colbert has been twice married. His first wife was Miss Mary J. Seets, a native of Tennessee, and to this marriage there were born the following children: Lucy A., wife of Jefferson Vinyard, of Hardin County; Allen B., who died at the age of ten years; Frances, wife of Robert Taylor, living near Harrisburg; Sarah, wife of Joseph Vinyard; James, who lives near his father; Mary L., who married Henry Hamp and afterward died; Aaron, who lives in the vicinity; Margaret, widow of Isaac Jennings, who was a farmer in Eagle Creek township; Thomas J.; Isabelle, who married Robert White and died some years ago as his wife; Prudence, wife of George Ledbetter, and John B., who died in 1893. The mother of these children died in 1875 and on Oct. 29, 1879, Mr. Colbert was married to Mrs. Mary A. Frohock, widow of Lucien Frohock, and a daughter of Josiah Hull. Three children have been born to this second marriage, viz.: Virgie, wife of George Blackman, of Eagle Creek township; Virgil, on the farm with his father, and Paul, at home.

— *Memoirs of the Lower Ohio Valley.*

Henry A. Cole, M.D. – 1876

HENRY A. COLE, M.D., son of Amos and Adeline (More) Cole, was born in Werthington, Massachusetts, April 9, 1825. His early life was characterized by earnest struggles to obtain and education. He attended three full courses of medical lectures at Pittsfield, Mass., and practiced medicine and dentistry at Adams and Snelburn Falls, Mass., where he was a leading member of the Methodist Church, and of the Sabbath school. January 1, 1852, he was married to Augusta V. Packard, by whom he had five children. During the past four years he has practiced dentistry and medicine in Shawneetown.

— *Illustrated Historical Atlas of the State of Illinois.*

G. W. Combs – 1887

G. W. COMBS, physician and surgeon, was born in February 1838, in Gallatin County, Ill. He is one of a family of nine children of Jonathan and Iayvilla (Dolan) Combs. The father was born in Kentucky, February 22, 1806; he came in about 1825, to Gallatin County, where he died in 1872. By occupation he was a farmer and blacksmith. The mother, a Virginian, born in 1812, died in 1876.

After his education in the schools of his native county, he followed teaching a few years, and then studied medicine under Dr. Campbell, of Equality, for three years, and for a time under Dr. Leacord of New Market. After practicing medicine for 12 years and frequently attending lectures during the time, he graduated from the Cincinnati School of Medicine in 1878. In April 1858, he married Hannah E., daughter of John F. and Mary E. Hemphill, and born in Pope County, Ill., in 1846. Their six children are W. F., Agnes A., Annie, Samuel M., Ellen E. and George E. Since 1870, when Dr. Combs located at Ridgway, he has been remarkably successful, and now owns 120 acres of land adjoining the town. He is a Republican in politics, and a member of the Masonic fraternity. He and his wife are members of the Cumberland Presbyterian Church.

— *History of Gallatin, Saline, Hamilton, Franklin and Williamson Counties, Illinois.*

George Washington Combs – 1905

GEORGE WASHINGTON COMBS, M.D., the oldest physician of Ridgway, Ill., was born about a mile and a half south of that place Feb. 23, 1838. His grandfather, Andrew Combs, was born in Pennsylvania, of German parentage, married in his native state, and at a very early date removed with his family and two brothers to Kentucky. His children were Jesse, Thomas, Priscilla, David and Jonathan. Jesse was a soldier in the war of 1812 and fought at the battle of New Orleans. Both parents died while the children were still young. Jonathan, the youngest of the family, was born in Muhlenberg county, Ky., Feb. 22, 1806. He learned the trade of blacksmith before he was twenty years of age and in 1826 went to Mount Vernon, Ind. After a short stay there he removed to Gallatin county, Ill., where he found employment as blacksmith for the salt works, remaining in that position for about three years. While working at the salt works he was married, and about 1830 he located about a mile and a half south of Ridgway and opened a shop of his own. This was the first blacksmith shop in that neighborhood and for nearly forty years he conducted it, building up a good trade. Soon after the war he went to New Market, where he remained about a year, then he occupied a place near Inman for a similar length of time. In 1871, while on a visit to the subject of this sketch, he was taken suddenly ill and died. His widow continued to live on the old home place until her death. He died in his sixty-sixth year, and she died at the age of sixty-four. Her maiden name was Isavilla Dolan, a daughter of Patrick Dolan, a native of Ireland, and she was born in either Virginia or Tennessee. Jonathan Combs and his wife had eleven children, viz.: Milton, Mary Jane, William, George W., Trenton, Martha, John, Thomas W., Calista E., Alice and Samuel. William lives at Dexter, Mo.; Dr. Combs is at Ridgway; Thomas and Samuel also live at Ridgway; and Calista, now Mrs. F. Drone, lives near Ridgway; Alice is a Mrs. Moore, of California, and the others are deceased.

Dr. Combs completed the course of study in the common schools and while still a young man took up the occupation of a teacher, which he followed for about seven years, reading medicine in the meantime. In 1858 he went into the office of Dr. Samuel Garry, near Ridgway, where he remained as a student until the death of his preceptor, when he went to Equality and continued his studies in the office of Dr. Lando Campbell. He then attended the Cincinnati College of Medicine and Surgery for one term in 1866, after which he studied and practiced with Dr. Secord of New Market until 1868, when he practiced in New Market and Ridgway until 1878 and then returned to the college and graduated from that institution in 1879. After receiving his degree he located at Ridgway, where he has ever since practiced his profession, and has won the distinction of being the oldest physician in the county. Besides his professional work Dr. Combs looks after the management of about 300 acres of land. For about three years he was special examiner, and in the course of his long professional career has visited nearly every home within a large radius from Ridgway. He is a Republican in politics, is a member of the Free and Accepted Masons, Lodge No. 816, and for over thirty years has been a member of the Cumberland Presbyterian church, in which he has for a long time held the office of elder.

On April 28, 1868, Dr. Combs was married to Miss Hannah, daughter of John F. and Eliza (Glass) Hemphill, of Pope county, and the following are the children born to this union: John M., Mary Jane, Milton H., Fuller, Eliza, Agnes, Anna, Samuel, Ella and George. Fuller is a teacher of Latin and Greek at Helena, Mont.; Agnes is a Mrs. Campbell, residing at Toledo, Ill.; Anna is a Mrs. Gahm at Thompsonville, Ill.; Samuel lives in Gallatin county; Ella and George are at home with their parents, and the others are deceased.

— *Memoirs of the Lower Ohio Valley.*

Charles Cook – 1883

CHARLES COOK, was born in White County, Ill., Feb. 1, 1830. He was the son of Zachariah Cook, who died when Charles was but five years of age. He then lived with his uncle, John Cook, till he was 19 years old, when he started out in the world for himself with a capital of $40. He worked at the Bailey Mills five years, at $5 a month. He bought a fourth interest in the mills. He, in company with Mr. Porter, built the flouring mills of Roland. Mr. Cook sold his interest and went on to his farm, where he resided till the War of the Rebellion.

In 1862 he enlisted under Captain Brill and served three years. He was in the battle of Holly Springs, Miss.; was one of Grant's men who ran by the batteries at Vicksburg, and participated in the battle of Grand Gulf. After the surrender of Vicksburg he was furloughed. He then went to New Orleans and Mobile. He was mustered out at New Orleans. He returned home and remained on his farm five years, when he came to Omaha, and engaged in the dry-goods business with his son Silas. He was also interested in a sawmill. Mr. Cook married Nancy J. Hedge. They have a family of two sons and four daughters. His educational advantages were limited, being only a few months in the early subscription school, yet by his energy and hard work he is at present worth $5,000.

— *History of White County, Illinois.*

Silas Cook – 1883

SILAS COOK, son of Charles and Nancy J. Cook, was born in White County, Ill., Feb. 20, 1854. He was very industrious and persevering both at home and in school. He graduated from the Evansville Commercial College at the age of 18, having attended only one term. His father started him in business, and, being very successful, his father went in partnership with him, the firm being C. Cook & Son.

Mr. Cook was married in 1879 to Surrilda E., daughter of J. Kinsall. They have two children — Lillie and Eula. Mr. Cook was elected, almost without opposition, on the Democratic ticket, in 1882, county clerk of Gallatin County. He already owns considerable property, and has the prospect of a bright future.

— *History of White County, Illinois.*

Silas Cook – 1887

SILAS COOK, county clerk of Gallatin County, was born in White County, Ill., in 1854. He is the son of Charles and Nancy J. (Hedges) Cook, the former of Irish origin, born in 1830 in White County, Ill., and the latter born in 1832 in Ohio. The grandfather, Zachariah Cook, was of White county, and the great-grandfather, John Cook, a native of Virginia, was a pioneer of southern Illinois. Married in 1851, the father bought 200 acres of White County land, and farmed until 1873, when he established a general store in Omaha, Gallatin County. In 1885 he bought his present home of 400 acres. Their six children are: our subject; Lettia A., wife of W. Beasley; Mollia A., wife of Dr. J. L. Harrel; Huldah; John, department clerk, and Lucinda.

Besides his common school education our subject graduated in the Evansville (Ind.) Commercial College in 1871. After a partnership with his father at Omaha, in November, 1882, he was elected county clerk and again re-elected in 1886. September 22, 1878, he married Sarilda E., daughter of Benj. and Sallie S. Kinsall, and born in 1856 in Gallatin County. Their three children are Lillie, Eula and Zella. Mr. Cook now owns 422 acres. He is a Democrat politically, a member of the F. & A. M., and both he and his wife belong to the Cumberland Presbyterian Church.

— *History of Gallatin, Saline, Hamilton, Franklin and Williamson Counties, Illinois.*

Prof. Thomas Jefferson Cooper – 1876

PROF. THOMAS JEFFERSON COOPER, Shawneetown, Gallatin County, son of Isaac and Lizpa F. Cooper, born at Shawneetown, April 15, 1848. Till the age of 18, he attended the district schools; he then entered McKendree College, where he remained till the spring of 1867, when he returned home and commenced teaching, resuming his college course in 1868, and remaining till the spring of 1869, when he again resumed the profession of teaching. During all this time he depended upon his own exertions. Feeling unable to continue his college course at McKendree, he entered the Branch Normal School in Southern Illinois, and continued at intervals, till 1874, when he was elected superintendent of public instruction for Gallatin County.

— *Illustrated Historical Atlas of the State of Illinois.*

John A. Crawford – 1887

JOHN A. CRAWFORD (1887) John A. Crawford, police magistrate, Ridgway, was born in Gallatin County, Ill., January 2, 1835, the son of William R. and Martha (Stevens) Crawford, natives respectively of North Carolina and Tennessee, the former born June 29, 1800, and the latter October 12, 1801. The father removed with his parents from South Carolina to Kentucky in 1803, and a few years later, to Illinois. Our subject's grandfather, John Crawford, located in Pope County, and later in life moved to Gallatin County, where he died. William R. settled near Cypress Junction on a farm in 1832, and, later, removed to another township, where he died January 24, 1857. The mother died June 10, 1851, and of eight children the following are living: Nancy J., widow of Jesse Kanaday; Hannah E., widow of William Engleton; Martha L., John A., and James S., of Pope County.

John A., reared on the farm with a common school education, left home in 1855 and farmed in Tazewell County, Ill., three years. He then returned home, and on May 13, 1858, married Mary Kanady, and settled on the old farm, where she died October 15, 1876. Their children are Sophronia A., wife of Edgar Mills; Susan E. and William H. June 13, 1883, he married Susan (Kanady) Yost, a native of this county. In April, 1884, he moved to Ridgway, where he now runs a first-class boarding-house. He has been a prominent Republican since the war, but never an official aspirant. In April 1886, he was elected to his present office, which he efficiently fills, and to the satisfaction of all concerned.

— *History of Gallatin, Saline, Hamilton, Franklin and Williamson Counties, Illinois.*

John Hart Crenshaw – 1905

JOHN HART CRENSHAW, the son of William Crenshaw and Elizabeth Hart, the daughter of John Hart of New Jersey, one of the signers of the Declaration of Independence, was born in the southern part of North Carolina on Nov. 19, 1797.[228] His parents moved to New Madrid, Mo., in 1809, and in the earthquake of 1811 their home was ruined. They then removed to Gallatin County, Ill., and settled on Eagle Creek, not far from the salt wells called the "Half Moon." His father died soon after coming to Gallatin County, leaving his mother and seven children.

John, being among the oldest children, went to the salt works and began drawing water for the company who were making salt. He continued in this business until after he married Miss Sina Taylor in 1817. He went to housekeeping in the "Half Moon," and in a few years rented the wells from the state and began to make salt, which industry he followed for many years. He bought a large body of land near Equality, and moved his salt works to his own land, which was heavily timbered. He used the wood in the salt works, and in that way cleared his land. When the production of salt became unprofitable, he turned to farming, which he continued to follow until his death, December 4, 1871.

He and his wife were members of the Methodist Episcopal church. His wife died Sept. 14, 1881, at the age of 82 years. They had ten children, five of whom lived to maturity, viz.: Mary, widow of John E. Hall; Elizabeth, widow of Gen. M. K. Lawler; William T., deceased; Margaret, who married Charles Lanphier, of Springfield, both now deceased; and Julia, widow of James Foster, a native of Bledsoe County, Tenn.

He [Foster] was born Dec. 14, 1827. On arriving at man's estate he became a dealer in livestock. This business made it necessary for him to make frequent trips to the North, and on one of these occasions he formed the acquaintance of Mrs. Julia A. Morris, nee Crenshaw, to whom he was united in marriage on April 6, 1858. From that time until the commencement of the Civil War he followed farming on what is now known as the old Crenshaw place.

At the beginning of the war he enlisted in the First Illinois Cavalry and was made captain of his company. In September 1861, he was captured at Lexington, Mo., and soon afterward was paroled. He returned home while on parole and never rejoined his command. He continued agricultural pursuits on the farm where his widow still lives until his death on Dec. 16, 1875. They had four children, three of whom died in infancy. Edward, their youngest son, lives on the old home place with his mother. He married Miss Mary Lamb, of St. Louis, and they have seven children.

— *Memoirs of the Lower Ohio Valley.*

Rev. Nathanlel Crow, D.D. – 1912

Nathaniel, son of John Harvey Crow, and Eleanor Pillow, was born near Shawneetown, Ill., Sept. 9, 1851, and died at Fairfield, Ill., March 12, 1912.

Dr. C. B. Spencer says: "Nathaniel Crow bore a given name that fitted his character, Nathaniel-in whom was no guile-was the key to his character." From a child he was

---

[228] John Hart Crenshaw was named for his grandfather John Hart, but his grandfather was a different John Hart than the signer of the Declaration of Independence.

ambitious to learn. He fought for an education. He won. Early in life he qualified himself for teaching, and for several years followed that profession, during which time he aspired to become a lawyer, but God had for him a different work. Accordingly, on August 6, 1868, he was converted and united with the Methodist Episcopal Church where he at once entered upon an active Christian life.

In the summer of 1878 he came face to face with his life work and resolved to preach the gospel of Jesus Christ. In this he was encouraged by his pastor, Rev. J. B. Thompson, and in the fall of that year was appointed a supply on the McLeansboro Circuit.

The following year, 1879, he was admitted into the Southern Illinois Conference on trial, and appointed pastor of New Liberty Circuit. Two year later he was received into full connection and ordained a Deacon, Sept. 4, 1881, by Bishop Hurst. Having completed the conference course of study he was elected and ordained an Elder, Sept. 23, 1883, by Bishop Bowman.

Besides the above, he served the following charges in the order named: Elizabethtown, Harrisburg, Vienna, Grayville, Carmi, Salem, Upper Alton, East St. Louis, Summit Ave., Mt. Vernon District, Vandalia, Centralia and Fairfield.

As a pastor, Rev. Crow began work in hard fields, but he cultivated well-his promotion was gradual-he served a number of the best charges in the Southern Illinois Conference. His appointment as Presiding Elder of Mt. Vernon District in 1897, was without doubt, Providential. He wrought well. He built up the work, opened up many new fields of labor, and at the close of a full term was elected a delegate to the General Conference which convened the following May, in Los Angeles, California.

As a minister, Rev. Crow was an able preacher, and a thorough Christian gentleman. He delivered sermons of great power. He had strong convictions, and was a defender of our common faith. He was industrious and studious. He devoured books and became a rich scholar. He was loyal and devoted to McKendree College. He urged young men to attend school — especially young preachers. The fact that, without any solicitation on his part, McKendree College conferred upon Nathaniel Crow the degree of Doctor of Divinity, was evidence of the value and appreciation of his work for that splendid institution.

Dr. Crow was literary. The work of his pen was no inconsiderate part of his ministry. A booklet, published by the American Citizens of Boston, on "The Bible, a Constructive Force in America" was in great demand and elicited commendation from many sources.

Nathaniel Crow was united in marriage to Miss Martha Asbury, of McLeansboro, Ill., Aug. 17, 1880. To them were born seven children, all of whom survive, and all are members of the Methodist Episcopal Church—a substantial evidence of early training. An "idyllic home."

Dr. Crow's last years were years of much suffering. He went to his last appointment-Fairfield-in broken health, but his reception was quite cordial. In appreciation of his ability, and services the quarterly conference gave him a handsome increase in salary, and when the people could do no more they literally covered his casket with flowers-not for show-but as an expression of love and devotion.

Dr. Crow was ambitious. He worked faithfully unto the end. His last week on earth was an unusually busy one. On Sunday, March 10th, he preached with more than his usual vigor and with much freedom. His sermons were full of thought and elicited many compliments.

His text at the evening hour was "Have Faith in God," and "There Remaineth a Rest to the People of God." At the close he announced the hymn "Forever here my rest shall be"

And sang the entire hymn with a clear resonant voice. It was his last hymn on earth. Here he laid down his armor. Hemorrhages come during the night, and Tuesday — a little past noon — the soul of Nathaniel Crow rested in the Paradise of God.

Funeral services were held in the church of his last pastorate, in charge of District Superintendent Poole, assisted by Revs. Whitlock, McCammon, Hall, Rodgers, Dr. Harmon, and J. A. Powell. Many pastor were present. The audience was concourse. All heads were bowed, and tears flowed from many faces.

Interment was at McLeansboro, in the Odd Fellows cemetery, beside the road he traveled when first he came to that city, thirty four years ago.

> Servant of God well done!
> Thy glorious warfares past;
> The battle's fought, the race is won,
> And thou art crowned at last.[229]

— *Minutes of the 61st Session of the Southern Illinois Conference, Methodist Church*

John Daily – 1905

JOHN DAILY, a farmer, living in what is known as the "Pond Settlement," near Ridgway, Ill., is of Irish descent. His father, William Daily, was a native of Queen's county, Ireland, a cousin of Gen. M. K. Lawler, and came to America about the same time. The voyage was made on a sailing vessel and he was nine weeks on the water. He reached Gallatin county, Ill., with something like $10 in his pocket, and commenced working by the month for the farmers living in the vicinity of. Shawneetown. After several years in this way he purchased a tract of 120 acres, about a mile from where the subject of this sketch now lives, and began farming for himself. At the time of his death in 1858 he was the owner of about 1,000 acres of good land and was one of the leading stock raisers of the county.

He was married three times. His first wife was Sylvelia Cusick, and to this union there were born the following children: Thomas, died young; John and Mary, twins, the latter of whom died at the age of twelve months; Sarah and Margaret, also twins, both deceased; William and Joseph. The subject of this sketch is the only one now living. William Daily's second wife was Martha Huston, by whom he had four children, Hannah, James. Samuel, and one who died in infancy. The mother of these children died from the effects of a mad dog's bite, and although John and his father were both bitten by the same dog, neither became affected with rabies. The third wife was a Mrs. Mary Luttrell, who is still living in White county, Ill., at the age of eighty years. She had one child, now deceased.

John Daily was born on the first farm his father ever owned, June 9, 1839. His first school was in a log house that stood on his father's farm. It had no floor and the seats were made of sassafras saplings split in halves with pins driven in the half-round sides for legs. The next school was a mile and a half away, but the house had a puncheon floor, which was at that time regarded as a luxury in a school house. The teacher of this school was a man

---

[229] J. C. Kinison and C. B. Whiteside. 1912. *Minutes of the 61st Session of the Southern Illinois Conference Methodist Episcopal Church*. Marion, Ill.: Stafford Print. 57-59.

named Watkins. When only nineteen years of age Mr. Daily commenced farming for himself, on the place where he now lives. The following year he was married to Miss Eleanora Stout, who was born near Mansfield, O., her parents being William and Mary (Van Horn) Stout. Mr. and Mrs. Daily began keeping house in a box frame dwelling with but one room and a kitchen, and only fifteen acres of cleared land upon which to raise a crop. But by the exercise of industrious habits and good judgment they have prospered until, in addition to his home place, Mr. Daily owns another farm of 80 acres. Politically he is a Democrat who always stands up for his principles, and with his family belongs to the Catholic church, of which his father before him was an honored member.

Mr. and Mrs. Daily have had the following children: William, who now has charge of the farm; Henry, who died in 1898; Aaron, who died at the age of twenty-three years; twins, who died in infancy; Mary A., wife of John Frey; John, Jr., who married Eunice Harrelson, and lives on a farm near his father; Sarah, wife of Leonard Frey; Thomas, an attorney at Shawneetown; Carrie, wife of Peter Zirkelbach, of Evansville, Ind., Charles, at home with his parents; and one who died in infancy. Mary A. and Sarah Frey are both living in the same neighborhood as their parents.

— Memoirs of the Lower Ohio Valley.

William S. Dale – 1883

WILLIAM S. DALE, JR., son of Wm. S. and Sarah (Eledge) Dale, natives of Illinois and Alabama, respectively, was born in Emma Township, White Co., Ill., Oct. 24, 1840. He lived on the home farm until his father's death in 1852, when the family, consisting of five sons, was moved to Cape Girardeau, Mo., afterward the spot where Marmaduke and the Federals had the skirmish. Mr. Dale moved to New Haven after the war.

He afterward settled in White County, and married Sarah R. , daughter of Rev. Wm. Slocumb, of White County. They returned to New Haven, where they have since resided. They have a family of four children — Edward L., Charles A., Maud and Cora L.

He enlisted in Company D, Marble City Guards, where General Jackson called for 50,000 men; was out six months, and then enlisted in Company D., Brown's Battalion. He was in the State service under General Price, and was transferred to the navy, on the gunboat Arkansas. He was wounded three times at Altoona Pass, — one shot in the head, one through the breast and one in the left leg. Of 125 who went out only seven came out alive, and with one exception, every man was wounded three times.

— History of White County, Illinois.

A. F. Davenport – 1887

A. F. DAVENPORT, merchant, was born near Equality, Ill., March 2, 1844. His father, R. W., was a native of Knoxville, Tenn., settled with his parents near Equality, and was always a farmer. He married Sarah, daughter of Abner Flanders, a farmer and manufacturer, and a native of New Hampshire. For ten years he was coroner, and filled an unexpired term as sheriff. His death occurred in December 1852. The mother, a native of New York, came with her parents to Illinois, settling near Equality; she died in 1875.

Our subject, the eldest of our children, was reared and educated in Equality, chiefly, and took a course at Bartlett's Commercial College, Cincinnati. Until two years ago he was a farmer and teacher, when he engaged in his present general merchandise business. February 13, 1878, he married Juliet, daughter of John W. Clifton, a merchant, formerly of Ohio. She was born in Gallatin County in June 1848. Their children are May, Delia, Martha J., Randall W., George A. and Robert C. Our subject is a Democrat, and he and his wife are members of the Presbyterian Church. Their home is in Equality.

— *History of Gallatin, Saline, Hamilton, Franklin and Williamson Counties, Illinois.*

Abner F. Davenport – 1905

Abner F. Davenport., of Equality, Ill., treasurer of Gallatin county, was born in the neighborhood where he now lives March 2, 1844. His grandfather, William Davenport., was one of the pioneers of the county, coming from Tennessee in 1825. At that time Randall W. Davenport., the father of Abner, was ten years of age, having been born in Knox county, Tenn., in 1815. In 1843 he married Sarah Flanders, a native of New York, and began farming near his father's home, where he lived until his death in 1852. He was a Democrat and took an active part in the political affairs of his day. They had four children: Abner F., Deborah, now Mrs. Purcell, of Equality; Sarah A., deceased, and George., who now lives at Eldorado in Saline county, Ill.

Abner F. Davenport obtained a good practical education in the public schools and remained at home until his mother's death in 1877, when he married Miss Juliett Clifton, a native of Gallatin county, and from that time until 1884 followed the vocation of a farmer in the vicinity of Equality. He then embarked in the general merchandise business at Equality and continued in that line until 1899, when be came connected with the bank of Equality. In 1901 he was elected treasurer of the county, which office he still holds. He is also school treasurer of Equality township, and is cashier of the First National bank of Equality.

In fraternal and church circles Mr. Davenport is a prominent figure about Equality, being a member of the Independent Order of Odd Fellows and a deacon in the Presbyterian church. Of the ten children born to Mr. and Mrs. Davenport; six are still living. May is the wife of a Mr. Farmer of Texas;[230] Mattie, William, George, Robert and Charles all live at home with their parents.

— *Memoirs of the Lower Ohio Valley.*

Rev. Robert Macklin Davis – 1883

REV. ROBERT MACKLIN DAVIS, son of Rev. William and Polly Davis, was born in White County, Ill., Mary 5, 1824. His parents were natives of North Carolina and Tennessee, of English descent, and came to Illinois in 1811. Both his grandfathers were in the Revolutionary War, and both were wounded. His father died when he was 13 years old. He was obliged to work hard on the farm, and his education was mostly obtained by home

---

[230] The Illinois Statewide Marriage Index shows May Davenport marrying Joseph D. Farmer. in Saline County on July 26, 1899.

study. He became a candidate for the ministry Oct. 29, 1843. He was licensed to preach on probation Sept. 28, 1844; ordained to the whole work of the ministry March 31 1849. He was married Feb. 27, 1844, to Mary Sharp. After his marriage and admission to the ministry he availed himself of the opportunity of attending school two winters. He preached at several places in the bounds of the Ewing Presbytery, and received a great many members into the church at Eagle Creek, Equality, Galatia, McLeansboro, New Haven and other places. He organized the Palestine church near his own residence in 1852, and has been its only pastor. He took charge of the village church in 1851, and preached there 26 years. He took charge of the Union Ridge church in 1855 and has continued as its pastor without intermission to the present time. He organized a church in New Haven in 1868, and one at Oak Grove in 1860, both offshoots of the Union Ridge church. He organized the church at McLeansboro, assisted by Rev. J. M. Miller, and took charge of it in 1876, and is still its pastor. He has had charge of the Norris City church since 1879. He has never had less than four churches under his supervision, and has taken about 1,500 members into the church.

Mr. and Mrs. Davis have four children — Prof. William Isaac Davis graduated at Lincoln in the classical course, and has been President of Hamilton College, and Principal at Mt. Vernon ten years, and is now teaching in Bryant, Iowa; M. M. and S. M. are in the dry-goods business in Omaha, the firm name being R. M. Davis & Sons; Jennie has attended Hamilton College, and is now attending school in Omaha and teaching music. Mr. Davis has been very successful in temporal affairs. He began on a farm in 1844 with nearly nothing, and now has 270 acres of fine farming land and also considerable town property. He is worth about $10,000. His first public speech was on temperance. He has never tasted liquor as a beverage. His wife has always been a helpmate to him, both in temporal and spiritual affairs.

— *History of White County, Illinois.*

Rev. Macklin Davis – 1887

REV. MACKLIN DAVIS (1887) – Rev. Robert Macklin Davis, son of Rev. William and Polly (Sebastian) Davis, was born in White County, Ill., Mary 5, 1824. His parents were natives of North Carolina and Tennessee, respectively, and of English descent. They came to Illinois in 1811. Both his grandfathers were wounded in the war of the Revolution. His father, Rev. William Davis, dying when he was 13 years old, he was thrown upon his own resources and was compelled to work upon the farm and obtain the of his education by hard study at home, though he attended school two winters after he was married.

He was received into the Cumberland Presbyterian Church October 21, 1839, and became a candidate for the ministry Oct. 29, 1843. He was licensed to preach September 28, 1844, and ordained to the whole work of the ministry March 31, 1849. Rev. Mr. Davis was sent as a home missionary to preach at several places within the limits of the Ewing Presbytery, and received many members into the church at Eagle Creek, Equality, Galatia, McLeansboro, New Haven and other places.

He organized the Palestine church near his own home in 1852, and has been its only pastor. He took charge of the village church in 1851, and preached there about 26 years. In 1855, he took charge of the Union Ridge Church, and has continued to be its pastor to the present time. He organized Oak Grove Church in 1860, and the New Haven church in 1868. Assisted by Rev. J. M. Miller he organized the church at McLeansboro, became its pastor in

1876, and resigned the position in 1883. In 1879 he took charge of the Norris City church, continuing its pastor until 1884. He organized the Hazel Ridge Church in 1883, assisted by Rev. William E. Davis, who afterward became its pastor. Since beginning his ministerial career he has not until recently had less than four churches under his charge and now he has three. He devotes nearly all of his time to reading, preaching and other church work, in which he has met with remarkable sucess, having received more than 2,000 into the church.

One of the most notable incidents in his career was the reunion of the Cumberland Presbyteiran Churches at the "Old Village Church," September 19, 1886, from which have sprung 13 other churches. At this reunion about 1,200 people were present, all "seeming to realize that this was the annual gathering at Jerusalem to worship the God of their fathers and to covent anew that they would continue in the good work." Rev. Mr. Davis officiated on that memorable occasion, reading Psalm lxxxiv, and taking for this text Isa. xxxii:20, upon the theme presented therein delivering an eloquent and thrilling discourse.

Rev. Mr. Davis was married to Miss Mary Sharp February 27, 1844, by whom he has four children: Prof. William Isaac Davis, a classical graduate of Lincoln University; was president of Hamilton College five years, of the main seminary at Tallequa, Cherokee Nation, three years, and while here engaged was appointed by the Government to organize an Indian school at Grand Junction, Colo., where he is still engaged; M. M. and S. M. Davis are in the dry-goods business in Omaha, Ill., and Jennie, the only daughter, is at home, studying and teaching music, and is also a very zealous worker in the W.C.T.U. has attended Hamilton College, and is now attending school in Omaha and teaching music.

— *History of Gallatin, Saline, Hamilton, Franklin and Williamson Counties, Illinois.*

Robert M. Davis – 1905

REV. ROBERT M. DAVIS, pastor of the Cumberland Presbyterian church of Omaha, Ill., is, in point of service, one of the oldest ministers of the gospel in the United States. He comes of that sturdy Scotch-Irish stock, a mere mention of which suggests courage, perseverance and rugged honesty. About the beginning of the Revolutionary war a Robert Davis, a native of the Emerald Isle, came to America and served under Washington in the struggle for independence. After the war he married a Miss McElroy, a native of North Carolina, settled in Tennessee, where he followed farming all his life, reared a large family, and lived to a good old age.

One of his sons, William Davis, was born in North Carolina in 1780, grew to manhood in Tennessee, there married Polly Sebastin, also born in North Carolina, and in 1814 came with his family to Gallatin county, Ill. About a year later they went to White county, where he entered 160 acres of land not far from where Norris City now is, and there lived until 1832. They then returned to Gallatin county, locating on a farm about four miles north of Omaha. In 1834 the family removed to a farm where Omaha now stands, where he died in 1838. The children of William and Polly Davis were Isaac S., Sarah., Margaret., Priscilla., Nancy., Elizabeth, Polly, Robert M., William P., Samuel and Cordelia. Sarah married a Dr. Pearce; Elizabeth married a man named Williams; Polly married a Mr. Riles; William P. lives in Omaha; Cordelia is now a Mrs. Hungate of McLeansboro, Ill. These with the subject of thus sketch constitute the living members of the family, the others all being deceased.

In 1824 William Davis entered the ministry of the Cumberland Presbyterian church and continued in the work in connection with his agricultural pursuits until his death on Aug. 25, 1838. The mother removed to White county and lived there until 1860, after which she made her home with her son Robert until her death in 1873. Robert M. Davis was born May 5, 1824, while his parents were living near Norris City. The death of his father left him at the age of fourteen years to not only fight his own way through the world, but to assist his widowed mother in the support of her large family. Under such circumstances his opportunities to attend school were very much restricted, indeed, but with a filial love and fortitude seldom equaled he took up his cross, toiling in the fields by day and in his books by night, the one to secure the physical comforts of life for himself and those dear to him, and the other in quest of knowledge.

In October, 1839, Mr. Davis became a member of the Cumberland Presbyterian church during the progress of a camp meeting at Village church, near Omaha. Soon after making a profession of religion he decided to enter the ministry and began studying to that end, farming and teaching in the meantime to support himself and his mother. On Sept. 29, 1843, his candidacy was announced to the church; he was licensed to preach on Sept. 28, 1844, and on March 31, 1849, was ordained to the whole work of the church, his ordination taking place at Hopewell, now Enfield, church in White county. From then until 1852 he preached at various places, assisting in revivals, etc., preparatory to the organization of a church at Omaha. His first effort in this direction was to found a Sunday school in 1850, with John Kinsall as superintendent. On Christmas day, 1852, the church was organized by Mr. Davis, assisted by Revs. John Crawford and Benjamin Bruce. It was first known as "Palestine" church, and since its organization has received into membership about 800 people.

The fiftieth anniversary was celebrated with appropriate ceremonies on Dec. 28, 1902, the sermon on that occasion being delivered by H. Clay Yates, D.D. During that entire half century the church had been under the pastoral charge of Mr. Davis and had enjoyed one unbroken era of peace and prosperity. His labors were not confined to this one congregation, however. In 1851 he took charge of the Village church and was its pastor for twenty-six years; has been pastor of Union Ridge church since 1855; organized Oak Grove church in 1860; the church at New Haven in 1868; the church at Hazel Ridge in 1870; supplied the church at Norris City for several years; reorganized the church at McLeansboro in 1876; was pastor there for eight years and built a new house of worship. Through all this long period of labor in the vineyard of the Master he has always been in favor of all the general enterprises of the church, the liberal endowment of the denominational colleges, and has been generous in his contributions to Lincoln college and Milliken university, as well as other colleges.

In 1872 Mr. Davis engaged in the merchandizing business as the head of the firm of R. M. Davis & Sons, an establishment that now occupies the best business block in Omaha. But he never permitted his personal interests in this house to interfere with his ministerial duties. Politically he is a Democrat, firm in his convictions, but always considerate for the opinions of others. He holds a dimit as a Master Mason, formerly being a member of Lodge No. 2, of Equality, Ill.

At the same time he united with the church Miss Mary, frequently called Polly Sharp, also became a member. She was a daughter of William and Lavina (Mason) Sharp, natives of South Carolina, who came to White county about 1827. Mr. Davis and Miss Sharp were married on Feb. 27, 1844, and moved to his farm, where Omaha is now situated, and remained there ever since. For nearly fifty years they lived together, happy in the companionship of each other. He has said that her noble assistance in his church work was one of the potent sources of his success as a minister. Her death occurred Dec. 13, 1893, and was the greatest bereavement of his life. Of their children, William I., who died a few years ago at Oxford, Miss., was a graduate of Lincoln university, an educator of far more than ordinary ability, and president of Cumberland Presbyterian Female college of Oxford at the time of his death. Millage M. and Samuel M. are members of the firm of R. M. Davis & Sons, of Omaha, and Jennie is the wife of H. P. Blackard, living in the old home with her father. Her husband is one of the leading Masons of Illinois.

Mr. Davis is now more than fourscore years of age, and over three-fourths of his long life has been spent in the active work of the ministry. He has spoken words of cheer from the pulpit, christened prattling babes, united fond hearts in the bonds of holy wedlock, and performed the last sad rites over the departed. He is now in good health, preaching at Palestine and Union Ridge churches as the regular installed pastor of each church, having served each one for fifty years or more without intermission. Through his ministrations many have been brought to Christianity, and now in his declining years he can enjoy the happy reflections consequent upon a well spent life, ready for the call of the Master whom he has served so well to enter upon the life eternal.

— *Memoirs of the Lower Ohio Valley.*

J. Louis Devous – 1905

J. LOUIS DEVOUS, a well-to-do farmer, living one mile east of the town of Ridgway, Ill., was born in Brown county, O., Sept. 5, 1852. His parents, Isadore and Catherine (Bartell) Devous, were both natives of France. (For an account of ancestry see the sketch of Joseph Devous elsewhere in this work.) When he was about six years of age his parents removed to Gallatin county, where he grew to manhood. He acquired his education in what is known as the Lane school house, in Equality township, and remained at home with his parents until 1880. On April 30, of that year, he married Miss Susanna Wargel and located on part of the farm that he now occupies, just across the road from his present residence. The house in which he went to housekeeping was an old school house, one of the first frame school houses in that part of the country. It is still standing. In 1885 he bought a tract of sixty acres where he now lives, and two years later built his present dwelling, which is one of the best in that part of the county. Altogether he owns 124 acres, well improved and nearly all under cultivation.

Mr. Devous is a Democrat in his political affiliations, though the only office he has ever held was that of school director, which he held for several years. The children born to him and his wife are Thomas, Julia, Leonard, Stella, Rosella, Isadore, Harry and Louis. Of these Thomas, Julia, Leonard and Stella are now living, the others being deceased. Mr. Devous and his family belong to the Catholic church and take a deep interest in its many worthy charities.

— *Memoirs of the Lower Ohio Valley.*

Joseph Devous – 1905

JOSEPH DEVOUS, of the firm of Devous & Rice, millers and grain dealers, Ridgway, Ill., is of French descent. In 1814, his grandfather, Isadore Devous, left his native province of Alsace-Lorraine and with his wife and two sons, Jacob and Isadore, came to America. For about a year the family lived at New Orleans, where Jacob died. They then removed to New Albany, Ind., where the grandfather followed the business of contractor and builder for many years, dying at the age of ninety-nine.

Isadore Devous, the father of the subject of this sketch, was about two years old when his parents came to America. He remained at home until he was thirteen years of age, when he started in to learn the trade of engineer. After serving his apprenticeship he was for two years an engineer on the *Alva Adams*, a steamboat running between Louisville and New Orleans. He then left the river and for about two years was engaged in peddling goods through the country, then a popular occupation and one in which there was considerable profit. His next venture was to establish a general store in Brown county, Ohio, which he conducted successfully for four years, when he came down the river to Gallatin county, and engaged in farming near Ridgway. Most of the land that he bought at from 50 cents to $10 an acre is still in the possession of his heirs, and is now worth about $100 an acre. He was a member of the Catholic church, and took an active interest in promoting its worthy charities.

While living in Brown county, Ohio, he was married to Catherine Bartell, a native of France, who came with her parents to this country in her childhood. To this union there were born fifteen children, eight of whom are still living. John is in Oklahoma; Joseph is the subject of this sketch; Sebastian, Louis and Charles live on the old home place; Leonia is Mrs. Hish, of Ridgway; Kate married a man named Mossman and lives in White county, Ill.; and Mary is the wife of a Mr. White, of Mount Vernon, Ind. The father of these children lived to the age of eighty-seven years and eight months, and the mother died in her eighty-third year.

Joseph Devous was born in Brown county, Ohio, Nov. 12, 1845. Up to the age of eleven years he attended St. Martin's academy there, which constituted his entire schooling. He then worked on the farm until he was twenty-six, when he engaged in farming for himself near his father's place. After five years in this occupation he embarked in the grain business. In 1889 he purchased an interest in the firm of Trusty & McDaniel, proprietors of the Ridgway flour mills, of which Mr. Devous is now the manager. The product of these mills, which is placed on the market under the names of Lily, Snow Bouquet and Red Rose flour, is known all over Southern Illinois, and even in other states. This firm also conducts the elevator at Ridgway and buys most of the grain from the farmers of the surrounding country.

Mr. Devous is a Democrat in his political views but is not an active politician. In his religious belief he clings to the faith of his father and belongs to St. Joseph's Catholic church. Of this church he was one of the founders and for twenty-five years he has been at the head of the board of trustees. Besides his interest in the firm of Devous & Rice he owns 500 acres of fine land, several pieces of town property, mining stocks and other investments. In 1872, Mr. Devous was married to Miss Anna Aman, a native of Posey county, Ind., and they had two children: Catherine, now a Mrs. Zirkelbach, of Ridgway, and Mary, wife of John Hansborough of Enfield, Ill. Mrs. Devous died on July 17, 1900, and Mr. Devous was subsequently married to Miss Emma Smith, of East St. Louis. Mrs. Devous is now one of the leading milliners of Ridgway.

— *Memoirs of the Lower Ohio Valley.*

Jonathan Dillard – 1905

JONATHAN DILLARD, a farmer living near Ridgway, Ill., is a descendant of one of the first settlers in that section of the state. About the time of the Revolutionary war Elisha Dillard, the grandfather of Jonathan, came from Ireland and settled in Tennessee, where he followed farming for many years. His son, Olsten Dillard served in the war of 1812 and fought at the battle of New Orleans, where he was severely wounded, carrying the ball to his grave. He married Eva Crumb, a native of Germany, and in 1817 came to Gallatin county, Ill., where he entered a tract of government land.

The following year his family joined him, coming with the Houstons, Eddys, Hutchinsons and others. Olsten Dillard built a log cabin and cleared part of his land. In 1826 he sold that place and bought another in White Oak township, where he lived until 1842, when he removed with his family to Missouri, and died there some years later. The children of Olsten and Eva Dillard were ten in number, only four of whom are now living. James lives in Shawneetown; Betsey is the widow of Jacob B. Hise and lives at Ridgway; Mary is the widow of Elijah Yates and also lives at Ridgway, and Jonathan is the subject of this sketch.

Jonathan Dillard is one of the oldest men in the county. He was born three miles southwest of Shawneetown March 15, 1824, and has lived his whole life in Gallatin county. When he was a small boy his mother died and his father married Anna Crumb, a sister of his first wife. To this marriage there were born several children, all of whom are now dead. Jonathan Dillard never went to school a day in his life, but by associating with educated people he has kept in touch with the doings of the world and is a well informed man. He lived with his parents until he was about sixteen years old, when he started in life for himself, working on farms and for five years was engaged in flat-boating to St. Louis.

In 1849 he came back to Gallatin county, married Roxana Boutwell, a native of the county, and commenced housekeeping on John Richeson's place. He continued to live on rented land until 1856, when he bought eighty acres, all wild land, where he now lives. This he has added to until he now has a farm of 160 acres, all good land, of which over 100 acres are under cultivation. This development has all been made by the labor of Mr. Dillard himself, who has been noted all his life for his industrious habits. Beginning life in a humble log cabin in the true pioneer style, he has kept up with the march of progress, improving his farm with better buildings as time passed.

Mr. Dillard is one of the active Democrats of his neighborhood, notwithstanding his age. For four years he was road supervisor, which is the only office he has ever sought or held. For thirty-two years he has been an active worker in the Presbyterian church, to which his wife also belongs. He has been twice married. After the death of his first wife he was united in marriage to Dicey Ann Harris, a native of Tennessee, who came with her father, Matthew Harris, to Illinois in 1863. To his first marriage there were born eleven children, viz.: Milbrey, Martha E., Celia, Mary, Elisha, Famariah, Albert, Jonathan, Eva, William and Harriet. Milbrey, Eva and William live in Missouri; Elisha and Harriet live near Ridgway;

Jonathan, is at home, and all the others are deceased. To his second marriage there were born: Viola, Fannie, Eliza, Jemima, Matthew and Aaron. Fannie married a man named Rambler and now lives with her parents: Jemima is in Missouri; Matthew and Aaron are at home, and Viola and Eliza are deceased. Mr. Dillard has passed the fourscore mark in age, and although he has reached that age when many men grow childish he still retains his faculties, remembering with vivid distinctness incidents that occurred three-quarters of a century ago. He is a popular man in his locality for his genial disposition and many sterling qualities, and "Uncle Jonathan Dillard," as he is familiarly called, is a welcome visitor in many homes.

— *Memoirs of the Lower Ohio Valley.*

Martin Doherty – 1905

MARTIN DOHERTY, a farmer and stock raiser, six miles east of Ridgway, Ill., was born on a farm in County Kilkenny, Ireland, not far from the city of Waterford, Dec. 19, 1838. He is the second of six children born to James and Nellie (Merry) Doherty. Mary the eldest, lives in Ireland; Ellen and Stephen came to America in 1863 and both died in this country; Richard died at the age of eighteen months, and one other died in Ireland.

When he was sixteen years of age Martin Doherty commenced learning the trade of ship carpenter. For the first year and a half he received no wages. Then he received a dollar a week, with an increase of twelve and a half cents a week each year during the rest of his four and a half years' apprenticeship. On June 29, 1860, he set sail for America, on one of the old sailing vessels of that day, and after a voyage of six weeks and four days he landed in Quebec. From there he came to the United States, working in the city of Cincinnati at anything he could find to do, then in the boat yards at Evansville, Ind., and in the spring of 1865 came to Shawneetown, Ill., where he helped to build a wharf-boat. He then went to Golconda, where he aided in the building of another wharf-boat, and in April, 1867, located on the farm where he now lives. However, he continued to work at his trade that year, not taking up farming for a livelihood until the following spring. Mr. Doherty now owns 408 acres of land in Ridgway township; 240 in New Haven township, and 40 in Gold Hill township. For the last twelve years he has been raising registered Hereford cattle, in which he has been quite successful. In politics he is a Democrat and for thirteen years held the office of justice of the peace. In 1904 he visited his native land, and by a coincidence sailed on June 29, the same day that he first left Ireland for America. Instead of a voyage of six weeks and four days he made the trip in six and one half days. After his return from Ireland he visited the great World's Fair at St. Louis.

Mr. Doherty has been twice married. His first wife, to whom he was united on Sept. 6, 1866, was Miss Mary McGuire. To this marriage there were born the following children: John, who attended Notre Dame university and now lives near Ridgway; Eliza, wife of Arthur Maloney, also in the vicinity; Hannah, educated at the St. Vincent convent, in Union county, Ky., now the wife of John Duffy; Stephen, a midshipman in the United States navy at Annapolis; James, who died at the age of nineteen years; Ella, who married William Maloney and died in September, 1896; May, who died at the age of fifteen months; Maggie, who died at the age of nine months, and Mary, who died at the age of six months. Stephen is a noted athlete. He is one of the football team of the naval academy and has won numerous medals for running, broad jumping, hurdle races, etc. The mother of these children died in

July, 1883, and in June, 1885, Mr. Doherty was united in marriage to Margaret, daughter of Thomas R. Lawler, and a niece of Gen. M. K. Lawler, whose sketch appears in this work.

— *Memoirs of the Lower Ohio Valley.*

Felix Downen (deceased) – 1905

FELIX DOWNEN (deceased), late a farmer near Ridgway, Gallatin County, Ill., was born near Mount Vernon, Posey County, Ind., May 20, 1858, and died on the farm now occupied by his widow, Oct. 22, 1900. He was reared to manhood in Posey County, received his education there in the public schools, and upon arriving at man's estate adopted the life of a farmer.

On Feb. 13, 1870, be was united in marriage to Miss Kate Allyn, who was born and reared in the same neighborhood, and in September of that year removed to Gallatin County, locating on the farm where he lived the remainder of his life. At the time he took possession of this farm there was but 80 acres, about half of which was cleared. He improved this place and added to it until at the time of his death he was the owner of 200 acres of land, well equipped with improvements, and which is now occupied and owned by his widow and her children. Mr. Downen did a general farming business in his lifetime and gave considerable attention to stockraising.

He was a member of the Court of Honor, a fraternal organization, and with his wife belonged to the Baptist church. In the ordinary affairs of life he was a consistent practitioner of the tenets of his religious faith, dealing fairly with his fellowman, sympathizing with the unfortunate and contributing to worthy charities as his means would permit. He and his wife had the following children — Lemuel, born Oct. 6, 1880, now deceased; Ora, born Sept. 15, 1882, now the wife of Charles Foster; Inez, born Nov. 9, 1884, now Mrs. Edward Barnett; Mattie, born Sept. 17, 1886, at home with her mother; Mary, born Sept. 9, 1889, and Hattie Olive, born Aug. 31, 1896.

— *Memoirs of the Lower Ohio Valley.*

Joseph Drone, Jr. – 1887

JOSEPH DRONE, JR. , farmer, was born in Ohio in 1842. He is one of ten children of Joseph and Margaret (Bartel) Drone, natives of France. The father, born about 1818, came to Ohio when about 12 years old with his father, Francis Drone, and in about 1839 was married.

Since 1857 he has been a resident of Gallatin County, and now one of the most extensive farmers in New Market Precinct. The mother is still living, and both are members of the Catholic Church. Our subject was married, January 22, 1865, to Mary C. , daughter of Christopher and Barbara Grazier, natives of France. Nine out of eleven children born to them are living: Charley F., Mary M., Christopher B., Barbara J., Sarah L., Jos. A., Geo. W., Edward and Henry. Leaving New Market Precinct in 1879, he came to his present fine farm of 160 acres about three and one-half miles west of Shawneetown. He and his wife are influential members of the Catholic Church.

— *History of Gallatin, Saline, Hamilton, Franklin and Williamson Counties, Illinois.*

Marion N. Drone – 1912

MARION N. DRONE. In naming those who have been identified with the business and financial interests of Gallatin county, mention should be made of Marion N. Drone, cashier of the First National Bank of Ridgway, and a native of that place, who has devoted his active business career to banking and enjoys the confidence and esteem of his fellow townsmen. Mr. Drone was born in Ridgway, December 9, 1885, and is a son of Alexander and Mary E. (Vilter) Drone, and a grandson of Joseph Drone. The latter came to Illinois from Ohio and settled two miles south of Ridgway, where he spent his life in agricultural pursuits.

Alexander Drone was born in Ohio, and as a young man started out on his own account by purchasing cheap land in this county. At first he met with a number of minor disappointments, and soon it seemed that he would fail disastrously, as within the space of a year his wife died and he lost his house and barn by fire. However, he made a fresh start, remaining single for seven years, and during that time had recovered his losses and started himself on the high road to success. For many years he was engaged in farming and stock raising at the edge of the village of Ridgway, where he owned 1,200 acres of land, and his fine roadsters and jacks were exhibited at a number of fairs, where they took numerous prizes.

In 1909 he was one of the organizers of the First National Bank, which was capitalized at $25,000, a new building erected for it and it now has $50,000 deposits and a surplus of $2,100. For the past eight years Mr. Drone has resided in Evansville, and now holds an official position with the Henneberger Ice and Cold Storage Company of Princeton, Indiana, and Mt. Carmel, Illinois.

A self made man in all that the word implies, Mr. Drone rose to his high position through his own ability, and his success in life should serve as an example to the aspiring youth of today and to show that a man may attain a comfortable competency and secure the esteem of his fellows through his own industry and integrity, and not through inherited advantages. He was very fond of out-of-door sports, and was never so happy as when off on an outing with his rod or gun. In political matters Mr. Drone was a Democrat, but he was never an office seeker, while in his religious views he was a life long member of St. Joseph's Catholic Church. Of his children, six still survive, namely: Marion N., Lucretia, Vincent P., Leonard, Madeline and Philip Alexander.

Marion N. Drone received his education in the public schools and Jasper College, Jasper, Indiana, from which he was graduated in 1904, at that time becoming bookkeeper of the Commercial Bank of Evansville. Subsequently he held a like position with the Mercantile National Bank, and rose to the position of receiving teller, but at the time of the organization of the First National Bank of Ridgway, in 1909, he came here as cashier of this institution, a position which he has held to the present time. Mr. Drone inherits his father's ability as a financier and businessman, and his pleasant personality has made him many friends among the bank's depositors, as it also has among his business associates. Also, like his father, he has been fond of out-of-door exercises, and is an expert at the game of tennis.

On July 14, 1908, Mr. Drone was united in marriage with Miss Etta Mary Zipp, of Evansville. They are members of St. Joseph's Catholic Church, and Mr. Drone is a member of the Knights of Columbus and is financial secretary of the local lodge.

— *History of Southern Illinois.*

Charles E. Dupler – 1887

CHARLES E. DUPLER, was born in Cincinnati, February 4, 1849. His father, C. E., a native of France, when 18, came to Cincinnati, was a merchant tailor several years, and then married Mary E., daughter of John J. Kopp, hotel-keeper and a native of Germany. Their two children are Louis G. and our subject. The father, while traveling for his health, died in Evansville, Ind., February 9, 1853. The mother, born in Germany September 22, 1822, died at Shawneetown, July 12, 1885.

Reared and educated at the latter place since his fifth year, our subject graduated from Notre Dame, Ind., and September 30, 1873, married at McLeansboro, Fannie A., daughter of Jas. M. Lasater, a miller and merchant, and a native of Virginia, and who, from his 18th year, was sheriff for twelve years. Our subject is a member of the firm Hargrave & Dupler, produce dealers, and one of the rising businessmen. His only daughter, Eva Dee, was born October 7, 1875. His wife was born July 19, 1850, at Shawneetown. He is a Democrat in politics, a member of the F.&A.M., and he and his wife are members of the Presbyterian Church. His home has one of the most elevated sites in Equality.

— *History of Gallatin, Saline, Hamilton, Franklin and Williamson Counties, Illinois.*

Notley Duvall – 1887

NOTLEY DUVALL, farmer, was born in Shawneetown Precinct in 1830, a son of William and Elizabeth (Timmons) Duvall, natives of Kentucky. The father, of French ancestry, spent the latter part of his life as a farmer in Gallatin County, and died in 1834. The mother died about 1840.

Left an orphan on his own resources at the age of ten, our subject had few advantages and worked hard at whatever he could find. The gold fever took him to California in 1852, and after three years of mining he returned to his native country. In 1858 he married a daughter of Henry and Carolina Gill, and a native of Gallatin County. Nine of their ten children are living: Henry, Addie (wife of E. Moore), Notley, Jr., Charley, Richard, Harry, Victor, Jacob and June. He has since lived on his present farm of 270 acres, improved, and about four miles from Shawneetown. Formerly a Whig, since his vote for Fremont has been a Republican. He is a member of the K. of H. and I.O.O.F. lodges.

— *History of Gallatin, Saline, Hamilton, Franklin and Williamson Counties, Illinois.*

Henry Earnshaw – 1887

HENRY EARNSHAW, farmer and merchant, was born in 1843 in Yorkshire, England, one of two children of Rollin and Mary Earnshaw. The father, born about 1820 in the same shire, was a carpenter and joiner, and died about 1846. The mother, born in 1825, still in the same shire also, is still living.

Educated in his native land, our subject came to America in 1864, and enlisted in the United States Navy as seaman on the steamer "Grand Gulf." He was honorably discharged in 1865, and, coming to Gallatin County, began his present mercantile life at Saline Mines, where he does a good business, and besides owns 200 acres of improved land. In 1869 he married Amelia, daughter of F. A. and Catherine Spieler, and born about 1853 in Auglaise

Couty, Ohio. Their seven children are Mary E., Annie, Joshua W., Emma, Willy, George H. and Raleigh. In politics he is a Republican, and is a Master Mason.

— *History of Gallatin, Saline, Hamilton, Franklin and Williamson Counties, Illinois.*

Lt. J. M. Eddy – 1887

LIEUT. J. M. EDDY was born in Shawneetown Precinct May 2, 1830, one of six children of Henry and Mary J. (Marshall) Eddy. The father was of English ancestry and born in Vermont.

He was one of the same family as Samuel and John Eddy, followers of Roger Williams. Henry was a son of Nathan Eddy, who was in the defense of Bennington in the Revolution. Reared in New York, when quite young Henry learned the printer's trade in Pittsburgh, Penn., and was in the war of 1812. He went to Shawneetown in 1818, and was there married.[231] For several years he was editor of the *Illinois Emigrant*, of Shawneetown, and while in Pittsburgh, having studied law under Judge Hall, he afterward became one of the first lawyers of Gallatin County. He died in 1848. The mother was born in Vincennes, Ind., and died about 1877, a member of the Presbyterian Church.

Educated at South Hanover, Ind., our subject served in 1862-63 as first lieutenant in Company C, 29th Illinois Infantry, mostly on Gen. McClernand's staff, and was his aide-de-camp at Belmont, Mo. On account of disability, he was discharged after the battle of Fort Donelson. In November 1868, he married Mrs. Minerva Fuller, daughter of James and Julia Butts. She was a native of Alabama, and died in 1870. They had one child, John F. Since 1881 Mr. Eddy has lived on his present fine farm of 70 acres near Shawneetown; elected sheriff of Gallatin County in 1862; has also served as provost-marshal. He is a member of the G. A. R. Formerly a Whig, he has since he voted for Douglas been a Republican. His son is in college.

— *History of Gallatin, Saline, Hamilton, Franklin and Williamson Counties, Illinois.*

Conrad O. Edwards – 1887

CONRAD O. EDWARDS, proprietor and publisher of *The Local Record* of Shawneetown, was born in 1844 in the same place, the son of William and Susan O. Edwards. The father, who was of Welsh descent, was born in 1800 on Chesapeake Bay, St. Mary's County, Md., married in 1831 and came to Shawneetown where he worked as cabinet-maker and carpenter. About 1851 he became editor and publisher of *The Southern Illinois Advocate*, but soon with new material, merged it with the *Southern Illinoisan* with the firm name of Edwards & Son, the son being associate editor.

Mr. Edwards, the elder, was deputy United States assessor for some time. He died in 1877. His wife, born in Jefferson County, Va., in 1811, died in 1876. Our subject, one of nine children born to them, was educated at Shawneetown, and since 12 years of age has been engaged in the line of printing office work almost entirely. July 1873, he established the

---

[231] Henry Eddy married Mary Jane Marshall, daughter of Shawneetown banker John Marshall, on Aug. 17, 1826.

Home News afterward enlarged and changed to *Shawnee News* with J. R. Ridlete as partner. A year later he sold and founded *The Local Record* in December 1877, which, started as independent in politics, became, what it now is, thoroughly Democratic. In 1879 he married Elizabeth A., a native of Illinois, and daughter of August Jam; their children are Bessie, Alice, John M. and Susan T.

The Edwards family are of old Revolutionary stock, coming originally from Wales and England under a Lord Baltimore. William's mother's brother, John Mills, was under Gen. Gates, at Camdem, and another brother under John Paul Jones. William's two aunts married husbands in the line of ancestry of Mrs. Gen. Grant.

— *History of Gallatin, Saline, Hamilton, Franklin and Williamson Counties, Illinois.*

George T. Edwards – 1905

GEORGE T. EDWARDS, a farmer and stock raiser of Ridgway township, Gallatin county, Ill., was born on Aug. 16, 1865 near Blairsville, Posey county, Ind. His great-grandfather is said to have been the first settler in that part of the Hoosier State, and his grandfather, Richard Edwards, was born there about 1809, some seven years before the state was admitted into the Union. Both Richard Edwards and his father became large landowners, the latter buying government land in that early day as low as twenty-five cents an acre. Richard Edwards lived to be seventy-five years of age, and in his day was an influential citizen of Posey county, where he passed his whole life. George T. Edwards now owns 166 acres of land that formerly belonged to his grandfather, who bought it years ago for $15 an acre.

Isom Edwards, the father of the subject of this sketch, was born on the same farm as his father, and there grew to manhood. On Feb. 2, 1854, he married Miss Esther, daughter of George T. and Lucetta (Culley) Downen, old residents of that section. Her grandfather, Timothy Downen, was one of the first settlers there. Isom Edwards and his family lived in Posey county until his death, when his widow removed to Gallatin county, Ill., and located on the farm where her son George now lives. On Aug. 11, 1891, she was married to Abner Crunk, who is now eighty-two years of age. The children born to Isom and Esther Edwards were George, Jane, wife of William Roark, living near Ridgway, and John, also a resident of Gallatin county.

George T. Edwards obtained his education in the common schools and lived with his mother until 1884. He was then united in marriage to Miss Ollie E. Downen, and soon afterward located on the farm where he now lives, a tract of 166 acres all under cultivation with the exception of about eleven acres. At the time he settled on the place there were only about thirty acres cleared. He has made all the improvements on the farm, devotes a great deal of his time to the raising of registered Hereford cattle, and is regarded as one of the progressive farmers of the county. Politically he is a Democrat and he and his wife are members of the regular Baptist church. They have had three children: Clara, Edith and one other who died in infancy and Cora, now living.

— *Memoirs of the Lower Ohio Valley.*

Leonard Edwards – 1905

LEONARD EDWARDS, farmer and stock dealer, living near Omaha, Ill., was born in the State of Tennessee, Nov. 25, 1836, while his parents, Lorenzo and Eliza (Broughton) Edwards, were visiting relatives and friends there, though they were at the time citizens of Gallatin county, Ill. Charles Edwards, the grandfather of Leonard, came to Southern Illinois at a very early date. There Lorenzo grew to manhood, married and commenced housekeeping in a little log cabin of the primitive type on the forty acres now owned by Mrs. M. C. Daniel. Later, a larger cabin of one room was erected, and it is still standing. Lorenzo Edwards died at the age of forty-eight years, and his wife survived until 1898, when she died at the advanced age of nearly ninety. Their seven sons and two daughters all lived to be married and reared families. Charles now lives in Saline county; Jeremiah lives at Omaha; William lives in Calhoun county; Washington died in 1899; Leonard is the subject of this sketch; Milton is in Arkansas: John is a resident of Gallatin county; Jane is the widow of C. R. Williams; and Harriet is the widow of Curtis Rowe.

Leonard Edwards grew to manhood in Gallatin county. In 1862 he enlisted as a private in Company B, First Illinois volunteer cavalry, and served about seven and a half months in Missouri, when he was mustered out as first sergeant of the company. After being discharged from the army he married Miss Sarah L. Abney, and to this union there were born the following children: M. H. , now living in Hamilton county, Ill.; William J., a farmer near Omaha (see sketch); Josie, wife of a Mr. Lawson, of Gallatin county; James, living in the same county; and Annie, wife of Archibald Yinn, of Hot Springs, Ark.[232] After the death of the mother of these children, Mr. Edwards married Mrs. Jane Foster, widow of John Foster. She had five children by her first husband, viz.: Sarah, wife of W. W. McReynolds; Alpha, wife of Noah Van Bibber; Charles, William and George. Mr. Edwards is one of the active Democrats of his township, and with his family belongs to the Cumberland Presbyterian church.

— *Memoirs of the Lower Ohio Valley*.

William G. Edwards – 1905

WILLIAM G. EDWARDS, a farmer living about two and a half miles south of Omaha; Ill., was born on the farm where he now lives, Sept. 8, 1867, his parents being Leonard and Sarah L. (Abney) Edwards, old settlers of Gallatin county. (See sketch of Leonard Edwards elsewhere in this work.)

William G. Edwards was educated in the public schools, and about the time he attained his majority was married to Miss Martha Garrett. She died in 1891 and he subsequently married Miss Lida Robb, a native of Indiana. Mr. Edwards owns 192 acres of fine land, all under cultivation except about four acres. He has lived upon his farm practically all his life, and the improvements, which are equal to those of any farm in the neighborhood, were all made by himself. As a farmer and stock raiser few men have a better reputation, or know more about the business. He takes a lively interest in public affairs and is one of the leading Democrats in his township, but has never been a candidate for office. In religious matters he

---

[232] The Illinois Statewide Marriage Index shows a Josie Edwards marrying a William W. Lawson on May 11, 1890, in Gallatin County.

is a consistent member of the Presbyterian church, and carries the tenets of his faith into his daily life. He has three children, Luther, Eval and Hurtis, living at home, and one deceased. Mr. and Mrs. Edwards are both popular in the neighborhood where they reside, their home being noted for its hospitality and good cheer.

— *Memoirs of the Lower Ohio Valley.*

Mathias Epley – 1883

MATHIAS EPLEY, born Feb. 17, 1840, in Baden, Germany, is a son of Martin and Barbara (Haman) Epley, who were large farmers for that county. They had a family of seven sons and one daughter. The parents, three sons and the daughter died in Germany. Joseph, Charles, Martin and Mathias came to this county in 1854, landing at Castle Garden June 1. From there they all went to Cincinnati, where Joseph and Charles are now living, both owning farms in Butler County, Ohio, Charles being married. Martin enlisted in the 69th Ohio, and died at New Orleans of fever.

Mathias lived in Butler and Hamilton counties, farming until 1865, when he came to Gallatin County and bought a farm, and has since resided here. He married Nancy E., daughter of James H. Lee, who moved here from Arkansas during the war. They had one child that died in infancy. His wife died in 1880. May 21, 1881, he married Susan A. Lee, a sister of his first wife. Besides carrying on his farm he is one of the firm of J. A. Hinch and Co., in the saloon and light grocery trade. He received a common-school education in Germany, but his English is pure and fluent.

— *History of White County, Illinois.*

James Farley – 1883

JAMES FARLEY, a son of Joseph and Indiana (McAllister) Farley, was born in White County in 1831. He was reared to the hardships and privations of a farm life. His father lived about three miles from New Haven. The family consisted of four children, of which three were half brothers. His father died when James was but three years old.

Mr. Farley has lived in New Haven for many years. He enlisted in the Seventh Illinois Calvary, and was in the service three years and three months. He married for his first wife Caroline Vines, of White County. One child was born — Margaret, afterward Mrs. Nelson. He married for his second wife Delila Elvira (Vaughn) Robinson, of White County. She was born April 21, 1830, and was a daughter of Benjamin and Elizabeth (Jackson) Vaughn. She was married to her first husband April 21, 1848, by whom two children were born. To the union of Mr. and Mrs. Farley has been born one child. He is present constable of New Haven, and has kept a hotel since 1878.

— *History of White County, Illinois.*

Maurice Feehrer – 1883

MAURICE FEEHRER was a son of Alexander and Mary (Droll) Feehrer. His father was of French nativity and his mother of German. They both came to this country when quite young. They were married at Shawneetown. Nine children were born to them, seven now living — John, Joseph (deceased), Alexander, Maurice, Mary (Mrs. Shockley-Raddick), Anthony, Charles, Laura and one that died in infancy. Mr. Feehrer was engaged in the general mercantile business in Shawneetown for many years. His widow still continues the business. Of his children, John is in the home store; Maurice established himself in a general grocery store in New Haven in 1875; Anthony and Charles are not yet located.

Maurice received a common-school education in Shawneetown and attended the Commercial College in Rockport, Ind. He clerked for his father three years and then opened his present store. He married Prudence H., daughter of I. J. and Nancy (Cross) Bozman, of Carmi, who has for several years been a teacher. She is now teaching in New Haven. She taught seven years in White County, averaging ten months a year.

— History of White County, Illinois.

William Ezra Ferrell – 1883

WILLIAM EZRA FERRELL was born near Independence, Saline Co., Ill, May 17, 1849. His early life was spent on the farm and in attending the public school. At the age of 20 he commenced teaching, and has since followed that avocation in connection with farming. He is now serving his fourth term as principal of the Omaha schools.

His grandparents were among the first settlers of this county, coming here from North Carolina in 1800. He was married Sept. 25, 1870, to L. J. Porter, daughter of Dr. J. A. Porter. They have one daughter — Effie J., aged nine years. Mr. Ferrell attended a select school in 1871 at Golconda, taught by Prof. Newcomb, one of the best Normal teachers in the State. In 1878 he attended Hamilton College, McLeansboro. He owns a good farm adjoining Omaha, and is now Township Treasurer. He has been a member of the United Baptist church since 1870.

— History of White County, Illinois.

Judge Ajax Fillingin – 1887

JUDGE AJAX FILLINGIN, farmer, an old resident of Gallatin County, was born in North Carolina in 1811. He is the son of Enoch and Hester (Campbell) Fillingin. The father, a native of Virginia, went to North Carolina when a boy, and some years later moved to Indiana, where he died in about 1822. The mother, of Irish origin, was born in North Carolina and died about 1853, nearly 77 years old. Our subject was educated near this home in North Carolina, and when a young man unmarried Nancy Moye, who died about 1843. They had four children, one living in Indiana and the others near their father. After his first wife's death he married her sister Louisa Moye, who died in 1880. They had two children.

Since 1856 our subject has been in Gallatin County as carpenter, and mason, but farmed chiefly. Mr. Fillingin has been a public worker in his county, and held the office of associate justice for a time. He is a Democrat. In November 1884, he married for the third time.

— History of Gallatin, Saline, Hamilton, Franklin and Williamson Counties, Illinois.

Capt. James Ford – 1883

CAPTAIN JAMES FORD, a native of Kentucky, was a son of Abraham Ford, an early pioneer of Kentucky. His early life was spent on Green River, in Ohio County, and his principal occupation after reaching maturity was that of a contractor on the river. He married a Miss Fox, of Ohio County. He came to New Haven in 1868 and contracted to put in the sixteen-foot dam, which he completed in 1869. After the acceptance of the work by the commissioners, Mr. Ford and A. C. Hess leased the privilege for a term of 50 years, and erected the mill, 40x40, four and a half stories high, three run of stones, with a capacity of 50 barrels of flour and 200 of meal per week, costing $18,000. After two years the partnership was dissolved, Mr. Hess going out, and Philip Garst succeeding him. Mr. and Mrs. Ford had eight children, five now living — Mary (Mrs. A. C. Hess), Lucy (Mrs. S. C. Hall), Thomas K., Charles L. and Grace. Mr. Ford received his title of Captain from his position on the river for about 20 years prior to his advent in New Haven. He was a member of the South Carrollton Lodge of Masons. He died in the fall of 1875, and Mrs. Ford in 1874.

— *History of White County, Illinois.*

Thomas K. Ford – 1883

THOMAS K. FORD was born in Ohio County, Ky., and was a son of James Ford. He spent his boyhood in South Carolina. He remained with his father til his death in 1875. He was married in December, 1878, to Kate, daughter of J. M. Reynolds, of Raymond, Hinds Co, Miss. Two children were born to them, but both died in infancy. In July, 1882, Mr. Ford leased the Eagle Mills, where he is doing a good business.

— *History of White County, Illinois.*

Isaac A Foster – 1905

ISAAC A. FOSTER, M.D., of New Haven, Ill., is one of the best-known and most popular physicians in Gallatin County. His ancestors originally came from England, and the Fosters were among the very first settlers of Southern Illinois.

About the beginning of the 19th century Asa Foster, the great-grandfather of Doctor Foster, came with his father from Virginia, and located in Pope County, where he married and reared one son. This son, Horace Foster, was born Jan. 8, 1811; married Phoebe Davis, born May 1, 1808, in that part of Pope County which afterward became a part of Hardin County; entered government land near Elizabethtown, and there they passed their lives. They were married on Sept. 29, 1826, and had four children: Asa, Horace, Lyman and Mary Jane. The mother of these children died comparatively young, the father on Dec. 1, 1834, married Mary or Polly Davis, a sister of his first wife, born May 9, 1819, and to this marriage there were born several children, all now deceased. He died about 1847, at the age of 35 years. The only one of the children of these two marriages now living is Horace Foster, the second child by the first wife. He was born on the farm near Elizabethtown, Nov. 18, 1829. He was married Dec. 9, 1848, to Miss Elizabeth Ann Hobbs, a native of Missouri. They began their married life on the old homestead on Rock Creek, in Hardin County, near where they now live. They had twelve children, five of whom are deceased. Those living are Thomas J., John

W., Isaac A., Hannah E., Julia A., Mary A. and Joseph A. Thomas and John W. live in White County; Harriet married M. L. Tyer, now county judge of Hardin County, and lives near Cave-in-Rock; Julia is a Mrs. Belt, living on Rock Creek; Mary is a Mrs. Patton, of White County, and Joseph lives at New Haven. The parents are both members of the Christian church.

Isaac A. Foster was born Oct. 4, 1867. As a boy he attended the public schools and improved his time so well that at the age of 19 he became a teacher, which occupation he followed for eight years. In 1888 he was elected surveyor of Hardin County and held the office for three years. While serving as surveyor he completed his course in medicine, and in 1891 graduated from the College of Physicians and Surgeons of St. Louis. After practicing on Rock Creek for about two years he located at New Haven, where he has built up a lucrative business and stands high in his profession. Doctor Foster is a member of the American Medical Association, the Illinois State and the Gallatin County Medical societies.

He is prominent in Masonic circles, being Worshipful Master of New Haven Lodge, No. 230; a member of Fairfield Chapter, No. 179, Royal Arch Masons, and deputy grand lecturer for the Grand Lodge of Illinois. He also belongs to New Haven Lodge, No. 7591, Modern Woodmen of America; Shawnee Tribe, No. 193, Improved Order of Red Men, and to Herald District, Court of Honor, No. 873. He and his wife belong to the Order of the Eastern Star, in which he holds the office of Worthy Patron and she is secretary. They are likewise members of Gallatin Camp, Royal Neighbors of America. In politics Dr. Foster is a Democrat and at this time holds the office of township collector. He belongs to the Christian church and his wife is a Methodist. He was married, in 1898, to Miss Belle Chastain, a native of White County, and for five years a teacher in the public schools. They have had the following children: Edward H., Paul, Alice B., and one who died in infancy.

— *Memoirs of the Lower Ohio Valley.*

Joseph Foster – 1905

JOSEPH FOSTER, a prominent farmer, living near Ridgway, Ill., is a native of the Buckeye State, having been born near Monterey, Clermont county, O., Oct. 17, 1844. He is one of a family of nine children, five sons and four daughters, born to Dennis and Abigail (Whitaker) Foster, natives of Ohio. Joseph Foster received a common school education and grew to manhood on his father's farm. When the One Hundred and Fifty-third regiment Ohio volunteer infantry was being organized he enlisted as a private in Company I, for the one hundred days' service, and was stationed with his regiment on the Potomac river guarding the line of the Baltimore & Ohio railroad. Prior to his enlistment in this regiment he had been a member of the Ohio State Guards. His brother Frank was also in the service.

In 1865 Dennis Foster removed with his family to Gallatin county, Ill., his son Joseph accompanying them. The father settled upon the farm adjoining the one where Joseph now lives, and there passed the remainder of his life, dying at the age of sixty-five years. In 1867 or '68 Joseph Foster bought a tract of forty acres where his residence now stands, though at that time the land was covered with timber. He built a hewed log house sixteen by eighteen feet, with one room and only one window, and in 1867 married Julia A. Moye. They began their married life in this humble home, but by a life of industry and frugality they have prospered, so that now in their declining years they can enjoy the fruits of their labors. Mr.

Foster now owns 400 acres where he lives, about 300 acres of which is in a high state of cultivation, and at other points in the county he owns 205 acres more. All this has been accumulated by his industry and foresight, and he is one of the finest examples of self-made men. He takes a laudable interest in public questions, and in political matters in identified with the Republican party. He and his wife are the parents of the following children: Alverson, living near Ridgway; Ida J., wife of Frank Miner, of Gallatin county; Abbie, wife of George Bell, residing near Ridgway; Charles, a farmer near his father; Lola, wife of Richard Alwalt, near Asbury; Lulu, wife of John Hardy, also near Asbury; Russell, Lane and George, the last named born March 23, 1892, and died September 22d, of the same year.

— *Memoirs of the Lower Ohio Valley.*

Thomas J. Frohock – 1905

THOMAS J. FROHOCK, a farmer living near Junction City, Ill., is a native of Tennessee, having been born in Smith county of that state, Feb. 28, 1841. He is one of a family of fourteen children, seven sons and seven daughters. All the sons and five of the daughters grew to maturity, but only three are now living. Those are Mrs. A. G. King, Thomas J., and David Franklin, a farmer not far from Junction City.

When the subject of this sketch was about fifteen years of age his parents removed to Kentucky, and there he grew to manhood. In 1866 he came to Gallatin county, Ill., where for about fifteen years he worked by the month for the farmers of Eagle Creek township. He then bought the farm where he now lives, consisting of 160 acres, though at the time there was but very little cleared land on the place. By his industry and good management he has now one of the best improved farms in the neighborhood, and in addition to his home farm owns 200 acres elsewhere, which he has accumulated by his thrift. Young men can learn from his career the lessons of economy and self-denial. Beginning life a poor boy, he had only his will and determination to succeed for a start in life. But by the proper exercise of these qualities, and by denying himself many of the so-called pleasures of youth, he is today one of the substantial citizens of the community in which he lives.

Mr. Frohock is a Democrat in his political opinions and takes a laudable interest in public questions. In 1869 he was married to Miss Mary S. Strickland, a native of Saline county, and to this union there were born the following children: John H., Thomas G., Dallas, Lee, Franklin, George, David, Charlie and Mary A., all living in the immediate vicinity, and all useful members of society.

— *Memoirs of the Lower Ohio Valley.*

Charles R. Galloway – 1883

CHARLES R. GALLOWAY, born Jan. 10, 1850, is a son of Dr. D. W. and Malinda J. Galloway. His father was reared in Kentucky, but when 21 came to Illinois, settling on a farm in White County, where he still resides. He has reared a large family of which Charles R. is the eldest. Charles R. was married July 16, 1868, to Brunett J. Pearce. She died, leaving one daughter — Virginia E. Jan. 30, 1875, he married Sylvestra J. McMurtry, of Roland. They have one child — Dora May, aged four years. In 1874 Mr. Galloway was employed as engineer in the flouring mill of D. M. Porter, and was afterward promoted to chief miller. In January 1882, he came to Omaha to take an interest in the mills of J. B. Latimer & Co. He is building a nice house here and intends making Omaha his permanent home.

— *History of White County, Illinois.*

J. B. Gates – 1887

J. B. GATES,[233] farmer, was born in 1840 in Saline County, the son of Squire and Sarah (Rice) Gates. The father, of Irish origin, went to Middle Tennessee in early life, and after his marriage, came to Gallatin County, and finally settled in Saline County where he died in 1854. The mother, born in Tennessee in 1806, died in 1875. Both were members of the United Brethren Church. Our subject, reared in Saline County was married, in February 1860, to Almira, daughter of Harvey and Maria Kanady, of Gallatin County, where she was born in 1837. Of their ten children, six are living: Hester E.; Mollie, wife of J. L. Ashly of Saline County, Jos. A., Walter B., Emma and Samuel M.

Mrs. Gates died in January 1875. He then married Sallie McCoo, a native of Gallatin County. Five of their six children are living: Gertrude, Bessie, Ethel, Frederick F. and Grover C. Since the first year of his married life in Saline County, Gallatin County has been his home. He purchased his present home of 40 acres in 1875. Enlisting in August 1862, in Company D, 120th Illinois Infantry, he was discharged eight months later on account of disability. He was township trustee for eight years. He is a Democratic in politics, a member of the G.A.R., and for several years deacon in the Baptist Church of which his wife is a member.

— *History of Gallatin, Saline, Hamilton, Franklin and Williamson Counties, Illinois.*

William Jefferson Gatewood – 1887

WILLIAM JEFFERSON GATEWOOD was born in Warren County, Ky., and moved to Franklin County, Ill., while yet a boy. He was of great buoyancy and elasticity of disposition, which enabled him to overcome a thousand obstacles. He was of a remarkably robust and vigorous constitution. About 1823 he moved to Shawneetown, having previously acquired a good English and classical education. In Shawneetown he taught school two or three years, devoting his leisure hours to the study of the law. Admitted to the bar in 1828, he rapidly rose to distinction in his profession. He represented Gallatin County in the Legislature several times, both in the House of Representatives and in the Senate. He possessed a kind and benevolent heart, and justice was always was always before his eye. So strongly was he attached to justice that he often combated the opinions of the judges, which were favorable to his own side of the case, because he believed them to be at variance with the law, which was to him the medium through which justice was to be attained. He died January 8, 1842, leaving a widow and four children.

— *History of Gallatin, Saline, Hamilton, Franklin and Williamson Counties, Illinois.*

---

[233] The Illinois Statewide Marriage Index lists him as Joseph B. Gates.

Richard Gill – 1887

RICHARD GILL, farmer, was born in Gallatin County in 1835, the son of Henry and Carolina (Thompson) Gill. The father, of Dutch-Irish ancestry, was born in 1810, a son of David Gill, a native of Pennsylvania. Moving with his father to Gallatin County, Henry soon married, in about 1828, and spent the rest of his life as a farmer. He died in 1866. The mother, still living, was born in Gallatin County in 1814. Both were members of the Baptist Church. Our subject received a common school education, and in 1858 married Mrs. Julia F. Thompson, daughter of Conrad and Luna Wagor, and born in New York in 1827. Mr. Gill has since lived on his present fine farm of 160 acres, three miles from Shawneetown. Always a Democrat, he cast his first vote for James Buchanan.

— *History of Gallatin, Saline, Hamilton, Franklin and Williamson Counties, Illinois.*

Thomas H. Glasscock – 1905

THOMAS H. GLASSCOCK, a farmer living near Omaha, Ill., was born in that county, March 26, 1845, on the site of the present village of Cottonwood, and has passed his whole life within two miles of his birthplace. His father, John J. Glasscock, was born in Virginia, but left that state in boyhood, removing with his parents first to Ohio and then to Gallatin county, Ill., being about nineteen years old when the family settled on the ground where William Wilson now lives. Both the grandfathers of Thomas H. Glasscock fought in the Black Hawk war and lived to be very old men. John J. Glasscock married Elizabeth Newman, and to this marriage were born the following children: Thomas H.; Jane, widow of James Bailey; Patsey, and John.

In 1862 the father of these children enlisted as a private in Company D, Twenty-ninth Illinois volunteer infantry, and took part in all the battles and skirmishes in which his command participated, serving until the close of the war. He and his wife were both members of the Methodist Episcopal church. Thomas H. Glasscock acquired his education in the old-fashioned log schoolhouse, with slab benches, puncheon floor, huge fireplace and only one window. Even to attend this school he was compelled to walk a mile and a half. His first teacher was a Mr. Dalton.

In 1865 he was married to Harriet Bryant, and to this union were born two children, James L. and John W. The former is deceased and the latter now lives near his father. Mrs. Glasscock died in 1869, and he subsequently married Miss Arminda Gwaltney. They have had three children: Clarence (deceased), Elma and Henry.

Mr. Glasscock owns 140 acres of fine land, all in a high state of cultivation and well improved. Politically he is a Republican, one of the kind who is always true to his convictions, though he has many personal friends of the opposite political faith. He is a member and one of the trustees of the Cumberland Presbyterian church, in which he has held the office of deacon the 'greater part of the time since 1863.

— *Memoirs of the Lower Ohio Valley.*

Lucien Winslow Gordon, M. D. – 1905

LUCIEN WINSLOW GORDON M.D., who for almost a quarter of a century has practiced his profession at Equality, Ill., can trace his ancestry back to Archibald Gordon, a native of Scotland, who was the leader of a powerful clan during the Stuart uprising about the middle of the eighteenth century, and was compelled in consequence to leave h i s native land to save his life. For a time he lived in France, but just before the beginning of the French and Indian war he came to America, settling either in South Carolina or Northern Georgia. He lived to a good old age, his death occurring about the time of the beginning of the Revolutionary war. His three sons, John, William, and Robert, all served under General Greene in the Revolution, the first named attaining the rank of colonel.

This John Gordon was the great-grandfather of Doctor Gordon, who is the subject of this sketch. He was born in Scotland, accompanied his parents to France and afterward to America. As a reward for his services during the Revolution he received the customary grant of land, located in what is now either Portage or Trumbull county, O., where he passed the remainder of his life. He married Susanna Bacon, a member of the old Virginia family of that name, and they had four sons: James, Robert, Archibald and Jonathan. (The names of the last two are not certain.)

Robert Gordon, the second son, was born at Warren, Trumbull county, Ohio, about the year 1794, and passed his whole life in that vicinity. At one time he was, one of the most prominent men in that section. He followed the vocation of making brick and erecting brick buildings, and did an extensive business. He was still in his minority when the war of 1812 broke out, but he enlisted as a "powder-monkey" in Commodore Perry's fleet, and served in the famous battle on Lake Erie. After the was he married Janet Porter, and they were the parents of the following children: Thomas Winslow, Isabella M., Anan Irwin, Robert Porter, George Washington, Maria, Alta, Zina, Etta C., William Wallace, and Samuel Quimby. Thomas died in 1901, aged eighty-two; Isabella now lives at Ravenna, O., as the widow, of John Wheatly; Anan lives at Cameron, Mo.; Robert died at Beaver Falls, Pa., where some of his descendants still live; George Washington was the father of the subject of this sketch; Maria married John Gottschell and died soon afterward; Alta also became the wife of John Gottschell and died at Waterloo, Ill.; Zina died single; Etta C., lives at Warren, O., as the widow of Walter Nichols; William Wallace served in the Second Iowa infantry during the Civil war and died at Trenton, Mo.; and Samuel is now living at Ravenna, O.

George W. Gordon was born at Warren, Sept. 23, 1830. He was educated in the high school of his native town and about 1856 graduated from the Cincinnati College of Medicine and Surgery. In 1852 he was united in marriage to Miss Sabine M. Tweed, of Ripley, O. Her father, John Tweed, was an ensign at the battle of Lake Erie, and his father was settled on a Revolutionary land grant in Brown county, O., in the Virginia Reserve. Soon after graduating from the medical college Dr. G. W. Gordon was elected demonstrator of anatomy in the institution and held that position until the death of his wife in 1859, when he removed to Little Rock, Ark.

Here he soon established a lucrative practice, but in 1861, on account of his pronounced opposition to secession, he again returned to the North, and at St. Louis enlisted in Foster's Independent Ohio cavalry. He was at once elected lieutenant and was later commissioned captain in Birge's Second Missouri sharpshooters. He was next commissioned assistant surgeon of the Eighteenth Indiana infantry by Gov. Oliver P. Morton, and subsequently rose to the position of surgeon with the rank of major.

In July, 1864, he was discharged for disability, came to Gallatin county, Ill., where he owned some land, and took up his residence there. As soon as he had sufficiently regained his health he resumed the practice of medicine, locating at Equality, and continued in that occupation until his death, Aug. 6, 1892. In November, 1864, he was married to Laura M. Campbell, widow of Lieut. Josiah Campbell. She was a daughter of Rev. Z. S. Clifford, who was chaplain of the Twenty-ninth Illinois infantry and a Lincoln elector in 1864. He was a native of New Hampshire and a cousin of Daniel Webster. Mrs. Laura Gordon died in 1888, and Major Gordon afterward married Flora R. Dively of Equality, who is still living. To the first marriage there were born two sons, John Robert and Lucien Winslow, the former of whom died in infancy and the latter is the subject of this sketch. To the second marriage five children were born, viz.: Laura, now the wife of Harry Huntsman, of Stamps, Ark.; George Ravenscroft, living at Acme, La.; Louise, wife of M. R. Moore, of Equality; and two who died in infancy unnamed. No children were born to the third marriage.

Dr. Lucien W. Gordon was born at New Hope, O., Aug. 9, 1858, and was but seven years of age when his father located at Equality. He received his education in the public schools, the Enfield college and the Southern Illinois Normal university at Carbondale. In 1877 he entered the Miami Medical college of Cincinnati, and graduated with the class of 1880. On June 26, of that year, he opened an office for the practice of medicine in Equality, and has followed up his profession there ever since. As a physician he is both successful and popular, enjoying the respect of his brother practitioners and the confidence of his patients. He is a member of the Masonic fraternity, and both himself and wife belong to the Methodist Episcopal church.

On Oct. 26, 1880, he married Miss Mollie Alexander Lewis, of Ripley, O., and they have one son, Frank Henderson, born Dec. 26, 1882, and graduated from the Cincinnati College of Pharmacy in 1902. Mrs. Gordon is the granddaughter of Capt. Enoch Lewis, who fought under Harrison at the battle of Tippecanoe. Her grandmother was Hannah Potts, of the old Quaker family that founded Pottsville, Pa.

— *Memoirs of the Lower Ohio Valley.*

Francis A. Gregg – 1905

FRANCIS A. GREGG, a farmer and stock dealer of Omaha, Ill., is of Irish ancestry. His grandfather, Hugh Gregg, was born in Ireland and in boyhood started with his parents to America. On the voyage both parents died and upon his arrival in this country, an orphan boy in a strange land, he was compelled to find a home with strangers. He grew to manhood in South Carolina, married there and followed the occupation of a farmer all his life. One of his sons, Francis Gregg, was born in, that state, May 28, 1791. Upon arriving at manhood's estate he married Nancy Riley and in 1832 removed to Gallatin county, Ill., settling near Texas City in White county. Of the fourteen children, born to Francis and Nancy Gregg but two are now living, the subject of this sketch and his brother John, both residents of Omaha. Their mother died while Francis was still in his boyhood and their father married a Mrs. Sarah Riley, also a native of South Carolina. To this second marriage there were born three children, all now deceased. The father and his second wife both lived to be seventy-five years of age. He was a prosperous farmer, an extensive dealer in livestock, a Democrat in politics, and both himself and wife belonged to the old side Presbyterian church.

Francis A. Gregg was born in Newberry county, S.C., April 3, 1829, received his education in the old fashioned subscription schools and grew to manhood on his father's farm. On Feb. 11, 1851, he was married to Nancy Caroline Eubanks, a native of White county, Ill., and commenced farming for himself not far from where his father lived. Some years later he removed to Hamilton county, where he lived for several years, then spent two years in Williamson county, at the end of which time he returned to Gallatin county. In 1876 he removed to his present residence in the edge of the town of Omaha, where he has ever since carried on the business of farming and dealing in stock.

Of the seven children born to him and his wife, Franklin K. and Elizabeth Ann are deceased; William E., John L., James, Emma and Eleanora all live in Omaha. Emma married a Mr. Humphries and Eleanora a Mr. Wilson. Mr. Gregg takes an interest in political matters and is one of the stanch Democrats of his township. His wife and daughters belong to the Presbyterian church.

— *Memoirs of the Lower Ohio Valley.*

H. C. Gregg – 1905

REV. H. C. GREGG, a well known Adventist minister of Eldorado, Ill., is a descendant of one of the oldest families in that section of the state. He is a great-grandson of Hugh Gregg, who came from Ireland in the Colonial days and settled in South Carolina. (See sketch of F. A. Gregg.) His son Francis married Nancy Riley, a native of North Carolina, and in 1832 came to Illinois, traveling by wagon through unbroken forests part of the way. They were the first settlers in the vicinity of the present town of Texas City in Saline county, where he took up government land and followed farming the remainder of his life. He and his wife both lived to be more than threescore and ten years of age. Of their twelve children, Francis and John, now living in Omaha, Ill., are the only survivors.

One of the sons, William R. Gregg, was born in 1821, married Elizabeth A. Cork, a native of Equality, Ill., and this couple were the parents of the subject of this sketch. They began their married life near Elba, in Gallatin county, and lived in that neighborhood until the death of William R. Gregg in 1859. Of their six children three are living, viz.: W. T., living near Eldorado; Mary E., now Mrs. Yost of Eldorado, and H. C., the subject. After the death of the father of these children Mrs. Gregg married Alexander G. Trousdale, and since his death has made her home with her children. To her second marriage there were born three children. Only one, John C., of Omaha, is now living.

Rev. H. C. Gregg was born in Gallatin, county, Sept. 8, 1856. He received a good education in the common schools and the colleges at McLeansboro and Carmi. When eighteen years of age he commenced teaching and followed that occupation for fourteen years. In, 1882 he was elected county superintendent of schools and served four years. Mr. Gregg has been somewhat active in political natters, and in 1888 was elected on the Democratic ticket to the legislature, serving one term.

On Sept. 14, 1890, he was united in marriage to Miss Eva A. Hopkins, daughter of Dr. N. E. Hopkins, of Mt. Carmel, and in 1894 moved upon his present farm two miles northwest of Elba. There he has 230 acres, all under cultivation with the exception of forty acres of timberland. He has his farm well improved, devotes much of his time to stock raising, and is one of the prosperous and influential citizens of the community where he lives. In 1899 he took up the work of the ministry in the Adventist church, and now has two congregations under his charge, Union Chapel and Bethel. He was one of the founders of the former church, which stands upon part of his land, and was one of the largest contributors toward building it. Mr. and Mrs. Gregg have the following children: Eleanora H., Hugh C., Raymond R. and Paul Jennings, all at home with their parents.

— *Memoirs of the Lower Ohio Valley.*

Hugh C. Gregg – 1883

HUGH C. GREGG, son of William R. and Elizabeth A. Gregg, was born in this county, Sept. 8, 1856. His father died in 1859, and his mother married Mr. Trousdale. His paternal grandparents were natives of South Carolina, and came to Illinois in 1832. His maternal grandparents (Cook) were natives of North Carolina, and removed to Tennessee, from there to Indiana, and in 1815 came to Gallatin County. His Grandfather Cook enlisted in the war of 1812, but his father objected on account of his age, and an older brother went in his place. He served as First Lieutenant in the Black Hawk War.

Mr. Gregg spent his youth alternately on the farm, and attending the district school. He attended a select school in Omaha two terms, and Hamilton College, McLeansboro, a short time; also attended the Normal School at Carmi one term. He has been a very successful teacher, having taught six years in one district. He owns a good farm of 150 acres, and it's worth about $2,500. Mr. Gregg is county superintendent of schools. Politically he is a Democrat.

— *History of White County, Illinois.*

William E. Gregg – 1883

WILLIAM E. GREGG, son of Franklin A. and Nancy C. Gregg, was born in Hamilton County, Ill., Dec. 24, 1857. His paternal grandparents were natives of Germany and immigrated to South Carolina early in the State's history, and from there to Illinois. His maternal grandparents were from Virginia, his Grandfather Eubanks being one of the pioneers of White County.

William E. attended school in the summer and worked on the farm in the winter, but being quick to learn and making good use of his time he always stood at the head of his classes. He was often advised to teach, but preferring a mercantile life he entered the dry-goods house of Henry Wakeford, Norris City. He afterward was employed by C. M. Ferrell & Co., Elizabethtown, Ill. About two years ago he came to Omaha to work in the branch store of Swafford Bros. A short time ago he left them and is now engaged in farming and dealing in stock.

— *History of White County, Illinois.*

Anthony Gross – 1887

ANTHONY GROSS, farmer, was born in Pennsylvania in 1838. He is the son of Andrew and Elizabeth (Whitmire) Gross, both natives of Germany. They came to Pennsylvania about 1835, and, after about twenty years' residence there, removed to Perry County, Mo., where the parents died, the father in the fall and the mother in the spring of 1876. In 1864 our subject married Zilpha Perry, a native of Tennessee, and who died in December 1876. Their five children are still living. In May 1878, he married Mary M., daughter of W. D. and Elizabeth C. Brown, born in Gallatin County in 1847. They have two children. Mr. Gross has always been successfully engaged in agriculture, and came to Gallatin County about 1870. He is a Republican in politics, and is wife is a member of the Methodist Episcopal Church. August 7, 1861, he enlisted in Company K, Eighth Missouri Infantry, under Col. M. L. Smith, and was mustered in at St. Louis. He participated in the battles of Forts Donelson and Henry, Shiloh, Corinth, and Arkansas Post, besides many minor engagements. Discharged on account of disability, he returned home in December 1863.

— *History of Gallatin, Saline, Hamilton, Franklin and Williamson Counties, Illinois.*

John Grumley – 1905

JOHN GRUMLEY, one of the best known and most popular farmers in the neighborhood of Ridgway, Ill., was born near Hopkinsville, Ky., Oct. 16, 1853, his parents being John and Mary (Jeffreys) Grumley. The father was killed in 1855 by the falling of a branch from a tree he was chopping down, and some years later the mother married a man named Posey Cisney and removed to Hamilton county, Ill. After a short stay there they returned to Kentucky, where Mr. Cisney died and the mother married a third time, her third husband being John D. Latham. They now live near Elkton, Todd county, Ky. Two children were born to John and Mary Grumley: Melissa, now a Mrs. Kelley, living in Kentucky, and the subject of this sketch.

Shortly after his father's death John Grumley was bound out to a Kentucky family by the name of Muckelwagner, with whom he lived until he was about nine years of age, when he started out to seek his fortune in his own way. He first went to Posey county, Ind., where he worked on a farm until he attained his majority. In 1872 he was married to Parthena Miller, a native of that county. She died in 1874, leaving one child, and he married Mary J. Mills, also a Posey county girl, and lived there until 1876, when he removed to Gallatin county, Ill., and bought eighty acres, three and a half miles northeast of Ridgway, most of which was in an uncultivated state.

With an energy and ambition worthy of the highest emulation he went to work, and from the first prospered. He now owns 180 acres, all under cultivation with the exception of about ten acres. As a farmer and stock raiser he is well known throughout the county as one of the most progressive and methodical of men. Mr. Grumley takes some interest in politics and is one of the solid Democrats of his township. He belongs to the Independent Order of Odd Fellows, Lodge No. 843, of Ridgway, and to the Court of Honor. In religious matters he is a member of the regular Baptist church, and for several years he has been one of the directors of the public schools. To his second marriage there have been born the following children: Roseander; now living in Saline county; Lura, now a Mrs. Rister, of Gallatin county, and Amelia, at home.

— *Memoirs of the Lower Ohio Valley.*

Amariah Gwaltney – 1905

AMARIAH GWALTNEY, a well known farmer and stock raiser, living near Omaha, Ill., was born Sept. 24, 1848, near Stewartsville, Posey county, Ind. His grandfather, John Gwaltney, was a native of England, but was banished from that country for picking up an apple under a tree that belonged to one of the nobility. In the course of time he settled in Posey county, where he became a well-to-do farmer.

One of his sons, Amariah, was born Feb. 9, 1804, married Sarah Reeder, July 24, 1828, and became one of the largest land-owners in the neighborhood where he lived. At the time of his death, July 7, 1848, he left his widow 600 acres, upon which she lived until her death, Oct. 17, 1867. Their children were John, Eliza, Elizabeth, Jeremiah, Anna, Emaline, Fanny, Marinda, Simon, Josephus, Adijah, Arminda and Amariah.

Amariah, the youngest of the family and the subject of this sketch, received a good education in his youth by attending the common schools and the Fort Branch academy. After his father's death he continued to live with his mother the remainder of her life. When she died he attended school for three winters, working on the farm in the summer time, and then commenced teaching. For three years he taught in the common schools. In the spring of 1872 he came to Gallatin county, and on August 22 of that year was married to Miss Mary E., daughter of Solomon Anderson. Soon after his marriage Mr. Gwaltney located in Ridgway township, where he bought eighty acres adjoining his present farm. Part of the tract was improved and a log cabin stood on the place. Here he and his wife lived for two years, when he sold out and bought the farm now occupied by J. B. Hale. Twelve years later he traded that farm for the one he now owns. When he took possession of this farm the improvements amount to almost nothing, but by his industry and good management he has now one of the best improved farms in the county.

Mr. Gwaltney is a Democrat in his political affiliations, takes an active interest in public affairs, and for two years served as justice of the peace. He and his wife both belong to the Primitive Baptist church. They have one daughter, Elsie, now the wife of Benjamin Kinsall.

— *Memoirs of the Lower Ohio Valley.*

J. W. Hales – 1905

J. W. Hales, dealer in general merchandise, Equality, Ill., was born two miles north of that town, July 5, 1840. He is the son of James and Matilda (Willis) Hales, the former a native of North Carolina and the latter of Tennessee. James Hales came to Illinois about the year 1830, married shortly afterward, and followed farming in the vicinity of Equality until his death, which occurred when the subject of this sketch was about five years old. After the death of his father, his mother bound him out to George W. Flanders, with whom he remained until he was nineteen years of age. His mother married a second time, her second husband being Leonard Haney. She died in Equality, the mother of four children, of whom the subject is the only survivor.

J. W. Hales received such an education as the district schools of his day afforded, and after leaving Mr. Flanders worked in a tobacco establishment at Equality until 1861. He was one of the first to answer the call for troops in that year and enlisted as a private in Company B, First Illinois cavalry. After about six months with this organization he was transferred to Company E, Fourteenth Illinois cavalry, in which he served until the close of the war, rising to the rank of sergeant. His regiment was with Sherman in the march to the sea; was at the siege of Knoxville; the surrender of the Cumberland Gap; and in numerous minor engagements. While engaged in a skirmish at Sunshine Church, near Hillsboro, Ga., Mr. Hales was captured and confined for four months in the famous Andersonville prison. In an attempt to escape he was severely hurt, but recovered and was exchanged. From that time to the end of the war he was with his command in all the principal engagements in which the regiment took part. He was discharged at Pulaski, Tenn., in July, 1865, returned to Equality, and for the following three years was a carder and spinner in the Equality woolen mills. Hen then clerked in a dry goods store for five years, and on Nov. 6, 1875, opened a store of his own, in which line of business he has ever since continued, in addition to which he looks after the management of his farms.

Mr. Hales is a Republican in his political affiliations and takes an active interest in promoting the success of his party. He is a prominent member of the Grand Army of the Republic and with is family belongs to the Methodist Episcopal church. He was married on April 15, 1874, to Miss Blanche E. Reed, a native of Tennessee, and they have two children: James E., who lives in Equality, and Hallie I., now Mrs. Burtie.

— *Memoirs of the Lower Ohio Valley.*

James Hall – 1856

JAMES HALL was born in Philadelphia August 19, 1793, and commenced the study of law in that city in 1811. At this period he saw something of military life. In 1813 he was one of a company of volunteers, the Washington Guards, commanded by Condy Raguet, Esq., afterwards United States Minister to Brazil, who entered the service of the United States and spent several months in camp, on the Delaware, watching the motions of a British fleet, performing all the duties of soldiers. At the close of that year he was commissioned a Third Lieutenant of Artillery, in the Second Regiment, commanded by Colonel Winfield Scott, who about that time became a Brigadier-General.

In the spring of 1814 he marched to the frontier with a company of artillery commanded by Captain Thomas Biddle, and joined the army at Buffalo under General Brown, in which Scott, Ripley, and Porter were Brigadiers. In the battle of Chippewa he commanded a detachment from his company, and had a full share of that brilliant affair. He was in the battle of Lundy's Lane (or Bridge-water), at Niagara, the siege of Fort Erie, and all the hard fighting and severe service of that campaign, and was commended afterwards officially, services.

At the close of the war, unwilling to be inactive, Mr. Hall went to Washington and solicited a Midshipman's warrant in the Navy, in the hope of going out in Decatur's squadron against the Algerines, but without success. Subsequently it was decided to send out with that expedition a bomb-vessel and some mortars to be used in the bombardment of Algiers, under the command of Major Archer of the artillery; and our author had the honor of being selected as one of four young officers who accompanied him. He sailed in September, 1815, from Boston in the United States Brig *Enterprise,* commanded by Lieutenant Lawrence Kearney, now the veteran Commodore. The war with Algiers was a short one, and after a brief, but to him most delightful cruise in the Mediterranean, he returned at the close of the same year and was stationed at Newport, Rhode Island, and afterwards at various other ports until 1818, when he resigned, having previously resumed the study of law at Pittsburgh, Pennsylvania, where he was then stationed, and been admitted to the bar.

In the spring of 1820, having no dependence but his own exertions, with great ardor and hopefulness of spirit, and energy of purpose, he resolved to go to a new country to practise his profession where he could rise with the growth of the population; but allured in fact by a romantic disposition, a thirst for adventure, and a desire to see the rough scenes of the frontier, he went to Illinois, then recently admitted into the Union as a State, and commenced practice at Shawneetown, and edited a weekly newspaper, called the *Illinois Gazette,* for which he wrote a great deal. The next winter he was appointed Circuit Attorney, that is public prosecutor for a circuit containing ten counties.

In a reminiscence of these journeyings, which were to supply the author with that practical knowledge of the people of the west, and the scenes of genial humor which abound in his pages, he remarks —

> Courts were held in these counties twice a year, and they were so arranged as to time that after passing through one circuit we went directly to the adjoining one, and thus proceeded to some twenty counties in succession. Thus we were kept on horseback and travelling over a very wide region the greater part of our time. There was no other way to travel but on horseback. There were but few roads for carriages, and we travelled chiefly by bridle-paths, through uncultivated wilds, fording rivers, and sometimes swimming creeks, and occasionally 'camping out.' There were few taverns, and we ate and slept chiefly at the log cabins of the settlers. The office of prosecuting in such a country is no *sinecure.* Several of the counties in my circuit were bounded by the Ohio river, which separated them from Kentucky, and afforded facilities to rogues and ruffians to change their jurisdictions, which allured them to settle among us in great gangs, such as could often defy the arm of the law. We had whole settlements of counterfeiters or horse thieves with their sympathizers, where rogues could change names, or pass from house to house, so skillfully as to elude detection, and where, if detected, the whole population were ready to rise to the rescue. There were other settlements of sturdy honest fellows, the regular backwoodsmen, in which rogues were not tolerated. There was, therefore, a continual struggle between these parties, the honest people trying to expel the others by the terrors of the law, and when that mode failed, forming *regulating* companies and driving them out by force. To be a public prosecutor among such a people requires much discretion and no small degree of courage. When the contest breaks out into violence, when arms are used, and a little civil war takes place, there are aggressions on both sides, and he is to avoid making himself a party with either;

when called upon to prosecute either he is denounced and often threatened, and it required calmness, self-possession, and sometimes courage to enable him to do his duty, preserving his self-respect and the public confidence.

In these cases Mr. Hall was a rigorous prosecutor, never flinching from duty, and on some occasions turning out himself and aiding in the arrest of notorious and bold villains.[234] He served in that office four years, and obtained also a large practice on the civil side of the court. He was then elected by the legislature Judge of the Circuit Court, the court having general original jurisdiction, civil and criminal. He presided in that court three years, when a change in the judiciary system took place, the circuit courts were abolished, and all the judges repealed out of office. At the same session of the legislature he was elected State Treasurer, and removed to Vandalia, the seat of government. This office he held four years, in connexion with an extensive law practice, and in connexion also with the editorship of the *Illinois Intelligencer,* a weekly newspaper, and of the *Illinois Monthly Magazine,* which he established, published, owned, edited, and for which he wrote nearly all the matter — tale, poem, history, criticism, gossip.

In 1833 Mr. Hall removed to Cincinnati, his present residence, having lived in Illinois twelve years. He has since 1836 been engaged in financial pursuits, having been at first the cashier of the Commercial Bank, and since 1853 the president of another institution bearing the same name.

The series of Mr. Hall's numerous publications commenced with his contributions to the *Port Folio* during the editorship of his brother, who took charge of that work. In 1820, when descending the Ohio, and afterwards during the early part of his residence in Illinois, Mr. Hall wrote a series of *Letters from the West,* which were published in the *Port Folio.* They were written in the character of a youth travelling for amusement, giving the rein to a lively fancy, and indulging a vein of levity and rather extravagant fun. They were intended to be anonymous, but having been carried by a friend to England, unexpectedly to the author appeared from the London press ascribed to "the Hon. Judge Hall" on the title-page. The English reviews had their sport out of the apparent incongruity. They acknowledged a certain sort of ability about it, and confessed that the author wrote very good English; but sneered at the levities, and asked the English public what they would think of a learned judge who should lay aside the wig and robe of office, and roam about the land in quest of "black eyes" and "rosy cheeks," dancing at the cabins of the peasantry, and "kissing the pretty girls." The *venerable* Illinois Judge they pronounced to be a "sly rogue," and wondered if the learned gentleman was as funny on the bench, &c. &c. The author never allowed the book to be republished.

Mr. Hall's subsequent literary productions may be classed under the heads of periodical literature, books written to exhibit the political and social character and statistics of the West, and an extensive series of works of fiction illustrating the romance, adventure, and humor of

---

[234] Hall led the raid on Sturdivant Gang of counterfeiters at Sturdivant's Fort in modern-day Rosiclare on June 28, 1822. Having made their arrests, Hall and his deputies nevertheless were forced to flee with supporters of the Sturdivants made a counter-attack. Hall and his group successfully made it to Potts Inn that night where they holed up. The next day, they found the coast clear and returned to Shawneetown. However, the raid proved in vain as in their haste to escape the fort, while they brought with them the suspects, the failed to gather the evidence.

the region. In 1829 he edited and secured the publication of the *Western Souvenir,* in imitation of the elegant annuals then in vogue. Half of the matter was written by himself. Though the appearance of the work suffered from mechanical defects, its spirit was admitted, and as a novelty it was quite successful.

In October, 1830, Mr. Hall published the first number of the *Illinois Monthly Magazine* at Vandalia, which was also a novelty, and judging from the numbers before us, quite a creditable one. In the worth and elegance of its matter it would not be out of place now in any of the leading cities of the country. Then it was a free-will offering of time, enthusiasm, and money (for the work was sustained by the author's purse as well as pen), to the cause of social improvement and refinement in a virgin state, the resources of which were as yet all to be developed. It was continued for two years, and served well its liberal purposes. This work was followed by the *Western Monthly Magazine,* published at Cincinnati for three years from 1833 to 1835, and sustained by a large subscription. Like the former it was not only diligently edited but mostly written by Mr. Hall.

A work of considerable magnitude, in which Mr. Hall soon engaged, involved vast labor and original research. In connexion with Col. Thomas L. M'Kenney he undertook to edit and write *A History and Biography of the Indians of North America.* The work, a costly one, was to be illustrated by a series of portraits taken at Washington by King, who had formed a gallery in the War Department of the various celebrated chiefs who visited the capital. It was proposed by Col. M'Kenney, who had been Commissioner for Indian Affairs, to publish one hundred and twenty portraits, with a memoir of each of the chieftains. The work appeared easy, but it was soon found sufficiently difficult to task the energies of Mr. Hall, upon whom the toil of composition fell, to the extent even of his accustomed diligence and pliant pen. The material which had been supposed to exist in official and other documents at hand had to be sought personally from agents of government, old territorial governors, and such original authorities as Governor Cass, General Harrison, and others. With the exception of a few facts from the expeditions of Long, Pike, and Schoolcraft, nothing was compiled from books. The testimony of actors and eye-witnesses was sought and sifted, so that the work is not only full of new and interesting facts but of a reliable character.

The expensive style of this publication, a copy costing one hundred and twenty dollars, has confined it to the public libraries or to the collections of wealthy persons. From the failure of the first publishers, the change of others, and the expense of the work, Messrs. M'Kenney and Hall, who were to have received half the profits, got little or nothing.

In 1835 Mr. Hall published at Philadelphia two volumes of *Sketches of History, Life, and Manners in the West,* and subsequently at Cincinnati, another pair of volumes entitled *The West, its Soil, Surface, and Productions; Its Navigation and Commerce.* The "Sketches" illustrate the social, the others the material characteristics of this important region.

During the canvass between General Harrison and Van Buren in 1836 Mr. Hall published a life of the former, the materials of which he had prepared for the *Sketches of the West.* It is a polished and interesting history.

The several volumes of Mr. Hall's tales include the separate publications, *The Legends of the West; The Border Tales; The Soldier's Bride and other Tales; Harpes Head, a Legend of Kentucky; The Wilderness and the War Path.* Many of these first appeared in magazines and annuals. They are characterized by a certain amenity and ease of narrative, a poetic appreciation of the beauties of nature, and the gentler moods of the affections; while the author's pleasing narrative has softened the rudeness without abating the interest of the wild border strife. The Indian subjects are handled with peculiar delicacy; the kindly sentiment of the author dwelling on their virtues, while his imagination is enkindled by their spiritual legends. His style, pure in sentiment and expression, may be aptly compared with the calm, tranquil aspect of his own Ohio river, occasionally darkened by wild bordering woods, but oftener reflecting the beauty of the azure heaven.

Several of Mr. Hall's family have engaged in literature. His mother, Mrs. Sarah Hall, the daughter of Dr. John Ewing, wrote *Conversations on the Bible,* which were republished abroad, and which have passed through several editions. She was a contributor to the *Port Folio* from the commencement and during the editorship of her son. A volume of her writings was edited and published by Harrison Hall in 1833, with a prefatory memoir by Judge Hall. She was born October 30, 1760, and died April 3, 1830.

John E. Hall, her eldest son, was born December, 1783. He was educated at Princeton, read law with Judge Hopkinson, was admitted to practice in 1805, and removed to Baltimore. He published the *American Law Journal* in Philadelphia from 1808 to 1817. He was elected Professor of Rhetoric and Belles Lettres in the University of Maryland. He collected and arranged an edition of the *British Spy*, to which he contributed several letters much to the gratification of Wirt the author. When the Baltimore riot broke out in 1811, he was one of the party of Federalists who aided in defending Hanson's house, and was one of the nine thrown on a heap as killed. He left Baltimore soon afterwards, removing to Philadelphia, where he assumed the editorship of the Port Folio in 1806. The memoirs of Anacreon in that journal were from his pen. They were a reproduction on this thread of narrative of Grecian manners and customs, supposed to be written by Critias of Athens, and the author was stimulated to their composition by the approval of the poet Moore, who was then creating a sensation in the literary circles of Philadelphia. Mr. Hall was the author of the life prefixed to the poems of his friend Dr. John Shaw, published in Baltimore in 1810. In 1827 he edited with biographical and critical notes, *The Philadelphia Souvenir,* a collection of fugitive pieces from the press of that city. The editor's part is written with spirit. In the same year was published in Philadelphia in an octavo volume, *Memoirs of Eminent Persons, with Portraits and Fac-Similes, written and in part selected by the Editor of the Port Folio.* In consequence of his declining health the Port Folio was discontinued in 1827. He died June 11, 1829. His brother, Harrison Hall, publisher of the *Port Folio*, is the author of a work on Distilling first published in 1815, which has received the commendation of Dr. Hare and other scientific men of the day.

Dr. Thomas Mifflin Hall, a younger brother, contributed poetry and some scientific articles to the Port Folio. In 1828 he embarked on board of a South American ship of war to which he was appointed surgeon. The vessel was never heard of after.[235]

— *Cyclopedia of American Literature.*

Mary H. Hall – 1912

Another name, Mrs. Mary H. Hall, has been stricken from the ever lessening roll of old settlers. She passed peacefully away at the home of her daughter, Mrs. J. W. Millspaugh, in

---

[235] Evert A. Duyckinck. 1856. *Cyclopaedia of American Literature.* New York: C. Scribner. 145-147.

this city Tuesday at 12:30 p.m.[236] Tender human ties cannot be severed without a pang, yet in such a death there is really no great cause for grief. Her life work was done, and well done. Wearied with life's duties and cares, weary of suffering and waiting, she lay down to rest. The end was peaceful. She had no fever; neither did she suffer a pain. She had been quite feeble for a month but only a week ago she was able to go out into the yard. She then expressed her desire to go and longed for the day when she would meet her Creator. She often said she "was hungry for heaven."

Mrs. Hall was the daughter of John and Sina Crenshaw and was born at the old salt works south of Equality, July 22, 1818. At the age of 16 – March 22, 1834, she was married to John E. Hall, a prominent young man of the county. Chas. Slocum performed the ceremony.

Eight children were born to them, four of whom survive – Mrs. Anna Dodds, of Waltonville, Ill., Mrs. J. W. Millspaugh, of Shawneetown Mrs. N. E. Raitt, of Cincinnati and John E. Hall of St. Louis. She is survived by 17 grandchildren, 26 great-grandchildren and four great great grand children. All of her surviving children excepting Mrs. Dodds, who is 77 years of age and quite feeble and unable to come, were here for the funeral. Most of the grandchildren, and some of the great grand children were also here.

The funeral was held from the M.E. church this morning (Thursday) at nine o'clock, conducted by Rev. Brown, and the remains were taken to the old family cemetery at Hickory Hill for internment. It was in this neighborhood that hours spent many of her happiest days and it was her request that beneath the shady trees of that silent little city should be the eternal abiding place of all that was mortal of her.

Mrs. Hall was a remarkable woman in many respects. Most of her long lifetime was present in Shawneetown, and for the past 33 years she has lived with her daughter, Mrs. Millspaugh, who has been faithful and cared for her like she would a child. Mrs. Hall was not a stout woman but she was healthy and hearty. She was from an aristocratic southern family and was highly cultured and refined, but regular in her habits and took no chances with her health. She has been a faithful member of the M.E. church since her childhood and never neglected her church duties for anything. She was in the truest since a Christian woman. She hated sin and there was no compromise with wrong doing. So true to these principles was she that whenever there was any doubt as to the correctness of her decision, she would not take a chance.

Mrs. Hall's life is linked with many important events of the past. She had a remarkable memory and often told with vivid recollection about the time that Gen. Lafayette was entertained in Shawneetown by the citizens in 1825. Nothing delighted her more than to sit down at home and talk about old times. She also told of her blood relation to John Hart, one of the signers of the Declaration of Independence of the U.S.[237] Mrs. Hall's grandfather, William Crenshaw, who died on Eagle Creek, Dec. 10, 1814, married Elizabeth Hart, who was the daughter of John Hart, was born in 1772 and died at the home of Mrs. Hall's father December 7, 1829. Mrs. Hall remembered her very well and often said that her grandmother

---

[236] July 16, 1912.

[237] As explained in a footnote in the John Hart Crenshaw biography. Her great-grandfather John Hart was not the John Hart who signed the Declaration of Independence.

would talk of her relationship to one of the signers of the Declaration of Independence with great pride.

Mrs. Hall's husband was assassinated by Robert C. Sloo, a son of Col. James G. Sloo, who was the recognized leader of the Democrats of this section at the time.

Nov. 11, 1856, Mr. Hall was Circuit Clerk of Gallatin county and had his office in the old frame building on the lot now occupied by the Peeples' building, in this city. The room was where the bookstore now is. Col. Bob Ingersoll was Mr. Hall's deputy. Sloo became enraged at an article published in a newspaper, attacking Col. Sloo and reflecting somewhat on his family and charged Hall with writing the article, and entered his office and killed him. Jr. Hall was sitting with his back to the door. Sloo fired one shot into his back and as Hall raised up and turned he fired another shot into his breast. Hall fell into Ingersoll's arms and died. Mrs. Hall kept the clothing which her husband wore when he was shot and at her request the shirt which she had made with her own hands and kept so carefully for 56 years, was put in the coffin with her and buried. The vest which Mr. Hall wore was also put in the casket with the shirt. Both garments bore the blood stains and the two bullet holes.

Through all the vicissitudes and sorrows of her life, and the death of her husband was perhaps the greatest, her faith in God never wavered and she died as she had lived — honored, trusted and loved, and now the grave hides from sight all that is mortal of this true and noble woman.[238]

— *Obituary.*

Charles S. Hanmore – 1883

CHARLES S. HANMORE, a native of New Albany, Ind., is a son of James and Sarah (Sprout) Hanmore. James was a son of Job and Mary Hanmore, afterward Sheridan. Charles S. spent his early life in St. Louis, his father being an engineer on one of the St. Louis and Paducah packets. His parents had two children — Charles S. and Sarah, now Mrs. Bradshaw. His mother died in 1847, and his father married Margaret Fowler, of New Albany. They had four children — John, William, James and Carrie, now a teacher in the New Albany High School. They moved from St. Louis to New Haven in 1858. Mrs. Hanmore died in 1862.

Mr. Hanmore had control of the large grist-mill for many years; part of the time with his brother Thomas, until his death in 1862, and afterward alone, until he sold out to the stock company. Charles S. received a common-school education in St. Louis and New Haven. He commenced work for himself in 1852, by going on one of the packets as steersman, and afterward as pilot. In 1866 he came to New Haven, and has since been engaged in the mercantile business. He married Sarah Harding, a daughter of Richard Harding (deceased), who was a Second Lieutenant in the Ninth Illinois Infantry. Her mother was a native of New York State, and, after Mr. Harding's death, married Elias R. Goad, of New Haven. To Mr. and Mrs. Hanmore have been born five children, two living — Claude and Capitola.

— *History of White County, Illinois.*

---

[238] July 18, 1912. "Mrs. Mary Hall" obituary. Unknown Shawneetown, Ill. newspaper.

Willis B. Hargrave – 1887

WILLIS B. HARGRAVE was born in White County, Ill., near Carmi, August 3, 1825. His father, George B., was born in Butler County, Ky., in 1798, and came to Illinois when seventeen years old. He lived in Gallatin County two years, White County fourteen years, and finally settled in Equality. He was sheriff of White County eight years, about after returning to Equality he preferred the privacy of farming, and died in December 1841. About 1819 he married Lucinda McHenry, a native of Kentucky. The mother died in 1836 near Equality.

Our subject, the third of nine children, received a good education in the common schools, and besides farming has been a member of the firm of Hargrave & Duplee, the leading produce dealers of the place, and is partner in a fine roller process flouring-mill. He served six months in the Mexican war, and was discharged at Camp Mear, on the Rio Grande. He enlisted in the Third Illinois Cavalry as private, afterwards as first lieutenant, and was at Pea Ridge, also near Vicksburg, and wounded at Champion Hill, disabling him a short time. After two years and a half he resigned his commission at Port Hudson on account of ill health. June 15, 1848, he married Sarah A., daughter of Richard Craw, a farmer and native of New York. Their children, Alma L. and George R., are both deceased. She was born in White County, January 6, 1831. He is a staunch Republican and was an active Odd Fellow. He and his wife are Methodists. He resides in Equality, and owns 325 acres near there.

— *History of Gallatin, Saline, Hamilton, Franklin and Williamson Counties, Illinois.*

W. C. and B. R. Harsha – 1887

W. C. and B. R. HARSHA, of the Shawneetown, were born, the former in 1852 in Beaver County, Penn., and the latter in 1861 in Washington County, Ohio. They are the sons of Dr. J. M. and Mary (Dawson) Harsha, the former of German descent, and born in Beaver County, Penn., in 1819.

The father was educated for engineering and surveying, but after graduating at Harrisburg Medical College, he practiced medicine at about the age of twenty years. After practicing in Beaver County, Penn., and Washington County, Ohio, in May 1873, he came to Shawneetown. In eighteen months he went to Reno County, Kas., where he died in 1885. The last forty years he also engaged in surveying and construction; was railway agent for the Marietta & Cincinnati Railroad at Cutler, Ohio, about seventeen years; county surveyor in Reno County, Kas., four years, and also in the lumber business in Ohio for several years; he was successful and enterprising in all. He was married three times, Mary Dawson being his second wife. She was born in 1828, in Beaver County, Penn., and died in 1861. She was Scotch in origin. Three sons: John P., William C., and Benoni R., are residents of Shawneetown. The first born in 1849 was appointed Ohio & Mississippi Railway agent in 1870. He married A. A. Campbell. Their four children are Ruth, May, John and Clyde. William C., proprietor of the wharf boat, and assistant agent for the Ohio & Mississippi Railway. He married Annie Egbert in September 1886. The brothers are Republicans in politics and solid citizens.

— *History of Gallatin, Saline, Hamilton, Franklin and Williamson Counties, Illinois.*

George Harrelson – 1905

GEORGE HARRELSON, a retail grocer of Shawneetown, Ill., was born in what is known as the "Pond Settlement" in that county, May 3, 1847. He is the second and only surviving child of George and Mary (Callicott) Harrelson. Rebecca, the eldest, married Henry Young and later died, and Joseph, the youngest, died at the age of twenty years.

George Harrelson, the father, was twice married. His first wife was a Miss Fleming, by whom he had four children, only one of whom is now living, viz.: Nancy, wife of Henry Young, of Omaha, Ill. When the subject of this sketch was about eight years of age his parents removed to New Haven, in Gallatin County, and there the father died the same year. The mother afterward married James Smith, who died in 1867.

George Harrelson lived with his mother until he was 21 years old, when he commenced working by the month for some of the neighboring farmers. After a few years passed in this way he bought out the other heirs to his father's estate and became the owner of the old homestead, consisting of 160 acres of land. He conducted this farm for three years, when he rented it and engaged in other pursuits for about four years, at the end of which time he returned to the farm and lived there until 1887. In that year he located in Shawneetown and embarked in the grocery business, in which he is still engaged. Mr. Harrelson has built up a good patronage by his close attention to business, studying the demands of his trade, and his correct business habits. Politically he is a Republican, although he is not particularly active in political work, and in religious matters he belongs to the Presbyterian Church. He has been twice married. His first wife, who died about a year after their marriage, was Mary Williams. His second and present wife was Sarah E. Hill.

To this marriage there was born one son, Joseph, who met his death by an accident. One day, during recess at school, a boy named Jesse Barr caught a schoolmate, Harry Docker, and bumped the back of his head against Joseph's right temple, causing an injury that resulted in his death.

— *Memoirs of the Lower Ohio Valley.*

James C. Harrell – 1883

JAMES C. HARRELL, M.D., was born in Bear Creek Precinct, Gallatin Co, Ill., Aug. 21, 1847. His father, Benton R. Harrell, was born and reared in Indian Creek Precinct; his grandfather, Cader Harrell, was born in North Carolina, but his parents removed when he was yet a child to Sumner County, Tenn., and from thence to Kentucky, and shortly after his marriage he moved to White County, Ill., at a very early period in its history, where he lived and died to a ripe old age, when by assiduous study he was qualified to teach, and began his life as one of the teachers of Gallatin County, which profession he followed with credit to himself and the profession in Gallatin and White counties, Ill., and Ballard County, in the meantime devoting himself earnestly and enthusiastically to the study of medicine.

After attending a course of lectures at Philadelphia in 1869-70, he graduated and returned home in the spring of 1870, and began his professional career in partnership with Dr A. R. Pearce, near Roland, which continued until January of the ensuing year. When the Springfield & Illinois Southeastern Railroad, as it was then called, was finished, he moved back to his native county, and built the first house in Omaha, since which time he has resided here. Feb. 6, 1871, he was married to Susan C. Keasler, a daughter of James Keasler, one of the pioneers of Gallatin County. Shortly after his building his new house at Omaha, he went to work with his usual zeal, and secured the establishment of a post office, and was himself appointed the first Postmaster. During his residence at Omaha, he has won for himself a reputation as a physician second to none in the town and county, the cause of education, churches, Sunday-schools and general progress.

He is ever to be found in the van, when the sanguine of the grand future of Southern Illinois, and is engaged in manufacturing brick and lumber, and looks forward with prophetic eye to the time when our part of the country will be full of manufacturing industries. Politically he is a Republican, and is an earnest worker in the ranks of that party. The Doctor is a fine specimen of a self-made man. He possesses a fine library; is an inveterate reader, fluent and scholarly public speaker, and a gentleman of whom Omaha may well be proud.

— *History of White County, Illinois.*

William Finley Harrell – 1883

WILLIAM FINLEY HARRELL, son of Benton R. and Dolly E. Harrell, was born in Gallatin County, in August, 1852. He was reared on a farm on the line between Gallatin and White counties. He was married in 1875 to Clara E. Blackard. He has a farm near that of his father. He moved to Omaha in 1880 and ran the Omaha House and a livery and feed stable in connection with his mother-in-law. He returned to his farm and engaged in farming and stock-raising until August, 1882, when he purchased a third interest in the Omaha flouring mills. Mr. Harrell has a family of two boys and one girl.

— *History of White County, Illinois.*

H. Harrington – 1887

H. HARRINGTON, junior member of the firm of Allen & Harrington, merchants, was born in Gallipolis, Ohio, in 1854, the son of M. and Jemimah (Irion) Harrington. The father, of English stock, born in 1815, in New York, was a farmer and trader, and when married lived in Gallia County, Ohio. In 1860 he located near New Haven, this county. He bought about 600 acres and was a prosperous farmer until his death in 1883. The mother was born in North Carolina in 1821 and is still living. Five of eleven children are living. Our subject, the seventh, was educated at Shawneetown and attended the normal at Lebanon, Ohio, for two years, and for seven year after was a successful teacher in Gallatin County. He clerked for T. B. Allen for three years from 1879, when the firm became Allen & Harrington, as above mentioned. They keep a first-class stock of general merchandise and are both able businessmen. He is a Republican, and first voted for Hayes. He is a Knight Templar, a member f the I.O.O.F. and Eastern Star.

— *History of Gallatin, Saline, Hamilton, Franklin and Williamson Counties, Illinois.*

John W. Harrington – 1905

JOHN W. HARRINGTON, a farmer living near Omaha, Ill., was born Feb. 4, 1859, on the farm adjoining the one on which he now lives. His father, Miro Harrington; was a native of Long Island, N. Y., where he was born in 1813. When he was a boy his parents removed to Ohio, locating near Gallipolis, where he grew to manhood and married Jemima Irion in the year 1840. For a number of years he followed boating to New Orleans and in 1857 he removed to Illinois, lived one year in Hardin county, and then came to Gallatin county. He bought 140 acres in what is now Ridgway township, the tract of land now being occupied by his daughter, Mrs. William Rogers. At the time he bought it there was a log cabin on the place and about forty acres cleared. He died on that farm in 1881, aged sixty-seven years. His wife survived until 1897, when she died at the age of seventy-five. They are buried side by side in Union Ridge cemetery, in White county. She was a member of the Methodist Episcopal church for many years prior to her death.

Their children were Amanda, Henry I., Hezekiah, Romelia, Ann, John W., Orlenia, Albina, Alice, Rosetta, Sarepta and Vienna. Amanda is the wife of a Mr. Holt; Henry lives in Ridgway; Hezekiah is in Kansas City, Mo.; Romelia is the widow of William Rogers and lives on the old home place; Ann is the wife of W. J. Sanders; John W. is the subject of this sketch, and the others are deceased.

John W. Harrington obtained a good practical education in the public schools, and at the age of twenty-one rented the old home place and began life on his own account. He now owns 200 acres, 160 of which is under cultivation, and is regarded as one of the foremost farmers of the community. Mr. Harrington is a Republican in his political views, and, although firm in his convictions, he has a large number of Democratic friends who value his friendship because of his many good qualities. He has been twice married, first in 1880 to Miss Mary E., daughter of James T. Ramsey of Indiana, and to this union there were born two sons, Leroy and Lawrence.

His first wife died in 1884, and in 1887 he was married to Cordelia Rogers, by whom he has three children: Clarence, Vera, and Henry. Mr. Harrington belongs to the Court of Honor, and is always interested in any and every movement for the betterment of the neighborhood where he has passed his whole life.

— *Memoirs of the Lower Ohio Valley.*

James H. Hemphill – 1887

JAMES H. HEMPHILL, agent and operator, Ohio & Mississippi Railway, Ridgway, Ill., was born in Gallatin County, in this township, July 8, 1860. He is the son of John F. and Mary E. (Glass) Hemphill, natives of Pope County, Ill. The father, a farmer and carpenter, came to the county in the fifties. He was a soldier in the Federal Army and died in service at Memphis, Tenn. The mother died July 3, 1884. Our subject was reared on the farmer with his mother, and secured a common school education. In 1881 he began telegraphy, and in 1882 was made operator at Ridgway, his present position, which he efficiently fills. After March 1, 1887, he was agent for the Baltimore & Ohio Express Company, until it was replaced by the Adams Company, whose agent he now is. May 1, 1887, he was made station agent which he ably fills. November 22, 1883, he married Maggie J., daughter of Jas. M. Bean. Their two children are Vesta Joy and Mary Irene. He is Republican in politics, and since April 1886, has served as village clerk. He and his wife are members of the Cumberland Presbyterian Church, and he is justly recognized as one of the leading young citizens of Ridgway.

— *History of Gallatin, Saline, Hamilton, Franklin and Williamson Counties, Illinois.*

Thomas B. Hick, M.D. – 1883

THOMAS B. HICK, M.D., was born Dec. 6, 1841, and was a son of Thomas S. and Fatima C. (Barger) Hick. He enlisted in the late war, in the Seventh Illinois Calvary. He was Postmaster for the Division. He was clerk for his father, and then attended Eastman's Commercial College at Poughkeepsie, N.Y. After his return he took up the study of medicine with F. M. Aldrich. He attended one course of lectures at Jefferson Medical College, Philadelphia, and graduated at the Western Reserve Medical College, Cleveland, Ohio. He went into the drug business the following year, with Mr. Mitchell, the firm name being Mitchell & Hick. Soon after they opened a drug store in Newport, Ark., associating with them a doctor named Gray, the firm name being Gray, Mitchell & Co., Dr. Hick being a silent partner, remaining in New Haven, practicing medicine. This partnership continued until Mitchell and Gray both died, when Dr. Hick went to Newport and settled up the business. He has been practicing in the vicinity of New Haven.

In 1876 he moved to Hawthorne Township, but remained there less than a year. In 1880 he opened a drug store. Of late years he has been engaged in bee culture, having the last summer about 150 hives. He was married in 1874, to Mary J. Slinger, daughter of Thomas Slinger. They had one child. His wife died in 1877. Dr. Hick is one in whom great confidence is reposed as a physician.

— *History of White County, Illinois.*

Thomas B. Hick, M.D. – 1905

THOMAS B. HICK, M.D., one of the best known physicians of Gallatin County, Ill., was born at New Haven, in that County, Dec. 6, 1841, and is now the oldest native resident of that place. He is the third in a family of five children born to Thomas and Fatima C. (Barger) Hick, the former a native of Yorkshire, England, and the latter of Gallatin County, where her father, Jacob Barger, was one of the early settlers. The other children were John, born in 1838 and died in 1875, a merchant during his lifetime; Mary J., who married George L. Hanna, and died in 1901; Elizabeth J., wife of Mathew Land, born Jan. 13, 1844, and one who died in infancy.

Doctor Hick's father came from England in his boyhood with his parents, settling near Golconda in the year 1816. He was bound out to a tobacconist until he was 21 years of age, but not liking the arrangement ran away before he completed his term of service. In 1835 he located at New Haven, where he engaged in mercantile pursuits. He took a prominent part, in political affairs and in 1845 and again in 1858 was elected to the legislature on the Democratic ticket. He continued in business until 1866, and upon his death his sons succeeded to the store. The mother of Doctor Hick died in 1855. Doctor Hick received his early education in the common schools, after which he took a course in the Eastman Business College, at Poughkeepsie, N.Y. On Dec. 1, 1861, he enlisted as a private in Company G, Seventh Illinois cavalry, joining the regiment at Bird's Point, Mo. He was at the siege of Vicksburg; participated in the battle of Arkansas Post, the military operations about Corinth, and was in a number of minor skirmishes. In 1862 he was promoted to sergeant, and in August of that year was detailed for special duty by order of General Grant. When the post office of the 13th Army Corps was created he was appointed a clerk in that department and remained in that capacity until August 1864. He was then transferred to the military post office at Cairo and served there until he was mustered out on December 19, at Nashville, Tenn. Before the war he had been associated with his father in the store and had spent some time in reading medicine. After being discharged from the army he again took up the study, though he continued in the store with his brother until 1869.

During the years 1870-71 he attended the Jefferson Medical College, of Philadelphia, and in 1872 graduated from the Cleveland Medical College. He located at New Haven, where he has been in continuous practice ever since. Although a third of a century has elapsed since Doctor Hick first received his degree of M.D. he has not allowed himself to fall behind in the progress of medical science. In the treatment of diseases he is looked upon as one of the successful physicians of his section of the state, and consequently has a large and lucrative practice. In addition to his professional interests he owns a farm of 160 acres, and has accumulated considerable town property. Like his father before him, he is an unswerving Democrat, though the only political position he could ever be prevailed on to accept was the post office at New Haven, where he served as postmaster for several years. Doctor Hick is a member of the Ancient Order of United Workmen; Rhodes Post, No. 586, Grand Army of the Republic, of New Haven, and belongs to the Cumberland Presbyterian church.

— *Memoirs of the Lower Ohio Valley.*

Thomas S. Hick (deceased) – 1883

THOMAS S. HICK (deceased) was one of New Haven's prominent citizens. He was of English nativity, and war born in November 1809. His father, having probably a large family, bound Thomas and his brother William to a man named Pickering till Pickering proved a hard task-master, and the boys left him, William settling in Equality, where he was successful as a merchant and miller, buying produce and provisions for the New Orleans market, and being interested in the salt wells leased from the State.

Thomas first went to Golconda, Pope County, where he learned the tobacconist's trade of John Raum, father of General Raum. From there he went to Shawneetown and assisted Kirkpatrick in business. He came to New Haven in 1836. He married Fatima C. Barger. They had four children — John (deceased), Mary (now Mrs. Geo. L. Hanna, of Emma Township), Thomas B. and Elizabeth (now Mrs. Matthew Land, of Hawthorn Township). Mrs. Hick died and he married Mrs. Sophia Staley, widow of Ahart Staley, of Carmi. She is still living in New Haven. From 1856 till his death he was engaged in general merchandising. He represented the district in the General Assembly, the last being in 1858, when Wm. R. Morrison was Speaker. He was President of the Illinois State Bank. He died Oct. 27, 1866.

— *History of White County, Illinois.*

Henry Hill – 1887

HENRY HILL, farmer and stock dealer, was born in 1846, in Saline County, Ill., one of nine children of James and Levina (Harris) Hill. The father, a farmer, was born in Tennessee in 1825, and came to Saline County, Ill., when a young man, and after marriage bought eighty acres of land where he lived at his death in 1869. He served four years as magistrate. The mother was born in 1825 and died in 1855. With common school advantages, and beginning as a poor boy, our subject has become the owner of 458 acres of fine land. In 1879 he married Mrs. Martha McCue, daughter of James and Mary Keurek, born in 1851 in Gallatin County. She has three children by her first marriage: James Y., Rachel S. and Mattie McCue. Mr. Hill served as county commissioner for three years after 1884. Politically he is a Democrat.

— *History of Gallatin, Saline, Hamilton, Franklin and Williamson Counties, Illinois.*

J. A. Hinch – 1883

J. A. HINCH, son of Benjamin P. and Rebecca S. (Barger) Hinch, was born May 29, 1851. His father was one of the prominent citizens of New Haven and Gallatin County. J. A. in early life helped to carry on the farm and afterward worked for the government on one of its river dredging boats. Also on the flat boats, on one trip going down the Ohio and Mississippi to the mouth of the Yazoo River, and selling the cargo to the farmers and residents of that region. He is now one of the firm of J. A. Hinch & Co., dealers in choice wines, liquors, cigars and small groceries, and he owns a farm in Emma Township, which he rents, and is altogether a businessman.

— *History of White County, Illinois.*

Lowry Hinch – 1883

LOWRY HINCH, son of Benjamin P. and Rebecca S. (Barger) Hinch, was born May 26, 1844. His father was a native of Christian County, Ky., and moved to Tennessee, and from there to Gallatin County in 1839. His mother was a native of Shawneetown and a daughter of Jacob Barger, who came to Shawneetown in 1813.

Benjamin P. Hinch was one of Gallatin's prominent men. He was a merchant, buying produce and provisions for the New Orleans Market. He was Justice of the Peace (precinct justice) eight years; county judge a year or two, having that office at the time of his death, and notary public from 1845 til his death. He was postmaster form 1845 till 1855, resigning to take his seat in the House of Representatives. He died May 19, 1861, in his 49th year. His family consisted of four children — Lowry, Fatima I. (Mrs. F. M. Aldridge, deceased), Julius A. and Amy (Mrs. J. G. Bunker, deceased). Mrs. B. P. Hinch died Oct. 1, 1877. July 19, 1874, Lowry Hinch married Lucinda, daughter of Harvey and Elizabeth (Dagley) Mitchell. Two children have been born to them — Rebecca C. (died in infancy) and Mary, born Oct. 8, 1877.

— *History of White County, Illinois.*

John T. Hogan – 1905

JOHN T. HOGAN, a prominent grain dealer and vice-president of the Exchange bank, of Omaha, Ill., was born near Dover, Stewart county, Tenn., Jan. 7, 1850. His grandfather, John Hogan, was a native of Virginia and of Irish parentage. On his return from the battle of New Orleans at the close of the war of 1812 he settled in Tennessee, married Sarah, daughter of Noah McGregory, who served with Washington during the Revolutionary war. To this marriage were born six children.

Edmund Hogan, father of the subject of this sketch, was born in Stewart county, Oct. 2, 1818. He married Alabama Owens, daughter of Major James Owens, a veteran of the war of 1812 and native of Virginia. After his marriage he followed farming in Tennessee until 1861, when he removed to White county, Ill., where his wife's parents had gone the preceding year. He bought a farm there and lived there until his death at the age of sixty-five years. His wife died at the age of forty-four. They were both members of the Cumberland Presbyterian church, and he was a Democrat in his political views. Their children were John T., the subject of this sketch; Thomas B., now living in Kansas; Bettie, now Mrs. Stevens, living in Missouri; James R., of Omaha; Charles F., who was captain of a company in the First California regiment in the Philippines and now living in that state; George, in Missouri; Waite, deceased; A. P. and Malinda, twins, both dead.

John T. Hogan was educated in the public schools and lived at home until twenty-two years of age, having charge of his father's affairs for some time on account of the latter's ill health. At the age of twenty-two he went to Nevada and California and remained there about three years, then returning to Illinois for a short time. In 1877 he again went to Nevada, where he followed farming and mining until 1880, when he came back to White county, married Martha C., daughter of D. W. and Jane (Riley) Galloway, and located on a farm near Roland. His wife died in 1884 and in 1887 he came to Omaha and engaged in the milling and grain business. Since 1893 he has devoted his attention to the grain business alone.

By his first marriage he has two children, Claudia and Harry, both living in Omaha, where the former is a teacher in the public school. In 1890 he was married to Mahala C. Kinsall, a native of Gallatin county, and they have two children, Althea and Harold, both at home. Mr. Hogan has been a prominent figure in Omaha business circles ever since coming to the town. In addition to his grain business he oversees his large farm; was one of the organizers of the Exchange bank, of which he is now vice-president; served six years as supervisor; was president of the board of school trustees for nine years, and is one of the active Democrats of Omaha. He is a prominent member of the Masonic fraternity, being a member of Lodge No. 723, and of Royal Arch Chapter, No. 165. In the lodge he has filled all the offices and is a representative to the Grand Lodge. In Lodge No. 472, Independent Order of Odd Fellows, he has also passed through the chairs and is a representative to the Grand Lodge. He and his wife both belong to the Cumberland Presbyterian church, in which he has been an elder for many years.

— *Memoirs of the Lower Ohio Valley.*

Richard M. Holland – 1905

RICHARD M. HOLLAND, a well known farmer of Gallatin county, Ill., living near the town of Omaha, was born Oct. 13, 1841, near Bowling Green, Warren county, Ky., his parents being Hezekiah and Sarah (Poole) Holland. Hezekiah Holland served in the Mexican war and in 1849 came with his family to Gallatin county, located about a mile and a half southwest of Cottonwood, where he built a log cabin twenty by twenty-four feet, on the place where Bennett Murphy now lives, and died there in 1853. After his death his widow married James Brockett and lived to be sixty years old. The children of Hezekiah and Sarah Holland were Thomas, Richard M., Shandy, Lambert P., James, George, Andrew, John, Sarah, Zachary and Josephus. Thomas lives in Norris City; Richard is the subject of this sketch; Shandy lives in Asbury township; Lambert lives at Omaha, and the others are deceased. Five of these brothers — Thomas, Zachary, John, Lambert and Shandy — enlisted at the beginning of the Civil war and served until the close taking part in numerous engagements.

At the age of eighteen years Richard M. Holland began working for the neighboring farmers at $13 a month. He then rented land on shares for two years. In 1862 he was married to Miss Tempy Sanders, and on October 9th of that year removed to the place where he still lives. His wife died July 20, 1868, leaving two children: Sidora J., wife of Lewis Murphy, and Parnesa A., who died in 1870.

On July 21, 1872, he was married to Miss Martha J. Hargrove, and to this union there were born four children: Annie B., Alonzo, and two who died in infancy. After the death of his second wife, he was married a third time, his last wife being Miss Sarah A. Pruitt, to whom he was married on Oct. 10, 1878. To this marriage there has been born one son, Lee A.

Mr. Holland has been successful in his farm life. Beginning with forty acres, on which stood a log cabin, he has gradually added to his farm until he is today one of the prosperous men of the community in which he lives. He is a staunch Democrat in his political views, and in 1891 assessed the property of his township. He is a member of the Cumberland Presbyterian church, and takes an interest in church work.

— *Memoirs of the Lower Ohio Valley.*

George L. Houston – 1905

GEORGE L. HOUSTON, of Shawneetown, Ill., state's attorney for Gallatin county, was born in that county June 8, 1870. His parents, Samuel and Nannie (Adams) Houston, were both natives of the county and there passed their whole lives. Samuel Houston received a common school education, and upon arriving at manhood became a farmer, which occupation he followed through life. When the Civil war broke out he enlisted in Company L, Sixth Illinois cavalry, and served until the close of hostilities. The exposure incident to army life affected his eyesight, and soon after the war he became totally blind. His general health was also impaired and he died on Dec. 24, 1874, his wife having died in the first week of the same month. They left three children: George L., the subject of this sketch; Alexander, who died in 1883; and Walter, now a farmer in Gallatin county.

George L. Houston was only about four years old when his parents died, and he was taken into the family of his father's brother, William Houston. About a year later his uncle died, and he then found a home with Martin Doherty, living about ten miles from Shawneetown, where he remained until he was about twenty years of age. Up to the time he was sixteen years old his opportunities to attend school were very much restricted by circumstances, and being without parents, or other intimate relatives to direct his course, his knowledge of books was quite limited. But, beginning when he was seventeen, he applied himself assiduously to his studies in the district schools for three seasons, and when he was twenty secured a teacher's certificate. After teaching a six months' term he attended the Hayward college at Fairfield, Ill., for a ten weeks' term, and then worked on a farm the remainder of the season until the school year opened. He taught another term, the following winter, and then attended a short term at the Southern Illinois college at Enfield, after which he again found work as a farm hand: In the spring of 1892, after teaching another term in the country schools, he went to Shawneetown, and in the following September was appointed to a position as deputy in the office of the county clerk. Mr. Houston filled this position very creditably for six years. During the first three years of that time he devoted his leisure hours to the study of law and in February, 1895, was admitted to the bar. Although engaged in the clerk's office he commenced the practice of his profession in a limited way and soon won the respect of both bench and bar by his earnestness and dignified bearing in the courts. In the spring of 1895 he was elected city attorney of Shawneetown, and was twice re-elected, serving six years in all. In 1900 he was nominated by the Democracy of Gallatin county for the office of state's attorney, and was elected to the position in November of that year. His record during his four years' term was so satisfactory that when the Democratic convention met in the spring of 1904 he was nominated for a re-election. Mr. Houston owes his success entirely to his own energy and determination to succeed. Left an orphan at a tender age he has fought the battle of life up to the present time against odds that would have discouraged one with less courage. Yet he never faltered, believing in the old adage that "Where there is a will there is a way," and his career is proof that such is the case.

He was married on July 6, 1901, to Miss Mabel, daughter of George Grater, an old resident of Gallatin county.

— *Memoirs of the Lower Ohio Valley.*

Will A. Howell – 1905

WILL A. HOWELL, of Shawneetown, Ill., master in chancery of Gallatin county, is a representative member of one of the oldest families in America. The Howells of Kentucky and Southern Illinois are of Irish extraction and can trace their ancestry back to one of three brothers who came from the Emerald Isle with Capt. John Smith's colony and settled at Jamestown, Va., in 1607. Much of the early history of the family is veiled in obscurity, but it is known that some of the descendants settled in Kentucky at a very early date, where they played an important part in wresting the "Dark and Bloody Ground" from the possession of the Indians. Some of the family finally located at Cynthiana, where Chester Howell, the immediate ancestor of that branch of the family now living in Shawneetown and vicinity, was born. He had three sons: Squire, James D., and one whose name has been lost. Squire Howell had two sons and two daughters: Thomas, Chester, Susan and Anna.

James D. Howell, who was the grandfather of the subject of this sketch, was born at Cynthiana, Jan. 27, 1809. He received his education in the schools of that period, the course of study being confined to the simplest rudiments of an English education. During his boyhood he engaged in hauling freight from Cynthiana to Cincinnati, but upon arriving at man's estate he removed to near Lexington, where he became a farmer. In 1840 he removed to Trimble county, Ky., where he lived for about twelve years, when he went to Union county, and there passed the remainder of his life, dying Aug. 23, 1894, at the advanced age of eighty-five years.

On Sept. 6, 1831, he was married to Miss Millicent, daughter of Alexander Breckenridge, living near Lexington. She was a member of the celebrated family of that name, and a first cousin to Gen. John C. Breckenridge. She died June 26, 1876. Her mother's maiden name was Wickliffe, a sister to George and Robert Wickliffe, who were among the Kentucky pioneers.

James D. and Millicent Howell were the parents of the following children: William A., who died young; Ann Martha, born Feb. 2, 1834, married Lemuel Holt, Nov. 26, 1857, and is now living a widow in Union county, Ky.; James Elmore, born April 27, 1830, and died Sept. 28, 1837; John Lloyd, father of the subject of this sketch; Nancy J., born Nov. 18, 1839, and died Feb. 21, 1886; Warren, born March 31, 1841, married Anna Harth, and now lives at Caseyville, Ky.; Harriet Matilda, born Nov. 23, 1842, and died Dec. 27, 1842; Harrison, born Nov. 22, 1844, now lives in Union county, Ky.; Walker T., born April 17, 1846, married Carrie Haskins in 1883, and now lives in Colorado; George W., born April 2, 1848, and died Aug. 21, 1893; Elizabeth Morris, born April 2, 1849, and died in 1885; Susan Howe, born Sept. 5, 1851, died July, 19, 1871; Thomas Henry, born in November, 1864, married Fannie Wall, and now lives in Morganfield, Ky.

John Lloyd Howell, the fourth child of this family was born at Lexington, Nov. 18, 1837. After such an education as the common schools of that day afforded he turned his attention to farming, and at the beginning of the Civil war was living near Hannibal, Mo. He returned home to Kentucky and enlisted in Company G, First Kentucky Confederate cavalry, which afterward became part of the famous "Orphan Brigade." After the war he located in Union county, Ky., and there followed farming and conducting a sawmill until 1885, when he became a pilot on the river, in which occupation he continued the rest of his active life. On April 25, 1867, he was united in marriage to Miss Mary L. Givens, of Trimble county, and she is now living in Shawneetown. To this marriage there were born four children: Nannie, widow of W. S. Callicott, and who for the last fourteen years has been a teacher in the Shawneetown public schools; Harry H., now a merchant in Shawneetown: Will A., the subject of this sketch; and Ray L., now the wife of C. L. Patterson, a post office inspector, living at Las Vegas, New Mexico.

Will A. Howell was born in Union county, Ky., Jan. 24, 1877. His parents removed to Shawneetown when he was about two years old, and here he grew to manhood, receiving his education in the public schools. In 1894 he was appointed deputy clerk of Gallatin county and filled that position for three years, at the end of which time he embarked in the real estate, abstract and loan business, in which line he has continued ever since with the exception of about four months. In April, 1899, he was elected city clerk of Shawneetown, and was re-elected in 1901, holding the office for four years. In October, 1903, he was appointed master in chancery for Gallatin county for a term of two years, and is now discharging the duties of that position.

Mr. Howell is prominent in the fraternal societies of Shawneetown, being a member of the Masonic fraternity, the Knights of Pythias, the Modern Woodmen of America, and the Fraternal Army of Loyal Americans. On New Year's day, 1900, he was married to Miss

Cleora L. Hite, of Peru, Ind., and to this union there has been born one son, Edward Hite, born Jan. 28, 1901.

— *Memoirs of the Lower Ohio Valley.*

Frederick Adolphus Hubbard – 1895

FREDERICK ADOLPHUS HUBBARD. No history of Gov. Coles administration [1822-1826] would be complete which failed to mention the part taken therein by the lieutenant-governor.

The name of this shining light in the political firmament of those days was Frederick Adolphus Hubbard, and Shawneetown enjoyed the distinction of being his place of residence. He seems to have been a lawyer by profession, of the kind, which only the day and age in which he lived could have produced. It is related of him that while engaged in the trial of a lawsuit, involving the title to a certain mill run by Joseph Duncan, the opposing counsel, David J. Baker, then recently from New England, had quoted from Johnson's "New-York Report," a case strongly against Hubbard's side. Reading reports of the decision of courts before juries was a new thing in those days, and Hubbard to evade the force of the authority as a precedent, coolly informed the jury that Johnson was a Yankee clock peddler, who had perambulating up and down the country gathering up rumors and floating stories against the people of the West and had them published in a book under the name of "Johnson's Reports." He indignantly repudiated the book as authority in Illinois, and clinched the argument by adding, "gentlemen of the jury, I as assure you will not believe anything that comes from such a source; and besides that, what did this Johnson know about Duncan's mill anyhow? Of course this was conclusive with the jury, and Hubbard gained his case.

Hubbard had been a member of the constitutional convention, and if in his subsequent career he did not attain to the utmost height of his "vaulting ambition," the failure can not be ascribed to any lack of effort on his part. At one time, after repeated and annoying application, he obtained from Gov. Edwards what he had reason to believe was a recommendation for a certain office. The more he thought about it however, the greater became his distrust of the contents of the governor's letter. In speaking of it afterward, in his lisping manner, he said: "contrary to the uthage amongst gentlemen he thealed it up, and contrary to the uthage amongst gentlemen I broke if open; and what do you think I found? Instead of recommending me, the old rathscal abused me like a pick-pocket."

At the time when Gov. Edwards resigned his seat in the United States senate in March, 1824, it happened that Hubbard was in Washington on a visit. Seeing as he supposed a splendid opportunity to advance his own political fortunes, he prevailed on the senator to allow him to deliver the letter of resignation to Gov. Coles in person. This he did, adding the gratuitous statement that Edwards and Cook [Illinois' lone Congressman] had selected him as the bearer of the document, in the belief that the governor would either resign, in which case he (Hubbard) as his successor to the gubernatorial power would appoint him (Coles) to fill the unexpired senatorial term, of that if the latter preferred the governor's chair, then in return for the general proposal, Coles should appoint no less a person than the aspiring Frederick Adolphus Hubbard to represent Illinois in the councils of the Nation! To his astonishment and chagrin, Gov. Coles was by no means favorably impressed with the suggestion. In plain words, he indignantly and contemptuously spurned the proposition, informing the ambitions politician that he declined to become a party to any such dishonorable dickering.

"Time brings its revenges," and Hubbard's opportunity to repay what he considered the insolence of his superior came within the following year. In 1825, the governor notified the lieutenant governor that circumstances would call him out of the State for a short period after July, and that during his absence the responsibilities of the executive office would devolve upon the latter. In the autumn, Gov. Coles returned, prepared to enter upon the discharge of his official duties. But Frederick Adolphus having once tasted the sweets of elevation of power, was loath to abandon the chair whose occupancy he had thoroughly enjoyed. Remembering the affront which he had suffered at the hands of Gov. Coles, his brilliant legal mind believed that it discerned an opportunity for gratifying at once his ambition and his desire for revenge. He therefore, under that clause of the constitution which provided that the lieutenant-governor should exercise all the power and authority appertaining to the office of governor in case of the latter's absence from the State "until the time pointed out by the constitution for the election of governor shall arrive," claimed that Gov. Coles by his absence had forfeited the office, and that he, the lieutenant-governor, had fallen heir to it. Finding a number of backers among those whom he fraternized, he determined to bring the question before the courts, and November 2, he appointed W. L. D. Ewing, paymaster-general of the Illinois militia, and requested Secretary-of-State George Forquer to issue the commission therefore, which he refused to do. Ewing, as had been arranged, applied to the supreme court for a writ of mandamus to compel the secretary to sign and issue the commission, and the motion was gravely argued at great length before a full bench. Judges Lockwood and Smith delivered separate opinions in the case "of great learning and research," the court unanimously reaching the conclusion that there was no ground on which to award the writ.

Not satisfied with this judicial determination of his claim, the redoubtable lieutenant-governor appealed to the legislature, where his application was equally unsuccessful, there being but one member in each house favorable to this pretensions; although Gov. Coles stated that there would doubtless have been more had there been a reasonable prospect of ousting himself. The wonder now is that a claim so unfounded should have been so seriously considered.

The occupancy of the governor's office for ten weeks, and the proceedings incident to his contest for its retention, had made the name of Adolphus Frederick Hubbard quite noticed and familiar in the State, of which celebrity, construing it to mean popularity with the people, he was not slow to take advantaged and accordingly offered himself as a candidate for governor in the general election of 1826. He canvassed the several counties and made speeches, a sample of which is given by Gov. Ford, as follows:

> "Fellow-citizens, I offer myself as a candidate before you for the office of governor. I do not pretend to be a man of extraordinary talents; nor do I claim to be equal to Julius Caesar or Napoleon Bonaparte, nor yet to be as great a man as my opponent Gov. Edwards. Nevertheless I think I can govern you pretty well. I do not think it will require a very extraordinary smart man to govern you; for to tell the truth, fellow-citizens, I do not believe you will be very hard to govern, no how."

The number of votes case for him, no doubt to his great surprise and dismay, was only 580, and the smallness of his poll was unquestionably the first convincing intimation he had received that his great abilities and aptitude for office were so much underrated by the people.

From this time forward the name of the Honorable Adolphus disappears from the page of history; but though "lost to sight it will long remain to memory dear," as an illustration of that peculiar class of men which was the outgrowth of the primitive times in which he lived.

— *Illinois: Historical and Statistical.*

Columbus M. Hudgins – 1883

COLUMBUS M. HUDGINS, M.D., was born Sept. 5, 1852, in Saline County, Ill. He was reared on a farm, and attended the public schools. He also attended one term at Hamilton College. He taught school four years and then commenced the study of medicine at Keokuk, Iowa. He was there two terms and then practiced until 1879, when he entered the Evansville Medical College, and graduated. He located at New Haven, and remained there two years and a half; them came to Omaha, where he has a good practice. Dr. Hudgins traces his paternal ancestors to England and his maternal to Germany. His parents were from North Carolina, and settled in Tennessee, and in 1826 came to Illinois, and settled in Saline County.

— *History of White County, Illinois.*

William Inman – 1905

WILLIAM INMAN, of Ridgway, Ill., one of the best known farmers in Gallatin county, was born in Lawrence county, Tenn., March 30, 1832. He is a son of William and Polly A. (Ware) Inman, both natives of Tennessee. His father was a wheelwright, who did a good business as chair maker for many years, picking up the trade himself without serving an apprenticeship. In 1847 he removed with his family to Gallatin county, coming by water, and located not far from Ridgway. About eighteen months later he removed to Union county, Ky., where he died about the year 1850. Soon after his death his widow returned to Illinois and died in Gallatin county at the age of sixty-three years. They had twelve children, only two of whom are now living. Thomas and Bartley, the two oldest sons, enlisted for the Mexican war, but saw no active service.

William Inman, the son, began working on a farm when a small boy, working for some time for $5 a month. He came to Illinois about six months after his parents, and though but fifteen years of age rented a farm on shares and gave his money to his father and mother. After the death of his father he continued to live with his mother and provided for her and for his younger brothers and sisters.

On Sept. 1, 1862, he enlisted in Company E, 131st Illinois infantry. His regiment was with Sherman in the first attack on Vicksburg; was at Arkansas Post; then in the siege of Vicksburg, at the close of which it numbered only 222 men, and was consolidated with the Twenty-ninth Illinois. Mr. Inman was discharged at Cairo in December, 1864, returned to

Ridgway, and became an extensive farmer. Since 1901 he has been a resident of the town of Ridgway. The town of Inman was named for him.

On Jan. 19, 1858, Mr. Inman was married to Miss Mary Johnson, a native of West Virginia. Of their children four died young; the others are James, Sarah, William, Mary, Jessie, Susan, Jennie L. and Thomas. The mother of these children died in January, 1887, and in December of the same year he was married to Mrs. Ellen Cox, widow of Isaac Cox and daughter of Medford and Malinda Shockley, of Monroe county, Ky. Two children, Marshall and Albert, were born to the second marriage, but both died in childhood. Mrs. Inman had, one daughter by her first marriage, now Mrs. Daniel Desper. Mr. Inman is a member of the Methodist Episcopal church, and belongs to the Grand Army of the Republic post at Ridgway.

— *Memoirs of the Lower Ohio Valley.*

Daniel Jacobs – 1876

DANIEL JACOBS, son of Jonathan and Susanna Jacobs, born in Marietta, Dauphin County, Pa., in September 1824. In his minority he learned the trade of millwright, and received 12 months' schooling in log school houses. Joined the Fourth Indiana and went to Mexico in 1847. Was married June 8, 1854, to Margaret A. Bradford, of Gallatin County, Illinois, having come to the State in 1852. His business, prior to this, had been building mills, milling and steam-boating on the Ohio and Mississippi Rivers. He built two large flouring-mills and two sawmills in Gallatin County, and also cleared 2000 acres of heavily timbered land, and raised a family of six children.

— *Illustrated Historical Atlas of the State of Illinois.*

Dr. M. S. Jones – 1887

Dr. M. S. JONES, physician and surgeon at Shawneetown, was born in 1840 in that place. He is the son of James M. and Artemesia (Wilson) Jones. The great-grandfather of our subject, exiled from Scotland, came to America with the Huguenots, and one son settled in Louisiana and the other in Virginia, of which branch comes our subject. The grandfather, Richard, lived in Virginia where his son James M. was born in 1793. James visiting Kentucky with an uncle in a surveying party was so pleased with the vicinity of Lexington, that he soon settled in Fayette County, Ky., where he was married. He was a tailor by trade, but began farming near Richmond, Ky., about 1826. He was an ensign in the Black Hawk War of 1832, and died in 1845. His wife, or English origin, was born in Kentucky in 1801, and died in 1851. She was an aunt of Maj.-Gen. Harrison Wilson and a descendant of ex-President Harrison.

Our subject, a mere boy when his father died, was reared and educated by J. W. Norton, a brother-in-law, and a native of Baltimore, Md. Mr. Norton, a shoe manufacturer and merchant, came to Shawneetown in 1844, and afterward was receiver of public money, in Fillmore's administration, and city judge. Dr. Jones graduated from Rush Medical College, Chicago, Ill., in 1865, and entered the regular United States Army as surgeon, and after spending two years on the Rio Grande in Texas he resigned, and for the past twenty years has been a physician in Gallatin County. He is a Republican politically, a member of the F. & A.M., being Sublime Prince of Royal Secret, and has taken twenty-two degrees in the same class as Gen. Logan. He is also Encampment member of the I.O.O.F. and for several years has been president of the Board of Examining Surgeons of the United States Pension office of Gallatin County.

— *History of Gallatin, Saline, Hamilton, Franklin and Williamson Counties, Illinois.*

Moses Kanady – 1887

MOSES KANADY, one of the leading farmers and stock dealers of South Shawneetown District, was born there in 1828, the oldest son of J. J. and Mary (Sherwood) Kanady. The father, of Irish origin, was born in 1804 in Kentucky, and died in 1875, and was the son of Moses Kanady. The latter was a native of Kentucky; was a pioneer of 1818 in Gallatin County. Mr. Kanady's great-grandfather, Peter Kanady, lived in a fort in Kentucky for a long time. He was married twice. One of his sons, Peter, was an Indian captive about thirteen years, after which he returned home and became a good citizen and father.

The father of our subject married in 1827, and became one of the self-made men of Gallatin County, serving several terms as associate judge and township treasurer. The mother was about the age of her husband, and was born in Maryland. She died in March 1859. Both were members of the Methodist Episcopal Church. Our subject was educated in the common schools at home; was married, in September 1849, to Elizabeth, daughter of Samuel and Sophia Seaton of Gallatin County, where she was born in 1826. Seven of their eight children are living: George W., Fatima (Wife of Nathaniel Floyd, of Union City, Ky.), Hester (now Mrs. Dr. J. Fair, of Shawneetown), Ida (wife of H. C. Strickland), Edgar, Johnson and U. Grant. He has since been a resident of his present farm of 240 acres in Section 29 and 32. He is a successful and valued citizen, and has been almost entirely a self-made man, inheriting but little of his fortune. He is a Democrat in politics, and his wife is a member of the Baptist Church.

— *History of Gallatin, Saline, Hamilton, Franklin and Williamson Counties, Illinois.*

Lt. Wash. Kanady – 1887

LIEUT. WASH. KANADY, one of the leading farmers and stock dealers of Shawneetown Precinct, was born there in 1839. He is the son of John J. and Mary (Sherwood) Kanady, for sketch of whom see the biography of Moses Kanady. Our subject, reared at home and educated at Pleasant Grove school, was married, in March 1861 to Ludica, daughter of John and Mary P. Reid of Shawneetown. They have six children: John R., Claudie, Washington J., Maud, Pearl and Moses.

He was first lieutenant in Company D, 120th Illinois Infantry; served at Vicksburg, Austin, Miss., and a number of skirmishes after the war's close. He has since lived on his fine farm of 120 acres in Section 29. Formerly a Democrat, he has been a Republican since the war. He is a member of the G. A. R. and of the Old School Presbyterian Church.

— *History of Gallatin, Saline, Hamilton, Franklin and Williamson Counties, Illinois.*

Victor Karcher – 1887

VICTOR KARCHER, contractor and builder, of the firm of Karcher and Scanland, was born in Baden, Germany, in 1832, the son of Baltaser and Anastasia (Reiling) Karcher, also natives of Baden. Their deaths occurred in 1850, at the age of seventy-six and seventy-five years respectively; the father was a farmer. Our subject, the youngest of nine children, was educated in his native land from six to fourteen years of age. He was then apprenticed for two and a half year as a cabinet-maker, and afterward was for four years a journeyman cabinet-maker in the various cities of Germany. He was drafted into a nine months' army service, and wounded in the left arm. After the war the soldiers went to Zurich, Switzerland, where he remained, working at his trade two years. In 1851, he went to France, and was in Paris when Louis Napoleon declared himself emperor. He left in six days for Havre, and then embarked for America. He was fifty-nine days afloat, and went from New Orleans to Shawneetown at once, where he resumed his trade.

In May 1856, he began contracting and building with his present partner, and also undertaking. In 1869, they started a planning-mill and sash, door and blind factory, and have now been in an undisturbed harmonious partnership for thirty-one years. They have erected most of the buildings now to be seen in Shawneetown, and are still doing nearly all that work. In 1861 he married Maggie, daughter of Peter McMurchy, born in Shawneetown. She died in 1871, and in October 1783, he married Mary R. Zachmeier, a native of Franklin County, Ind. Their children are Thomas, Victor and Carl. He is a conservative Democrat, and was the first Knight Templar in Shawneetown. He and his wife belong to the Catholic Church. In 1881, they went by way of Washington, receiving the passport from Secretary Blaine, and made a four months' visit to their fatherland across the ocean.

— *History of Gallatin, Saline, Hamilton, Franklin and Williamson Counties, Illinois.*

Benjamin Kinsall – 1883

BENJAMIN KINSALL, son of John and Elizabeth Kinsall, was born in White County, Ill., Sept, 30, 1824. His parents were natives of Virginia, but removed to Tennessee, and from there to Illinois in 1818. His maternal grandfather, John Hancock, was a soldier in the Revolutionary war, and was with Jackson at New Orleans, in the War of 1812. He also fought the Indians at Horseshoe Bend, Miss., where he was wounded in the leg, carrying the ball to his grave. Mr. Kinsall was Justice of the Peace 22 and Associate Justice of the County Court of Gallatin County six years. Aug. 19, 1845, he married Sarah A. Davis, a native of Tennessee. They have two children — Maurice and Surrilda E., the wife of Silas Cook, County Clerk of Gallatin County. Mr. Kinsall has been an Elder in the Cumberland Presbyterian church of Omaha 22 years. He resides on a fine farm of 700 acres a mile south of Omaha. He is worth $10,000.

— *History of White County, Illinois.*

Benjamin Kinsall – 1887

BENJAMIN KINSALL was born in 1824, the son of John and Elizabeth B. (Hancock) Kinsall, natives of Tennessee and Kentucky respectively. The father was in the Creek Indian war, and wounded in the leg, unnoticed until his attention was called to it. He afterward served in the War of 1812, and with Jackson. The grandfather, of English descent, came from North Carolina to Tennessee. The mother was of Irish descent, the daughter of John Hancock, a native of Virginia. The father, when about eighteen, left the farm and engaged at Weed's Salt Works as wood-chopper, and with two friends bought a barge load of salt on credit to ship South, but on the way the barge was sunk by a snag and the three and a negro swam to shore, Mr. Kinsall saving his hat and the negro an overcoat belonging to one of them; the rest lost their hats. The debt of $300 which this disaster left for Mr. Kinsall, threatened to disarrange his plans for marriage which was to be consummated on his return. He soon saved enough money at the salt works to clear himself, and moved into White County and rented a farm, and two years later to near Shawneetown where he farmed two years, and finally settled east of Omaha, where he and his wife died within six months of each other, both in their sixty-third year. The family were educated in the pioneer subscription schools of that day in log houses.

Our subject, however, educated himself mostly after his marriage with books at home, and taught school about eight years and farming with his brother. He was a member of the county court from 1869 to 1875, and is the present postmaster of Omaha, appointed in 1887. August 20, 1845, he married Sarah, daughter of John and Elizabeth (Shaw) Kinsall, natives of Tennessee. Two of their seven children are living: Monroe, teaching in Gallatin County, and Sarilda, wife of Silas Cook, county clerk. He encouraged war measures and assisted in looking after the wants of the sick and helpless. He and his wife are members of the Cumberland Presbyterian Church. He is a worthy citizen and in politics a Democrat.

— *History of Gallatin, Saline, Hamilton, Franklin and Williamson Counties, Illinois.*

D. M. Kinsall – 1887

D. M. KINSALL.[239] State's Attorney of Gallatin County, was born in the southwest part of White County in 1852, the son of Thomas and Malinda E. (Harrell) Kinsall, the father a farmer and of German origin was born in 1827 in Gallatin County. The grandfather, John Kinsall, a native of Tennessee, came very early to Gallatin County with two brothers, Benjamin and William, and all settled in the northern part of the county. John was one of the first commissioners of the county, was in the Battle of New Orleans in 1815, where he received a ball in his leg from a gun of the enemy, which he carried until his death in the year 1853.

In 1851 Thomas married and settled in the southwest of White County. In 1853 he removed to Bear Creek Township, Gallatin County, where he has since resided on his farm, excepting four years past he has resided in Omaha. His wife was born in White County, Ill., in 1829, and died in 1876. Their five living children are our subject; Alvin H., a teacher, John H., a farmer, Samuel S., a farmer and Jennie.

Educated in the common schools, our subject, in 1870, began teaching, and continued four sessions. In 1872 he attended five months at Fairfield High School. Then at different times from 1872 to 1875 he was deputy assessor of Gallatin County during which he studied law also. In 1874 he entered the law department at Bloomington (Ind.) State University and

---

[239] The Illinois Statewide Marriage Index gives his name as David M. Kinsall.

continued one year, then after teaching one term, he entered the law office of Hon. R. W. Townshend and studied one year. In 1877 he was admitted to the bar at Mt. Vernon, Ill., and began the practice in the above office while Hon. R. W. Townshend was in Congress. In April, 1879, he was elected city attorney of Shawneetown, Ill., for two years. In September of same year he was appointed master in chancery for two years. November 3, 1880, he was elected State's attorney and re-elected without opposition in 1884. He is one of the ablest lawyers in the county. November 27, 1883, he married Edith, daughter of A. K. and Cassandra J. Lowe, of Shawneetown. He is a Democrat, first voting for Tilden. He is a Mason. His wife is a member of the Presbyterian Church.

— *History of Gallatin, Saline, Hamilton, Franklin and Williamson Counties, Illinois.*

David M. Kinsall – 1905

David M. Kinsall, of Shawneetown, Ill., ex-judge of Gallatin county, and one of the leading members of the Southern Illinois bar, is of English descent, the first of the name in this country having come from England some years prior to the Revolutionary war and settled in North Carolina. Later he removed to Tennessee, where he reared a large family of children, among whom was John Kinsall, the grandfather of this sketch.

John Kinsall was born in Tennessee about 1791, was reared on a farm, received such an education as the schools of that day afforded and at the age of eighteen years began life on his own account as a wood chopper at Werd's salt works. After working at this for sometime he, in company with two friends, bought a barge load of salt and started south with it. The barge struck a snag and sank, the three young salt traders barely escaping with their lives. This unfortunate termination of his first business venture left him considerably in debt, but with courage characteristic of the early pioneers he returned to the salt works and by strenuous efforts and rigid economy succeeded in clearing up his indebtedness. Soon after this he was married to Miss Elizabeth, daughter of John Hancock, of Virginia, a representative of one of the oldest and most prominent families of the Old Dominion, and removed with his young wife to White county, Ill., the region at that time being on the frontier. For two years he lived upon a rented farm in White county, at the end of which time he rented another farm near Shawneetown, and lived there until he entered government land a short distance east of Omaha, where he passed the remainder of his life, he and his wife both dying in 1854, within six months of each other. He took a keen interest in political affairs in his day, his house frequently being the place of holding the election, and he was one of the first commissioners of Gallatin county. Both he and his wife were earnest church workers.

He fought in the war with the Creek Indians, and at the beginning of the war of 1812 he enlisted as a private under General Jackson. At the historic battle of New Orleans he received a bullet which he carried to the day of his death. John and Elizabeth Kinsall were the parents of seven children, viz.: Hiram, William, Benjamin, Thomas. David, Moses and Jane. Moses lives on the old home farm, Jane is the widow of Sterling Edwards, and now lives in Omaha, and all the others are deceased.

Thomas Kinsall, the fourth son, was born in 1827, in Gallatin county, and passed his whole life in that part of the state. From the subscription schools of that day he acquired a meager education, which he supplemented by self-study and reading, becoming one of the leading citizens of the community in which he lived. In 1850 he was married to Malinda E. Harrell, and soon afterward settled in the southwest part of White county, where he followed farming for two years, and then removed to Bear Creek township, in Gallatin county, where he lived the remainder of his active life. Upon retiring from the active conduct of the farm he removed to Omaha, where he lived until his death in 1889. His wife, who was born in 1829, died in 1876. They were both members of the Cumberland Presbyterian church, and in politics he was always a consistent Democrat. Their children are all living. David M. is the subject of this sketch; Alvin H. is a banker at Eldorado, Ill.; John H. is a farmer in Clinton county of the same state; Samuel S. is a merchant and farmer in Colorado, and Jennie is the wife of B. L. Rodgers of Harrisburg, Ill.

David M. Kinsall was born near Omaha, May 6, 1851, and has always lived in Gallatin county. After attending the public schools until he was eighteen years old he became a teacher, and for four terms taught in the common schools. In 1872 he attended the Fairfield high school for five months, and from that time until 1875 worked at different times as deputy assessor of Gallatin county. While there employed he devoted his spare time to the study of law. In 1874 he attended the law department of the Indiana State university at Bloomington for the entire school year, and then, after teaching one term, entered the office of Hon. R. W. Townshend, who was at that time a member of Congress. In April, 1879, he was elected city attorney of Shawneetown for a term of two years and in September of the same year was appointed master in chancery for Gallatin county. This appointment was for two years, and in November, 1880, he was elected state's attorney for the county and was re-elected in 1884, without opposition, holding the office for eight years and making an enviable record as a public official. In 1890 he was elected to the office of county judge, was re-elected at the close of the first term, making eight years that he discharged the duties of this position.

Since his retirement from the judgeship he has devoted all his time to the practice of his profession and in looking after his large landed interests. His clientage is one of the largest in Southern Illinois, embracing all classes of law, in which Judge Kinsall is thorough versed. In politics he is one of the strong Democrats of his section of the state, and stands high in the councils of his party. He was married on Nov. 27, 1883, to Miss Edith, daughter of A. K. and Cassandra J. Lowe, of Shawneetown, and to this union there has been born one daughter, Edna, who is at home with her parents.

— Memoirs of the Lower Ohio Valley.

Monroe Douglas Kinsall – 1883

MONROE DOUGLAS KINSALL was born in Bear Creek Precinct, Gallatin Co, Ill., June 12, 1860. He is the only surviving son of Benjamin and Sarah S. Kinsall. He spent his boyhood days working on the farm and attending the district and village schools in the vicinity of Omaha. He also attended Hamilton College, McLeansboro, Ill., one term. He taught school two terms. He is at present employed as a bookkeeper and salesman for C. Cook & Son. He is unmarried.

— History of White County, Illinois.

Prof. William M. Kinsall – 1887

WILLIAM M. KINSALL was born June 3, 1821, the son of John and Elizabeth B. (Hancock) Kinsall, for an account of whose life and ancestry see the biography of Benjamin Kinsall. Our subject was married to Eliza J., daughter of James K. and Susan Abney, in March 1844. One of their three children is living, Eliza J., who married Robert Whittington in May 1872, and after his death married J. Carsey; James A., died in August, 1880, and one child in infancy. Our subject's wife died, October 1851.

In November 1853, he married Polly M., daughter of Cader Harrell, a prominent farmer of White County. Their ten children are Hiram C., Barbara A., Mary E. (wife of Alex. McGehee, farmer), Edgar B., Rosetta E., Margaret S., Mahala C., Laura M., Benjamin and Nellie. Mr. Kinsall was reared on his father's farm and educated in White County. He has been a farmer all of his life and owns a fine farm east of Omaha, Ill. He is a member of the Cumberland Presbyterian Church and likewise his family. He is a Democrat and a worthy citizen.

— *History of Gallatin, Saline, Hamilton, Franklin and Williamson Counties, Illinois.*

Christian Kratz – 1905

CHRISTIAN KRATZ, prominently identified with the lumber and sawmill interests of Shawneetown, Ill., was born Aug. 6. 1864, in the city of Evansville, Ind. His parents, Christian and Philipine (Krug) Kratz, were both born in Germany. The father learned the trade of machinist in his native land, and in 1858, when about sixteen years of age, came to America. Soon after reaching this country he located at Evansville, where he followed his trade until he retired from the active pursuits of life. He was married at Evansville, his wife having come over in 1853. They had eight children, all living. All except the subject of this sketch live at Evansville. Mary is a Mrs. Hartman; Tillie a Mrs. Wade; Philip; Edward; Elizabeth is a Mrs. Smith, and Emma is at home with her father. The mother died in 1896. The family belongs to the German Lutheran church.

Christian Kratz was educated in the public schools and in 1881 graduated from the Evansville Commercial college. He then served an apprenticeship as a machinist and followed that trade several years, after which he engaged in the planning mill and hardwood lumber business at Evansville. In 1898 he came to Shawneetown and commenced operating a sawmill on the Wabash river, later dealing in lumber in the town. Since then he has built several mills in the county, and has recently erected a new one at Shawneetown. He is also connected with the dressed lumber and commission business as a member of the firm of Kratz & McMurchy. Mr. Kratz is a member of the Masonic fraternity and the Knights of Pythias, and belongs to the Presbyterian church. Politically he is a Republican, and while living in Evansville served two terms as councilman at large. In 1886 he was married to Miss Ella Casper, and they have three children, Christian, Walter and Elenora, all at home with their parents.

— *Memoirs of the Lower Ohio Valley.*

Prof. R. A. Lamb – 1887

R. A. LAMB, farmer, near Ridgway, Ill., was born in Gallatin County in 1836. He is one of five children of John and Elizabeth (Dillard) Lamb. The father was a blacksmith and farmer and came to Gallatin County when a young man, and there spent his life. He died in September 1846, about forty-one years of age. The mother was born in 1816, and now resides in New Market Precinct.

Our subject received the education of the schools near his home, and in December 1853, he was married. His wife was Maria, daughter of John W. and Elender Hancock, born in Gallatin County in 1834. Her death occurred in September 1885. Their eight children are all living. Mr. Lamb located where he now resides in 1865, and has 130 acres of valuable, improved land. He is a public-spirited man, is politically a Republican, and is a member of the Cumberland Presbyterian Church.

— *History of Gallatin, Saline, Hamilton, Franklin and Williamson Counties, Illinois.*

Marshall E. Lambert – 1905

Marshall E. Lambert, city attorney of Shawneetown, Ill., is a native of Union county, Ky. His grandfather, David Lambert, was a Virginian, but came with his brother to Kentucky at an early date, locating near Skaggs' Mill, a short distance from Bowling Green, in Warren County. There he married, reared a family of children, and passed the remainder of his life as a farmer. There John M. Lambert, the father of the subject of this sketch, was born Oct. 9, 1836. When he was about twelve years of age he went with his brother Josiah to Henderson county, where he found employment as a farm hand. For ten years he worked for John S. McCormick, and was then employed by other farmers until 1864, when he went to Union county, Ky., as manager of the David R. Burbank estate, and remained in that position for three years.

In 1866 he was married to Elizabeth Ann, daughter of John and Caroline Sprague, and went to housekeeping on a farm directly opposite Shawneetown. The Sprague family was one of the oldest in Union county, and had its beginning there in John Sprague, a millwright of Pittsburgh, Pa., who married Margaret Fleming of that city and came down the river in a flatboat to Union county, where he entered government land and passed the remainder of his life. Their son, John Sprague, married Caroline McKinney and they had three children: Elizabeth, who became Mrs. Lambert; Ellen, who married a man by the name of McKinney, and John.

In 1884 John Lambert removed with his family to Shawneetown, and there died in 1901. In 1891 he, in connection with his son Marshall, engaged in general merchandizing at Blackburn, Ky., just across the river from Shawneetown, and they conducted this business until 1896, when he retired from active pursuits. His first wife died in 1875 and he was married in 1876 to Lavinia Waggener Jones, widow of Nat Jones, who is still living at the old home in Shawneetown.

Marshall E. Lambert was born Jan. 17, 1873, and is the only one of five children born to John M. and Elizabeth Lambert now living. After attending the public schools of Shawneetown and private university at Louisville, Ky., he entered the law department at the University of Michigan in 1896 and graduated in 1899. Upon leaving college he formed a partnership for the practice of law with C. N. Hollerich of East St. Louis, and practiced there until 1900, when he returned to Shawneetown and opened an office there. In addition to his law practice he assumed the management of his father's business, which consisted of large landed interests, and upon the latter's death became the sole heir to the large estate, as no children were born to his father's second marriage.

Mr. Lambert, like his father before him, takes a great interest in politics, and is regarded as one of the coming men of his section of the state. In 1901 he was elected city attorney of Shawneetown, which position he still holds. This selection was a tribute to both his ability and his personal popularity. He belongs to the Knights of Pythias, and is always a welcome visitor at the meetings of his lodge, because of his genial disposition and general good-fellowship. On May 15, 1901, he was united in marriage to Miss Katherine I., daughter of Judge James Marshall of Spokane, Wash., and they have two children: Elizabeth Sprague and William Payne.

— *Memoirs of the Lower Ohio Valley*.

James S. Lasater – 1883

JAMES S. LASATER, born Feb. 22, 1837, is a son of Absalom and Louisa (Vickers) Lasater, the father a native of Hamilton County, Ill., and the mother of Virginia. His parents moved to Tennessee after their marriage, and James was born there. They lived there a year and then returned to Hamilton County. Their family consisted of five children, James S. being the second. His father died about the time of the birth of his youngest sister.

When he was 13 years old he was obliged to take care of himself, and worked several years for $4 a month. His schooling was necessarily limited, but by self-application and observation he acquired a good education. At the time of the Kansas excitement he went to that Territory, but finding it unprofitable and unsatisfactory he returned to Illinois. The next two years he traded in chickens in Shawneetown and New Orleans. At that time the Pike's Peak gold fever broke out, and he, in company with half a dozen others, started with ox teams for the Peak. When they reached Fort Kearney they met men coming back, and a few miles further on, more men, there being no gold. They then retraced their steps and returned to White County. Mr. Lasater worked the rest of the year in a sawmill and the next year went to farming in Hamilton County. He remained there a year, and then moved to White County and remained two years; then moved to Gallatin County where he has since resided. He is on the county line, so his interests are still with White County. He married Mrs. Mary (Mills) Boyd, daughter of Charles and Julia (Pierce) Mills. They have two children — Lucy and Edgar. He has 80 acres under good cultivation, gained by energy and hard work.

— *History of White County, Illinois*.

John B. Latimer – 1883

JOHN B. LATIMER was born in White County, Ill., May 12, 1832. He is a son of Benjamin A. Latimer, for several years a County Commissioner of White County. He was a life-long member of the Cumberland Presbyterian church, of which he was an Elder several years, and was sent several times to represent his society in the General Assembly.

Mr. Latimer's grandfather was one the minutemen from Connecticut. He served as Orderly under his father, Colonel Latimer, in many important engagements of the Revolution. He was the Orderly who was sent to New London, Conn., to inform the minutemen of the approach of the British. He was wounded in the thigh, which prevented further active service. He was afterward engaged in a severe personal combat with a Tory alone in the woods, whom he captured after receiving a severe wound in the hand by a broadsword. Mr. Latimer's great-grandfather came from England about the middle of the last century. He traces his genealogy direct from Bishop Latimer, who was martyred during the reign of Queen Elizabeth for his belief in the Protestant religion. Mr. Latimer's father came to White County in 1844. He was married in 1854 to Martha Bryant, of White County. They have three children. Mr. Latimer served three years in the late war under Grant, participating in the battles of Fort Donelson and Fort Henry and Shiloh. He was engaged in farming til 1871, when he moved to Omaha and ran the Latimer House. He served one year as Justice of the Peace. He is at present one of the proprietors of the Omaha flouring mills.

— *History of White County, Illinois.*

Raphael E. Lawler – 1905

RAPHAEL E. LAWLER a farmer, living three and a half miles east of Equality, was born in December 1858, on the spot where he now lives, though the house in which he was born was destroyed some years ago by fire.

His father, Gen. Michael K. Lawler, was born in County Kildare, Ireland, Nov. 16, 1814. When he was about a year old his parents, John and Elizabeth (Kelly) Lawler came to the United States. After about a year in Baltimore, Md., they came to Gallatin County, Ill., making the greater part of the journey by way of the Ohio River in a flatboat. John Lawler was the first Catholic to settle in that part of the state, and was regarded with some curiosity by his neighbors for this reason. He first bought land in what is known as the Pond, or Irish Settlement, which land is still in the possession of his descendants. It was largely through big influence that the first Catholic Church was established in that section. The old hewed log house with puncheon seats has long since been replaced by a more modern structure, and many of the Catholics now living in the vicinity are descendants of men who were induced to come there by John Lawler. He and his wife both died comparatively young. Their children were Mary, Margaret, Michael and Thomas, all now deceased.

Michael K. Lawler grew to manhood in Gallatin County. On Dec. 20, 1837, he was united in marriage to Miss Elizabeth, daughter of John and Sina Crenshaw, old residents of the county. At the time of the marriage her father was the largest landowner in the county, and gave the young couple the farm where Raphael E. now lives. They commenced their married life in a log cabin of one room, later built a cheap frame house, then one of more modern character — the one that was burned.

When the Mexican War broke out M. K. Lawler was bookkeeper for his father-in-law. He gave up his position, organized a company, of which he was elected captain, and was immediately sent to the front. At Cerro Gordo the company distinguished itself, and from that time until the close of the war was in several of the fiercest engagements. After the war Captain Lawler took up the occupation of farming which he followed until the commencement of the Civil War. Then the old military spirit revived and he organized the

18th Illinois volunteer infantry, afterward known as the "Bloody Eighteenth," of which he was commissioned colonel. The regiment was in many of the hottest engagements of the war, particularly in Tennessee, Alabama and Mississippi. At Fort Donelson Colonel Lawler was severely wounded in the arm, but after a short time rejoined his command and remained in the field until the end. On April 15, 1863, he was made brigadier-general by President Lincoln, and on April 17, 1866, received the rank of brevet major-general from Andrew Johnson.

At the close of the war he was appointed commandant of the post at Baton Rouge, and while there bought a cotton plantation, but soon afterward sold it, having been appointed to a position as government storekeeper at San Antonio, Tex., where he remained for two years. He then returned home and lived on his farm until his death, July 26, 1882. Since his death his widow has made her home with the subject of this sketch. The children of Michael and Elizabeth Lawler were Margaret, deceased; Sina, now Mrs. Evans, in Mexico; John C., deceased; Mary, who married a man named Riley and now deceased; Addie, Mrs. Walters, of Equality; Judith, also a Mrs. Walters, now dead; Michael, Elizabeth and William, all three deceased, and Raphael E. The parents were both members of the Catholic Church, in which General Lawler took great interest. He was also active in politics and was one of the best known Democrats in Southern Illinois. Raphael E. Lawler attended different colleges in his youth, but left college to assume the management of his father's business, on account of the latter's failing health. On Jan. 10, 1881, he was married to Elizabeth, daughter of Lewis and Elvira Fowler, and a native of Gallatin County.

After his marriage he lived with his parents until the death of his father, and since then has had full control of the farm, which he now owns. Like his father, he is a Democrat and a Catholic, now being one of the trustees of the church. The children born to him and his wife are: Margaret A., now Sister M. Veronica, O.S.M., of St. Mary's convent at Enfield, Ill.; Mary E., now Mrs. Luckett, living near Equality; Michael K., Louis F., Raphael E., John C., Lawrence C. and George F., at home; Elizabeth, deceased; Mary R., Paul, and Judith A., at home; Philip, deceased; Anthony, deceased; Mary, at home; Mary N., deceased, and Monica A., deceased.

— *Memoirs of the Lower Ohio Valley.*

Prof. C. J. Lemen – 1887

PROF. C. J. LEMEN, superintendent of public schools of Shawneetown, was born in Madison County, Ill., in 1843. He is the son of Josiah and Laurine (Gay) Lemen, natives of Madison County, Ill. The great-grandfather, James Lemen, of Scotch-Irish descent, came to Illinois when his son Robert was three years old, and settled near Waterloo. He was with Gen. Washington at Yorktown. The grandfather, Robert, was a native of Virginia. The father lived his whole life in Madison County, a farmer by occupation. The mother, after his death, married W. Berry, of St. Louis, and is yet living.

Our subject was an only child. Educated at St. Louis, he became a teacher at seventeen in St. Clair County. Enlisting August 27, 1862, in Company G, 25th Regiment, Iowa Infantry, for three years or for the war, he took part in Arkansas Post, Haynes Bluff, Vicksburg, Lookout Mountain, Atlanta and "March to the Sea." With the exception of six years as druggist in Collinsville, Ill., he has been teaching since the war: principal at Caseyville three years, at Belleville, two years, and since 1883 in his present position. In April 1868, he married Sarah Caswell Smith, of Ottawa, a native of New York. Their children are Mary L., Mabel C., and William C.

Prof. Lemen is one of the leading educators of southern Illinois, and in his especial study of ornithology has made a fine collection of over 100 different varieties. He has been observer for the Smithsonian Institute for four years, and for the State weather service in connection with the United States Signal Service. He and his wife are members of the Presbyterian Church.

— *History of Gallatin, Saline, Hamilton, Franklin and Williamson Counties, Illinois.*

Samuel D. Lewis – 1883

SAMUEL D. LEWIS, son of Philip and Hester L. Lewis, was born in Lawrence County, Ill., in 1852. His grandparents were from England and Scotland, and settles in North Carolina in early colonial times. His parents moved to Kentucky, and from there in 1815 to Illinois. His father was one of the pioneers of Eastern Illinois, being one of the earliest settlers of Lawrence County.

Mr. Lewis was educated in the pubic schools. When 21 years of age he commenced the study of telegraphy, at Farmington, Iowa. His health failing, he returned to the farm and remained two years. He then went to Texas and taught penmanship in Wilderville, Snowsville and Hampton; then worked on a cotton farm awhile, after which he returned to Lawrenceville, Ill., and continued the study of telegraphy, and also dealt in grain. May 1, 1876, he took charge of the telegraph office at Omaha, where he still remains. He is a very faithful agent, attending to all the duties of his office, and has had charge of several mail routes; is also dealing in grain, game, etc. Jan. 21, 1876, Mr. Lewis married Maggie Lane, of Bridgeport, Ill. They have three children — Luella, Carrie and Pearl, ages, six, four and one.

— *History of White County, Illinois.*

David A. Logan – 1905

DAVID A. LOGAN, a farmer near Junction City, Ill., and trustee of the township in which he resides, was born, March 11, 1843, in what is now West Virginia. When he was about twelve years of age he came with his parents to Gallatin county, Ill., and lived there with them until Aug. 15, 1862, when he enlisted as a private in Company D, One Hundred and Twentieth Illinois volunteer infantry. The regiment was mustered in at Springfield for "three years or during the war," and soon afterward sent to Memphis on guard and patrol duty. There Mr. Logan contracted smallpox and before he fully recovered he was taken ill with typhoid fever. The two maladies kept him in the hospital for nearly five months. A few days after the fall of Vicksburg he reported there for duty and rejoined his regiment at Lake Providence, La., where it was stationed on guard duty. In September, 1863, it was ordered back to Memphis, after which it was at Corinth, Miss., Lagrange, Tenn., again at Memphis, then on the Guntown raid through Mississippi, and up the Tennessee river. It was mustered out at Memphis, Sept. 10, 1865, and the men returned to their homes.

Since the war he has devoted his attention and energies to farming, and although he has but 100 acres he has one of the best-improved farms in the neighborhood. In his political convictions Mr. Logan is a stalwart Republican, and for the last twenty years has held the office of township trustee. No better recommendation of his honor, popularity, and trustworthiness is needed than this long record as a public official, during which he has ever maintained the confidence and respect of the citizens who have entrusted him with the administration of township affairs. He is a charter member of M. K. Lawler Post, Grand Army of the Republic, at Junction. Shortly after the war he was married to Miss Elizabeth Munch, and to this union there have been born the following children: Alfred, Moses, Arthur, Chester, Harrison, Walter, Clarence, and twins who died in infancy. Alfred and Arthur are in the State of Washington, Chester is at home, and the others live in the vicinity. Mr. Logan has lived on the farm he now occupies ever since his marriage.

— *Memoirs of the Lower Ohio Valley.*

John R. Logan – 1905

JOHN R. LOGAN, a farmer near Junction City, Ill., was born near Moundsville, Marshall county, W. Va., though at the time of his birth the county was in the Old Dominion. He is a son of James and Belle (St. Clair) Logan, and is one of a family of seven children, five sons and two daughters. In 1855, he came with his parents and brothers and sisters to Gallatin county, Ill., being at the time about fifteen years of age. They settled in Gold Hill township, where the father died in the year 1876.

On Aug. 15, 1862, John R. Logan enlisted as a private in Company D, One Hundred and Twentieth regiment Illinois volunteer infantry, and was mustered in at Camp Butler "for three years or during the war." For some time the regiment was assigned to the unromantic duty of guarding railroads, its first real service being at the siege of Vicksburg during the latter part. After the fall of Vicksburg it was sent back to Memphis and there did provost duty until the men were discharged in 1865.

After the war he returned to Gallatin county, where he has ever since lived. In 1872 he was married to Miss Mary Munch, and commenced farming for himself. He and his uncle bought 80 acres, all in timber, for $5 an acre, and built a hewed log house. Mr. Logan now owns a well improved farm of 100 acres, and although other men may own more land few have their farms in a higher state of cultivation than he. He is a member of the Grand Army of the Republic, belonging to the post at Shawneetown. Mr. and Mrs. Logan have had the following children: James, Charles, Annie, Edward, John A., David, Minnie, Fred and Bertha. James is in Minnesota; Annie is the wife of Edgar Kanady; John is a school teacher; Edward and Bertha are deceased, and the others live at home.

— *Memoirs of the Lower Ohio Valley.*

J. E. Logsdon – 1887

J. E. LOGSDON, farmer and stock dealer, was born in Shawneetown Precinct in 1853. He is one of eight children of Thos. and Margaret Logsdon. The father was born in Ripley County, Ind., in 1820, the son of Thos. Logsdon, Sr., of Irish ancestry. Coming to Gallatin

County when a young man the father was married in 1843, and spent the remainder of his life there, the most extensive land holding in the county, and a large stock dealer. He died in 1864. The mother was born in Gallatin County in 1828 and is still living, a member of the Cumberland Presbyterian Church. Our subject finished his education at Notre Dame, Ind. In 1883 he married Edith, daughter of John E. and Lucy Rearden, of Gallatin County, where Mrs. Logdson was born. Their two children are Eugene and Maud. He is now living on the farm on which he was reared. He owns about 2,600 acres of land, one of the largest landowners in the county. He is also largely interested in stock dealing, and is a successful financier. He is a Democrat, casting his first vote for Tilden.

— *History of Gallatin, Saline, Hamilton, Franklin and Williamson Counties, Illinois.*

J. J. Logsdon – 1887

J. J. LOGSDON, farmer, was born in Ripley County, Ind., in 1838, the eldest of five children of Thos. B. and Mary (Muir) Logsdon. The father, a native of Gallatin County, who died when our subject was nine years old, went, when a young man, to Ripley County, Ind., where he married and passed his life as farmer and grocer, as the latter of which he was buying goods in Cincinnati at the time of his death. The mother was also born in Ripley County in 1818, and about nine years her husband junior; she died in 1881, a member of the Methodist Episcopal Church.

With few educational advantages our subject, when nineteen, came to Gallatin County and engaged for some time as a farm hand. With the exception of the years from 1865 to 1868 in Kentucky, Gallatin County has been his home. March 21, 1861, he married Nancy A., daughter of Jos. and Margaret Logdson. They had two children, both dead. Mrs. Logsdon died in 1863, and in 1865 he married Mrs. Prudence James, daughter of Jos. L. and Jane Muir. Seven of their nine children are living: Mary M., Prudence A., Fannie M. and William (deceased), Robert and Rosa (twins), Jos., Thomas, and James, Jr. With the exception of about two years in Kentucky in the grocery business our subject has been on his present farm of 840 acres since 1869. He is extensively engaged in stock dealing also. He has always been a Democrat, voting first for Douglas.

— *History of Gallatin, Saline, Hamilton, Franklin and Williamson Counties, Illinois.*

James J. Logsdon – 1905

JAMES J. LOGSDON, one of the largest farmers and land owners of Gallatin county, Ill., living on the New Haven road, five miles from Shawneetown, was born on May 14, 1838, near Napoleon, Ripley county, Ind. His father, Thomas B. Logsdon, was born on what is known as "Sandy Ridge," near Shawneetown. When he was about nineteen years of age he went to Ripley county, where he married Miss Mary Muir, and was for some time engaged in conducting a general store at a place called Tall Bridge, not far from Napoleon. He died there in October, 1846.

James J. is the eldest of five children. Joseph M. was killed in 1872, by the recoil of a gun; Thomas B. is a retired farmer of Shawneetown; Prudence is the wife of J. W. Gregor, of Indianapolis, Ind.; and Mary lives with her brother James. When about eight years of age

James J. Logsdon had the misfortune to lose his father by death, and about three years later his mother remarried, her second husband being William Love.

In the spring of 1861 James went to Indianapolis, and in the fall of that year came to Gallatin county. On March 21, 1861, he was married to Nancy A., daughter of Joseph Logsdon, and a native of Gallatin county. (For a more extended account of the family genealogy see the sketch of Joseph Logsdon.) To this marriage there were born two children, both of whom died in infancy. His wife died early in 1863, and about a year afterward he went back to Indiana. There he was married in the spring of 1865 to Miss Prudence Elizabeth Muir, and soon after his marriage returned to Shawneetown. They remained there but a few weeks, however, going to Raleigh, Ky., where he conducted a general store for about two years. At the end of that time he again returned to Shawneetown, rented a farm from his brother for one year, and in October, 1869, settled on the farm where he now lives. To his second marriage there have been born the following children: Margaret, Robert L., James J., Jr., William, Joseph, Rosa, Thomas B., Fannie M., and Annie. Margaret is the wife of James Gray, living near her father; Robert also lives in the vicinity; James J. is at home, and the others are deceased. Annie was the wife of Douglas Case.

Mr. Logsdon owns 800 acres in his home farm, 500 of which is under cultivation; 60 acres near Round Pond; 96 acres in another tract; a half interest in another farm of 160 acres; and is one of the heirs to 1,400 acres in the river bottoms, 600 of which is under cultivation. One of the farms he owns is that where his father was born. Until quite recently he was active in buying and selling live stock, but in more recent years has devoted most of his time and attention to looking after his farming interests. In politics he is a Democrat, and was for ten years the supervisor of the poor. He is a member of the Shawneetown Lodge, No. 838, Independent Order of Odd Fellows, and is always a welcome attendant at the lodge meetings.

— *Memoirs of the Lower Ohio Valley.*

Joseph Logsdon – 1905

JOSEPH LOGSDON, a farmer, living five miles southwest of Shawneetown, Ill., is of German extraction, and a descendant of one of the first settlers in that section of the Lower Ohio Valley. His great-grandfather came from Germany some time prior to the Revolutionary war, settled in Maryland, and there passed the remainder of his life. He married there and reared a family of children, one of whom, a son named Joseph, served with Braddock in the French and Indian War, and afterward fought in the Revolution. This Joseph Logsdon married Susan Durban, whose father owned the ground upon which a part of the city of Baltimore now stands, and who leased it for a period of 99 years. The leases have long since expired and the tenants remain in possession, though the land rightfully belongs to the Durban heirs.

Soon after his marriage Joseph Logsdon packed his worldly goods upon horses, and with his wife made his way to Virginia, then to Kentucky, next to Indiana, and finally to Southern Illinois, settling in what is now Gallatin County. The region was at that time the extreme frontier, and troubles with the Indians were of no uncommon occurrence. After a short stay in his new location he and his wife were compelled to seek the protection of old Fort Massac, in what is now Massac County, and there he passed the rest of his days. Most of his life was spent on the frontier and he had frequent brushes with the Indians. While living in Kentucky he was attacked by two Indians, one of whom shot him from his horse, but the ball glanced and saved his life. In the hand-to-hand fight which followed he killed one of the Indians with his knife, and wounded the other so badly that he committed suicide afterward. He was known as "Big Joe" or "Bulger Joe" Logsdon, the latter name having been given to him while he was with Braddock. Although a man of great physical strength he was not quarrelsome, and few of the pioneers had more friend. During the latter part of his life he took great interest in encouraging immigration to Southern Illinois.

He and his wife had the following children: Thomas, Polly, Prudy, Peggie, Susan and Joseph. Thomas married in Ripley County, Ind., while the family were living there, and his descendants still live in that state. Polly married Isaac Williams, and Prudy married James Meyer, both of Ripley County. Peggie married a man named Cox, after the family came to Illinois, and died at Shawneetown. Susan died young and Joseph was the father of the subject of this sketch. He was born near Covington, Ky., Aug. 19, 1795. After the death of his father at Fort Massac he returned with his mother and one sister to Gallatin County, and bought a farm near Shawneetown, where his mother died some years later.

On Dec. 16, 1829, he was married to Matilda Thompson, who was born Aug. 13, 1802, and they commenced their married life on the farm above mentioned. He no doubt inherited some of his father's liking for a military life, for he served in the Black Hawk War. In the cholera epidemic of 1832 he, his mother and his sister Peggie all fell victims to the dread disease. His widow afterward married Richard Tarlton, a native of Gallatin County, and lived until 1837. Joseph and Matilda Logsdon had four children: Eliza married a man by the name of Rogers and is deceased; Peggy lives north of Shawneetown; Joseph is the subject of this sketch, and Thomas died in Oregon from the effects of a kick from a horse. Joseph Logsdon, the third to bear that name, was born about a mile southwest of Shawneetown, Oct. 22, 1825. In his boyhood he attended the old subscription schools for six months, which constituted his entire schooling. After the death of his mother he went to Indiana, where he lived with relatives for four years, at the end of which time he returned to Gallatin County. For some time he was employed as a farm hand, after which be followed the river for a while, making nine trips to New Orleans.

In 1850 be made the trip overland to California. Leaving Fort Leaven-worth on May 22, he reached Hangtown, Cal., on August 22d, which was then the quickest trip on record. After working in the mines and in Sacramento for about 18 months he returned to Illinois in 1852, and took up the occupation of a farmer, which he has followed ever since. In 1859 he bought 185 acres where he now lives, and the following year built the house he occupies. He now owns 435 acres, all under cultivation but about forty acres, and is one of the successful farmers of the County. In 1853 he was married to Mary A. Rogers, who was born Feb. 10, 1835, and died Jan. 23, 1892, leaving no children. On April 23, 1896, he was married to Mrs. Ann Lacey, widow of George Lacey. Mr. Logsdon is an ardent Democrat; has been an Odd Fellow since 1866; and he and his wife belong to the Cumberland Presbyterian church in which he has been either deacon or elder for the last 28 years.

— *Memoirs of the Lower Ohio Valley.*

Joseph E. Logsdon – 1905

JOSEPH E. LOGSDON, one of the most prominent farmers and stock raisers of Gallatin County, Ill., living one mile west of Shawneetown, is a native of that County, having been born on a farm about one and a half miles west of Shawneetown, Dec. 11, 1854.

His father, Thomas Logsdon, was a son of one of the old pioneer settlers. (See sketches of Joseph and James Logsdon) After an education as the common schools afforded Joseph E. Logsdon attended Notre Dame for one year. At the age of 22 years he engaged in general farming and stock raising upon the farm owned by his mother until 1899, when he removed to the farm where he now lives. He does an extensive business in raising and feeding stock and is interested in various other enterprises, being generally recognized as one of the leading businessmen of the County.

In 1883 he was united in marriage to Miss Edith Riordan. Two children born to this union are deceased, viz.: Arthur and Edward. Those living are Eugene, Maude, Thomas, Lucy, Isabelle, Horace, Frederick and Bluford. In politics Mr. Logsdon is a Democrat and he takes a lively interest in all questions of public policy. He is in favor of good roads, good schools, good local government, and in fact is one of the most progressive men in his vicinity.

— *Memoirs of the Lower Ohio Valley.*

Thomas B. Logsdon – 1905

THOMAS B. LOGSDON, a retired farmer of Shawneetown, Ill., was born in Ripley County, Ind., Oct. 21, 1841, his parents being Thomas B. and Mary (Muir) Logsdon.

When the subject, of this sketch was about 17 years of age he commenced his business career as a farmer, but in 1859 went to Indianapolis, Ind., where he secured a position as clerk in a grocery, and worked there until 1862. He then worked on the railroad for about a year, at the end of which time he came to Shawneetown and engaged in business. A year later he entered the service of the Illinois Central Railroad Company as a sleeping-car conductor, and continued in that capacity for about 18 months. Then for something over a year he was a night watchman in the railroad yards and in the fall of 1868 again located in Gallatin County.

On Jan. 19, 1869, he was united in marriage to Mrs. Margaret Logsdon, widow of Carter Logsdon and daughter of Solomon and Nancy Brown, and went to farming near Bowlesville, four miles west of Shawneetown. In 1891 he removed to Shawneetown, where he now lives retired, though he still owns his farm of 327 acres. When he came to Shawneetown in 1891 he went into the store of Jacob Bechtold as a clerk and remained there for four years. Mr. Logsdon is one of the active Democrats of Gallatin County. For two years he was postmaster at Bowlesville, at the end of which time he resigned. From 1870 to 1886, he held the office of justice of the peace; was appointed County commissioner to fill a vacancy caused by the death of Dr. Harmon, and served almost a full term; was then twice elected to the office, serving nearly six years in all; and served as police magistrate for two years. Since 1872 he has been a member of the Independent Order of Odd Fellows, and since 1894 a Knight of Pythias.

Mr. Logsdon and his wife both belong to the Cumberland Presbyterian church at Bowlesville, where he was for some time superintendent of the Sunday school. (See sketches of Joseph and James J. Logsdon for extended account of ancestry.)

— *Memoirs of the Lower Ohio Valley.*

William Hick Loomis – 1887

WILLIAM HICK LOOMIS, postmaster of Shawneetown, appointed by President Cleveland August 16, 1886, is the son of James R. and Eleanor L. Loomis, both of Scotch and English descent, the former born April 9, 1836, in Mount Vernon, Ind., and the latter at Equality, Ill., in November, 1837. After marriage, when living in Equality, the father served as clerk in the adjutant-general's office at Springfield, and from 1863 was appointed for a part of one and elected for two terms as circuit court clerk of Gallatin County. Before his second term expired he was elected to the State Legislature, but soon died in 1874, and was buried on his thirty-eighth birthday. Of his seven children five are living: Lucy, wife of Thomas Patterson, our subject, James, Nellie, and Guy, assistant postmaster.

Our subject born in Equality February 4, 1861, and educated in Shawneetown, began life for himself at thirteen, being compelled to do so by the death of his father, and to help his mother raise the large family of children, he being the eldest boy, clerking in T. S. Day's book store. After two years here, in 1877, he began a five years' clerkship for J. D. Richeson, dealer in general merchandise. In 1882 he was appointed deputy county clerk, and in eight months was made assistant postmaster under Mrs. S. Edwards, who commission as postmaster expired August 7, 186, and Mr. Loomis assumed the duties of the office August 21, 1886. He is a member of K. of H. Lodge, No. 1708, and belongs to the Presbyterian Church. September 13, 1883, he married Maggie, daughter of T. J. Spivey, who was born near Bowlesville, June 10, 1862. Her father, T. J. Spivey, was a native of North Carolina. William R., their only child, was born June 25, 1884. While filling the position of assistant postmaster, he made the race for the Democratic nomination for circuit clerk of Gallatin County in 1884. Although unsuccessful, he had just cause for being proud of the race he made, he being the second out of five candidates running for the office, and only twenty-three years of age at the time.

— *History of Gallatin, Saline, Hamilton, Franklin and Williamson Counties, Illinois.*

John Marshall – 1883

JOHN MARSHALL, post office, Marshall's Ferry is the son of John and Amira (Leech) Marshall, natives of County Armagh, Ireland, and Jefferson County, Ky., respectively. His mother was reared in Knox County, Ind. Her husband came to the United States in 1801, and located in Knox County, Ind., where he followed farming some years, marrying Oct. 21, 1806.[240]

---

[240] For more on the Leech family and the banker John Marshall's early life, see the biography of his brother-in-law Isaac White later in this section.

He began mercantile life at Shawneetown, making frequent trips to Philadelphia for goods coming by water or flat-boats. He was Judge of the Court of Common Pleas in 1814, appointed by Territorial Governor Edwards; also represented the county in the first State Legislature; was Postmaster at Shawneetown — a distributing office for many years — appointed by Monroe, and resigned during Van Buren's administration. He was President of the Bank of Illinois for many years, and died at Shawneetown, May 23, 1858. His wife died Aug. 17, 1874, at the residence of her son in White County, Ill. There were seven children in this family, two of whom are now living — John, and Sarah L., wife of Judge John J. Hayden, of Washington, D.C.

John was born at Shawneetown, Ill., May 15, 1820. He was educated here, and before twenty years of age he went into full partnership with his father in the mercantile business, and remained in this trade till the spring of 1852, when he moved to White County and located on his present farm on the bank of the Wabash, on section 18, where he owns over 200 acres of land; he also owns about 1,300 acres of adjoining lands.[241]

April 20, 1843, in Shawneetown, Ill., he married Joanna G., daughter of William and Sarah (Ruddick) Stevenson, of Ireland, where they died. Joanna G. was born in Ireland, Parish Kilmore, County Armagh, Aug. 10, 1823. She was reared by her uncle, Thomas Ruddick, Esq., where she married, in Shawneetown, April 20, 1842. By this union there were born ten children, four living — Elizabeth, Genevieve, May and Daniel. John Jr., Georgianna, Francis L., Samuel D., Jr., William S., and Amy, or Amira, are dead.

Mrs. Marshall died Jan. 4, 1871. Mr. Marshall votes the Democratic ticket, having voted ten times for the Democratic candidate for President, but was himself never a candidate for any office.

His Grandfather Marshal died in Ireland; his grandmother came to the United States with her son Daniel, and died at the house of her son John, at Shawneetown. His grandfather George Leech, came to the United States in 1776, and settled at Bordentown, N.J., where he married Achsah Applegate. George Leech died at Shawneetown, Ill., and Achsah died at Fairfield, Ill.

— *History of White County.*

Thomas Martin – 1883

THOMAS MARTIN, born in West Franklin, Posey County, Ind., Oct. 1, 1836, is a son of Alfred and Rachel Martin. His grandfather Martin immigrated to Indiana from South Carolina in 1810. He lived on his father's farm, attending the subscription schools during his early life. He followed flat boating and trading on the Ohio River three years. In 1863 he commenced buying stock in Illinois and driving it to Indiana. He thus made acquaintances in White County and located at Brockett's Mill. After a residence there of about eight years he came to Omaha and is at present one of the partners of the firm of Martin & Rice.

He first married Sarah V. Riley, daughter of Charles Riley, editor of the Cairo Sun. She died in 1863, leaving a daughter — Ratie, now assistant teacher in the Omaha schools. He next married Nancy C. Rice, of White County. Mr. Martin's maternal grandfather was a

---

[241] Marshall's home is in Emma Township, White County.

member of the Constitutional Convention that drafted the Constitution of Indiana, and was a member of the Indiana State Legislature.

— *History of White County.*

Judge Angus M. L. McBane – 1887

JUDGE ANGUS M. L. MCBANE, merchant at Shawneetown, was born in 1837 in Parkersburg, W. Va. He is the son of Dr. A. M. L. and Ellen (Willard) McBane. The former, of Scotch descent, was born in 1808 in Cannonsburg, Penn., and the latter, of English and French descent, was born in New York. The father, after graduating in medicine and traveling in Europe, began practicing in Louisville, Ky. Here he married about 1836 and moved to Parkersburg, W. Va., and in 1842, with his brother, William McBane, bought 1,600 acres of land where Metropolis City now is, and 600 acres on the Kentucky side, where he died July 3, 1860. He had an extensive practice and influence in his profession. The mother's father, Rev. Joseph Willard, a descendant of Maj. Simon Willard, of Boston's early history, was an Episcopal minister in Newark, N.J., in 1806, and died at Marietta, Ohio. Their children were William A., Marietta and Angus, now living, our subject, who was five years old when they came to Metropolis City.

"Bob" Ingersoll was his instructor, whose letter of inquiry for the schools, May 16, 1853, is in Mr. McBane's possession. "Bob" allowed our subject to the greater part of the teaching, while Latin and history occupied his own attention. Princeton Academy (N.Y.) was one of his educators also. After studying law under Hon. Cyrus G. Simons and W. H. Green, of Cairo, Ill., he graduated from the law department of Louisville, Ky., in 1860, and immediately began practice at Metropolis City. After a year in Shawneetown, he was elected county judge in 1865. Since 1877 he has been devoted to his profession and present extensive business. In 1862 he married Mary, daughter of John D. Richeson, of Shawneetown, her native place. She is a member of the Methodist Episcopal Church, while Mr. McBane is an Episcopalian, a member of the K. of H., and in politics a Douglas Democrat.

His war history is as follows: he organized two Federal companies, one from White County, Ill., Capt. Goslin, the other from Ford's Ferry, Ky., Capt. Young, and placed them with the 48th Illinois at Camp Butler. On account of his father's death leaving him in charge of the family, he was able only to go South with the Adams Express Company from Paducah to Pittsburg Landing with Grant's forces, and consequently was at the great battle of Shiloh.

— *History of Gallatin, Saline, Hamilton, Franklin and Williamson Counties, Illinois.*

Angus M. L. McBane – 1905

ANGUS M. L. McBANE, a retired lawyer and merchant of Shawneetown, Ill., and ex-judge of Gallatin county, is justly entitled to be classed as one of the foremost citizens of the city. The McBane family is of Scotch origin, the grandfather of judge McBane coming from Scotland in the early part of the nineteenth century and settling at Cannonsburg, Pa., where he reared a family of children. One of his sons, Dr. A. M. L. McBane, was born at Cannonsburg in 1808. He received a fine literary education, which was supplemented by a complete course in the science of medicine. After graduating from medical college he traveled extensively through Europe, and upon returning to America located at Louisville, where he soon won eminence as a physician. In 1836 he went to Parkersburg, W. Va., and practiced there until 1842, when, in company with his brother William, he came to Illinois. The two brothers bought 1,600 acres of land where Metropolis City now stands, and 600 acres on the opposite side of the Ohio river in Kentucky. Here Dr. McBane passed the remainder of his life, in the practice of his profession and in looking after his large landed and commercial interests. His death occurred July 3, 1860.

In 1836, while living in Louisville, he was married to Miss Ellen Willard of that city, though a native of New York. She was of English and French extraction, her father, Rev. Joseph Willard, having been an Episcopal minister at Newark, N. J., as early as 1806. Later he came West and died at Marietta, Ohio. He was a descendant of Maj. Simon Willard, who was somewhat famous in the early history of Boston. Dr. McBane and his wife had five children, viz.: Angus M. L., the subject of this sketch; Joseph, a graduate of the New Orleans Medical college, died on shipboard while crossing the Atlantic and was buried at sea; Ellen, deceased; Marietta, widow of William Ward, living in Chicago, the mother of three children, one son, Frank, being a traveling man and secretary of the Standard club; and William A., who was a real estate and insurance man of Metropolis City at the time of his death in 1903.

Angus M. L. McBane was born at Parkersburg, W. Va., Sept. 8, 1837. He was but five years of age when his parents came to Illinois. Ever since that time he has resided in that state and has been identified with the growth and development of Massac and Gallatin counties. He obtained his early education in the schools of Metropolis City, one of his teachers being Robert G. Ingersoll, who afterward achieved a world-wide reputation as an exponent of Agnosticism. Although nominally a student at this time young McBane was really an assistant teacher, Mr. Ingersoll devoting most of his time to Latin and history, leaving the greater part of his other school work to McBane. Later Judge McBane graduated from Princeton college of New York, after which he returned home, took up the study of law under Hon, C. G. Simons and W. H. Green, and in 1860 graduated from the law department of the Kentucky State university, at Louisville.

He began practice at Metropolis City, but scarcely established himself when the Civil war broke out. His desire was to enter the service of his country, but the recent death of his father made it necessary for him to remain at home to look after the large estate and to care for the family. However, he organized two companies, one in White county, Ill., and the other at Ford's Ferry, Ky., both of which were mustered into the army as part of the Forty-eighth Illinois infantry, of which he was made adjutant, but for reasons already stated he was compelled to resign the position. He accompanied Grant's forces from Paducah to Pittsburg Landing, and in the capacity of expressman for Grant's army was present at the historic battle of Shiloh.

In 1864 he removed to Shawneetown, where he was elected county judge the following year and held the position for four years. In addition to his large law practice judge McBane became interested in the mercantile affairs of Shawneetown. For several years he conducted one of the largest general stores there and was a large buyer of grain. In 1877 he practically retired from both professional and commercial life, and since then has devoted his time to the management of his large and varied investments. He was married in 1862 to Miss Mary, daughter of John D. Richeson, whose sketch appears elsewhere in this work. They have no children. Judge McBane is a member and past dictator in the Knights of Honor; has been president of the Business Men's association ever since it was organized in 1890, was once a candidate for state senator, and is always active in promoting the general welfare of the community in which he lives. His wife is a member of the Methodist Episcopal church.

— *Memoirs of the Lower Ohio Valley.*

John A. McClernand – 1912

MAJ. GEN. JOHN ALEXANDER McCLERNAND was born in Breckinridge County, Ky., May 30, 1812, died at Springfield, Ill., September 20, 1900.

The Black Hawk War (1832) found young McClernand occupied in the study and practice of law in Shawneetown, Ill., but with the instincts of a born soldier, and with a patriotism that burned fiercely until the hour of his death, he volunteered for this Indian war, which meant so much to the safety of the pioneers and to the progress of Illinois. This service brought him a well-earned reputation for energy, fearlessness and skill, and cultivated a natural aggressiveness, which later became so strikingly prominent in his career in the Civil War.[242]

Appointed a Brigadier General, while serving as a Representative in Congress, he took the field for the Union at Cairo, Ill., in September, 1861, and under Grant bore the principal subordinate part at the battle of Belmont in the following November. Here his coolness under fire, the resourcefulness of his active and aggressive mind in combating and overcoming seemingly insurmountable obstacles, and his marked ability to inspire the enthusiasm of victory where others saw only defeat, gained for him the loyalty and confidence of his soldiers that he ever afterwards maintained, and which served him and his cause such signal service on many a hard-fought field to follow.

Advanced to the command of a division, McClernand led in the attacks upon Forts Henry and Donelson in February, 1862, and beyond question largely contributed to those decisive victories. His skill in posting his troops on February 13 and 14 in front of the enemy's entrenchments at Donelson, and the desperateness with which he fought his command on the 15th prevented the Confederates, who had massed practically their entire force against the Union right, commanded by McClernand, from cutting their way out and

---

[242] Another biography fills in more of the pre-Civil War period of McClernand's life noting he had been brought to Shawneetown in 1816: " [He] was admitted to the bar in 1832 and engaged in journalism for a time. He served in the Black Hawk War, and was elected to the Legislature in 1836, and again in 1840 and '42. The latter year he was elected to Congress, serving four consecutive terms, but declining a re-nomination, being about to remove to Jacksonville, where he resided from 1851 to 1856. Twice (1840 and '52) he was a Presidential Elector on the Democratic ticket. In 1856 he removed to Springfield, and, in 1859, re-entered Congress as Representative of the Springfield District; was re-elected in 1860, but resigned in 1861 to accept a commission as Brigadier-General of Volunteers from President Lincoln, being promoted Major-General early in 1862. [Source: 1912. *Encyclopedia of Illinois and History of Sangamon County.* Chicago: Munsell Publishing Co. 1:359.]

McClernand's move to Jacksonville probably had something to do with his marriage to Sarah F. Dunlap of Morgan County on Nov. 7, 1843. After her death, he married her sister Minerva Dunlap on Dec. 23, 1862, in Morgan County. Both girls were daughters of Col. James Dunlap of Jacksonville. [Source: Illinois Statewide Marriage Index].

escaping. During the sanguinary conflict that occurred at this time an unfortunate combination of circumstances came near depriving the Army and Naval Commanders, Grant and Foote, of the full fruits of their well-planned campaign.

His army being in position, Grant left the field to consult with Foote on the latter's gun boat. Not foreseeing that the enemy would attempt to force his way out, he gave orders to part of the line, at least, and certainly to Smith, who commanded the left division, not to bring on an engagement without further orders. Doubtless he contemplated arranging with Foote for a combined and simultaneous attack by land and river, and assuming that the enemy had remained on the defensive, the measures adopted would seem to have been wise, but the enemy did not remain on the defensive; on the contrary he hurled nearly his entire force on McClernand's Division; hence its desperate fighting, while other parts of the Union line, with minor exceptions, stood looking on. As events developed, the order referred to was unfortunate, costly, and nearly enabled the Confederates to escape. On General's Grant's return he ordered Smith to assault. This, of course, relieved the pressure on McClernand and, indeed, nailed victory to the Northern standards. If this battle had been fought later in the war, probably neither Smith nor Wallace, commanding left and center, able and gallant soldiers, would have hesitated to set aside orders given to cover conditions that no longer existed, and at once moved to the assault when the roar of the battle on their right reached them.

The battle of Shiloh, April 6 and 7, 1862, one of the most desperately fought of the war, and, indeed, of all times, came near being a great Southern victory. That it was not is due wholly to the stubborn gallantry on the first day of the better elements of the Army of the Tennessee. As the enemy unexpectedly advanced on the 6th under the able leadership of Albert Sidney Johnston, surprise and terror passed rapidly through the Union ranks, and swept a great mass of panic-stricken men back to the vicinity of the steamboat landing. Many were seized with terror who, on previous and later battlefields, fought with courage. During all that long and terrible first day when the Northern troops were driven from position to position, and when those who appreciated the situation prayed for Buell or night, none fought harder, with death and panic surrounding them on all sides, than McClernand and the greater part of his gallant division. These are facts, and are susceptible of proof to any lover of truth who will put aside a lot of trash written under the name of history, and turn to the Rebellion Records, officially published by the Government. An intelligent and diligent reader will have little difficulty in sifting the wheat from the chaff if he will read those "Records," where the dispatches, orders and reports of the war are found verbatim, with the comments and criticisms they called forth at the time by men who were actually participating in the great drama. Nearly twenty years later General Buell told a son of General McClernand that, when he arrived on the field in person on the evening of the 6th, McClernand's Division was the only one with any fair organization left.

With Grant and Sherman, and other officers of high rank who were present, McClernand must share the just criticism of permitting the Army to be surprised; but his share is materially less than that of the two named, because Grant commanded and it was his bounden duty to prevent surprise, which could have been done, and Sherman's division being nearer the enemy, the importance of proper reconnaissance and outpost by his division was more evident.

In September, 1862, McClernand submitted to the President and Secretary of War a plan to capture Vicksburg from the rear, by ascending the Yazoo, and thus open the Mississippi, and later to cut the Confederacy in two parts by advancing from the Mississippi River eastward, and from Mobile, which he would seize, toward Opelika, and in this way permanently break the only rail communications left open between the eastern and western States of the Confederacy.

The Vicksburg proposition, at least, was favorably considered, and McClernand was ordered to Illinois to raise the necessary troops therefore. He raised and forwarded, principally from Illinois, Indiana and Iowa, some forty thousand. He expected to command this expedition, and a perusal of the official records will show he was fully justified in this assumption. However, in the end he did not.

McClernand assumed command at Milliken's Bend, La., January 4, 1863. The troops there had a few days before been repulsed under Sherman at Chickasaw Bayou, in an attempt to take Vicksburg from the rear. In order to encourage the beaten troops, as well as to deal the enemy a heavy blow, McClernand moved the Army against Fort Hindman, a strongly fortified position on the Arkansas River, more generally known as Arkansas Post. Here, on the 11th, he met with complete success, capturing the fort with five thousand prisoners, a number of cannon, small arms, and munitions of war. President Lincoln congratulated the successful General and his troops for the victory gained at a time when "disaster after disaster was befalling our arms." Governor Yates, of Illinois wrote, "Your success on the Arkansas was both brilliant and valuable, and is fully appreciated by the country and the Government."

Subsequently McClernand returned to the Mississippi and was assigned to the Thirteenth Army Corps, under Grant, who assumed immediate command of all the forces operating against Vicksburg. The time until March 29 was mainly spent in digging a canal in the attempt to deflect the Mississippi away from Vicksburg, but without success. Finally Gen. Grant decided to run the batteries at Vicksburg with sufficient vessels to cross his Army to the east bank of the river, below the enemy's stronghold. The Thirteenth Corps initiated the movement across the peninsula from Milliken's Bend to New Carthage. Many obstacles, with considerable fighting, were met and overcome. The Army was finally landed on the east bank of the Mississippi, and the struggle for Vicksburg commenced in terrible earnestness. This is generally and justly considered Grant's most brilliant campaign. All the honors that pertain to the position of the General-in-Chief are his, and they are great, but the responsibility for any failures that followed honest, skillful and gallant attempts to execute his orders is likewise his, and must be so assigned.

In the marches and battles that followed the crossing of the Mississippi, McClernand and his corps (Thirteenth) did their full duty and did it well. The long list of honored dead, the testimony of many eye-witnesses, and the official "Rebellion Records" all attest this. Port Gibson, fought mainly by the Thirteenth Corps, was skillfully won, and caused the enemy to evacuate Grand Gulf, and retire upon Vicksburg and Edward's Station.

When the objective point of Grant's army was changed May 12 from Edward's Station to Jackson, Miss., to beat back the Confederates in that direction before closing in on Vicksburg, McClernand's Corps, facing the enemy at Edward's Station, had to be withdrawn with great care. Grant states that McClernand accomplished this delicate movement with skill. On May 15, McClernand's and McPherson's Corps won an important battle at

Champion Hill, and on the following day the Thirteenth Corps beat the enemy at the Big Black River, capturing some 1500 prisoners and 18 cannon, with a loss of only 373 killed, wounded and missing.

After brilliantly driving the foe within his entrenchments at Vicksburg, Grant thought to carry that stronghold by assault. With this purpose in view he ordered two assaults all along the line, the first on the 19th and the second on the 22nd. Both failed, with heavy losses. The first assault was ordered before the army had gained a favorable position from which to make it.

On the evening of the 21st Grant notified McClernand that "a simultaneous attack will be made tomorrow, at ten o'clock a.m., by all the army corps of this Army." It was made, as ordered, and gallantly made too. Had success been achieved the laurels would have justly belonged to Grant. It failed, and no amount of argument can shift the responsibility from his shoulders. In his memoirs he expresses a regret that he ordered the assault. Where all failed, the Thirteenth Corps came nearer gaining success than any other. McClernand's men carried the ditch and slope of a heavy earthwork, and planted their colors on the latter. The enemy began concentrating against them to check their advance, and the battle there raged with great fury. At noon McClernand notified the Commanding General that he was in partial possession of two forts. Re-enforcements were ordered to him, but did not arrive in time to be useful. Upon receiving McClernand's reports, Grant ordered the assault to be renewed along other parts of the line, but nothing substantial was gained.

Viewing the conflict in the calmness that comes with passing years, it appears that McClernand should have been promptly and heavily re-enforced, or that Gen. Grant should have suspended operations along his entire line. That McClernand did make a considerable impression the enemy's position is an established fact. Maj. Bluford Wilson, who first carried the news of this success to the Corps Commander, still lives, and is an honored and respected citizen of Springfield, Ill., and one of that city's foremost men.

A controversy later arose about the amount of the success gained by McClernand, and as to whether or not the renewal of the assault along other parts of the line should have been ordered. In this connection it is important to bear in mind that Grant himself ordered the renewed assault; he commanded, and the responsibility is his. It is also important to note that he states that, from his position, he thought he could observe the action along McClernand's front as well as that Corps Commander. Nevertheless, he ordered the renewed assault, the responsibility for which cannot be shifted to another.

It was also claimed that the contents of McClernand's congratulatory order to his Corps, or the fact that a copy was not sent to Army Headquarters, was sufficient reason for relieving him from his command on June 18. An oversight of his Adjutant General explains the fact that a copy of the order was not sent to Gen. Grant's Headquarters. As to the congratulatory order itself, it can be found in the Rebellion Records, and will bear favorable comparison with many other such orders found there.

McClernand's Corps lost in killed, wounded, and missing before Vicksburg, 1487 men. Of the missing there were but few. To say that that Corps and its Commander did not do their whole duty intelligently, manfully, and nobly, is a direct contradiction of historical facts.

McClernand was later assigned to duty in Texas along the Rio Grande, observing the French occupation of Mexico. He also served under Banks in the expedition against the Confederates on the Red River, where he became dangerously ill, and was sent North to recuperate. No further opportunity offered for him to continue his valuable military services to his country.[243]

The lustre of his fame will continue to brighten as the impartial historian seeks for facts to replace the prejudices that usually accompany contemporary history.[244]

— *Encyclopedia of Illinois and History of Sangamon County.*

Josiah McCue – 1905

JOSIAH McCUE, a farmer living five miles southwest of Shawneetown, Ill., was born near Saline Mines, in the same county, Oct. 2, 1859. His grandfather, John McCue, was a native of Ireland, a collier by occupation, who came to the United States in his early manhood, located in Marion county, O., where he married and continued to reside until 1844, when he came to Gallatin county and located near Saline Mines. There he was employed in the mines until his death. He and his wife had four children, none of whom are now living. One of the sons, John Y. McCue, was born in Marion county in 1838, and was six years of age when his parents came to Illinois. His mother died when he was twelve years of age, and for the next three years he made his home with an uncle, after which he went to work in the mines and continued in that occupation for about four years.

Toward the close of the Civil war he enlisted in the Union army, but never got any further than Shawneetown, where he was when the news came that Lee had surrendered and the war was over. When he was about nineteen years old he was married to Nancy Marble, a native of Tennessee, and from that time until his death followed farming in the neighborhood of Saline Mines. They had four children: John W. (deceased); Josiah, the subject of this sketch; Sarah, a Mrs. Oxford, of Hardin county; and Mary A., now Mrs. Hill, also living in Hardin county.[245] The mother of these children died in 1867, and the father married Martha Kendrick. To this union there were born three children: Y. Y., in St. Louis; Rachel Robinson, at home; and Mattie (deceased).

Josiah McCue received his education in the common schools, and at the age of twenty years began farming on his own account on his father's farm. In 1886 he bought a place of 157 acres, where he now lives. This he has added to until he now owns 275 acres, all under cultivation and well improved. Mr. McCue, like his father before him, takes some interest in politics, and has been elected on the Democratic ticket to some of the township offices. He belongs to the Farmers' Social and Economic Union. In 1881 he was married to Elizabeth Shaffer, a native of Evansville, Ind., and their children are: Joseph A., Clara, George, Katie,

---

[243] The 1911 edition of *Encyclopedia Britannica* presented the following information on one on of McClernand's children: "His son, Edward John McClernand (b. 1848), graduated, at the U.S. Military Academy in 1870. He served on the frontier against the Indians, notably in the capture of Chief Joseph in October 1877, became lieutenant-colonel and assistant adjutant general of volunteers in 1898, and served in Cuba in 1898-99. He was then ordered to the Philippines, where he commanded various districts, and from April 1900 to May 1901, when he was mustered out of the volunteer service, was acting military governor.

[244] 1912. *Encyclopedia of Illinois and History of Sangamon County.* Chicago: Munsell Publishing Co. 2:1429.

[245] The Illinois Statewide Marriage Index shows a Sarah F. McCue marrying a James A. Oxford on July 11, 1880 in Gallatin County. A Mrs. Martha Ann McCue is shows marrying a Henry Hill on Nov. 6, 1879, also in Gallatin County.

Bessie, Raymond, Rachel, Frankie and John. Joseph is in St. Louis, Clara married a Mr. White and lives in the neighborhood, and the others are at home.

— *Memoirs of the Lower Ohio Valley.*

C. W. McGehee – 1887

C. W. MCGEHEE,[246] farmer and stock dealer in South Shawneetown Precinct, was born in Gallatin County in 1820. He is one of twelve children (only two living) of William and Catherine (Little) McGehee. The father, born in North Carolina, the son of Thomas McGehee, a native of Ireland, left North Carolina at about fifteen years of age, and went to Tennessee. With three years there and one in Kentucky he came, a pioneer, to Gallatin County. Here he married at about his twenty-fifth year, and died in 1844. The mother, a native of South Carolina, died in 1852; she was a member of the Old School Baptist Church.

Our subject was married, in February 1840, to Mahala, daughter of Vincent and Elizabeth Moreland, of Gallatin County, who was born in White County in 1821. Six of their eleven children are living: Emily J., wife of William Miller; Francis M., Elizabeth A., wife of B. J. Smith; William S., Charles W., Jr., and John. Mrs. McGehee was a member of the General Baptist Church, and died in March 1865.

Our subject has one of the best farms in Gallatin County, consisting of about 700 acres five miles west of Shawneetown, and finely improved. He is a self-made man, and one of the most progressive financiers and citizens. Since the dissolutions of the old Whig party he has been identified with the Republicans.

— *History of Gallatin, Saline, Hamilton, Franklin and Williamson Counties, Illinois.*

F. M. McGehee – 1887

F. M. MCGEHEE,[247] farmer, of south Shawneetown Precinct, was born there in 1842. He is one of ten children of Charles W. and Mahala (Moreland) McGehee, whose biography see elsewhere. With common-school advantages our subject enlisted, in August 1864, in Company C, 29th Illinois Infantry, operating in Alabama, Mississippi, Louisiana and Texas, and was in a number of severe engagements. After the war he resumed farming, and in April 1869, married Elizabeth E., daughter of James and Isabelle Logan, of Gallatin County, who was born in Virginia in 1848. Four of their seven children are living: Francis M., Alex. C., Anna I. and Wright W. Since his marriage he has been a resident of this vicinity, and is now the owner of 180 acres of fine land within six miles of Shawneetown. A Republican in politics, his first vote was for Lincoln.

— *History of Gallatin, Saline, Hamilton, Franklin and Williamson Counties, Illinois.*

---

[246] From the biographies of his sons, it's clear his name is Charles W. McGehee.

[247] His father's biography gives his name as Francis M. McGehee. He's probably named after Revolutionary War Gen. Francis "Swamp Fox" Marion.

W. S. McGehee – 1887

W. S. MCGEHEE, farmer and stock dealer, was born in Gallatin County in 1850. He is one of eleven children of Chas. W. and Mahala (Moreland) McGehee, whose biography see elsewhere. Reared in his home surroundings, in September 1873, he married Jennie, daughter of John and Sarah Pellin, who was born in Gallatin County in 1854.[248] Four of their five children are living: Hattie E., Eddie S., Effie E. and Andrew G.

Our subject has since lived on his present fine farm of 160 acres, about five miles west of Shawneetown, and in connection with which he has also been a large dealer in cattle, horses and mules, handling from fifty to 100 head a year. In politics a Republican, he has also been an ardent Prohibitionist. He is a member of the K. of H.

— *History of Gallatin, Saline, Hamilton, Franklin and Williamson Counties, Illinois.*

W. Smith McGehee – 1905

W. SMITH McGEHEE, a farmer, living four and a half miles west of Shawneetown, Ill., was born April 16, 1850, on the farm adjoining the one where he now lives. His grandfather, William McGehee, was born in Scotland, but came to America in his early manhood, locating in Maryland. There he married Catherine Little and in 1806 settled in Gallatin county, Ill. He entered a tract of land 320 acres in extent, paying twelve and a half cents an acre for it. Game was plentiful in Southern Illinois at that time and he made quite a reputation as a hunter and marksman. He died when about fifty years of age, but his wife lived to the age of eighty-four. They had eleven children, all of whom grew to maturity. One of these children was Charles W., the father of the subject of this sketch. He was born on Gold Hill, Gallatin county, Sept. 10, 1820, not far from where his son, W. Smith, now lives, and there grew to manhood. He married Mahala Moreland, who was born in the same neighborhood in 1823, and followed farming all his life. His wife died in March, 1865, and he passed away in 1887. She was a member of the Baptist church and he was a Presbyterian. They always lived in Gold Hill township, where he was a successful farmer and stock raiser, owning at one time 900 acres of land. They had the following children: Angeline, Samuel, George, Catherine and Nora, all deceased; Emily, wife of William Miller, living in the vicinity; Francis M., living at Cisne, Ill.; Lizzie, wife of Benjamin Smith; W. Smith; Charles, a farmer of Gold Hill township; and John, also a farmer in that township.

W. Smith McGehee was educated in the common schools and has followed agricultural pursuits all his life. On Sept. 23, 1873, he was married to Miss Jennie Pellum, of Ridgway, and about a year later settled on the farm where he now lives. He owns 400 acres, more than three-fourths of which lies in the valley, and devotes considerable attention to raising stock. He is a member of the Knights of Honor and is a Republican politically. His wife and children belong to the Presbyterian church. Their children are Hettie, Mrs. Edward Dale; Nora, who died in infancy; Edward S. of Junction City; Ethel and Gilbert, at home.

— *Memoirs of the Lower Ohio Valley.*

---

[248] The Illinois Statewide Marriage Index lists William Smith McGehee marrying Jannie Pellam on September 25, 1873. Thus it's unclear the correct spelling of McGehee's wife's maiden name.

Dr. J. T. McIlrath – 1887

DR. J. T. MCILRATH, of Ridgway, was born at Harrisburg, Saline Co., Ill., February 27, 1858. His father, John McIlrath, was born in County Down, in the north of Ireland, and was of that remarkable Scotch-Irish stock which has furnished so many men of sterling worth and character to the world. He received a classical education in his native country, and for some time there followed the profession of teaching. He came to the United States in 1855, at the age of twenty-five landing in New York, and came to Harrisburg, Ill., by the way of Pittsburgh, Penn.; arriving there early in 1856, he taught the first school in Harrisburg under the common school law of 1855, and followed teaching until 1870.

Hugh McIlrath, father of John McIlrath, died in Ireland about 1860; the wife of Hugh McIlrath, and grandmother of Dr. J. T. McIlrath, who was also of Scotch-Irish descent, lived until 1886. John McIlrath married, in 1856, Miss Martha A. Pickering, daughter of Thomas Pickering of Saline County. Mrs. McIlrath died in 1872, leaving two children: Annie and J. T.

The subject of this sketch attended school in Harrisburg, Ill., for a short time, and then attended school about three years in New Haven, Gallatin County, when that village had good schools, in 1867-69, after which he came to Ridgway. In 1878-80 he studied medicine at Evansville, Ind., graduating in the spring of 1881, when he began the practice of medicine in Ridgway, where he is still located. In the spring of 1887 he opened a drug store in connection with his profession.

— *History of Gallatin, Saline, Hamilton, Franklin and Williamson Counties, Illinois.*

William McIntire – 1905

WILLIAM McINTIRE, senior member of the firm of McIntire & Son, brick and tile manufacturers, Equality, Ill., was born near Laconia, Washington county, Ind., June 4, 1844. When he was about seven years of age his father died and the following year the mother removed with her family to Equality. Here he grew to manhood and obtained a good practical education in the common schools. While still a boy he commenced working on a farm at $6 a month during the summer seasons, and when only ten years old began to learn the coopers' trade. He worked at this until 1862, enlisted when he as a private in Company G, One Hundred and Thirty-first Illinois infantry, and was mustered in at Metropolis City. The regiment took part in the siege of Vicksburg and was at Arkansas Post, after which it was consolidated with the Twenty-ninth Illinois infantry, and fought at Natchez, New Orleans, Mobile, at various points in Texas, and was mustered out in November, 1865. Mr. McIntire held the rank of corporal at the time he was discharged.

After the war he worked at his trade in Paducah, Ky., for some time, then came back to Equality and in 1869 started a cooper shop of his own, which he conducted until 1880, when he established a brick yard in connection with Mr. Proctor. Two years later he bought out his partner and in 1885 located where he now is. In 1903 he took his son Thaddeus into partnership and added lumber to his business. The yards have a capacity of twenty-five thousand brick and a car load of tile every day, and the trade in lumber is constantly increasing.

Mr. McIntire is a director in the First National bank, is a Republican in his political affiliations, and was for several years president of the town board. In 1868 he was united in marriage to Miss Sarah A. Seeley and they have two children: Lizzie is the wife of R. E. Reed, of Equality, and Thaddeus is in partnership with his father as the junior member of the firm.

— *Memoirs of the Lower Ohio Valley.*

William R. McKernan – 1905

WILLIAM R. McKERNAN a prominent lawyer of Shawneetown, Ill., is of Irish extraction, his great-grandparents coming from County Cavan, Ireland, and settling in what is now West Virginia. They had a family of twelve sons and as these sons grew to manhood they scattered to different parts of the country. Three of them, Peter, Charles, and Reuben, went to Kentucky, and subsequently settled in Gallatin county. Here Reuben McKernan (the original Irish spelling of the name was McKiernan) engaged in farming for the remainder of his life. He was born in Ireland, and coming to the New World in early life the privilege of attending school was practically denied him, yet he developed into a man of strong character and fixed convictions, a leader among his neighbors and highly respected by all who knew him. He married a Miss Addison of Gallatin county and they had a family of four children, only one of whom is now living.[249] Henry, Elizabeth, and Julia are all dead and Charles is living in Kansas. Elizabeth married a man named Calvert.

Henry McKernan, the eldest son, was born in 1829, and passed his whole life in Gallatin county, where he followed the occupation of a farmer. He was a man of fair education. On Nov. 28, 1852, he was married to Miss Lydia, daughter of Thomas Spivey, an old resident of Gallatin county. To this marriage were born the following children: Maria, deceased; William R., the subject of this sketch; Mollie, living in Louisville, Ky.; and Charles Henry, a farmer living near Equality, in Gallatin county. The father of these children died in February, 1864, and the mother died in 1871.

William R. McKernan, the eldest son of Henry and Lydia (Spivey) McKernan, was born May 27, 1856. He was therefore but eight years old when his father died, and only fifteen when his mother passed to her final resting place. Consequently, the responsibilities of a man were thrust upon him early in life. The care of a younger sister and baby brother was thrown upon him and his elder sister, who was his senior by a little more than a year, but with true Irish spirit they accepted the responsibility, and with heroic sacrifice they kept the little family together. William worked for the neighboring farmers for twenty-five cents a day, taking his pay in provisions, while his sister spun and wove the cloth, from which she made the clothing for the orphaned children, the wool being the product of ten head of sheep that had been left by the parents. Under these conditions attendance at school was out of the question. But the boy made up his mind to secure an education. With such assistance as his sister could give him he studied of evenings and at odd times until he was twenty years of age, when, with not more than six months altogether in school, he secured a teacher's certificate and commenced teaching. He taught for two years, saving all the money he could, and then attended the Illinois academy at Enfield for a year. Again he entered the schoolroom as a teacher for a year, after which he went to Ewing college for a year. From

---

[249] This is wrong. The Illinois Statewide Marriage Index shows Reuben McKernon marrying Nancy Murry on Oct. 28, 1830. It was Charles McKernan who married a Miss Addison — an Emeline Addison on Oct. 27, 1853.

that time until 1888 he taught continuously in the school at Waltonborough, studying law in the meantime, as opportunity offered, under the directions of Judge E. D. Youngblood, of Shawneetown. In 1887 he was admitted to the bar and in 1888 was nominated by the Democracy of Gallatin county for the office of state's attorney, and at the ensuing election was victorious by a decisive majority. In 1892, at the close of his first term, he was re-elected, serving two terms of four years each. In 1891 he was appointed master in chancery for Gallatin county, and served with signal ability for four years. Mr. McKernan is a splendid example of a self-made man, a worthy son of an honored sire, whose family were among the pioneers of the Lower Ohio Valley.

The young man who reads this sketch of his life may find in it an inspiration to make a mark in the world. In fraternal circles Mr. McKernan is a prominent figure, belonging to the time-honored Masonic fraternity, the Independent Order of Odd Fellows, and the Knights of Pythias. He has been twice married. In June, 1892, he was married to Miss Margaret Smith, of Indianapolis, Ind., but she died without issue in October, 1893. In 1901 he was married to Miss Grace Phile, daughter of William Phile, an old resident of Shawneetown. Mr. and Mrs. McKernan are both members of the Presbyterian church and take an interest in its good works.

— *Memoirs of the Lower Ohio Valley.*

Franklin McLain – 1887

FRANKLIN MCLAIN, farmer, was born in Hopkins County, Ky., March 15, 1831. His father, Samuel, formerly from South Carolina, in early life settled in Hopkins County, and here married Lurania Warson. He was a farmer, and died while on a prospecting tour in Missouri, a few months before the birth of our subject, the youngest of three children. The mother, a subject of South Carolina, came in 1850 with our subject to Gallatin County, and settled on their present homestead. She died in Jefferson County, in September 1877. Reared on the farm, and with a limited education, our subject has been chiefly devoted to agriculture.

November 11, 1852, he married Mary, daughter of Owen Riley, in Saline County. They had but one child (deceased). After his wife's death, December 9, 1853, he married in Gallatin County, September 2, 1855, Nancy, daughter of Nicholas Purcell, a millwright and farmer, a native of New York, and who died in 1842 from injuries received while employed at his trade. From this marriage are the following children: Jessie M., Francis M., Calvin B., Lucy A., Ellen, Clara, Lewis V., Guy, Viola and Iva. His wife was born in Gallatin County, October 10, 1836. Our subject is a Democrat, first voting for Pierce. He has a fine home and farm of 180 acres, three miles north of Equality, devoted chiefly to wheat and clover seed.

— *History of Gallatin, Saline, Hamilton, Franklin and Williamson Counties, Illinois.*

Peter McMurchy – 1887

PETER MCMURCHY, of the firm of McMurchy & Bahr, proprietors of the City Mills, Shawneetown, is the son of James McMurchy, who came from Scotland to Clermont County, Ohio, in 1820, with his seven boys and two girls, his wife Margaret having died in

1815. James, the father, died in 1826. With the sisters married and the brothers now scattered, our subject in 1831 went to live with his uncle, Andrew Harvey, two miles north of Cincinnati, and was apprenticed in the blacksmith business. After his instructor's death by cholera in the fall of 1832, he worked in various places in the South, and being accidentally left twelve miles south of Shawneetown by the grounded steamer "Tuscarora" while on her way from Natchez in February 1838, he walked to the former place and started a blacksmith and wagon shop. He continued until 1869, and in 1870 went into the tanning business four miles to the north, but sold out a year later and engaged in his present successful business. He has been married twice, and of his eleven children three daughters and two sons are dead. The remaining daughters are married, and his only son, twenty years of age, is still at home.

— *History of Gallatin, Saline, Hamilton, Franklin and Williamson Counties, Illinois.*

Edgar Mills – 1887

EDGAR MILLS, of Ridgway, was born in Shawneetown, Ill., August 31, 1843, the son of Edgar, Sr., and Sarah J. (Ridgway) Mills. The father, with four brothers, came from New York in 1838. He located in Shawneetown and married a sister of Thos. S. Ridgway; she died in 1863. He was a merchant and died in 1846, after which the mother married Silas Hemingway, by whom she had one daughter, Harriett. Our subject's only brother died July 4, 1862, at Memphis, Tenn., a soldier of the Sixth Illinois Cavalry.

With a fair education gained in his native place, our subject when a youth became a clerk for his uncles, the Ridgways. He served four months in Company B, 18th Regiment Illinois Infantry, in the quartermaster's de-partment, and for the four years after 1866, he was traveling salesman for a wholesale dry goods house in Evansville, Ind. In 1870, in company with B. W. Waggener, he started a general merchandise store in Shawneetown, but after four years a Mr. Peeples became his partner, and in 1877, Mr. Mills withdrew and began merchandising in Ridgway. Since 1885 he has been devoted to the grain business, and was postmaster from 1881 to 1886. He is a Republican in politics, and was for several years member of the city council of Shawneetown, and its mayor for four years. He is the only Republican ever elected commissioner in this county; he was elected in 1875, and served the unexpired term of his predecessor and a term of his own. In 1865 he married Miss Z. Hunter, a daughter of Mathew Hunter, a well-known contractor of Shawneetown. January 16, 1872, he married Eva, sister of his first wife. She died October 23, 1884, and August 24, 1886, he married Sophronia, daughter of J. A. Crawford, of Ridgway. By his second marriage he had five children: Hunter (deceased), Ridgway, Ruth, Ella and Laura. He has been identified with public enterprises for the last twenty-five years.

— *History of Gallatin, Saline, Hamilton, Franklin and Williamson Counties, Illinois.*

Edgar Mills – 1905

EDGAR MILLS, proprietor of the Mills Hotel and postmaster, Ridgway, Ill., was born at Shawneetown in the same county, Aug. 3, 1843. His father, whose name was also Edgar, was a native of New Jersey, of English descent, and came to Shawneetown about 1840, and there engaged in mercantile pursuits, in which he continued until his death in 1846. He married Miss Sarah Ridgway, a native of White county, Ill., and a daughter of John and Mary (Grant) Ridgway. To this union there were born two sons: Edgar and Walter. The latter died at Memphis in 1863, while serving in the Union army. After the death of the father the mother in 1852 married Silas Hemingway, and by this marriage had one daughter, Harriet, now a resident of Chicago. The mother died in 1863 and Mr. Hemingway in 1854.

Edgar Mills was educated in the Shawneetown public schools and the Spencerian business college of Cincinnati. In 1855 he began life as a clerk in the store of John & George A. Ridgway, and remained with them until 1861, when he enlisted as a private in Company B, Eighteenth Illinois infantry, commanded by Col. M. K. Lawler. The regiment was first ordered to Cairo, where it was assigned to the command of Gen. John A. McClernand, but was later attached to the Army of the Tennessee. Mr. Mills took part in the first battle of Fort Donelson, was at the battle of Shiloh, and in a number of skirmishes. After seven months of service he returned to Shawneetown, his brother taking his place.

From the time he left the army until 1865 he was engaged as a clerk in a store in Shawneetown. He then married Miss Zue E. Hunter, daughter of Matthew Hunter, a native of Pennsylvania. By this marriage he had one child, now deceased. His wife died in 1866, and Mr. Mills went to Evansville, Ind., and remained there until 1871, when he returned to Shawneetown and became a member of the firm of Waggener & Mills. In addition to their store at Shawneetown the firm established one at Ridgway, and when the partnership was dissolved some four years later the latter establishment fell to Mr. Mills. He continued in the mercantile line until 1884.

In 1880 he was appointed postmaster of Ridgway by President Hayes. He continued to serve under the administration of Garfield and Arthur and during Cleveland's first term, up to Jan. 15, 1886. On June 10, 1889, he was again appointed postmaster under President Harrison, and in 1897 was appointed by President McKinley, having held the position ever since. Mr. Mills is one of the leading Republicans of Gallatin county, and is one of the two members of that party that have been elected to county office. In 1876 he was elected a member of the board of county commissioners and was re-elected in 1879. For fourteen years he has served as justice of the peace of Ridgway township; was twice elected mayor of Shawneetown; and served two terms on the board of aldermen of that city. Since 1876 he has been nearly half of the time chairman of the Republican county central committee, and has always been active in behalf of his party.

After the death of his first wife, already mentioned, he married her younger sister, Eva, in 1872, and they had four children, two of whom are living. Ridgway is a merchant in the town of the same name, and Ella is the wife of Professor Blackard, superintendent of the public schools of Gallatin county. The second Mrs. Mills died in 1884, and in 1886 he was married to Sophronia Crawford, a daughter of John and Mary Kanada. No children have been born to this union. Mr. Mills has been proprietor of the hotel that bears his name since 1895, and in that time he has made it one of the popular hostelries of Southern Illinois. He and his wife are both members of the Presbyterian church.

— *Memoirs of the Lower Ohio Valley.*

Albert C. Millspaugh – 1912

ALBERT C. MILLSPAUGH. The entire career of Albert C. Millspaugh has thus far been marked with many honors, which as a public man the people have bestowed upon him. As city clerk, city attorney. mayor of his city for two terms, then chief clerk of the Southern Illinois Penitentiary for a number of years and clerk of the appellate court since 1902, Mr. Millspaugh has been a man of affairs since he began the practice of law in 1889. In addition to the many public offices he has filled so admirably he has been honored in diverse ways as a private citizen, and the esteem in which he is generally held in his community is evidenced by the many important positions of trust he holds in connection with financial and other organizations in Mount Vernon.

Albert C. Millspaugh was born on September 26, 1858, in White County, Illinois. He is the son of John and Sarah (Bogan) Millspaugh, of Dutch and Irish descent. John Millspaugh was a native of Orange county, New York, born there in 1815. He was a member of the medical profession and passed his life in the practice of medicine. He was the son of Daniel G. Millspaugh, born December 26, 1781, in Orange County, New York, and the grandson of John Millspaugh, born January 22, 1758. The latter was a soldier in the Revolutionary war, and fought and was wounded at Bunker Hill, and his father was Peter Millspaugh, who emigrated from Germany to America in about 1750.

When quite a young man Dr. John Millspaugh went to Kentucky, thence to White County, Illinois, where he remained for some years engaged in the practice of medicine, and later, in 1876, he removed to Gallatin county, where he spent the remainder of his life, passing away there in 1898. Dr. and Mrs. Millspaugh reared a family of nine children, including: J. W., in Shawneetown; Mrs. Margaret A. Joyner, of Equality; Daniel, a farmer in Gallatin county; Mrs. Emma Fowler, also of Gallatin county; Robert L., of Shawneetown; J. M., a farmer and stock breeder of Equality; William L., of Equality; and Albert C., clerk of the appellate court of the fourth district.

The preliminary education of Albert C. Millspaugh was obtained in the schools of Shawneetown, which he attended after he was 21 years of age, paying for the privilege five cents per day as tuition. After leaving his studies he was employed for some years in the offices of the circuit clerk and the county sheriff, reading law in his spare moments. In 1889 he had so far advanced with his studies that he was admitted to the bar, and in that same year he was elected to the office of city attorney. For a number of years he served the city as clerk, and in 1894 he was elected mayor of Shawneetown. He discharged the duties of his office in such a manner that he was again elected in 1896, serving from April of that year to January 1897, at which time he was appointed chief clerk of the Southern Illinois Penitentiary at Chester, and he re signed from the mayoralty to assume the duties of his new position. He held that office for a period of six years, and was still in office when he was elected clerk of the appellate court of the fourth district, which comprises the thirty-four southern counties of the state. He resigned his position as clerk of the Southern Illinois Penitentiary to assume, as in former years, the place higher up, and after six years of praiseworthy service in that berth was re-elected in 1908. He bears the honor and distinction of being the first and only Republican ever elected to that office since the court was established in 1877. Following his resignation at the State Penitentiary and his election to the clerkship, he moved to Mount Vernon, where he has since been a resident. In January 1912, Mr. Millspaugh was elected to the directorate of the Third National Bank of Mount Vernon, and he has been variously connected with the leading enterprises of that city since he established his residence in it. In 1906 he was one of the leaders in the organization of the Jefferson County Fair Association, and served as president of that organization until 1911, when he resigned, owing to the pressure of other matters of a more important nature. Mr. Millspaugh is a member of the Poultry Raisers' Association, which he has assisted very materially in financial and other ways. He bears an enviable reputation not only in Mount Vernon and Jefferson County, but throughout all Southern Illinois, where he has a wide acquaintance. Mr. Millspaugh is in line for further honors at the hands of the people and his party, if popular sentiment is any criterion as a guide to the future. In addition to the many calls upon his time and attention he has been able to give some consideration to the claims of the many fraternal organizations extant in Mount Vernon, and has become affiliated with the A. F. & A. M., being a member of the Blue Lodge, H. W. Hubbard Chapter of the Royal Arch Masons, and Patton Commandery, No. 69, Knights Templar, of Mount Vernon. He is also a member of the Knights of Pythias of Mt. Vernon and the Benevolent and Protective Order of Elks of East St. Louis, and a member of the Council at Mt. Vernon.

On January 14, 1894, Mr. Millspaugh married Miss Julia Scanland, of Shawneetown, the daughter of William Scanland, at one time a leading business man and prominent citizen of that city.

— *History of Southern Illinois.*

James W. Millspaugh – 1887

JAMES W. MILLSPAUGH, ticket and freight agent of the Louisville & Nashville Railway of Shawneetown, was born in 1840, the eldest son of Dr. John and Sarah (Bogan) Millspaugh, for history of whom see sketch of R. L. Millspaugh.

James W., after his education in the public schools of White County, at 16 became a teacher and so continued for five years. In 1861 he came to Shawneetown and clerked for Martin & Inman one year, and the following three years for Chester & Powell, wholesale grocers and liquor dealers. He was in Cairo one year, and he and Mr. Powell in 1866 started a grocery. He sold out the following year, and until 1881 was wharfboating. In 1872 he was elected circuit clerk and recorder of Gallatin County for four years. In 1882 he began speculating in grain, and in November was appointed to his present position.

In 1867 he married Sina, daughter of John E. Hall, who was born in Equality in 1847. The children are John W., Giles W., Frank, Charles and James H. He has been a trusted citizen of Shawneetown for 26 years, serving as alderman several years, and was elected mayor in 1881 and re-elected in 1883, during the most trying period of the floods of '83 and '84. He is a Democrat, a Master Mason and a K. of H. He and his wife are members of the Methodist Episcopal Church.

— *History of Gallatin, Saline, Hamilton, Franklin and Williamson Counties, Illinois.*

R. L. Millspaugh – 1887

R. L. MILLSPAUGH, circuit clerk and recorder of Gallatin County, was born in White County in 1850, and is the son of Dr. John and Sarah (Bogan) Millspaugh, the former, of

German descent, born in 1815 in Simpson County, Ky., and the latter, of Irish descent, in the same county in 1814. The grandfather Daniel Millspaugh, was a native of Orange County, N.Y., came to Kentucky in 1808, and was in the war of 1812. After his marriage in 1836, Dr. John Millspaugh moved to White County, Ill, in 1838 and finally settled near Equality, Ill., in 1876. After eight years' merchandising in White County he began his practice of medicine. As the Doctor was nicknamed "Shad" the settlement about his store received its present name of Shadville. His grandfathers were both soldiers of the Revolution, one having his arm shot off.

Of 12 children, these are living: James W., grain dealer; Margaret E., wife of Thos. Joyner; Cynthia A., wife of A. A. Gosset; Emily; Danl. S., farmer; John M., farmer; William L., farmer, and Albert C., deputy circuit clerk. Our subject came to Gallatin County in 1869, and in 1871 became superintendent of Levee Improvement at Shawneetown. In 1874, he was appointed deputy sheriff, and served eight years, and in 1876 also elected constable, serving six years, then in 1884 elected to his present position.

In 1879 he married Jennie, daughter of Sidney Addison, who was born in 1861 in Gallatin County. They have two children: May and Volney. His wife is a member of the Methodist Episcopal Church, and he is not a member of any church. Politically he is a Democratic, and a good officer.

— *History of Gallatin, Saline, Hamilton, Franklin and Williamson Counties, Illinois.*

James Mitchell – 1905

JAMES MITCHELL, a farmer of Gallatin County, Ill., living five miles southwest of Shawneetown, is a native of Ireland, having been born on Dec. 20, 1838, in County Londonderry. His father, John Mitchell, was a farmer, but died when James was about eleven years of age, and from that time the son was thrown upon his own resources. In 1855 he came to America and made his way directly to Cincinnati, where he had uncles. These relatives found him a place in a machine shop, where he served his apprenticeship, becoming an expert machinist.

He was working at his trade when the Civil War broke out, but left the bench to enlist in Company B, 6th Ohio infantry, and was mustered into service at Camp Dennison. The regiment was first assigned to duty in Western Virginia, but was soon transferred to the Department of the Tennessee and took part in the engagements at Pittsburg Landing, Stone River, Chickamauga, and a number of minor engagements and skirmishes. At Stone River Mr. Mitchell was wounded in the shoulder, and at the battle of Chickamauga his left leg was shattered and he was left on the field. In his helpless condition he was captured and held a prisoner for ten days, when he was exchanged and sent to the hospital. Altogether he served for three years and three months, being mustered out at Camp Dennison, June 1, 1864.

After the war he returned to work at his trade in Cincinnati and remained there until 1868, when he came to Gallatin County, as engineer and machinist for the Bowlesville Coal Company, and remained in the employ of that corporation for 17 years. In 1885 he gave up his position with the mining company and began farming. In 1901 he bought the place of 100 acres where he now lives, and where he has been successful as a farmer and stock raiser on a modest scale.

Mr. Mitchell was married in 1864, to Miss Minnie Heitzelman, a native of Germany, and to this union have been born twelve children, seven of whom are yet living — Mary Ann, William, Robert, and Rena are all married and live in Gallatin County, and Minnie, Jennie and James are at home. Mr. Mitchell is an unswerving Democrat in his political views, and with his family belongs to the Cumberland Presbyterian church.

— *Memoirs of the Lower Ohio Valley.*

John G. Mobley – 1905

JOHN G. MOBLEY, a farmer living two and a half miles south of New Haven, Gallatin county, Ill., was born in that neighborhood; Nov. 11, 1855. He is a son of William Mobley, who was born in White county in 1818, his father being one of the pioneers of that part of Southern Illinois. William Mobley married Cynthia Hughes, a native of Hamilton county, and lived in the Wabash bottoms for several years, after which he went to Iowa for two years, but at the end of that time returned to Gallatin county and settled on what is known as "The Knoll," where he died in 1866. Of the children born to William and Cynthia Mobley, Francis, James E., Sarah J., and two who died unnamed are deceased. Those living are Alexander, who resides in Jefferson county, Ill.; Mary, married and living near New Haven; Martha, wife of William A. Smith, of New Haven; John G., the subject of this sketch; and Rebecca, wife of James D. Radsner, living in Missouri.

John G. Mobley attended the common schools in his boyhood and while still in his teens commenced working out by the month, which he continued for three years. He then went back home and took charge of the farm for his mother, and has lived on the old home place ever since. His mother died in 1892, at the age of seventy years and he has bought the interests of the other heirs, now being the sole owner of the old homestead of 300 acres, 100 of which are in the Wabash bottoms, and 250 under cultivation. Mr. Mobley has a fine residence, good barns and out-buildings, and is one of the live farmers of his part of the county. Politically he is a Republican, has served one term as township commissioner and three years as director. In 1882 he was married to Miss Eliza Moye, and to this union have been born the following children: Essie, Raymond, Mattie, Willie, Horace, Lemuel and two who died in infancy unnamed. Lemuel is also deceased, Essie is the wife of Lawrence Givens, and the others are at home.

— *Memoirs of the Lower Ohio Valley.*

George W. Moore – 1905

GEORGE W. MOORE, a grain and seed dealer of Equality, Ill., is of Scotch extraction, his ancestors belonging to the same family as Sir John Moore, the celebrated British general who was killed at the battle of Corunna, Jan. 16, 1809. George Moore, the father of the subject of this sketch, was born at the little village of Montgomery, Hamilton county, O., in 1799. While still in his boyhood he had the misfortune to lose his father by death, and he became the chief support of his widowed mother. Consequently his opportunities to acquire an education were very much restricted, yet by his own efforts he mastered the intricacies of the profession of civil engineer and surveyor, and followed that occupation for several years upon arriving at manhood's estate.

In 1845 he removed to Lawrenceburg, Ind., and in 1852 to Gallatin county, Ill., where he bought a farm three miles east of Equality. Here he passed the remainder of his life in farming and surveying. He died in 1863. His wife was a Miss Mary Ann Cross, a native of Kentucky, who survived him until 1884. They had six children, viz.: Ludwell G., who died in 1853; Dr. Thomas H., who died in Hopkins county, Ky., at the age of forty-four years; James and William, twins, now living in Gallatin county; Jennie, widow of C. C. Smith, of Equality; and George W., the subject of this sketch.

George W. Moore was born Sept. 4, 1846, while his parents were living at Lawrenceburg. He was therefore but six years old when the family removed to Illinois. He grew to manhood in Gallatin county, received his education in the public schools there, and has lived all his life in the vicinity of Equality. Upon arriving at his majority he became a farmer and followed that occupation until 1884. In 1886 he engaged in the grain and seed business, in which he has continued ever since. Mr. Moore has always taken an active interest in local public affairs, and he has served several terms as mayor of Equality.

In 1870 he was married to Miss Martha, daughter of Owen Riley, an old citizen of Gallatin county, and to this union there have been born three children, two sons and a daughter: Marshall R. and Harry, the two boys, are partners in the drug business at Equality, and Pet is the wife of Charles W. Turner, a sketch of whose family appears elsewhere in this work.

— *Memoirs of the Lower Ohio Valley.*

John S. Moore – 1887

JOHN S. MOORE, farmer and stock dealer in South Shawneetown, was born in Clermont County, Ohio, in 1838. He is one of ten children — six living — of James and Elizabeth (Smith) Moore, natives of Clermont County, Ohio. The father, born in 1810, died in 1874, and was the son of Joseph Moore, a native of Virginia, the latter of whom was a pioneer of Ohio when a lot in the center of Cincinnati cold be bought for $50. James was married about 1832, and died in his native county in 1874. The mother, of German origin, was born in 1809 and died in 1883. Both were members of the Baptist Church.

Receiving a common-school education, our subject was married, December 20, 1860, to Elizabeth, daughter of Jackson and Sarah Turner, both natives of Ohio. She was born in Clermont County, Ohio, in 1842. Eight of their eleven children are living: Edwin W., James H., Sarah E., John T., Michael, Minnie, Charley and Andrew.

Mr. Moore served four months in 1864 in Company I, 153rd Ohio Infantry, on guard duty along the line of Baltimore & Ohio Railway, and was in several severe skirmishes. In 1870 he came to Gallatin County and the next year located on his present improved farm of ninety-one acres, four miles from Shawneetown, and also bought 132 acres nearby. In politics he is Republican. Mrs. Moore is a member of the Baptist Church.

— *History of Gallatin, Saline, Hamilton, Franklin and Williamson Counties, Illinois.*

Joseph H. Moore – 1883

JOSEPH H. MOORE, M.D., was born in Catawba County, N.C., in January, 1856. His great-grandfather came from Scotland in early colonial days. His grandfather was one of the early pioneers of Western North Carolina, and was one of the minutemen in the Revolution.

Mr. Moore was educated at Rutherford College, Happy Home, N.C. He taught school a year and then went to South Carolina, and worked in a sawmill, and ran a cotton gin, by which he earned the money to begin his medical education. He studied with Dr. Ferrell, of New Jersey, eighteen months, and then attended the United States Medical College at New York City. After practicing a year at home, in Hickory, N.C., he attended the American Medical College, St. Louis, Mo., where he graduated in May 1879. After settling up his business at home, he went to Lincoln County, Ky., and practiced a few months. In September 1880, he bought the property of I. M. Asbury, in Omaha, and has since resided here. He has built a fine drug store, and is running it in connection with his practice. May 18, 1881, he married America J. Bradford of Pendleton Co., Ky.

— *History of White County, Illinois.*

Fredrick Mossman – 1887

FREDRICK MOSSMAN was born near the French line, in Switzerland, March 6, 1828, the fifteenth of seventeen children of Anthony and Mary (Stoker) Mossman, natives of Switzerland, and who died when sixty-two and seventy years of age respectively.

Our subject learned the trade of butcher after his education was over, and worked at his trade in Germany, France and Italy. In 1849 he came directly to New Orleans, and the winter following went to Cincinnati and engaged in his trade. June 11, 1850, in St. Mary's Church, Cincinnati, he married Margaret, daughter of Michael Morris, a native of France. Their children are Jacob F., August V., Frank X., John N., Minnie and Emma. She was born in Germany, May 3, 1831, and came with her parents to America when five years old.

Our subject enlisted in the 47th Ohio Infantry June 15, 1861, and was made wagon-master. He was injured while on duty at Colfax Ferry, Va., on account of which he was discharged May 30, 1862. Since February 6, 1869, he has lived in Equality. He is independent in politics, voting for the man rather than party. He is an Odd Fellow, has been commander of Post No. 351, G. A. R., and his entire family are members of the Catholic Church. Besides his residence in Equality he owns 250 acres within two miles.

— *History of Gallatin, Saline, Hamilton, Franklin and Williamson Counties, Illinois.*

William T. Moxley – 1887

WILLIAM T. MOXLEY was born in Hickman, Ky., January 12, 1850. His father, Nathaniel, was a native of Virginia and settled at Hickman when a young man, and was in the livery business part of his life. He went to Franklin County, Mol, seventy-one miles west of St. Louis, and here enlisted in Company I, 29th Missouri Infantry (Federal). He was wagon-master, and died sixty miles below Vicksburg in 1864. The mother, Amanda (Burges), was born near Nashville, Tenn., in 1827, and is still living on the old homestead in Missouri.

Our subject, the second of seven children, was reared on the farm and educated in the home schools, and has been a liveryman and stock dealer ever since he began for himself. February 12, 1879, he married Ada, daughter of Pleasant Sipes, a blacksmith, native of Kentucky. She was born in Union County, Ky., October 8, 1858. Their children are Charles W., born in Webb City, Mo., November 13, 1879; Bessie E. and Thomas, born in Shawneetown September 28, 1881, and December 4, 1884 respectively, and Ada M. in Equality January 18, 1886. Our subject is a Democrat, and is now engaged in his business successfully at Equality.

— *History of Gallatin, Saline, Hamilton, Franklin and Williamson Counties, Illinois.*

Frederick Naas – 1905

FREDERICK NAAS, a farmer living one and a half miles west of Ridgway, Ill., was born near St. Wendell's in Vanderburg county, Ind., May 10, 1852. He is a son of Frederick and Malinda (Weiss) Naas, both natives of Germany, where the father was born in 1817. When he was about ten years of age, or in 1827, he came with his father, Jacob Naas, to America and settled in Posey county, Ind., where Jacob Naas took up government land and followed farming the rest of his life. His four children, Fred, Christ, Jacob and Sally, are all deceased. Jacob Naas lived to be ninety-two years old, and his wife died at the age of seventy.

Frederick Naas, the father of the subject of this sketch, lived with his parents until after his marriage, when he went to farming in Vanderburg county. In 1860 he removed to Gibson county, Ind. When the war broke out he enlisted in the Union army and was killed at the battle of Shiloh. Of their ten children four are now living. Mary is a Mrs. Wormit of Evansville, Ind.; Joseph lives in Poseyville in that state; Peter still lives in Gibson county, and Frederick is the subject of this sketch. After the war Mrs. Naas married again, her second husband being Leonard Cole, and they lived in Gibson county the rest of their lives.

Fred. Naas attended the public schools in his boyhood, and at the age of sixteen years started in to learn the blacksmith trade. He worked at this occupation for eight or nine years, at the end of which time he became a farmer in Vanderburg county. In 1884 he bought a farm near Omaha, in Gallatin county, Ill., and lived there until he purchased his present place of 232 acres near Ridgway. Mr. Naas has spent considerable time and money in improving his farm since it came into his possession, and has one of the best dwellings in the neighborhood — a comfortable two-story frame house, with all con-veniences usually found in the homes of the most progressive farmers. In 1874 he was married to Barbara Wormit of Gibson county, and they have the following children: George, Emil, Mary, Fritz, Edward, Barbara, John, William, Katie and Maggie. George is in Evansville; Mary is married and lives near her parents; Maggie is dead, and the others are all at home. The family all belong to the Catholic church.

— *Memoirs of the Lower Ohio Valley.*

J. F. Nolen – 1887

J. F. NOLEN, sheriff of Gallatin County, was born in Wilson County, Tenn., in 1844. He is the son of Daniel and Lucinda (Joplin) Nolen, the former of Irish descent, born in 1808 in North Carolina, and the latter also a native of North Carolina. The dates of their deaths are 1856 and 1878 respectively. The father, a shoemaker and afterward farmer, went to Wilson County, Tenn., and about 1854 moved to Franklin County, Ill.

Our subject, one of thirteen children, with few educational advantages, no schooling after his tenth year, left home August 2, 1863, to join Company A., 110th Regiment Illinois Infantry. He was sent home after being in service for several weeks, and having "enlisted for the war," again enlisting twice afterward in the 13th Illinois Cavalry as recruit in the one hundred days' service of Col. Fred. A. John's regiment, and in October 1864, he was in several minor actions in the first, and the surrender occurred soon after the second.

After farming some he went to Equality, Ill., engaging in the retail liquor and grocery business for three years, since when he has been in Shawneetown. Appointed deputy circuit clerk in 1870, he served six years, and then was elected clerk, serving until 1884. He then established his present grocery business, and in 1866 was elected to his present office of sheriff.

In 1864 he married Artimissa Beeves, a native of Arkansas, born in 1844. They had two children: Ellen, wife of G. A. Harmon and Millard, he being divorced from his first wife in 1866, married Elizabeth Holley in 1871, born in Gallatin County in 1837. Their two children are Edward and Harry. Mr. Nolen is a Republican, a member of the I.O.O.F., F.&A.M. and G.A.R., and his wife is a member of the Methodist Episcopal Church.

— *History of Gallatin, Saline, Hamilton, Franklin and Williamson Counties, Illinois.*

James O'Rourke – 1905

JAMES O'ROURKE, a farmer of Gallatin County, Ill., living six miles west of Shawneetown, was born in County Limerick, Ireland, Sept. 5, 1849. His father was a peasant farmer, but died when James was only about two months old. He remained on the farm with his mother until 1865, when he came to this country with an uncle, William O'Rourke, who had previously been here, and who is now living in Evansville, Ind., about 86 years of age.

James found employment as a teamster in Evansville, and continued to work at that occupation until 1872. He then came to Gallatin County, where for several years he worked in the mines. Upon leaving the mines he rented a farm near Bowlesville, and lived there nearly 20 years, when he bought 80 acres of what is known as the "Old Huston Place," where he now resides, and where he carries on a successful farming business. Mr. O'Rourke has the true Irish sentiment, and the love for the Emerald Isle that has been celebrated in song and story by men like Carleton and Tom Moore. He has made two trips to his native land since first coming here, and on the occasion of each visit has come back to his labors refreshed by happy recollections of his old home. In politics he is a steadfast Democrat, and in his religious faith is a member of the Catholic Church.

On April 23, 1880, he was married to Miss Belle Pettery, daughter of James and Rachel (White) Pettery, of Gallatin County, and to this union have been born the following children: Henry, Kate, James, Willie, George, Mayme, and Charles. Henry Willie and Charles are deceased and the others are living at home with their parents.

Mr. O'Rourke is a fine example of what industry and frugality will accomplish. Coming to this country at the age of 16, an orphan and almost penniless, he has, by his energy and good management, become one of the successful farmers of the community in which he lives, while by his genial and generous disposition he gas made friends in whatever walk of life his lot has been cast.

— *Memoirs of the Lower Ohio Valley.*

Granville R. Pearce – 1883

GRANVILLE R. PEARCE, son of Elisha and A. J. Pearce, was born July 31, 1849, in Indian Creek Township, White Co., Ill. He was educated in the public schools of Roland. He remained on the farm till 18 years of age, when he engaged in the wool-carding business with his father, at Roland. He then worked on the farm three years, after which he was in the flourmill of Porter & Rice, Roland; came to Omaha and built the flour mill here under the firm name of G. R. Pearce & Co. Since retiring from the flouring mill, he has been engaged in wheat threshing and running a sawmill. Mr. Pearce was married in 1860 to Margaret J. Winfrey, of White County.

— *History of White County, Illinois.*

J. McKee Peeples – 1887

J. MCKEE PEEPLES (deceased),[250] banker of Shawneetown, Ill., born in 1826, was the son of Robert and Elizabeth (Maxwell) Peeples, natives of western Pennsylvania. Mr. Peeples attended school a year and a half in Perry County, Ill., after which he entered the store of E. H. Gatewood, at Shawneetown, and remained with him until he was seventeen, at which time he entered the counting-house of O. Pool at $200 a year and board. At twenty he and Thos. S. Ridgway,[251] were admitted as partners, and the firm remained O. Pool & Co. until 1850, when he and Mr. Ridgway bought Mr. Pool. The business continuing as Peeples & Ridgway until 1864, when they established the First National Bank, with a capital stock of $200,000 paid up; Mr. Peeples becoming president and Mr. Ridgway cashier, and so it remained until Mr. Peeples' death in 1879.

He was an elder in the Presbyterian Church, and a devoted Sunday-school worker, giving much times and money to the cause. He was president of the State Sunday-school Convention of 1872. He married Harriet, daughter of W. A. Docker, a leading merchant of Shawneetown in 1846. Mrs. Peeples was born in 1827. They have three sons living: John, William and Henry.

— *History of Gallatin, Saline, Hamilton, Franklin and Williamson Counties, Illinois.*

---

[250] The biography in the 1887 history incorrectly lists Mr. Peeples's name as I. McKee Peeples. His full name is John McKee Peeples.

[251] Besides their business ties, marriage also connected Peeples and Ridgway, as they both married daughters of W. A. Docker.

W. A. Peeples

W. A. PEEPLES, merchant at Ridgway, Ill., began his business in 1881. He is a large dealer, and keeps a general stock of dry goods, groceries, notions, etc., and carries a stock from $7,000 to $10,000. His annual business would probably reach from $25,000 to $30,000. He also buys and ships large quantities of grain in connection with his merchandise, and does the leading business in Ridgway.

— *History of Gallatin, Saline, Hamilton, Franklin and Williamson Counties, Illinois.*

W. S. Phillips – 1887

W. S. PHILLIPS, attorney at law, was born in Bedford County, Tenn., January 20, 1854. He is one of six children of James B. and Agnes C. (Wise) Phillips. The father was born in 1820 in Tennessee, came to Williams[252] County, Ill., in 1863, where he resides, engaged in farming. The mother was born in Mississippi in 1823, and died in 1864. After his academic education in Pope County, he began teaching, when nineteen years of age, and continued six consecutive terms, two of which were in Pope and the rest in Gallatin County. During this time he read law, and afterward began study under J. H. Clark, prosecuting attorney, at Golconda, Ill., and also a year under D. M. Kinsall of Shawneetown. July 8, 1880, he was admitted to the Mount Vernon, Ill., bar, and then removed to Ridgway, where he has since become an esteemed and able lawyer, with an extensive practice. He is a Republican in politics and a member of the Cumberland Presbyterian Church. In May 1879, he married Luella, daughter of Capt. B. C. Porter of Ridgway, Ill., born in Covington, Ky. They have two children: Sarah A. and William B.

— *History of Gallatin, Saline, Hamilton, Franklin and Williamson Counties, Illinois.*

Winfield Scott Phillips – 1905

WINFIELD SCOTT PHILLIPS, lawyer and bank president, of Ridgway, Ill., is a native of Tennessee and a descendant of one of the old pioneer families of that state. Several generations have lived in Tennessee, though the family came originally from Virginia. Richard Newton Phillips, the grandfather of the subject of this sketch, was a man of considerable influence in his county. He was a large land owner and at the breaking out of the war possessed eight slaves. Notwithstanding this he was a pronounced opponent of secession and cheerfully gave his negroes their freedom. He died about 1878 or 1879. He married a Miss Margaret Poole and they had a family of six children: William, Samuel Poole, James B., John Milton, Sarah, and Eliza Word. The last named is the only survivor of the family and now lives at Shelbyville, Tenn.

John Milton was a captain in one of the Union Tennessee regiments during the war, and afterward held the position of deputy internal revenue collector for some time. Subsequently he removed to Macon, Ga., and after living there awhile started for California. The last heard of him was when he was near Salt Lake City, and it is supposed that he met his death by foul play. James B. Phillips, the third son, was born in Rutherford county, Tenn., in 1819. He was

---

[252] This probably should be Williamson County since there isn't a Williams County in Illinois.

given a good common school education and upon reaching manhood became a farmer, which occupation he followed through life, though he was a natural mechanic and did a great deal of work in the construction of cotton gins and wool carding machines. While still a young man he removed to Bedford county, Tenn. In politics he was a Whig, and during the life of the American party affiliated with that organization.

When the war broke out he organized an independent company, and for about two years was engaged in drilling newly enlisted troops. In December, 1863, he removed with his family to Golconda, Ill., making the trip by way of the Cumberland and Ohio rivers on the Argonaut. He bought a farm six miles west of Golconda and lived there until 1884, when he removed to Creal Springs, in Williamson county, and farmed there until his death in November, 1897. He was twice married. His first wife was Miss Agnes Caroline Wise, a native of Monroe county, Miss., and a distant relative of Gov. John S. Wise, of Virginia. To this marriage there were born the following children: Radford Reedy, now living at Puxico, Mo.; Virginia, wife of James A. Adams, of Southeastern Texas; Clay and Epiminondas, both of whom died in infancy; Tennessee Belle and Campbell, also died young; Alice, wife of John F. Glass, of Marion, Ill.; Winfield Scott, the subject of this sketch; William Monroe, now living at Chanute, Kan.; and Melissa Ellen, wife of Robert M. Morrison of Ridgway. The mother of these children died in January, 1864, and the father married Margaret Zerinda Crawford, of Pope county, Ill. To this union there were born five children, viz.: Eugene B., now at Morrell, Ark.; Ida, died at the age of sixteen years; Horace Poole, died in childhood; Ethel, wife of Oscar Williams, of Marion, Ill.; and Irenæus, who died in infancy. The mother is still living and makes her home with her daughter Ethel.

Winfield Scott Phillips was born at Normandy, Bedford county, Tenn., Jan. 20, 1854, and was about nine years old when his parents removed to Illinois. His mother died on his tenth birthday, and he went to live with an uncle, Samuel P. Phillips, in Pope county. Here he remained until his father remarried, when he returned to the parental roof. In the public schools he secured a good practical education, one of his teachers being James A. Rose, afterward secretary of state, of Illinois. When he was about twenty years of age he began teaching and taught for six successive terms in Pope and Gallatin counties. While thus engaged he devoted his spare time to the study of law under Thomas H. Clark, of Golconda, and finished his studies with D. M. Kinsall, of Shawneetown. On July 8, 1880, he was admitted to the bar and at once opened an office in Ridgway, where he has continued in practice ever since. Mr. Phillips is prominently identified with the financial interests of Gallatin county, being president of the Gallatin County State bank, and the Exchange bank at Omaha. He is one of the active Republicans of the county, and in 1902 was the candidate for county judge. Although the Democratic majority for the state ticket that year was 620 in the county, Mr. Phillips was defeated by only 217. By appointment of Governor Yates he is one of the trustees of the Southern Illinois Normal school at Carbondale, and he is also a trustee of the James Milliken university at Decatur. He is a member of the Masonic fraternity and the Independent Order of Odd Fellows, and both himself and wife belong to the Cumberland Presbyterian church, in which he holds the office of elder.

On May 11, 1879, he was united in marriage to Miss Luella, daughter of Braxton Carter Parter, an old resident of the State of Illinois. To this union there have been born the following children: Sarah Agnes, wife of Otis C. Moore, of Ridgway, who was one of the

Jefferson Guards during the St. Louis exposition; William Braxton, cashier of the Exchange bank of Omaha; Anna Alice and Clyde Winfield, at home.

— *Memoirs of the Lower Ohio Valley.*

Winfield S. Phillips – 1912

WINFIELD S. PHILLIPS. The records of Gallatin county show that never before have there been so many able members of the bar within its confines. With so many important matters before the country which involve serious problems of jurisprudence, it is exceedingly necessary for the lawyer of today to be able to cope with them and lend his aid in obtaining justice. Because of the necessity for successful qualifications, the present day lawyer is being asked to occupy positions of trust and responsibility, and among those heading large institutions where the interests of many are to be conserved, the proportion of lawyers is large. One of those representatives of this learned calling who has attained to considerable prestige both as a lawyer and financier is Winfield S. Phillips, of Ridgway, Illinois, president of the Gallatin County State Bank. Mr. Phillips was born at Normandy, Bedford county, Tennessee, January 20, 1854, and was nine years of age when brought by his parents to Golconda, Pope County, Illinois.

At the age of 20 years Mr. Phillips began to teach in the country schools near Golconda, continuing therein for six years, and pursuing his law studies with Thomas H. Clark, of Golconda and D. M. Kinsall, of Shawneetown. He came to Ridgway in 1880, and on July 8th of that year was admitted to practice, in which he has continued here to the present time with great success. The general high esteem in which Mr. Phillips is held was made manifest in 1906 when, in a Democratic county of 6,000 majority, he was elected county judge on the Republican ticket, and at the end of four years was presented by the bar association with a beautiful gold-headed cane, an honor never before conferred at the end of four years, although on two occasions it has been given to others after eight years of service. He has been prominent in conventions of his party, served as chairman of the county central committee for 15 years, was chairman of the congressional committee for a long period, and is now state central committeeman for the 24th district. He was appointed a trustee of the Southern Illinois State Normal University by Governor Yates and re-appointed by Governor Deneen, serving in that capacity for eight years, and was also one of the first trustees of James Milliken University at Decatur, Illinois. He is a prominent member of the State Bar Association. Mr. Phillips has been equally prominent in financial circles being president of the Gallatin County Bank, of which he has been the head since its organization as a state institution. This bank, which has its own handsome building and is equipped with modern fixtures throughout, is known as one of the solid and substantial banking businesses of the southern part of the state and its officials are men of the highest integrity and standing in the business and financial world. Mr. Phillips is also one of the original stockholders of the Norris City State Bank, of White county, and he and his son have owned the controlling interest in the bank at Omaha, Gallatin County, for two years.

On May 11, 1879, Mr. Phillips was married to Leuella Porter, of Gallatin county who was born in Covington, Kentucky, daughter of Captain B. C. Porter, an old steamboat captain who is now deceased. Mr. and Mrs. Phillips have had the following children: Sarah Agnes, who married Otis C. Moore, of Chester, Illinois; W. Braxton, a graduate of the business college at Quincy, and now assistant cashier of the Gallatin County Bank; Anna Alice, who resides at home with her parents; and Clyde W., who like his brother completed his education in the Quincy Business College. Mr. Phillips is a Master Mason and belongs to the Odd Fellows. He and Mrs. Phillips hold membership in the Presbyterian Church, with which he has been connected since boyhood. He has been active in church work for a number of years, and is now acting in the capacity of elder. Mr. Phillips has associated himself with every movement that would tend to advance Ridgway in any manner, and in every field of endeavor his standing has been high. His popularity is not confined to the members of his profession or his business associates, but extends throughout this section of the state, where he is well known and highly esteemed.

— *History of Southern Illinois.*

M. M. Pool – 1887

M. M. POOL,[253] banker, is the son of Orval and Madeline (Snider) Pool. The father, of Scotch stock, was born in 1809, in Union County, Ky. His father, John, a native of Virginia, moved to Kentucky, and in 1816 finally settled in Shawneetown, where his son, Wilson, was the first white child born in Gallatin County.[254]

Orval was seven years old when he came to Shawneetown and in his "teens" he went to Smithland, Ky., and served several years as a saddler's apprentice. He then started a shop of his own in Shawneetown successfully, and several years later sold and for three years was a merchant, when he began pork-packing and tobacco speculation. In one year he packed 33,000 hogs. After ten years the war caused him to abandon this, and in 1871 he organized and was elected president of the Gallatin National Bank, and died in June of that year. He was an esteemed pioneer, and an able financier. The mother was born in 1814, in Strasburg, Germany, and five years old when they reached Shawneetown. She is still living. The children of our subject, Mary A., (wife of H. C. Docker),[255] Hester M. (wife of Hon. R. W. Townshend, congressman for the 19th District) and Ellen (wife of J. J. M. Peeples).[256]

Our subject was born in 1843 in Shawneetown, and educated in Danville, Ky., with one year also at Michigan University, Ann Arbor. In November 1864 he was commissioned captain and aide-de-camp by Gov. Yates, on Gen. Wilson's staff, with whom he was in his raid through Alabama and Georgia, and one of those who captured Jefferson Davis at Macon. From the latter part of 1865 to 1868, he was in the commission business in Cincinnati, but returned and began speculating in grain at Shawneetown. On his father's death he was elected president of the bank, which in April 1874 went into voluntary liquidation, and he and W. B. Henshaw started a private bank, the firm being M. M. Pool & Co., and Mr. Pool the manager.

---

[253] The Illinois Statewide Marriage Index lists his name as Marshall M. Pool.

[254] It's doubtful Wilson was really the first white child born in Gallatin County if he wasn't born until 1816 or later.

[255] The Illinois Statewide Marriage Index shows Mary A. Pool marrying Henry A. Docker on December 22, 1859.

[256] The Illinois Statewide Marriage Index shows Ellen Pool marrying John McKee Peeples, Jr. on March 31, 1870.

In 1868 he married Amanda C., daughter of Judge A. M. Grant, of Mount Vernon, Ill., her native place. Gertrude, Marshall and Grant are their children. Mr. Pool has inherited his father's ability, and is an esteemed and respected citizen of high standing.

— *History of Gallatin, Saline, Hamilton, Franklin and Williamson Counties, Illinois.*

Marshall Mason Pool – 1876

MARSHALL MASON POOL, son of Orval and Madeline (Snider) Pool, Banker, Shawneetown, was born in Shawneetown, Illinois, October 9, 1843. He received a common school education. From 1867 to 1871, was engaged in packing pork and dealing in grain. Was president of the Gallatin National Bank, Shawneetown, till the bank went into voluntary liquidation in 1874, when he organized a private bank under the name of M. M. Pool & Co.

He has been President of the Gallatin County:Agricultural Board since its organization in 1872. Served one year in the Union Army, and was captain and aide-de-camp on Gen. H. H. Wilson's staff. He has three children, the fruit of his marriage in April 1868, to Caroline, daughter of Judge A. M. Grant, of Mt. Vernon.

— *Illustrated Historical Atlas of the State of Illinois.*

Orval Pool (deceased) – 1876

ORVAL POOL, (Deceased), Banker, Shawneetown, was born in Union County, Kentucky, seven miles east of Shawneetown, Illinois, February 17, 1809. Was the son of John and Cecilia (Wilson) Pool, both born near Culpepper Court House, Virginia.

Mr. Pool received a good common school education, commenced saddle and harness business in 1829, merchandise in 1843, went into produce business in 1850, becoming the largest dealer in pork and leaf tobacco in Southern Illinois. He retired from business in 1863, and in July 1871, organized the Gallatin National Bank, of which he was President at the time of his death, June 30, 1871. He was a man of strong will and untiring energy, and was successful in all his speculations.

— *Illustrated Historical Atlas of the State of Illinois.*

General Thomas Posey (deceased) – 1912

GENERAL THOMAS POSEY was born 1750 in Virginia. He was captain and lieutenant colonel in the Revolutionary war. He was at Stony Point and at Yorktown. He held the position of lieutenant governor of Kentucky, U.S. senator from Louisiana, territorial governor of Indiana, made his home in Shawneetown and lies buried in Westwood Cemetery, Shawneetown.

— *History of Southern Illinois.*

George H. Potter – 1887

GEO. H. POTTER, farmer and stock dealer, was born in 1841 in Muskingum County, Ohio. He is one of fourteen children of Thomas and Sarah (Cheney) Potter. The father was born in Stokesley, England. A minister of the gospel, he came to near Zanesville, Ohio, in 1832, and, in 1860, to Effingham, Ill.; then, in 1863, to Gallatin County, where he remained with his son, our subject, until his death, in 1885, after years' service as minister. The mother was born in Kingston, England, in 1807, came with her husband, and died in Tuscarawas County, Ohio, in 1852.

Educated in the common and high schools of Muskingum and Loraine Counties, Ohio, in 1857 he became a teacher, and, in 1859, began teaching in Illinois, continuing up to 1863, when he became manager of Joseph Bowles' store, at Bowlesville Mines. In 1865 he began a ten years' partnership with Robert and David Reid in the coal business, after which he purchased his present farm of 330 acres.

In 1861 he married Annie R., daughter of Robert and Agnes Campbell, born in 1843. Their two children were Thomas (deceased October 10, 1872) and Sarah (deceased November 3, 1871). Mr. Potter is a Presbyterian elder and local evangelist, of which his wife is also a member. He is a Republican.

— *History of Gallatin, Saline, Hamilton, Franklin and Williamson Counties, Illinois.*

Joseph L. Purvis – 1883

JOSEPH L. PURVIS, born in Chatham County, N.C., Dec. 6, 1816, was a son of William Purvis. His father was a wealthy planter, and gave Joseph a classical education. He taught in North Carolina previous to his coming to this county. He has taught in various districts of Gallatin and White counties; also in Shawneetown. He came here in 1841.

He married Nancy Maria, daughter of Thomas and Nancy A. (Perryman) Abshier, natives of North Carolina. She was born in Murray County, Tenn., Feb. 2, 1822. To this union have been born nine children — Matilda, born Aug. 7, 1817, now Mrs. J. A. Bennett; John M. born July 1, 1849, deceased; James G., born Nov. 19, 1850, married Emma R. Butts; William L., born Jan. 24, 1853; Clarinda, born Mary 19, 1855, deceased; Clarissa, born Aug. 17, 1856; Manna A., born April 12, 1859, deceased; Andrew, born April 16, 1862, deceased; Mary E., born Aug. 25, 1864. Mr. Purvis raised Company E, 131st Illinois Infantry, in and about this town and precinct. He was in the service for 14 months.

— *History of White County, Illinois.*

Simon Baptiste Questell (deceased) – 2000

SIMON BAPTISTE QUESTELL, son of Lewis Questell, was born on 22 Nov. 1850, in Gallia County, Ohio, and moved to Illinois in 1856. On 25 Feb. 1879, he married Theresa Isabelle Bonner and they had 8 children. On 17 April 1889 he was appointed postmaster at Herald, Illinois, in White County, and on 28 March 1897 he was appointed postmaster at New Haven, Illinois, in Gallatin County. Simon died 28 March 1923 and is buried in the Union Ridge Cemetery in White County, Illinois.

Simon's great-grandfather, Nicholas Questel, came over from France in 1790. His wife, Jeanne Claude LeMont, died aboard ship while giving birth to a son, John Baptiste Questel. The son survived and the ship landed at Alexandria, Virginia. From there they went to Pittsburg, Pennsylvania, and boarded flatboats to go down the Ohio River to the place where they founded Gallipolis, Ohio.

The son of John Baptiste Questel was Lewis Questell, who moved from Ohio to White County, Illinois, in 1856. Lewis began spelling the name as Questell instead of Questel. A year later his brother, Alexander, joined them.

— Compiled from e-mail messages sent by Nick Questell to Jon Musgrave on July 18, 2000, and July 20, 2000. Nick is the great-grandson of Simon Baptiste Questell.

James A. Quick – 1905

JAMES A. QUICK, manufacturer of vehicles, agricultural implements, pipe, brass goods, mill supplies, etc., Shawneetown, Ill., is one of the representative businessmen of that city. He was born at Taunton, Somersetshire, England, Oct. 28, 1831, his parents being James and Emma (Summers) Quick, both natives of Somerset. The father was a farmer and contractor, and lived to be 75 years of age. The mother died at the age of 80. They had 24 children, six of whom are now living: Eliza is a Mrs. Martin, of Bridgewater, England; James is the subject of this sketch; Charles is at Sacramento, Cal.; Elizabeth married a man named Bufford and lives in England; Stephen and Simeon live at Taunton and Edwin lives at Bristol, England.

James A. Quick attended the common schools of his native land, and at the age of nine years started in to serve his apprenticeship at the wheelwrights' trade, at which be worked for seven years, receiving 25 cents a week the first year, with an increase of twelve and a half cents a week for each succeeding year during his period of service. He boarded with his parents and walked a mile and a half to and from his work. After learning his trade he received good wages as a journeyman for about two years, when he and his brother Charles set sail for America, and landed at New York on June 18, 1854. Mr. Quick worked one summer in Philadelphia, then the following winter in Cincinnati, after which he went to Cleveland, where he worked until 1860. He then came to Shawneetown, arriving there on, October 6th, and has ever since been a resident of the place. For two years he was employed by Mr. McMurchy, whom he succeeded in business. Mr. Quick has been successful in his business, has one of the best-equipped and largest machine shops in this part of the country, and owns other property in Shawneetown. His practical training in youth, although a hardship then, has been of great value to him in his undertakings, and he is a splendid example of a self-made man. In politics he is a Republican, and he has served with credit as one of the board of aldermen. He was married in 1861 to Margaret Welsh, a native of Indiana, and they have had four children.

— Memoirs of the Lower Ohio Valley.

Leonard E. Quigley – 1883

LEONARD E. QUIGLEY was born in Gallatin County, Ill., Nov. 27, 1835. He remained on the farm till 21 years of age and then attended the public schools and obtained a good education. He then taught till the breaking out of the late war. In August 1861, he entered the service of the United States as a private; was promoted four times, and when discharged was First Lieutenant. He was in all the important battles of the army of the Mississippi, including Fort Donelson, Shiloh, Vicksburg, Spanish Fort and Fort Blakely. He was mustered out Dec. 6, 1865. He then returned home and engaged in farming and teaching school till 1874, when he came to Omaha and bought out a hotel. In 1882 he built the finest hotel and residence in this part of the country, where he now resides. He was married Aug. 22, 1866, to Edna, daughter of Dr. James Porter. Mr. Quigley's great-grandfather was from Ireland. His grandfather was a soldier in the Revolutionary war. His maternal grandfather came from Scotland and settled in North Carolina.

— *History of White County, Illinois.*

Philip C. Quigley – 1883

PHILIP C. QUIGLEY, son of Aaron Quigley, was born in Gallatin County, Oct. 7, 1841. He was reared on a farm and received a common-school education. He enlisted in the late war when 20 years of age. He was with Grant at the battles of Fort Henry, Fort Donelson and Shiloh. He was afterward with Thomas at Spanish Fort and Fort Blakely. He was captured at Holly Springs, Miss., and sent to St. Louis, Mo., when he was paroled and exchanged, arriving at Vicksburg on the day of the surrender. He was with the land forces who supported Farragut at Mobile, Ala.; went from there by ship to Galveston, Texas, and from there to Houston; from there to Springfield, Ill., where he was mustered out, having served four years and five months. Mr. Quigley was married at the age of 26 to Nancy J. Eubanks. They have three children. Mr. Quigley owns a farm of 70 acres. He is also engaged in the manufacture of wagons, buggies, plows, etc.

— *History of White County, Illinois.*

Moses M. Rawlings – 1883

GEN. M. M. RAWLINGS was born in Virginia in 1793, his parents moving to Newcastle County, Ky., in 1794. When a boy he left his father's house and on foot made his way to Shawneetown, Ill., reaching that place without a dollar in the spring of 1809.

At that early day, the Saline salt works were being operated, and directly and indirectly gave employment to a number of laborers. Young Rawlings took hold of whatever came in his way to do. The result was he soon accumulated more than a bare living. He invested in produce, furs, or anything out of which he thought a profit might be the result.

Gen. Rawlings was married three times. He married his first wife, Miss Sarah J. Seaton, of Breckinridge County, Ky., in 1811, long before he had reached his majority, and by whom he had ten children. All died before he came to Mound City but Sarah J., wife of Dr. Henry F. Delaney, and now a widow, living on Rose Hill, six miles north of Mound City, and Francis M. Rawlings, a brilliant young lawyer, a man of imposing appearance, thoroughly educated and an orator not equaled in the State. He represented Union, Alexander and Pulaski Counties in the Legislature in the years 1854-55. He died in 1858, which greatly distressed his father and friends.

After his marriage with Miss Seaton, Gen. Rawlings enlarged his business, and in a few years he had the largest wholesale and retail dry goods and grocery establishment in the southern part of the State. He seems to have dealt in any and everything. Parties came down from Louisville and agreed to pay him a certain price for all the pecans he could deliver to them at Louisville by a mentioned time. The result was the General loaded a steamboat with pecans, which resulted in the financial ruin of the company. A similar transaction occurred with salt.

Gen. Rawlings was a large and powerful man, full six feet tall, and often weighed 300 pounds. He had a great force of character; his energy and determination never failed him, and whatever he engaged in brought into action all his intellect and energy. He had received no education in his youth, no free school to attend in his boyhood. He was strictly a self made man. He had a large amount of natural ability, and while employed in his active business life, he sought any moment he could spare to educating himself; while he did not excel in book learning, he did as the judge of character of his fellow-man. He was always exceedingly courteous, dignified and polite to ladies. No man living had greater respect or admiration for them. His kindness to little children was proverbial, and, while he was eccentric and irritable, and would often give vent to a whirlwind of words, not couched in Bible language upon slight provocation, yet the storm was soon over and he would be as calm as a May morning, but under all this worry and excitement, his heart was tender and yielded in sympathy and relief to distress wherever he found it. But his eccentricities got him into many episodes; while they were not injurious to any one or himself, they were at times a source of annoyance to his friends and even to himself.

The anecdotes told of him and about him would fill a volume. He suffered periodically with the gout. A friend one day every injudiciously asked him if gout was painful. After exhausting himself on the absurdity of the question, he wound up by saying, "My God, my friend, put your big toe in a vise, have an able-bodied man turn the crank until it seems he can turn it no more, but have him turn it again. That, my God, my friend is gout."

He married his second wife, Miss Henrietta B. Calmes, daughter of Gen. Calmes, who lived near Hopkinsville, Ky., in 1829. She died in 1833, leaving two children — Florida, who became the wife of Dr. N. R. Casey, and died in Mound City, August, 1878, and Carroll H. Rawlings, who never married, and died in Texas in 1877.

Gen. Rawlings was one of the three Internal Improvement Commissioners. In 1839, Col. Oakley, Gen. Rawlings, two of the Commissioners, in company with ex-Governor Reynolds, one of the Governor's agents, went to Europe to negotiate canal and improvement bonds, etc. Judge R. M. Young, also an agent of the Governor's, subsequently joined them in London, and while the internal improvement system of that day, as viewed at this date, was not the thing to do, for negotiating bonds and for whatever success the Commissioners had financially, was admitted to be due to Gen. Rawlings.

Among the many enterprises the General engaged in was that of steam boating. He owned at one time the side-wheel steamboat *Tuskina* that ran between Louisville and New Orleans. He made one or more trips as her Captain, and when she made a landing and when she backed from a landing was invariably accompanied with a storm of commands, which kept the pilot busy ringing the bells and the engineers working their engines and the passengers apprehensive she was on fire.

Gen. Rawlings moved from Shawneetown in 1840, purchasing a magnificent resident, surrounded by 200 acres of land, highly improved, four miles from Louisville, Ky. In 1832, he was appointed by Gov. Reynolds Major General of the State militia. In 1840, he married Miss Ann H. Simms, of Washington City. She died in 1849, without children. In 1846, he sold his country place and moved into Louisville. Gen. Rawlings never attached himself to any church, but was always ready and willing to aid in building churches, and for several years before hotels were built in Mound City, the ministers who visited the place found a welcome at his house. He read the Bible much, and was familiar with its teachings. He was baptized in the Catholic Church by Mother Angela, of the Holy Cross, a few hours before his death, which occurred January 11, 1863, aged seventy. Having an admiration for the State that had been his home for nearly forty years, had much to do in his location of Mound City in 1854.

The original plat of Mount City was made by William J. Spence, Surveyor of Pulaski county, for Gen. Moses M. Rawlings' property, April 1854. At that time, a log cabin stood on the banks of the river, and fifteen or twenty acres of land cleared was all the evidence of civilization to be seen. The General utilized the cabin as hotel, boarding house and residence. During rain-storms, it sheltered them, but when the days and nights were pleasant they staid and slept upon the Mound, on which had grown many locust trees, making a delightful shade, while the gentle south breeze from off the broad Ohio, from here to its mouth, only six miles away, made it a pleasant place of resort in the day time and delightful at night, and during the days and nights when the mosquitoes congregated, which they did in the early history of Mound City, the mound was about the only place of safety, or where you could stay and with any degree of confidence say your life was your own…

Gen. Rawlings built the first house in Mound City. It was a frame, two stories high, 25x100 feet. It was framed in Louisville, Ky., and brought to Mound City on steamboats; this was in 1854. He filled the lower story with dry goods, groceries, hardware, etc., and used the second story for a residence… The first brick house built in Mound City was F. M. Rawlings', in 1856; it was a fifty feet square two stories, with a thirty-foot ell — a very fine building, that succumbed to the great fire of 1879.

…[I]n June, 1856, a post office [at Mound City] was established, receiving two mails a day, with Gen. Rawlings Postmaster, a position he had to take for the want of any other available man to fill it. In 1858, Gen. Rawlings resigned, much to his relief, and equally so to the public. He kept the office in his storeroom. While his clerks were deputies and attended to the office, there were times when persons would call for their mail, when the clerks were out and the General alone. We are sure he never opened or distributed a mail, neither did he ever find a letter or paper for any one. When he made the effort to do so, he never knew where to look for them, and after considerable worry, he would discharge the applicant with "Who would write you a letter, anyhow?"[257]

— *History of Alexander, Pulaski and Union Counties, Illinois.*

---

[257] William Henry Perrin, ed. *History of Alexander, Union and Pulaski Counties, Illinois.* Chicago: O. L. Baskin & Co., Historical Publishers. 539-544. Dr. N. R. Casey, Rawlings' son-in-law, wrote the chapter that included Rawlings biography.

Dent Reid – 1905

DENT REID, dealer in general merchandise, Ridgway, Ill., was born near Saline Mines, in the county where he now lives, Sept. 14, 1860. He is a son of the Rev. Robert and Elizabeth (Campbell) Reid, both natives of Scotland, who came to America on the same ship, and were married some time after their arrival in this country. (See sketch of Rev. Robert Reid, elsewhere in this work.) Dent Reid is the fifth in a family of twelve children. He received a good common school education and up to the time he was twenty-five years of age lived at home with his parents.

On Feb. 18, 1885, he was married to Miss Laura Dossett, who was born near Cave in Rock, in Hardin county, where her parents, I. F. and Minerva Dossett, were old settlers. Before his marriage Mr. Reid had been engaged in farming, and he continued to follow that occupation afterward until 1890 when he opened a store at Saline Mines. The venture proved a successful one, and in 1894 he removed to Ridgway, where he enlarged his stock and soon became one of the successful merchants of the place. In his political affiliations Mr. Reid has followed in the footsteps of his honored father, who at one time was one of the only eight Republicans in Gallatin county. His success in business is largely due to that persevering disposition so characteristic of the Scotch people, which he possesses to a marked degree, and to his rugged honesty.

He is a member of Ridgway Lodge, No. 816, Free and Accepted Masons, and with his family belongs to the Cumberland Presbyterian church, in which he holds the office of elder. Mr. and Mrs. Reid's children are Robert Ila D. and Wiley, all at home with their parents.

— *Memoirs of the Lower Ohio Valley.*

Rev. Robert Reid – 1905

REV. ROBERT REID, a retired Presbyterian minister, living at Saline Mines, Ill., is a native of Scotland, having been born at Paisley, Nov. 6, 1822. His father, whose name was also Robert, was born in 1799. In early life he was for a time engaged in the manufacture of shawls for which Paisley is noted all over the world, but the greater part of his life he followed the occupation of mining. He married Ann Wiley and in 1839 they left Scotland for America. They first settled in Nova Scotia, where they lived until 1842, when they came to the United States. They lived in Pennsylvania until 1850, then removed to Maryland, where the father died and the widow came with her family soon afterward to Gallatin county, Ill. Of their ten children Anna and the subject of this sketch, both living at Saline Mines, are the only survivors.

Rev. Robert Reid received the greater part of his schooling in the common schools of his native land. At the age of twenty-eight he married Elizabeth Campbell, a native of Scotland, who came over on the same ship with him in 1839, being at that time but eight years of age, and afterward removing to Maryland about the same time he did. They began their wedded life at Minersville, Pa., where he was employed in the mines. Later they removed to Maryland, and in 1854 to Gallatin county. Mr. Reid took charge of the mines for the Saline Coal Company, and settled at Saline Mines, in which locality he has ever since lived. He continued as superintendent of the mines until 1859, when he engaged in mercantile pursuits. This business he carried on for about fifteen years, though he was also interested in mining operations most of the time, either in connection with the Saline Coal

Company or the Martha Iron and Furnace Company, of Gallatin and Hardin counties. He is still associated with the Saline Coal Company. In addition to his interests in the mines he owns about 160 acres of land near Saline Mines, which for years he has managed.

In 1856 he took up the work of the ministry, having been an elder in the Presbyterian church for some time previously, and since 1884 he has devoted most of his time to the church, preaching at Equality, Harrisburg, Saline Mines and for other churches. Mr. Reid is a Republican in politics, and in his earlier years took an active interest in public affairs. He has served as justice of the peace and has been identified with many movements for the upbuilding of the community in which he lives. He and his wife had the following children: Agnes, now Mrs. Hamilton, of Victor, Col.; Wiley, living at Carbondale, Ill.; Walter, who lives at Danville in the same state; George, deceased; Dent (see sketch); Thomas, now in Oklahoma; Bessie, at home; May (deceased) ; Millie, now Mrs. Wiederhold, of Gallatin county; Clara, at home; William (deceased); Robert (deceased).[258] The mother of these children died in January, 1894. In the spring of 1904 Mr. Reid met with an accident that disabled him to such an extent that he has been compelled to forego the active work of the ministry, though he still preaches at times. He has a large circle of acquaintances, with all of whom he is popular, and who esteem him for his many good qualities of both mind and heart.

— *Memoirs of the Lower Ohio Valley.*

James August Rensmann – 1887

JAMES AUGUST RENSMANN, rector of St. Joseph's Church, Ridgway, was born in Westphalia, Germany, June 8, 1845. Reared and educated in his native land, he passed through the regular college course at Essen, Rheinland, and absolved his philosophical and theological studies at the University of Muenster, Westphalia, whereupon he was ordained a priest in 1872. He then came in the fall to Mattoon, Ill., and took charge of the church, then at Vandalia, and, in 1874, came to Shawneetown where he labored in the church and school five years, and also established Saint Joseph's. He came to Ridgway in 1879, and has since succeeded in building up a large and wealthy congregation. There is also a parochial school in operation, in which, since 1884, he has been assisted by two Sisters.

— *History of Gallatin, Saline, Hamilton, Franklin and Williamson Counties, Illinois.*

Edward Rice – 1883

EDWARD RICE, son of Archibald B. and Nancy M. Rice, was born June 26, 1845. his great-grandfather, Ebenezer Rice, was a native of Wales, and was a missionary to the Chickasaw Indians near Memphis in 1799. He put his goods on a flat-oat at the head of the Ohio and floated down that river and the Mississippi to his destination. His grandfather, Joel Rice, was born in Vermont; the first word he spoke was in the Indian language. He was in the Black Hawk War and went to California in 1848, during the gold excitement. He made

---

[258] The Illinois Statewide Marriage Index shows an Agnes H. Reid marrying a William H. H. Hamilton on July 3, 1873 in Gallatin County.

money and returned via New Orleans in 1850 to his home in White County, Ill. He named Sacramento, Ill., in honor of the Sacramento Valley.

Edward was reared on a farm and attended the public-schools. At breaking out of the late war he was undecided whether to enter the army or go to the High School. His father settled the matter by sending him to Hamilton College, McLeansboro. In 1868 he attended the Evansville Business College, where he graduated; then entered the dry-goods house of Martin & Rice, as bookkeeper, remaining with them three years. He then went to Omaha, Neb., and kept books for J. J. Brown and Bro. two years, when he returned to Roland, Ill., and was employed by Porter & Rice. In 1878 he came to Omaha, and engaged with his brother-in-law, Thomas Martin, in the dry-goods business, the firm name being Martin & Rice. He is a very energetic worker and a prominent political man in a quiet way. June 26, 1872, he married Grace G. Mount, of Tennessee. They have four children — Rollo, Estella Florence, Mabel Claire and Laura Edith.

— *History of White County, Illinois.*

Edward Rice – 1905

EDWARD RICE, grain dealer and miller of Ridgway, Ill., is a native of White county, that state, having been born on a farm near Enfield. When he was twelve years of age his parents removed to Sacramento, in the same county, where he completed the course in the common schools, after which he attended commercial college at Evansville, Ind., where he completed his education. When he was eighteen he commenced clerking in a store at Sacramento, which position he held for seven years. He then went to Enfield as a bookkeeper for two years, at the end of which time he was engaged as bookkeeper by a wholesale house at Omaha, Neb. After two years with this concern he returned to White county, and obtained a situation, as bookkeeper at Roland, but about a year later went to Omaha, Ill., as a partner of Thomas Martin in the grain business. This partnership lasted for seven years, or until 1886, when Mr. Rice sold out his interests in Omaha and removed to Ridgway as bookkeeper for W. A. Peeples. Six years later he again engaged in the grain business and has continued in that line ever since. In 1894 he built one of the nicest residences in the town, occupying one entire block.

Mr. Rice has been married twice. His first wife, to whom he was married in 1872, was Miss Grace J. Mount. Of their children, Grace F. and Clarence M. are deceased the others are Estella F., D. R., Mabel C., Laura E. and Edward H. His first wife died in 1888 and in 1889 he was married to Mrs. Laura Porter, widow of Capt. D. M. Porter and a sister to his first wife. Mr. Rice is a Republican in his political affiliations, is a prominent member of the Masonic lodge at Ridgway and a trustee in the Methodist Episcopal church.

— *Memoirs of the Lower Ohio Valley.*

George W. Rich – 1887

GEORGE W. RICH, farmer, was born in Alabama in 1839, and is one of eight children of William and Mary (Simms) Rich. The father, a native of Florida, died about 1850, about ninety years of age. He was married twice: first in his native state and after his wife's death he removed to Alabama, where he settled, and married the mother of our subject. The mother, a native of Alabama, was also married twice, her first husband being a Mr. Caudle. She died, about one hundred years old, in 1872. When seventeen our subject spent a year and a half in Indiana, and then came to Shawneetown, where he married, in 1860, Ellen, daughter of Samuel and Nancy Andrews, born in Gallatin County in 1841. Six of their children are living: Isabelle, George, Minnie and May (twins), Daisy and Lewis. Beginning as a tenant, in 1870, he bought his present improved farm of eighty acres, six miles from Shawneetown. Politically a Democrat, his first vote was for Douglas. Mrs. Rich was a member of the Baptist Church and died in 1876.

— *History of Gallatin, Saline, Hamilton, Franklin and Williamson Counties, Illinois.*

Albert G. Richeson – 1905

ALBERT G. RICHESON, proprietor of the Pioneer Store, one of the leading mercantile establishments of Shawneetown, Ill., is a native of Gallatin county. He can trace his ancestry on both sides back to old Virginia families, some of whom played important parts in establishing the independence of the United States. John Richeson, his grandfather, was a farmer in Amherst county, Va., and married Nancy A. Dickinson, whose father, David Dickinson, was a commissary for the Virginia troops during the Revolutionary war.

One of his sons was John D. Richeson, who was born in Amherst county, May 16, 1810. At the age of sixteen years he started out for himself. Making his way to Charlestown he hired out to some flatboatmen named Mays for $8 a month. That was on the first day of March, 1826. His first trip was down the Kanawha and Ohio rivers to Cincinnati, then a town of less than ten thousand inhabitants. He continued flatboating until the fall of 1832, when he returned to Virginia and for the next four years followed trading in live stock and slaves and looking after a farm. He was then engaged in contracting on some public work at Louisville for about a year. In 1837 he came to Shawneetown, where he secured contracts for paving the levee in front of the town, and for grading the Shawneetown & Alton railroad to Equality, a distance of eleven miles. Being favorably impressed with the future prospects of Shawneetown he engaged in the general merchandizing business in 1838, and conducted it on both a wholesale and retail basis until his death in 1893, a period of more than fifty years.

In 1839, he was married to Mrs. Judith M. Carroll, *née* Williamson, the widow of James Carroll, and to this marriage there were born three children: Albert G., Mary, wife of Judge McBane, and Eleanora, who married Judge J. D. Turner and died in 1900. Both parents were active workers in the Presbyterian church.

Albert G. Richeson received his education in the public schools and at Notre Dame, South Bend, Ind. Upon leaving college he engaged for about a year in conducting a saw and grist mill at Equality. He was then for a time in the stock trading business; was next in partnership with Henry Richeson in operating a saw mill at Cypress in Johnson county; after which he embarked in the hardware business at Shawneetown and continued in that line until 1887. For the next three years he farmed and traded in stock, and in 1890 formed a partnership with his father, under the name of J. D. Richeson Co., for general merchandizing. Upon the death of his father he succeeded to the business and is now the sole proprietor of one of the oldest and best known mercantile establishments in Gallatin county. In addition to his merchantile interests Mr. Richeson owns about 1,500 acres of land is extensively connected with the saw mill business about Shawneetown. He is a member of the Independent Order of Odd Fellows and Knights of Honor.

On April 15, 1875, he was married to Miss Mattie L., daughter of Andrew and Mary McCallen, of Shawneetown. Her father was at one time the law partner of Abraham Lincoln, and Mrs. Richeson has in her possession a great many keepsakes in the way of letters, etc., that have passed between her father and Mr. Lincoln. Mr. and Mrs. Richeson have had four children: May, Judith and Johnnie are deceased, and Helen is a student in school.[259]

— *Memoirs of the Lower Ohio Valley.*

John D. Richeson – 1876

JOHN D. RICHESON, Merchant, Shawneetown, son of John and Nancy N. Richeson, natives of Virginia, was born in Amherst County, Virginia, May 16, 1810. His grandfather, on his mother's side, was David Dickinson, of Virginia, who was Commissary for the troops of that colony during the Revolution; came west in 1826, located on the Ohio and Mississippi River, traded in Virginia and Louisville, Kentucky, and came to Shawneetown in 1837. He contracted for paving the riverbank in front of the city, and grading the Shawneetown & Alton Railroad bed to Equality — 11 miles. After several years in Kentucky, in farming and tanning business, he returned and, in 1843, established the mercantile business, which he still continues.

— *Illustrated Historical Atlas of the State of Illinois.*

John D. Richeson – 1887

JOHN D. RICHESON, merchant, Shawneetown, Ill., son of John and Nancy A. Richeson, natives of Virginia, was born on his father's farm, in Amherst County, Va., on the 16th of May 1810.[260] His grandfather on his mother's side was David Dickinson of Virginia, who was commissary for the troops of that colony during the Revolution. In the spring of 1826, boy-like and being desirous of making something for himself, Mr. Richeson started west, arriving at Charleston, W. Va., the first day of March, 1826, and hired to a flat-boatman by the name of Mays, at the wages of $8 per month, an started down the Kanawha into the Ohio River to Cincinnati, Ohio, which at that time was a place of less than 10,000 inhabitants. Thence he went South flat-boating, etc., until the fall of 1832, when he returned to Virginia, where he began farming and trading in stock and Negroes until 1836, when he

---

[259] All of Richeson's riches would soon be wasted in a few years. Helen, his only heir would later marry J. B. Holbrook, but it's her relationships with two of Southern Illinois' most notorious gangsters in the 1920s is how she's most remembered. Her flings as the 'Shawneetown Dame' included escapades with both Charlie Birger and Carl Shelton.

[260] The Illinois Statewide Marriage Index shows John D. Richeson marrying Mrs. Mary E. Dupler in Gallatin County on July 19, 1858. The biography of Charles E. Dupler lists Mary E. Kopp as the wife of Mr. Dupler's father, C. E. Dupler. The elder Dupler died in 1853. His widow and Mr. Richeson's later wife, died at Shawneetown on July 12, 1885.

went to Louisville and contracted on public works till 1837, when he contracted for paving the river bank in front of Shawneetown, and grading the Shawneetown & Alton Railroad to Equality, eleven miles west. Being well pleased with the outlook surrounding this place, in 1838 he went into the wholesale and retail mercantile business, which he has continued successfully ever since, now enjoying the fruits of a large and well established trade. Mr. Richeson is now in his seventy-eighth year, is in good health and is the first man on duty for business every morning.

— *History of Gallatin, Saline, Hamilton, Franklin and Williamson Counties, Illinois.*

Edgar Rider – 1905

EDGAR RIDER, a farmer living near Shawneetown, Ill., was born on June 3, 1839, in what is now Harrison county of West Virginia. At the age of twenty-one years he left his father's farm and went to Cincinnati, where he worked with an uncle in a blacksmith shop one winter, and in March, 1861, came to Gallatin county. During the spring and summer of that year and also a part of the following year he worked on a farm.

In the fall of 1862 he helped to organize the First Illinois heavy artillery, but as one hundred and fifty men were required and that number could not be easily obtained the organization was merged into the Fifty-sixth infantry. The officers who could not get positions in the infantry were released, Mr. Rider being one of the number. He then enlisted as a private in Company K, One Hundred and Thirty-first Illinois volunteer infantry. He was soon afterward made corporal and went through the entire war with that rank. His first engagement was at Chickasaw Bayou, after which he was at Arkansas Post, the first battle of Vicksburg, the siege of that place that followed, Spanish Fort, Fort Blakely, and was then in Texas until September, 1865, when he was discharged. After the siege of Vicksburg, where his regiment and the Twenty-ninth both suffered severe losses, the two were consolidated, afterward being known as the Twenty-ninth.

After the war he returned to Shawneetown and opened a retail meat market, which he conducted successfully for seventeen years. He was then engaged in buying and shipping stock for a while, after which he turned his attention to farming. In this line he has been successful, being the owner of 170 acres of good land which he cultivates according to the most approved methods. Mr. Rider is a Republican and while living in Shawneetown was a member of the board of aldermen for eight years. He also served nine years as road commissioner. He is a member of the Independent Order of Odd Fellows and the Grand Army of the Republic.

On May 10, 1867, he was married to Miss Isabelle O. Seeley, and their children are Emma, wife of William Rosolott; Oliver, John, Bertha, wife of Edward Slaton; Med; Jessie, wife of James Logsdon; Edith, who married Charles Martin and afterward died; June, the youngest, who died in early childhood, and one who died in infancy.

— *Memoirs of the Lower Ohio Valley.*

Thomas S. Ridgway – 1876

THOMAS S. RIDGWAY, was born on a farm in White County, Illinois, August 30, 1829, as the son of John Ridgway. In 1832, Mr. Ridgway, Sr., removed to Shawneetown with his family but died a short time after. Thomas Ridgway worked in Mr. McCracken's printing office for some time, meanwhile studying hard. In 1839, he became a store boy at E. H. Gatewood's; in 1845, a junior partner of O. Pool & Co. In 1850, the firm changed to Peeples & Ridgway, and their business amounted often to a million dollars annually. The mercantile business of Peeples & Ridgway closed in 1865, and they opened the First National Bank of Shawneetown. Mr. Ridgway was elected state treasurer in 1874, and the wealth of his bondsmen, in total, was five million dollars, a sure testimony to his honesty and business talents.

— *Illustrated Historical Atlas of the State of Illinois.*

Hon. Thomas S. Ridgway – 1887

HON. THOMAS S. RIDGWAY was born August 30, 1826, on a farm in White county, Ill. His father, Hon. John Ridgway, was born in New Jersey, and was a descendant of a Quaker family. In his earlier days he was engaged in mercantile life in Philadelphia, but in 1818, yielding to the imaginary fascinations of a life in the western wilds, he started for Illinois with his family, household goods and merchandise, traveling to Pittsburgh in Conestoga wagons, and to Shawneetown in a keelboat. From Shawneetown to Carmi, then in Gallatin County he traveled again by wagon and having arrived at his destination he immediately engaged in merchandising and trading. His wife, who previous to marriage was Miss Rebecca B. Olden, died soon after reaching Illinois, and in 1822 Mr. Ridgway was married to Miss Mary Frazier Grant, daughter of John Grant. The Grant family was originally Scotch Presbyterians, and after immigrating to the United States resided for a time in Philadelphia. About 1818 they likewise moved to White County, Ill. By this marriage with Miss Grant, Mr. Ridgway had six children: Sarah, Harriet, John G., Thomas S., Eliza and George A.

In 1832 Mr. Ridgway moved to Shawneetown, where his second wife soon afterward died, firm in the religious convictions of her entire life, and John Ridgway, who had served in the Legislature when it convened at Vandalia, did not long survive his wife, and thus, Thomas S., the subject of this sketch, was left without the loving, guiding hand of either or father or mother. But he had been so thoroughly instructed an inculcated with the principles of integrity and with reverence for Christianity, which had always been the guiding star of his parents' lives that his character was formed, and he at once began a life of usefulness and honor.

At the age of twelve he earned his first dollar in the printing office of John S. McCracken of Shawneetown. In 1839 he entered the dry goods establishment of Col. E. H. Gatewood as store boy, remaining there until 1843. In this year he made his first trip east to Philadelphia to buy a stock of goods, and while there paid a visit to this grandfather, John Ridgway, Sr., then over ninety years of age. In 1845 he became the junior member of the firm of O. Pool & Co. (Orval Pool, John McKee Peeples and himself). In 1850 Mr. Pool retired from the firm and Messrs. Peeples & Ridgway succeeded to the business. The house of Peeples & Ridgway became the leading house in southern Illinois, their sales amounting to between $200,000 and $300,000 per year. It was no uncommon thing for them to supply farms and other living from fifty to seventy-five miles away. They were also heavy purchasers of tobacco, sometimes to the extent of half a million dollars in a year; and of pork, grain and other products which they shipped to New Orleans, New York and Europe. In 1865 they closed up their business, and organized the First National Bank of Shawneetown.

In December 1867, Mr. Ridgway was made president of the Springfield & Illinois Southeastern Railway Company, and owing largely to his capacity and energy, the railway was completed in an incredibly short space of time from Shawneetown to Beardstown, a distance of 226 miles. He retired from the presidency of this company in 1874, much poorer in purse but much richer in experience. In 1874 he was elected state treasurer of Illinois, being the only candidate on the republican ticket that was successful. He assumed the duties of the office January 13, 1875, and served his term with credit to himself and the state. In 1874 he became president of the board of trustees of the Southern Illinois Normal University at Carbondale, and has ever since held that position. The first building erected for the use of this institution burned down, and in the spring of 1887, an elegant new building of brick an stone, 115 x 215 feet in size, an three stories high, was completed and dedicated, Mr. Ridgway making the principal address on that occasion. The building cost $250,000, and is one of the finest structures devoted to educational uses in the United States. It is in connection with this institution that Mr. Ridgway had rendered his most important service to mankind.

Mr. Ridgway was married September 20, 1849, to Miss Jane Docker, daughter of W. A. Docker, an early merchant of Shawneetown. He is a man of strong religious convictions, has been a member of the Presbyterian Church since 1858, and a ruling elder since 1860. He is also superintendent of the Sunday-school, and the superlatively important causes of religion and education have always found in him an earnest and able supporter and champion.

— *History of Gallatin, Saline, Hamilton, Franklin and Williamson Counties, Illinois.*

Blueford Robinett – 1905

BLUEFORD ROBINETT, a retired farmer, of Shawneetown, Ill., was born in that County, not far from Ford's Ferry, Jan. 18, 1833. His father, Joseph Robinett, was a native of Bourbon County, Ky., where he was born in 1785. In 1819 he came with his wife and four children to Gallatin County, Ill., making the journey by wagon, entered 280 acres of government land, for which he paid $1.25 an acre. On this land Mr. Robinett built a hewed log house of two rooms, and there passed the remainder of his life as a farmer. This farm is the one where the subject of this sketch was born. Joseph Robinett was twice married, His first wife was a Miss Hughes; by whom he had four children, all born in Kentucky. John was a soldier in the Black Hawk War; Irene married John Potts: Phoebe married Joseph Potts, and Matilda married James Barlow. The second wife was Clarissa Nighswonger, a native of Ohio, who came down the Ohio, river with her brother in a flatboat, about 1824, and settled in; Gallatin County. To this marriage there were born the following children: James, who died at the age of 78 years; Louisiana, who married Todd Dunn and died at the age of 40; Allen, who died when he was about 30 years-old; Cynthia A., who married Jeremiah Potts and died at the age of 40; Blueford, the subject of this sketch; Rachel, now living in Gallatin

County as the widow of Henry Rose; Joseph a farmer of Gallatin County, and Alfred, who died when but nine years of age. The mother of these children died at the age of 84 years and the father when he was about 66.

Blueford Robinett was about 19 years of age at the time of his father's death and he was called on to take charge of the farm and conduct it for his mother. He continued to live on the farm until 1892, when he removed to Shawneetown. Although in his boyhood be was denied the privilege of attending school as much as most of the boys of the present generation enjoy, he has succeeded in life. At one time he owned over 1,000 acres of land. Much of this has been divided among his children, but he is still the owner of a fine farm of 200 acres. In politics Mr. Robinett has always been a Democrat, one of the kind who always have the courage of their convictions and ready to defend their principles, but he has never been a seeker for public office.

In 1853 he was married to Miss Eliza J. Rose and to this union were born the following children: Charlotte, wife of John C. Brinkley, of Shawneetown; Lucy, wife of J. W. Rogers, a well known farmer of Gallatin County; Cynthia, who died at the age of six years; Minerva, wife of J. B. Hellington, a stock dealer of Harrisburg, Ill., and John, who died at the age of 24 years. The mother of these children died a few years ago, and since that time Mr. Robinett has made his home in Shawneetown.

— Memoirs of the Lower Ohio Valley.

George W. Robinson – 1883

GEORGE W. ROBINSON is a son of Enos and Polly Ann (Perkins) Robinson. His mother was a daughter of Stephen and Margaret Perkins. Both mother and daughter were well known throughout this settlement, the mother being a woman of strong mind, kind and generous heart, philanthropic, a devout Methodist and a skillful nurse. Stories are told of her skill as a rider and her unselfishness in riding miles to attend to cases. Her daughter was no doctress but was a woman of marked beauty. The husband and father came from Christian County, Ky., to Gallatin County, at an early day, and settled on what is now known as the Perkins farm. His father, Enos Robinson, was a native of Pennsylvania and came to this county when 19 with his mother and stepfather. He married Polly Ann Perkins. They had four children — Margaret (deceased), Delilah A. (deceased), Lucian M. and George W. He married for his second wife, Mrs. Martha Haney. They had no children. His third wife was Rebecca, daughter of James Patterson, of Clermont County, Ohio. Their children were Martha J. (Mrs. James Luther) and Etta (deceased). Mr. Robinson moved to Ohio about 1850. He married his fourth wife, Elizabeth Haines, there. They had three children. Mr. Robinson died in 1879.

George W. married Mrs. Sarah (Buchanan) Prichard, a native of East Tennessee, and a daughter of Elihu and Elizabeth (Parks) Buchanan. Her parents moved to Indiana when she was young. They had a family of 10 children, the most of whom grew to man and womanhood near Mount Vernon.

Mr. Robinson is at present keeping a hotel. The stranger and traveler is always hospitably received and entertained. He is also quite extensively engaged in farming, having about 300 acres, with 200 under cultivation.

— History of White County, Illinois.

Hon. Carl Roedel – 1887

HON. CARL ROEDEL, attorney at law, and mayor of Shawneetown, was born in Van Wert County, Ohio, and son of Jacob and Barbara Roedel, natives of Germany and born in 1806 and 1809 respectively, and their deaths occurring likewise in 1867 and 1866. The father, a potash manufacturer, came to America about 1838, and bought eighty acres of the site of Cleveland, Ohio. About 1840, he married and settled in Van Wert County, and in 1848 moved to Decatur, In., where he passed his life.

Our subject, the eldest of four children, began at eleven years of age working for his father in the potash factory, so continuing until the age of sixteen. His education was received in Vermillion Institute, Ohio, by an attendance of three years. In 1865 he was elected superintendent of the Mount Carmel (Illinois) schools, in which position he served three years with flattering success, and then for one year had charge of the Shawneetown schools. During the last two of these years he was studying law, and in 1871, was admitted, under the examination of Congressman Townsend.

He at once began practice with marked success, and for the past fifteen years he has had a most lucrative practice, and has been one of the leading lawyers of the county, especially able in civil and chancery law. In 1884 he became a partner with Eugene R. Sission in the firm of Roedel & Sission.

In 1869 he married Fannie Koser, of Mount Carmel, Ill. Their children are Ida M., Rose, William K., Sarah, Emma, Charles, Lillie and Jacob. He is a Republican, and first voted for Lincoln. Since 1885 he has been mayor. For six years past he has been president of the school board. He is an Odd Fellow, Knight of Honor and has been an elder in the Presbyterian Church for ten years. His wife also is a Presbyterian, and both are highly esteemed people.

— *History of Gallatin, Saline, Hamilton, Franklin and Williamson Counties, Illinois.*

Carl Roedel – 1912

CARL ROEDEL. Unless the modern lawyer is a man of sound judgment, possessed of a liberal education and stern training, combined with a keen insight of human nature, there is not much chance of his meeting with success. The reason for this lies in the spirit of the age, with all its complexities. Modern jurisprudence has become more and more intricate because of new conditions and laws and in their interpretation. Years of experience, constant study and natural inclination are superinduced upon a careful training in the case of Carl Roedel, whose career as an attorney-at-law has been marked with many successful out comes for his clients. His heart is in his work and he brings to it an enthusiasm and belief in its importance which would probably result in his being raised to the bench were it not that his political convictions have made him a member of the party now in the minority in his section of Illinois. Mr. Roedel, whose field of practice is the city of Shawneetown, Gallatin county, was born in Van Wert county. Ohio. September 30, 1842, and grew to manhood at Decatur, the county seat of Adams county, Indiana, whence his parents had removed when he was a child.

Mr. Roedel was educated in Vermilion Institute at Hayesville, Ohio, taught school awhile in Indiana, and for a period of three years was principal of the schools of Mt. Carmel, Illinois. In 1868 he came to Shawneetown as principal of its schools for one year, and even at that time the attendance was about what it is today, although the school buildings were poor and the system had not advanced to its present efficiency. Miss Joanna Golden, who was one of his assistants, has taught school here for more than half a century and is still engaged in the profession here. Later Mr. Roedel taught at Grayville, in the meantime assiduously studying law, and in 1871 he was admitted to practice, locating in Shawneetown the year following.

Since that time he has devoted himself unreservedly to his profession and has been very successful in his chosen line, that of civil practice. He has served as counsel in almost every case of any importance in Gallatin county during this time, and several with which he has been connected have attracted widespread attention, especially the famous "Riverside Tax Title Case," involving title to the widely-known Riverside Hotel, the only case on record that has had three rehearings before the supreme court. The former state treasurer Ridgway and the then member of congress Townshend were the leading spirits in this case, which gave opportunity to fight out long existing personal, political and business animosities, the questions involved interesting the profession generally. For some five or six years Mr. Roedel's son, Charles K., a graduate in law from Wesleyan College at Bloomington, Illinois, has been his partner. An earnest Republican, casting his first vote in 1864 for President Lincoln, Mr. Roedel has been an active and earnest worker for his party, the campaign of 1896 especially demanding his efforts on the rostrum to counteract the Free Silver movement. He stands high in his profession, many of the members of which would be pleased to see him occupy a seat on the circuit bench, but an overwhelming Democratic district leaves little chance for a Republican to be elected.

Mr. Roedel was married at Mt. Carmel, Illinois, to Miss Sarah Frances Koser, and they have reared a family of seven children. He is an elder in the Presbyterian church and has been active and liberal in his support of religious and charitable movements, especially in the Sunday-school, of which he has been the head for many years. Mr. Roedel belongs to the old school of lawyers, although progressive in his methods and ideas, and is of gracious and genial personality and courteous bearing. Widely acquainted throughout Gallatin county, he has hosts of friends both in and out of his profession, regardless of political views, and is justly regarded as one of this section's most eminent attorneys.

— *History of Southern Illinois.*

John W. Rogers – 1905

JOHN W. ROGERS, farmer and stock raiser near Junction City, Ill., was born near Harrisburg Saline county, of that state, Jan. 31, 1851. His father was horn at Chattanooga, Tenn., in 1807. In 1845 be removed to Saline county and bought a farm not far from the present Eagle post office and lived there until the fall of 1851, when he came to Gallatin county and bought 160 acres adjoining the farm on which John W. now lives. Only a few acres were cleared at that time, but he improved the farm and brought most of it under cultivation before his death, which occurred on Jan. 18, 1889. He was twice married. Before leaving Tennessee he was married to Elizabeth Booten, and two daughters, Catherine and Polly, both now deceased, were born to that union. His wife died after coming to Illinois and he was married to Mrs. Eliza A. Colbert, widow of Allen Colbert and a daughter of Joseph Logsdon, whose sketch appears elsewhere. His second wife survived him, dying Feb. 19, 1903, at the age of eighty years. She had two children by her first husband Margaret, now the wife of Thornton Bennett, of Denver, Col., and Allen, who died in infancy.

John W. Rogers is the eldest of a family of four children: William T. died June 28, 1897; Matilda is the widow of George Borroughs of Shawneetown; and Marinda is the wife of James White of Gallatin county. The parents of these children were both members of the Presbyterian church.

John W. Rogers received his education in the district schools near his father's home, and spent one year in the schools of Ewing, Franklin county. At the age of twenty he commenced teaching and followed that occupation for nine years, also assuming the management of his father's farm after he had reached the age of twenty-two years. On Jan. 25, 1880, he was united in marriage to Miss Lucy, daughter of Bluford and Amanda J. (Rose) Robinett, and since then has devoted the greater part of his time to farming. He owns in all 600 acres, 550 of which are under cultivation. One of his farms is that formerly belonging to his father, and which adjoins the one on which he lives. All the improvements have been made since the land came into his possession. In recent years he has given considerable attention to the breeding of fine horses, Polled Angus and Hereford cattle, and he is generally regarded as one of the most intelligent and progressive farmers in his neighborhood.

Mr. Rogers is a Democrat and for eight years held the office of justice of the peace. He and his wife are both members of the Presbyterian church, in which he holds the position of deacon. The church to which they belong stands on his farm. Mr. and Mrs. Rogers have had ten children. Bluford was drowned when he was four years of age; three died in infancy; Daisy is the wife of Casper Fink, of Equality; Joseph, John, Virgil, James and Tessie are at home with their parents.

— Memoirs of the Lower Ohio Valley.

Robert Monroe Rudolph – 1905

ROBERT MONROE RUDOLPH, a prominent grain dealer and president of the town board of Omaha, Ill., is of German lineage. The origin of the family in this country is traced back to one Peter Rudolph, who came from the Fatherland just before the Revolutionary war and settled in North Carolina. When the contest for independence was commenced he cast in his lot with the patriots and was murdered by some of his Tory neighbors. About the year 1800 one of his descendants, Joseph Rudolph left North Carolina and located near Clarksville, Tenn. There he followed farming until 1823, when he removed with his family to Illinois and settled in White county, where he continued to farm until his death about 1855. He was considered a man of more than average intelligence and was an influential citizen in his community.

Before leaving North Carolina he was married to Miss Rachel Lowe, to which union eleven children were born; Peter, David, Margaret, Elizabeth, John, Phoebe, Jane, Andrew, Robert, Frederick and Sarah. All are now deceased.

Frederick Lowe Rudolph, the tenth child of the family, was born at Clarksville in 1821, and was therefore but two years old when his parents located on a farm in White county, a few miles northeast of Carmi. There he grew to manhood, received a good common school education and passed his entire life on a farm a few miles from his father's old homestead, dying in 1889. Farming and stock raising was his occupation and he was looked upon as a model farmer and good business man. At the commencement of the Civil war he enlisted in Company K, Eighty-seventh Illinois infantry, and was elected captain of the company; but the serious illness of his wife compelled him to resign his commission. He was married about 1844 to Elizabeth Graham, a native of White county, and they had the following children: Sarepta, George, Robert, Ella, one who died in infancy, Daniel, Benjamin, Harlan, Thompson and Jacob. Sarepta, George and Harlan are deceased; Robert is the subject of this sketch; Ella is the wife of Horace Cleveland and lives at Ridgway, Ill.; Daniel lives on a farm in White county; Thompson is postmaster at Thomaston, Ga., and Jacob is a merchant and grain dealer at Crossville, Ill. The parents died within a week of each other in 1899.

Robert M. Rudolph, the oldest living child of Frederick L. and Elizabeth Rudolph, was born in White county, Sept. 4, 1849, and there grew to manhood, receiving a good common school education in the public schools. Upon arriving at his majority he became a farmer and followed that occupation for about ten years, after which he was for five years engaged in the manufacture of brick and tile at Crossville. In 1885 he removed to Gallatin county, where he engaged in farming and dealing in grain at Omaha until 1889, since which time he has given all his attention to the grain business. While living in White county he was elected to various local offices, and for some time has held the position of president of the Omaha town board. For ten years he taught school during the winter months. Mr. Rudolph is a member of the Free and Accepted Masons and the Independent Order of Odd Fellows, and both himself and wife belong to the Methodist Episcopal church.

He was married in 1870 to Miss Anna Dickens, a native of White county, Ill., and to this union there have been born ten children. Charles Dickens died at the age of seventeen years; Frederick L. and Harold L. both live at Crossville; Amy is the wife of Otis Bruce, of Gallatin county; Nellie is the wife of Thomas Bruce, of Harrisburg, Ill.; Mark is at Los Angeles, Cal.; Robert M., Jr., Jessie, Laura and Hubert are at home.

— *Memoirs of the Lower Ohio Valley.*

Frank N. Sanders – 1905

FRANK N. SANDERS, a well-to-do and popular farmer, living near Cottonwood, Ill., was born in the vicinity where he now resides Feb. 15, 1850. He received his education in the common schools, married Jemima McGhee, daughter of D. W. and Polly McGhee, who were natives of Tennessee. At the time of his marriage Mr. Sanders was only about twenty years of age. They began their married life on the old home place, but three years later he bought a sixty-acre tract where he now lives, only about six or seven acres being under cultivation, built a hewed log house, and removed to his new home. Since then he has prospered by his industry, owning at the present time about 140 acres, all of which is under cultivation, and has a modern house, together with other good improvements on his farm. He carries on a general farming business and devotes considerable time and attention to stock raising. Mr. Sanders is one of the leading Democrats in his locality and has held some of the minor offices in the township. For several generations his ancestors have been affiliated with the Democratic party.

The following named children have been born to Mr. and Mrs. Sanders: Lowry A., deceased; William S., a teacher, and lives at home with his parents; Hezekiah, a teacher in White county; Evolia J., deceased; Carrie B., now Mrs. Holland, living near Cottonwood; Lillie R., wife of a Mr. McDonald, of Arkansas; Ratie May, now Mrs. Clark, living in

Missouri; Lulu, Annie, Roscoe and Luther are at home.[261] Ever since they were fifteen years of age Mr. Sanders and his wife have been members of the Cumberland Presbyterian church and interested in promoting its good works.

— *Memoirs of the Lower Ohio Valley.*

William J. Sanders – 1905

WILLIAM J. SANDERS, farmer and stock raiser, living two miles southwest of Cottonwood, Ill., was born Feb. 11, 1850, on the exact spot where his house now stands. His great-grandfather was a native of England, who came to this country before the Revolutionary war and settled in North Carolina, where he reared a large family. He and his son James, the grandfather of the subject of this sketch, both served in the war of 1812. James Sanders married in North Carolina and soon afterward removed to Tennessee, where he followed farming and stock raising until 1821, when he brought his family to Gallatin county, Ill., and entered government land, not far from the site of the present town of Cottonwood, upon which he lived until his death at the age of eighty-four years.

One of his sons was Eli Sanders, who was born on Christmas day in 1810. He came with his parents to Illinois and continued to live with them until 1836, when he married Nancy J. McGill, a native of Tennessee, and they began their married life on the farm where William J. Sanders now lives. Eli Sanders was the first to enter land having a black soil. He became a very successful farmer and at one time was one of the largest land owners in the vicinity of Cottonwood. Then he made a venture in merchandizing that proved disastrous, bringing him to the verge of bankruptcy. He died on Oct. 29, 1884, his wife having passed to her last rest on Sept. 2, 1876. During their lives they were active in church work and were known far and wide for their charity and hospitality. They had twelve children. Those living are Mary Ann, widow of David Rogers; Margaret J., now Mrs. Hale of Cottonwood; Juda, now Mrs. Millspaugh; Frank N. and William J.

William J. Sanders received his education in the public schools and lived at home until he was thirty-two years old. He was married at the age of twenty-two to Miss Ann, daughter of Miro and Jemima Harrington, and a native of Gallatin county. They commenced housekeeping on the old home place, where they have lived ever since. Mr. Sanders is one of the foremost farmers in his neighborhood, and takes an active interest in public affairs. He makes a specialty of Poland-China hogs and Jersey and Hereford cattle. His farm consists of 200 acres, all under cultivation and well improved, the new improvements having been made by him to take the place of the old buildings erected by his father some years before. He and his wife are both members of the Cumberland Presbyterian church, in which he has been an elder for twenty-five years. Their children are Stella, now Mrs. Holland, living in the neighborhood; Claudie, married and living on the home place; Vernon and Cyrus, who are still at home.

— *Memoirs of the Lower Ohio Valley.*

---

[261] The Illinois Statewide Marriage Index shows Carrie Bell Sanders marrying S. A. Holland on Feb. 11, 1900, and Lillie R. Sanders marrying George L. McDonald six months later on Aug. 12, 1900. Both marriages took place in Gallatin County.

Henry G. Sanks – 1905

HENRY G. SANKS, of Shawneetown, Ill., clerk of the court of Gallatin County, is a native of Indiana, having been born near Lawrenceburg in Dearborn County, May 7, 1851. His grandfather, Joshua Sanks, was in early life a farmer near Baltimore, Md. From there he removed to Virginia and later to Indiana, locating near Lawrenceburg, where he lived to the age of 89 years. He was married three times and reared a large family of children.

George D. Sanks, the father of Henry G., was born near Winchester, Va., Sept. 2, 1813. After his parents removed to Indiana he became interested in flat-boating on the Ohio and Mississippi rivers and followed that occupation for a number of years. About 1849 he was married to Mary Evans, a native of Dearborn County, and they went to housekeeping at Aurora, in that county, where he engaged in the manufacture of brick. Mary Evans was a daughter of Samuel Evans, who was born in the city of Philadelphia, Pa., Feb. 7, 1781, and removed to Dearborn County, Ind., in 1807, where he lived the rest of his life. His father was born in Wales, but came to American some time between 1720 and 1750. They were both ship carpenters and the subject of this sketch now has in his possession a try-square that formerly belonged to one of them.

In 1853 George D. Sanks took his family and their effects aboard a flatboat and floated down the river to Shawneetown. Nine miles west of the town he purchased a farm and followed agricultural pursuits the remainder of his life. His wife died in 1873 and he afterward married Nancy J. Leighliter, who is now also deceased. By his first wife his children were Henry G., the subject of this sketch; Tamson V., Sarah E., and Martha E., all deceased. By his second wife he had four children: Susanna V., now Mrs. Turner, of Danville, Ill.; David R. and George D., who now live on the old home place; and Mary, now Mrs. Riley, of Bowling Green, Ky. He died in 1894.

Henry G. Sanks was educated in the common schools and lived with his parents until his marriage, when he engaged in farming near Ridgway for one year, after which he removed to Shawneetown, but after living there a while returned to the farm and lived there until 1883. He then removed to Ridgway and lived there until 1890, when he was elected sheriff of Gallatin County and again took up his residence in Shawneetown. After serving four years as sheriff he was elected county treasurer and held that office for four years. He was then appointed deputy clerk and continued in that position until 1902, when he was elected clerk, which office he now holds.

Mr. Sanks probably inherited his love for political affairs from his father, who was active in politics the greater part of his life. He is now chairman of the Democratic central committee of Gallatin County, and as a political organizer has few equals in Southern Illinois. He is a good mixer and his genial disposition wins friends for him even among his political opponents. In a knowledge of county affairs he is well qualified to transact any of the official business of any office, his long connection with the different offices he has held rendering him thoroughly familiar with the business. His wife was Miss Mary E. Lawler, a native of Gallatin county and a niece of Gen. M. K. Lawler. Of their five children three are living, George D., Margaret E. and Mary E., all at home with their parents. He is a member of the Catholic Church and is in every way one of the representative men of his county.

— *Memoirs of the Lower Ohio Valley.*

Willliam M. Satterley – 1905

WILLIAM M. SATTERLEY, a farmer and stock raiser, living about five miles from Shawneetown, Ill., is one of those men who begin life at the bottom of the ladder, and who, by industry, good judgment and correct habits, win for themselves places among the successful and reputable citizens of the community in which their lots may be cast. He was born in Monroe County, Mo., March 9, 1860, and there grew to manhood on a farm. Circumstances prevented him from securing a first-class education in school and he commenced life as a farm hand, studying in favorable moments those needful branches of a business education. For several years he continued to work on farms by the month, saving his money in the hope that some day he could own a farm of his own.

In 1878 he came to Gallatin County, Ill., where he worked for some time for various farmers. All of his old employers speak of him as a faithful and trustworthy man. In 1880 he was married to Miss Elma James, and in 1883 he located on the farm where he now lives. This farm consists of 160 acres, about one-half under cultivation and the rest in timber. All the improvements on the place have been made by Mr. Satterley since the farm came into his possession. He carries on a general farming business, studies how to secure the best results through the rotation of crops, etc., and devotes considerable time and attention to stock breeding. Politically he is a Democrat, and although he takes a keen interest in all those questions that affect the general welfare and is always ready to discharge his duty as a citizen, he is not what could be called an active politician. Mr. and Mrs. Satterley have had two children, Roy F. and Charles A., but both died in infancy.

— *Memoirs of the Lower Ohio Valley.*

F. H. Sellers – 1887

F. H. SELLERS,[262] civil and mining engineer, was born in Philadelphia in 1835, and is one of six children of George E. and Rachel B. Sellers. He was educated at Woodward College, Cincinnati, and came to Gallatin County in 1857, and engaged with the Saline Coal & Manufacturing Company, and two years after was employed in paper-making in Hardin County for five years. He then returned to Bowlesville, leased the mines, and operated them for six years, when he became their superintendent for eleven years. In 1875 he married. Mrs. A. L. Dennis, daughter of Frank and Lydia Smith, who was born in 1843 in Pennsylvania. In politics Mr. Sellers is a Republican, casting his first presidential vote for Fremont. His wife is a member of the Presbyterian Church.

His father, George E. Sellers, was married March 6, 1833, to Rachel B., daughter of Robert A. and Eleazer Parish, the mother's birth occurring in Philadelphia July 18, 1812. She died in Hardin County, Ill., September 11, 1860. She bore her husband these children: Frederick H., born February 26, 1834; Eleanor P., November 23, 1835, died August 21, 1855; Lucy, April 3, 1837, died September 21, 1860; Charles H., August 26, 1838, and two others, who died in infancy.

In politics the father is a Republican, and himself and children are members of the Swedenborg Church, while his wife is an Episcopalian. He has led an active and useful life. From 1834 to 1839 he was engaged in building locomotive engines, paper machinery, and

---

[262] The Illinois Statewide Marriage Index gives his name as Frederick H. Sellers.

machinery for the mints at Charlotte, N.C., Dahlonega, Ga., and New Orleans. In 1841, he removed to Cincinnati, and engaged in making lead pipes by pressure from fluid melted lead. With his brother and Josiah Tourease he erected the Globe Rolling & Wire Works. From 1847 to 1849 inclusive he was engaged in getting up his direct traction and forge hammer, and heavy grade locomotive works, and then accepted the presidency of the Saline Coal Company, and moved to the Saline Mines in 1858. In 1859 he removed to Sellers' Landing, in Hardin County, and was there engaged in the manufacture of paper from cane. He removed to Bowlesville about 1879, and is now principally engaged in archaeological researches among the prehistoric earthworks of southern Illinois.

— *History of Gallatin, Saline, Hamilton, Franklin and Williamson Counties, Illinois.*

Amaziah Morgan Sergeant – 1876

AMAZIAH MORGAN SERGEANT, Postmaster, Shawneetown was born in Rush County, Indiana, April 22, 1829; son of Thomas and Isavella Sergeant. Raised on a farm, he was educated at the common schools, and followed farming and school teaching until 1857, then contracting and building until 1864, when he removed to Clay County, Illinois and retired from business. In 1870, he was appointed to take the census of Clay County. In 1871 he was appointed United States Mail Agent, and continued in that capacity till October 1875. October 16, he was commissioned postmaster of Shawneetown, and confirmed by the Senate, January 7, 1876.

— *Illustrated Historical Atlas of the State of Illinois.*

J. P. Siddall – 1905

J. P. Siddall, tinner and dealer in hardware, Equality, Ill., is a grandson of William Siddall, a native of England, who came to Equality in his early manhood. Having learned the tinners' trade in his native land, he opened the first tin-shop and hardware store in Equality. The business he established has been in the family for three generations. Sometime after coming to America he married Martha Maltby, and to this union there were born five children: John M., now in Texas; William, in Iowa; Elizabeth, now a Mrs. Hine, living in Florida;[263] Joseph and Parmenas, deceased.[264]

Both parents lived to be very old. Parmenas Siddall, after obtaining a common school education, learned the trade with his father, and upon the latter's death succeeded to the business, which he conducted through life. He married Johanna A. Probasco, whose acquaintance he formed while she was on a visit to friends in Equality. They had three children, all living. Florence is now a Mrs. Friend, living in Missouri; Etta is a Mrs. McDonald, of Texas; and the son is the subject of this sketch. Parmenas Siddall was an

---

[263] The Illinois Statewide Marriage Index shows Elizabeth A. Siddall marrying Miller J. Hine in Gallatin County on Feb. 16, 1864.

[264] Parmenas Siddall was likely named for Parmenas Redman who, according to the Illinois Statewide Marriage Index, married Mary Siddall in Gallatin County on Feb. 14, 1822. It's not certain how Mary is related to J. P. Siddall.

active Democrat in his day, and both himself and wife were devout Presbyterians. He gave the lot upon which the Presbyterian church of Equality stands, and always took an active part in church work. He died in 1885 and his wife in 1889.

J. P. Siddall was born Aug. 20, 1869. He grew to manhood in Equality, received a good practical education in the public schools of the town and after leaving school became associated with his father in business. Since the death of his father he has continued the business, which was founded by his grandfather three-quarters of a century ago. Mr. Siddall takes an active part in political affairs and is now local committeeman of the county central committee. He has served three terms as assessor, one term as village treasurer, and two terms on the school board. He is a member and trustee of the Odd Fellows Lodge, No. 19; a member of Lodge No. 581, Daughters of Rebekah, and of Lodge No. 381, Court of Honor. In Odd Fellowship he has been through the chairs and is now grand representative.

He was married June 10, 1896, to Miss Emma, daughter of Mr. and Mrs. William F. Yost, of Equality, and they have two children, Halton and Kelly, both at home. The family occupies one of the coziest homes in Equality and are members of the Presbyterian church, in which Mr. Siddall is a deacon and trustee.

— *Memoirs of the Lower Ohio Valley.*

Amos L. Siebman – 1905

AMOS L. SIEBMAN, one of the most progressive farmers in the neighborhood of Ridgway, Ill., is of Pennsylvania Dutch ancestry, his parents, William and Rachel (Pisal) Siebman, both being natives of the Keystone state and of German lineage. William Siebman was born about the year 1810, and while still a young man learned the trade of shoemaker, which he followed for several years in Pennsylvania after his marriage. He then went to Cincinnati, O., where he worked at his trade until about 1848, when he came with his family to Gallatin County, Ill., and settled near Equality. There he took up farming for a livelihood, adding carpentering some time later, and worked at these occupations the rest of his life. He died at the age of 55 years and his wife at the age of 62. They had eight children, three of whom are still living. Sarah is now Mrs. Fox, of Shawneetown; Amos is the subject of this sketch, and Theodore lives with his brother.

Amos L. Siebman was born May 5, 1852, on what is known as the Dan Woods farm near Equality, in the same County where he now lives. As a boy he attended the common schools and spent much of his spare time in study at home, a habit he kept up even after reaching manhood. In 1874 he was married to Miss Philomine Brazier, and began life for himself on the place where he now lives. Mr. Siebman has two farms: one of 280 acres, most of which is under cultivation, and the other of 82 acres, part of which lies within the corporate limits of Ridgway. His larger farm was nearly all wild land when it came into his possession, and has been brought to its present improved state by his own industry and good management. Mr. Siebman believes in education, and for eleven years was a member of the school board. Politically he is a Democrat, and in religious matters is a consistent member of the Catholic Church. Four children have been born to him and his wife, all of whom are living. Rachel is a Mrs. Luckett, of Ridgway; Emma is a Mrs. Beatty and Mary a Mrs. McCormick, both living in that vicinity, and Walter is at home with his parents.

— *Memoirs of the Lower Ohio Valley.*

Virginius W. Smith – 1912

VIRGINIUS W. SMITH. The man who buys land today in Gallatin county has no idea of the obstacles which confronted the ones who began developing this property. Now fertile fields yield banner crops, the ground once covered with mighty forest trees smiles beneath cultivation, and where worthless swamps gathered green slime and sent forth pestilential fevers, the rich soil eagerly responds to the modern methods of the farmer. All this was not attained without endless hard work through all seasons. When summer crops did not require effort the fences had to be repaired, there were new buildings to be erected, and other improvements to be inaugurated. No man who has brought out success from his years of endeavor ever attained it unless he was ready and willing to make any kind of sacrifice of inclination or strength to bring it about, and one who has through his efforts in this way become more than ordinarily prosperous and has developed some of the best land of Gallatin county is Virginius W. Smith, of Ridgway, Illinois, who is widely known and highly respected. Mr. Smith was born at Cincinnati, Ohio, March 20, 1842, and was brought to Illinois by his parents Joseph and Eliza Jane (Akins) Smith.

Joseph Smith was a farmer by occupation, and on first settling in Illinois located at Equality, where he had friends. Subsequently he rented the Crenshaw farm, three miles south of Ridgway, but during the fall of 1849 came to the present farm of Virginius W. Smith, located one mile east of Ridgway, where he purchased eighty acres of land, for about $500. Fifteen acres of this land was cleared, and a small log cabin had been erected thereon, and here Mr. Joseph Smith started to develop a farm, it being very conveniently located, as it was but a two or three-hour journey to Equality, about eight miles, and three or four hours to New Haven, which was ten miles away, although the land at that time was all a wilderness and there had not yet been a settlement made at Ridgway. Joseph Smith started a store at New Market, one-half mile south of his home, but later all the business there was removed to Ridgway. He continued to operate his farm, putting a great deal of it under cultivation, and served for some years as justice of the peace, to which office he had been elected as a Democrat. His death occurred in May, 1863, when not must past fifty-five years, his widow surviving until 1895 and being seventy-three years old at the time of her death. They had the following children: Virginius W.; Dennis, a soldier, a member of the 131st Illinois Regiment, who died at Vicksburg, Mississippi, in 1863; Margaret, who died as a young married woman; John F., a farmer, who died at 1911, at the age of 55 years; Catherine, who married John Hammersley and died at the age of 30 years; Christopher, a farmer near Eldorado, Illinois; and Lucinda, who married Thomas Riley and died when about 40 years of age.

Virginius W. Smith received his education in the public schools of the vicinity of the home farm, and remained with his parents until the outbreak of the Civil war. In August 1861, he enlisted in Company D, 29th Regiment, Illinois Volunteer Infantry, a company recruited about New Haven by Captain Whiting, and with this organization he served until securing his honorable discharge, November 20, 1864. This regiment saw some of the hardest fighting of the war, and among its battles may be mentioned Belmont, Missouri; Columbus, Kentucky; Paducah and Forts Henry and Donelson, Shiloh, Corinth, Jackson, second Corinth, Holly Springs and Coldwater. The regiment was captured at Holly Springs but his company, with another, was sent back on detail to Jackson, Tennessee. In April 1863, the regiment was sent to Vicksburg to man the gunboat "Tyler," as sharpshooters, on the Mississippi and Yazoo rivers, and this boat was constantly in the severest part of each action.

At the battle of Vicksburg the vessel was sent to the Arkansas side to ward off the Confederate Generals Marmaduke and Price, and after this engagement Mr. Smith and his companions rejoined their regiment, which in the meantime had been exchanged. They were on guard at Vicksburg and on the Black river until Sherman's Atlanta campaign, as far as Jackson, but eventually were sent back to Vicksburg, and Mr. Smith then became a member of a scouting party which went to Natchez, and at that point he received his honorable discharge. He had been twice wounded, in the left side and right leg, and the effects of these injuries did not entirely pass away for a long period.

On his return to Illinois he again took up farming, and for five years rented a property, then purchased forty acres, which he sold after developing, and eventually purchased 120 acres, to which from time to time he added until he now has a magnificent tract of 340 acres, including the old family homestead. For some of this land he paid only ten dollars per acre, and when he bought the homestead it cost him only forty-three dollars per acre, this land now being all worth upwards of $100 per acre. His large, comfortable home is situated on a hill one mile east of Ridgway, and his other buildings are well built and modern in equipment. Mr. Smith raises wheat and corn, and gives a good deal of attention to the raising of purebred stock.

He was one of the original stockholders of the First National Bank of Ridgway, but outside of this has given most of his time and attention to his farm. He has done more than one thousand dollars worth of tiling, and his land is perfectly drained an ditched, although at first much of it was swampy and unproductive. Modern methods, however, have done much for this property, and it is nearly all now black soil. Mr. Smith is a Republican in politics, cast he first vote for Abraham Lincoln in 1864, and for ten years has served as supervisor of his township. He is a popular comrade of Loomis Post, Grand Army of the Republic. On the breaking out of the Spanish-American War in 1898, a regiment was organized and Virginius W. Smith was appointed captain, awaiting the call of his country, but the service was not require, there being no more calls necessary for troops.

In 1875 Mr. Smith was united in marriage with Miss Sarah McDermott, who died less than two years later, leaving one child: Joseph, who is now engaged in cultivating a part of the home farm.[265] In 1900, he was married to Orvilla Shain, a native of Gallatin county, and three children has been born to them: Susie, Eliza and Virginius, Jr. Mr. and Mrs. Smith have numerous friends in this part of Gallatin County. He is remembered as a brave and faithful soldier during the war, and he has discharged his duties just as faithfully as a private citizen. His success has been the result of his own efforts and his career is typical of the successful American agriculturist.

— *History of Southern Illinois.*

---

[265] Joseph, later known as Joe "Peck" Smith, killed his wife and step-aunt Orpha (Shain) Smith at his farm on Nov. 2, 1926. His hanging on Feb. 16, 1927, was the last legal hanging in Gallatin County.

J. E. Speer – 1887

J. E. SPEER,[266] farmer and stock dealer, was born near Nashville, Tenn., in 1826, the eldest of four children of Andrew and Elizabeth (Williams) Speer. The father, of Irish origin, was born in Davidson County, Tenn., about 1798. The grandfather, Moses Speer, was one of the earliest pioneers and settlers of Davidson County, where he reared his family In 1830 he removed to Texas where he spent the rest of his life on the frontier. Reared and married in his native county, Andrew, a farmer, moved to Arkansas Territory, where he died about 1834. The mother, born in Virginia in 1805, is still living with our subject, and is a member of the Methodist Episcopal Church.

Our subject spent about five years of his early life in the tanning business. In 1853 he came to Gallatin County, and the next year was married to Phoebe Berry. Six of their seven children are living: Andrew, of Moultrie County, Ill.; David, of Minnesota; William; Robert, Allan, and Mary, wife of J. Munch, of Moultrie County. The next year he located on his present farm of 200 acres, 160 acres of which are improved, producing over 5,000 bushels of corn annually. Formerly a Whig, he has, since his vote for Gen. Scott, been a Republican. Mrs. Speer is a member of the Baptist Church.

— *History of Gallatin, Saline, Hamilton, Franklin and Williamson Counties, Illinois.*

Allen T. Spivey – 1905

ALLEN T. SPIVEY, editor and proprietor of the Shawneetown, Ill., *News-Gleaner*, was born six miles west of that town April 5, 1875. He is a son of Thomas and Sallie (Smyth) Spivey, and a grandson of Thomas S. Spivey, who was born in North Carolina, of English ancestry, and who was one of the pioneers of Southern Illinois, settling in Gallatin county in 1832. There he took up a tract of government land and followed farming all his life. He was an influential man, in his clay and one of the leading Democrats of the county, serving as justice of the peace and in other minor offices until 1850, when he was elected county judge for one term. He was also active in building up the Presbyterian church. At the time of his death he was sixty-two years of age, but his wife lived to the advanced age of eighty-four. They reared a family of three sons and seven daughters, only two of whom now survive, viz.: Carrie Spivey, of Shawneetown, and Louise, who is a Mrs. Kanady, of New Albany, Ind.

Thomas J. Spivey was born in North Carolina in 1830. He came to Gallatin county with his family when two years of age. When about nineteen years of age he crossed the plains to California, where he followed mining for about two years, when he returned home via the isthmus, and for the rest of his life followed farming with the exception of the last four years. His wife died in 1879, aged forty-five years. In 1893 he removed to Junction City. He died in Shawneetown in 1897. Like his father before him, he was an unswerving Democrat and a member of the Presbyterian church. Of the children born to him and his wife Quinton is in Alaska; Minnie is a Mrs. Smyth of Gallatin county; Margaret is Mrs. Loomis, of Evansville, Ind.; Addie married a Mr. Willis and lives at Mt. Vernon, Ill.; Anna married a Mr. Kanady and is now deceased; Walter W. lives at Shawneetown: Samuel S. is at Paducah, Ky.;

---

[266] The Illinois Statewide Marriage Index lists Mr. Speer as John E. Spears who married Phoebia Berry on January 6, 1854.

Gertrude is a Mrs. Kanady and lives in Gallatin county; Allen T. is the subject of this sketch and Marshall lives at McLeansboro, Ill.

Allen T. Spivey received his education in the public schools, graduating from the Shawneetown high school in 1893. He then went to Evansville, Ind., and took a complete course in the commercial college of that city graduating in 1895. For about a year he was employed as a bookkeeper, but in 1896 started in to learn the printers' trade in the office of the *Gallatin Democrat*. After three years in that office he went to Henderson, Ky., where he became the city editor of the *Daily Gleaner*. In 1900 he went to St. Louis for a short time, but returned to Shawneetown where for a few months he was employed as a reporter on the Democrat. Next he served as a bookkeeper in a hardware store for a short time, but the journalistic instinct had been developed in his make-up, and in November, 1901, He started the *Shawneetown Gleaner*. The following March he bought out the *News* and consolidated the two papers under the present name. Mr. Spivey is one of the youngest and most aggressive journalists in Southern Illinois. His paper is fearlessly Republican in its politics, and it is the official organ of the party in Gallatin county. Personally he has been somewhat active in political affairs, and held the office of city treasurer for one term. He is a member of the Modern Woodmen of America and the Presbyterian church. On Christmas Day in 1901 he was married to Miss Mollie Wright, a native of McLeansboro, and they have one child, Mittase Wright, born Sept. 10, 1902.

— *Memoirs of the Lower Ohio Valley.*

Allen Thomas Spivey – 1912

ALLEN THOMAS SPIVEY, the active and efficient postmaster of Shawneetown, Illinois, has not had an easy row to hoe in life. He, however, is endowed with that gift from Pandora's box, Hope, and with this and his indomitable courage he has been able to win success in spite of all obstacles. He occupies a position of considerable influence in this part of the state through his editorship of the *Shawneetown News-Gleaner*, and in the columns of his paper his voice is continually heard on the side of good government and progress. Through this paper he has accomplished much for the public good, and the citizens of this section realize that if the *Shawneetown News-Gleaner* can be persuaded to espouse a cause it is a long step towards its success. As a politician Mr. Spivey has always taken a prominent part in the work of his party, and is everywhere recognized as one of the leaders of the Republican Party in Southern Illinois. As a businessman he is also progressive and up-to-date, as will be seen in a further account of his career.

Allen Thomas Spivey is the son of Thomas Jefferson Spivey, who was born in Gates County, North Carolina, February 18, 1830. His father was the founder of the family in this country, having been brought to America at the age of two years. This rather young pioneer was Thomas Sawyer Spivey, and was born in England, February 25, 1799. When quite a young man he married Teresa Eason, his wife being still younger, her age being fourteen. She was of Scotch descent. He received a fairly good education for those times and came to Illinois in 1832, his profession being that of a schoolteacher. He settled in Shawneetown and taught school for a number of years. He was greatly respected in the community, both for his learning and for his good common sense. He was elected justice of the peace, and in 1856 was elected to the higher position of county judge. He served in this capacity for four years.

In 1860 he moved out to a farm near Shawneetown, and there he died in 1862. His wife survived him for many years, and for a long time before her death was a living example to all around her of the beauty of Christian patience and fortitude, for she was blind for many years. She died in 1888, having reared the large family of ten children. Sallie, Murray, Lydia and Thomas Jefferson were all born in North Carolina. Annie Henry, Mollie, Caroline and Louise were all born in Shawneetown. Of these many children all have passed into the Great Beyond save two. Caroline is unmarried and lives in Shawneetown and Louise is a widow and lives in New Albany, Indiana.

Thomas Jefferson Spivey came to Shawneetown with his parents in 1832 He grew up here and received his education in the public schools. When the gold fever swept over the country in 1849, he was seized with the ambition to go to the west and try his fortune at picking up the nuggets. He went to California, but returned two years later, having suffered disappointment in his search, like so many others. On his return he bought a farm seven miles west of Shawneetown, and settled down to the quiet life of the farmer. He was married March 12, 1857, to Sallie Annie Smyth, born January 27, 1841, a daughter of Samuel Marshall Smyth, who was a native of Londonderry county, Ireland, and has settled in Gallatin county in youth. Success came to Thomas Jefferson Spivey. His farm prospered and he won many friends through his public activities. He was a Democrat, and although he never sought office, yet he served conscientiously in several minor offices of the community. He and his wife were both members of the Presbyterian church, and for twenty-five years he was an elder in the Ringold Presbyterian church, while his wife was a leader in many of the church activities. Ten children were born to this couple: Quentin E., Minnie, Marguerite, Addie, Annie, William Walter, Samuel Simon, Gertrude, Allen Thomas and Marshall.

Allen Thomas Spivey was born on the Spivey farm, seven miles west of Shawneetown, on the 5th of April 1875. He was educated in the country schools until he was of high school age, when he was placed in the Shawneetown high school. He attended school during the winters and during vacations he worked on the farm, so life did not have much play time for this youngster. In 1894 he finished school, but he did not feel that he was as well equipped for the world which, from his youthful experience, he knew was not one of ease, so he entered a commercial college in Evansville. He remained there during the winter of 1894-1895 and until 1896 he worked at various occupations, gathering a broad, general knowledge of different phases of business. In December of 1896 he commenced work as an apprentice in a printing office, having decided that journalism was the profession which had the strongest attraction for him. He did not believe that he could ever become a successful journalist unless he possessed some practical knowledge, and furthermore he had no powerful friends to get him a position as "cub" reporter. After his apprenticeship he followed the trade, working in various offices, but it was not long before his chance came to get into the real work of journalism. In 1897 he formed a partnership with A. C. Clippinger, and they published the Norris City, Illinois, *Record*. This venture not proving to be as successful as he had hoped, he sold out his interest and returned to Shawneetown in 1898. Here he again took up his trade, and worked at it until the winter of 1899, when he went to Henderson, Kentucky, continuing to work as a printer. No opening seemed to be in sight and, as nearly discouraged as it is possible for Mr. Spivey to become, he gave up his trade and in the spring of 1900 went to St. Louis and entered the employ of a wholesale sash and door company. The call of the printer's ink was too strong for him, however, and when a chance came to go back to his old trade he accepted it gladly. In this capacity he returned to Shawneetown in the fall of 1900. He only remained in news paper work for a few months, however, becoming a bookkeeper in a hardware store in the spring of 1901. He also served as the assessor of the Shawnee Township during the spring of 1901, and in April of that year he was elected city treasurer of Shawneetown for a term of two years.

He had always been economical, and had denied himself many comforts in the hope that some day he might be able to buy a paper of his own. Now his dream was realized, for with his small savings he invested in a Washington hand press and some type, bought a little printing office, and November 8, 1901, the first issue of the *Shawneetown Gleaner* was on the streets. This was the turning point of his career. He was no longer to knock about from pillar to post, for the paper was a success from the start. So prosperous was it, in fact, that on the 2nd of March 1902, almost exactly five months since the first issue, Mr. Spivey was able to announce his purchase of the *Shawnee News*, a Republican newspaper. The *Gleaner* had been the third newspaper in Shawneetown, and while the size of the place scarcely warranted the publication of three papers it could easily support two. Mr. Spivey, therefore, consolidated the papers of which he was the owner, under the title, The *Shawneetown News-Gleaner*. The paper continued to grow and prospects looked brighter every day. The debts were all about paid off on the plant when suddenly disaster came in the shape of a fire that destroyed the whole thing on the morning of the 4th of June 1904. The insurance was small and the loss was heavy, but success had once come to Mr. Spivey and now nothing could discourage him. Taking the insurance money as a nucleus he began all over again; bought another plant and continued to publish the paper without missing an issue. His confidence was fully justified, for now the paper is one of the most influential in Southern Illinois. He is now president of The Southern Illinois Editorial Association, an organization composed of almost every editor in Southern Illinois. He has the confidence and respect of all of them and was the only person ever elected to the office without opposition.

He was appointed postmaster of Shawneetown on the 21st of January 1907, and is now serving his second term. Now that the Democratic Party is beginning to show its strength, the Republican Party should congratulate itself upon the fact that such a loyal worker as Mr. Spivey is to be found among its ranks.

Mr. and Mrs. Spivey are both members and active workers of the Presbyterian Church in Shawneetown, and in the fraternal world Mr. Spivey is a member of the Modern Woodmen of America, affiliating with Warren lodge, and of the Masonic order, Chapter No. 14, of Shawneetown.

Mr. Spivey was married in McLeansboro, Illinois, on the 25th of December 1901, to Mary O'Neal Wright, a daughter of T. B. Wright. The latter was a soldier in the Union army during the Civil war, and her mother was Mary O'Neal, who was the daughter of John William O'Neal. Her father was the nephew of a man who was a political leader in Democratic circles in Southern Illinois for many years. This man was Judge Samuel Marshall, who was congressman for six terms, the first time in 1855-1857, and the last time in 1873-1875. Mrs. Spivey was educated in the common schools of McLeansboro and later attended college in Nashville, Tennessee. Mr. and Mrs. Spivey are the parents of two children: Mittase Wright Spivey was born on the 10th of September, 1902, and their son, Allen Thomas Spivey, Jr., was born on the 1st of October, 1911.

Mr. Spivey possesses those characteristics that make a man loved and honored by the community. He is straightforward and conscientious in all of his business dealings. His prosperity has been built up not through snatching the bread from the mouths of someone else, but by his own honest industrious efforts. He is known for his generosity and his charity to all who are in need, and he is a man to whom his family, his God and his home mean more than all of the wealth and fame in the world He has added much to the material prosperity of the town, not only in the erection of his beautiful modern home which is both commodious and attractive, but also in the business block occupied by the post office and other offices, which he owns. He is also the owner of other property throughout the town. He feels that although he has had a stiff battle with life, yet in his ambition to succeed he has not torn down the work of others, for his philosophy is, "Work and application to this work, and you will find that the world has room for us all."

— *The History of Southern Illinois.*

Capt. W. H. Stiles – 1887

CAPT. W. H. STILES was born in Hartford, Conn., in 1828, the son of Hyas and Harriet L. Stiles, both natives of Connecticut. He received an academical education in the public schools of Lancaster, Ohio, after his tenth year when his parents removed there, and when eighteen years old went to Louisville, Ky., and served as apprenticeship in the foundry business. After two years' work at Cincinnati he was likewise employed at Detroit, Mich., then at New Orleans eight months. For two years thereafter he was on the river between Cincinnati and New Orleans, when he returned to Ohio and worked at his trade. For about four years he was engaged in training and dealing in horses and mules.

In 1861 he enlisted in Company G, Seventh Illinois Cavalry, as second lieutenant, under Col. Edward Prince, and two years later was promoted directly to captain. He took part in some of the most severe cavalry engagements of the war, and in three years returned home on account of broken down health. August 8, 1847, he married Catherine Smith of New Boston, Ohio, who died April 27, 1881. Their five children are living in Gallatin County. In December 1884, he married July Stull, a native of Georgia, by whom he had one child. After the war he returned to his family in Gallatin County, where they have lived since 1857. He has since been engaged in the sawmill business and looking after his farm interests. For seven years he had been correspondent and reporter for the United States Agricultural Society, is an ardent Republican, and a member of the G.A.R.

— *History of Gallatin, Saline, Hamilton, Franklin and Williamson Counties, Illinois.*

William Henry Stiles – 1905

CAPT. WILLIAM HENRY STILES of Ridgway, Ill., was born at Windsor, Conn., on Oct. 22, 1828. His ancestry dates back to John Stiles, who was born in Bedfordshire, England, Dec. 25, 1595 and who came to America in 1635, settling at Windsor, Conn., where he died on June 4, 1662 John Stiles had a son, John, who was born in 1633 and died at Windsor, Conn., Dec. 8, 1863. He was married to Dorcas, a daughter of Henry Burt, of Springfield, Conn., and they had a son, John, who was born at Windsor on Dec. 10, 1663.

This son died at New Haven, Conn., on May 20, 1753. His wife was a Miss Ruth Bancroft, of Westfield, Mass., who died at Windsor in 1714. To this union was born, at Windsor, on July 30, 1697, Isaac Stiles, who was twice married, his second wife being Ester Hooker of Farmington, Conn. She died at North Haven on Jan. 2, 1779. Isaac was a minister and was educated at Yale university, where he graduated with the degree of B.A. in 1722 and A.M. in 1725.

The union of the Rev. Isaac Stiles and Ester Hooker was blessed with a son, Ashbel, who was born at North Haven on Aug. 30, 1734, and died at Norwich, Mass., in October, 1810. Ashbel Stiles married his cousin, Hannah Stiles, who died at Norwich in September, 1810. They had a son, Job, who was born on Jan. 12, 1765, and died at Windsor April 15, 1813. He married Mary Drake of Windsor, who died on March 16, 1839. Their son, Hylas, was born at Windsor, June 11, 1793, and married Harriet L. Roberts, of Sandersdale, Mass. To this union was born a son, William Henry, the subject of this sketch. Hylas Stiles removed with his family to Cleveland, O., and later to Lancaster in the same state, where Captain Stiles received his education, numbering among his schoolmates Gen. William T. Sherman and Gen. Phil Sheridan.

While still a young man, Captain Stiles moved to Cincinnati, and later to New Market, Gallatin county, Ill., in which county he has since resided, following successfully the occupation of farming. He now lives at Ridgway in that county. Captain Stiles was married at New Boston, Ohio, on Aug. 8, 1847, to Catherine Smith, of Owensville, Ohio, and they had the following children: Harriet Louise, born Oct. 6, 1848 William Andrew, born Jan. 6, 1850; Mary E., born Dec. 7, 1851; Catherine M., born Oct. 10, 1853; Hylas C., born Aug. 27, 1835; Joseph F., born July 27, 1858; John D., born May 26, 1861; Theoba J., born Dec. 11, 1863; George Trafton, born Jan. 6, 1866; Laura E., born Jan. 26, 1868; Edwin L., born Nov. 11, 1870; and Adaline, born May 3, 1874. His wife died on May 27, 1881, and he was again married on Sept. 1, 1884, his second wife being Julia A. Fulks of New Market. To this union was born one child, Clemma L., born June 13, 1885.

At the outbreak of the Civil war Captain Stiles enlisted from Gallatin county, on Aug. 12, 1861, and was mustered into the service on Sept. 13, at Camp Butler, Ill., as second lieutenant of Capt. George W. Trafton's company, G, Seventh regiment Illinois volunteer cavalry, Col. William Pitt Kellogg commanding. In the latter part of October, 1861, the regiment was ordered to Birds Point, Mo., and in January, 1862, moved to Cape Girardeau, where it performed scout and guard duty until the following spring. At New Madrid, Mo., the regiment was recruited, forming a part of Hatch's division, Army of the West, and participated in the following engagements: New Madrid, Mo.; Island No. 10, Farmington, siege of Corinth, Iuka, battle of Corinth, Summersville, pursuit of Price, Coffeeville, Miss.; Grierson's raid, Plains store, Port Hudson, La.; Byhalia Road, Miss; Moscow, Campbellsville, Harts Crossroads, Franklin, Brentwood Hills, the routing of Hood's army at Nashville, Tenn., and numerous scouting expeditions and raids.

At the close of the war the regiment received its final muster out at Camp Butler. Captain Trafton having been promoted to major, Second Lieutenant Stiles, by petition from the entire company, was promoted to captain and was mustered in with that rank on Nov. 8, 1863. He received honorable discharge at Springfield, Ill., Oct. 15, 1864, his term of service having expired. He was wounded by gunshot in the right thigh and by a piece of shell in the right ankle on Dec. 3, 1863, and was confined to the hospital for one month. He was also injured in the engagement at Colliersville, Tenn., Nov. 3, 1863, causing the loss of hearing in his left ear. He was at all times with his command, participating in all its engagements, and by gallant and meritorious service he achieved a proud record for bravery and proficiency in action. Captain Stiles is a member of and past post commander of R. Loomis Post, No. 583, Department of Illinois, Grand Army of the Republic; also member of the American Protective association. Although past seventy-five years of age, the captain is hale and hearty and active for one of his years.

— *Memoirs of the Lower Ohio Valley.*

Gen. Joseph Montfort Street – 1918

Joseph Montfort Street was born in Lunenburg County, Virginia, on the 18th day of December, 1782. His father, Anthony Street, was a Virginia planter, of English ancestry. His mother, Mary (Stokes) Street, was a sister of Gov. Montfort Stokes, of North Carolina. Anthony Street was a soldier in the Continental army from the commencement to the close of the Revolutionary war, and retired a colonel in command of a regiment. He was then made sheriff of Lunenburg County, holding the office for many years.

Joseph was appointed deputy sheriff before he was of age. His early educational advantages must have been meager, for we soon find him employed in a commercial house in Richmond, Virginia. Little is known of his migration to Kentucky. He read law in the office of Humphrey Marshall and with the great Henry Clay, and for a brief period practiced law in the courts of Kentucky and Tennessee.[267]

Young Street and John Wood began in Frankfort the publication of a politically independent weekly newspaper named *The Western World.* The World one day startled its readers by boldly charging Aaron Burr, Judge Innis, one Sebastian and others with conspiracy against the Government. Kentucky was alive with sympathizers with Burr, some of them erroneously believing that the proposed expedition to the Southwest was secretly sanctioned by the Government. Judge Innis sued the publishers for libel. The editors pleaded justification, proving that Innis had transmitted sealed documents to New Orleans, documents prepared and sent by Burr. Innis, taken by surprise, fainted and was carried from the courtroom. Street was challenged by several of Burr's allies, but he paid no attention to their challenges further than to publish them as items of news, editorially remarking that they were on file and the writers would severally be attended to!

One of the challengers was not thus easiliy dismissed. One day as Street was passing a hotel, a man confronted him and, holding a copy of *The Western World* in his hand, asked him if he had written the offending article. Street replied:

"I am responsible for all that appears in that paper."

With an oath the man said he proposed to "cowhide the man who wrote it," and with that he drew a whip from his sleeve. He raised his arm; but Street swung his cane and struck his assailant on the elbow. He struck a second time and the man was felled to the ground. Before friends could interfere, the aggressor was severely punished.

---

[267] An original footnote provides the source: "Gen. Joseph M. Street," by William D. Street, *Annals of Iowa*, July-October, 1895.

On one occasion Burr's friends undertook to thrust Street from a ball-room, and they would doubltess have succeeded had not Colonel Posey come to the rescue.

A third attack was made by a young lawyer named Adams. He placed two men in an alley, and, as the offending editor passed, they seized and held him until Adams fired a shot at him. The ball struck a button on his coat, glanced from its course and broke the lower part of the breast-bone. Street drew a dirk and pursued the fleeing assassin. Overtaking him, he slit the man's coat from the collar to the skirt. Adams ran into a bank and closed the door. Weak from the loss of blood, Street sat down upon the steps in front of the bank. Adams stepped out of a rear door of the bank, ordered the crowd to stand aside that he might shoot, but Humphrey Marshall wrested the pistol from Adams' hand.

For many weary weeks Street lay in bed. When Burr's trial came on he was unable to quit his bed. The fact that he did not appear as a witness was distorted by Burr's champions as a backing down from the original charge. Adams, in his *History of Jefferson's Second Administration*, describes Street as "the fighting editor of *The Western World*," but, making no note of his serious illness, declares that he, like his partner, Wood, "was similarly reticent as a witness."

We next learn of Street's marriage to Eliza Maria, daughter of Maj.-Gen. Thomas Posey of Revolutionary fame, and of his retirement from the State of Kentucky. In Shawneetown, Illinois, Street served for sixteen years as clerk of the court. During much of that time he served also as postmaster and recorder of deeds.

In the year 1827, President John Quincy Adams appointed Joseph M. Street agent for the Winnebago Indians at Prairie due Chien, on the Wisconsin side of the upper Mississippi.

The appointment was due to the influence of Street's friend, Henry Clay. In a letter announcing that he had been appointed to the Indian agency, Clay expressed his conviction that the appointment would redound to the welfare of the Indians and the honor of the Government.

The appointment was followed by Street's resignation as brigadier-general of militia, September 2, 1827. The title of "General" so well fitted his intrepid nature and his military bearing that it clung to him to the last.

The newly appointed agent entered upon his duties in November, 1827. Early the next year he moved his family to Prairie du Chien.

Street's predecessor had proved himself inefficient and a tool of corrupt traders. The new agent found the Indians addicted to intoxicants, and otherwise decadent. His first "case" was that of Chief "Red Bird," who, with two other Indians, had been found guilty of shooting two men and then scalping a girl, leaving her for dead. He had been condemned to be hung. Street investigated and found there were extenuating circumstances which in his judgment would justify the pardon of the criminals, and on his recommendation President Adams pardoned them.

Agents and employees of the American Fur Company, finding they could not use Street, conspired to effect his removal. President Jackson, who had known Street in Kentucky, informed the conspirators that there would be no change while he was president. President Van Buren also continued him in office.

The exasperated agents involved Street in many complications and in two vexations and costly lawsuits, but could not break his spirit nor lessen his growing influence with the Indians.

Conforming to the custom of the time and place, Street at first kept liquor in his house and was wont to treat his friends, but, finding he could not safely give whisky to the Indians, he banished intoxicants from his home.

Finding the mission at Prairie du Chien was doibng little or nothing for the moral instruction of the Indians, Street started Sunday meetings in his home to which the Indians were invited. In these meetings he avoided theology, giving only plain, practical lessons on right living.

Street's control of the Indians had a marked effect on the Black Hawk war. Rounding up a company of Winnebagoes, he turned them over to an officer, a son of Alexander Hamilton, who marched them against the Sacs and Foxes. After the battle of Bad Axe, his Winnebagoes brought Black Hawk and "the Prophet" to Street, who replied to the speech of their chief, assuring them that they had done well in bringing the prisoners to him. He, himself, would accompany the prisoners to Rock Island and take with him such chiefs and warriors as they might select. The prisoners, about fifty in number, were temporarily turned over to Col. Zachary Taylor, then in command at Fort Crawford.

Street met Gen. Winfield Scott at Rock Island and, with his permission, took his Winnebagoes with him to participate in the Rock Island treaty of the Sacs and Foxes. Colonel Taylor placed Lieut. Jefferson Davis in command of the guard escorting Street with his Indians and the prisoners to Rock Island. On the boat Street shook hands with all the prisoners. Confronting Black Hawk in irons, he called Lieutenant Davis to him and said:

"Lieutenant Davis, have these irons removed."

Davis thought it might not be safe. Street dignifedly responded:

"Sir, I hold myself personally responsible for this man's safety and good conduct."

"If you direct it, General," was the lieutenant's response, and he ordered the irons removed.

Street's treatment of his prisoners was so generous that to the last black Hawk entertained the warmest friendship for him. No higher praise was ever given him than that which Black Hawk paid him in his fragment of autobiography:

"I called on the agent of the Winnebagoes (Gen. J. M. Street), to whom I had surrendered myself after the battle of Bad Axe, who received me very friendly, ... I hope he will not forget his promise (to return a medicine bag which the chief valued highly), as the whites generally do, because I have always heard that he is a good man, and a good father, and made no promises that he did not fulfill."

...The next move of the superintendent, in 1835, was the transfer of General Street from the Winnebago agency to that of the Sacs and Foxes, with a change of residence from Prairie du Chien to Rock Island. This change was a great loss to the Winnebagoes, but a corresponding gain to the Sacs and Foxes.

From 1835 to 1837 General Street and his family resided in Rock Island. Then, at no little personal sacrifice, he removed to Prairie du Chien that he might place the Government school which he had founded upon a permanent basis.

Accompanied by Chief Poweshiek and a body-guard of Sac and Fox braves, General Street penetrated the wilderness of the lower Des Moines, to locate an agency at a point most accessible from the principal villages of the tribe. The site was duly selected — early in 1838 — and the general contracted for the erection of the necessary buildings, including a council house, a dwelling for his family, a business office, stables and a blacksmith shop.

The site selected, Street contracted with a builder from Missouri and imported a force of mechanics, laborers and negro slaves. The council house was first erected and after that the blacksmith shop. In April, 1939, General Street moved his family and household effects to the new agency, and, with many plans for the future, settled down to the final work of his career.

While deeply engaged in work for his wards, he was warned by failing health that his end was near. He was taken ill in November, 1839, and lingered on until the 5th of May, 1840. Drs. Enos Lowe of Burlington and Volney Spaulding of Fort Madison attended him during his last illness, their ride extending over seventy-five miles each way. Doctor Posey, of Shawneetown, his wife's brother, came to their relief as soon as possible.[268] While his death was attributed to apoplexy, his son was of the opinion that he was afflicted with paralysis attended with aphasia. While he found difficulty in expressing himself, "his mind was clear and his faith bright. A short time before his death he called his family together and spoke of his probable death with his customary fearlessness, and charged them to meet him in Heaven."[269]

In a picket enclosure in the woods not far from Agency City, near Ottumwa, Iowa, are three vaults each covered with a marble slab. One of these contains the mortal remains of Chief Wapello; another, those of the Indian's "father and friend," General Street, and the third, the remains of the widow and those of her children who have passed away.

These graves may be seen on the south side of the railroad track about a half-mile east of Agency City. As a local historian has well said, "This spot is classic ground in Iowa's aboriginal history."

Now, three-quarters of a century removed from the period made glorious by this man's fidelity to a sacred trust, we of the twentieth century should be proud of the fact that away back in the thirties there lived in Iowa a man who in his long career as Indian agent was, and will remain for all time, an ideal public servant whom the spoils of office could not buy.[270]

— *Iowa: Its History and Its Foremost Citizens.*

---

[268] The doctor's full name is Alexander Posey.

[269] Another account provides more details of Street's last day: "In April, 1839, Gen. Street removed his family from Prairie du Chien to the new agency. In the meantime his health had been gradually declining, and before the close of this year he had become almost totally disabled, owing to a complication of obstinate maladies. On the 5th day May, 1840, he was out riding with his brother-in-law, Dr. Posey, who had been attending him professionally. On returning home he alighted from the carriage, and seating himself in the door, called for a cup of cold water. When the servant brought it he remained motionless in the chair. Dr. Posey was immediately called, and came without the delay of a minute, but too late. The general had died while sitting in his chair." The same account also described Street as a "strict Presbyterian." [Source: A. R. Fulton. 1882. *The Red Men of Iowa: Being a History of the Various Aboriginal Tribes*. Des Moines, Iowa: Mills & Co., Publishers. 349-351.]

[270] Brigham Johnson, ed. 1918, Rev., Home and School Ed. *Iowa: Its History and Its Foremost Citizens*. Des Moines, IA: The S. J. Clarke Publishing Company. 1:46. Taken from online version at the Iowa Biographies Project edited and condensed by Tamara Jorstad.

H. C. Strickland – 1887

H. C. STRICKLAND, farmer and trader, was born in Gallatin County in 1852. He is one of seven children — three living — of John D. and Ariminta (Dobbs) Strickland. The father of English origin, was a native of Montgomery County, Ohio. Since his youth he was a resident of Gallatin County, where he lived in 1859. A bookkeeper in his early years, he became a hatter, and for a time was in the grocery business. The later years of his life were devoted to general trading and stock shipping to southern ports. The mother, born in Gallatin County, January 3, 1825, died in April 19, 1878.

Educated through his mother's care at common schools, and at the Southern Normal at Carbondale, our subject engaged in successful teaching for several years in the same place, and for several years agent for agricultural machinery also. April 4, 1881, he married Ida, daughter of Moses and Elizabeth Kanady, born in Gallatin County in 1859. They had two children, both dead. Since his marriage he has lived on his present finely improved farm of forty acres four miles from Shawneetown.

One of the best educators of Gallatin County, his school, where he taught for nine terms, was awarded three premiums in 1886, by the Gallatin County Agricultural Society, for the best schoolwork, and that in competition with Shawneetown High School. In politics he is a Republican, voting first for R. B. Hayes. His wife is a member of the Methodist Episcopal Church.

— *History of Gallatin, Saline, Hamilton, Franklin and Williamson Counties, Illinois.*

E. L. Tadlock – 1905

E. L. TADLOCK, one of the leading farmers of Gallatin County, Ill., was born near Battery Rock, Hardin County, of that state, March 18, 1848. His parents, Michael and Sarah (Baer) Tadlock, were both natives of that county, where the father was a farmer and passed his whole life. They had three children. Isaac and Nancy are both deceased, the subject of this sketch being the only surviving member of his family. Michael Tadlock died while the subject was still a small boy, and his widow married William A. Scroggins. E. L. Tadlock continued to live with his mother and stepfather until his marriage to Miss E. J. Benson, a native of Saline county, and rented a farm near Shawneetown, where he lived for four or five years, when he bought 90 acres where he now lives, six miles west of Shawneetown. Since then he has prospered and now owns 400 acres of land, most of which is in a high state of cultivation and well improved. For the last ten years Mr. Tadlock has been conducting a general store on his place in connection with his agricultural pursuits. His success in life is due mainly to his energy and foresight, and he is regarded as one of the best businessmen in his locality. Mr. and Mrs. Tadlock have had the following children born to them: Laura E., Charles, Mamie, Kate, Maud, Edgar, William C., Clarence and Lewis. Charles and Lewis are deceased and the others are all married and live near their parents. Mrs. Tadlock is a member of the Baptist church.

— *Memoirs of the Lower Ohio Valley.*

Joseph W. Towle – 1912

JOSEPH W. TOWLE. Prominent among the early and honored pioneers of Harrisburg was the late Joseph W. Towle, who was an active factor in developing and advancing the material interests of this section of Saline county, having for a full quarter of a century carried on an extensive business as junior member of the firm of Mitchell & Towle, general merchants.

A son of Israel D. Towle, he was born April 9, 1838, in Equality, Gallatin county, Illinois. He was a lineal descendant in the sixth generation of Philip Towle, the immigrant ancestor, who was born, it is supposed, in Ireland, the family name on the other side of the Atlantic having been O'Toole. Philip Towle was for many years a resident of what is now Hampton, New Hampshire, where he reared several sons, four of whom took part in King William's wars. The line of descent was continued through Benjamin Towle, born in 1669; Benjamin Towle, born in 1713; and Jacob Towle, born in 1744, who spent a large part of his early life in Loudon, New Hampshire, but subsequently removed to Danville, Vermont, where he spent his remaining years.

Born in Loudon, Merrimack County, New Hampshire, April 13, 1787, Israel D. Towle served as a soldier in the war of 1812. About 1831 or 1832 he migrated with his family to Gallatin County, Illinois, locating at Equality, where he became a citizen of prominence and influence, remaining there until his death, April 3, 1875, at a ripe old age. Active in religious and fraternal circles, he was one of the petitioners for the organization of the Presbyterian church of Harrisburg, and a charter member of its Masonic Lodge. He married, in Greenboro, New York, in 1816, Eliza Pearce, who was born in Westminster, Massachusetts, in October 1798, and died July 20, 1876, in Illinois.

Brought up and educated in Gallatin County, Illinois, Joseph W. Towle began life for himself as a clerk, and while yet a young man obtained a practical insight in regard to the details of the mercantile trade. Locating in Harrisburg, Saline county, he embarked in business on his own account, and for 25 years was in partnership with Dr. Mitchell, under the firm name of Mitchell & Towle building a large business as a general merchant. He was also one of the pioneers in the development of the coal interests of Southern Illinois, which his keen foresight told him would become one of the leading industries of this section of the state. A cripple throughout his life, Mr. Towle was unable to serve his country during the Civil War, and was never an aspirant for political honors, his business requiring his entire time and attention.

Mr. Towle married, May 26, 1867, at McLeansboro, Illinois, Minerva J. Rathbone, who was born in that city April 7, 1839, a daughter of Dr. Lorenzo Rathbone, and niece of Dr. Valentine Rathbone, of whom a brief sketch may be found on another page of this work.[271] Dr. Rathbone was for many years engaged in the practice of medicine until his death, November 25, 1885, at the venerable age of 84 years and nine months. He belonged to the Rathbone family of England that was prominent in the mercantile affairs of Liverpool for upwards of 200 years, and was also active in military affairs. Captain John Rathbone, one of his ancestors, took an active part in the Revolutionary War; having had command of the

---

[271] Actually Dr. Rathbone's biography is not found in this work since it primarily deals with his time in Saline County. However, it can be found in George W. Smith's *History of Southern Illinois* published in 1912 on page 849 of the second volume.

sloop "Providence," while in the War of 1812 he was a large contributor towards the general fund raised for paying expenses. About 1820 Dr. Lorenzo Rathbone began the practice of medicine in McLeansboro, and in addition to his work as a physician and surgeon was a preacher in the Presbyterian church. He married, in 1824, Pamelia Anderson, who outlived him a few years.

Mrs. Towle is still living in Harrisburg. Of the four children born of the union of Mr. and Mrs. Towle one son and one daughter have passed to the life beyond, and two sons are living, namely: Ralph S., engaged in the real estate business at Louisville, Kentucky, and Herman T.

Herman T. Towle was for several years engaged in the mercantile business with his brother Ralph, to whom he subsequently sold his interests in the general store which they conducted in partnership. In 1904 Mr. Herman T. Towle embarked in the clothing business in Harrisburg, and has since built up a thriving trade, carrying in his well-equipped store a large and varied stock of fine goods. He married, in 1900, Loudene Karnes, of Galatia, Saline County, a daughter of J. W Karnes, a retired agriculturist, and into their pleasant home three children have been born, Bernice, John Warren and Herman Edwin.

— *History of Southern Illinois.*

Richard Wellington Townshend – 1876

HON. RICHARD WELLINGTON TOWNSHEND, son of Samuel H. and Catharine O. Townshend, was born in Prince George County, Maryland, April 30, 1840; educated in Washington, D.C., where he was a page in the House of Representatives in 1857-8, and moved to Illinois in March 1858. In that year he clerked in the Post Office at Cairo; in 1859 and 1860, taught school; in 1857, he began the study of law at Washington, D.C., was licensed to practice while studying under Hon. S. S. Marshall, at McLeansboro, Illinois; in 1862, was elected clerk of the Circuit Court of Hamilton County, serving from 1863 to 1868, when he was elected state's attorney for the 12th Circuit, and moved to Shawneetown in 1873, where he has since practiced law.

— *Illustrated Historical Atlas of the State of Illinois.*

Richard W. Townshend – 1887

RICHARD W. TOWNSHEND, representative in Congress from the 19th District of Illinois, is a native of the State of Maryland, a point in Prince George County eighteen miles south of Washington, being the place, and April 30, 1840, the day when he first saw the light. His father, Samuel H. Townshend, was a planter, and died when Richard was but two years of age, leaving the mother with the care of nine children, one of whom was younger than Richard. The Townshend family is one of the oldest in southern Maryland, the first representative immigrating thither from England in 1746, and settling in the immediately vicinity of the place where nearly one hundred years later his distinguished great-grandson was born. On the maternal side Mr. Townshend comes from Virginia stock, his mother being a Miss Lumsden, daughter of a prominent merchant of Alexandria, and sister of Dr. William O. Lumsden, who was a healer of a spiritual as well as physical man, having occupied the pulpit as a minister of the Methodist Church, and prior thereto practiced medicine in the city of Baltimore.

In the course of a few years, after her husband's death, Mrs. Townshend removed with her family to this city (Washington, D.C.), and here the future congressman received his education. He was employed for some time in Col. Jo Shillington's bookstore, which was a general rendezvous for the distinguished men of that day — Benton, Cass, Douglas, Gen. Scott and others — who always found an attentive auditor in young Townshend. During the sessions of 1856-57 and 1857-58 he was employed as a page on the floor of the House of Representatives, an occupation which was in every way desirable to him, as it afforded him the coveted opportunity of witnessing the great struggle on the Kansas question as embodied in the Lecompton constitution, probably one of the most exciting events in National legislation that had occurred up to that time. It was during this service in the House that the young statesman in embryo made the acquaintance and friendship of Hon. Samuel S. Marshall, a representative from Illinois, who was eminent alike for his ability as a statesman and rank as a jurist. Taking an interest in the ambitious young page, he encouraged him to anticipate the later advice of Horace Greeley and "go West."

Accordingly, in the year 1858, westward young Townshend's star of empire took its way, beckoning him on to the brilliant future which southern Illinois had in store for him; his first abiding place being the modern Cairo, thence to McLeansboro, and then he removed to Shawneetown, on the Ohio River, his present place of abode. His energies were at once devoted to completing his law studies, which he pursued energetically under the guidance and direction of his friend, Mr. Marshall, teaching school in winter to be able to meet his expenses. In 1862 he was admitted to the bar and almost immediately sprang into a lucrative practice. In 1864 he was elected clerk of the circuit court of Hamilton County, a position which he filled for four year, and in 1868 was chosen prosecuting attorney for the Twelfth Judicial District of Illinois, comprising six counties, in which capacity he served with marked distinction and ability until 1872, the expiration of the term for which he had been elected. During the period from 1872 to 1876 he devoted himself to the business of national banking as well as practice of law, in which he acquired an experience which has been valuable to him as a national legislator.

In the political campaign of 1876 the Democrats of the 19th District of Illinois, anxious to regain the ascendancy which they had lost in the previous contest in 1874, when a Greenbacker was elected to Congress, agreed with remarkable unanimity upon Mr. Townshend as their standard-bearer to lead them to victory. Right gallantly did he justify their trust and fulfill their high expectation. In every town and hamlet and at every crossroads his voice was heard in advocacy and support of the eternal principles of Democratic faith, and when the day of reckoning in November came he was triumphantly elected by a handsome plurality vote of more than 4,000, and the district was again safe in the Democratic column. His services during his first term in Congress pleased his constituency so well that he was re-nominated in 1878 and elected by an increased vote of 6,000 plurality and a clear majority over both his opponents of nearly 3,000. Since then he has been re-elected by constantly increasing majorities, making the district now one of the most reliably Democratic districts in the State of Illinois.

During the time that Mr. Townshend has been in Congress he has not been idle. Few representatives, indeed, on their first participation in legislation take such a wide and practical view of their duties and responsibilities as he has done. Within his range of vision came not only the interests of his own people, but the welfare and prosperity of the country at large, broadly and wisely recognizing that what whatever tended to promote the latter would certainly inure to the benefit of the former; and this it is that constitutes true statesmanship. Some of the most prominent and important measures which now demand the attention of Congress an vitally affect the National well-being were first urged and insisted upon by him.

Early in the first session of the XLV Congress he introduced "a bill to regulate interstate commerce and to prohibit unjust discriminations by common carriers," which was one of the first measures introduced in Congress looking to the settlement of that important question and upon which have been framed some of the principal features of the Reagan bill reported in the present Congress from the committee on commerce. At the same session he brought the attention of the House to the dangerous encroachments of the Federal judiciary upon the powers of the State courts in a bill to regulate the removal of causes from state to federal tribunals, but it was crowded out by other business in the last Congress. One of the first things he did at the commencement of the present Congress was to re-introduce this all-important measure and have it referred to the committee on the revision of the laws, by which committee it was returned to the House with a favorable report; but by filibustering against it for weeks during the extra session the Republicans prevented action at that time. During the last Congress a substitute for this measure was adopted which has greatly restricted the jurisdiction of the Federal courts. Thus after years of persistent effort this important measure of Mr. Townshend's has been crowned with a large degree of success. To his efforts in Congress the Mexican soldiers are more largely indebted for the recent law granting them pensions than perhaps to any one else. And indeed he has signalized his friendship for the Union soldiers of the Republic by effective service in Congress.

The most important measure of which he is the author and creator is the bill looking to the establishment of an American Zollverein, or customs union of all the American nations. It provides for the same freedom of trade between the nations of North, Central and South America as exists among the States of this Union, and if finally accepted by the countries concerned, will no doubt greatly developed the resources of the Western Hemisphere, and bring to this country the immense commerce of the Southern countries which are now monopolized by European nations. It has already met with such favorable progress in Congress as renders it very probably that it will be adopted at the next session. Other important measures have been introduced by him which we have not the space to mention.

During his service he has been a member of several of the most important committees in Congress, including that of the Judiciary and Appropriations. Each one of these important questions which Mr. Townshend has had the energy and perseverance to bring before the body of which he is a member, has been advocated by him in speeches which, for strength or argument and depth of reasoning, it would be difficult to surpass. As an orator he is graceful, fluent and forcible, expressing his thoughts in simple and appropriate language, and with a beauty of diction and power of logic which go straight to the understanding, carrying conviction to the hearer. He never rails to command the respect and attention of the House, and he justifies the compliment by never uttering what is not worth hearing. His public career has been most promising, and it is not too much to say that we regard him, in every essential, as one of the men to whom the country must look for safe guidance and counsel in the future.

In 1869 Mr. Townshend married a daughter of Orville Pool, Esq., a prominent banker and leading merchant of Shawneetown. She is a lady of rare good sense, of accomplished manners and retiring demeanor, happy in the companionship of her husband and children, and fitted to adorning position in life.

The writing of this brief sketch of the life of Richard W. Townshend was conceived as a pleasant duty, typifying, as that life does, the possibilities and opportunities which wait at the door of every young man under the glorious institutions of free America. The youth who left the hall of the House of Representatives as a humble page returned in a few years a peer of its ablest members. And as he has been the first of former page boys to reach a seat in Congress, it is to be hoped many more may achieve equal success should they make as able and efficient legislators as he has done.

— *History of Gallatin, Saline, Hamilton, Franklin and Williamson Counties, Illinois.*

L. F. Tromly – 1887

L. F. TROMLY, editor, publisher and proprietor of the *Shawnee News*, was born October 30, 1846, in Mount Vernon, Ill., and is the son of Michael and Jane (Bouton) Tromly.

The father, of French descent and born in 1800 in Vincennes, Ind., lived there until he lost his first wife, about 1832, then lived in Burlington, Iowa, where he married Jane Bouton November 19, 1835. After 1840, Mount Vernon, Ill., was his home. He was first a cabinet-maker, and then for 35 years a silversmith. His father, Isaac Tromly, ran the first ferry at Vincennes. He (Michael) died May 26, 1878. His second wife, born in New Jersey and reared in New York City, went to Burlington, Iowa, when a young lady. She died August 26, 1855.

Our subject, one of ten children, was educated at Mount Vernon, Ill, and since his 14th year was an apprenticed or journeyman printer until 1871 with the exception of 18 months in the grocery business, the senior member of Tromly & Ellis, at Mount Vernon, Ill. After eight months as editor and publisher of the *Mount Vernon News*, he and his brother Theodore became its owners. It was the first successful Republican paper in the county. After three and a half years with this, Mr. Tromly sold out and retired from business for two years to recuperate his failing health, but in 1880 bought the *Shawnee News*, and is now sole owner and manager. A fearless Republican, his paper is quote by the State press frequently. Mr. Tromly's first teacher was "Bob" Ingersoll.

February 25, 1877, he married Miss Iva E. Phillips, born in Anna, Union Co., Ill., June 4, 1856. She is a member of the Christian Church. Their two children are Herbert H. and Mabel.

— *History of Gallatin, Saline, Hamilton, Franklin and Williamson Counties, Illinois.*

Isaac T. Trusty – 1883

ISAAC T. TRUSTY, son of Henry and Elizabeth Trusty, was born in Tennessee, July 31, 1825. His parents moved to White County, Ill., when he was two years of age. Isaac T. was reared to the hardships of a pioneer farmer, having but a limited education. He was married Dec. 23, 1848, to Elizabeth Wilson.

He moved to Gallatin County in 1850 and entered 80 acres of government land. He now has a large and valuable farm. Mr. Trusty has always taken an active part in all public improvements. He united with the Methodist church in 1841. He is a member of the Omaha Lodge, I.O.O.F. He has been constable several years. Mr. and Mrs. Trusty have reared a family of eight children. The eldest, William C., was a schoolteacher several years, and is at present one of the proprietors of the flouring mills at Equality, Ill.

— *History of White County, Illinois.*

James B. Turner (deceased) – 1905

JAMES B. TURNER (deceased), late a resident of Equality, Ill., was born at Oswego, N.Y., Nov. 27, 1837. While still in his early boyhood his parents, Charles W. and Sally (Spencer) Turner, removed to Kenosha, Wis., where the mother died a few years later and James went to St. Louis to live with an elder brother, Dr. Carlos Turner. When he was about sixteen or seventeen years old he went to New Orleans on a flatboat and spent some months in visiting different places in the South. He then located at Elizabethtown, Ill., where he became interested in the study of law. After a preliminary course of reading he entered the law department of the Indiana State university at Bloomington in 1857. Two years later he completed his legal education and began practice in Shawneetown. Shortly after locating there he formed the acquaintance of Miss Eleanora, daughter of John D. Richeson, a prominent merchant of that city and about a year later they were married.

He continued to practice in Shawneetown for ten or twelve years, when he removed to Mount Vernon, Ill. After four years there he went to Ewing, in Franklin county, and took charge of a large general store, a woolen mill and a flour mill. Here he organized the Farmers' bank and was president of it for some time. After a residence of sixteen years at Ewing he located at Equality, where he practiced law until his death in 1893. While living at Shawneetown he filled the position of city judge for one term. Judge Turner and his wife had the following children: One who died unnamed in infancy; John D. R., who now lives in Springfield, Mo.; Spencer and Judith Mimms, both deceased; James B., Charles W., and Jesse M., all now living at Equality; Minnie T.; Mary, who died in infancy; Albert R., also deceased, and Eugene Ambrose, now living at Niagara Falls, N.Y. The mother of these children died in 1899.

Charles W. Turner, the sixth child of the family, was born at Shawneetown, Dec. 13, 1869. While living at Ewing he attended the college there, after which he attended the Southern Illinois Normal school at Carbondale, and took a course in the Bryant & Stratton business college at St. Louis. After the death of his father, in 1893, he took charge, with his brother, John D. R., of the large mercantile establishment at Equality, and the farming interests of the estate. Upon the death of his mother, six years later, he was appointed executor of the estate. In 1900 he went to Grand Rapids and assumed the management of an aunt's business matters during the last years of her life. In the fall of 1903 he returned to Equality, where now resides.

Mr. Turner has been successful as a business man. Just before going to Grand Rapids he built the Turner business block and opera house in Equality, which building he still owns. This marked his public spirit and enterprising disposition and shows that he is one of the progressive men of his town. He is a member of the Independent Order of Odd Fellows, the Modern Woodmen of America, and the Court of Honor, and both himself and wife belong to the Presbyterian church. Politically he is a Democrat, with Prohibition sympathies, though he never "dabbles" in politics. On Dec. 26, 1900, he was united in marriage to Miss Pet, daughter of George W. Moore, an old resident and grain dealer of Equality. Mrs. Turner was born near Equality, Sept. 26, 1877.

— *Memoirs of the Lower Ohio Valley.*

Peter J. Valter – 1912

PETER J. VALTER, vice-president of the Gallatin County Bank, of Ridgway, Illinois, and one of his section's leading capitalists, has been engaged in various lines of business for a number of years in Ridgway, has associated himself with enterprises for the development of Gallatin county land, and is now the owner of much valuable real estate in this part of the state. Mr. Valter is a product of Brown County, Ohio, and was born December 26, 1864, a son of Nicholas and Barbara (Pfarr) Valter.

Nicholas Valter was a native of the province of Alsace, France, and came to the United States as a young man, settling in Ohio, where he was married to Barbara Pfarr, a native of Bavaria, Germany. During the spring of 1883 he came to Gallatin County, Illinois, and purchased a tract of 60 acres of farming land adjoining the village of Ridgway, erecting the present family home during that same year. He also owned a farm near Bartley Station, and the remainder of his life was devoted to clearing and cultivating these properties, on which he erected four tenant houses. His death occurred in 1887, when he was 58 years of age, in the faith of the Catholic Church. His widow survived her husband three years and was also 58 years old at the time of her death. Three of their children grew to maturity, as follows: Mary, wife of Alexander Drone, of Evansville, Indiana, whose son, Marion, is cashier of the First National Bank of Ridgway; Peter J.; and Katie, who is the widow of Henry Zirkelbach.

Peter J. Valter assisted his father to clear the home farm until he was 20 years of age, and then, having secured a good public school education in Ohio, became a teacher and continued as such for four years. At the time of his father's death he returned home and took charge of the farm, being appointed administrator of the estate, and subsequently laid out Valter's Addition to Ridgway, a tract of nine acres. He acquired the Bartley Station farm and a part of the old homestead, and subsequently sold the addition, on which the public school now stands. In 1890 Mr. Valter embarked in the lumber and building material business at Ridgway, but after five years of successful operation sold his interests and rented his farms. He had been one of the original stockholders when the Gallatin County State Bank was organized in 1895, and since that time he has served as its vice president and also acted for a time as assistant cashier. In 1898 the Ridgway Dry Goods Company was organized, and Mr. Valter was its president for three years, devoting a part of his time to the store, but eventually sold his interest and began to invest in land. He added to the Bartley farm and secured 20 acres inside of the corporation limits, which has subsequently become the Citizens Addition to Ridgway. This farm is operated by tenants, as is also his 280-acre tract situated east of Ridgway, and both are in an excellent state of cultivation. This land, which cost Mr. Valter from 22 to 70 dollars per acre, is now all worth in excess of 100 dollars an acre. Mr. Valter is possessed of the happy faculty of recognizing an opportunity and being able to grasp it, and his large operations have made him known in the business, realty and financial fields. No man stands higher in the esteem of his business associates and fellow towns men, and any enterprise with which his name is connected has the en tire confidence of the people.

On June 20, 1906, Mr. Valter was married to Miss Celia Zirkelbach, who was born in Indiana and reared in Illinois and they have had two children: Arnold, who is four years old; and Dolores, who is two. The family is connected with St. Joseph's Catholic Church. Mr. Valter is a Democrat in his political views, and has served very acceptably as village clerk and as a member of the board of trustees.

— *History of Southern Illinois.*

George J. Vineyard – 1887

GEO. J. VINEYARD, farmer and pension agent, was born in 1834 in Hardin County, Ill., one of nine children of Eli P. and Sarah (Hill) Vineyard. The father, a farmer, was born November 15, 1806, in Virginia, came to Hardin County in 1811 when a child. After his marriage he purchased 200 acres of land on which he still resides. The mother, born in Georgia in 1808, came to Hardin County in 1824 with her parents. She died in August 1874.

With common-school advantages our subject began life, and became owner of his present fine farm of 200 acres in 1861. In 1855 he married Sarah, daughter of Jackson and Mary Moore, born in Gallatin County in 1838. Their six children are John T., Benjamin F., Margaret, Mary, George A. and Lucretia. Since 1877 he has served as justice, and since 188- has been pension agency, and has collected about $50,000 for soldiers.[272] Politically a Republican, his first vote was for Buchanan.

— *History of Gallatin, Saline, Hamilton, Franklin and Williamson Counties, Illinois.*

John B. Walters – 1905

JOHN B. WALTERS, farmer and justice of the peace, living about six miles west of Shawneetown, Ill., was born in that County, Sept. 25, 1846, on the farm now owned B. A. Meyer, in Bowlesville Township.

His grandfather, Hiram Walters, was a Virginian, who went to Tennessee when he was a young man and located near Sparta. There he married and had one son, John T., who was the father of the subject of this sketch. Hiram Walters' wife died soon after the birth of this son, and the widowed husband returned to Virginia, carrying the infant all the way on a pillow. There he made his home with a sister until 1834, when he came with his son to Gallatin County, entered government land in Bowlesville Township, and followed farming there until

---

[272] "188-" is in the original history.

his death. After coming to Illinois he was married to a Mrs. Kinsall, but no children were born to this second marriage.

John T. Walters was born at Sparta, Tenn., in 1820, and was therefore about fourteen years old when his father brought him to Gallatin County. A year or two later he began life on his own account as a farm hand, and continued in this occupation until he married Eliza Brown, a native of South Carolina, and commenced farming on part of the old home place. There they both lived until death overtook them, with the exception of a short time they lived in Shawneetown. He was prominently identified with the affairs of the County, served as constable, sheriff, and county commissioner, as well as school treasurer and other minor officers. He was for many years regarded as one of the leading Democrats of the county, and was a member of the Independent Order of Odd Fellows. Generous to a fault, he went security for his friends, and in the latter part of life was made almost bankrupt from this cause. He and his wife had three children: Hiram, living at Equality, Ill.; John B., the subject; and William, residing at Shawneetown. John T. Walters died at the age of sixty-two and his wife lived to be seventy-four years of age.

John B. Walters was educated in the common schools and at Notre Dame, South Bend, Ind. He married Nannie, daughter of James M. and Rebecca Wathen, of Gallatin County, and commenced life on his own account as a farmer near where he now lives. In 1878 he bought his present place of 100 acres, 40 of which were under cultivation. Since then he has added by purchase another 50 acres, and nearly all of his farm is now under cultivation and well stocked and improved. Mr. Walters has been for years one of the Democratic wheel horses of Gallatin County. With the exception of about eighteen months he has served as justice of the peace for the last twenty-six years. Of the children born to him and his wife Bertha, Mattie and one who died in infancy are deceased; Estella and Lydia are married and live in Gallatin County; John T., Edith, Hiram, William I., Rebecca, and James are at home. Mrs. Walters died on Nov. 23, 1900.

— Memoirs of the Lower Ohio Valley.

William H. Walters – 1883

WILLIAM H. WALTERS, son of Charles and Nancy Walters, was born in Montgomery County, Tenn., March 21, 1849. His parents came to Illinois in 1861. Mr. Walters received a common-school education. He is one of Gallatin County's most industrious farmers. He has served very acceptably as constable five years, and deputy sheriff three years. He resides on his farm one-half mile west of Omaha.

— History of White County, Illinois.

John T. Wathen – 1887

JOHN T. WATHEN, farmer, was born near Shawneetown, Ill., December 21, 1842. His father, James M., born in Union County, Ky., in 1818, came to Illinois with is parents when one year old. Joseph, the grandfather, formerly of Maryland, and at an early age in Kentucky, early in life renounced the Catholic faith and became an earnest member of the Baptist Church. A pioneer from taste, he came to Illinois in 1819, and when this State became settled, moved to Iowa, where he died in 1856. The father, James M., reared in Gallatin County, when of age married Rebecca Pilkington, a native of North Carolina, and with her parents an early settler in Illinois. She died in Gallatin County in 1866. They had ten children. By his second marriage he had two daughters. He was a cooper, but later in life a farmer, dying in June 1874, on the farm on which he was partly reared.

Our subject received an ordinary education, and although he taught school in early life, he has made farming his chief business. March 10, 1864, he marred Catherine, daughter of William Byrne, a native of Dublin, Ireland. She was born near Equality, April 10, 1844. Their children are Hettie A., Mary E., William M., John A. and Willis G. Our subject is a staunch Republican, but cast his first vote for McClellan. He owns 375 acres of land, 175 of which is in the home place west of Equality.

— *History of Gallatin, Saline, Hamilton, Franklin and Williamson Counties, Illinois.*

Ellen B. White – 1887

ELLEN B. WHITE, teacher, was born in 1860, in Gallatin County, Ill., one of eleven children of Thornton and Margaret (Colbert) Barnett. The father, born in 1826, in Gallatin County, is one of the foremost farmers of his native county, owning 400 acres of land. The mother was born in 1843, in the same county, where she is still living on the old homestead.

Educated at St. Vincent's Academy, Union County, Ky., our subject has been one of the first teachers in Gallatin County. November 27, 1881, she married Wiley F. White, son of Don and Sarah White, and born in Smith County, Tenn., August 8, 1856. He was a farmer, and owner of 200 acres of lend, and lived on his farm an influential young man until his death in 1883. Their one child, Willie, died when but six months old. Since the death of her husband, Mrs. White has been engaged in teaching, living with her parents. She is a member of the Social Brethren Church.

— *History of Gallatin, Saline, Hamilton, Franklin and Williamson Counties, Illinois.*

Isaac White (deceased) – 1889

ISSAC WHITE.

To the Knox County Historical Society,

Sirs: In response to a request made to me some time since by my brother-in-law, Major Albert G. Sloo, the present Clerk of the Knox County Circuit Court. I take pleasure in submitting to you, for whatever use you may think proper to make of it, a short memoir of my grandfather, Col. Isaac White, one of the early citizens of your county.

Much of the information contained in this memoir I obtained orally from my father; some I got from my Virginia cousins, the descendants of Mrs. Katy Davis, my grandfather's sister; some, again, from letters and other family papers in my possession; and some from very interesting manuscript notes written by Mrs. Sarah M. Hayden, concerning the Leech branch of my family, and kindly loaned to me for my information.

The sketch, as you will no doubt perceive, is very imperfect, but it is as nearly complete as I have been able to make it. Such as it is. I present it to you with the hope that it will be of some interest to the members of your Society, in bringing before them the career of a brave, intelligent, and honorable man, who aided greatly, during the time he was a citizen of Indiana Territory, in dignifying its history, and in laying the foundations of that greatness and prosperity, which our beloved State has since reached.

Yours respectfully, &c.,
Geo. F. White.

The subject of this sketch, Isaac White, was born in Prince William County, Virginia, shortly after the beginning of the Revolutionary War. The exact year of his birth is not now positively known, bur from the record of his initiation, in 1811, as a member of Masonic Lodge, No. 1, of Vincennes, Indiana, in which is age is stated to be 35 years, and from certain interesting family notes written by Mrs. Sarah M. Hayden, which are as yet unpublished, it is altogether likely that he was born in the year 1776. His father, who probably was of English origin, was a man of education and good family, and prior to this settling in Virginia, had held a captain's commission in the British Merchant Marine service. Surrendering this office, he purchased a large tract of land in Prince William County, and successfully devoted himself to farming until the war of the Revolution began, when, taking up arms against the tyranny of the British Government, he lost his life near the end of the war nobly fighting for the independence of his adopted country. The old house where his patriot lived — a substantial, roomy stone structure, indication in all its arrangements that it was t home of a cultured and hospitable gentleman — is still standing, in an excellent state of preservation, near Brentsville, the county seat of Prince William County. In this house Isaac White was born, as was his elderly brother, Thomas, and one younger sister, Katie, and here he continued to live with his mother, assisting her, as he grew in age and experience, in the management of the estate, until he had nearly reached his twenty-four year, when an unhappy event in his mother's life impelled him and his brother to seek a new and more adventurous career in the great Northwest territory. It seems that on an occasion when the two sons and all the male servants of the plantation were absent from home, a strange man called at the house and asked for something to eat — a request which, in accordance with the hospitality of those days, was at once complied with; but not satisfied with this kind treatment, and seeing only women about, he demanded the keys of the drawers where the family treasure was kept, and on being refused them by Mrs. White, he endeavored by ruffianly violence to take them from her person. Her screams attracted the attention of a neighbor-a bachelor gentleman — who being out on a hunting expedition, and fortunately passing at the time, rushed in and brained the would-be robber on the spot! The gratitude of Mrs. White to her gallant rescuer (who after judicial inquiry was not only exonerated from all blame but extolled for his bravery), and no doubt the appreciation of the gentleman, who was in rather needy circumstances, for Mrs. White's comfortable home and broad acres, brought about in little time a marriage; which, while it may have given happiness to the contracting parties, gave eminent displeasure to the two sons; so much so that they remained with their mother only long enough to see their sister happily and eligibly married, when, without any great superfluity of money, they bade adieu to the old homestead, and made their way to Vincennes, soon afterwards to be the seat of government of Indiana Territory. This was in the beginning of 1800.

Naturally the advent of an enterprising man — handsome, brave, well-bred, and full of spirit, such as young White was at this time — was calculated to create some little excitement in any village of a sparsely settled country; and so it did at Vincennes. He won his way at once to the hearts of everybody whose goodwill was worth having. Not only was he welcomed by the elders of the village, but he was a special favorite with the young ladies. In Mrs. Hayden's unpublished notes, before referred to, the following statement occurs regarding the family of Judge George Leech, then living at Vincennes, and particularly of his eldest daughter, Sallie, who soon became young White's wife, Mrs. Hayden's statement is substantially a repetition of the artless recital of her mother, formerly Miss Amy Leech, a sister of Sallie, and the wife of Hon. John Marshall, for many years the President of the Bank of Illinois at Shawneetown:

> "The eldest daughter, Sallie," Mrs. Hayden says, "was now approaching a marriageable age, and her beauty and loveliness of manner attracted the attention and won the affections of a young Virginian, who had recently moved to their vicinity, Mr. Isaac White. Like the natives of his State, he had a courtly, aristocratic bearing, which some of the country people, in their inaccurate dialect, called pompous. He was quite a beau, and considered the best prize in the matrimonial field at that time. But while he rode with, and visited, and went to the simply merry-makings of the day with _____ _____ and other gay and dashing girls, it was not from among them that he cared to selected a wife. * * * He required in the one who should be the companion of a lifetime the tender graces of a truer womanhood. * * * Many were surprised that this modest unassuming girl should have won the love of so gallant a young man, or that, with his aspirations, he should have been willing to marry a poor girl. It was the source of gratification to the parents that their sweet wild-wood blossom had made so excellent a match, and they accordingly set to work to do the best they possibly could in the momentous affair."

Mrs. Hayden says further:

> "A wedding dinner was prepared, to which most all the people of the surrounding country were invited; but mother smilingly added, when narrating this (alluding to the smallness of the population), that the guests were not very numerous after all. I do not know who officiated, but presume Judge Decker, because when my mother was married, a few years later, grandfather with to have him perform the ceremony; but she refused, preferring her own father, who was then a judge of probate."

The gentleman, Judge George Leech, into whose family Isaac White thus entered, had emigrated to Vincennes from Louisville, Kentucky, with his brother Francis and other relatives and friends, in the year 1784, and they had all selected homesteads in Knox County; but after a three-years sojourn, and owning to Indian depredations and barbarities (Judge

Leech having his house burned over his head by them), they all, with the exception of Francis Leech, who had died, moved back to Louisville. Nine years later, in 1796, Judge Leech again emigrated to Vincennes; but the governor of the Northwest Territory refused him permission to reoccupy the land on which he had formerly lived, although it was still vacant, and he was therefore compelled to occupy the land which had belonged to his brother. Afterwards, when General Wm. Henry Harrison was appointed governor of Indiana Territory, Judge Leech was granted 100 acres more, and this tract, which he gave as a marriage present to his daughter, and which is now a part of what is known as the White-Hall Farm in Knox County, was the nucleus of a very considerable estate, which Col. White acquired after his marriage.

Like all pioneers in a new county, Isaac White and his wife had plenty of hardships to encounter; but they had also the sympathy and friendship of their neighbors — characteristics that are so often met among people who have left the comforts of civilization to brave the privations of new life in the forest or on the prairie. An illustration of the friendly help which the settlers in a new country are so ready to give one another when necessary is shown in the fact that on one occasion when the home of the Whites was burned to the ground, their friends and neighbors from all parts of the country, with one accord "pitched in," to use the vernacular of the West, and in a few weeks reared them a larger, more substantial, and altogether more comfortable home (of hewn logs, be it understood) than the one that had been burned. In this house the eldest child of the young couple, George W. L. White, was born; here they gravely struggled year after year for the advancement of their earthly interests, not forgetting their spiritual ones; and here they enjoyed that happiness which, whether in the log-house or in the palace, can come only form love and the exercise of virtue and industry. They were reckoned among the best people of the Territory, and their friendliness of character, charity, and public spirit were conspicuous traits. Among others, they became friends of Governor Harrison and his family, and the friendship thus begun was transmitted to their children.

A striking evidence of this friendship of the Governor is shown in his appointment of Mr. White as Agent of the United States at the Salt Works on Saline Creek, in Illinois, contiguous to the present village of Equality, in Gallatin County. The following is a copy of this appointment:

>Indiana Territory.
>
>William Henry Harrison, Governor and Commander-in-Chief of the Indiana Territory,
>
>[seal.] To all who shall see these presents, Greeting:
>
>Know ye, that in pursuance of instructions from the President of the United States, I have constituted and appointed, and do by these presents constitute and appoint, Isaac White, of Knox County, to be agent for the United States, to reside at the Salt Works on Saline Creek, for the purpose of receiving and selling the salt and to perform such other acts and things as the Government of the United States may think proper to charge him with. This commission to continue during pleasure.
>
>Given under my hand and seal of the Territory, at Vincennes, this 30th day of April, 1805, and of the Independence of the United States the Twenty-ninth.

Willm. Henry Harrison.
By the Governor:
Jno. Gibson, Secretary.

Among the persons employed by Isaac White, in his capacity of Government agent of these salt works was John Marshall, a man of the most sterling character, and who afterwards, as a banker, acquired a great reputation both in Indiana and Illinois. In the following year their connection became closer still – Marshall having married Mrs. White's younger sister, Amy Leech. The following reference to this interesting event occurs in Mrs. Hayden's notes, before mentioned:

> The marriage occurred on the 21st of October, 1806, and accompanied by Colonel White and her sister (Mrs. White), they "—that is, young Marshall and his bride—" set out next day for the salt works, where their home was to be for the present — he (Marshall) being employed a book-keeper by Colonel White.

Mrs. Hayden has unconsciously fallen into a slight anachronism in referring here to Isaac White as "Colonel." He had not as yet reached that honor, but have had, a little more than a month before, been appointed a captain in the Knox County militia, as the following copy of his commission will show:

> William Henry Harrison, Governor and Commander-in-Chief of the Indiana Territory, to Isaac white, Esq., of the County of Knox, Greeting:
> Reposing special trust and confidence in your fidelity, courage, and good conduct, I have appointed you a captain of the company in the ___ battalion of the ___ regiment of the militia of the County of Knox, and you are hereby appointed accordingly. You are, therefore, carefully and diligently to discharge the duty of a captain, in leading, ordering, and exercising the said company in arms, both inferior officers and soldiers, and to keep them in good order and discipline; and they are hereby commended to obey you as their captain, and you, yourself, to observe and follow such orders and instructions as you shall from time to time receive from me or your superior officers.
> In testimony whereof I have hereunto caused the seal of the Territory to be affixed the eighth day of September, in the year of our Lord one thousand eight hundred and six, and of the Independence of the United States of America the Thirty-first.
> [Territorial Seal.] Willm Henry Harrison.
> By the Governor's command:
> Jno. Gibson, Secretary.
> [Endorsement]: Wm. H. Harrison to Isaac White. Commission in militia. Captain.
> On the 10th day of September, 1806, personally came before me the within-named Isaac White, and had administered unto him the oath to support the Constitution of the U.S.
> Given under my hand and seal the day and year above given.

Willm H. Harrison.
Isaac White, Esq. Captain. Militia. Knox County.

How long the Salt-Works Agency lasted cannot be stated: it is presumed not very long, however, for, from the papers now in the hands of Colonel White's descendants, it would seem probably that, under a statute of the United States then in existence — the act of Congress of March 3, 1803 — which authorized the leasing of Salt Springs belonging to the Government, Col. White had in 1807 acquire a private interest in the Salt Works, which he held until shortly before his death, finally disposing of it, with other business interests, to Wilkes, Taylor & Co., and returning to Vincennes. As lessee of the Springs, he acquired considerable wealth, the manufacture of salt being quite lucrative, and the celebrated Kanawha salt springs in Virginia not being then discovered so that the Illinois Works supplied the whole Territory.

While residing at these Salt Works Colonel White had two daughters born to him — Harriet Grandison, on June 12, 1808, and Juliet Greenville, on July 30, 1810. While there, also, he was appointed a colonel, probably in the militia of Illinois Territory, which was organized under the act of Congress of February 3, 1809. The commission of Colonel White is unfortunately lost, but the evidence of his having received it is conclusive, and, indeed, undisputed.

At a public installation of the officers of a Masonic Lodge at Evansville many year ago, Hon. John Law, in a closing address to the Lodge, made the following reference to the death of these two brave men, which, though inaccurate in its statement that Daviess came to Vincennes in command of a corps of mounted Kentucky rangers, and that Colonel White commanded a regiment at the battle of Tippecanoe, is sufficiently interesting to quote in this place:

> "On the 18th day of September, 1811," Judge Law said, "Joseph H. Daviess, grand Master of the Grand Lodge of Kentucky came to Vincennes, commanding a corps of mounted rangers then on their route to the battle-field of Tippecanoe, where the battle was fought with the Indians in November of the same year, and where Daviess was killed while making a brilliant and successful charge on his savage foes. His remains now rest, where they properly should, on the bloody field where he fought so bravely, and where, after the battle, I saw then nearly half a century since, deposited under a majestic oak of the forest near where he fell, on the soil of Indiana, fattened with the best blood of our people, and mingled with that of our friends and neighbors from the south side of the Ohio, who came to our assistance, and to whom we owe a debt of gratitude which should never be forgotten to the latest generation. The County of Daviess was named after him. While at Vincennes with his regiment he acted as Master of the Lodge there, and conferred the degree of Master Mason on Colonel Isaac White, the grandfather of our esteemed friend, Isaac White, now a citizen of Evansville, and named after him. Colonel White also commanded a regiment from Knox County, and fell on the same field. It is a singular fact that these noble men, the Master and the Neophyte — he who gave the Masonic Degree of Master Mason, and he who receive it — in less than two months after, felon the same battle-field, killed by

the same foe, and were buried side by side, with their martial cloaks around them. Two more noble men or braver soldiers, or true and faithful Brethren of the Order, never sacrificed their lives in the defense of their country. May we not hope and believe that both these true and loyal Brothers have been transferred from earth to heaven?"

Lieutenant George Leech, the brother-in-law of Colonel White, and who was a participant of the battle, is also authority for the statement that Daviess and White were buried side by side, under an oak tree which he had marked, but which an inability to revisit the battle-ground had afterwards prevented him from permanently identifying.

Colonel White was in the 36th year of his age when he died. He was widely known, and universally beloved. Liberal and charitable — not the least bit penurious or avaricious — he yet amassed a considerable fortune for that day, his lands amounting to several thousand acres in extent, and his personal property being not insignificant. His character was without reproach — treachery and cowardice, deceit, and all forms of meanness, being hateful to him. A loving husband and father, a kind and steadfast friend, a good and enterprising citizens, and a patriotic can gallant soldier — he, like hundreds of others of the pioneers of Indiana, who settled within her boarders to hew their way to fame and fortune, has left a name which should not be permitted to be soon forgotten. This, indeed, is not likely to happen; for two great States — Indiana and Illinois — in order to perpetuate his memory, have, as will appear from the historical notices below, given his name to two prosperous counties within their respective borders.

He left a widow, who in 1816 married again, her second husband being Samuel Marshall, the brother of John Marshall; but she died three years after, in 1819. He also left three children — George Washington Leech White, afterwards a prominent citizens of Indiana, who, by commission from Governor Coles, of Illinois, served as lieutenant-colonel and aide-de-camp to Major-General Willis Hargrave in the Black-Hawk War;[273] Harriet Grandison White, who married Mr. Albert Gallatin Sloo, at White Hall farm, in Knox County; and Juliet Greenville White, who married Mr. James Huffman. From Colonel White's son, who married Miss Eliza Griffin Fauntleroy, of Kentucky, are descended Colonel George Fauntleroy White, now a citizen of Knox County (who has participated in two wars, the Mexican War and the late War of the Rebellion), and Dr. Isaac T. White, for many years a prominent citizens of Evansville, Indiana. From the eldest daughter of Colonel White are descended, among others, Major A. G. Sloo, now clerk of the Knox County Circuit Court, his brother Thos. Sloo, a citizen of the same county, and his sisters. Sarah E. Sloo, who married Col. Francis E. McIlvaine, Mary Frances Sloo, who married her cousin, Col. Geo. F. White, before mentioned, Juliet White Sloo, who married Hon. R. J. Corwine, and Harriet White Sloo, who is still unmarried — the father of all these being Colonel Albert G. Sloo, who in his day, as a man of immense enterprise and at one time of great wealth, was known from one end of the United States to the other.

— George Fauntleroy White (grandson of Col. Isaac White). 1889. *Sketch of the Life of Colonel Isaac White, of Vincennes, Indiana. Killed at the Battle of Tippecanoe, November 7, 1811.* Washington: Gibson Bros., Printers and Bookbinders.

---

[273] The author has the wrong governor at this point.

J. W. Wilkins – 1905

J. W. WILKINS, who conducts a blacksmith and general repair shop at Shawneetown, Ill., was born in Muhlenberg county, Ky., Feb. 19, 1859. His father was born in Muhlenberg county, though the ancestors came originally from England, and were among the early settlers of Kentucky. James W. Wilkins, the father of the subject of this sketch, married Margaret J. Latham in Muhlenberg county and lived there until 1860, when they went to Union county of the same state and lived there until 1871, when they came to Gallatin county, Ill., bought a farm near Kedron and lived there until the death of the father at the age of sixty-three years. The mother died in Shawneetown at the age of forty-eight. Of their ten children only three are living: Jefferson D., who lives near Kedron; Nathaniel, who is in Columbus, O., and the subject of this sketch.

J. W. Wilkins received a very limited education in his youth, but he has managed to gather a valuable fund of information by self-study and by associating with well-informed men. In 1875 he left home and went to White county, where he found employment in a sawmill. Some time later he went to Hamilton county and took charge of a sawmill there until 1884, when he returned to Gallatin county and followed farming until 1897. He then removed to Shawneetown and engaged in his present line of business, in which he had just got a good start when the great flood came and swept away everything he had accumulated. With commendable enterprise he started over again, and by industry honest dealing and a close attention to business has built up a good trade, requiring the assistance of two workmen all the time to keep up with the demand. Much of his success is due to his personal popularity, as few men in Gallatin county are more universally liked.

In 1879 he was married to Mrs. Margaret Sullivan Hoskins, a native of Hamilton county and a widow with one child, Sarah Elizabeth. Mr. and Mrs. Wilkins have five children living, viz.: William, Oma, Virginia, Paul, and Wilmer. Mr. Wilkins takes considerable interest in political affairs as a Democrat, but is not a seeker for office. His wife belongs to the Methodist Episcopal church.

— *Memoirs of the Lower Ohio Valley.*

W. J. Wilks – 1905

W. J. WILKS, a farmer near Shawneetown, Ill., was born on March 10, 1860, not far from Madisonville, Hopkins county, Ky. He is the youngest of twelve children, six sons and six daughters, born to H. J. and Pauline Wilks. Only two of the family are now living. When lie was about two years of age his mother died and in 1866 his father came with the family to Gallatin county, Ill., where he bought 120 acres of land in the river bottoms and died there the following year. After the death of his father the subject of this sketch lived with a family named Duvall, working for his board and clothes, with the privilege of attending school a few months each year, until he was seventeen years old. He then commenced life on his own responsibilities as a farm hand, which occupation lie followed for several years, saving his money with a view to some day becoming a farmer on his own land.

On Aug. 12, 1888, he was united in marriage to Mrs. Laura Meek, a daughter of Thomas Logsdon, and for the next four years was the manager of Charles Carroll's farm. At the end of that time he bought the farm where he now lives, five miles from Shawneetown, and began farming on his own account. Since then he has bought and paid for 80 acres in New Haven township. On the two farms he has 150 acres under cultivation.

Mr. Wilks is a Democrat in politics; though the only office he has ever held was that of school director, which he occupied to the entire satisfaction of his neighbors for three years. He is a modest, unassuming gentleman, whose chief aim in life seems to be to mind his own business, and it is to this trait of character that much of his success in life is due. Naturally such a man possesses the confidence and respect of the people around him, and few men in the community stand higher in a general way than Mr. Wilks.

— *Memoirs of the Lower Ohio Valley.*

Aaron Wilson (colored) – 1887

AARON WILSON (colored), farmer, was born in Kentucky in 1834, a son of Aaron, Sr., and Queenie (De Ball) Wilson. They father is supposed to have been a slave in Virginia of E. Wilson, afterward a resident of Kentucky. He remained in bondage about 50 years, during which time he was married and had several children. He finally obtained his freedom, and purchased his wife and three children, the rest of whom continued slaves until the emancipation. He then went to Illinois, where he died in 1848 in Gallatin County. The mother was born in Union County, Ky., and died in 1858, about 80 years old.

Our subject has been twice married, having left home at 21. In 1854 he married Flora Eddy. Five of their six children are living: Flora, wife of John Dimmett; Queenie, wife of George Wilson; Mary, wife of James Stephens; Laura, wife of E. Dickerson, and Davis. Mrs. Wilson died in 1860. In 1875 he married Susan Nash, by whom he had two children, one living — John.

Since his 11 years as drayman in Shawneetown, he has been farming, and is owner of 178 acres of improved land, five miles west of Shawneetown. His first wife, a native of Virginia, was a member of the Methodist Episcopal Church. Mr. Wilson is a Republican and a Mason.

— *History of Gallatin, Saline, Hamilton, Franklin and Williamson Counties, Illinois.*

Bluford Wilson – 1904

BLUFORD WILSON — There is something akin to poetic justice in the fact that Bluford Wilson is recognized as a distinguished and prominent citizen of the state in which his ancestors were pioneers. They aided in laying the foundation of the great commonwealth of Illinois and from an early period in its development the name has been closely interwoven with its history in connection with progress, upbuilding and advancement. Furthermore the family has a notable record for patriotism and for military service and General Wilson of this review has added new lustre to the record made by his father, his grandfather and great-grandfather. Isaac Wilson, the last named, was a soldier of the war of the Revolution, serving for three years in the Virginia State Line as a sergeant under command of Captain Augustine Tabb. When the war was over and the independence of the nation was assured he removed with his family from the Old Dominion and became a resident of Fayette county, Kentucky.

Alexander Wilson, the grandfather of our subject, established his home in Union county, Kentucky, and afterward came to Illinois, settling in Gallatin county in 1808. The work of reclaiming this wild district had scarcely been begun. There was a little fort upon the present site of the city of Chicago for protection for a few scattering settlers against an Indian attack. A few settlements had also been made in the southern portion of the state, but the greater portion of the broad prairies remained as they came from the hand of nature. Alexander Wilson was a man of influence who left the impress of his individuality upon the public life of the locality. He was a member of the first council of the territory of Illinois and was the personal friend of Governor Ninian Edwards and Governor Ford, enjoying the confidence and esteem of those distinguished men to an unusual degree. He was sent to the territorial legislature which met in Kaskaskia, then the capital of the state, but in recent years the town has become entirely obliterated, remaining only as a memory in the minds of the early settlers. While in the legislature, Mr. Wilson served as chairman of various committees and speaker of the house, and largely aided in molding public policy in those, its territorial days. He died in January 1814, and the legislature in subsequent session showed its appreciation of the man and his service by granting to his heirs the privilege of ferry franchise at Shawneetown, which has ever since remained in the family.

Harrison Wilson, the father of our subject, was born in Culpepper county, Virginia, and he too rendered his country valiant service by becoming a soldier of the war of 1812. While in the Black Hawk war he was captain of a spy battalion. He married Catherine Schneider, who was born in Gambsheim, near Strasburg, Alsace, whence she came to America in the early part of the nineteenth century with her father, Augustus Schneider.

A new chapter was added to the military history of the family during the period of the Civil war. General James Harrison Wilson, a brother of our subject, was a graduate of West Point and became one of the celebrated officers of the Union service, was a distinguished member of General Grant's staff and was one of Sheridan's division commanders. He afterward commanded Sherman's cavalry and was largely instrumental in securing the decisive victory over Hood in the engagement at Nashville. He led his corps to victory when opposing Forrest, the noted cavalry commander of the south and closed the war by the capture of Jefferson Davis.

He was also a major general in the war against Spain and is now a retired brigadier general of the United States army and his life record forms a part of the history of his country. His brother, Major Henry S. Wilson, distinguished himself as an officer in the Eighteenth Illinois Volunteer Infantry, in which he successfully served as adjutant, captain and major, and our subject was also a veteran in the Civil war, so that the three sons of Harrison Wilson nobly maintained the fighting prestige of their Revolutionary and pioneer sires.

Colonel Bluford Wilson was born near Shawneetown, Gallatin county, Illinois, November 30, 1841, and for a short period was a student in the public schools there. He afterward conducted the ferry which has always been in possession of the family and with money earned in this and other ways he was enabled to continue his education as a student in McKendree College, which he entered in 1859. Desirous of becoming a member of the bar he entered the University of Michigan, but after the outbreak of the Civil war he could no longer content himself to continue his studies while the preservation of the Union was in doubt and in 1862 he enlisted in the One Hundred and Twentieth Illinois Infantry, becoming a member of the company commanded by Captain P. B. Pillow. However, before the regiment took the field he was made adjutant and in May, 1863, he was promoted to the rank of captain and became assistant adjutant general on the staff of Brigadier General Michael K. Lawler. He bore an active part in the Vicksburg campaign, participating in the battles of Champion Hills, Black River and the siege of Vicksburg, and he served on the staffs of Generals Dana and Eugene A. Carr, in Texas, Louisiana and Alabama. During the Red River campaign he was adjutant general of the Thirteenth Corps, then commanded by General Lawler, and for gallant conduct he was breveted major, in pressing the siege and assault of Spanish Fort, continuing to serve on General Carr's staff until the close of the war.

When hostilities had ceased Major Wilson returned to the north with a most creditable military record and continued the study of law in the University of Michigan until his admission to the bar in Shawneetown, in 1867. The following year he was made the candidate of the Republican party for the office of state's attorney and in 1869 he was appointed by President Grant United States district attorney for the southern district of Illinois, acting in that capacity until the re-election of General Grant, when in May, 1874, he was made solicitor of the treasury. The position was a very responsible one and he a young man of but thirty-three years of age, but the same loyalty, determination and comprehensive understanding of duty that marked his military services were also manifest in his official career.

In Washington he was the main support of General B. H. Bristow, secretary of the treasury, in the famous contest against the Whiskey Ring, which was the most powerful and extensive combine of public plunderers that ever disgraced the civil service of the country. In this combine were not only many distillers, but also collectors and supervisors of internal revenue and men high in political authority who had gained the confidence of the president and then betrayed their trust in a most infamous manner. Owing to the work of Major Wilson, General Bristow and others, this combine was completely crushed out and its ringleaders were sent to the penitentiary. In recognition of the services of Major Wilson, General Bristow wrote to him the following letter:

> Washington, D. C., June 20, 1876.
>
> My Dear Wilson: I can not take leave of the treasury department without expressing to you my great gratitude for the earnest and able support you have given me throughout my term of service. Whatever has been accomplished in the direction of enforcing law and bringing to merited punishment those who for a considerable time had plundered the public revenue and debauched the public service, is due more to your courageous, able and efficient conduct than to any effort of my own. The government owes you more than it is likely to pay. I beg you to be assured that I carry with me into private life, the most grateful remembrance of your fidelity, zeal and capacity with which you have met all your official duties and obligations, as well as the uniform kindness and friendship extended to me during our official relations. May heaven bless and prosper you in all your undertakings. Sincerely and gratefully your friend, B. H. Bristow.
>
> Hon. Bluford Wilson, Solicitor of the treasury.

In the meantime Major Wilson had become actively connected with his brother, General Wilson, in the development and building of railroads in the southern portion of Illinois and as the result of their efforts the St. Louis & Southeastern Railroad, from East St. Louis to Shawneetown and to Evansville, Indiana, came into existence. The line was afterward extended to Nashville, Tennessee, and this property now constitutes the St. Louis end of the Louisville & Nashville Railroad, and has been a most important element in the development of southern Illinois and southern Indiana. The brothers also constructed the Cairo & Vincennes Railroad, now an important part of the Cleveland, Cincinnati, Chicago & St. Louis Railroad, and they organized the company which built the Louisville, Evansville & St. Louis Railroad, now the St. Louis connection of the great Southern Railway system. In this regard the work of Major Wilson is deserving of special commendation. He was perhaps in advance of his time in the recognition of the possibilities and opportunities for railroad building. For a few years his work did not produce a remunerative return, but in the course of time these various railroad lines became of the greatest value in opening up different sections of the country to trade relations and thereby promoting the commercial prosperity and welfare of the localities through which they passed.

On resigning his official position in Washington in 1876, Major Wilson became a resident of Springfield, and has gained distinction as a member of the bar of this city. He is particularly well known as a practitioner in the United States courts and as a corporation lawyer. He is now general solicitor for the Chicago, Peoria & St. Louis Railway Company, general counsel for the Illinois Southern Railway Company, in which he is a stockholder, and is controlling an extensive private practice as a member of the firm of Wilson & Warren, his partner being his son-in-law, Philip Barton Warren. Few of the members of the Illinois bar have a more comprehensive and accurate understanding of the principles of jurisprudence than does Bluford Wilson. He is especially well informed in the department of law concerning corporations and the character of his clientage indicates his high standing as a representative of the legal profession.

From the time of the organization of the Republican party down to the present Major Wilson has been a Republican, although he differed radically from the polity of the party in 1892 and cast his ballot for Grover Cleveland. He announced his intention of doing so and also made the statement that Judge Gresham would follow the same course. This was vigorously denied by men prominent in the ranks of the Republican party and as a vindication of his statement Major Wilson published the following:

> To the public: The truth of the statement made by myself and others, that Judge Gresham said he intended to vote for Mr. Cleveland at the coming election, has been persistently denied, not only by the Republican press, but also by the Republican national committee and upon the stump. It is due to Judge Gresham and his friends that the truth should be known, and I therefore take the responsibility of giving to the public his letter of the 27th of October, addressed to me. Bluford Wilson.

> Chicago, Ill., Oct. 27, 1892
> Hon. Bluford Wilson, Springfield, Ill.

Dear Major: I have your letter of the 21st inst. I did tell you, at Springfield, that, after mature reflection, I had determined to vote for Mr. Cleveland this fall, because I agreed in the main with his views on the tariff and did not believe in the principles embodied in the McKinley bill. I adhere to that determination and have said nothing indicating a change of purpose. It is not true that with my knowledge or consent the president was asked to appoint me to any office. It is not true that I requested any one to say or do anything to obtain the Republican nomination this year. It is not true that I voted for Mr. Cleveland in 1888. I voted the Republican ticket at every presidential election since the party was organized, except in 1864, when I was not able to go to the polls. Republicans were pledged to a reduction of the war tariff long before 1888 and during the campaign of that year the pledge was renewed with emphasis again and again. Instead of keeping that promise the McKinley bill was passed, imposing still higher duties. It was in the interest of the favored classes and not for the benefit of the whole people. It neither enhanced the price of farm products nor benefited labor. Wages are and ever will be regulated by supply and demand. Duties were imposed upon some articles so high as to destroy competition and foster trusts and monopolies. I think you will agree with me that this was an abandonment of the doctrine of moderate, incidental protection. The tariff is now the most important question before the people and whatever others may do I shall exercise the right of individual judgment and vote according to my convictions. I think with you that a Republican can vote for Mr. Cleveland without joining the Democratic party. How I shall vote in the future will depend upon the questions at issue. Yours very truly, W. Q. Gresham.

With this exception, however, Major Wilson has been a firm and unfaltering Republican, although he has never failed to support his honest convictions when occasion warranted. He differed radically from his party concerning the Hawaiian question as treated during the Cleveland administration, strongly opposing the lowering of the American flag, which he believed to be lawfully floating over the islands. By telegram, letter and in personal conference he insisted that the act of annexation had been completed in President Harrison's administration; that it accorded in all respects with the traditional and patriotic aspirations of the great majority of the American people regardless of party and that the law of *stare decisis* in the administration of the state department should be as inviolable in American cabinets as in England, where no matter who is premier the state department always stands "four square" to the outside world. It is a matter of history that Major Wilson's views were not accepted in Washington and it is also known that no act of President Cleveland during his second term of office did more to re-establish Republican supremacy.

Patriotism may well be termed the keynote of the character of Major Wilson. It was again strongly manifest when the Spanish-American war was inaugurated, for at that time he offered his services to the governor of the state, who gave him authority to raise a regiment of infantry on the 22d of April, 1898. Three days later his regiment had more than the full quota of men and he tendered his aid to the governor. In the meantime, however, the governor had decided to give the militia organizations preference, and Colonel Wilson was therefore obliged to hold his regiment until the militia organizations who desired so to do were sent to the field. Then came the order for the Eighth Illinois, a colored regiment, to supersede the First Illinois in the field and again political reasons interfered with an order that would send Bluford Wilson's Provisional Regiment to the front, the Ninth Illinois being sent in its place. This regiment, however, would have been the next in order of muster had not the close of the war crushed his hopes for active service. All of this time Major Wilson had from fifteen hundred to three thousand men ready to respond to his call and many of these were sent to the front. A member of Mitchell Post, No. 450, G.A.R., he has served as its commander and is also identified with the Loyal Legion, Illinois Commandery.

On the 3^d of July, 1865, occurred the marriage of Colonel Wilson and Miss Alice Warren Mather, a daughter of Captain James Mather, of Louisville, Kentucky, and the became the parents of five children: Harry, who died in infancy; Jessie, the wife of Philip Barton Warren; Lucy, the wife of Ralph Vance Dickerman; Bluford, who was the champion wrestler and wing shot at Yale as well as an excellent student during his senior year; and Arthur Harrison, who is now a cadet at West Point.

The family attend the services of Christ church, protestant Episcopal, at Springfield, which Major Wilson aided in organizing in 1888, since which time he has served as senior warden. He is also a member of the standing committee of the diocese and of the board of trustees.

He was a delegate to the general convention in Washington in 1898, while in 1901 he was a delegate to the convention which met in San Francisco. Perhaps we can not better close this sketch of the life of Colonel Wilson than by quoting the opinion of his work and character as given by one of his friends who has known him long and intimately, and said of him:

> When he was appointed United States district attorney by President Grant he was only twenty-seven years of age and came to Springfield a stranger to the members of the Sangamon county bar. He soon made a favorable impression by his prompt, business like methods and his close application to every case that came before him. From that day to this his record has been one of conscientious devotion to his chosen profession. He has been so long and prominently connected with railroads that he is most widely known as a corporation lawyer and his reputation as such is of the highest character. Colonel Wilson was for many years the trusted and confidential friend of the late Judges Allen and Gresham of the United States Court, being one of their masters in chancery. In many of their most important receiverships they appointed him special commissioner and they would often act upon his conclusions both as to law and fact in these important cases. By members of his profession he is held in the highest respect for the thoroughness of his legal training and learning. He displays as complete a familiarity with fundamental principles of the law as with precedents. A profound lawyer as well as an accomplished scholar, he is moreover a singularly effective speaker, the charm of his diction being enhanced by a graceful delivery and a dignified bearing which at once makes a favorable impression upon his audience. There is a sort of vigor and a glow to what he says that holds the attention and controls juries. All those who have encountered him in the arena of forensic debate have had occasion to acknowledge the soundness of his judgment in dealing with large and important interests and his perfect fairness

toward opposing counsel. It is the careers of such distinguished men as Colonel Wilson that should be an inspiration to the student and younger members of the Illinois bar.[274]

— *Past and Present of the City of Springfield and Sangamon County, Illinois.*

Alois Winterberger – 1905

ALOIS WINTERBERGER a farmer and grain dealer, living near Junction City, Ill., is a native of the historic province of Alsace-Lorraine, where he was born April 4, 1845, of French parentage. In 1854, in company with his parents, two brothers and two sisters, he came to the United States. For about a year after arriving in this country his father followed his trade of gunsmith in Cincinnati, at the end of which time they came on to Shawneetown, Ill. There the father worked at his trade until about 1856, when he bought a farm of fifty acres near Junction, and died there Sept. 21, 1899, aged seventy-nine years. The mother died on April 4, 1902, in the eighty-fourth year of her age.

Alois was eleven years of age when the family settled at Shawneetown. He attended the common schools and on Aug. 15, 1862, enlisted in Company D, One Hundred and Twentieth Illinois volunteer infantry, as a private. In May, 1863, he was made a corporal, and on April 6, 1864, was promoted to orderly sergeant, which rank he held for the remainder of his service. The regiment was mustered in at Springfield; sent to Memphis, Tenn., on patrol and provost duty, then to Vicksburg, where it participated in the siege. After the fall of Vicksburg it was on guard duty at Lake Providence, La., Memphis and Lagrange, Tenn., Corinth, Miss., and in, June, 1864, took part in the famous Guntown raid. He was once severely wounded by a ball which struck him in the back of the head, passed under the scalp, and killed the next man in the line. On Sept. 10, 1865, he was mustered out with the regiment at Memphis and returned to Gallatin, county. He soon returned to Memphis, however, where for three years he worked at the trade of carpenter. From that time until 1880 he was engaged in contracting and building in Gallatin county. During the next five years he worked as a millwright in different parts of the country. In 1885 he built what is known as the "Little Gem" Flour mill at New Haven and conducted it in connection with a grain buying business until 1892. He then removed to the farm where he now lives, though he still does considerable business as a grain buyer at Junction City.

Mr. Winterberger owns 165 acres in the home farm, and fifty acres in another tract. He has made all the improvements on his farms, among which may be especially mentioned several thousand rods of tile drain, his farm in this respect being one of the best supplied in the county. Politically he is a Republican and from 1898 to 1902 held the office of township supervisor. At the present time he is one of the three drainage commissioners for the Cypress special drainage district. He is a Royal Arch Mason and Knight Templar; served as Worshipful Master of Warren Lodge, No. 14, Free and Accepted Masons, of Shawneetown in 1876; and is a Past Commander of Rhodes Post, No. 586, Grand Army of the Republic, of New Haven.

---

[274] Joseph Wallace. 1904. *Past And Present of the City Of Springfield and Sangamon County, Illinois.* Chicago: The S. J. Clarke Publishing Co. 916.

In 1877 Mr. Winterberger and Miss Kate Wallace were united in marriage and they had two sons: Louis, deceased, and Ralph, now in the United States navy on board the steamship *Tacoma*. He attended the State university for two years before entering the navy. The mother of these two boys died in 1881 and in 1883 Mr. Winterberger was married to Miss Mary Krauser, a native of Portsmouth, O.

— *Memoirs of the Lower Ohio Valley.*

Marshall Wiseheart – 1905

MARSHALL WISEHEART, of Shawneetown, Ill., county judge of Gallatin county, was born in that county, June 25, 1865. The family is of German origin, though the Wisehearts of Gallatin county are of Pennsylvania ancestry. The first of the name to come to Illinois was John Wiseheart, a native of Pennsylvania, who came West in the twenties, entered a tract of land in Gallatin county, and there passed the remainder of his life as a farmer. He married before leaving Pennsylvania and reared a family of seven children, only one of whom is now living. Richard was a minister of the Christian or Campbellite church; John followed farming and merchandizing; William, the only survivor of the family, is now a farmer of Gallatin county; Samuel was a merchant; Ellen married William Bird; Hannah married Alvin DeWitt; and Mary was the wife of James Rice.

William Wiseheart was born in Gallatin county, Ill., Jan. 7, 1832, and has always lived in the county. He received a common school education and upon reaching manhood adopted the occupation of farming, which he has followed all his life. He married Sarah, daughter of Henry Gill, an old resident of the county, and to this union there have been born the following children: Laura, widow of William Mattingly; Albert, a farmer of Gallatin county; Anna, wife of James Purcell, of Equality, Ill.; Marshall, the subject of this sketch; and Lucy, wife of William Powell, of Gallatin county.

Marshall Wiseheart, familiarly known as "Marsh," has always lived in Gallatin county. As a boy he worked on his father's farm, attending the district schools during the winter months. At the age of nineteen years he commenced teaching and followed that occupation for three years, when he was appointed to a position as deputy in, the circuit clerk's office at Shawneetown. Later he went into the sheriff's office as deputy, remaining in the two positions until 1892. While thus employed he spent his spare time in the study of law, and in May, 1892, he passed the examination before the state supreme court and was admitted to the bar. He then commenced the practice of his profession at Gallatin and continued in it until August, 1894, when he was appointed postmaster at Shawneetown and held the office for a little over four years, retiring in September, 1898. In November of that year he was elected treasurer of Gallatin county on the Democratic ticket, and served a full term of four years. In 1902 he received the nomination of his party for county judge, and at the election in November was chosen by a handsome majority to administer the affairs of that office for a term of four years. He is now serving in that position. Judge Wiseheart is prominent in fraternal circles, being a member of the Independent Order of Odd Fellows, the Knights of Pythias, the Court of Honor, and the Loyal Americans.

He was married on April 4. 1894 to Miss Fannie Boyd, a daughter of John R. Boyd, an old and honored resident of Gallatin county, who at the time of his death in 1896 was a member of the Illinois State board of equalization from the Twenty-fourth Congressional district. Mr. and Mrs. Wiseheart have four sons, viz.: Malcolm William, Raymond and Marshall Clarence.

— *Memoirs of the Lower Ohio Valley.*

R. J. Wiseheart – 1887

R. J. WISEHEART, a pioneer farmer and stock raiser, was born in Hardin County, Ky., in 1819, the son of John, Sr., and Elizabeth (Miller) Wiseheart, natives of Kentucky. The father, of German-Scottish ancestry, and reared and married in Kentucky, soon went to Indiana, and then finally in 1829 settled in Gallatin County. On account of ill health he was compelled to quit service in the Black Hawk War, and died in 1836, about 46 years of age. The mother died in 1872, about 87 years old.

December 25, 1838, our subject was married to Nancy Parks. Three of their six children are living: Emily, wife of John Weber, of Evansville, Ind.; Rebecca, wife of L. Raber, of Henderson County, Ky., and Harrison. Mrs. Wiseheart died in 1871. In December 1872, he married Sarah Boswell. Their two children are Richard and William.

He is still living on the old homestead, the owner of 316 acres of improved land. He began life with a suit of good clothes and 50 cents in money after his marriage. After making a thorough study of eye diseases, he practiced his profession for ten years, and at the same time was a minister of the Christian Church, which latter service he was compelled to abandon on account of old age and ill health. Besides his own family he has reared and educated seven orphan children. Formerly a Whig, he has been a Republican since his vote for Harrison in 1840. Mr. Wiseheart organized the first Sunday-school in Gallatin County, and baptized over 200 persons during his ministry.

— *History of Gallatin, Saline, Hamilton, Franklin and Williamson Counties, Illinois.*

Richard J. Wiseheart (deceased) – 1905

RICHARD J. WISEHART (deceased), who in his day was a well known and influential citizen of Gallatin County, Ill., was born Sept. 11, 1819, in the State of Kentucky, and died on the farm where his widow and one son now live, three and a half miles from Shawneetown. While he was still in his boyhood he came with his parents, John and Elizabeth Wiseheart, to Gallatin County, crossing the Ohio on a flatboat, and settled on a farm. There he grew to manhood, receiving his schooling in the old fashioned subscription schools of pioneer times, which he supplemented by a course of reading and home study until he became a well informed man. While he was still of tender age he had the misfortune to lose his father by death and was thus thrown on his own resources at an early period in his life. At the time he was married the first time his entire possessions were a two-year-old colt and one dollar and a half in money. But by a life of industry and sterling honesty he accumulated considerable property, the home farm consisting of 200 acres of fine land. He also did an extensive business in stock raising, and was for many years a minister of the Christian church.

His first marriage was to Nancy Parks, and they had four children: Harrison and Emily are living and Rebecca and John Henry are deceased. Emily is the wife of Levi Weaver, of Evansville, Ind.

After the death of his first wife he was married on Dec. 15, 1872, to Sarah J. Boswell, a native of Bristol, England, who came with her parents, John and Sarah (Harris) Boswell, to America, while still in her girlhood. Her father was an expert in mineralogy and upon locating in Hardin County, Ill., he opened up some lead mines there. Subsequently he went to Kentucky and opened some coal mines, but later returned to Gallatin County, and opened the old Saline Mines, which are still running. In his day he did perhaps more than any other one man to develop the mineral resources of Southern Illinois. He died at Shawneetown about 1864. Richard and Sarah Wisehart were the parents of two children: Richard, who now lives with his mother on the old homestead, and William S., who died in the 20th year of his age.

— *Memoirs of the Lower Ohio Valley.*

Samuel Wiseheart (deceased) – 1887

SAMUEL WISEHEART (deceased), merchant, was born in 1829 in Gallatin County, and son of John, Sr., and Elizabeth (Miller) Wiseheart, for whose history see sketch of R. J. Wiseheart. November 10, 1859, our subject married Mary, daughter of Washington and America (Turner) Sherwood, the former a farmer near New Haven, this county, who died in 1857 at the age of forty, and the latter in 1851, aged 33.

Their children are Alfred D., Thomas, Mollie and Gertrude. He then purchased 160 acres in Shawneetown Precinct and began farming and speculation in stock, most successfully, until he became owner of about 1,000 acres. After 1879 he was merchandising in Shawneetown until his death, April 16, 1880, and his wife then continued his business until 1882 and for a time kept boarding house. He was a successful financier, was an Odd Fellow, and his wife is an esteemed member of the Presbyterian Church.

— *History of Gallatin, Saline, Hamilton, Franklin and Williamson Counties, Illinois.*

James W. Young (deceased) – 1905

JAMES W. YOUNG (deceased), who in his day was a well known resident of Gallatin County, Ill., was born in Wilson County, Tenn., Aug. 39, 1843, there grew to manhood, and died on the farm where his widow now lives, Sept. 18, 1901.

On Nov. 26, 1890, he married Laura Boyd, a daughter of William J. Boyd, who was born near Maysville, Mason County, Ky., [on] April 30, 1824. In 1846 he came with his parents, John and Leah C. Boyd, to Gallatin County, located at New Haven, where he carried on a tan yard for about seven years, and also did considerable business as a boot and shoe manufacturer. He then removed to a farm in what is known as "Nettle Bottom," about five miles from Shawneetown, where he bought 80 acres of wild land. Subsequently he removed to the farm where Mrs. Laura Young now lives.

William J. Boyd was a man of fine appearance, weighing over two hundred pounds. He was a Democrat in politics; was a prominent member of the Masonic fraternity; served several years as justice of the peace, and was a man of affairs generally.

On March 24, 1847, he was married to Mrs. Jane Hooker, widow of Hiram Hooker, a daughter of Robert Bradford, and a native of Ireland. The children born to this marriage were Leona, Charles W., Rebecca, Walter and Laura C. Rebecca is the widow of James Rice; Laura C. is the widow of James Young and the others are deceased. The mother of these children died Aug. 9, 1887, aged 72 years. During the greater part of her life she was a devoted member of the Presbyterian Church. William J. Boyd died on Aug. 4, 1887. At the time of his death he was the owner of several hundred acres of land, besides some city property in Shawneetown, where for several years he was in the livery business.

After the marriage of James W. and Laura C. Young they lived on the farm where she now resides, and where he carried on a general farming and stock raising business. Since his death Mrs. Young continues to manage the farm, which consists of 160 acres. She also owns 80 acres in another tract. The children of James W. and Laura C. Young were Charles W., aged 12 years, now living on the old homestead with his mother, and Irene, Susie and Mary Frances, all deceased.

— *Memoirs of the Lower Ohio Valley.*

Edmund D. Youngblood – 1876

HON. EDMUND D. YOUNGBLOOD, lawyer, Shawneetown, was born at Paradise Prairie, Perry County, Illinois, October 21, 1838; son of Isaiah I. and Electa Youngblood, who died respectively in 1842 and 1850. He followed farming till 1865, meanwhile studying considerably through the aid of his wife, formerly Miss Emmie M. Kennie. In 1865, he moved to Benton, Illinois, and read law at leisure hours; in 1867, was admitted to practice; practiced in Harrisburg till 1871, when he removed to Shawneetown, where he soon attained a successful practice. In 1873, he was elected Judge of the City Court, and ranks among the leading lawyers of Southern Illinois.

— *Illustrated Historical Atlas of the State of Illinois.*

Hon. E. D. Youngblood – 1887

HON. E. D. YOUNGBLOOD, county judge of Gallatin County, was born in Perry County, Ill., in October, 1838, and is the son of Isaiah and Electa (Jones) Youngblood, the former of German descent, born in Georgia in 1794, and the latter in New York in 1801.

The father, a farmer, was a soldier of the War of 1812, and located at Mobile when peace was declared. Then after a residence in the county of his marriage, Franklin County, Ill., he went to Perry County in 1835, and there died in 1850. His wife died in 1841. They had ten children; these mentioned are living: Corvina I., wife of Geo. W. Sturdevant, Jefferson County, Ill.; Louisa H., wife of J. P. Ford, Los Angeles County, Cal.; Lovina C., wife of M. C. Hawkins, Carbondale, Ill.; Sarah A., wife of J. R. Hawkins, Perry County, Ill.; William J., Franklin County; Francis M., lawyer, Benton, Ill.; E. D. and Rachel, wife of W. W. Robertson, Franklin County.

With a limited amount of common-school education our subject began life as farmer in Perry County and Saline County, and in 1866 began the study of law with his brother at Benton, and caring for his family, as clerk and otherwise, he sought admission to the bar in Mount Vernon, Ill., began practice at Harrisburg, Ill., and in 1871 changed to Shawneetown. In 1871 he attended the law school of Judge A. D. Duff, of whose character and manhood he was a great admirer. In April 1857, he married Eunice M., a native of Pennsylvania and reared in Indiana, daughter of Geo. N. Kinne, a teacher. Only one of their four children is living, Eva, wife of Dr. J. F. Barton, of Inman, Gallatin Co., Ill. For the last 12 years a leading attorney of his home, our subject was elected city judge in 1873, in 1876 elected state's attorney of Gallatin County, in 1880 a Hancock and English elector, in 1882 elected county judge, and re-elected in 1886; in 1881 appointed master in chancery by Judge Conger, and re-appointed in 1883 and 1885. He is an able speaker and debater and a skillful criminal lawyer, a member of the A.F.&A.M., I.O.O.F. and K.H., and the Presbyterian Church.

— *History of Gallatin, Saline, Hamilton, Franklin and Williamson Counties, Illinois.*

Christian Zinn – 1887

CHRISTIAN ZINN, farmer and carpenter, was born in Germany in 1835, one of nine children of Otto F. and Anna E. (Bernhardt) Zinn. The father, born in the same place in 1802, and a machinist, remained there until his death in 1841. The mother, born in Germany in 1804, died in 1847.

Educated in his native land, our subject came to New Orleans in 1853, and six months later to Kentucky. In 1870 he came to Gallatin County, where he now lives on his fine farm of 280 acres, with coal under it. In 1856 he married Mary J., daughter of James B. and Frances McMurtry, and born in Wayne County, Ill., in 1840. Their eleven children are Elizabeth, James F. , Fanny (deceased), Mary J., Charles C., Henry J., George B., Nora (deceased), William B., Bertha L., and Crystal (deceased). Politically, Mr. Zinn is a Democrat, and a member of the I.O.O.F. He is a Presbyterian, and his wife is a member of the Christian Church.

— *History of Gallatin, Saline, Hamilton, Franklin and Williamson Counties, Illinois.*

William J. Zirkelbach – 1905

WILLIAM J. ZIRKELBACH, a farmer and stock raiser near Ridgway, Ill., is a son of Andrew and Katherine (Leutzhuick) Zirkelbach, both natives of Germany, the former of Bavaria and the latter of Prussia. Andrew Zirkelbach was born June 24, 1827, came with his parents to America when he was about ten years of age, settled in Vanderburg county, Ind., where the father carried on farming until his death at the age of seventy-five years. Before coming to this country he followed the trade of baker, but never worked at it after. His wife came with her parents about the same time. They were married in Vanderburg county and lived on the same farm, near St. James, for about thirty-five years. She lived to be eighty-seven years old. Of their children, William J., Andrew, George, Frank and Lena live in Gallatin county, Ill.; Rachel, Mary, Maggie and Peter live in Evansville, Ind.; Barbara, Mena and Mathias are deceased. Andrew Zirkelbach was always somewhat active in political affairs and was one of the prominent Democrats in his neighborhood. His children were all brought up in the Catholic faith, of which church both himself and wife were members.

William J. Zirkelbach was born in Vanderburg county, Nov. 14, 1854. He was educated in the parochial and district schools and lived with his parents until his marriage to Anna K. Wencel of Vanderburg county. They continued to live in that county until 1885, when they removed to Gallatin county, locating on a farm, which Mr. Zirkelbach bought, near Ridgway. For sixteen years he lived on this place, one year of that time being engaged in mercantile pursuits in Ridgway. In 1901 he sold the farm and bought his present place, three-fourths of a mile west of Ridgway, where he has a well improved farm of eighty acres, upon which he carries on a general farming business, devoting much of his time to breeding Aberdeen and Polled Angus cattle. Like his father before him, he is a Democrat and a Catholic, and takes an interest in both political and church matters. The children born to William J. and Anna K. Zirkelbach are Andrew, George, Cecilia and Katherine, living in the vicinity of Ridgway; Josie, William M., Eleanora and Rudolph, at home, and one who died in infancy.

— *Memoirs of the Lower Ohio Valley.*

Gallatin County Bank – 1912

GALLATIN COUNTY BANK. The standard of every community is measured by the character of its financial institutions, for unless they are stable the credit of the municipality and its people is impeached. The Gallatin County Bank, of Ridgway, Illinois, is an institution which has grown out of the needs of its locality, and was organized by men of exceptional standing, whose interests have been centered in it, and whose honor and personal fortunes are bound up in its life. Under such desirable conditions a bank is bound to maintain a high standard and to make money for its stockholders, while at the same time safeguard the interests of its depositors.

The Gallatin County Bank of Ridgway, Illinois, was organized as a state bank in January 1895, with a capital of $25,000, which was eventually increased to $35,000. It had been originally started in 1893 by Robert Mick, president, and David Weidemann, cashier, with William Gregg and T. W. Hall, as a private institution. Mr. Weidemann is now cashier of the First National Bank of Henry, Illinois; Mr. Gregg is cashier of the City National Bank of Harrisburg, and T. W. Hall is president of the First National Bank of Carmi. Shortly after the death of President Mick, the bank became a state institution, with Judge Phillips as president and Mr. Weidemann as cashier, and the former still holds office, although the latter was succeeded in July, 1897, by George L. Land, who has continued as cashier to the present time. The present home of the bank was erected in 1910, and was fitted out with the latest improvements, and now boasts of deposits of $140,000, and $125,000 loans, is continually paying dividends and has a surplus of $6,000. This is considered one of the strongest banking institutions of Southern Illinois and does business with some of the largest houses in its part of the state. The assistant cashier is W. B. Phillips, son of the Judge. George I. Land, the able cashier of this bank, was born at Carmi. White county, Illinois, July 10, 1865, and is a son of John and Ann Eliza (Crane) Land, and a grandson of Yearby Land and his wife, who bore the maiden name of Rupert. Yearby Land was born in North Carolina, and was brought to Illinois when two years old in 1809. He spent a number of years in Wayne county, but eventually moved to White county, where he and his sons, John and David Land, were engaged in a mercantile business under the firm name of Y. Land & Sons. His death occurred at his home in Carmi at the age of 90 years, and for some years the sons continued to carry on the business, which is still in existence at Carmi, being conducted by a son of John, E. A. Land, and is the oldest mercantile business in White county.

John Land, the father of George L., was for a number of years engaged in farming in connection with the mercantile business, which in 1879 became known as D. R. & J. Land, and he finally retired in 1885 and still resides at Carmi, as does his wife. He was succeeded by his son, George L., as D. R. Land & Company, which continued until the death of D. R., and George L. was then joined by his two brothers, E. A. & H. C. Land, but subsequently George L. Land left the firm to become cashier of the Gallatin County Bank, and H. C. became cashier of the Bank of Omaha, Gallatin county, which was organized as the Exchange Bank of Omaha by David Weidemann, and of which George L. Land has been president for some time. He has not been active in political matters, preferring to give his attention strictly to his banking business, although he is also interested in a coal business at Eldorado, Illinois.

Mr. Land was married at the age of 27 years, to Miss Mollie B. Hick, of Carmi, daughter of John Hick, of New Haven, who died when she was a child. Three children have been born to this union, all residing at home: Walter H., Madeline E. and Louise. Mr. and Mrs. Land are well-known members of the Missionary Baptist church, and have been active in its work. They have numerous friends throughout this community, where members of both families have been prominent in various walks of life.

— *History of Southern Illinois.*

Bibliography

1843. *Minutes of the Colored Baptist Association... August 11, 12, 13, & 14, 1843*. Alton, Ill.: Alton Telegraph.

1878. *American Biographical History of Eminent and Self-made Men*. Michigan Volume. Cincinnati: Western Biographical Pub. Co.

1883. *History of White County, Illinois*. Chicago: Inter-State Publishing Co.

1886. *History of Union County, Kentucky*. Evansville, Ind.: Courier Co., Printers, Binders and Engravers.

1887. *History of Gallatin, Saline, Hamilton, Franklin and Williamson Counties, Illinois*. Chicago: Goodspeed Publishing Company.

1889. *History of the Pacific Northwest: Oregon and Washington*. Portland, Ore.: North Pacific History Co.

1905. *Memoirs of the Lower Ohio Valley*. Madison, Wis.: Federal Publ. Co.

1912. *Encyclopedia of Illinois and History of Sangamon County*. Chicago: Munsell Publishing Co.

Lewis Caleb Beck. 1823, 1975 Reprint. *A Gazetteer of the States of Illinois and Missouri*. New York: Arno Press.

Clarence Bonnell, ed. 1947. *Saline County: A Century of History, 1847-1947*. Harrisburg, Ill.: Saline County Historical Society.

Samuel R. Brown. *Western Gazetteer; or Emigrant's Directory*. Auburn, N. Y.: H. C. Southwice, 1817.

Jane W. Crichton. 1965. *Michael Kelly Lawler: A Southern Illinois Mexican War Captain and Civil War General*. Master's Thesis. SIU-Carbondale.

George Ticknor Curtis. [1864-1865]. *The True Conditions of American Loyalty*. New York.

Alexander Davidson and Bernard Stuvé. 1876. *A Complete History of Illinois from 1867 to 1873*. Springfield, Ill.: Illinois Journal Company.

Myron D. Dillow. 1996. *Harvesttime on the Prairie*. Illinois State Baptist Association. Franklin, Tenn.: Providence House Publishers.

Evert A. Duyckinck. 1856. *Cyclopaedia of American Literature*. New York: C. Scribner.

Logan Esarey, ed. 1922. *Governors Messages and Letters: Messages and Letters of William Henry Harrison. Vol. 1. 1800-1811*. Indianapolis: Indiana Historical Commission.

Executive Relief Committee. 1900. *The Shawneetown Flood, April 3rd, 1898: Final Report of the Executive Relief Committee*. Shawneetown, Ill.: Executive Relief Committee.

Milo Erwin. 1876. Reprint 1976. *The History of Williamson County, Illinois*. Marion, Ill.: Williamson County Historical Society.

Timothy Flint. 1832, 2nd Ed. *The History and Geography of the Mississippi Valley*. Cincinnati: E. H. Flint and L. R. Lincoln.

A. R. Fulton. 1882. *The Red Men of Iowa: Being a History of the Various Aboriginal Tribes*. Des Moines, Iowa:Mills & Co., Publishers.

James Hall. 1828. *Letters from the West*. London.

Hiram H. Hunter. 1839, Reprint 1904. *The Story of Isaac Knight, Indian Captive*. Overbrook, Kan.: The Overbrook Citizen.

Shadrach "Shady" L. Jackson. 1888. *The Life of Logan Belt*.

Adam R. Johnson. *The Partisan Rangers of the Confederate States Army: Memoirs of Adam R. Johnson*. Louisville, Ky.: G. G. Fetter.

Brigham Johnson, ed. 1918, Rev., Home and School Ed. *Iowa: Its History and its Foremost Citizens*. Des Moines, IA: The S. J. Clarke Publishing Company.

J. C. Kinison and C. B. Whiteside. 1912. *Minutes of the 61st Session of the Southern Illinois Conference Methodist Episcopal Church*. Marion, Ill.: Stafford Print.

William T. Lawler. 1978. *The Lawlers from Ireland to Illinois*. Privately Published.

Gen. Usher F. Linder. 1879 2nd Ed. *Reminiscences of the Early Bench and Bar of Illinois*. Chicago: The Chicago Legal News Company.

D. W. Lusk. 1884. *Politics and Politicians: A Succinct History of the Politics of Illinois from 1856 to 1884*. Springfield, Ill.: H. W. Rokker.

John Moses. 1895 (2nd Ed. Rev.). *Illinois: Historical and Statistical*. Chicago: Fergus Printing Co.

Ronald L. Nelson, Doris Nelson and Ralph S. Harrelson. 1996. *History of Liberty Baptist Church*. Utica, Ky.: McDowell Publications.

Frederick Palmer. 1930. *Clark of the Ohio: A Life of George Rogers Clark*. New York: Dodd, Mead & Co.

John Mason Peck. 1837, 2nd Ed. *A Gazetteer of Illinois*. Philadelphia: Grigg & Elliot, 1837.

William Henry Perrin, ed. *History of Alexander, Union and Pulaski Counties, Illinois*. Chicago: O. L. Baskin & Co., Historical Publishers.

John Reynolds. 1852, 2nd Ed. 1887. *Pioneer History of Illinois*. Chicago: Fergus Printing.

———— 1879. 2nd Ed. *My Own Times*. Chicago: Chicago Historical Society.

Glenn Sneed. *Ghost Towns of Southern Illinois*. Johnston City, Ill.: A.E.R.P., Publisher.

George W. Smith. 1912. *A History of Southern Illinois: A Narrative Account of its Historical Progress, its People, and its Principal Interests*. Chicago, Ill.: Lewis Publishing Co.

Edmund L. Starling. 1887. *History of Henderson County, Kentucky*.

Wilson Thompson. 1873. *Autobiography of Elder Wilson Thompson*. Cincinnati: Wilstach, Baldwin & Co., Printers.

Christiana Holmes Tillson; Milo Milton Quaife, ed. 1919, Reprint 1995. *A Woman's Story of Pioneer Illinois*. Carbondale, Ill.: SIU Press.

United States. Naval War Records Office. *Official Records of the Union and Confederate Navies in the War of the Rebellion*. Washington: Government Printing Office.

United States. War Department. *The War of the Rebellion: A Compilation of the Official Records of the Union and Confederate Armies*. Washington: Government Printing Office.

John A. Wall. 1909. *Wall's History of Jefferson County, Illinois*. Indianapolis: B. F. Bowen & Co., Publishers

Joseph Wallace. 1904. *Past and Present of the City of Springfield and Sangamon County, Illinois*. Chicago: The S. J. Clarke Publishing Co.

Warner & Beers. 1876. *Illustrated Historical Atlas of the State of Illinois*. Union Atlas Co.

George Fauntleroy White (grandson of Col. Isaac White). 1889. *Sketch of the Life of Colonel Isaac White*. Washington: Gibson Bros.,

Paul Wilhelm, Duke of Wurttemberg. *Travels in North America, 1822-1824*. Norman, Okla.: U. of Oklahoma Press, 1973.

James Harrison Wilson. 1912, reprint 1971. *Under the Old Flag*. Westport, Conn.: Greenwood Press Publishers.

Index

When looking for Civil War soldiers, don't forget to look at the roster of men from Gallatin County on pages 178-203. Those names, which are listed alphabetically in the text, are not included in this index.

All other names should be included in the list; under whatever spelling they appeared in the original text. Be creative when looking for certain names. They may have been spelled phonetically. Women are listed twice when the maiden name is known; once under their maiden name and again under the married name.

Abbott, William W. 70
Abner, Henry 170
Abney
   Eliza J. 299
   James K. 299
   Matthew 170
   Sarah L. 258
   Susan 299
Abshier
   Anderson 208
   Elias 208
   Elizabeth 208
   Frances 208
   Jackson 69, 140, 208
   Malinda 208
   Milly L. 208
   Nancy A. (Perryman) 208, 340
   Nancy Maria 340
   Spencer 208
   Thomas 208, 340
   W. P. 69, 140
   Washington 208
Abshier & Stone 68
Adams
   (lawyer) 372
   Eli 22, 33
   J. 169
   James A. 336
   John Quincy 372
   L. H. 63, 65, 77
   Maria 14, 218
   Mr. 23
   Nancy Jane 14
   Nannie 287
   Virginia (Phillips) 336
Adams Company 282
Adams Express Co. 312
Addison
   Emeline 322
   Jennie 328
   Sidney 328
   Sidney, Sir 172
   Thomas 38
Aden, Varner 170
Adkinson, Joseph 47
Adventist churches 269
   Bethel 269
   Union Chapel 269
African M.E. churches
   Shawneetown 129
Agency City, Iowa 374
Aiken
   Eliza N. "Aunt Lizzie" (Atherton)
   176
   George 42
   John 42, 43
Aiken Gang 43
Akers
   Thomas 38
   William 8
Akins, Eliza Jane 363
Aldrich
   F. M. 283
   T. W. P. 69
   W. P. 69, 140
Aldridge
   Clara B. 209
   Eli 208
   Eliza 209
   F. M. 208, 285
   Fatima I. (Hinch) 285
   George D. 209
   Harriet 209
   Harriet (Downes) 209
   John 209
   Lavina (Kivit) 208
   Mary (Hanchel) 209
   Mary J. (Black) 208
   Minnie R. 209
   Patsy 209
   Permelia 209
   Peter 208
   Russell D. 208, 209
   Sarah 209
   Sarah (Smith) 208
   W. P. 51, 69
   Warren 208
   William P. 208, 209
Alexander
   John 80
   Mastin 171
   Rheubin 171
Algiers 273
Allen
   ___ 41
   Enos T. 21
   James C. 41
   John L. 147
   Judge 398
   Samuel 204
   T. B. 281
   William G. 77
   William J. 23, 25, 127
   Willis 22
Allen & Harrington 281
Allyn
   ___ 26
   Kate 253
Alshear, Anderson 170
Alsop, Joseph 74
Alston, Phillip 91
Altoona Pass, Battle of 244
Alva Adams 250
Alwalt
   Lola (Foster) 263
   Richard 263
Aman, Anna 250
Ambers, Sister 133
American Fur Co. 372
American Knights, Order of 178
American Medical Coll. 331
Anderson
   Asa C. 209
   Audrey 210
   Bertha 210
   Capt. 46
   Dora 210
   Elias 209
   Hannah (Downen) 209
   James 209
   John 209
   John C. 209
   Julia H. 210
   Lt. 49
   Margaret 209
   Margaret (Williams) 209
   Martha 209
   Mary A. 210
   Mary A. (Rusher) 209
   Mary E. 209, 271
   Miss ____ 230

Nancy 209
Pamelia 377
Polly 209
Solomon 209, 271
Stella M. 210
Urbane 209
W. B. 25
William B. 23, 25
William L 210
William N. 209
Andersonville Prison 50, 272
Andrews
   Ellen 348
   Nancy 348
   Samuel 348
Angela, Mother 344
Applegate, Achsah 311
Arbuckle, widow 96
Archer, Maj. 273
Arcola 177
Armstrong
   Abraham 8, 136
   Abraham L. 210
   E. F. 52, 60, 64
   Elias A. 204
   J. W. 210
   Lancelot 210
   Margaret S. (Blackard) 210
   Samuel A. 49
Arthur, Chester A. 325
Artman, Henry 49
Artus, Capt. 100
Asbery, I. M. 138
Asbury
   I. M. 69, 210, 331
   J. M. 72
   Martha 242
   Susan M. (Mitchell) 210
   Wesley 210
Asbury Precinct 224
Ashly
   J. L. 264
   Mollie (Gates) 264
Ashworth
   Mary F. 214
   William 214
Atherton, Eliza N. 176
Awalt, Scott 49
Aydelotte, Zadock 38
Ayres, James 48
Bacon, Susanna 266
Bad Axe, Battle of 373
Badger, William 38
Badollet
   John 229
   Sarah 229
Baer, Sarah 375
Bagsley, Samuel 47, 48
Bahr, Charles 204
Bahr, McMurchy & 64, 323
Bailey
   ____ 26
   Alice M. 89

Bowdoin 223
E. D. 73
James 265
Jane (Glasscock) 265
L. C. 223
Winslow 131
Bailey & Hinch 68
Bailey Mills 239
Bain
   Mary Ann 221
   Miranda 221
   Riley 221
Baker
   Adam 64
   Calvin 236
   Calvin M. 211
   Caroline 211
   Covington 211
   David J. 57, 290
   David P. 172
   Edmon 170
   Effie 211
   Elizabeth 211
   Felix 211
   Frances (Colbert) 236
   Henry 211
   James 171, 211
   Lt. 49
   Lucy 211
   M. A. 71
   Mary 211
   Peter 10
   Phoebe 211
   Phoebe (Collinsworth) 211
   Rena 211
   Sarah 211
   William 211
Baldwin
   Isaac 8, 33
   M. V. 73
   Martha J. 229
   Mary F. (Leavell) 229
   William 229
Baldwin Family 79
Baltes, Bishop 82
Baltimore & Ohio Express Co. 282
Baltimore & Ohio R.R. 330
Baltimore & Ohio S.W. R.R. 222, 233, 234
Baltimore Blues 223
Bancroft, Ruth 370
Bandy, Dr. 43
Banewood, Baston 10
Bank of Illinois .. 38, 52, 56, 311, 387
Bank of Omaha 406
Banks
   City National 405
   Commercial 274
   Commercial, of Evansville 254
   Exchange 286, 336
   Exchange (Omaha) 406
   Farmers (Ewing) 381
   First Nat'l (Carmi) 405

   First Nat'l (Equality) 245, 321
   First Nat'l (Henry) 405
   First Nat'l (Ridgway) 254, 364, 382
   First Nat'l (Shawneetown) 58, 334, 351, 352
   First National (Shawneetown). 57
   Gallatin Co. 337, 382, 405
   Gallatin Co. State 336, 382
   Gallatin National 58, 338, 339
   Illinois State 139, 284
   Illinois, Bank of 38, 56, 387
   Illinois, of 52
   Illinois, of 311
   New Haven 139
   Norris City State 337
   Omaha, Bank of 406
   Peeples & Ridgway 334
   Pool, M. M., & Co. 338
   Pool, O., & Co. 334
   State B. of Illinois 213
   State Bank of Illinois 56, 212, 230
Bankston's Fork Church 132, 133
Bankstone's Fork 107
Bantam, Sallie 227
Baptist churches
   Bankston's Fork 132
   Bethel's Creek 132
   Big Creek 132
   Block House Creek 133
   Coal Bank Springs 134
   Concord Regular Old Side, for People of Color .. 130, 134
   Indian Camp 134
   Island Ripple 132, 133
   Lick Boundary 133
   Lick Creek 133
   Middle Fork Saline 132
   Wolf Creek 132
Baptist churches, Emancipation
   Big Saline 134
   Eagle Creek 134, 135
   Grassy Creek 133
   Hurricane Creek 133
   Liberty 133
   Mineral Springs 134
   Rock Creek 134
   Shawneetown (Colored) 129, 134
Barbour
   James 113
   Phillip 113
Barbre, Eli 133
Barbrey, ____ 150, 157
Barger
   Anna Lawler 213
   Elizabeth 213
   Elizabeth (Seaton) 211, 212, 213
   Fatima C. 283, 284
   George 211, 212, 213
   George D. 211

H. C. 63
Harrison O. 213
Isaac..170
Jacob..........7, 52, 211, 212, 213,
   283, 285
James Ella (Parks).....................213
James S. 213
Jos. T. 212
Joseph B. 22, 64, 84, 87, 213
Josephine...................................213
Louisa M. (Carter) 212, 213
Louise 213
Lucy E. (Floyd) 212
Lucy G. 212
Maud E. 212
Nathaniel B. 212
Rebecca S. 285
Richard 213
Richard A. S. 171
Barker
   James B. 128
   Jessee G...................................169
   Lewis.........................28, 29, 31
   William 169
Barker's Ferry.........................28, 31
Barley, Milton................................ 22
Barlow
   James 352
   Matilda (Robinett) 352
   Thomas 132
Barnett
   Albert C. 214
   David C. 172
   Edward 253
   Ellen B. 385
   George 145
   Inez (Downen) 253
   John T. 214
   Joseph 214
   Malinda (Choat)......................214
   Margaret (Colbert)..................385
   Mary 214
   Mellie M. 214
   Sarah J. 214
   Sidney A. (Patton)...................214
   Thornton..................................385
Barnhill, Alexander....................... 38
Barr
   Isaac L. 80
   Jesse 280
Barrett, George J. 80
Barry, David................................210
Bartel, Margaret.........................253
Bartell, Catherine 249, 250
Barter
   Authur......................................214
   Charles A.................................214
   Charles F. 70
   Ella 214
   Emma M. 214
   Ethel May 214
   Fred 214
   John A. 214

John F...214
John H. 214
Mary F. (Ashworth) 214
Mattie (Hutcherson) 214
William 214
William A. 214
Barter & Kinsall.............................138
Barter, John H., & Son.................214
Barter, John H., & Sons 214
Bartlett, Michael............................33
Bartlett's Commercial College.....245
Bartley
   ___ 26
   Milton 22, 25, 26, 37, 51, 64
Bartley & Son..................................44
Bartley Station 382
Bartley, Ill. 74
Barton
   Dr. J. F. 404
   Eva (Youngblood).....................404
Barton & Co..................................69
Bate
   James S. 113
   James Smally..........................113
   John 112, 113
Bates, John 113
Battery Rock......................105, 375
Battleford Creek...................133, 161
Battles, Black Hawk War
   Bad Axe...................................373
Battles, Civil War
   Altoona Pass 244
   Arkansas Expedition.................46
   Arkansas Post.......215, 221, 270,
      283, 292, 303, 321, 350
   Atlanta.................225, 303, 364
   Austin, Miss.............................294
   Belmont............... 256, 314, 363
   Big Black River 221, 317
   Black River 395
   Brentwood Hills 370
   Byhalia Road...........................370
   Cache River 221
   Camp Cetico.............................49
   Campbellsville 370
   Cape Girardeau 244
   Champion Hill 279, 317
   Champion Hills 395
   Chickamauga..........................328
   Chickasaw Bayou..........316, 350
   Coffeeville, Miss. 370
   Colliersville, Tenn. 371
   Columbus 363
   Coldwater........................ 49, 363
   Corinth 46, 48, 230, 270,
      283, 363, 370
   Corinth (2nd).............................363
   Corinth, Miss...........................304
   Cotton Plant, Ark..........216, 221
   Cumberland Gap 272
   Dyersburg..................................49
   East Point, Miss. 228
   Edward's Station 316

Farmington.................................370
Florence, Ala. 49
Fort Blakely 231, 235,
   342, 350
Fort Donelson........45, 46, 47, 48,
   230, 231, 235, 256, 270,
   302, 303, 314, 325, 342,
   363
Fort Henry.........46, 48, 230, 302,
   314, 342, 363
Fort Hindman 316
Fort Morgan 48
Fort Sumter................................174
Franklin.......................................370
Georgetown, Mo. 174
Grand Gulf..............48, 221, 239
Grierson's Raid 49, 370
Guntown 228, 231, 304, 399
Haine's Bluff 46
Harts Crossroads 370
Haynes Bluff 303
Holly Springs............48, 235, 239,
   342, 363
Island No. 10..............................370
Iuka..370
Jackson 363
Jackson, Miss. 216, 221
Jackson, Miss., 2nd.....................221
Jackson, Tenn............................. 46
Knoxville 272
La Grange, Tenn. 49
Lagrange, Tenn. 304
Lexington, Mo. 175, 241
Lookout Mountain 303
Magnolia Hill..............................221
March to the Sea 272, 303
Milliken's Bend 316
Mobile..321
Moscow.......................................370
Moscow, Tenn............................. 49
Nashville 49, 221, 370
Natchez.......................................321
New Madrid, Mo........................370
New Orleans 321
Olive Branch 49
Paducah......................................363
Pea Ridge 216, 221, 279
Pittsburg Landing............... 46, 48,
   230, 231, 328
Plains Store................................370
Port Gibson 221, 316
Port Hudson.......................49, 370
Red River Expedition................216
Ripley 228
Saline Bar 177
Shiloh 45, 47, 235,
   302, 312, 313, 315, 325,
   332, 342, 363
Spanish Fort 231, 235,
   342, 350, 395
Stone River 328
Summersville 370
Sunshine Church, Ga. 272

413

Vicksburg 47, 48, 215, 216, 221, 228, 229, 231, 239, 279, 283, 292, 294, 303, 305, 316, 321, 342, 350, 363, 364, 395, 399
Wilson's Raid 338
Battles, Mexican War
   Cerro Gordo 171, 302
   Chapultepec 44, 218
   Contreras 44, 218
   Horcasitas 172
   Molino del Rey 44, 218
   Vera Cruz 171
Battles, Revolutionary War
   Bennington 256
   Brandywine 114
   Bunker Hill 326
   Stony Point 339
   Yorktown 230, 303, 339
Battles, War of 1812
   Chippewa 272
   Fort Erie 272
   Horseshoe Bend 295
   Lake Erie 266
   Long Ridge 164
   Lundy's Lane 272
   New Orleans 238, 251, 286, 295, 296, 297
   Niagara 272
   Tippecanoe 156, 267, 390
Baugh, Downing 41
Baugher, John J. 172
Bayley, C. B. 139
Bays
   David, Jr. 170
   John 170
Beal, James 33
Beale, Robert 38
Bean
   Belle 216
   Catherine 215
   Catherine (Skeef) 215
   Charles 215
   Elizabeth 215
   F. M. 79
   Fastina Ellen 216
   General F. M. 50, 204
   George 215
   George L. 215
   Henry 214, 215
   Henry M. 214
   Jacob 215
   James 215
   James M. 214, 215, 282
   Jane 215
   Jasper 215
   Jemima (Kimbrough) 215
   Jerome 216
   John 215
   Jonathan 215
   Joseph M. 50
   Josephine 216
   Laura 215

Logan Grant 216
Maggie J. 282
Margaret 215
Margaret (Hise) 215
Margaret (Rise) 214
Marshall H. 215
Mary (Glass) 216
Monroe 216
Nancy 215
Nazarene 216
Sherman 216
Stella 215
Susan Catherine 216
Turana 215
William 215
William C. 50
Bean, J. "Jimmy" M. 145
Bear Creek 107
Bear Creek Twp. 136
Bearce, Henry 137
Bears, black 18, 94
Beasley
   Lettia A. (Cook) 239
   W. 239
Beatty, Emma (Siebman) 362
Beaumont, James S. 52
Beaver Creek 33
Beaver Pond 1
Bechtold & Webber 64
Bechtold, Jacob 64, 309
Beck, George 63
Bedford, Wilmer 46
Beecher
   Charles A. 234
   Edwin 41
Beeves, Artimissa 333
Beggs, Joshua 29
Behan, John 47
Bell
   Abbie (Foster) 263
   George 263
   Henry 129
   James M. 45
   Reuben 29
   Robert 25
Bellah, Thomas F. 204
Beller, Reuben 8
Belt (Logan) faction 93
Belt, Julia (Foster) 262
Bender, Lucy iii
Bennett
   Alonzo 50
   J. A. 340
   John 80
   Joseph C. 172
   Margaret (Colbert) 355
   Matilda (Purvis) 340
   Thomas I. 172
   Thornton 355
Benson, E. J. 375
Bently, Osborn 130
Benton Barracks 48, 175, 176
Bernhardt, Anne E. 404

Berry
   Benjamin F. 47
   John 39
   Laurine (Gay) 303
   Phoebe 365
   Phoebia 365
   W. 303
Bethel's Creek Church 132, 133
Bethlehem M.E. Church 81, 137
Beveredge, Gov. 93
Biddle, Thomas 272
Big Bend 43
Big Creek 32, 131
Big Creek Church 132
Big Creek Twp. 29, 31
Big Eagle Creek 17
Big Fish Lake 1
Big Lake 1
Big Muddy River .. 20, 149, 150, 156
Big Prairie 159, 166, 209
Big Prairie Precinct 209
Big Prairie Settlement 166
Big Saline Church 134
Big Slough 34
Bikeman, Father 141
Binkley, J. T. 65
Birbeck, Morris 59
Bird
   Ellen (Wiseheart) 400
   Samuel 129
   William 400
Bird's Point, Mo. 46
Birger, Charlie 349
Birkbeck, Mr. 105
Bish, George 169
Bishop
   James M. 216
   Mary (Davis) 216
   William 216
Black
   James 208
   John 9, 33
   Mary J. 208
   Nancy 208
Black Hawk War 164, 314, 373, 394
Black Hawk, Chief 373
Black Laws 126
Blackard
   A. H. 71
   A. M. 71
   Alexander H. 216
   Alfred 216, 217
   Edward S. 204
   Ella (Mills) 325
   Emma 216
   Felix G. 216
   H. P. 71
   Harvey P. 216, 217, 249
   J. H. 71
   Jennie (Davis) 249
   Jennie V. (Davis) 217
   John 137
   Leroy 217

Mansford W. ...217
Margaret S. ...210
Mollie ...216
Prof. ...325
Reece L. ...217
Sarah ...216
Thomas ...216
W. L. ...22
William L ...23, 50
Blackburn, Archibald ...128
Blackburn, Ill. ...74
Blackford
  Ephraim ...152
  Reuben ...152
Blackman
  George ...237
  Josiah ...170
  Stephen ...40
  Virgie (Colbert) ...237
Blades, W H. ...51
Blairsville, Ill. ...42, 156
Blairsville, Ind. ...257
Blanchard, ___ ...26
Blewett, James G. ...178
Block House Creek Church ...133
Blockhouse Creek ...133, 161
Bloomfield, Mo. ...46
Blue
  Bessie (Hughes) ...218
  Bessie G. ...218
  Camille ...218
  Charles David ...218
  George E. ...218
  James ...217
  James Barber ...218
  James S. ...217
  John R. ...217
  Lou (Hughes) ...218
  Pemesia (Glenn) ...217
  Sarah McGoodwin ...218
  Solomon ...94
  Willis ...218
Bogan, Sarah ...326, 327
Bogardus
  Adeline (Smith) ...218
  Edgar ...44, 218
  Egbert ...218
  Elizabeth (Whiting) ...219
  Elsie (Comfort) ...218
  Francis Pembrook ...219
Boggs, Carroll C. ...42
Bond
  George ...170
  Stephen ...170
  William ...172
Bonham, Edward ...25
Bonnell, Clarence ...iii, 123, 124, 151, 161, 407
Bonner, Theresa Isabelle ...340
Bonpas Creek ...166
Boone
  ___ ...140
  Daniel ...67

Jonathan ...67
Joseph ...67
Boone Settlement ...163
Boone's Lick ...105
Boone's Mill ...21, 67
Booten, Elizabeth ...355
Borroughs
  George ...356
  Matilda (Rogers) ...356
Boswell
  John ...402
  Sarah ...401
  Sarah (Harris) ...402
  Sarah J. ...402
  William ...47
Botright, Daniel ...170
Boultinghouse Prairie ...159, 167
Boultinghouse, Daniel ...159
Boultinhouse, Daniel ...167
Bourland
  Allie ...220
  Anita G. ...220
  Bernardine ...220
  Ebenezer ...219
  Elizabeth ...220
  Ella A. (Greer) ...220
  Emma ...220
  Francis ...219
  Frank ...220
  Gabriel A. ...220
  Gertrude ...220
  Herbert C. ...220
  Isaac ...73
  Isaac N. ...219, 220
  James A. ...219
  John ...219
  John A. ...220
  Nancy (Strong) ...219
  Rachel (Slaten) ...219
  Susan ...219
  Timothy D. ...220
  William ...219
Bouton, Jane ...380
Boutwell, Roxana ...251
Bowles
  Joseph ...74, 340
  Mr. ...74
Bowles family ...83
Bowlesville ...1, 4, 74, 333, 383
Bowlesville Coal Co. ...233, 328
Bowlesville Mines ...340
Bowling
  Abraham L. ...222
  Addie ...222
  Albert Leslie ...222
  Anna M. ...221
  Benjamin H. ...221
  Edwin ...222
  Eliza (Davis) ...222
  Elizabeth (Roman) ...220
  Emory Emmons ...222
  Ethel Gail ...222
  Eudora ...222

Flora ...221
Florence B. ...221
Hattie ...222
Helen ...222
James ...220
Jane (Stinson) ...222
Jasper ...42, 221
John ...220
John E. ...221
John M. ...50, 220, 221
John W. ...222
John William ...221
Julia Ann ...221
Maggie ...221
Mary (Ransbottom) ...221
Miranda (Bain) ...221
Pauline (row) ...222
Philip S. ...222
W. H. ...70
William ...220
William H. ...221
Bowman
  ___ ...26
  Bishop ...242
  J. Winston ...222
  Jesse ...152
  Mary ...222
  William G. ...26, 37, 63
  William Granville ...222
Bowman & Pillow ...44
Bowman & Wasson ...64
Boyd
  Archibald ...223
  Arthur L. ...223
  Charles W. ...403
  Ethel ...223
  Fannie ...400
  J. ...223
  J. L. ...51, 70
  J. R. ...65
  Jane (Bradford) ...403
  John ...223, 402
  John R. ...64, 223, 400
  Julia ...131
  L. C. ...223
  Laura ...402
  Laura C. ...223, 403
  Leah C. ...402
  Leona ...403
  Lizzie ...130
  Martha (Landford) ...223
  Mary (Mills) ...301
  Mrs. ...223
  Rebecca ...223, 403
  Robert A. ...172
  Samuel O. ...223
  Thannie ...223
  Thompson ...223
  Thompson, Jr. ...223
  W. J. ...223
  Walter ...403
  William J. ...5, 64, 402, 403
Boyd's Mound ...5

415

Boyde
  Jane (Bradford) 224
  John 224
  Leah C. 224
  William James 224
Boyer
  ____ 26
  Henry 9, 34
Boyers, Henry 22, 39
Boyle, Thomas M. 81
Bozarth
  Alice 226
  Bryant 225
  Charles Edwin 225, 226
  Elihu 225
  Finis 225
  Franklin 224
  Franklin P. 225, 226
  Fred D. 227
  George 227
  Grandfather 224
  H. C. 89
  H. P. 87, 89, 137, 138
  Harmon Pinnell 224, 225, 226
  Israel 225
  John A. 226
  John W. 226
  Jonathan 225
  Jonnie 225
  Lillian 227
  Lucretia (Pinnell) 224
  Lucy 226
  Mary 225
  Minnie May 227
  Nicinda 225
  P. 137
  Pearl 227
  Pinnell (Lucinda) 225
  Polley (Wilson) 225
  Sarah M. (Wolfe) 224, 226
  Stephen 225
  Tilford 225
  William Franklin 226
  Willie 225
Bozeman
  Prudence H. 131
  Richard M. 47
Bozman
  I. J. 260
  Nancy (Cross) 260
  Prudence H. 260
Braddock, Gen. 307
Bradford
  America J. 331
  J. S. 172
  James 223
  Jane 223, 224, 403
  Margaret 223
  Margaret A. 293
  Robert 403
Bradolette, John 20
Bradshaw
  James 47, 113

John 20, 113
  Sarah (Hanmore) 278
Bramlet, Alfred J. 172
Branch, John 78
Brannon, Hiram T. 83, 135
Brasier, Ferd 144
Brayman
  Mason 47
  Moses 47
Brazier
  Philomine 362
  Riley 172
Brazier family 83
Breckenridge
  Alexander 289
  John C. 289
  Millicent 289
Briant, John B. 170
Brick clay 3
Bridgeman, Daniel 37
Bridges
  James 170
  Thomas L. 170
Brill, Capt. 239
Brinkley
  Charlotte (Robinett) 353
  John C. 353
Brinkly, R. E. 88
Bristow, B. H. 395
Brocket, H. A. 227
Brockett
  A. D. 137, 138
  Alanson F. 227
  B. F. 64
  Benjamin F. 77
  James 227, 287
  Sarah (Poole) 287
Brockett's Mill 311
Brooks, Jennie 65
Broughton, Eliza 258
Brounnelhouse, W. A. 69
Brown
  Coleman 33, 38, 161, 167
  Daniel 170
  Edward 47
  Effie (Baker) 211
  Eliza 384
  Elizabeth C. 270
  Gen. 272
  John 211
  John T. 170
  M. 79
  Margaret 309
  Martin 80
  Mary 78
  Mary M. 270
  Nancy 309
  Rev. 277
  Samuel 170
  Sarah 78
  Solaman 171
  Solomon 309
  Thomas C 95

W. D. 270
Wesley 41
William 50
Brown, J. J., and Bro. 347
Browne, Thomas C. 24, 32, 37,
                                              38, 39, 40, 44
Browning
  Gilbert 149
  James 151, 157
  John 150, 151, 157
  Levi 151, 157
  Mollie (Jordan) 151, 157
  Sanford 41
  William 150, 151, 157
Brownlee, James H. 88
Bruce
  ____ 26
  Amy (Rudolph) 357
  Benjamin 23, 248
  Benjamin F. 80, 228
  Eslie 228
  Franklin 229
  George W. 227
  Henry 227
  Hulda C. (Campbell) 228
  Huldah C. (Campbell) 227
  Isaac T. 228
  James M. 204
  John N. 144
  John T. 228
  Margaret J. 228
  Maria 227
  Nellie (Rudolph) 357
  Oscar F. 228
  Otis 357
  Otis T. 228
  Robert 227, 229
  Robert J. 22, 227, 228
  Sallie 228
  Sallie (Bantam) 227
  Sallie (Millspaugh) 228
  Sarah 228
  Sarah M. 228
  Solomon S. 228
  Thomas 72, 229, 357
  Tillis 228
  Walker 227
  William M. 227, 228
Bruce & Young 138
Bruns-Bowersox Lumber 233
Bryan, Simon P. 204
Bryant
  Harriet 265
  Martha 302
  Mr. 137
  William 96
Bryant & Stratton Bus. Coll. 381
Bryant, Latimer & 71, 137
Buchanan
  Elihu 353
  Elizabeth (Parks) 353
  James 66, 212, 265, 383
  Sarah 353

Buck
  Frederick............8, 11, 32, 33, 38
  Warren.....................................9, 10
Buell, Gen. 315
Buffalo, Ill. 74
Bufford, Elizabeth (Quick).............341
Bunker
  Amy (Hinch)..................................285
  J. G. 285
  J. S. 73
  Joseph G. 73
Bunker Hill, Battle of 326
Bunn, Walter H...............................131
Burbank, David R............................300
Burch, J..172
Burchum, Joseph 170
Burges, Amanda..............................331
Burgess, Thomas H. 45
Burks, Duncan & 138
Burlingame, George 89
Burnet, Hirun 171
Burnett
  C. 26
  W. 22
  William 33
Burns, John 79
Burnt Mill 72
Burr, Aaron 371
Burrell, Charles 204
Burroughs
  Caroline D. 229
  Charles R. 229
  Emily N. 229
  George 229
  James M. 229
  Martha (Coleman 229
  Martha E. 229
  Martha J. (Baldwin)......................229
  Mary 229
  T. W. M...229
  Victoria 229
  William H. 229
Burt
  Dorcas 369
  Henry...369
Burtie, Hallie I. (Hales) 272
Butler
  Capt. 110
  Peter 57
  William W. 204
Buttram, J. C. 69
Butts
  Emma R. 340
  James 256
  Julia 256
  Minerva 256
Byrne
  Catherine 385
  William 385
Cache River.....................................154
Cade, Simon 96
Cader, Polly M. 299
Cahokia, Ill. 19, 20

Cain, James M................................. 172
Cairns, James 39
Cairo & Vincennes R.R.................. 396
Cairo Sun 311
Cairo, Ill. 176
Caldwell
  A. G. 44
  A. P. 138
  Achsah 76
  Achsah 76
  Albert G. 67, 74, 234
  Albert Gallatin 21, 229
  C. A. 73
  Eleanor (Castle) 230
  Eliza 229
  Eliza J. 229
  H. P. 72
  James 40, 73, 169
  John 11, 21, 32, 64, 171, 229, 230
  John B. 230
  Margaret 230
  Martha 230
  R. P. 71
  Sarah (Badollet) 229
  William L. 65, 230
California Gold Rush...................... 218
Callahan, Stephen 69
Callicott
  ___ (Anderson) 230
  Aggie 230
  Beverly 230
  Beverly, Jr. 230
  Claiborne 230
  Dicey 230
  Eliza (Hamilton) 231
  F. E. 88
  Frank E. 230, 231
  Harrison 230
  Hester (Kanady) 231
  John 230
  John A..47, 51, 63, 64, 142, 230, 231
  Jordan 230
  Mary 231, 280
  Mrs. W. C. 142
  Nancy 230
  Nannie (Howell) 289
  Polly 230
  Polly Ann 230
  Rebecca 231
  Samuel 230
  Sarah (Ellis) 231
  Talitha 230
  W. C. 142
  W. S. 289
  Wade 230
  Washington 231
  William 230
  William B. 231
Callicott Cemetery 230
Callicott, J. A. & Son 64
Calmes

Gen. 343
  Henrietta B. 343
Calvert
  Elizabeth (McKernan) 322
  Frances 211
Camp Butler................. 46, 48, 49, 50, 221, 228, 370
Camp Mear 279
Campbell
  A. A. 279
  Agnes 340
  Agnes (Combs) 238
  Ann V. 78
  Annie R. 340
  Dr. 237
  Elijah 134
  Elizabeth 345
  Hester 260
  Hulda C. 228
  Huldah C. 227
  J. M. 172
  James R. 131
  John L. 77, 78
  John S. 78
  Josiah 50, 267
  Lando 238
  Laura M. (Clifford) 267
  Mary 76
  Mary 233
  Mary (Guard) 232
  Mrs. 76
  Nancy... 76
  Nellie 233
  Nora 233
  Robert 340
  Rose (Norcross) 233
  Sallie (Gillette) 232
  Sarah 340
  Thomas 340
  William 232
  William A. 233
  William C. 78, 232
Canady, Washington 49
Cane Creek 33
Cannon family 166
Cannon, Townsend 38
Carder, James K............................170
Carey, Samuel K. 65
Carlin, Thomas 57
Carmi 29, 42, 80, 96, 117, 120, 122, 260, 405, 406
Carnoy
  Belle Ward 234
  Charles H. 234
  David 170
  Ellen 233
  John 233, 234
  Josephine 233
  M. 233
  Margaret (Euright) 233
  Mary 233
  William 233
  William F. 234

Carpenter, William 172
Carr, Eugene A. 395
Carrie 177
Carroll
   Bessie 235
   Charles 64, 76, 234, 392
   Charles, Jr. 234
   Elizabeth K. (Eddy)........234
   Henry D. 204
   James 234
   John 234
   Judith M. (Williamson)..234, 348
   Judith Mimms........................234
   Patrick 234
Carruth, Lee 140
Carsey
   Eliza J. (Kinsall) 299
   J. 299
Carter
   Emriah J. 50
   J. C. 55
   James M. 88
   John 10, 37, 212
   Louisa M. 212, 213
   William 130
Cartwright, Peter 80
Caruth, Lee 69
Case
   Annie (Logsdon)........................307
   Douglas 307
Casey
   Florida (Rawlings)........................343
   Isaac 28, 31
   N. R. 343, 344
   Robert 134
   Thomas S. 42
   Zadock 26
Cash
   Robert B. 235
   Serena (Hall)........................235
   William T. 235
Casper, Ella 299
Cass, Lewis 211, 275
Cassidy
   ___........................64
   Bridget 235
   Claudia 236
   George P. 235
   Grattan 236
   J. F. 89
   John 84
   John A. 235
   Olive (Grattan) 236
Castle
   Charles 230
   Eleanor 230
   Joseph 230
   Joseph G. 74
   Joseph J. 27, 73
   Judith 76
   Sarah 230
   William 10
Castle & Temple 2, 7

Castle Garden 259
Castleman, Nicholas 92
Catamounts 18
Catholic churches
   Equality 83
   Shawneetown 36
   St. Joseph's 346
Catlin, H. C. 68
Caton, W. W. 172
Caudle, Mr. 348
Cave Township 157
Cave-in-Rock 19, 20, 29, 104, 163
   Outlaws 91
Cayton, George W. 77, 129
Central Star, The 70
Cerro Gordo, Battle of 171, 302
Chambers, Jesse 130
Charlesworth, Firth 49
Charmer 177
Chastain, Belle 262
Cheek, William 30, 37
Chenoworth, James 43
Cheney, Sarah 340
Chester & Powell 327
Chester limestone 2
Chicago, Peoria & St. Louis R.R. ..396
Chickasaw Indians 346
Childs, J. Webster 89
Choat, Malinda 214
Choate, Zadok 214
Choisser
   Attallas 172
   Edmund 172
   John 39, 95
   Marianna (Labuxiere)........95
Cholera Epidemic of 1832 308
Chossier, William 170
Choudin, John 133
Christian, Valentine 18
Church of Sharon 75
Church, C. F. 89
Cincinnati College of Medicine 232, 238, 266
Cincinnati Eclectic Med. Coll. 210
Cincinnati School of Med. 237
Cisney
   Mary (Jeffreys) 270
   Posey 270
Citizens Add. to Ridgway 383
City National Bank (Harrisburg) ..405
Civil War
   Confederate activity 17
   Secession movement 45
Clamhit, Nathan 32
Clara Poe 177
Clark
   Annesley 10
   George Rogers 109, 162
   J. H. 335
   Joel 209
   John J. 49
   Ratie May (Sanders) 357
   Samuel 10

Thomas 6
Thomas H. 336, 337
Clautau, Stephen 10
Clay
   Dennis 32
   Henry 121, 371, 372
   Isham 30, 132
   Porter 57
Clayton
   Alex 204
   Charles, Sr. 142
   Gertrude 142
   Grant 142
   Jesse 142
   Mrs. Charles, Sr. 142
   Myrtle 142
   William 42
Cleminson, J. M. 22
Cleveland
   Ella (Rudolph) 357
   Grover 217, 325, 396, 397
   Horace 357
Cleveland Medical College 284
Cleveland, Cincinnati, Chicago
   & St. Louis R.R. 396
Cleveland, Grover 216, 310
Clifford
   Laura M. 267
   Z. S. 81, 267
Clifton
   J. W. 73, 78
   John W. 245
   Juliet 245
   Juliett 245
Clippinger, A. C. 367
Cluck., Joseph E 204
Coad, G. W. 45
Coal 3
Coal Bank Springs Church 134
Coal Hill 1, 3
Coal mines 223, 406
Coffee, Horatio 171
Coffey, Archilaus 170
Colbert
   Aaron 236
   Allen 355
   Allen B. 236
   Allen, Jr. 355
   Drury 236
   Elisha 236
   Elisha C. 50
   Eliza A. (Logsdon) 355
   Frances 211, 236
   Henry 236
   Hiram 236
   Isabelle 237
   James 211, 236
   James T. 37, 236
   John B. 237
   Lucy A. 236
   Margaret 237, 355, 385
   Mary A. (Hull) 237
   Mary J. (Seets) 236

Mary L.	236	
Nancy J.	236	
Paul	237	
Prudence	237	
Sarah	236	
Thomas	236	
Thomas J.	237	
Virgie	237	
Virgil	237	
William	236	
Coldwater, Battle of	49	
Cole		
A. H.	64	
Adeline (More)	237	
Amos	237	
Augusta V. (Packard)	237	
Henry A.	237	
Leonard	332	
Malinda (Weiss)	332	
Coleman, Martha	229	
Coles		
Edmund	291	
Edward	290, 291	
Collard, Franklin	45	
College of Physicians and Surgeons of St. Louis	262	
Collinsworth, Phoebe	211	
Colvard		
Charles	204	
E. C.	64	
Combs		
Agnes	238	
Agnes A.	237	
Alice	238	
Anna	238	
Annie	237	
Calista E.	238	
David	238	
Eliza	238	
Ella	238	
Ellen E.	237	
Fuller	238	
George	238	
George E.	237	
George Washington	237, 238	
Hannah (Hemphill)	238	
Hanneh E. (Hemphill)	237	
Iayvilla (Dolan)	237	
Icavilla (Dolan)	238	
Jesse	238	
John	238	
John M.	238	
Jonathan	237, 238	
Martha	238	
Mary Jane	238	
Milton	238	
Milton H.	238	
Priscilla	238	
Samuel	238	
Samuel M.	237	
Thomas	238	
Thomas W.	238	
Trenton	238	
W. F.	237	
William	238	
Comet of 1811	54	
Comfort, Elsie	218	
Commercial Bank	274	
Commercial Bank of Evansville	254	
Concord C.P. Church	79	
Concord Regular Old Side Baptist Church for People of Color	130, 134	
Cone, Sylvester R.	48	
Conestoga, USS	176	
Conger		
Chauncey S.	42	
Judge ____.	404	
Conklin, Isaac N.	219	
Conkling, Roscoe	74	
Conner, James	89	
Connor House	64	
Connor, Mr.	52	
Contraband Negroes	126, 127, 128, 129	
Cook		
A. H.	41	
Bethuel	41	
C., & Son (firm)	298	
Charles	239	
Cullen	170	
Elizabeth A.	269	
Eula	239, 240	
Grandfather	269	
Joel	22	
John	13, 239	
John T.	35	
Joseph	73	
Jourdan	170	
Lettia A.	239	
Lillie	239, 240	
Lucinda	239	
Mollia A.	239	
Nancy J. (Hedge)	239	
Nancy J. (Hedges)	239	
Sarilda (Kinsall)	296	
Sarilda E. (Kinsall)	240	
Silas	22, 26, 127, 239, 295, 296	
Surrilda E. (Kinsall)	239, 295	
Turner	34, 36, 169	
Zachariah	239	
Zella	240	
Cook, C., & Son	138	
Coolley, W. J.	134	
Coon		
George	30	
Phillip	28, 30, 31	
Coop		
John M.	63	
William	171	
Cooper		
Isaac	36, 240	
Lizpa F.	240	
Thomas J.	65, 87	
Thomas Jefferson	240	
Corder, A. P.	22, 129	
Corinth, Tenn.	230	
Cork, Elizabeth A.	268	
Cormick, Joseph T.	46	
Cornwallis, Lord	230	
Cortwright, George W.	131	
Corwin, Thomas	74	
Corwine		
Juliet White (Sloo)	391	
R. J.	391	
Cossitt, T. H.	65	
Cotner, Duncan	170	
Cottage	177	
Cottonwood, Ill.	115, 223, 358	
Council		
Elizabeth	159	
Hardy	159	
Country Hampton, Ill.	74	
Covey, George	48	
Covington, John	170	
Cowan, Andrew J.	41	
Cox		
Charles D.	204	
Ellen (Shockley)	293	
George	43	
Isaac	293	
John	170	
Peggie (Logsdon)	308	
William	171	
Coy, John	170	
Crabb, "Aunt Rit"	160	
Crabtree		
Connie	71	
George T.	71	
Isaa	171	
Jackson	50	
W. J.	71	
Crabtree, Quigley &	138	
Craig		
Samuel	32	
Thomas E.	37	
Warner	88	
Cralley, L. B.	70	
Crandle		
Benedict	49	
Benjamin	49	
Crane, Ann Eliza	405	
Craw		
Richard	279	
Sarah A.	279	
Crawford	74	
F. C.	58	
George R.	47	
Hannah E.	240	
J. A.	324	
James S.	240	
John	80, 240, 248	
John A.	70, 240	
M. C.	22	
Margaret Zerinda	336	
Martha (Stevens)	240	
Martha L.	240	
Mary (Kanady)	240	
Nancy J.	240	

419

Sarah 78
Sophronia 324, 325
Sophronia (Kanada) 325
Sophronia A. 240
Susan (Kanady) 240
Susan E. 240
W. H. 73
William H. 240
William R. 47, 240
Crawford's Campground 80
Crebs, John M. 23, 25
Creed
   James 172
   Robert 172
Creek Indians 162, 297
Creek War 296, 297
Cremeens
   Charles 72
   William 72
Crenshaw
   Abraham 172
   Abraham (son of Thos.) 172
   Elizabeth 241, 302
   Elizabeth (Mary) 241
   Francine "Sina" (Taylor) 130, 241, 277
   John Hart .. 6, 13, 14, 26, 39, 53, 72, 80, 95, 121, 130, 134, 175, 211, 218, 241, 277, 302
   Johnny 124
   Julia A. 241
   Margaret 241
   Mary 241
   Mary H. 277
   Sina (Taylor) 302
   W. T. 63
   William 277
   William C. 241
   William F. 22
   William T. 22, 241
Crenshaw Farm 363
Crenshaw rascals vi
Crenshaw, Bogardus & Co. 218
Crenshaw's Mill 133
Crest
   Kathie vi
   Vernon H. .... iii, vi
Crest, Vernon H. 162
Crews, Seth F. 25
Crichton, Jane W. 173, 407
Crockett, ____ 41
Croghan, George 149
Cromwell, Richeson & 88
Cross, Nancy 260
Crow
   Eleanor (Pillow) 241
   John H. 42
   John Harvey 241
   Martha (Asbury) 242
   Nathaniel 241
   Pauline 222
Crumb

Anna 251
Eva 251
Crunk
   Abner 257
   Esther (Dowden) 257
   John M. 138
Cuba 318
Cubbage, L. P. 69
Culley, Lucetta 257
Cullom
   Gov. 93
   S. M. 26
Cumberland College 234
Cumberland Presbyterian churches
   Concord 79
   Hazel Ridge 79
   Hazel Ridge 137, 248
   Liberty 79
   McLeansboro 248
   New Haven 79, 139, 248
   New Pleasant 80
   Norris City 248
   Oak Grove 80, 248
   Omaha 295
   Palestine 79
   Palestine 136, 248
   Pisgah 79
   Union Ridge 248
   Village 248
Cummings, Jacob 172
Cummins, Jacob 40
Cummons, William M. 170
Cunningham
   John M. 64
   Mary F. 64
Curlew Mines, Ky. 177
Curtail, The 21
Curtin, Dan 162, 163
Curtis
   Elijah P. 47
   Sarah 130
Cusick, Sylvelia 243
Cypress Creek 107
Cypress Junction, Ill. 26, 72, 240
Cypress Mills, Ill. 72
Cypress, Ill. 72
Cypress, Ill. (Johnson Co.) 348
Cypressville, Ill. 13, 44, 72, 218
Dagley
   Catherine 223
   Elizabeth 285
   James, Jr. 68
   Jonathan B. 223
   Samuel 21, 69, 140
   Samuel, Jr. 68, 139
   Samuel, Sr. 67
Dagley & Co. 68
Dagley estate 69
Dagley, Samuel, & Co. 68
Dagney, Virginia 223
Dailey
   James 49
   John 50

Daily
   Aaron 244
   Carrie 244
   Charles 244
   Eleanora (Stout) 244
   Eunice (Harrelson) 244
   Hannah 243
   Henry 244
   James 243
   John 92, 243
   John, Jr. 244
   Joseph 243
   Margaret 243
   Martha (Huston) 243
   Mary 243
   Mary A. 244
   Samuel 243
   Sarah 243, 244
   Sylvelia (Cusick) 243
   Thomas 243, 244
   William 243, 244
Daily Gleaner 366
Daily Register, The 66
Daimwood
   Boston 10, 38
   J. G. 24
   John G. 22, 32, 33
Dake, A. B 52
Dale
   Charles A. 244
   Cora L. 244
   Edward 320
   Edward L. 244
   Hettie (McGehee) 320
   Maud 244
   Sarah (Eledge) 244
   Sarah R. (Slocumb) 244
   W. S. 69
   William S., Jr. 244
   William S., Sr. 244
Dalton, Mr. 265
Daly family 82
Damron
   C. M. 22
   C. N. 22
Dana, Gen. 395
Daniel, M. C., Mrs. 258
Darr, John 38
Davenport
   ____ 95
   A. F. 73, 244
   Abner F. 245
   Adran H. 170
   Adrian 8
   Charles 245
   Delia 245
   George 245
   George A. 245
   James 8, 22, 36, 37, 52
   Joseph A. 49
   Juliet (Clifton) 245
   M. S. 26
   Marmaduke S. 22, 32, 33, 38, 52

Martha J. ...245	W. E. ...137	Julia ...249
Mattie ...245	W. I. ...224	Kate ...250
May ...245	William ...8, 136, 245, 246, 247, 248	Leonard ...249
R. W. ...244		Leonia ...250
Randall W. ...245	William E. ...79, 247	Louis ...249, 250
Robert ...245	William I. ...249	Mary ...250
Robert C. ...245	William Isaac ...246, 247	Rosella ...249
Sarah (Flanders) ...244, 245	William M. ...226	Sebastian ...250
Sarah A. ...245	William P. ...47, 247	Stella ...249
William ...73, 172, 245	Davis, R. M., & Sons ...138, 217, 246, 248	Susanna (Wargel) ...249
David		Thomas ...249
Hezekiah ...166	Daws, Edmund ...172	Devous & Rice ...250
Jennie ...247	Dawson	Dewel, Robert R. ...169
R. M. ...79	John ...170	DeWitt
Davidson, W. W. ...70	Mary ...279	Alvin ...400
Daviess, Joseph H. ...154, 155, 390	Thomas ...10	Hannah (Wiseheart) ...400
Davis	Day	DeWolf, James ...76
___ ...41	John S. ...45	Dhu, Roderick ...164
Cordealia ...247	Samuel ...130	Dickens, Anna ...357
Eliza ...222	T. S. ...310	Dickenson
Elizabeth ...247	De Ball, Queenie ...393	Nancy A. ...349
Francis ...171	De Witt, Alfred ...47	Nancy N. ...349
Isaac S. ...247	Dean, John J. ...169	Dickerman
James ...40	Dearinger, Lowell ...95	Lucy (Wilson) ...398
James B. ...166	Decatur, Stephen ...272	Ralph Vance ...398
James M. ...171	Decker Bros. ...68	Dickerson
Jefferson ...338, 373	Decker, J. P. ...69	E. ...393
Jennie ...71, 246, 249	Delaney	Laura (Wilson) ...393
Jennie V. ...217	Henry F. ...342	Dickey
Jesse P. ...81	Sarah J. (Rawlings) ...342	T. Lyle ...25
Jessee ...93	Delap, Robert ...80	W. A. ...70
John ...30, 50, 154	Delaware Indians ...152	Dickinson
John B. M. ...172	Demming, Anton ...82	David ...348, 349
John W. F. ...204	Dempsey	Nancy A. ...348
Katie (White) ...385	Mary (Campbell) ...233	Dillard
Lucy (Bozarth) ...226	Michael J. ...48	Aaron ...252
M. M. ...71, 137, 138, 246, 247	DeNeal, Gary ...v, vi	Albert ...251
Margaret ...247	Deneen, Gov. ...337	Anna (Crumb) ...251
Mary ...216	Denning family ...150	Betsey ...251
Mary "Polly" ...261	Denning, William A. ...22, 41	Celia ...251
Mary (Sharp) ...246, 247	Dennis, Mrs. A. L. (Smith) ...360	Dicey Ann (Harris) ...251
Millage M. ...249	Dent	Elisha ...251
Nancy ...247	Captain ...97	Eliza ...252
Phoebe ...261	Frederick Fayette ...97	Elizabeth ...300
Polly ...245, 247	Julia Boggs ...97	Eva ...251
Polly (Sebastian) ...246	Depriest, Elizabeth J. ...214	Eva (Crumb) ...251
Polly (Sebastin) ...247	Derham, A. ...138	Famariah ...251
Polly (Sharp) ...217	Desper, Daniel ...293	Fannie ...252
Priscilla ...247	Devil's Anvil ...107	Francis M. ...50
R. M. ...79	Devon family ...83	George ...215
R. M. ...71, 72, 79, 80, 246	Devous	Harriet ...251
Richard ...166	Anna (Aman) ...250	James ...10, 251
Robert ...247	Catherine ...250	James, Sr. ...80
Robert ...217	Catherine (Bartell) ...249, 250	Jemima ...252
Robert Macklin ...136, 137, 139, 245, 246, 247, 248	Charles ...250	Jonathan ...251
	Emma (Smith) ...251	Margaret (Bean) ...215
S. M. ...246, 247	Harry ...249	Martha E. ...251
Samuel ...71, 137, 247	Isadore ...249, 250	Mary ...251
Samuel M. ...249	Isadore, Jr. ...250	Matthew ...252
Sarah ...247	J. Louis ...249	Milbrey ...251
Sarah A. ...295	Jacob ...250	Olsten ...251
T. A. ...73	John ...250	Roxana (Boutwell) ...251
Thomas G. ...204	Joseph ...249, 250	Viola ...252

421

William 251
Dillard Settlement 107
Dillard's Place 79
Dimmett
   Flora (Wilson) 393
   John 393
Dively, Flora R. 267
Dixon
   J. S. 72
   John 73
Dobbs, Arminta 375
Docker
   H. C. 338
   H. O. 63
   Harriet 334
   Harry 280
   Henry A. 338
   James 63
   Jane 352
   Jean 88
   Mary A. (Pool) 338
   S. N. 55, 64
   W. A. 55, 57, 61, 334, 352
Docker & Peeples 64
Dodd, Jackson 128
Dodds
   Anna 277
   Thomas 170
Doe, John 39
Doherty
   Eliza 252
   Ella 252
   Ellen 252
   Hannah 252
   James 252
   John 252
   Maggie 252
   Margaret (Logsdon) 253
   Martin 252, 287
   Mary 252
   Mary (McGuire) 252
   May 252
   Nellie (Merry) 252
   Richard 252
   Stephen 252
Doherty brothers 82
Dolan
   layville 237
   Isavilla 238
   Patrick 238
Dolph, Hiram 204
Donahue, Maggie (Bowling) ... 221
Donald, William 154
Donley, Edward 47
Donohue, John 73
Donovan, Andrew J. 47
Donovon, James 172
Dorris, Thomas M. 10, 11, 30, 38, 53
Dorsey
   Preston 211
   Sarah (Baker) 211
   William 211

Dossett
   I. F. 345
   James 69
   Laura 345
   Minerva 345
Douglas, Stephen A. 73, 256
Downen
   Esther 257
   Felix 253
   George T. 257
   Hannah 209
   Hattie Olive 253
   Inex 253
   Kate (Allyn) 253
   Lemuel 253
   Lucetta (Culley) 257
   Mary 253
   Mattie 253
   Ollie E. 257
   Ora 253
   Timothy 257
Downes
   Harriet 209
   Mary 209
   William 209
Downey, Joel F. 145
Drake, Mary 370
Droll, Mary 259
Drone
   Alexander 254, 382
   Barbara J. 253
   Calista E. (Combs) 238
   Charley F. 253
   Christopher B. 253
   Edwards 253
   Etta Mary (Zipp) 254
   F. 238
   Francis 253
   George W. 253
   Henry 253
   Joseph 254
   Joseph A. 253
   Joseph, Jr. 253
   Joseph, Sr. 253
   Leonard 254
   Lucretia 254
   Madeline 254
   Margaret (Bartel) 253
   Marion 382
   Marion N. 254
   Mary (Valter) 382
   Mary C. (Brazier) 253
   Mary E. (Vilter) 254
   Mary M. 253
   Sarah L. 253
   Vincent P. 254
Drone family 83
Dryden
   Mr. 43
   Mrs. 43
Dubois
   J. K. 57
   Toussaint 112

Duckworth
   Charles 138
   Solomon 71
   William 71
Duff
   Andrew D. 22, 41, 129, 404
   John 91
Duff the counterfeiter 7, 91
Duff's Mercantile College 220
Duffy
   Hannah (Doherty) 252
   John 252
Duffy family 82
Dugger, Allen 8, 79, 136
Duncan
   Joseph 26, 56, 290
   Stephen 172
   Thomas 170
Duncan & Burks 138
Dunlap
   ____ 166
   James 57, 314
   James E. 47
   John 153
   Minerva 314
   Sarah F. 314
Dunn
   Isham 170
   James 169
   Louisiana (Robinett) 352
   Mr. 8, 136
   Squire 170
   Tarlton 169
   Todd 352
Duplee, Hargrave & 279
Dupler
   C. E. 73, 255, 349
   Charles E. 255, 349
   D. L. G. 65
   Eva Dee 255
   Fannie A. (Lasater) 255
   Louis G. 255
   Mary E. (Kopp) 255, 349
Dupler, Hargrave & 255
Dupont, George W. 47
DuQuoin, John 150
Durban, Susan 307
Durbin
   E. J. 36, 82
   W. J. 36
Dutton
   Lydia, Jr. 76
   Lydia, Sr. 76
Dutton's Mound 5
Duvall
   Addie 255
   Charley 255
   Elizabeth (Timmons) 255
   Harry 255
   Henry 255
   Jacob 255
   June 255
   Notley 255

Notley, Jr. 255
Richard 255
Victor 255
William 255
William M. 49
Duvall family 392
Duvall's Bluff, Ark. 46
Dyersburg, Battle of......................... 49
Eagle Creek...1, 2, 3, 17, 18, 31, 33,
    79, 107, 237, 241
    Presbyterian Church................... 78
Eagle Creek Bridge 78
Eagle Creek Church 134
Eagle Creek Emancipation Baptist
    Church....................................135
Eagle Creek settlement..................116
Eagle Creek Township 1
Eagle Creek Valley 134
Eagle Mills 261
Eagle Mountain 116, 134
Eagle post office 355
Earnshaw
    Amelia (Spieler).........................255
    Annie 256
    Emma 256
    George H. 256
    Henry 255
    Joshua W. 256
    Mary 255
    Mary E.......................................256
    Raleigh 256
    Rollin 255
    Willy 256
Easley
    Elizabeth 225
    Joseph 133
    Sister 133
Eason, Teresa.................................366
Eastern Star, Order of the 71
Eastman Business College 283
Eastwood, Mary 142
Eaton
    George F. 131
    Major 46
    Samuel 45
Eckert, Carl..................................... 83
Eddy
    Alice 64
    Elizabeth K. 234
    Flora 393
    Henry....... 13, 14, 39, 44, 55, 57,
        65, 95, 115, 116, 118, 121,
        122, 234, 256
    J. M. 256
    John 230, 256
    John F..256
    John M. 22, 47
    Mary 234
    Mary J. (Marshall)......................256
    Mary Jane (Marshall) 256
    Minerva (Butts) 256
    Mrs. Frank 231
    Nathan......................................256

Safford B. 172
Samuel 256
Eddy family 251
Edwards
    Alice 257
    Alice (Bozarth) 226
    Annie 258
    Bessie 257
    Charles..................... 8, 72, 258
    Charles M................................. 45
    Charles, Sr. 8, 136
    Clara 257
    Conrad O. 66, 256
    Cora 257
    Edith 257
    Eliza (Broughton) 258
    Elizabeth A. (Jam) 257
    Eval 259
    George T. 257
    Harriet 258
    Hurtis 259
    Isom 257
    J. B. 79
    J. W. 71
    James................... 69, 140, 258
    Jane 257, 258
    Jane (Kinsall) 297
    Jeremiah.................................. 258
    John 8, 64, 136, 257, 258
    John M. 257
    Josie 258
    Leonard 258
    Lida (Robb) 258
    Lorenzo 258
    Luther 259
    M. H. 258
    Martha (Garrett)....................... 258
    Milton 258
    Mrs... 64
    Ninian............. 19, 20, 23, 28, 32,
        37, 56, 112, 113, 164, 290,
        291, 311, 394
    Oliver 89
    Ollie E. (Downen) 257
    Peter 71, 138
    R. M. 226
    Richard 257
    S. 310
    Sarah L. (Abney)....................... 258
    Sterling................. 41, 72, 84, 297
    Susan O..................................... 256
    Susan T..................................... 257
    W. 66
    Washington 258
    William 37, 256, 258
    William G. 258
    William J. 258
    William, Sr................................... 37
Edwards & Son............................. 256
Egbert, Annie 279
Egypt, the horse 51
Eherwine, E. 64
El Dorado Co., California 218

Elba, Ill...........................74, 115, 268
Elder
    ____. 26
    John..170
    Samuel 86
    Samuel C. 78
Eledge, Sarah 244
Elizabeth, Queen 302
Elizabethtown, Ill. 116
Elliott
    Cornelius. 45
    Richard 39
Ellis
    ____. 95
    Abner 231
    Benjamin 231
    Caleb..231
    James 231
    John 40, 68, 231
    John B....................................... 40
    Letitia (McCool) 231
    Nancy 231
    Sarah 231
    Spencer..................................... 38
    William 171, 231
Ellsworth, A. 64
Elstun, William 150, 157
Elwell, W. J. 64
Emma, Ill. 159
Emory, Jacob 172
Enfield College 267
England, Anderson 47
Engleton
    Hannah E. (Crawford) 240
    William 240
Ensminger
    E. 95
    Emanuel 34
    Samuel 72
Epley
    Barbara (Haman) 259
    Charles.....................................259
    Joseph 259
    Martin 259
    Mathias 69, 259
    Matthias 69
    Nancy E. (Lee) 259
Epley, Hinch & 69
Equality 34, 72, 107
    First Addition 130
    First brick house......................219
    Jail 34
    Presbyterian Church 78
    Social Brethren Church............ 83
    Woolen Mills 272
Erwein, Ambrose 64
Eskew, John 42
Estes
    Absalom 32
    Chism 28, 33
    Joseph 150, 157
Etter, Peter 31
Eubanks

423

Grandfather	269	
John	16	
Joseph	132	
Nancy C.	269	
Nancy Caroline	268	
Nancy J.	342	
Shannon	16	

Euright, Margaret 233
Evans
- Charles 70
- George W. 49
- Mary 359
- Samuel 359
- Sina (Lawler) 303
- William G. 172

Evansville & So. Ill. R.R. 27
Evansville Business Coll. 347
Evansville Commercial College.. 239, 240, 299
Evansville Medical College 292
Evansville Telephone Exchange ..209
Evansville, Carmi & Paducah R.R. Co. 27
Everett, C., Jr. 171
Ewing
- James 89
- John 11, 276
- W. L. D. 291
- William L. O. 38

Ewing College 226, 322
Ewing High School 224
Ewing Presbytery 246
Exchange Bank 286, 336, 406
Fair
- Hester (Kanady) 294
- J. 294
- Jacob 64

Fairbank, Daniel 81
Farley
- Caroline (Vines) 259
- Delila Elvira (Vaughn) 259
- Edward 10
- Indiana (McAllister) 259
- James 69, 259
- Joseph 259
- Margaret 259

Farm Fort 158
Farmer
- ____ 26
- G. W. 81
- Joseph D. 204, 245

Farmers Bank 381
Farmers' Hotel 64
Farrell, George 47
Fauntleroy, Eliza Griffin 391
Feehrer
- Alexander 259, 260
- Anthony 260
- Charles 69, 260
- John 260
- Joseph 260
- Laura 260
- Mary 260
- Mary (Droll) 259
- Maurice 69, 131, 259, 260
- Maurice, Jr. 260
- Prudence H. (Bozeman) 131
- Prudence H. (Bozman) 260

Feehrer Bros. 64
Ferrell
- Dr. 331
- Effie J. 260
- John G. 131
- L. J. (Porter) 260
- W. E. 71, 89, 137
- William Ezra 260

Ferrell, C. M., & Co., ...269
Ferries
- Barker's 28, 31
- Buck's 158
- Flynn's 132
- Ford's 132
- Rheburne's 32
- Shawneetown 30, 32, 94, 95, 394
- Vincennes 380
- Williams' 159

Ferrill, Charles M. 47
Ferry, Robert 113
Field, A. P. 117, 120
Fields
- G. B. 141
- James 5, 38
- Mr. 81
- Rev. 139
- Stephen 5, 8, 11, 38

Fillingin
- Ajax 260
- Enoch 260
- Hester (Campbell) 260
- Louisa (Moye) 260
- Nancy (Moye) 260

Fills, Thomas S. 80
Fink
- Casper 356
- Daisy (Rogers) 356

Finley, John Evans 75
First Nat'l Bank (Carmi) 405
First Nat'l Bank (Equality) 321
First Nat'l Bank (Henry, Ill.) 405
First Nat'l Bank (Ridgway) 254, 364, 382
First Nat'l Bank (Shawneetown) ...57, 59, 334, 351, 352
Fish, John M. 45
Fisher
- Meredith 33
- Meredith K. 10

Fissinger's Hotel 64
Fitzgibbon, John 42
Fitzsimmons, ____ 131
Flack, W. R. 69
Flanders
- ____ 26
- Abner 6, 78, 244
- Abner, Sr. 78
- Apphia 78
- Deborah 78
- George W. 271
- Sarah 244, 245

Flannigan, Samuel 25
Flat-boating 124, 212, 213, 251, 282, 285, 311, 348, 349, 359
Fleck, Mrs. Edward F. 142
Fleming
- James 80
- Margaret 300
- Miss 280
- Zachariah 170

Fletcher
- ____ 68
- Elizabeth (Abshier) 208
- Housan 11
- John 47
- Wesley 170, 208

Flinn's Ferry 33
Flitter Ford 108
Flood of Shawneetown 141
Floods
- 1832 59
- 1847 59
- 1853 59
- 1858 59
- 1867 59
- 1875 60
- 1882 60
- 1883 .... 60, 327
- 1884 .... 60, 140, 327
- 1898 ...141, 142, 231, 233, 392
- 1913 143

Floyd
- Ann 212
- Fatima (Kanady) 294
- Henry A. 212
- Lucy E. 212
- Nathaniel 294

Flynn's Ferry 132
Fogle, Martin 45
Foliart, Mr., Sr. 116
Ford
- Abraham 261
- Capt. 69
- Capt. James 261
- Charles L. 261
- Clarence T. 204
- Gov. Thomas 171
- Grace 261
- J. B. 89
- J. P. 403
- James 29
- James (of Ohio Co.) 261
- Kate (Reynolds) 261
- Louisa H. (Youngblood) 403
- Lucy 261
- Mary 261
- Thomas 26, 394
- Thomas K. 261

Ford's Ferry 107, 132
Ford's Ferry Road 78, 158

Ford's Ferry, Ky. 312, 313	Julie A. (Crenshaw) 241	Lee 263
Forester, William 38	Lane 263	Lucien 237
Forman, Col. 44	Lola 263	Mary A. 263
Forman, F. 171	Lulu 263	Mary A. (Hull) 237
Forquer, George 291	Lyman 261	Mary S. (Strickland) 263
Forrest, Nathan Bedford 49, 216	Mary 262	Thomas 42
Forrester, John 10, 29, 33	Mary "Polly" (Davis) 261	Thomas G. 263
Fort Blakely 231	Mary (Lamb) 241	Thomas J. 263
Fort Crawford 373	Mary A. 262	Fromley, William 47
Fort Dearborn 109	Mary Jane 261	Fugate, John M. 172
Fort Donelson 230, 231, 303	Ora (Downen) 253	Fugitive Slave Act 17
Fort Henry 230	Paul 262	Fulk, M. E. 88
Fort Hindman 316	Phoebe (Davis) 261	Fulkerson, Laura (Bean) 215
Fort Kearney 301	Russell 263	Fulks, Julia A. 370
Fort Madison, Wis. 374	Sarah 258	Fuller
Fort Massac 7, 307, 308	Thomas 92, 262	Jesse 130
Forts/Blockhouses	Thomas J. 261	Minerva (Butts) 256
Battleford 161	William 258	Gaddes, Daniel 47
Boone's 160	Fowler	Gahm, Anna (Combs) 238
Brown's 151, 161	E. P. 146	Galagher, ____ 68
Davis' 154	Elizabeth 303	Galbraith, Dr. 139
Frank Jordan's 153, 157	Elvira (Riggs) 303	Galbreath, R. C. 78
Gasaway's 161	Emma (Millspaugh) 326	Galbrieth, Jones 68
Hardin Co. 158	Lewis 303	Galena lead mines 67
Humphreys' 156	Margaret 278	Gallagher
Jordan's 156, 160	Fox	____ 68
Jordan's (Franklin Co.).. 150, 157	John 80	Mr. 64
Karnes' 151, 161	Miss 261	Gallatin Academy 73
Old Station 153	Sarah (Siebman) 362	Gallatin County 20
Pankey's 160	Fox Indians 373	Agricultural and Mech. Assoc.. 27
Pond Settlement Fort 158	Frame	Agricultural Board 339
Rude's 160	Roger 130	Agricultural Soc. 144, 375
White Co. 159	William H. 47	Agriculture Board 234
Foster	Franklin County 21	Attempts to divide 115, 116
(military leader) 209	Franklin, Isom 40	Fairgrounds 27
Abbie 263	Frazier	Historical Society 102
Abigail (Whitaker) 262	John 40	Medical Society ... 220, 222, 233, 236
Alice B. 262	Lord 149	Unit School District 116
Alpha 258	Martin 43	Veteran Association 50
Alverson 263	Martin P. 11	Gallatin County Bank 337, 338, 382, 405, 406
Asa 261	Free Silver movement 355	Gallatin County Cavalry 174
Belle (Chastain) 262	Freeher, Maurice 69	Gallatin County Democrat 178
Charles 253, 258, 263	Freeman, ____ 41	Gallatin County State Bank 336, 337, 382
Dennis 262	Fremont, Charles 255	Gallatin Democrat 366
Edward 241	French and Indian War 149	Gallatin National Bank 58, 338, 339
Edward H. 262	French, Augustus C. 172	Gallatin, Albert 20, 229
Elizabeth Ann (Hobbs) 261	Frenchman, Capt. 152	Gallaway, C. R. 71
Frank 262	Frey	Gallipolis, Ohio 281
George 258, 263	John 244	Galloway
Hannah E 262	Leonard 244	Brunett J. (Pearce) 263
Harriet 262	Mary A. (Daily) 244	C. R. 137
Horace 261	Sarah (Daily) 244	Charles R. 263
Ida J. 263	Friar, Noah 49	D. W. 263, 286
Isaac A. 261, 262	Friend, Florence (Siddall) 361	Dora 142
James 174, 175, 241	Frizzel, William 31	Dora May 263
Jane 258	Frohock	G. R. 141
John 258	Charlie 263	Jane (Riley) 286
John W. 262	Dallas 263	Malinda J. 263
Joseph 262	David 263	Martha C. 286
Joseph A. 262	David Franklin 263	
Julia 262	Franklin 263	
Julia A. 262	George 263	
Julia A. (Moye) 262	John H. 263	

Mary	142	
Mrs. C. R.	142	
Sylvestra J. (McMurtry)	263	
Virginia E.	263	
Garden of the Gods	158	
Gardner, William	38	
Garfield, James A.	325	
Garland, Griffith	68	

Garner
- Garret 170
- John 170

Garret, William 170

Garrett
- George F. 50
- J. L. 72
- Martha 258

Garrison, James 152
Garry, Samuel 238
Garst, Philip 261
Gasaway, William 161
Gaskins, William H. 170

Gaston
- E. W. 69, 140
- Wesley W. 172

Gasway, Hamilton 170

Gates
- Almira (Kanady) 264
- Bessie 264
- Emma 264
- Ethel 264
- Frederick F. 264
- Gen. 257
- Gertrude 264
- Grover C. 264
- Hester E. 264
- J. B. 264
- Joseph A. 264
- Joseph B. 264
- Mollie 264
- Sallie (McCoo) 264
- Samuel M. 264
- Sarah (Rice) 264
- Squire 264
- Walter B. 264

Gatewood
- ____ 67
- E. H. 55, 57, 334, 351
- Ephraim H. 68
- Mr. 25
- W. J. 26
- William J. 24, 44, 73, 169
- William Jefferson .. 117, 120, 264
- William Thomas 118

Gattu, Edward 11
Gay, Laurine 303
Gazaway, Hamilton 170
Gem 177
Georgetown, Mo. 174
Gerley, G. W. 69
Germania Hotel 64
Gevney, George W. 69
Gholson, George 204
Giberson, William 171

Gibson
- A. M. 79
- John 389
- S. K. 73
- Simeon K. 26
- Sullivan N. 89

Giles, William 170

Gill
- Carolina 255
- Carolina (Thompson) 265
- David 38, 265
- Henry 255, 265, 400
- Richard 265
- Sarah 400

Gillette, Sallie 232

Gilpin
- Dr. 139
- W. B. 147

Ginger, Lacy Lee 204

Givens
- Essie 329
- Lawrence 329
- Mary L. 289

Glass
- Alice (Phillips) 336
- Eliza 238
- James 216
- John F. 336
- Mary 216

Glass, Mary E. 282

Glasscock
- Arminda (Gwaltney) 265
- Clarence 265
- Elizabeth (Newman) 265
- Elma 265
- Harriet (Bryant) 265
- Henry 265
- James L. 265
- Jane 265
- John 265
- John J. 265
- John W. 265
- Patsey 265
- Thomas H. 265
- William 69, 140

Glenn
- David 217
- Pemesia 217

Glide
- Allen 43
- Charles 42
- Charley 43
- Henry 42

Globe Rolling & Wire Works 361

Goad
- Elias R. 278
- Sarah (Harding) 278

Goetzman Bros. 64
Goetzman, L. W. 63
Golang, (Frenchman) ... 152

Golconda
- Presbyterian Church 76
- Wharfboat 252

Gold
- Calvin 1, 22, 36, 64
- Hannah 76

Gold Hill 1, 2, 3, 91, 132, 320
Gold Hill Ridge 1, 3
Gold Rush 255, 301, 308, 346, 365, 367

Golden
- Joanna 88, 355
- Mike 144, 146

Goodell, R. E. 58

Goodpaster
- Franklin 204
- John 204

Goodwin, Adeline 213

Gordon
- Alta 266
- Alta (Gordon) 266
- Anan Irwin 266
- Archibald 266
- Etta C. 266
- Flora R. (Dively) 267
- Frank Henderson 267
- George Ravenscroft .. 267
- George Washington .. 266
- Isabella M. 266
- James 266
- Janet (Porter) 266
- John 266
- John Robert 267
- Jonathan 266
- Laura 267
- Laura M. (Clifford) .. 267
- Louise 267
- Lucian 73
- Lucien Winslow 266, 267
- Maria 266
- Mollie Alexander (Lewis) .. 267
- Robert 266
- Robert Porter 266
- Sabine M. (Tweed) .. 266
- Samuel Quimby 266
- Susanna (Bacon) 266
- Thomas Winslow 266
- William 266
- William Wallace 266
- Zina 266

Gordon, Sterling & Greer 64
Goshen Road 96, 153
Goslin, Capt. 312

Gosset
- A. A. 328
- Cynthia A. (Millspaugh) .. 328

Gottschell
- John 266
- Maria (Gordon) 266

Grable, David A. 170
Grable's Settlement 107

Grady
- J. H. 69
- Joel H. 69

Graham, Elizabeth 357
Granpier Township 29, 30

Grant
  A. M. ...339
  A. S. ...67
  Alexander F. ...40
  Amanda C. ...339
  Caroline ...339
  George W. ...46
  John ...351
  Judge ...40
  Julia Boggs (Dent) ...97
  Mary ...325
  Mary Frazier ...351
  Mrs. U. S. ...257
  R. H. ...68
  Robert ...68
  Roswell H. ...21, 67
  Ulysses S. ...46, 51, 97, 174, 176, 284, 314, 315, 317, 395, 398
Grassy Creek Church ...133
Grater
  George ...288
  Mabel ...288
Grattan, Olive ...236
Gray
  James ...307
  Margaret (Logsdon) ...307
Gray, Mitchell & Co. ...283
Grayson
  Elizabeth ...162
  Jesse F. ...172
  Joseph ...41
Grazier
  Barbara ...253
  Christopher ...253
  Mary C. ...253
Great Cave ...19
Great Chicago Fire ...57
Great Salt Springs ...vi, 132
Greathouse, Gabriel ...28, 30
Greeley, Horace ...378
Green
  Andrew H. ...74
  Eli W. ...47
  Harvey ...34
  J. M. ...77
  M. ...79
  Reuben ...170
  Samuel ...10
  W. H. ...312, 313
Green House Inn ...158
Green Valley Church ...83
Greene, Gen. ...266
Greenlee, J. L. ...69
Greenup, William C. ...31
Greer
  Ella A. ...220
  George W. ...50
  J. S. ...73
  Reivas W. ...45
Greetham, William D. ...6
Gregg
  ___ ...26

Eleanora ...268
Eleanora H. ...269
Elizabeth A. (Cook) ...269
Elizabeth A. (Cork) ...268
Elizabeth Ann ...268
Emma ...71, 268
Eva A. (Hopkins) ...268
F. A. ...268
Francis ...267, 268
Francis A. ...268
Franklin A. ...269
Franklin K. ...268
H. C. ...268
Hugh ...267, 268
Hugh C. ...87, 269
James ...268
James G. ...204
James M. ...71
John ...138, 267, 268
John L. ...268
M. C. ...71
Mary E. ...268
Nancy (Riley) ...267, 268
Nancy C. (Eubanks) ...269
Nancy Caroline (Eubanks) ...268
Paul Jennings ...269
Raymond R. ...269
W. E. ...71
W. T. ...268
William ...64, 405
William E. ...268, 269
William R. ...268, 269
Gregor
  J. W. ...306
  Prudence (Logsdon) ...306
Gregory, Mr. ...85
Gresham, Judge ...396, 398
Grierson's Raid ...49
Griffee, Thomas ...154
Griffin
  James S. ...170
  John ...170
Griggs, Hubbard A. ...172
Grimes, William T. ...78
Grindstaff, Samuel ...93
Griswold
  Judge ...75
  Stanley ...37
Gross
  Andrew ...270
  Anthony ...270
  Elizabeth (Whitmire) ...270
  Mary M. (Brown) ...270
  Zilpha (Perry) ...270
Grove, Capt. ...29
Groves
  John ...10, 21, 33
  John B. ...47
  Squire ...140
Grumley
  Amelia ...271
  John ...270
  Lura ...271

Mary (Jeffreys) ...270
Mary J. (Mills) ...270
Melissa ...270
Parthena (Miller) ...270
Roseander ...271
Grundy, (atty) ...39
Guard
  Alexander ...78
  C. C. ...78
  Chalon ...95
  Elizabeth (Bourland) ...220
  Martha E. ...78
  Mary ...232
  Seth ...95
  Timothy ...26, 39, 57, 73, 78, 95
  Timothy A. ...45
Guard, Choisser & Co. ...95
Gulley, Thomas ...170
Guy, George L. ...88
Gwaltney
  Adijah ...271
  Amariah ...271
  Anna ...271
  Arminda ...265, 271
  Eliza ...271
  Elizabeth ...271
  Elsie ...271
  Emaline ...271
  Fanny ...271
  Jeremiah ...271
  John ...271
  Josephus ...271
  Marinda ...271
  Mary E. (Anderson) ...271
  Sarah (Reeder) ...271
  Simon ...271
Hackleton, S. ...172
Hadley, James ...80
Hagan, Isaac ...10
Hagerman, William ...91
Hahr, John ...49
Haines, Elizabeth ...353
Hair
  Jennie ...64
Hale
  ___ ...26
  J. B. ...271
  Margaret J. (Sanders) ...358
  Robert ...204
Hales
  Blanche E. (Reed) ...272
  Hallie I. ...272
  J. W. ...271
  James ...271
  James E. ...272
  John W. ...73
  Matilda (Willis) ...271
  Mrs. J. W. ...73
Haley
  Lt. ...174
  Thomas A. ...69
Half Moon Lick ...4, 96, 108, 112, 132, 158, 241

427

Hall
- Anna 277
- Dr. 139
- Dr., Mrs. 69
- Harrison 276
- J. C. 72
- James 38, 39, 40, 55, 113, 165, 272, 408
- James P. 48
- Jesse 170
- John 170
- John E. 22, 34, 35, 41, 60, 241, 276, 277, 327
- John E., Jr. 277
- Johnathan 170
- Judge 256
- Lucy (Ford) 261
- Lulu S. 71
- Mary 71
- Mary (Crenshaw) 241
- Mary H. (Crenshaw) 278
- Rev. 243
- S. C. 261
- Sarah 276
- Serena 235
- Sina 327
- T. W. 405
- Thomas Mifflin 276

Hall & Pemberton 71, 137
Halley
- Cornelius W. 50, 174
- John H. 41
- Mrs. John 142
- William L. 63

Haman, Barbara 259
Hamesly, John 70
Hamilton
- (Alexander's son) 373
- A. W. 37
- Agnes H. (Reid) 346
- Alexander 113, 152, 373
- Eliza 231
- Henry 171
- James 172
- Mollie 88
- William H. H. 346

Hamilton College 246, 247, 260, 269, 292, 298, 347
Hamilton County 21
Hammersley
- Catherine (Smith) 363
- John 363

Hamons, William 170
Hamp
- Henry 236
- Mary L. (Colbert) 236

Hampton
- David 170
- Edward 170
- Jonathan 32

Hampton, Ill. 74
Hanchel
- George 209

Mary 209
Hancock
- Elender 300
- Elizabeth 297
- Elizabeth B. 295, 299
- John 295, 296, 297
- John W. 300

Handmore & Galagher 68
Haney
- Leonard 272
- Martha 353
- Matilda (Willis) 271

Hanmore
- ___ 68
- C. S. 69
- Capitola 278
- Carrie 278
- Charles S. 278
- Claude 278
- J. B. 69, 140
- James 278
- Job 278
- John 278
- Mary 69, 278
- Sarah 278
- Sarah (Harding) 278
- Sarah (Sprout) 278
- Thomas 278
- William 278

Hanmore & Gallagher 68
Hanna
- Brice 99, 100
- Celia (Tade) 101
- Dolphes Brice 101
- F. F. 70
- George 159
- George L. 283, 284
- John 159
- Mary (Hick) 284
- Mary J. (Hick) 283

Hannah
- A. M. 42
- Brice 33
- F. H. 70
- Isaac N. 80
- John 30

Hansborough
- John 250
- Mary (Devous) 250

Hantchel, Emily 209
Hardin 14
- Ben. (of Ky.) 14, 118, 119
- Benjamin 14, 169
- Jephtha/Jephthah 9, 11, 14, 26, 30, 32, 38, 39, 40, 44, 117, 118, 119, 120, 121
- John J. 119
- Joseph 172
- Martin D. 119
- Peter 40
- Richard 174
- William 38

Hardin County 21, 115

Hardin Creek 43
Harding
- Richard 278
- Robert 38
- Sarah 278

Hardy
- John 263
- Lulu (Foster) 263
- Thomas 72

Harget
- Betsy 133
- Israel 50
- William 133

Hargrave
- Alma L. 279
- E. B. 73
- George B. 279
- George R. 279
- George W. 50
- J. R. 73
- James R. 73
- Lucinda McHenry 279
- Sarah (Craw) 279
- Seth 29
- William 41
- Willis ... 32, 56, 72, 73, 162, 163, 164, 169, 391
- Willis B. 279

Hargrave & Duplee 279
Hargrave & Dupler 255
Hargraves
- Carter 170
- Robert 69
- Willis, Jr. 170

Hargrove
- Martha 287
- Willis 95

Harlan, Justice 40
Harlt, G. C. 112
Harmon
- Dr. 243, 309
- Ellen (Nolen) 333
- G. A. 333

Harmons, George 172
Harper, Mr. 140
Harpool, Fountain E. 50
Harrel
- J. L. 239
- Mollia A. (Cook) 239

Harrell
- Benton R. 280
- C. 138
- Cader 280, 299
- Dolly E. 281
- J. C. 71, 72, 137, 138
- James C. 137, 280
- Malinda E. 296, 298
- Mary 71
- W. F. 71, 137
- William Finley 281

Harrell & Johnson 137, 138
Harrell Bros. 138
Harrell, Latimer & 137

428

Harrelson
- Eunice 244
- George 280
- Joseph 280
- Mary (Callicott) 280
- Mary (Williams) 280
- Miss (Fleming) 280
- Nancy 280
- Rebecca 280
- Sarah E. (Hill) 280

Harrington
- Albina 282
- Alice 282
- Amanda 282
- Ann 282, 358
- Clarence 282
- Cordelia (Rogers) 282
- H. 281
- Henry 282
- Henry I. 282
- Hezekiah 282
- Jemima 358
- Jemima (Irion) 282
- Jemimah (Irion) 281
- John W. 281, 282
- Lawrence 282
- Leroy 282
- M. 281
- Mary E. (Ramsey) 282
- Miro 281, 282, 358
- Orlenia 282
- Romelia 282
- Rosetta 282
- Sarepta 282
- Vienna 282

Harrington, Allen & 281

Harris
- Aulsey 170
- Dicey Ann 251
- Gen. 175
- Gillam 170
- Lee Sullivan 46
- Levina 285
- Matthew 251
- P. P. 69
- Pinckney B. 47
- Sarah 402

Harris Creek 31
Harris's Creek 107
Harrisburg Chronicle 128
Harrisburg Medical Coll. 279
Harrisburg schools 321

Harrison
- Benjamin 325
- Gabriel 68
- Leonard 29
- William Henry . 19, 26, 152, 154, 155, 156, 158, 267, 275, 293, 388, 389, 407

Harsha
- A. A. (Campbell) 279
- Annie (Egbert) 279
- Benoni R. 279
- Clyde 279
- J. M. 279
- James 80
- John 279
- John P. 279
- Mary (Dawson) 279
- May 279
- Ruth 279
- William C. 279

Hart
- Charles C. 77
- Elizabeth 241, 277
- J. H. 63
- James B. 47, 174
- James H. 63, 64
- John 241, 277

Harth, Anna 289
Hartman, Mary (Kratz) 299

Harvey
- Andrew 324
- John 211
- Lewis 47
- Phoebe (Baker) 211

Haskins
- Carrie 289
- James R. 169

Hatfield
- Susan Catherine (Bean) 216
- William 216

Hause, D. O. 63

Hawkins
- J. R. 403
- James 170
- Lovina C. (Youngblood) 403
- M. C. 403
- Sarah A. (Youngblood) 403

Hawse, Peter 170
Hay, Lowery 38

Hayden
- ____ 60
- John J. 311
- Sarah L. (Marshall) 311
- Sarah M. 385, 386

Hayes
- Elizabeth 78
- Joseph 7, 22, 34, 86
- Rutherford B. 325
- Samuel 7, 33, 38, 52, 68
- Samuel Snowden 121
- Solomon 52
- Thomas 10

Hayle, J. 134
Hays, Solomon 169
Hayward College 288
Hazel Ridge C.P. Church 79, 137
Hazen, W. S. 63
Heacock, Russell E. 32, 44
Head, Betty vi

Heath
- T. J. 89
- Thomas S. 204

Hedge
- James 170
- Nancy J. 239

Hedges, Nancy J. 239
Heitzelman, Minnie 329
Hell's Half Acre 74

Hellington
- J. B. 353
- Minerva (Robinett) 353

Helm, Christian 73

Hemingway
- Harriet 325
- Harriett 324
- Sarah (Ridgway) 325
- Sarah J. (Ridgway) 324
- Silas 324, 325

Hemphill
- Eliza (Glass) 238
- Hannah 238
- Hannah E. 237
- Harvey 216
- J. H. 70
- James H. 282
- John F. 237, 238, 282
- Josephine (Bean) 216
- Maggie J. (Bean) 282
- Mary E. 237
- Mary E. (Glass) 282
- Mary Irene 282
- Rufus M. 204
- Vesta Joy 282

Hemphill, Massey & 70

Henderson
- Benjamin 170
- Claiborne 170
- Robert 39

Hendricks, Stephen 69
Henekin, George W. 166
Henneberger Ice & Cold Storage Co. 254
Henrick, Americus 172

Henry
- Charles M. 50
- Edward 88

Henshaw
- W. B. 338
- William B. 59

Hensley, William 22
Henson, John 45
Heraldson, William 169
Herman, S. F. 64

Herod
- John W. 169
- Thomas G. S. 48, 49

Herod, Ill. 116
Herrein, James 156
Herritt, Emily 78
Herrod, John 8

Hess
- A. C. 261
- James H. 69
- Mary (Ford) 261

Hewitt
- Emily 162
- Henry 45

429

Sallie (Gillette) 232
William 232
Hicco, Tenn. 16
Hick
  Dr. 69
  Elizabeth 284
  Elizabeth J. 283
  Fatima C. (Barger) 283, 284
  George B. 22
  John 140, 283, 284, 406
  Mary 284
  Mary J. 283
  Mary J. (Slinger) 283
  Mollie B. 406
  Sophia 284
  Thomas 283
  Thomas B. 69, 140, 283, 284
  Thomas S..26, 68, 69, 139, 140, 283, 284
  William 73, 284
Hick & Hinch 68
Hick, Mitchell & 283
Hickey, Michael 47
Hickman, Benjamin 48
Hicks, Thomas S. 26
Hide, William 170
Hidger, David 72
Higgins
  Bessie (Carroll) 235
  William R. 235
Hill
  Albert 42
  Allen 170
  Charles 32
  Henry 37, 285
  James 172, 285
  Levina (Harris) 285
  Martha (Keurek) McCue 285
  Mary A. (McCue) 318
  Sarah 383
  Sarah E. 280
Hilton
  John 52, 54
  Mr. 54
Himple, W. F. 72
Hinch
  Amy 285
  B. P. 69, 140, 285
  Benjamin P. 208, 285
  Fatima 208
  Fatima I. 285
  J. A. 285
  Julius A. 285
  Leroy 69
  Lowry 69, 131, 285
  Lucinda (Mitchell) 285
  Mary 285
  R. P. 37
  Rebecca C. 285
  Rebecca S. (Barger) 285
Hinch & Epley 69
Hinch & McDaniel 68
Hinch, Bailey & 68

Hinch, Hick & 68
Hinch, J. A., & Co. 259, 285
Hine
  B. F. 73
  Elizabeth A. Siddall) 361
  Miller J. 361
Hise
  Betsey (Dillard) 251
  George W. 86
  Jacob 215
  Jacob B. 251
  Margaret 215
Hish, Leonia (Devous) 250
Hitchcock
  Levi. H. 130
  Martin 33
Hite, Cleora L. 290
Hobart, Norris 80
Hobbs
  Elizabeth Ann 261
  Mr. 81
Hodge, ____ 68
Hodge, Ulen & Nelson 68
Hoelzle, Benjamin 64
Hogan
  ____ 231
  A. P. 286
  Alabama (Owens) 286
  Althea 286
  Bettie 286
  Charles F. 286
  Claudia 286
  David 220
  Edmund 286
  Elizabeth 220
  Elizabeth (Roman) 220
  George 286
  Harold 286
  Harry 286
  Isaac 38, 50
  J. T. 138
  James 220
  James R. 286
  Jasper 220
  John 286
  John M. 220
  John T. 286
  Mahala C. (Kinsall) 286
  Malinda 286
  Martha C. (Galloway) 286
  Mary 220
  Sarah (McGregory) 286
  Thomas B. 286
  Waite 286
  William 220
Hogan Graveyard 231
Hogg
  ____ 96
  Stephen 32
Hogin, Richard 171
Hoit, Fritz, ferry 31
Holbrook
  Helen (Richeson) 349

J. B. 349
W. H. 146
Holderby, N. P. 86
Holderly
  Nathaniel 89
  Winifred 89
Holey, Henry 171
Holland
  Alonzo 287
  Andrew 287
  Annie B. 287
  Carrie B. (Sanders) 357
  George 287
  Hezekiah 287
  James 170, 287
  John 287
  Josephus 287
  Lambert P. 287
  Lee A. 287
  Martha J. (Hargrove) 287
  Parnesa A. 287
  Richard M. 286, 287
  S. A. 358
  Sarah 287
  Sarah (Poole) 287
  Sarah A. (Pruitt) 287
  Shandy 287
  Sidora 287
  Stella (Sanders) 358
  Tempy (Sanders) 287
  Thomas 287
  Zachary 287
Holleman, Henry H. 204
Hollerich, C. N. 300
Holley, Elizabeth 333
Holliday, Joel 169
Holly Springs, Miss. 49
Holms, Jacob 170
Holt
  Amanda (Harrington) 282
  Ann Martha 289
  Lemuel 289
  Mr. 282
  William 135, 172
Home News 66, 257
Honey Moore Pond 1
Hood, Charles 171
Hooker
  Ester 370
  Hiram 403
  Jane (Bradford) 403
  John 50
Hope, James 170
Hopkins
  Eva A. 268
  Joseph H. 80
  N. E. 268
Hopper
  ____ 26
  John 64
  John P. 63
Horcasitas, Battle of 172
Horsehoe Bend, Battle of 295

Hoskins
    Margaret (Sullivan) 392
    Sarah Elizabeth 392
Hoter, Bernard 109
Housek, Farley 69
Houston
    Alexander 287
    George L. 287
    Mabel (Grater) 288
    Nannie (Adams) 287
    Samuel 287
    Walter 287
    William 287
Houston family 251
Houts, Christopher J. 80
Howard, John 172
Howe, James 153
Howell
    Ann Martha 289
    Anna 288
    Anna (Harth) 289
    Carrie (Haskins) 289
    Chester 288
    Cleora L. (Hite) 290
    Edward Hite 290
    Elizabeth Morris 289
    Fannie (Wall) 289
    George W. 289
    Harriet Matilda 289
    Harrison 289
    Harry H. 289
    James D. 288
    James Elmore 289
    John 170
    John L. 89
    John Lloyd 289
    Mary L. (Givens) 289
    Millicent (Breckenridge) 289
    Nancy J. 289
    Nannie 289
    Ray L. 289
    Riley 170
    Squire 288
    Susan 288
    Susan Howe 289
    Thomas 288
    Thomas Henry 289
    W. A. 64
    Walter T. 289
    Warren 289
    Will A. 288, 289
    William A. 289
Howell, Millspaugh & Co. 64
Hubbard
    ____. 95
    A. F. 95
    Adolphus F. 24, 291
    Ephraim 11, 22, 33
    Frederick Adolphus 290
Hubbs
    Bani 169
    Beni 169
    James 172

Hudgins
    C. M. 72, 138
    Columbus M. 292
    Dr. 139
    James 172
Huffman
    James 391
    Juliet Greenville (White) 391
Hughes
    Bessie 218
    C. G. 63
    Cynthia 329
    George 47
    John 69
    John H. 140
    John W. 49
    Lou 218
    Miss 352
Hughston, Jonathan 169
Hull
    Joseph P. 64
    Josiah 237
    Mary A. 237
Humphrey
    Betty 156
    Charles 156
    Mrs. E. J. 89
Humphreys, Charles 156
Humphries
    Emma (Gregg) 268
    Mr. 268
Hungate, Cordelia (Davis) 247
Hunter
    Alice 88
    Eva 324, 325
    Mary 88
    Mathew 324
    Matthew 63, 77, 325
    Mayor 177
    W. G. 72
    Z. 324
    Zue E. 325
Hunter & Keister 68
Huntsman
    Harry 267
    Laura (Gordon) 267
Hurd, Mr. 8, 136
Hurricane Creek Church 133
Hurricane Island 104
Hurst, Bishop 242
Huse, John H. 68
Huston
    Even 171
    Martha 243
Huston Place, Old 333
Hutchcraft, Elijah 169
Hutcherson
    Mattie 214
    Philo 214
Hutchinson family 251
Hutchison, William G 170
Hutson, John 170
Hyatt, Peter 88

Hyde, Maurice 8
Illinois & Michigan Canal 121
Illinois & Southeastern R.R. 234
Illinois Academy 322
Illinois Advertiser 108
Illinois Central R.R. 309
Illinois Emigrant 65, 256
Illinois Gazette 23, 65, 273
Illinois Intelligencer 274
Illinois Iron Furnace 157
Illinois Iron Works 211, 236
Illinois Monthly Magazine ... 274, 275
Illinois Republican 14, 15, 66
Illinois River 19
Illinois Southern R.R. 396
Illinois State Bank 139, 284
Immaculate Conception, Church
    of the 82, 83
Independent Coal Co. 2
Indian Camp Baptist Church 134
Indian Camp Creek 158
Indian Creek Twp. 167
Indian mounds 5
    Battle 149
    Boyd's 5
    Dutton's 5
    Shawneetown 76, 130
    Sugar Loaf 5
Indian trails 5
Indiana State U. 381
Indians
    at Shawneetown 95
    Attacks 151, 157, 159, 162,
        164, 166, 167
    Black Hawk 373
    Captives 210, 294
    Chickasaw 346
    Creek 162, 296, 297
    Delaware 152
    Fox 373
    Joseph, Chief 318
    Kaskaskia 8, 149, 150
    Kickapoo 152, 156
    Miahues 152
    Muscoega 152
    Muscoga 152
    Piankeshaw 152
    Poweshiek, Chief 373
    Red Bird, Chief 372
    Sacs 373
    Salt Boilers 149
    Shawnee 8, 51, 149, 150,
        152, 156, 163
    Trails 158
    Wapello, Chief 374
    White River tribe 152
    Winnebago 372, 373
Ingersoll, Robert G. 44, 73, 82,
    278, 312, 313, 380
Ingram
    John W. 172
    Timothy 170, 172
Inman

431

Albert...................................293	Zephrania.............................8	Joyner
Bartley.................................292	Johnson	Margaret A. (Millspaugh)........326
Ellen (Shockley)....................293	Adam................................177	Margaret E. (Millspaugh)........328
James..................................293	Andrew..............................303	Thomas................................328
Jennie L...............................293	Col..91	Junction City, Ill................146, 399
Jessie...................................293	George A...........................204	Junction, Ill...............................72
Marshall...............................293	James B.............................169	Justice, John.............110, 111, 112
Mary....................................293	Jesse...................................41	Kanada
Mary (Johnson)....................293	Mary..................................293	John..................................325
Polly A. (Ware)....................292	William..............................170	Mary..................................325
Sarah...................................293	Johnson County......................20	Sophronia..........................325
Susan..................................293	Johnson, Harrell &...........137, 138	Kanaday
Thomas.........................292, 293	Johnston, John J...................170	Jesse.................................240
William..........................292, 293	Joiner, Robert W..................204	Nancy J. (Crawford)............240
Inman, Ill........................238, 293	Jolly	Kanady
Inman, Martin &.....................327	Benjamin............................132	Almira................................264
Innis, Judge..........................371	Mary..................................132	Anna..................................365
Internal Improvement Act.......343	Jones	Annie (Logan)....................305
Irion	Artemesia (Wilson)..............293	Claudie..............................294
Jemima..............................282	Edward...............73, 169, 172	Edgar..........................294, 305
Jemimah............................281	Electa................................403	Elizabeth...........................375
Irish Settlement.....................302	Elias W...............................45	Elizabeth (Seaton)..............294
Irish Store, Ill...........................74	Fawntainee........................171	Fatima...............................294
Iron industry.........................223	Henry.................................152	George W..........................294
Iron works...............211, 236, 346	J. M.....................................61	Gertrude (Spivey)...............366
Island Riffle..............................1	James..........................39, 204	Harvey..............................264
Island Ripple...............18, 30, 132	James A..............................42	Hester.........................231, 294
Island Ripple Church......132, 133	James M.......................52, 293	Ida...........................294, 375
Isom, Richard.......................170	John Paul...........................257	John J................................294
Jackson	John T..................................55	John R...............................294
Andrew.............75, 159, 210, 231, 296, 297, 372	John W..............................172	Johnson......................236, 294
Elizabeth............................259	Jonathan............................169	Louise (Spivey)..................365
Gen. (CSA)........................244	Lavinia (Waggener).............300	Ludica (Reid).....................294
John....................................29	M. S..............................64, 293	Maria.................................264
Josiah E..............................86	Michael........8, 9, 11, 24, 25, 26, 30, 38, 120	Mary..................................240
Jacobs	Nat 300	Mary (Sherwood)................294
Daniel..........................126, 293	Richard........................52, 293	Maud.................................294
Jonathan............................293	W.......................................134	Moses..........................294, 375
Margaret A. (Bradford).........293	Washington C......................45	Nancy J. (Colbert)..............236
Page..................................171	William.........................131, 132	Pearl..................................294
Susanna.............................293	William C.............................42	Peter..................................294
Jam	Jones Cemetery.....................134	Peter, Jr.............................294
August...............................257	Jonny, Capt..........................151	Sandford B..........................47
Elizabeth A.........................257	Joplin, Lucinda......................333	Susan................................240
James	Jordan	U. Grant.............................294
Almira..................................65	Elias.............................151, 157	Washington.......................294
Elma..................................360	Frank...........................153, 157	Washington J.....................294
Prudence (Muir)..................306	James.................................157	Kanady Graveyard................231
Jaques, James F......................80	Joseph................................157	Kanawha Springs..................390
Jasper College......................254	Mollie............................151, 157	Kane
Jefferson Co. Fair Assoc........327	Moses...........................151, 157	Elias Kent............................44
Jefferson Med. Coll.........283, 284	Jordan Brothers................150, 157	Michael...............................52
Jefferson, Thomas.........117, 229	Jordan Settlement.................153	Kane Creek..........................136
Jeffreys, Mary......................270	Jordan's Fort........................156	Kannady
Jenkins, Jesse........................41	Jorstad, Tamara....................374	Sanford B............................47
Jennings	Joseph, Chief.......................318	Thomas..............................204
Isaac.................................237	Jourdan	Karbers Ridge......................157
Joshua D.............................49	Elias................................31, 32	Karcher
Margaret (Colbert)..............237	Francis.................................28	Anastasia (Reiling)..............295
John, Frederick A................333	James.................................157	Baltaser.............................295
Johns	Joseph.................................28	Carl...................................295
Zephaniah..........................136	Joy, Ephraim..........................81	Maggie (McMurchy)...........295
		Mary R. (Zachmeier)..........295

Thomas 295	King William's War 376	Sarilda 296
Victor 295	King, A. G. 263	Sarilda E. 240
Karcher & Scanland 64, 295	Kingston, Jeff 204	Surrilda E. 239, 295
Karcher, Peeples & 64	Kinne	Thomas 138, 296, 297
Karnes	Eunice M. 404	William 296, 297
Alfred 172	George N. 404	William M. 299
David B. 172	Kinney, William 26	Kinsall, Barter & 138
J. W 377	Kinnie, Emmie M. 403	Kinsoll, James 131
Jacob 161	Kinsall	Kirkham
Loudene 377	A. H. 89, 137	____ 67
Karns	Alvin H. 296, 298	Jesse 55, 68
George 170	Barbara A. 299	Robert 126
John 170	Benjamin 37, 71, 136, 137,	Kirkindol, Robert 171
Samuel 170	169, 240, 271, 295, 296,	Kirkman, Col. 177
Kaskaskia Indians 8, 150	297, 298, 299	Kirkpatrick
Kaskaskia, Ill. 19, 75	Benjamin, Sr. 8, 136	Alexander 52, 55, 57, 77,
Kate Robison 177	D. M. 22, 44, 63, 296,	130, 229
Kaufman family 83	335, 336, 337	Eliza J. (Caldwell) 229
Kaufman, Charles A. 51	Dan M. 204	J. 11
Keagy, Charles 204	David 169	James 52
Keane family 82	David M. 296, 297, 298	John 77
Kearney, Lawrence 273	Edgar B. 299	Mr. 76, 284
Kearny, David 170	Edith (Lowe) 297, 298	Mrs. 76
Keasler	Edna 298	Thomas 20
David 8, 136	Edward J. 204	Kirkpatrick, Peeples & 38, 52
James 280	Eliza J. 299	Kiser, William 137
Mary 71	Eliza J. (Abney) 299	Kivit, Lavina 208
Susan C. 280	Elizabeth 295	Knight, George B. 131
Keath, George P. 170	Elizabeth (Hancock) 297	Knights of the Golden Circle 176
Keaton, William 171	Elizabeth (Shaw) 296	Knox Co., Ind. Terr. 20
Keeny, Jonathan 169	Elizabeth B. (Hancock)..295, 299	Knox County militia 389
Keiser, Daniel M. 71	Elsie (Gwaltney) 271	Kopp
Keister, Hunter & 68	Hiram 297	John J. 255
Keith, Robert 39	Hiram C. 299	Mary E. 255, 349
Kelley, Melissa 270	J. 239	Koser
Kellogg, William Pitt 370	J. M. 89, 137	Fannie 354
Kelly	James A. 299	Sarah Frances 355
Elizabeth 302	Jane 297	Kratz
Mordecai B. 45	Jennie 71, 296, 298	Christian 299
William 10	John 8, 79, 136, 137, 248,	Edward 299
Kendrick, Martha 318	295, 296, 297, 299	Elenora 299
Kenrick, James 170	John H. 296, 298	Elizabeth 299
Kent	Laura M. 299	Ella (Casper) 299
Loren 47, 72	Mahala C. 286, 299	Emma 299
Lt. Col. 48	Malinda E. (Harrell) 296, 298	Mary 299
Ketchum, J. C. 64	Margaret S. 299	Philip 299
Keurek	Mary E. 299	Philipine (Krug) 299
James 285	Maurice 295	Tillie 299
Martha 285	Monroe 296	Walter 299
Mary 285	Monroe Douglas 298	Kratz & McMurchy 299
Kickapoo Indians 152, 156	Moses 8, 136, 297	Krauser, Mary 400
Kidnappings 12, 18, 41, 52	Mrs. 384	Krug
Kielbraid, John 45	Nellie 299	Philipine 299
Kilgore, ____ 93	Polly M. (Harrell) 299	William 82
Killis, William 12	R. D. 89, 137	Kunn, John 70
Kimball, Gen. 46	R. S. 71	Kuykendall
Kimberly, Samuel W. 11	Rosetta E. 299	Andrew J. 25
Kimbrough	Sallie S. 240	Lewis 10, 13, 14, 218
Calvin 215	Samuel S. 296, 298	Peter 152
Jemima 215	Sarah 296	Robert 171
Nancy 215	Sarah (Kinsall) 296	Kuykendall Valley 1
Kimmel, ____ 65	Sarah A. (Davis) 295	La Bauissier, ____ 95
Kincade, McDonald 69	Sarah S. 298	Labuxiere, Marianne 95

Lacey
　Ann..................................308
　George.............................308
Lackins, Isaac.........................47
Lacy, Jordan..........................38
Lafayette, Marquis de....55, 66, 113, 225, 277
Lafferty
　Benjamin......................13, 34
　Cornelius...............10, 30, 33
　William...........................169
Lamb
　Elizabeth (Dillard).............300
　John..........................210, 300
　Maria...............................300
　Maria (Hancock)................300
　Mary........................210, 241
　Mr. 228
　R. A.................................300
　Sarah (Bruce)...................228
Lambert
　David...............................300
　Elizabeth (Sprague)...........300
　Elizabeth Ann (Sprague)....300
　Elizabeth Sprague..............301
　John.................................300
　John M.............................300
　Josiah...............................300
　Katherine I. (Marshall)........301
　Lavinia (Waggener)...........300
　Lewis...........................45, 82
　Marshall............................300
　Marshall E........................300
　William Payne...................301
Lamburth, James...................172
Land
　Ann Eliza (Crane)...............405
　D. R.................................406
　D.R., & Co........................406
　David...............................406
　E. A.................................406
　Elizabeth (Hick).................284
　Elizabeth J. (Hick)..............283
　George I...........................405
　George L. 405, 406
　H. C.................................406
　John..........................405, 406
　John.................................406
　Louise..............................406
　Madeline E. 406
　Mathew............................283
　Matthew....................159, 284
　Mollie B. (Hick).................406
　Mrs. (Rupert)....................405
　Robert.......................152, 159
　Walter H..........................406
　Yearby.............................405
Land, D. R. & J......................406
Land, Y., & Sons....................406
Lane
　____...................................26
　J. A...................................37
　John.............22, 33, 34, 72, 95

Joseph A..............................23
　Maggie.............................304
Lane School..........................249
Langford, Martha..................223
Lann, Robert..........................30
Lanphier
　Charles.............................241
　Margaret (Crenshaw)........241
Lasater
　Absalom...........................301
　Edgar...............................301
　Fannie A...........................255
　James M....................255, 301
　James S............................301
　Louisa (Vickers).................301
　Lucy.................................301
　Mary (Mills) Boyd..............301
Latham
　John D..............................270
　Margaret J........................392
　Mary (Jeffreys).................270
Latimer
　Benjamin A. 301
　Bishop..............................302
　Clemma.............................71
　Col. 302
　J. B..................71, 137, 138, 264
　John B..............................301
　Martha (Bryant)................302
Latimer & Bryant..............71, 137
Latimer & Harrell..................137
Latimer House.......................302
Latimer, J. B., & Co................264
Lauderbaugh, Myra................65
Laughlin, Andy.......................38
Law, John............................390
Lawler
　Addie...............................303
　Anna................................213
　Anthony...........................303
　Elizabeth..........................303
　Elizabeth (Crenshaw)..241, 302, 303
　Elizabeth (Fowler).............303
　Elizabeth (Kelly)................302
　George F...........................303
　John...................81, 82, 302
　John C..............................303
　Judith...............................303
　Judith A...........................303
　Lawrence C. 303
　Louis F. 303
　Lucille...............................iii
　Margaret.............253, 302, 303
　Margaret A. 303
　Mary.........................302, 303
　Mary E......................303, 359
　Mary N.............................303
　Mary R.............................303
　Michael Kelly.........16, 44, 45, 46, 51, 73, 81, 171, 172, 213, 230, 241, 243, 253, 302, 303, 325, 359, 395

Michael Kelly......................303
　Micheal.............................303
　Monica A..........................303
　Patrick................................46
　Paul.................................303
　Philip................................303
　Raphael E. 302, 303
　Raphael E., Jr....................303
　Sally.................................213
　Sina.................................303
　Thomas......................81, 302
　Thomas B.........................213
　Thomas R.........................253
　William.............................303
Lawler family.........................82
Lawler, Ill.............................74
Lawrence, G. H. W..................51
Lawson
　Josie (Edwards).................258
　Mr. 258
　William W........................258
Lawyer, Michael K..................73
Leach, L. B. 58
Leacord, Dr. 237
Lead....................................402
Lead mines at Galena.............67
Leamington, Ill.......................74
Leavell
　Benjamin............................18
　Edward, Jr..........................18
　Lewis................................18
　William G...........................18
Leavell Family.......................79
Leavell Hill....................18, 132
Ledbetter
　Asa.............................29, 33
　George.............................237
　Henry...........................8, 31
　Prudence (Colbert)............237
Ledford, John.......................128
Lee
　Buzel................................37
　James..............................132
　James H...........................259
　Nancy E...........................259
　Priscilla............................132
　Susan A...........................259
Leech
　Achsah (Applegate)...........311
　Amira...............................310
　Amy..........................387, 389
　Francis........111, 112, 387, 388
　George..........111, 112, 311, 387, 391
Leffler, B..............................78
Leich, Humphreys...................8
Leighliter, Nancy J................359
Lemen
　C. J...........................88, 303
　James..............................303
　Josiah..............................303
　Laurine (Gay)....................303
　Mabel C............................304

Mary L	304
Robert	303
Sarah Caswell (Smith)	304
William C.	304
Lemon, Dr.	139
LeMont, Jeanne Claude	341
LeRhodes, F.	177
Letters from the West	274
Leufgen, Adam	82
Leutzhuick, Katherine	404
Level Hill	18
Levell, Peter	45
Levil, Lewis	170
Leviston, ___	26

Lewis
Abraham	170
Carrie	304
Charles	172
David W.	50
Enoch	267
Hester L.	304
Louisa	130
Luella	304
Maggie (Lane)	304
Mollie Alexander	267
Pearl	304
Philip	304
S. D.	138
Sam	151
Samuel D.	304

Lewis, A. M. & Bro.	64
Lewis, S. B. & Co.	72
Liberty C.P. Church	79
Liberty Church	133
Lick Boundary Church	133
Lick Creek Church	133

Lincoln
Abraham	44, 303, 314, 349, 364
John	40

Lincoln College	248
Lincoln University	247
Linder, Usher P.	120
Line, Henry S.	68
Linn, William	57
Lippincott, Thomas	54
Little Fish Lake	1
Little Gem Flour mill	399
Little Jim Roller Mill	69
Little Mackinaw Creek	19
Little Saline Creek	107
Little Wabash River	21
Dam at New Haven	261
Little, Catherine	319, 320
Livery business	223, 403
Livingston, George	73
Local Record	66, 256, 257
Lockhart, John	132
Locklar, Samuel	204
Lockwood, Samuel D.	40

Logan
Alfred	305
Annie	305
Arthur	305
Belle (St. Clair)	305
Charles	305
Chester	305
Clarence	305
David	305
David A.	304
Edward	305
Elizabeth (Munch)	305
Elizabeth E.	319
Harrison	305
Isabelle	319
James	38, 305, 319
John	305
John A.	22, 23, 25, 41, 44, 45, 64, 73, 125, 126, 294
John R.	305
Mary (Munch)	305
Moses	305
Moses M.	204
Walter	305

Logan's Settlement	107

Logsdon
"Peggy"	53
Ann	308
Annie	307
Arthur	309
Bluford	309
Butler	53
Carter	309
Edith (Rearden)	306
Edith (Riordan)	309
Edward	309
Eliza	308
Eugene	306, 309
Fannie M.	306, 307
Frederick	309
Horace	309
Isabelle	309
J. J.	306
James	309, 350
James J.	306
James J., Jr.	307
James, Jr.	306
Jessie (Rider)	350
John	53
John W.	204
Joseph	52, 53, 306-308, 355
Joseph "Bulgar Joe"	307
Joseph E.	309
Joseph M.	306
Laura	392
Lucy	309
Margaret	53, 305, 306, 307
Margaret (Brown)	309
Mary	306
Mary (Muir)	306, 309
Mary A. (Rogers)	308
Mary M.	306
Matilda (Thompson)	308
Maud	306
Maude	309
Nancy	53
Nancy A.	306, 307
Nancy A. (Logsdon)	306
Peggie	308
Peggy	308
Polly	308
Prudence	306
Prudence A.	306
Prudence Elizabeth Muir	307
Prudy	308
Robert	306
Robert L.	307
Rosa	306, 307
Susan	308
Susan (Durban)	307
Thomas	74, 305, 308, 309, 392
Thomas B.	37, 306, 307, 309
Thomas, Sr.	305
William	306, 307

Logston
John	171
Joseph	171

Lollard's Settlement	107

Long
___	275
Addie A.	65
Jacob	47

Long Ridge, Battle of	164

Loomis
Eleanor L.	310
Guy	310
J. R.	26
James	310
James R.	22, 213, 310
Lt. Col.	48
Lucy	310
Maggie (Spivey)	310
Margaret (Spivey)	365
Nellie	310
William Hick	310
William L.	64
William R.	310

Lopas, Thomas C.	80
Louis Napoleon	295
Louisville & Nashville R.R.	26, 27, 72, 222, 327, 396
Louisville, Evansville & St. Louis R.R.	396
Love, William	307
Lovejoy, Elijah P.	54
Low, Mr.	53

Lowe
A. K.	58, 63, 64, 297, 298
Cassandra J.	297, 298
Edith	297, 298
Enos	374
George A.	27
Rachel	356

Lower Lick	vi
Lowrey, Charles	172

Luckett
Mary E.	303
Rachel (Siebman)	362

Lumsden

435

Miss 377
William O. 377
Lurguy, A. J. 68
Lusk Creek 20
Lusk, D. W. 17, 63, 66, 121, 126,
    127, 130, 177, 408
Luther
    Ezra G. 169
    George 69
    James 353
    Martha J. (Robinson) 353
    Mr. 69
Luttrell, Mary 243
Lutz, George A. 71, 137
Lynch, Logan 172
Lyon, M. 64
M. Veronica, Sister 303
Mace, Edward 204
Mack, John 77, 78
Magazines
    Illinois Monthly 274
    Port Folio 274
Malden, John 131
Malingly, Z. 17
Maloney
    Arthur 252
    Eliza (Doherty) 252
    Ella (Doherty) 252
    William 252
Maloney family 82
Maltby, Martha 361
Manesse, John 154
Mangrum, Jackson J. 47
Mann, John 172
Mansker, John G. 46
Mapes
    ____ 118
    Thomas 172
Marble, Nancy 318
March to the Sea 209, 210
Margrave, Eliza J. 216
Marietta & Cincinnati R.R. 279
Marion, Francis 230, 231
Marion, Ill. 154
Marks, Samuel B. 45
Marmaduke, Gen. 364
Marmaluke Legion 172
Marshal, Grandfather 311
Marshall
    Amira 76, 311
    Amira (Leech) 310
    Amira L. 76
    Amira L. "Amy" (Leech) 389
    Daniel 311
    Elizabeth 230, 311
    Francis L. 311
    Genevieve 311
    Georgianna 311
    Humphrey 371, 372
    James 301
    Joanna G. (Stevenson) 311
    John 7, 14, 21, 32, 33, 52, 55,
        56, 64, 76, 95, 102, 112,
        122, 256, 310, 387, 389,
        391
    John, Jr. 311
    Katherine I. 301
    Mary J. 256
    Mary Jane 256
    May 311
    S. S. 377
    Samuel 22, 45
    Samuel D. 14, 22, 23, 35, 44,
        55, 66, 118, 122, 171, 391
    Samuel D., Jr. 311
    Samuel S. 22, 23, 25, 36, 41,
        368, 378
    Sarah L. 311
    William S. 311
Marshall House 76
Martha Iron & Furnace Co. 346
Martin
    ____ 25, 26
    Alfred 311
    Charles 350
    Edith (Rider) 350
    Eliza (Quick) 341
    Horace 64
    Jason 170
    Jesse L. 47
    John 8
    Nancy C. (Rice) 311
    R. 89, 137
    Rachel 311
    Ratie 311
    Sarah V. (Riley) 311
    Thomas 42, 71, 138, 311, 347
Martin & Inman 327
Martin & Rice 311, 347
Mason, Lavina 248
Masonic Lodge 154, 376, 386
Massachusetts & Connecticut
    Missionary Society 75
Massachusetts Missionary Society
    75
Massey & Hemphill 70
Massey, James M. 80
Mather
    Alice Warren 398
    James 398
Mathes, A. R. 77
Matteson, Joel A. 58
Mattice, Daniel D. 46
Mattingly
    Laura (Wiseheart) 400
    William 400
Maxwell, Elizabeth 334
May
    Belam 30
    Daniel G. 88
Mayer, A. 64
Mayfield, John L. 204
Mayhew
    ____ 26
    W. W. 23
Mayhue, Adam 50
Mays
    ____ 348
    Mr. 349
McAlister, John 38
McAllister
    Elias 45
    Ellen 142
    Indiana 259
    Mary 142
    Samuel 129
McBane
    A. M. L. 27, 64, 65, 312
    Angus M. L. ... 37, 234, 312, 313,
        348
    Ellen 313
    Ellen (Willard) 312, 313
    Joseph 313
    Marietta 313
    Mary (Richeson) .. 234, 312, 313,
        348
    William 312, 313
    William A. 312, 313
McCabe
    A. K. 63
    Arad R. 23
McCaleb
    E. H. 73
    Edward H. 50
    P. H. 73
McCallen
    ____ 41
    Andrew 349
    Andrew J. 64
    Mary 349
    Mattie L. 349
McCammon, Rev. 243
McCartney
    ____ 26
    John F. 47
McCaslin, James B. 170
McCauley, ____ 72
McCauslin, John 172
McCay, William 10
McChiskey, Hiram 172
McClain, F. 37
McClellan
    George 48
    George B. 385
McClelland, John 169
McClernand
    Edward John 318
    Fatima 52
    John A. 23, 24, 26, 44, 48, 51,
        52, 212, 213, 230, 256, 325
    John W. 84
    Minerva (Dunlap) 314
    Sarah F. (Dunlap) 314
McClintock
    Mr. 99
    Samuel 24
McComb
    J. B. 78
    William H. 78

McConnell, Hugh 33	McDouglass, T. L. 89	McGill, Nancy J. 358
McCoo, Sallie 264	McElduff, John 7	McGoffin, Col. 174
McCool	McElroy	McGregory
A. T. 39	Alexander 33	Noah 286
Abraham 231	Miss 247	Sarah 286
Abraham T. 8	McFadden, Roley 69	McGuire family 82
Abraham, Jr. 231	McFadden's Bluff, Ind. 214	McGuire, Mary 252
Letitia 231	McFarland, James 29, 31	McHenry
Marion 47, 231	McFarland's Ferry 31, 32	Capt. 29
William 231	McGee, Charles W. 320	Daniel 152
William H. 50	McGehee	Lucinda 279
McCord	Alex. C. 319	William 152
Cave 148	Alexander 299	William B. 159, 163, 164
J. M. 77	Andrew G. 320	McIlrath
McCormick, Mary (Siebman) 362	Angeline 320	Annie 321
McCoy	Anna I. 319	Hugh 321
Ezekiel 158	C. W. 27, 319	J. T. 321
Wade W. 49	Catherine 320	J. T., Jr. 321
William 22, 33, 34	Catherine (Little) 319, 320	John 70, 321
McCracken	Charles 320	Martha A. (Pickering) 321
John S. 351	Charles W. 319, 320	McIlreth, John 131
Mr. 351	Charles W., Jr. 319	McIlvaine
McCracken W. H., & Co. 66	Eddie S. 320	Francis E. 391
McCready, James 75	Edward S. 320	Sarah E. (Sloo) 391
McCue	Effie E. 320	McIlvane, Mr. 73
Bessie 319	Elizabeth A. 319	McIntire
Clara 318	Elizabeth E. (Logan) 319	Lizzie 322
Elizabeth (Shaffer) 318	Emily 320	Sarah A. (Seeley) 322
Frankie 319	Emily J. 319	Thaddeus 321, 322
George 318	Ethel 320	William 73, 321
James Y. 285	F. M. 319	McIntire & Son 321
John 318, 319	Francis M. 319, 320	McKee, Thomas 42
John W. 318	George 320	McKendree College 240, 242
John Y. 318	Gilbert 320	McKenney
Joseph A. 318	Hattie E. 320	Elizabeth (Baker) 211
Josiah 318	Hettie 320	Thomas L. 275
Katie 318	Jennie (Pellin) 320	Wallace 211
Martha (Kendrick) 318	Jennie (Pellum) 320	McKernan
Martha (Keurek) 285	Jesse 216	Charles 322
Mary A. 318	John 319, 320	Charles Henry 322
Mattie 285, 318	L. L. 71	Elizabeth 322
Nancy (Marble) 318	Lizzie 320	Emeline (Addison) 322
Rachel 319	Mahala (Moreland) 319, 320	Grace (Phile) 323
Rachel Robinson 318	Mary E. (Kinsall) 299	Henry 322
Rachel S. 285	Nora 320	Julia 322
Raymond 319	Polly 216	Lydia (Spivey) 322
Sarah 318	Polly A. 216	Margaret (Smith) 323
Sarah F. 318	R. S. 72	Maria 322
Y. Y. 318	Rachael 11	Mollie 322
McCullogh, John 73	Samuel 320	Nancy (Murry) 322
McDaniel	Thomas 9, 319	Peter 322
Edward T. 204	W. S. 320	Reuben 322
William 209	W. Smith 320	William R. 322
McDaniel & Hinch & 68	William 132, 319, 320	McKinley
McDaniel, Hinch & 68	William S. 319	Daniel 10
McDermott, Sarah 364	William Smith 320	William 325
McDonald	Wright W. 319	McKinney
Etta (Siddall) 361	McGhee	Carolina 300
George L. 358	D. W. 357	Ellen (Sprague) 300
Lillie R. (Sanders) 357	James 38	McLain
Moses 42	Jemima 357	_____ 26
Mr. 357	Polly 357	Addie (Bowling) 222
McDonald, Seelinger & 64	Rebecca (Callicott) 231	Calvin B. 323

Clara 323
Ellen 323
Francis M. 323
Franklin 323
Guy 323
Iva 323
Jessie M. 323
Lewis V. 323
Louis 222
Lucy A. 323
Lurania (Warson) 323
Mary (Riley) 323
Nancy (Purcell) 323
Samuel 323
Viola 323
McLaughlin, John 101
McLean, John 23, 24, 32, 39, 44, 52, 92, 95
McLin, David W. 80
McMasters, ____ 131
McMintry, James H. 22
McMullen
 N. 209
 Permelia (Aldridge) 209
McMurchy
 George 41
 James 323
 Kratz & 299
 Maggie 295
 Mr. 341
 Peter 295, 323
McMurchy & Bahr 64, 323
McMurtry
 Frances 404
 James B. 404
 Mary J. 404
 Sylvestra J. 263
McQuay, Franklin 137
McReynolds
 Sarah (Foster) 258
 W. W. 258
Meador, J. W. 138
Medling, Nedum 170
Meek, Laura (Logsdon) 392
Melvar, Gen. 226
Melville, Andrew 68
Melville, Nelson & 68
Melvin
 Andrew 79
 Augustus H. 47
 James 69, 140
 John 68
 Victor 69, 140
Mercantile National Bank 254
Merry, Nellie 252
Methodist churches
 Bethlehem 81, 137
 Carmi 242
 Centralia 242
 East St. Louis 242
 Elizabethtown 242
 Fairfield 242
 Grayville 242

Harrisburg 242
Mt. Vernon Dist. 242
New Haven 81, 139
Omaha 81, 137
Salem 242
Summit Avenue 242
Upper Alton 242
Vandalia 242
Vienna 242
Mexican War 44, 302
Meyer
 B. A. 383
 James 308
 Prudy (Logsdon) 308
Miahues Indians 152
Miami Medical Coll. ... 220, 235, 267
Miami War 7
Michelson, Edmond J. 129
Mick
 Charles 34
 Robert 405
Middle Fork Saline River Church 132, 133
Milburne, ____ 92
Miles' Trace 20, 156
Military units
 "Whang-Doodle" Reg. 42
 10th Ky. Cav. (CSA) 177
 110th Ill. Inf. 333
 120th Ill. Inf. ... 49, 228, 229, 236, 264, 294, 304, 305, 394, 399
 128th Ill. Inf. 42
 131st Ill. Inf. 48, 50, 145, 174, 215, 292, 321, 340, 350, 363
 13th Army Corps 284
 13th Corps 316, 395
 13th Ill. Cav. 333
 13th Ill. Inf. Reg. 77
 13th Mo. Inf. 175
 14th Ill. Cav. 49
 14th Ill. Inf. 174, 272
 14th U.S. Inf. 218
 153rd Ohio Inf. 262, 330
 18th Ill. Inf. 45, 303, 324, 325
 18th Ind. Inf. 267
 1st Cal. Reg. 286
 1st Ill. Cav. 174, 175, 241, 258, 272
 1st Ill. Heavy Art. 350
 1st Ill. Reg. 398
 1st Ky. Cav. (CSA) 289
 25th Iowa Inf. 303
 29th Ill. Inf. 45, 47, 145, 174, 215, 230, 235, 256, 265, 267, 292, 319, 321, 350, 363
 29th Mo. Inf. (Fed.) 331
 29th U.S. Col. Inf. 45
 29th U.S. Inf. 226
 2nd Iowa Inf. 266
 3rd Ill. Cav. 216, 221, 279

 3rd Ill. Inf. 171
 3rd Ill. Reg. 44
 3rd Ind. Co. Ill. Vol. 173
 47th Ohio Inf. 331
 48th Ill. Inf. 312, 313
 4th Ill. Inf. 171
 56th Ill. Inf. 48, 174, 350
 60th Ill. Inf. 210
 65th Ind. Inf. 209
 69th Ohio Inf. 259
 6th Ill. Cav. 45, 48, 174, 176, 214, 287, 324
 6th Ohio Inf. 328
 7th Ill. Cav. 174, 259, 283, 369, 370
 87th Ill. Inf. 174, 356
 8th Ill. Reg. 397
 8th Ky. Cav. 178
 8th Mo. Inf. (USA) 270
 9th Ill. Inf. 278
 9th Ill. Reg. 398
 Army of the Tennessee 325
 Army of the West 370
 Baltimore Blues 223
 Birge's 2nd Mo. Sharpshooters 266
 Brown's Battalion 244
 Chenoweth's Reg. (CSA) 177
 Foster's Ind. Ohio Cav. 266
 Gallatin Co. Cavalry 174
 Gov. Yates' Legion 176
 Hatch's Division 370
 Irish Brigade 175
 Knox Co. militia 389
 Marble City Guards 244
 Marmaluke Legion 172
 McClernand's Division 315
 Ohio State Guards 262
 Orphan Brigade 289
 Shawneetown Artillery 177
 Sypert's Reg. (CSA) 177
 Washington Guards 272
Mill Slough 1
Miller
 Elizabeth 401, 402
 Emily (McGehee) 320
 Emily J. (McGehee) 319
 J. M. 246
 Parthena 270
 William 319, 320
Milligan, Elihu 48
Milliken University 248, 336, 337
Mills
 Charles 301
 E. 63, 70
 Edgar 37, 240, 324
 Edgar, Jr. 325
 Edgar, Sr. 324
 Ella 324, 325
 Eva (Hunter) 324, 325
 Hunter 324
 John 257
 Julia (Pierce) 301

Laura 324	Capt. 174	James H. 330
Mary 301	Dr. 376	Jennie 330
Mary J. 270	Elizabeth (Dagley).......... 285	John 329
Ridgway.....................324, 325	Harvey............................ 285	John "Leather"................... 15
Ruth 324	Ichabod 210	John S................................330
Samuel J. 75	James.....................328, 329	John T.................................330
Sarah (Ridgway)..................325	Jennie 329	Jonathan B........................... 6
Sarah J. (Ridgway)...............324	John 328	Joseph 330
Sophronia (Crawford)...........324	John Vergel......................50	Joseph H............................331
Sophronia (Kanada)..............325	John W. 17, 127, 128, 129	Louise (Gordon) 267
Sophronia A. (Crawford).........240	Lucinda 285	Ludwell G. 330
Walter 325	Mary Ann 329	M. J. 70
William 39	Minnie 329	M. R. 267
Z. (Hunter) 324	Minnie Heitzelman 329	Marshall R. 330
Zue E. (Hunter) 325	Mr. 283	Martha (Riley) 330
Mills Hotel...........................324	Rena 329	Mary 383
Mills, Waggener &................ 64	Robert 329	Mary Ann (Cross) 330
Millspaugh	Stephen F. 170	Michael 330
A. C. 63	Susan M. 210	Minnie 330
Albert C. 326, 328	William 329	Mrs. 153
Charles 327	Mitchell & Hick 283	Otis C. 204, 336, 337
Cynthia A. 328	Mitchell & Towle 376	Pet 330, 382
Daniel 326, 328	Mize, Benjamin T. 79	Ransom..............................172
Daniel G. 326	Mobley	Sarah 383
Daniel S. 328	Alex................................. 148	Sarah Agnes (Phillips)...336, 337
Emily 328	Alexander 69, 329	Sarah E. 330
Emma 326	Cynthia (Hughes) 329	Susan (Bourland) 219
Giles W. 327	Eliza (Moye) 329	Thomas H. 330
J. M. 326	Essie 329	William 330
J. W. 63, 326	Francis 329	Moore family........................ 83
James H. 327	Horace 329	Moore's Prairie 153
James W.22, 65, 276, 277, 327, 328	James E. 329	More, Adeline 237
Jennie 328	John G. 329	Moreland
John 326, 327, 328	Lemuel 329	Elizabeth 319
John M. 328	Martha 329	Gardner........................... 38
John W. 327	Mattie 329	Hazel 1, 68
Juda (Sanders) 358	Raymond 329	Hazle 9, 10, 30, 40, 68
Julia (Scanland) 327	Rebecca 329	James 10
Margaret A. 326	Sarah J. 329	Mahala 319, 320
Margaret E. 328	William 329	Vincent 319
Peter..................................326	Willie 329	Moreland Hill 1
R. L. 327	Mock, Charles.....................42	Morgan, Stephen 49
Robert L. 22, 326	Monroe Township.................33	Morris
Sallie 228	Moody	____ 26
Sarah (Bogan) 326, 327	John 172	A. W. 81
Sina (Hall) 327	Mr. 142	B. S. 58
William L 326, 328	Moore................................. 15	C. W. 81, 137
Milne, John 39, 53	Addie (Duvall)................. 255	Elijah 45
Miner	Alice (Combs) 238	James 10
Frank 263	America J. (Bradford).............331	Julia A. (Crenshaw) 241
Ida J. (Foster) 263	Andrew...................153, 330	Margaret 331
Mineral Springs Church..............134	Charles........................... 138	Michael 331
Mines	Charley........................... 330	Mr. 139
Coal 2, 223, 333, 340, 360, 402	E. 255	Richmond 170
Curlew 177	Edwin W. 330	Stephen 68
Gold 308	Elizabeth (Smith) 330	Thomas 55
Lead 402	Elizabeth (Turner) 330	Morrison
Rees, T., & Co.'s.................. 2	George W. 73, 329, 330, 382	____ 96
Salt 223	Harry 330	James 112
Mitchel, Robert 170	Henry W.......................... 35	Melissa Ellen (Phillips)............336
Mitchell	J. H. 72, 138	Robert M. 336
	Jackson 383	William J. C. 135
	James 330	William R. 284

439

Morrow
  Forquer 169
  Robert H. 35
  Thomas 169
Morton, Oliver P. 267
Mosley
  Ada (Sipes) 332
  Nathaniel 331
Mossman
  _____ 250
  Anthony 331
  August V. 331
  Emma 331
  Frank X. 331
  Fredrick 331
  Jacob F. 331
  John N. 331
  Kate (Devous) 250
  Margaret (Morris) 331
  Mary (Stoker) 331
  Minnie 331
Mound City, Ill. 46, 162, 342, 344
Mount
  Grace G. 347
  Grace J. 347
  Laura 347
Mount Etna 105
Mount Vernon News 380
Moxley
  Ada M. 332
  Amanda (Burges) 331
  Bessie E. 332
  Charles W. 332
  Thomas 332
  William T. 331
Moye
  Eliza 329
  Julia A. 262
  Louisa 260
  Nancy 260
Moyers, W. N. 156
Mt. Carmel, Ill., schools 354
Mt. Pleasant No. 2 Church 136
Muckelwagner family 270
Muddy River Association 132
Muddy River Baptist Assoc. 132
Muir
  Jane 306
  Joseph L. 306
  Mary 306, 309
  Prudence 306
  Prudence Elizabeth 307
Mulligan, James 175
Munch
  Elizabeth 305
  J. 365
  Mary 305
  Mary (Speer) 365
Mundine, Thomas J. 170
Munn, David W. 25
Munsell, Charles W. 81
Murphy
  Bennett 287

John, Sr. 80
Lewis 287
R. C. 48
Sidora J. (Holland) 287
Murphy family 82
Murrap, Ed. C. 204
Murray, Samuel 130
Murry, Nancy 322
Musceoga Indians 152
Muscoga Indians 152
Musgrave, Jon vi
Mustering Oak 163, 164
Naas
  Barbara 332
  Barbara (Wormit) 332
  Christ 332
  Edward 332
  Emil 332
  Fred 332
  Frederick 332
  Fritz 332
  George 332
  Jacob 332
  John 332
  Joseph 332
  Katie 332
  Maggie 332
  Malinda (Weiss) 332
  Mary 332
  Peter 332
  Sally 332
  William 332
Napier, Lt. Col. 177
Napoleon, Ind. 306
Nash, Susan 393
Nation, Thomas C. 204
Neal
  Aaron 132
  Nancy 132
Neel, Samuel H. 94
Neele, David M. 94
Negro Salt Well 4, 5
Nelson
  _____ 68
  Elijah 216
  J. L. 68
  Margaret (Farley) 259
  Nazarene (Bean) 216
  Ron .... v, vi, 36
  Stephen 169
Nelson & Melville 68
Nettle Bottom 224, 402
New Haven 66, 115
  C.P. Church 79, 139
  Civil War 174
  M.E. Church 81
  Methodist Church 139
  Mill 261
  Mills 95
  Physicians 139
  Post office 140, 209
  Saloons 68
  Schools 130

Stage route 140
New Hotel 73
New Madrid Earthquakes .. 113, 241
New Madrid, Mo. 241
New Market Precinct 253
New Market, Ill. 74, 79, 115, 237,
  238, 253, 363
New Orleans, Battle of 295, 296
New Pleasant C.P. Church 80
Newcomb, Prof. 260
Newell, Nathan L. 45
Newman
  Elizabeth 265
  John 169
Newspapers
  Cairo Sun 311
  Central Star 70
  Daily Gleaner 366
  Gallatin Co. Democrat 178
  Gallatin Democrat 366
  Home News 66, 257
  Illinois Advertiser 108
  Illinois Emigrant 65, 256
  Illinois Gazette 65, 273
  Illinois Intelligencer 274
  Illinois Republican 66
  Local Record 66, 256, 257
  Mount Vernon News 380
  News-Gleaner 365
  Record (Norris City) 367
  Shawnee Herald 66
  Shawnee News 66, 257, 368,
    380
  Shawneetown Gleaner 366, 368
  Shawneetown Intelligencer 66
  Shawneetown Mercury 66
  Shawneetown News 366
  Shawneetown News-Gleaner
    366, 368
  Southern Illinois Advocate 66,
    256
  Southern Illinoisan 66, 256
  Western Expositor 222
  Western Voice 66
  Western World 371
Nichols
  Etta C. (Gordon) 266
  Walter 266
Nicholson, E. J. 77
Nickerson, J. E. 81
Nigger Spring v
Nigger Works 2
Nighswonger, Clarissa 352
Niglas, Maj. 176
Niswonger, Jefferson 170
Noel, Joseph F. 64
Nolen
  _____ 26
  Artimissa (Beeves) 333
  Capt. 232
  Daniel 333
  Edward 333
  Elizabeth (Holley) 333

Ellen 333	Olney, John 63	William K. 22, 25
Harry 333	Omaha 8, 71, 137	Parrish Bros. 44
J. F. 22, 69, 333	Businesses 138	Parter
Joseph F. 22, 213	C.P. Church 295	Braxton Carter 336
Lucinda (Joplin) 333	Flour mills 216	Luella 336
Millard 333	Flouring Mills 71, 281, 302	Pate
Norcross, Rose 233	M.E. Church 81	Amster B. 50, 174
Normal School at Carmi 269	Post office 217	Andrew 47
Norman, John 40	Schools 137	Philip A. 50, 174
Norris City State Bank 337	Omaha House 138, 227	Patilloe, Alexander 169
North, Richard J. 46	Omaha, Ill. 115	Patterson
Northern Precinct 153	O'Niel, J. 171	C. L. 289
Norton	Orr	George 10
___ 60	James 45	James 353
Alexander 47	Mr. 8, 136	Lucy (Loomis) 310
J. W. 293	Oskins, Robert 47	Mr. 52
Notre Dame 235, 252, 255, 309, 348	Ottumwa, Iowa 374	Ray L. (Howell) 289
Notsom, John N. 65	Overton, George W. 131	Rebecca 353
Noye, Hiram 45	Overton, Ill. 74	Thomas 310
Nye, Bill 144	Owen	Patton
O'Brien, William 45	Carr 50	James H. 45
O'Melvaney, Samuel 28	George W. 50	Lutitia 214
O'Neal	Joseph 113	Mary (Foster) 262
Joe 16	Owens	Sidney A. 214
John William 368	Alabama 286	Thomas 214
Mary 368	Anna 160	Pavey, C. W. 25
O'Neill	James 286	Peankeshaw Indians 152, 167
James 69	Joseph 113	Pearce
Joseph E. 69	Oxberry, James 172	A. J. 334
O'Rourke	Oxford	A. R. 280
Belle (Pettery) 333	James A. 318	Brunett J. 263
Charles 333	Sarah (McCue) 318	Dr. 247
George 333	Packard, Augusta V. 237	Edward V. 22
Henry 333	Page, William. 172	Elisha 334
James 333	Paine, Gen. 178	Eliza 376
Kate 333	Paisley, Joseph P. 172	G. R. 71, 334
Mayme 333	Palestine C.P. Church ... 79, 136, 248	G.R., & Co. 71, 334
William 333	Palestine Cemetery 227	Granville R. 334
Willie 333	Pankey	Hosea 159, 167, 168
O'Toole family 376	Betty 32	Margaret J. (Winfrey) 334
Oak Grove C.P. Church 80	Hampton 160	Sarah (Davis) 247
Oakley, Col. 343	John 160	W. D. 71, 138
Odum Ford 154	William 170	Pearce, G. R., & Co. 137
Ogden, William B. 74	Panthers 18	Pearson
Oglesby, R. J. 46, 48	Paper making 360, 361	Harry 211
Ohio & Mississippi R.R. 26, 27, 60, 70, 71, 72, 146, 279, 282	Paradise Prairie 403	Mary (Baker) 211
Ohio County 116, 261	Parish	Peck, John Mason 133
Ohio River	Eleazer 360	Peebels Family 79
Low water mark 60	Rachel B. 360	Peeples
Ohio Saline 95	Robert A. 360	Elizabeth (Maxwell) 334
Okaw Bottom 168	Parker	Ellen (Pool) 338
Okaw River 157, 168	John 172	H. M. 147
Old School Presbyterians 76	Nathaniel 172	Harriet (Docker) 334
Old Station 153	Parks	Henry 334
Olden, Rebecca B. 351	Adeline (Goodwin) 213	I. McKee 334
Oldenburg, Mary 76	Elizabeth 353	J. J. M. 338
Oldham	James Ella 213	J. M. 77
Henry 30	James S. 213	James C. 171
Thomas 170	Mr. 153	John McKee 52, 58, 77, 177, 334, 351
Oldham faction 93	Nancy 401, 402	John McKee, Jr. 334
Olive Branch, Battle of 49	William 67	John McRoy 52
	Parrish	Mr. 324
	Braxton 64	

441

R. 11
Robert 11, 33, 52, 334
W. A. 70, 335, 347
William 334
Peeples & Karcher 64
Peeples & Kirkpatrick 38, 52
Peeples & Ridgway 334, 351
Peeples, Docker & 64
Pellam, Jannie 320
Pellin
   Jennie 320
   John 320
   Sarah 320
Pellum, Jennie 320
Pemberton, Gen. 46
Pemberton, Hall & 137
Penberton, James A. 204
Perkins
   James S. 131
   Polly Ann 353
Perry
   Commodore 266
   J. B. 63
   Mr. 8
   Zilpha 270
Perryman, Nancy A. 208, 340
Peter (Indian) 152
Peter, James A. 50
Petigrew, Isaiah W. 170
Pettery
   Belle 333
   James 333
   Rachel (White) 333
Pettigrew
   Isaiah W. 80
   James M. 8, 10
Pfarr, Barbara 382
Phalen
   Minnie 142
   Mrs. Paul 142
Phar, George H. 131
Phelps Prairie 154
Phelps, John 154
Philadelphia Bible Society 75
Phile
   Grace 323
   Mira 65
   W. D. 65
   William 323
Philippines 226, 318
Phillips
   ____ 16
   Agnes C. (Wise) 335
   Agnes Caroline (Wise) 336
   Alice 336, 337
   Anna 337
   Anna Alice 338
   Campbell 336
   Clay 336
   Clyde W. 338
   Clyde Winfield 337
   David L. 25
   Eliza Word 335

   Epimonondas 336
   Ethel 336
   Eugene B. 336
   Horace Poole 336
   Ida 336
   Irenæus 336
   Iva E. 380
   James B. 335
   John Milton 335
   Judge ____ 405
   Leuella (Porter) 337
   Luella (Parter) 336
   Luella (Porter) 335
   Margaret (Poole) 335
   Margaret Zerinda (Crawford) 336
   Melissa Ellen 336
   Radford Reedy 336
   Richard Newton 335
   Samuel P. 336
   Samuel Poole 335
   Sarah 335
   Sarah A. 335
   Sarah Agnes 336, 337
   Tennessee Belle 336
   Virginia 336
   W. B. 405
   W. Braxton 337
   W. S. 70, 88, 335
   William 335
   William B. 335
   William Monroe 336
   Williams Braxton 337
   Winfield S. 337
   Winfield Scott 335, 336, 337
Physicians, female 225
Pickering
   Martha A. 321
   Mr. 284
   Thomas 40, 170, 321
Pickett, Francis M. 66
Pierce
   Gertrude (Bourland) 220
   Julia 301
   Polly (McGehee) 216
   Polly A. (McGehee) 216
Pierson, Henry 170
Pike, Zebulon M. 275
Pike's Peak 301
Pilkington, Rebecca 385
Pillow
   Eleanor 241
   George W. 63
   Gideon 12
   Parker B. 49, 395
   Parker E. 22
Pillow, Bowman & 44
Pinnell
   Ambrose 225
   Carlin 225
   Carroll 226
   Elizabeth (Easley) 225
   Gilbert 225
   Green 225

   Harmon 225
   Juda 225
   Lucretia 224, 225
   Nancy 225
   Wesley 225
   Wiley 225
   William A. 225
   Willis 225
Pinney
   Sidney 140
   Sidney A. 50
Pinson
   Nancy J. (Colbert) 236
   Robert 236
Pioneer Store 348
Pisal, Rachel 362
Pittsburg Landing 46, 230, 231
Pleasant Grove School 294
Pleasant Grove Social Brethren
   Church 136
Pogue, James 170
Polk, James K. 44, 212, 213, 224
Pomeroy, Ohio 6
Pond Creek 153
Pond Settlement 167, 230, 243,
   280, 302
Pond Township 29
Pond, John 167, 168
Pool
   Alexander W. 172
   Amanda C. (Grant) 339
   Carolina (Grant) 339
   Cecilia (Wilson) 339
   Ellen 338
   Gertrude 339
   Grant 339
   Hester M. 338
   John 338, 339
   M. M. 27, 58
   Madeline (Snider) 338, 339
   Marshall 339
   Marshall Mason 338, 339
   Mary A. 338
   Orval 51, 52, 58, 144, 338,
      339, 351, 380
   Orvel 171
   Thomas 69
   Wilson 338
Pool, M. M., & Co. 59, 338, 339
Pool, O., & Co. 334, 351
Poole
   ____ 243
   Margaret 335
   Orvil 230
   Sarah 287
Pope, Nathaniel 19, 20
Port Folio 274
Port Hudson, Battle of 49
Porter
   B. C. 335, 337
   B. F. 70
   D. M. 69, 264, 347
   David 50

Edna 342	Prather, Martha 16	Clarissa 340
Gen. 272	Presbyterian churches	Emma R. (Butts) 340
J. A. 260	"Old Village Church" 247	J. L. 139, 208
J. H. 138	Cabin Creek 224	James G. 340
James 72, 138, 342	Church of Sharon 75	John M. 340
Janet 266	Eagle Creek 78	Joseph L. 79, 174, 340
L. J. 260	Eagle Creek 246	Manna A. 340
Laura (Mount) 347	Equality 78, 246, 362	Maria (Abshier) 208
Leuella 337	Galatia 246	Mary E. 340
Luella 335	Golconda 76	Matilda 340
Mr. 239	Harrisburg 376	Nancy Maria (Abshier) 340
Robert 130	Hazel Ridge 247	William 340
Robert W. 172	McLeansboro 246	William L. 340
Thomas I. 42	New Haven 246	Questel
Porter & Rice 137, 334, 347	Norris City 246, 247	Jeanne Claude LeMont 341
Posey	Oak Grove 246	John Baptiste 341
___ 41	Palestine 246	Nicholas 341
Alexander 52, 374	Saline Mines 77	Questell
Col. 372	Shawneetown .. 76, 77, 129, 130	Alexander 341
Dr. 374	Union Ridge 246	Lewis 340, 341
Eliza Maria 372	Presbytery of Cairo 77	Nick .... vi, 341
Fayette 12	Presbytery of Kaskaskia 78	Simon Baptiste 340
Thomas 12, 339, 372	Presbytery of Saline 77	Theresa Isabelle (Bonner) 340
Thomas L. 52	Price	Quick
W. A. G. 52, 55, 57	B. R. 81	Charles 341
Washington A. G. 77	Berry 172	Edwin 341
Poston, Joseph 83	Eli 79, 137	Eliza 341
Potter	Lewis M. 71	Elizabeth 341
Annie R. (Campbell) 340	Stirling 244, 364	Emma (Summers) 341
George H. 65, 77, 78, 340	William F. 138	J. A. 64
Sam 166	Prichard, Sarah (Buchanan) 353	James 341
Sarah (Cheney) 340	Prier, Anderson 170	James A. 64, 341
Thomas 340	Prince, Edward 369	Margaret (Welsh) 341
Potter, John S. 92	Prison bounds 32	Simeon 341
Potters' clay 3	Pritchett, William T. 50	Stephen 341
Potts	Probasco, Johanna A. 361	Quick-lime 3
Alfred D. 147	Proctor	Quigley
Billy 217	___ 26	Aaron 342
Cynthia A. (Robinett) 352	Emma (Bourland) 220	Edna (Porter) 342
Hannah 267	Ephraim 78	L. E. 51, 71, 72, 137, 138
Irene (Robinett) 352	Giles 172	Leonard E. 342
Isaiah L. 217	J. M. 77	Nancy J. (Eubanks) 342
Jeremiah 352	Littlepage 10	Philip C. 342
John 352	Mr. 321	Quigley & Crabtree 138
Joseph 352	Samuel L. M. 172	Quigley House 72, 138
Phoebe (Robinett) 352	Samuel. S. M. 172	Quigly, Aaron 169
Potts Inn 217, 274	Thomas J. 87	Quincy Business College 338
Powell	Prohibition 320	Raber
H. P. 68	Prohibitionists 217	L 401
Henderson B. 58, 77	Prophet, the Shawnee 154, 155	Rebecca (Wiseheart) 401
J. A. 243	Pruit, James 170	Radaner
John 172	Pruitt, Sarah A. 287	James D. 329
Lucy (Wiseheart) 400	Pruney, Sidney 69	Rebecca (Mobley) 329
Major 68	Puckett, E. B. 169	Raguet, Condy 272
Mr. 327	Purcell	Railroads 223
Thomas 169	Anna (Wiseheart) 400	Baltimore & Ohio 330
William 400	James 400	Baltimore & Ohio S.W. 222, 233, 234
Powell, Chester & 327	Nancy 323	Cairo & Vincennes 396
Powell's cabins 33	Nellie (Campbell) 233	Chicago, Peoria & St. Louis 396
Poweshiek, Chief 373	Nicholas 323	Cleveland, Cincinnati, Chicago
Prairie du Chien, Wis. 372	Purvis	& St. Louis 396
Prairie Township 29, 30	Andrew 340	Evansville & So. Ill. 27
Prather Negroes 16	Clarinda 340	

443

Evansville, Carmi & Paducah .. 27
Illinois 396
Illinois & S.E. 234
Illinois Central 309
Louisville & Nashville 26, 27,
  72, 222, 327, 396
Louisville, Evansville & St. Louis
  396
Marietta & Cincinnati 279
Ohio & Mississippi 26, 27,
  71, 72, 146, 279
Shawneetown & Alton 218,
  348, 349, 350
Shawneetown & Eldorado 27
Springfield & Ill. S.E. 352
Springfield & Illinois S.E. 146,
  233, 280
St. Louis & S.E. 27, 62,
  71, 137, 396
Raitt, Nathan E. 277
Raleigh Social Brethren Church ..136
Rallings, Moses M. 95
Rambler
  Fannie (Dillard) 252
  Mr. 252
Ramsey
  James T. 282
  John J. 43
  Mary E. 282
  Thomas 113
Randolph County 19
Randolph, J. H. 71
Ransbottom, Mary 221
Rathbone
  Dr. Lorenzo 376, 377
  John 376
  Minerva J. 376
  Pamelia (Anderson) 377
  Valentine 376
  W. R. 70
Rau, V. A. 71
Raum
  Green Berry 23, 25, 284
  John 284
Rawlings
  Ann H. (Simms) 344
  Carroll H. 343
  Florida 343
  Francis M. 342, 344
  Henrietta B. (Calmes) 343
  Moses M. 11, 33, 37, 38,
    52, 54, 57, 95, 342, 344
  Sarah J. 342
  Sarah J. (Seaton) 342
Rawlings Hotel 55, 66
Rawlings House 52, 54, 97
Rawlings' Brick 60
Rawls, Nathaniel 169
Reaf, J. J. R. 81, 137
Rearden
  Edith 306
  James S. 47, 63, 172
  John E. 306

Lucy 306
Record (Norris City) 367
Rector
  John 151, 164
  Nelson 164, 165
Rector Creek 151
Rector Township. 151
Rector's Fork 107, 165
Red Banks, Ky. 7
Red Bird, Chief 372
Redden
  J. W. 63, 64
  Joseph W. 77
Reddick, A. D. 64
Redman
  Allen 73, 77
  Mary (Siddall) 361
  P. 57
  Parmenas 361
Reed
  Blanche E. 272
  Eliza J. (Caldwell) 229
  Elizabeth (Marshall) 230
  Green 170
  James 229
  Lewis 169
  Lizzie (McIntire) 322
  Ludica 294
  R. E. 322
Reeder
  Sarah 271
  Simon 37
Reef, Mr. 139
Rees, T., & Co.'s mines 2
Reeves
  John C. 52
  William D. 204
Regulators 13
Reid
  Agnes H. 346
  Alexander 9
  Bessie 346
  Clara 346
  David 340
  Dent 345, 346
  Elizabeth (Campbell) 345
  George 346
  Ila D. 345
  John 8, 9, 11, 39, 52, 294
  Johnson 172
  Joseph 52
  Laura (Dossett) 345
  Mary P. 294
  May 346
  Millie 346
  Mrs. 9
  Robert 77, 78, 340, 345, 346
  Thomas 346
  Walter 346
  Wiley 345, 346
  William 346
Reiling, Anastasia 295
Rensmann

J. 82, 83
  James August 346
Reubenacher, Mrs. 65
Reynolds
  J. M. 261
  John 26, 36, 150, 343, 408
  Joseph 39
  Joseph L. 73, 169
  Kate 261
  Thomas 172
Rheburne, John 32
Rheburne's ferry 32
Rheinhold
  Annie 142
  Charles 142
  Ella 142
Rhoades, ____ 26
Rhoads
  F. L. 64, 69
  Silas 64
Rhyon
  John 170
  William 170
Rice
  ____ 26
  Archibald B. 346
  Benjamin 22, 204
  Chief Engineer 27
  Clarence M. 347
  D. R. 347
  Ebenezer 346
  Edward 71, 138, 346, 347
  Edward H. 347
  Estella F. 347
  Estella Florence 347
  Grace F. 347
  Grace G. (Mount) 347
  Grace J. (Mount) 347
  Jacob 50
  James 223, 403
  Joel 346
  Laura (Mount) 347
  Laura E. 347
  Laura Edith 347
  Mabel C. 347
  Mabel Claire 347
  Mary (Wiseheart) 400
  Nancy C. 311
  Nancy M. 346
  R. G. 71
  Rebecca (Boyd) 223, 403
  Robert 204
  Rollo 347
  Sarah 264
  T. W. 69
Rice, Devous & 250
Rice, Martin & 311, 347
Rice, Martin, & Co. 138
Rice, Porter & 137, 347
Rich
  Daisy 348
  Ellen (Andrews) 348
  George 348

George W. 347	Rebecca B. (Olden) 351	Blueford 352, 353
Isabelle 348	Robert 81	Bluford 356
Lewis 348	Sarah 325, 351	Charlotte 353
Mary (Simms) 347	Sarah (Castle) 230	Clarissa (Nighswonger) 352
May 348	Sarah J. 324	Cynthia A. 352
Minnie 348	Thomas 70, 351	Eliza J. (Rose) 353
William 347	Thomas J. 355	Irene 352
Richardson, ___ 68	Thomas S. ... 25, 27, 58, 77, 234,	James 352
Richeson	324, 334, 351	John 352, 353
___ 26	William 235	Joseph 352, 353
A. G. 65, 84	Ridgway and Carroll 60	Louisiana 352
Albert G. 234, 348, 349	Ridgway Dry Goods Co. 382	Lucy 353, 356
Eleanora 348, 381	Ridgway flour mills 250	Matilda 352
Elenora 234	Ridgway, Peeples & 334, 351	Minerva 353
Henry 348	Ridlete, J. R. 257	Miss (Hughes) 352
John 348, 349	Rieling, Thomas 47	Phoebe 352
John D. 27, 58, 64, 234, 251,	Right, Linzey 169	Rachel 352
310, 312, 313, 348, 349,	Riles	Robinnet, John 170
381	Mr. 247	Robinson
Johnnie 349	Polly (Davis) 247	___ 41
Judith 349	Riley	Christopher 33
Judith M. (Williamson) .. 234, 348	___ 303	Delila Elvira (Vaughn) 259
Mary 234, 312, 313, 348	Charles 311	Delilah A. 353
Mary A. 127	Charles E. 50	Elizabeth Haines 353
Mary E. (Kopp) 349	Flora (Bowling) 221	Enos 353
Mattie L. (McCallen) 349	J. L. 128	Etta 353
May 349	Jane 286	Felix 68
Nancy A. (Dickenson) 349	Joseph 33	Franklin 141
Nancy N. (Dickinson) 349	Lucinda (Smith) 363	George 22, 69
Richard 22	Martha 330	George W. 69, 353
Richeson & Carroll 234	Mary 323	Hugh 33
Richeson & Cromwell 88	Mary (Sanks) 359	J. A. 81
Richeson & Winner 64	Nancy 267, 268	J. P. 138
Richeson, J. D., & Co. 348	Owen 323, 330	J. S. 78
Richeson's Place, John 251	Sarah 267	James 22
Richey, John P. 170	Sarah V. 311	John D. 27
Ricker, ___ 26	Thomas 363	John L. 27
Rider	Rineholdt, George 204	John McCurdy 77
Bertha 350	Ringold, Ill. 79	John, Sr. 30
Edgar 350	Riordan, Edith 309	Laban 38
Edith 350	Ripley, Gen. 272	Lucian M. 353
Emma 350	Rippetoe, Olin B. 81	M. M. 89, 137
Isabelle O. (Seeley) 350	Rise, Margaret 214	Margaret 353
Jessie 350	Rister, Lura (Grumley) 271	Mark 170
John 350	Ritchy, Joseph 30	Martha Haney 353
June 350	Riverside Hotel 64, 76, 142, 223,	Martha J. 353
Med 350	355	Mary A. 78
Oliver 350	Roark	Michael 7, 11, 33, 52
Ridgway 70	Jane 257	Paddy 67
Businesses 405	William 257	Polly Ann (Perkins) 353
Eliza 351	Robb, Lida 268	Prof. 84
George 230	Roberts	Rebecca (Patterson) 353
George A. ... 58, 64, 77, 325, 351	Hanson Q. 172	Sarah (Buchanan) 353
Harriet 351	Harriet L. 370	William 38
Jane (Docker) 352	Roberts, Archibald 9	Robinson Bros. 64
John 325, 351	Robertson	Robinson House 68
John G. 351	Rachel (Youngblood) 403	Rochell, James 47
John, Jr. 351	W. W. 403	Rock and Cave 28, 29, 31, 33
John, Sr. 351	William 170	Rock and Cave Twp. 29, 33
Judith Mimms (Carroll) 234	Robinet, Ill. 74	Rock Creek 261, 262
Mary (Grant) 325	Robinett	Rock Creek Church 134
Mary Frazier (Grant) 351	Allen 41, 352	Rock Island, Ill. 373
Post office 324	Amanda J. (Rose) 356	Rocky Branch Church 83

Rodgers
    ____ 26
    A. C. 89
    B. L. 298
    H. L. 71, 72
    Jennie (Kinsall) 298
    Rev. 243
Roe, Richard 39
Roedel
    Barbara 354
    C. K. 113
    Carl . 22, 63, 64, 65, 77, 88, 354
    Charles K. 355
    Charles, Jr. 354
    Emma 354
    Fannie (Koser) 354
    Ida M. 354
    Jacob 354
    Lillie 354
    Rose 354
    Sarah 354
    Sarah Frances (Koser) 355
    William K. 354
Roedel & Sission 354
Roedel & Sisson 44
Rogers
    Benjamin 132
    Bluford 356
    Cordelia 282
    D. B. 137
    Daisy 356
    David 358
    Eliza (Logsdon) 308
    Eliza A. (Logsdon) 355
    Elizabeth (Booten) 355
    J. W. 353
    James 356
    John 356
    John W. 355, 356
    Joseph 356
    Lucy (Robinett) 353, 356
    Marinda 356
    Mary A. 308
    Mary Ann (Sanders) 358
    Matilda 356
    Romelia (Harrington) 282
    Tessie 356
    Virgil 356
    William 282
    William T. 356
Rohrer
    John 52
    William R. 37
Roleman, William 49
Rollman
    Sallie (Bruce) 228
    William T. 204
Roman, Elizabeth 220
Rood, Harvey 170
Roper, David 128
Rose
    Amanda J. 356
    Eliza J. 353

Henry 158, 353
James A. 336
Rachel (Robinett) 352
Sarah (Baker) 211
Wiley 211
Rose Hill 342
Rosolott
    Emma (Rider) 350
    William 350
Ross
    ____ 26
    George C. 25
    Lewis W. 125
Ross' Mill 2
Rouche, Julius de 149
Round Pond 1, 307
Routh, William V. 204
Rowan
    Mrs. S. C. 9, 52
    Stephen R. 17, 64
Rowan, L., & Son 64
Rowe
    Curtis 258
    Harriet (Edwards) 258
    Lucy 130
Rubennaker, Josephine 162
Ruddick
    Sarah 311
    Thomas 311
Ruddick, Mrs. 76
Rude, Hankerson 33, 160
Rudolph
    Amy 357
    Andrew 356
    Anna (Dickens) 357
    Benjamin 357
    Charles Dickens 357
    Daniel 357
    David 356
    Elizabeth 356
    Elizabeth (Graham) 357
    Ella 357
    Frederick L. 357
    Frederick Lowe 356
    George 357
    Harlan 357
    Harold L. 357
    Hubert 357
    Jacob 357
    Jane 356
    Jessie 357
    John 356
    Joseph 356
    Laura 357
    Margaret 356
    Mark 357
    Nellie 357
    Peter 356
    Phoebe 356
    Rachel (Lowe) 356
    Robert 356
    Robert M., Jr. 357
    Robert Monroe 356, 357

Sarah 356
Sarepta 357
Thompson 357
Running Slough 34
Rupert, ____ 405
Rush Medical College 293
Rush, Capt. 46
Rusher
    Jerry 209
    Mary A. 209
Russell
    David B. 170
    J. W. 128
    James W. 128
    John 170
    William 46
Ryan, Ebenezer Z. 61
Sac Indians 373
Sacramento, Ill. 347
Safford
    A. B. 58, 87
    A. D. 87
    Mary E. 87
Salina Creek 96
Saline Association 133
Saline Bar 177
Saline Coal & Mfg. Co. 74, 360
Saline Coal Co. 345, 361
Saline County 21, 36
Saline County Register 66
Saline Landing 177
Saline Mines
    Presbyterian Church 77
Saline Mines Road 43
Saline Mines, Ill.147, 255, 345, 361,
    402
Saline Reservation 115
Saline River 1, 2, 4, 5, 20, 34, 51,
    62, 74, 107
    Mouth 177
    North Fork 229
Saline Salt Works 153, 156
Saline Tavern 33
Saline Township 29, 33
Saline Well ....v, vi
Salt mines 223
Salt War 149, 150
Salt War, 2nd 150
Salt works... 2, 4, 6, 30, 51, 72, 125,
    156, 236, 238, 241, 389
    Boone's Lick 105
    Castle & Temple 7
    Crenshaw's, John 211
    Hargrave's, Willis. 32
    Kanawha 6, 105, 390
    Ste. Genevieve 105
    Weed's 296
    Werd's 297
Salt, prices 6
Sampson, William 169
Samson, William 169
Sanders
    Ann (Harrington) 282, 358

446

Annie 358
Carolina 12, 127
Caroline 126, 127
Carrie Bell 357, 358
Claudie 358
Cyrus 358
Eli 358
Evolia J. 357
Frank N. 357, 358
Hezekiah 357
James 358
Jemima (McGhee) 357
Juda 358
Lillie R. 357
Lowry A. 357
Lulu 358
Luther 358
Margaret J. 358
Mary Ann 358
Nancy J. (McGill) 358
Ratie May 357
Roscoe 358
Stella 358
Tempy 287
Vernon 358
W. J. 282
William J. 358
William S. 357
Sanderson, Thomas 50
Sands
  James 133
  Sister 133
Sands, John 170
Sandy Ridge 53, 306
Sanks
  David R. 359
  George D. 204, 359
  Henry G. 359
  Joshua 359
  Margaret E. 359
  Martha E. 359
  Mary 359
  Mary E. 359
  Mary E. (Lawler) 359
  Nancy J. (Leighliter) 359
  Sarah E. 359
  Susanna V. 359
  Tamson V. 359
Sargent
  A. M. 64
  Winthrop 19
Sarver, John 71, 138
Satterley
  Charles A. 360
  Elma (James) 360
  Roy F. 360
  William M. 360
Scanland
  Julia 327
  William 45, 327
Scanland, Karcher & 64, 295
Scarborough, John 172
Scates

Henry 64
Walter B. 40, 41
Schermerhorn, John F. 75
Schneider
  Augustus 394
  Catherine 394
Schoolcraft, Henry 275
Schools 83
  African-American 129
  Early descriptions 243
Scott
  ____ 16
  Joseph 10
  Samuel T. 75
  Winfield 171, 229, 272, 373
Scroggins
  John 8
  William A. 375
Scrogins, Bartin 171
Scudmore
  Caroline (Baker) 211
  Thomas 211
Scully, Patrick 172
Seabolt, Mr. 166
Seabolt's Row 76
Seat, Alexander 47
Seaton
  Elizabeth 211, 212, 213, 294
  Peter C. 52
  Samuel 52, 294
  Sarah J. 342
  Sophia 294
Seaville, Ill. 74
Sebastian
  ____ 371
  Polly 246
Sebastin, Polly 247
Secord, Dr. 238
Seebold, John 39
Seebolt, John 38
Seeley
  Isabelle O. 350
  Sarah A. 322
Seelinger & McDonald 64
Seets, Mary J. 236
Selam, the horse 51
Self, Jacob 132
Sellers
  A. L. (Smith) 360
  Charles H. 360
  Eleanor P. 360
  F. H. 74, 360
  Frederick H. 360
  George E. 4, 74
  George Escol 360
  Lucy 360
  Rachel B. (Parish) 360
Sellers' Landing 361
Sellers' paper-mill 2
Sergeant
  Amaziah Morgan 361
  Isavella 361
  Thomas 361

Sexton
  George 11
  Jacob 33
  Joshua 52
  Orval 34
  Orville 52
Seymour, ____ 223
Shackleford, Garland W. 46
Shadowen, John 133
Shadville, Ill. 328
Shaffer, Elizabeth 318
Shain
  L 79
  Orpha 364
  Orvilla 364
Shannon, Dr. 52
Sharp
  Lavina (Mason) 248
  Mary 246, 247, 248
  Polly 217
  William 248
Shaw
  ____ 26
  Elizabeth 296
  John 276
  Margaret J. (Bruce) 228
Shawannaetown 97
Shawanoe Township 29, 33
Shawnee Herald 66
Shawnee Indians 8, 51, 105, 150,
  152, 156, 163
Shawnee News 66, 257, 368, 380
Shawneetown 7, 11, 20, 29,
  51, 108
  1872 City Directory 63
  A.M.E. Church 129
  Artillery 177
  City Court 403
  City Mills 323
  Colored Emancipation Baptist
    Church 134
  Confederate raids 177
  County Seat 35
  Courthouse 35
  Descriptions of 53
  Early descriptions 54, 105
  Early settlement 95
  Ferries 394
  Floods .. 59, 143, 231, 233, 327,
    392
  Front Street 76
  Incorporation 24, 61
  Indians 95
  Jail 34
  Lafayette's visit 55, 113, 277
  Land office 9, 229
  Levees 59, 60, 143, 328, 348
  M.E. Church 81
  Market St. 76
  Newspapers 66
  Post office 213, 361, 368
  Post Office 64
  Presbyterian Church 76

447

Regulator raid 15
Schools 85, 87, 354
Seabolt's Row 76
Wharf boat 279
Shawneetown & Alton R.R. ...25, 218, 348, 349, 350
Shawneetown & Eldorado R.R. 27
Shawneetown Gleaner 366, 368
Shawneetown Intelligencer 66
Shawneetown Mercury 16, 66
Shawneetown News 366
Shawneetown News-Gleaner 365, 366, 368
Shawneetown-Kaskaskia Trail..... 161
Shearer, John 34, 52
Shearwood, Edward 38
Shelby
    Catharine 52
    Edmund.. 52
Shelton, Carl 349
Sheridan
    John, Mrs. 68, 69
    Johnny 68
    Mary 278
    Phil 370
Sherman
    Frank.. 122
    William Tecumseh 49, 143, 176, 209, 292, 315, 316, 370
Sherrod, Robert W. 47
Sherwood
    America (Turner) 402
    Edward 50
    Hugh B. 169
    John 50
    John V. 80
    Mary 294, 402
    Thomas 169
    Washington 35, 402
Shields, James 171
Shillington, Jo. 378
Shoat, Levi 170
Shockley
    Ellen 293
    Malinda 293
    Medford 293
Shockley-Raddick, Mary (Feehrer) 260
Shoemaker
    John B. 38
    William 169
Siddall
    Elizabeth A. 361
    Emma (Yost) 362
    Etta 361
    Florence 361
    Halton 362
    J. P. 361
    Johanna A. (Probasco) 361
    John 56, 58, 72, 73, 77, 129
    John M. 361
    Joseph 361

Kelly 362
Martha 78
Martha (Maltby) 361
Mary 361
P. 73
Parmenas 361
William 6, 22, 361
Sidle, Robert 171
Siebman
    Amos L. 362
    Emma 362
    Mary 362
    Philomine (Brazier) 362
    Rachel 362
    Rachel (Pisal) 362
    Sarah 362
    Theodore 362
    Walter 362
    William 362
Sils, T. H. 64
Sim, William 57
Simmons, Robert P. 49
Simms
    Ann H. 344
    Mary 347
Simons
    C. G. 313
    Cyrus G. 312
Simpkins, Samuel 42
Simpson settlement 95
Singleton, Myers 158
Sipes
    Ada 332
    Pleasant 332
Sisk
    Albert 172
    Benjamin 172
    George vi
Sission, Eugene R. 354
Sisson
    E. R. 234
    Ida 8
    Mary (Eddy) 234
Sitles, Henry 172
Skaggs Mills, Ky. 300
Skeef, Catherine 215
Skelton, William J. 172
Sketo, Albert N. 50
Sketoe, Isaac M. 172
Slack, Andrew 8, 11, 34
Slaten, John 6
Slaten, Rachel 219
Slater
    P. 116
    Peter 21, 68
Slaton
    Bertha (Rider) 350
    Edward 350
Slave trading 349
Slavens, A. Calvin 172
Slavery 6, 11, 17
Slayton, Samuel S. 204
Slinger

David 48
Mary J. 283
Thomas 283
Sloan, Wesley................................. 41
Slocumb
    Charles 80, 159, 277
    J. C. 28
    John C. 28, 30, 32, 159
    R. B. 26
    Samuel 159
    Sarah R. 244
    William 244
Sloo
    Albert Gallatin 385, 391
    Harriet Grandison (White) 391
    Harriet White 391
    James C. 57, 64
    James G. 278
    John 52
    Juliet White............................... 391
    Mary Frances 391
    Robert C. 41, 278
    Sarah E. 391
    Thomas 32, 52, 64, 391
    Thomas, Jr. 52
Smith
    _____... 26
    A. J. 216
    Adeline 218
    Andrew P. 69
    B. J. 319
    Benjamin 320
    Bryant 13
    C. C. 330
    C. W. 73
    Catherine 363, 369, 370
    Daniel 75
    David 88
    Dennis 363
    E. M. 37, 145
    Eliza 364
    Eliza Jane (Akins) 363
    Elizabeth 330
    Elizabeth (Kratz) 299
    Elizabeth A. (McGehee) 319
    Emma 251
    Frank 360
    G. E. 88
    George C. 49
    George W. .... iii, 204
    George Washington.................. 143
    Isaac 37
    James 280
    Jennie (Moore) 330
    Jobe... 230
    John 170, 172, 288
    John F. 363
    John H. 170
    Joseph 363, 364
    Lizzie (McGehee) 320
    Lucinda 363
    Lydia 360
    M. L. 270

Margaret 323, 363
Martha (Mobley) 329
Mary 13
Orpha (Shain) 364
Orvilla (Shain) 364
Peter 58, 169
S. M. 213
Samuel Marshall 367
Sarah 208
Sarah (McDermott) 364
Sarah Caswell 304
Susie 364
Theodore S. 69
Theophilus W. 40
Thomas 22, 132
Virginius W. 363, 364
Virginius, Jr. 364
William A. 329
William T. 172
Smithsonian Institute 304
Smothers
   John 39, 170
   Thomas 170
Smyth
   _____ 26
   Minnie (Spivey) 365
   S. M. 23
   Sallie 365
   Sallie Annie 367
Smyth & Wiseheart 64
Snake bite remedies 19
Snakes
   Copperheads 18
   Rattlesnakes 18
   Water moccasins 18
Sneed, Eldridge 172
Snider, Madeline 338, 339
Social Brethren churches
   Equality 83
   Green Valley 83
   Mt. Pleasant No. 2 136
   Pleasant Grove 136
   Raleigh 136
   Rocky Branch 83
Social Brethren, history 83, 135
Soils 3
Solomon, Josiah 34
Somerset 134
Sons of Liberty 8, 74, 136
Southern Illinois Advocate 66, 256
Southern Illinois Editorial Association
.... 368
Southern Illinois Normal 226, 240, 267, 336, 352, 381
Southern Illinois Penitentiary 326
Southern Illinois University 224
Southern Illinoisan 66, 256
Sowerheaver, Michael 134
Spafford, Dwite 89
Spanish Fort, Battle of 342
Spanish-American War 226, 318, 364, 397

Sparks, William A. J. 65
Spaulding, Volney 374
Spears
   John E. 365
   Phoebia (Berry) 365
Speer
   Allan 365
   Andrew 365
   David 365
   Elizabeth (Williams) 365
   J. E. 365
   Mary 365
   Moses 365
   Phoebe (Berry) 365
   Robert 365
   William 365
Spence, William J. 344
Spencer
   E. V. 208
   Sally 381
Spencer, C. B. 241
Spieler
   Amelia 255
   Catherine 255
   F. A. 255
Spielman, Benjamin F. 75, 76
Spilman
   Ann B. 76
   B. F. 76, 87
   B. J. 87
   Benjamin F. ... 73, 75, 76, 77, 78, 129
   O. P. 73
   Thomas A. 33
Spivey
   Addie 365, 367
   Allen T. 365, 366
   Allen Thomas 366, 367
   Allen Thomas, Jr. 368
   Anna 365
   Annie 367
   Caroline 367
   Carrie 365
   Gertrude 366, 367
   Henry 367
   Louise 365, 367
   Lydia 322, 367
   Maggie 310
   Margaret 365
   Marguerite 367
   Marshall 367
   Mary (O'Neal) 368
   Mary O'Neal (Wright) 368
   Minnie 365, 367
   Mittase Wright 366, 368
   Mollie 367
   Mollie (Wright) 366
   Murray 367
   Quentin E. 367
   Quinton 365
   Sallie 367
   Sallie (Smyth) 365
   Sallie Annie (Smyth) 367

   Samuel S. 365
   Samuel Simon 367
   T. J. 310
   Teresa (Eason) 366
   Thomas 322
   Thomas J. 365
   Thomas Jefferson 366, 367
   Thomas Sawyer 365, 366
   Walter W. 365
   William Walter 367
Sprague
   Caroline 300
   Caroline (McKinney) 300
   Elizabeth 300
   Elizabeth Ann 300
   Ellen 300
   John 300
   Margaret (Fleming) 300
Sprigg, William 37
Springfield & Illinois S.E. R.R. 146, 233, 280, 352
Sprinkle
   George 7
   John 7
   Michael 7, 10, 52
   Peter 7
Sprout, Sarah 278
Spruel, Pleasant 170
Squirrels 94
St. Clair
   Arthur 19
   Belle 305
St. Clair County 19, 20
St. Joseph's Catholic Church 346
St. Louis & Southeastern R.R. 27, 62, 71, 137, 396
St. Mary's Convent 303
St. Mary's School 82
St. Vincent's Academy 385
St. Vincent's Convent 252
Staff, Mathew H. 49
Staley
   Ahart 284
   Sophia 284
Standefer, Job 84
Stanley
   R. H. 88
   Thomas 170
Stanton, Solomon 46
Stapp, J. T. B. 171
Stark, Andrew 33
Starkey place 159
Starkey, H. K. 41
State Bank at Shawneetown 230
State Bank of Illinois 40, 56, 58, 61, 212, 213
Stave factory 137
Ste. Genevieve, Mo. 105
Steel, Capt. 29
Steele, James 29
Stephens
   James 393
   Mary (Wilson) 393

449

Nathan 69
Stephenson
   Andrew 78
   James 38
   Mr. 84
   William K. 37
Stevens
   Bettie (Hogan) 286
   Martha 240
Stevenson
   Joanna G. 311
   Sarah (Ruddick) 311
   William 311
Stewart
   alias 16
   Augustus 42
Sticklin, William 172
Stickney
   ____ 26
   John 64
   Mr. 119
   William H 22, 77, 118
Stiff
   David 128
   Lewis 170
   Nathaniel 172
   Richard 169
Stiles
   Adaline 370
   Ashbel 370
   Catherine (Smith) 369, 370
   Catherine M. 370
   Clemma E. 370
   Dorcas (Burt) 369
   Edwin L. 370
   Ester (Hooker) 370
   Francis 370
   George Trafton 370
   Hannah 370
   Harriet L. 369
   Harriet L. (Roberts) 370
   Harriet Louise 370
   Hyas 369
   Hylas 370
   Hylas C. 370
   Job 370
   John 369
   John D. 370
   John, III 369
   John, Jr. 369
   Joseph F. 370
   Julia A. (Fulks) 370
   July (Stull) 369
   Laura E. 370
   Mary (Drake) 370
   Mary E. 370
   Ruth (Bancroft) 370
   Theoba J. 370
   William Andrew 370
   William H. 174
   William Henry 369
Stilley, Stephen 131, 132, 134
Stilly, George B. 42

Stinson
   Adam 51
   David 21
   James 85
   Jane 222
stocks 124
Stoker, Mary 331
Stokes
   Mary 371
   Montfort 371
Stokes settlement 95
Stone
   Captain 131
   E. P. H. 131
   Eberlee P. H. 47, 174
   Henry 68
   T. N. 89
Stony Point, Battle of 339
Storms, John 21
Stout
   Aaron B. 177
   Aaron R. 47
   Eleanora 244
   Henry 49
   Mary (Van Horn) 244
   Mr. 33
   William 244
Stovall, John B. 31
Street
   A. J. 26
   Anthony 371
   Eliza Maria (Posey) 372
   Joseph Montfort ...11, 12, 22,
      28, 30, 32, 33, 37, 39, 52,
      73, 79, 95, 371
   Mary (Stokes) 371
Stribling, G. W. 80
Strickland
   Ariminta (Dobbs) 375
   H. C. 294, 375
   Henry 170
   Ida (Kanady) 294, 375
   John D. 375
   Mary S. 263
   William 170
Stricklin
   J. Garner 172
   Willis 170
Strong, Nancy 219
Stull, July 369
Sturdevant
   Corvina I. (Youngblood) ...403
   George W. 403
Sturdivant Gang 274
Sturdivant, Merrick 92
Sturdivant's Fort 274
Sturgis, Gen. 176
Sturman, Robert L. 204
Styles, Lt. 174
Sugar Grove 9
Sugar Loaf Mound 5
Sullivan, Margaret 392
Summers, Emma 341

Sumner, W. S. 69
Sumners & Co. 69
Surgery, A. J. 69
Surguy, A. J. 140
Swafford Bros. 52, 68, 69, 138, 269
Swager, Charles 70
Swan
   B. C. 78
   Benjamin C. 77
   Walter N. 204
Swayne, Dr. ____ 16
Swearengin, Thomas V. 169
Sweeney, Richard 42
Swett, ____ 41
Switzer, James 43
Swoffard Bros. 64
Tabb, Augustine 393
Taburn, Jefferson 45
Tade
   Celia 101
   David 101
Tadlock
   Charles 375
   Clarence 375
   E. J. (Benson) 375
   E. L. 375
   Edgar 375
   Green 170
   Isaac 375
   Katie 375
   Laura E. 375
   Lewis 375
   Mamie 375
   Maud 375
   Michael 375
   Nancy 375
   Sarah (Baer) 375
   William C. 375
Talbot, Dr. 74
Talbott
   Benjamin 24
   Cass 147
Tall Bridge, Ind. 306
Talley, Thornton 10
Tally
   Amos 169
   Pleasant 38
   Thornton 8
Tally's Ferry Road 43
Talton, Richard 171
Talty
   Eugene 204
   Lawrence 204
Tanner
   John 34
   Judge 22
   Tazewell B. 41, 42
Tanquary land 159
Tarleton
   ____ 53
   Richard 308
Tate
   Thomas J. 37

William R.	42
Tavern rates	30
Taylor	
Edmund Dick	121
Frances (Colbert)	236
Francine	302
Francine "Sina"	241
George	130
Giles	121
Henry	172
Jonathan	112
Merritt	21
Robert	236
Washington	171
Zachary	119, 171, 373
Tecumseh	154
Telephone Exchange	140
Temple, Broughton	4
Terry, Robert	113
Texas City, Ill.	267
Thacker's Gap	116
Thatcher, Kathie (Crest)	vi
Third National Bank (Mt. Vernon)	326
Thomas	
Abe	16
Benjamin	22
Gen.	342
Jesse B.	9, 23, 37
John M.	42
Thomas	306
William	130
Thomason, William	38
Thomley, Ira	65
Thompson	
Alexander	50
Carolina (Gill)	265
F. L.	81
J. B.	81, 242
Jeff.	46
Julia F. (Wagor)	265
Matilda	308
Matthew	169
Mr.	76
Mrs.	76
Neil	33
W. W.	71
William	50
Wilson	156, 409
Thorn Thicket	227
Thorn, Alexander	170
Thornton, Gen.	119
Throop, J. D.	150
Tilden, Samuel J.	74
Tillson, Mrs.	54
Timmins, Elijah J.	47
Timmons, Elizabeth	255
Tippecanoe, Battle of	109, 155, 156, 390, 391
Tobart, Mr., Sr.	116
Tong, Thomas	22, 34
Tongue, Thomas	170
Tourease, Josiah	361
Towle	

Benjamin	376
Bernice	377
Chalon A.	46
Eliza	78
Eliza (Pearce)	376
Herman Edwin	377
Herman T.	377
Israel D.	78
Israel D.	35, 376
Jacob	376
John Warren	377
Joseph W.	376
Loudene (Karnes)	377
Philip	376
Ralph S.	377
Towle, Mitchell &	376
Towles, Thomas	38
Town Mount Prairie	150
Townshend	
Catharine O.	377
Hester M. (Pool)	338
Mrs. (Lumsden)	377
Orval P.	204
R. W.	355
Richard W.	23, 25, 26, 44, 59, 297, 298, 338, 354, 377, 380
Richard Wellington	377
Samuel H.	377
Trafton, George W.	174, 370
Trammel	
Jerrett	10
Philip	24
Phillip	6, 28
Trammell, Philip	162
Travis, R. W.	81
Tromley, L. F.	66
Tromly	
Herbert H.	380
Isaac	380
Jane (Bouton)	380
L. F.	380
Mabel	380
Michael	380
Theodore	380
Tromly & Ellis	380
Trousdale	
____	167
Alexander G.	268
Capt.	29
Elizabeth A. (Cork)	268
James	8, 136, 169
James A.	50
James T.	36
John A.	147
John C.	268
John W.	23
Mr.	269
Robert M.	37
Sandy	84
son of	168
Trumbull, Lyman	26
Trusty	

Elizabeth	381
Henry	381
I. T.	72
Isaac T.	381
W. C.	37, 72
William	71
William C.	137, 381
Trusty & McDaniel	250
Trusty & West	71
Tuck, N. F.	77, 88
Turner	
Albert R.	381
America	402
Carlos	381
Charles W.	330, 381
Eleanora (Richeson)	348, 381
Elenora (Richeson)	234
Elizabeth	330
Eugene Ambrose	381
H. L.	146
J. B.	63, 64
J. D.	234, 348
Jackson	330
James B.	12, 17, 26, 126, 127, 381
Jesse M.	381
John D. R.	381
Judith Mimms	381
Mary	381
Minnie T.	381
Pet (Moore)	330, 382
Sally (Spencer)	381
Sarah	330
Spencer	381
Susanna (Sanks)	359
Turney	
D.	171
L. J. S.	22, 66
Turney, L. J. S.	66
Turrentine, John	224
Tuscarora (riverboat)	324
Tuskina	343
Tweed	
John	266
Sabine M.	266
Tyer	
Harriet (Foster)	262
M. L.	262
U.S. Agricultural Soc.	369
U.S. Medical College	331
U.S. Saline Springs	28
U.S. Salines	30, 31, 32, 96, 115, 388
U.S. Signal Service	304
Ulen, ____	68
Ulmsnider, Joseph	143
Ulmsnider, Joseph, & Son	64
Underground Railroad	123
Union Springs, Ky.	112
Upchurch	
John	170
Johnathan	170
Thomas	170

Upton, Thomas..................152
Usselton, G. W.....................51
Utly, J. H............................71
Valter
   Arnold................383
   Barbara (Pfarr)................382
   Dolores................383
   Katie................382
   Mary................382
   Nicholas................382
   Peter J................382, 383
Valter's Add. to Ridgway..............382
Van Bibber
   Alpha (Foster)................258
   Noah................258
Van Buren, Martin..............26, 372
Van Cleve, J. W......................81
Van Dorn, Gen....................48, 49
Van Horn, Mary....................244
Vanlandingham, O. C.........8, 52, 57
Vaughn
   Benjamin................259
   Delila Elvira................259
   Elizabeth (Jackson)................259
   Thomas................170
Vaught
   Claiborne C.................47
   J. H.................65
Venters, Pete....................204
Vera Cruz, Battle of................171
Vermilion Institute..............354
Veterans
   Black Hawk War....72, 208, 236, 265, 269, 293, 308, 346, 352, 391, 401
   French & Indian War................307
   King William's War................376
   Mexican War.........51, 209, 225, 230, 279, 287, 292, 302, 391
   Revolutionary War.........210, 223, 230, 231, 245, 247, 256, 257, 266, 286, 295, 302, 307, 328, 331, 339, 342, 349, 371, 376, 393
   War of 1812....210, 219, 223, 238, 256, 266, 269, 286, 295, 296, 297, 328, 358, 403
Vickers, Louisa................301
Vicksburg, Miss..................231
Vigilantes................16
Villars, Mary H....................65
Vilter, Mary E................254
Vincennes land office..............229
Vincennes, Ind.................75, 380
Vines, Caroline................259
Vineyard
   Benjamin F................383
   Eli P.................383
   George A................383
   George J................383
   John T.................383
   Lucretia................383
   Margaret................383
   Mary................383
   Sarah (Hill)................383
   Sarah (Moore)................383
Vinson
   Charles................36, 169
   Charles E.................47
   Edmund................134
   Edward................170
   Stokely................172
Vinyard
   Daniel................158
   Jefferson................236
   John T.................204
   Joseph................236
   Lucy A. (Colbert)................236
   Sarah (Colbert)................236
Wabash Precinct................224
Wabash River................20
Wabash, Ill.................74
Wade, Tillie (Kratz)................299
Wadle, Andrew................171
Waggener
   B. W.................324
   Lavinia................300
Waggener & Mills................64, 325
Waggoner, John................170
Wagner, S.................82
Wagor
   Conrad................265
   Julia F.................265
   Luna................265
Wakeford, Henry................269
Walden, John................8
Walker, Z. T.................80
Wall, Fannie................289
Wallace
   Kate................400
   William................131, 169
Wallers, William................50
Walls, John................38
Walsen
   Charles................211
   Lucy (Baker)................211
Walsh family................82
Walters
   Addie (Lawler)................303
   Bertha................384
   Charles................384
   Edith................384
   Estella................384
   Hiram................52, 53, 383, 384
   James................384
   John B.................42, 384
   John T.................22, 37, 383, 384
   Judith (Lawler)................303
   Lydia................384
   M. H.................71
   Mattie................384
   Nancy................384
   Nannie (Wathen)................384
   Rebecca................384
   W. H.................138
   William................384
   William H.................384
   William I.................384
Waltonboro, Ill.................146
Waltonborough................323
Wamack, Shepherd F.................172
Wapello, Chief................374
Ward
   Belle................234
   Frank................313
   Josephine (Carney)................233
   Marietta (McBane................313
   William................313
Ward, Pleasant L.................64
Ward's Mill................154
Ware
   Polly A.................292
   Robert................170
Warford, William M.................58
Wargel, Susanna................249
Warren
   Charles M. C.................172
   Jessie (Wilson)................398
   Philip Barton................398
Warrick, Needham A.................50
Warson, Lurania................323
Washington Guards................272
Washington, George................247, 286, 303
Wasson
   J. M.................26
   J. N.................63
Wasson, Bowman &.................64
Waters
   Pleasant G.................47
   W. H.................138
Wathen
   Catherine (Bryne)................385
   Hettie A.................385
   James M.................384
   John A.................385
   Joseph................132, 384
   Mary................88
   Mary E.................385
   Nannie................384
   Nora (Campbell)................233
   Rebecca................384
   Rebecca (Pilkington)................385
   William M.................385
   Willis G.................385
Wathen family................83
Watkins
   _____................131
   J. E.................26
   Lewis................31, 32
   Mr.................244
Watson
   Emri C.................45
   James H.................50
   Robert................33
Wattles
   E.................39
   James O.................40

Weaver
    Cornelius C. 45
    Emily (Wiseheart) 402
    Levi 402
    Stokeley 172
Webb
    E. B. 57
    John 210
    Mary 210
    Miss 140
    Robert 133
Webber, S. T. 138
Weber
    Emily (Wiseheart) 401
    John 401
    Lewis 64
Webster
    Daniel 267
    J. D. 74
Weddle
    Andrew 172
    William 172
Weed, George M. 172
Weed's Salt Works 296
Weidemann, David 405, 406
Weigant, William A. 204
Weir & Vanlandingham 52
Weir, James 10
Weiss, Malinda 332
Welch, James J. 146
Welsh
    Margaret 341
    Mrs. Noah 142
    Noah 142
Wencel, Anna K. 405
Werd's salt works 297
Wesley, Bogarth 47
Wesleyan College 355
West
    E. A. 71, 137
    H.H. 57
    Lewis 79, 137
    Matthew 37
Westbrooks, Samuel 169
Western Expositor 222
Western Gazetteer 97, 407
Western Mining Co. 74
Western Reserve Medical College
    .... 208, 283
Western Voice 66
Western World, Tho 371
Wheatly
    Isabella (Gordon) 266
    John 266
Wheeler
    Erastus 32
    William 10
Whiskey Ring 395
Whitaker
    Abigail 262
    W. J. 81
White
    Benjamin 26
    Betsy 111
    Capt. 162, 163
    Charles 111, 112
    Clara (McCue) 319
    Don 385
    Eliza Griffin (Fauntleroy) 391
    Ellen B. 385
    George F. 386, 391
    George Fauntleroy 112, 156, 391, 409
    George W. L. 388
    George Washington 111
    George Washington Leech 391
    Harriet G. 111
    Harriet Grandison 390, 391
    Henry 69
    Isaac 95, 109, 110, 112, 154, 155, 156, 163, 385, 386, 387, 388, 389, 390, 391, 409
    Isaac T. 154, 391
    Isabelle (Colbert) 237
    James 356
    James J. 47
    Joseph 47
    Juliet 111
    Juliet Greenville 390, 391
    Katie 385, 386
    Leonard .. 22, 24, 28, 29, 32, 40, 73, 95, 109, 162, 163, 164
    Marinda (Rogers) 356
    Mary (Devous) 250
    Mary Frances (Sloo) 391
    Mr. 250, 319
    Rachel 333
    Robert 237
    Sally 110
    Sarah 111, 385
    Thomas 111, 386
    Varanda J. 78
    Wiley F. 385
    Willie 385
White County 21
White, Dawson & Brown 10
White's Mill 17
Whiteside, Thomas 170
Whiting
    Capt. 363
    Elizabeth 219
    John S. 47
Whitlock, Rev, ... 243
Whitmire, Elizabeth 270
Whitney, Jasper 46
Whittington
    Eliza J. (Kinsall) 299
    Robert 299
Wickliffe
    Charles A. 119
    George 289
    Robert 289
Wiederman, E. M. 73
Wight
    A. G. S. 39
    A. P. S. 39
Wilbanks
    D. P. 36
    Daniel P. 35
Wilburn, William 13
Wild, John H. 204
Wildcat Hills 18
Wilde, John 42
Wiley, A. 172
Wilkes, Taylor & Co. 390
Wilkins
    ____. 96
    Andrew 32
    Charles 30, 112
    J. W. 392
    James W. 392
    Jefferson D. 392
    Margaret (Sullivan) 392
    Margaret J. (Latham) 392
    Nathaniel 392
    Oma 392
    Paul 392
    Virginia 392
    William 392
    Wilmer 392
Wilkins, Charles, & Co. 30
Wilks
    H. J. 392
    Laura (Logsdon) 392
    Pauline 392
    W. J. 392
Willard
    A. P. 125
    Ellen 312, 313
    Joseph 312, 313
    Simon 312, 313
Willbanks, J. 171
Willey, W. W. 171
Williams
    Aaron 159
    C. R. 258
    Ebenezer 170
    Elizabeth 365
    Elizabeth (Davis) 247
    Ethel (Phillips) 336
    Henry B. 169
    Herbert 204
    Isaac 308
    James 169
    James J. 42
    Jane (Edwards) 258
    John 172, 204
    Margaret 209
    Mary 280
    Mr. 247
    Oscar 336
    Polly (Logsdon) 308
    Price 42
    Roger 256
    Thomas 159
    W. H. 157
    William 41
    William F. 48

453

Williams' Ferry 159
Williamson
    Daniel 204
    Judith M. 234, 348
Williamson County 21
Williamson County Airport 154
Williamson, John 22
Willing, S. E. 88
Willis
    Addie (Spivey) 365
    Fastina Ellen (Bean) 216
    Hepsy 133
    Jacob 171, 204, 216
    James 10, 38
    James, Sr. 38
    John 10, 171
    Mary (Hogan) 220
    Matilda 271
    Merrel 10
    Mr. 220
    William 42
Wilson
    ____ 95
    Aaron 393
    Aaron, Sr. 393
    Alexander 24, 30, 31, 39, 52, 394
    Alice Warren (Mather) 398
    Artemesia 293
    Arthur Harrison 398
    Bluford 317, 393, 394, 395, 396, 398
    Bluford, Jr. 398
    Catherine (Schneider) 394
    Cecilia 339
    Charles H. 46
    Davis 393
    E. 393
    Eleanora (Gregg) 268
    Elizabeth 381
    Flora 393
    George 393
    Harrison 13, 26, 40, 125, 171, 394
    Harry 398
    Henry S. 45
    Isaac 393
    J. H. 71
    James Harrison 51, 125, 293, 338, 339, 394, 396, 409
    James M. 293
    Jessie 398
    John 393
    John A. 39
    John G. 37
    Laura 393
    Lt. 49
    Lucy 398
    Mary 393
    Miss 131
    Mr. 268
    Polley 225
    Queenie 393

Queenie (De Ball) 393
Queenie (Wilson) 393
Thomas 22
William 38, 40, 265
Wilson & Warren 396
Wilson Bros. 64
Winfrey, Margaret J. 334
Wing, William 38
Winnebago Indians 372, 373
Winner, Richeson & 64
Winterberger
    Alois 69, 399
    Kate (Wallace) 400
    Louis 400
    Mary (Krauser) 400
    Ralph 400
Wise
    Agnes C. 335
    Agnes Caroline 336
    John S. 336
Wiseheart
    Albert 400
    Alfred D. 402
    Anna 400
    Elizabeth 401
    Elizabeth (Miller) 401, 402
    Ellen 400
    Emily 401, 402
    Fannie (Boyd) 400
    Gertrude 402
    Hannah 400
    Harrison 401, 402
    John 400, 401
    John Henry 402
    John, Sr. 401, 402
    Laura 400
    Lucy 400
    Malcolm 401
    Marshall 400
    Marshall Clarence 401
    Mary 400
    Mary (Sherwood) 402
    Mollie 402
    Nancy (Parks) 401, 402
    R. J. 401
    Raymond 401
    Rebecca 401, 402
    Richard 400, 401
    Richard J. 401
    Richard, Jr 402
    Samuel 400, 402
    Sarah (Gill) 400
    Sarah J. (Boswell) 401, 402
    Thomas 402
    William 148, 400, 401
    William S. 402
Wiseheart, Smyth & 64
Wolf Creek Church 132, 133
Wolfe
    A. A. 226
    Sarah M. 224, 226
Wolves 17, 18

Women's Christian Temperance
    Union 65
Wood
    Daniel 57, 170
    John 68, 69, 140, 169, 371
    Mason 169
    Walter W. 204
Woods
    Dan 362
    John 73, 170
Woods Pond 1
Woodward, M. 74
Wooten, J. C. 131
Wormit
    Barbara 332
    Mary (Naas) 332
Wright
    Francis 135
    Mary O'Neal 368
    Mollie 366
    Newton E. 16
    Robert 77
    Robert E. 204
    T. B. 368
Wrinkle, George 170
Wurttemberg, Duke of 105, 409
Yale University 370
Yates
    Elijah 251
    H. Clay 248
    Mary (Dillard) 251
    Richard 61, 125, 126, 336, 337, 338
Yehie, Willibald 49
Yellow Bank Slough 1
Yinn
    Annie (Edwards) 258
    Archibald 258
Yorktown, Battle of 303, 339
Yost
    ____ 26
    Emma 362
    John 22
    Mary E. 268
    Susan (Kanady) 240
    William F. 362
Young
    Arthur G. 33
    Benjamin F. 48
    Capt. (48th Inf.) 312
    Charles W. 403
    Edward 42
    Henry 280
    Irene 403
    James 403
    James W. 402, 403
    Laura (Boyd) 402
    Laura C. (Boyd) 403
    Mary Frances 403
    Mr. 227
    Nancy (Harrelson) 280
    Nathan 152
    R. M. 343

Rebecca (Harrelson) 280
Susie 403
Thomas A. 38
Young, Bruce & 138
Youngblood
____ 26
Corvina I. 403
E. D. 22, 26, 37, 44, 323, 403
Edmund D. 403
Electa (Jones) 403
Emmis M. (Kinnie) 403
Eunice M. (Kinne) 404
Eva 65, 404
F. M. 22
Francis M. 403
Isaiah 403
Isaiah I. 403
Louisa H. 403
Lovina C. 403
Rachel 403
Sarah A. 403
William J. 403
Ypsilanti, Mich. 219

Zachmeier, Mary R. 295
Zinn
Anna E. (Bernhardt) 404
Bertha L. 404
Charles C. 404
Christian 404
Crystal 404
Elizabeth 404
Fanny 404
George B. 404
Henry J. 404
James F. 404
Mary J. 404
Mary J. (McMurtry) 404
Nora 404
Otto F. 404
William B. 404
Zipp, Etta Mary 254
Zirkelbach
Andrew 404, 405
Anna K. (Wencel) 405
Barbara 404
Carrie (Daily) 244

Catherine (Devous) 250
Cecilia 405
Celia 383
Eleanora 405
Frank 404
George 404, 405
Henry 382
Josie 405
Katherine 405
Katherine (Leutzhuick) 404
Katie (Valter) 382
Lena 404
Maggie 404
Mary 404
Mathias 405
Mena 404
Peter 244, 404
Rachel 404
Rudolph 405
William J. 404
William M. 405

455